MANAGERIAL ACCOUNTING
Concepts for planning, control, decision making

MANAGERIAL ACCOUNTING

Concepts for planning, control, decision making

RAY H. GARRISON, D.B.A., C.P.A.
Brigham Young University

1979 Revised Edition

Business Publications, Inc.
Dallas, Texas   75243

Irwin-Dorsey Limited
Georgetown, Ontario L7G 4B3

ISBN 0-256-02209-7
Library of Congress Catalog Card No. 78–70982
Printed in the United States of America

7890   654321

To
Leslie, Kimberly, Jimmy, Jana, LeAnn

Preface

This text is designed for a one-term course in managerial accounting, to be used by students who have already completed one or two terms of basic financial accounting. Its emphasis is on uses of accounting data internally by managers in directing the affairs of organizations, both business and nonbusiness. As in the first edition, the revised edition of *Managerial Accounting* is consistently managerial in thrust, looking at accounting data through the eyes of those who must use it in setting plans and objectives, in controlling operations, and in making the myriad of decisions involved with the management of an enterprise. Looking at accounting data from this perspective provides a solid managerial base on which to build concepts. It also makes it easier for the instructor to portray the internal accountant in his true role—that of a key participant in the basic functions of management.

Although the emphasis of the book is on uses of accounting data, care has been taken to not sacrifice the student's need for basic technical understanding. To this end, topics are covered in enough depth to insure full comprehension of basic concepts. The student is then able to proceed with confidence and understanding in the application of these concepts to organizational problems.

A paramount objective in writing this book has been to make a clear and balanced presentation of relevant subject material. Effort has been made to draw examples and homework problems, where appropriate, from service-oriented as well as from profit-oriented situations, and from nonmanufacturing as well as from manufacturing situations.

New in this edition

In the revision process, great care has been taken to retain all of the strengths favorably commented upon by users of the first edition. The book has been thoroughly updated, however, with about 70 percent of the exercise and problem material either completely new or thoroughly revised. In addition, users will find more problem material in this edition, as well as a greater range of problems in terms of level of difficulty. Other additions or changes include:

1. A section titled "Key Terms for Review" has been added at the end of each chapter. Altogether, over 250 key terms are thus highlighted for the reader.

2. The book has been shortened from 19 to 17 chapters.

a. Old Chapter 16, Inventory Planning and Control, has been eliminated. That material in old Chapter 16 which dealt with the Economic Order Quantity and with the Reorder Point has been condensed and placed in an appendix to Chapter 7, Profit Planning. This is a more logical placement, since it permits the EOQ material to be integrated with other budgeting concepts.

b. Old Chapter 17, Quantitative Decision Techniques, has also been eliminated. That material in old Chapter 17 which dealt with linear programming has been condensed and placed in an appendix to Chapter 11, Relevant Costs in Nonroutine Decisions. Again, this is a more logical placement, since it allows the instructor to integrate linear programming with other decision making concepts, if desired.

3. Old Chapter 4, Cost Allocation for Planning and Control, has been completely rewritten, retitled "Service Department Cost Allocations," and moved to Chapter 15 in the text. Great care has been taken to retain the strengths of old Chapter 4, but the material has been clarified and integrated more fully with flexible budgets and other managerial accounting tools. Moving the chapter toward the end of the text makes it easier for those instructors who prefer to omit this chapter, while at the same time makes it more convenient for those instructors who prefer to cover this material after covering basic budgeting concepts.

4. Old Chapter 6, Cost-Volume-Profit Relationships, has been largely rewritten to focus more directly on contribution analysis. The material in its rewritten form has been extremely well received by students in classroom testing. This chapter becomes Chapter 5 in the revised edition.

5. Old Chapter 9, Control through Standard Costs, has been largely rewritten to include more material on the setting of standards. In addition, a columnar approach to variance analysis is used in this edition, along with the formula approach, to permit the instructor to focus more directly on input/output analysis, if desired. Also, an appendix illustrating journal entries for the recording of variances has been added, for those instructors who wish to cover this material.

6. Old Chapter 19, How Well Am I Doing?—Statement of Changes in Financial Position, becomes Chapter 17 in the revised edition. This chapter has been rewritten to clarify the material and to tie it to actual funds statements extracted from annual reports. An appendix has been added to the chapter illustrating the adjustment of the income statement to a cash

basis, for those instructors who prefer this approach to preparing a cash flow statement.

7. Behavioral issues have been given more consideration in both text and problem material.

Using the text

Flexibility in meeting the needs of courses varying in length, content, and student composition has been a prime concern in the revision process. Sufficient text material is available to permit the instructor to choose topics and depth of coverage as desired. Appendixes, parts of chapters, or even whole chapters can be omitted without adversely affecting the continuity of the course. An instructor's manual is available which gives a number of alternate assignment outlines, and which gives suggestions as to the problems to be assigned from the various chapters.

Although the book has been shortened by two chapters, the question, exercise, and problem material has been expanded to some 700 items in the revised edition. A study guide is available, as is a test bank containing both objective and problem-type questions.

Acknowledgments

Ideas and suggestions have been received from many faculty members who used the first edition of the book. Each has my thanks, since the book is a better product as a result of their insightful comments.

The following professors spent considerable time providing in-depth reviews of the first edition: Mark F. Asman, Bowling Green State University; Paul E. Fertig, The Ohio State University; Sanford C. Gunn, State University of New York at Buffalo; James A. Hallam, Illinois State University; Philip A. Jones, Sr., University of Richmond; Robert D. MacDonald, University of Wisconsin; M. Nelson, McMaster University; Thomas J. O'Neil, American International College; Ray M. Powell, University of Notre Dame; Lloyd Seaton, Jr., University of Arkansas; Donald E. Stone, University of Massachusetts; George D. Welch, Drake University; and Jeffrey L. Williams, University of New Haven.

My appreciation is extended to the National Association of Accountants and to the American Institute of Certified Public Accountants for permission to quote from their publications. Selected materials from the Uniform CPA Examinations, copyright © 1950 through 1976 by the American Institute of Certified Public Accountants, Inc., are used and adapted by permission. These problems bear the notation (CPA) in the text. Material from the Certificate in Management Accounting Examinations, copyright © 1973 through 1977 by the National Association of Accountants, is reprinted (or adapted) by permission. These problems bear the notation (CMA) in the text. I also acknowledge, with appreciation, permission from the Society

of Management Accountants of Canada to incorporate its examination
questions in this text. Problems from the examinations administered by
the Society of Management Accountants of Canada are designated (SMA).

Finally, my thanks to Standard Brands Incorporated and Pet Incorporated for permission to use excerpts from their annual reports.

January 1979   **Ray H. Garrison**

Contents

1. **Managerial accounting — A perspective** **1**

Organizations and their objectives: *Setting objectives. Strategic planning. The work of management. The planning and control cycle. Organizational structure. The controller. Organizations have basic similarities.* The manager's need for information: *Accounting information. Information must be in summary form.* Comparison of financial and managerial accounting: *Differences between financial and managerial accounting. Similarities between financial and managerial accounting.* The expanding role of managerial accounting: *Increased needs for information. The certificate in management accounting (CMA).*

PART ONE
MANAGERIAL ACCOUNTING FUNDAMENTALS

2. **Cost terms, concepts, and classifications.** **23**

General cost classifications: *Manufacturing costs. Nonmanufacturing costs. Period costs. Product costs.* Cost classifications on financial statements: *The income statement. The balance sheet. Product costs — A closer look.* Further classification of labor costs: *Idle time. Overtime premium. Payroll fringe benefits.* Costs and control: *Variable and fixed costs. Direct and indirect costs. Controllable and noncontrollable costs.* Other cost concepts: *Differential costs. Opportunity costs. Sunk costs.*

3. **Cost accumulation for product costing** **55**

The need for factory unit cost data. Types of costing systems: *Process costing. Job order costing.* Job order costing — The general outline: *Measuring direct materials cost. The job cost sheet. Measuring direct labor cost. Application of manufacturing overhead. Computation of unit costs. A summary of document flows.* Job order costing — The flow of costs: *The purchase and issue of materials. Labor costs. Manufacturing overhead costs. The application of manufacturing overhead. Nonmanufacturing costs. Cost of goods finished. Cost of goods sold. A summary of cost flows.* Problems of overhead application: *The concept of underapplied or overapplied overhead. Disposition of under and overapplied overhead balances. A general model of product cost flows. Multiple overhead rates.* APPENDIX A: PROCESS COSTING AND THE CONCEPT OF EQUIVALENT UNITS. APPENDIX B: NORMALIZED OVERHEAD RATES.

4. **Cost behavior patterns — A closer look** **119**

Types of cost behavior patterns: *Variable costs. True variable versus step-variable costs. The linearity assumption and the relevant range. Fixed costs. The trend toward fixed costs. Types of fixed costs. Fixed costs and the relevant range. Mixed costs.* The analysis of mixed costs: *The high-low method. The scattergraph method. The least squares method. The use of judgment in cost analysis. Multiple regression analysis. Engineering approach to cost study.* The contribution format: *Why a new income statement format? The contribution approach.* Review problem on cost behavior. APPENDIX: ALTERNATE APPROACH TO LEAST SQUARES.

5. **Cost-volume-profit relationships** **161**

The basics of cost-volume-profit analysis: *Contribution margin. Contribution margin ratio. Cost structure. Operating leverage. Some applications of CVP concepts. Importance of the contribution margin.* Break-even analysis: *Break-even computations. Cost-volume-profit relationships in graphical form. Target net profit analysis.* Further CVP applications: *Structuring commissions to salespersons. The concept of sales mix.* Limiting assumptions in cost-volume-profit analysis.

PART TWO
USES OF MANAGERIAL ACCOUNTING DATA

6. **Segmented reporting, and the contribution approach to costing** . . . **207**

Segmented reporting: *Differing levels of segmented reports. Basic allocation concepts. Variable expenses and contribution margin. The importance of fixed costs. Direct and common costs. Segment margin. Common costs and net income. Varying breakdowns of total sales.* Inventory valuation under the contribution approach — Direct costing: *Direct costing. The controversy over fixed costs. Comparison of absorption and direct costing. The definition of an asset. Extended comparison of income data. Sales constant, production fluctuates. Cost-volume-profit analysis and absorption costing. External reporting and income taxes.* Advantages of the contribution approach.

7. **Profit planning.** **253**

The basic framework of budgeting: *Definition of budgeting. Nearly everyone budgets. Difference between planning and control. Advantages of budgeting. Responsibility accounting. Choosing a budget period. The self-imposed budget. The matter of human relations. The budget committee. The master budget — A network of interrelationships. Sales forecasting — A critical step.* Preparing the master budget: *The sales budget. The production budget. The direct materials budget. The direct labor budget. The manufacturing overhead budget. Cost of a unit of product. The selling and administrative expenses budget. The cash budget. The budgeted income statement. The budgeted balance sheet.* Zero-base budgeting. The need for further budgeting material. APPENDIX: ECONOMIC ORDER QUANTITY AND THE REORDER POINT.

8. **Control through standard costs** **305**

Standard costs — Management by exception: *Who uses standard costs?* Setting standard costs: *Ideal versus practical standards. Setting direct materials standards. Setting direct labor standards. Setting variable overhead standards. Are standards the same as budgets? Advantages of standard costs.* A general model for variance analysis: *The general model.* Using standard costs — Direct material variances:

Materials price variance — A closer look. Materials quantity variance — A closer look. Using standard costs — Direct labor variances: *Labor rate variance — A closer look. Labor efficiency variance — A closer look.* Using standard costs — Variable overhead variances: *Overhead variances — A closer look.* Graphical analysis of the price and quantity variances. Variance analysis and management by exception: *Criteria for determining "exceptions." Statistical analysis of random variances.* Review problem on standard costs: *Materials variances. Labor variances. Variable overhead variances.* APPENDIX: GENERAL LEDGER ENTRIES TO RECORD VARIANCES.

9. **Flexible budgets and overhead analysis** **347**

Flexible budgets: *Characteristics of a flexible budget. Deficiencies of the static budget. How the flexible budget works. The measure of activity — A critical choice.* The overhead performance report — A closer look: *The problem of budget allowances. Spending variance alone. Both spending and efficiency variances.* Fixed costs and the flexible budget. Fixed overhead analysis: *Flexible budgets and overhead rates. Overhead application in a standard cost system. The fixed overhead variances. The budget variance — A closer look. The volume variance — A closer look. Graphical analysis of fixed overhead variances. Cautions in fixed overhead analysis.* Summary problem on overhead analysis.

10. **Control of decentralized operations** **389**

Responsibility accounting: *The functioning of the system. The flow of information. Expanding the responsibility accounting idea. Investment, profit, and cost centers. Measuring management performance.* Rate of return for measuring managerial performance: *The ROI formula. Factors underlying rate of return. Operating income and the asset base.* Controlling the rate of return: *Increase sales. Reduce expenses. Reduce operating assets. The problem of allocated expenses and assets.* The concept of residual income. Transfer pricing: *The need for transfer prices. Transfer prices at cost. Transfer prices at variable cost. Transfer prices at market price. Illustrating the market price approach. The problem of a change in market price. Transfers at negotiated market prices. The matter of opportunity cost. Divisional autonomy and suboptimization.*

11. **Relevant costs in nonroutine decisions** **431**

Cost concepts for decision making: *Identifying relevant costs. Cost relevance versus cost precision.* Sunk costs are not relevant costs: *Book value of old equipment.* Future costs that do not differ are not relevant costs: *An illustration. Why isolate relevant costs?* Adding and dropping product lines: *An illustration of cost analysis. A comparative format. Beware of allocated fixed costs.* The make or buy decision: *The advantages of integration. An example of make or buy. The matter of opportunity cost.* Utilization of scarce resources: *Contribution in relation to scarce resources. The problem of multiple constraints.* Joint product costs and the contribution approach: *The pitfalls of allocation. The contribution approach to the problem.* APPENDIX: LINEAR PROGRAMMING.

12. **The pricing decision** **483**

The economic framework for pricing: *Total revenue and total cost curves. Marginal revenue and marginal cost curves. Elasticity of demand. Limitations to the general models.* Pricing standard products: *Cost-plus pricing formulas. The absorption approach. The contribution approach. Using cost-plus data. Why use cost data in pricing?*

Pricing new products: *Test marketing of products. Pricing strategies. Target costs and product pricing.* Special pricing decisions: *Pricing a special order. The variable pricing model.* Criticisms of the contribution approach to pricing. The Robinson-Patman Act.

13. Capital budgeting decisions. **521**

Capital budgeting — An investment concept: *Typical capital budgeting decisions. Characteristics of business investments.* The concept of present value: *The theory of interest. Computation of present value. Present value of a series of cash flows.* Discounted cash flows — The net present value method: *The net present value method illustrated. Emphasis on cash flows. Recovery of the original investment. Limiting assumptions. Choosing a discount rate. An extended example of the net present value method.* Discounted cash flows — The time-adjusted rate of return method: *The time-adjusted rate of return method illustrated. The problem of uneven cash flows. The process of interpolation. Using the time-adjusted rate of return.* The cost of capital as a screening tool. Comparison of the net present value and the time-adjusted rate of return methods. Expanding the net present value approach: *The total-cost approach. The incremental-cost approach. Least-cost decisions.* APPENDIX: PRESENT VALUE TABLES.

14. Further aspects of investment decisions **565**

Income taxes and capital budgeting: *The concept of aftertax cost. The concept of depreciation tax shield. The best depreciation method. Comprehensive example of income taxes and capital budgeting.* Preference decisions — The ranking of investment projects: *Time-adjusted rate of return method. Net present value method. Comparing the preference rules.* Other approaches to capital budgeting decisions: *The payback method. Evaluation of the payback method. Payback and uneven cash flows. The simple rate of return method. Criticisms of the simple rate of return. The choice of an investment base.*

PART THREE
SELECTED TOPICS FOR FURTHER STUDY

15. Service department cost allocations **603**

The need for cost allocation: *The predetermined overhead rate revisited. Equity in allocation.* Guidelines for cost allocation: *Selecting allocation bases. Interdepartmental services. Allocating costs by behavior. Pitfalls in allocating fixed costs. Should actual or budgeted costs be allocated? Guidelines for allocating service department costs.* Implementing the allocation guidelines: *Basic allocation techniques. An extended example. No distinction made between fixed and variable costs. Should all costs be allocated? Beware of sales dollars as an allocation base.*

16. "How well am I doing?" — Financial statement analysis **639**

The importance of statement analysis: *Importance of comparisons. The need to look beyond ratios.* Statements in comparative and common-size form: *Dollar and percentage changes on statements. Common-size statements.* Ratio analysis — The common stockholder: *Earnings per share. Extraordinary items and earnings per share. Fully diluted earnings per share. Price earnings ratio. Dividend payout and yield ratios. Return on total assets. Return on common stockholders' equity. Book value per share.*

Ratio analysis — The short-term creditor: *Working capital. The current ratio. Acid-test ratio. Accounts receivable turnover. Inventory turnover.* Ratio analysis — The long-term creditor: *Times interest earned. The debt / equity ratio.*

17. "How well am I doing?" — Statement of changes in financial position   681

The purpose of the statement: *An example of the statement. Alternate titles to the statement.* Sources and uses of working capital: *Sources of working capital. Uses of working capital. Summary of sources and uses. No effect on working capital.* The funds statement — An illustration: *Three basic steps to the funds statement. Statement of changes in working capital. Changes in noncurrent balance sheet accounts. The completed funds statement. Uses of the funds statement.* A working paper approach to the funds statement: *The statement of changes in working capital. The T-account approach. The completed funds statement.* Focusing on changes in cash: *What activities have an impact on cash? Sources of cash. Uses of cash. The cash flow statement — An illustration.* APPENDIX: MODIFIED CASH FLOW STATEMENT

INDEX **725**

Chapter 1

Managerial accounting — A perspective

Managerial accounting is concerned with providing information to *managers;* that is, to those who are *inside* of an organization and who are charged with directing and controlling its operations. Managerial accounting can be contrasted with financial accounting, which is concerned with providing information to stockholders, creditors, and others who are *outside* of an organization.

Because it is manager oriented, any study of managerial accounting must be preceded by some understanding of the management process and of the organizations in which managers work. Accordingly, the purpose of this chapter is to examine briefly the work of the manager, and to look at the characteristics, structure, and operation of the organizations in which this work is carried out. The chapter concludes by examining the major differences and similarities between financial and managerial accounting.

ORGANIZATIONS AND THEIR OBJECTIVES

An organization can be defined as a group of people united together for some common purpose. A bank providing financial services is an organization, as is a university providing educational services, and the General Electric Company producing appliances and other products. An organization consists of *people,* not physical assets. Thus, a bank building is not an organization; rather, the organization consists of the people who work in the bank and who are bound together for the common purpose of providing financial services to a community.

The common purpose toward which an organization works is called its *objective.* Not all organizations have the same objective or objectives. For some organizations the objective is to produce a product and earn a profit. For other organizations the objective may be to render humanitarian service (the Red Cross), to provide aesthetic enrichment (a symphony orchestra), or to provide government services (a water department). To assist in our discussion, we will focus on a single organization, the Discount Furniture Marts, Inc., and look closely at this organization's objectives, structure, and management and at how these factors influence its need for managerial accounting data.

Setting Objectives

The Discount Furniture Marts, Inc., is a corporation, and its owners have placed their money in the organization with the thought in mind of earning a return, or profit, on their investment. Thus, one objective of the company is to earn a profit on the funds committed to it. The profit objective is tempered by other objectives, however. The company is anxious to acquire and maintain a reputation for integrity, fairness, and dependability. It also wants to be a positive force in the social and ecological environment in which it carries out its activities.

The owners of the Discount Furniture Marts, Inc., prefer not to be involved in day-to-day operation of the company. Instead, they have outlined the broad objectives of the organization, and have selected a president to oversee the implementation of these objectives. Although the president is charged with the central objective of earning a profit on the owners' investment, he[1] must do so with a sensitivity for the other objectives which the organization desires to achieve.

Strategic planning

The implementation of an organization's objectives is known as strategic planning. In any organization strategic planning occurs in two phases:

1. Deciding on the products to produce and/or the services to render.
2. Deciding on the marketing and/or manufacturing methods to employ. That is, deciding on the best way to get the intended product and/or service to the proper audience.

The set of strategies emerging from strategic planning is often referred to as an organization's *policies,* and strategic planning itself is often referred to as *setting policy.*[2]

PHASE ONE STRATEGY.   In deciding on the products to produce or the services to render, there are several strategies that the president of the Discount Furniture Marts, Inc., could follow. The company could specialize in office furniture. It could specialize in appliances, it could be a broad "supermarket" type of furniture outlet, or it could employ any one of a number of other product and/or service strategies.

After careful consideration of the various strategies available, a decision has been made to sell only home furnishings, including appliances. The president, for one reason or another, has rejected several other possible strategies. He has decided, for example, not to service appliances. He has also decided not to sell office furniture, or to deal in institutional-type furnishings.

PHASE TWO STRATEGY.   Having decided to concentrate on home furnishings, the president of the Discount Furniture Marts, Inc., is now faced with a second strategy decision. Some furniture companies handle only the highest quality home furnishings, thereby striving to maintain the

---

[1] The English language lacks a generic singular pronoun signifying he *or* she. For this reason the masculine pronouns he and his are used to some extent in this book for purposes of succinctness and to avoid repetition in wording. As used, these pronouns are intended to refer to both females and males.

[2] For an expanded discussion of strategic planning, see Harold Koontz and Cyril J. O'Donnell, *Management,* 6th ed. (New York: McGraw-Hill Book Co., 1976); and William H. Newman and E. Kirby Warren, *Process of Management,* 4th ed. (Englewood Cliffs, N.J.: Prentice-Hall, Inc., 1977).

image of a "quality" dealer. Markups are usually quite high, volume is quite low, and promotional efforts are directed toward a relatively small segment of the public. Other furniture dealers operate "volume" outlets. They try to keep markups relatively low, with the thought that overall profits will be augmented by a larger number of units sold. Still other dealers may follow different strategies. The selection of a particular strategy is simply a matter of managerial judgment; some companies make a profit by following one strategy, while other companies are equally profitable following another. In the case at hand, the Discount Furniture Marts, Inc., has decided to operate "volume" outlets, and to focus on maintaining a "discount" image.

Every organization must make similar strategy decisions. The set of strategies resulting from these decisions may not be written down, but they exist nonetheless and are a central guiding force in the organization's activities and in its need for accounting information.

The work of management

The work of management centers around what is to be managed—the organization itself. Essentially, the manager carries out four broad functions in an organization:

1. Planning.
2. Organizing and directing.
3. Controlling.
4. Decision making.

These activities are carried on more or less simultaneously and often under considerable stress, urgency, and pressure. Rarely (if ever) will managers stop to examine which function they are engaged in at that particular moment. Perhaps they couldn't tell even if they tried, since a specific action might touch on all four.

PLANNING.   In planning, the managers outline the steps to be taken in moving the organization toward its objectives. We saw the planning function in operation in the Discount Furniture Marts, Inc., as the president decided on a set of strategies to be followed. The president's next step will be to develop further, more specific plans, such as store locations, methods of financing customer purchases, hours of operation, discount policies, and so forth. As these plans are made they will be communicated throughout the organization, and will serve to coordinate, or to meld together, the efforts of all parts of the organization toward the company's objectives.

ORGANIZING AND DIRECTING.   In organizing, the managers decide how best to put together the organization's human and other resources in order to carry out established plans. As a customer enters one of the Discount Furniture Marts, Inc.'s stores, the results of the managers' organizational efforts should be obvious in several ways. Certain persons will be performing specific functions, some directly with the customer, and some not. Some persons will be overseeing the efforts of other persons. The store's physical assets will be arranged in particular ways, and certain procedures will be followed if a sale is made. These and a host of other things, seen and unseen, will all exist to assure that the customer is assisted in the best way possible, and that the company moves toward its profit objectives.

In sum, the organization that is apparent in most companies doesn't simply happen; it is a result of the efforts of the manager who must visualize and fit together the structure that is needed to get the job done, whatever the job may be.

In directing, managers oversee day-to-day activities, and keep the organization functioning smoothly. Employees are assigned to tasks, disputes between departments or between employees are arbitrated, questions are answered, on-the-spot problems are solved, and numerous small routine and nonroutine decisions are made involving customers and/or procedures. In effect, directing is that part of the managers' work which deals largely with the routine and with the here and now.

CONTROLLING. In controlling, managers take those steps that are necessary to ensure that every part of the organization is functioning at maximum effectiveness. To do this they study the accounting and other reports coming to them, and compare these reports against the plans set earlier. These comparisons may show where operations are not proceeding effectively, or where certain persons need help in carrying out their assigned duties. Control, in large part, is a function of obtaining useful *feedback* on how well the organization is moving toward its stated objectives. This feedback may suggest the need to replan, to set new strategies, or to reshape the organizational structure. It is a key ingredient to the effective management of any organization. As we shall see in chapters following, the generation of feedback to the manager is one of the central purposes of internal accounting.

DECISION MAKING. In decision making, the manager attempts to make rational choices between alternatives. Decision making isn't a separate management function, per se; rather, it is an inseparable part of the *other* functions already discussed. Planning, organizing and directing, and controlling all require that decisions be made. For example, when first establishing its organizational strategies, the Discount Furniture Marts, Inc., had to make a decision as to which of several available strategies would be followed. Such a decision is often called a *strategic decision,* because of its long-term impact on the organization. In organizing and in directing day-to-day operations, as well as in controlling, the manager must make scores of lesser decisions, all of which are important to the organization's overall well-being.

All decisions are based on *information.* In large part, the quality of management's decisions will be a reflection of the quality of the accounting and other information which it receives. Simply put, bad information will generally lead to bad decisions. Thus the need for a course in managerial accounting, in which we deal directly with the informational needs of management in carrying out decision-making responsibilities.

The planning and control cycle

The work of management can be summarized very nicely in a model such as shown in Exhibit 1–1. This model, which depicts the planning and control cycle, illustrates the smooth movement of management activities from planning through organizing, directing, and controlling, and then back to planning again. All of these activities are shown as turning on the hub of decision making.

Exhibit 1–1
The planning and control cycle

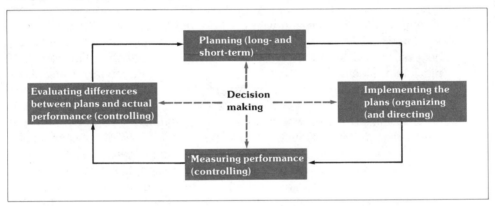

Organizational structure

Just as organizations are made up of people, management accomplishes its objectives by working *through* people. The president of the Discount Furniture Marts, Inc., could not possibly execute all of the company's strategies alone. The president must rely on other people to carry a large share of the management load. This is done by the creation of an organizational structure that will permit a *decentralization* of management responsibilities. For example, the Discount Furniture Marts, Inc., has three stores, with each store having a furnishings department and an appliances department. Each store has a store manager, as well as a separate manager over each department. In addition, the company has a purchasing department and an accounting department. These organizational relationships are shown in Exhibit 1–2.

Exhibit 1–2
Organization chart, Discount Furniture Marts, Inc.

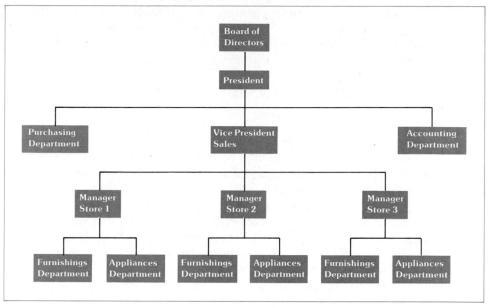

The arrangement of boxes shown in Exhibit 1–2 is commonly called an *organization chart.* Each box depicts an organizational unit, as discussed above, and the lines between the boxes show the relationship of one organizational unit to another. The chart tells us, for example, that the managers of the stores are responsible to the vice president in charge of sales. In turn, the latter is responsible to the company president, who in turn is responsible to the board of directors. The purpose of an organization chart, therefore, is to show formal responsibility relationships between managers of an organization. If the manager of Store 3 has a problem, he or she should not go directly to the company president, but rather should take the problem to the sales manager who is the immediate superior.

In very large organizations informal relationships and channels of communication often develop which are not shown on the formal organization chart but which may be helpful in maintaining a smooth flow of activity. These informal relationships are discussed at length in textbooks on general management.[3]

An organization chart also depicts *line* and *staff* authority in an organization. Any organizational unit whose activities are *directly* related to the basic objectives of the organization is a line unit. Refer to Exhibit 1–2.

---

[3] For further discussion, see W. Jack Duncan, *Essentials of Management* (Hinsdale, Ill.: The Dryden Press, 1975), chap. 13.

One of the objectives of the Discount Furniture Marts, Inc., is to earn a profit through sales of furnishings and appliances to customers. Therefore, the furnishings and appliances departments in each store are line units. Moving upward on the chart, the stores themselves are line units, as is the position of the vice president in charge of sales. The units represented by these boxes are all *directly* involved in meeting the company's stated objectives.

A staff unit is one which provides services and assistance to other units in the organization. The purchasing department in the Discount Furniture Marts, Inc., is in a staff position, since its only function is to support and serve the line departments by doing their purchasing for them. The company has found that better buys can be obtained by having one central unit purchase for the entire organization. Therefore, the purchasing department has been organized as a staff department to perform this service function. It cannot be called a line department, since it is involved only *indirectly* with the basic objectives of the organization, and since its role is *supportive* in nature. By this line of reasoning, the accounting department is also a staff department, since its purpose is to provide specialized accounting services to other departments.

The Discount Furniture Marts, Inc.'s organization chart shows only two staff departments. In a larger organization there would be many more staff departments, including perhaps finance, engineering, medical services, cafeteria, personnel, advertising, and research and development.

The distinction we have drawn between line and staff is an important one, since the role of staff persons is basically advisory in nature, and they have no authority over line units. By this we mean that in most organizations policy is not formulated by persons occupying staff positions. Rather, policy setting and the making of key operating decisions is done by line managers with staff units either providing input or carrying out other duties as directed by top line management.

Since accounting is in a staff position, where does it get the authority to set policy in accounting and financial reporting matters? The answer is simple. Top line management *delegates* to the accounting department the right to prescribe uniform accounting procedures and the right to require reports and other information from line units. In carrying out these duties, the accounting department is not exercising direct authority over line departments; it is simply acting for top line management as its delegated voice.

The controller

The manager in charge of the Accounting Department is known as the *controller*. He or she is a member of the top management team, and is an active participant in the planning, control, and decision-making processes. Although the controller does not "control" in terms of line authority (remember, accounting is a staff function), as chief information officer he or she is in a position to exercise control in a very special way. This is through the reporting and interpreting of data needed in decision making. By the supplying and interpreting of relevant and timely data, the controller exerts an influence on decisions and plays a key part in directing an organization toward its objectives.

Because of the position as a member of the top management team, the controller's time generally is kept free of technical and detailed activities. The controller oversees the work of others, directs the preparation of special reports and studies, and advises top management in special problem situations. The organization of a modern controller's office is shown in Exhibit 1–3.

Since the focus of this book is on managerial accounting, we are particularly interested in the work of the controller and the department he or she manages. The information which the accounting department generates is used throughout an organization in many different ways, as we shall see in chapters following.

Organizations have basic similarities

Organizations can be classified into three basic groups:

1. Profit-oriented business enterprises that are privately owned and operated as corporations, partnerships, and proprietorships.
2. Service-oriented agencies and associations that are either publicly or privately controlled, such as the Red Cross, the YMCA, and the Salvation Army, and that are usually operated as nonprofit corporations.
3. Service-oriented agencies such as the Department of Defense, a state university, and a city water department that are created and controlled by government bodies.

Each of these groups contains thousands of organizations. Each organization may be unique in its own right, but nearly all will share the following basic similarities:

1. Each will have an objective or group of objectives toward which it is working.
2. Each will have a set of strategies designed to assist in achieving the basic objective or objectives.
3. Each will have a manager or managers who plan, organize, direct, and control the organization's activities, and who make numerous decisions of both a long- and short-term nature.
4. Each will have an organizational structure that shows responsibility relationships between various managers, and that shows line and staff relationships.

Exhibit 1–3
Organization of the controller's office

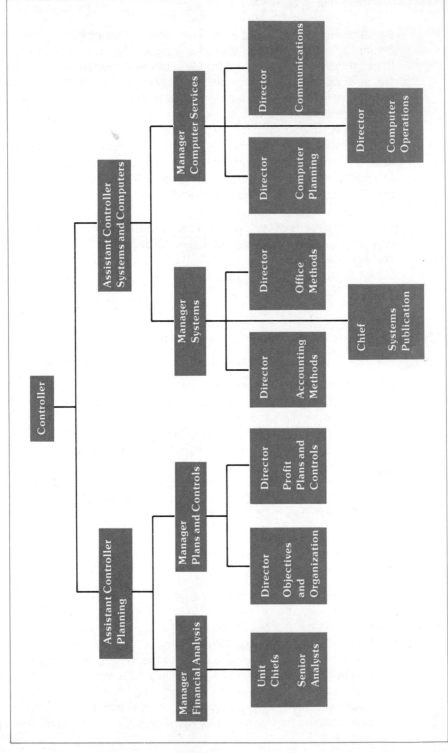

Source: W. Joseph Littlefield, "Developments in Financial Organizations: 1915–1965." *Financial Executive*, vol. 33, no. 9 (September 1965), page 14, supplement. Reproduced by permission from the Financial Executives Institute, Inc.

5. Each will have an insatiable need for information to assist in the execution of its strategies.

Because of these basic similarities, much of what we say in this book about managerial accounting and its uses will have almost universal application among organizations. To the extent that organizations differ, some of our topics will of necessity be more narrow in their focus. It is our intent, however, to be concerned with the nature and uses of managerial accounting data in all types of organizations; for this reason, the reader will find chapter examples and problems relating to organizations that are service-oriented as well as to those that are profit-oriented.

THE MANAGER'S NEED FOR INFORMATION

Information is the "motor" that makes management go. In the absence of a steady flow of information, management would be powerless to do anything. Fortunately, a large part of management's information needs are satisfied within the structure of the organization itself. As suggested by the organization chart in Exhibit 1–2, there are channels of communication extending throughout an organization through which the various levels of management can communicate. Through these channels, policies and instructions are submitted to subordinates, problems are discussed, formal and informal contacts are made, reports and memos are transmitted, and so on. Without these channels of communication, it would be impossible for management to function effectively.

The management of an organization also depends on specialists to provide a large part of its information needs. Economists, marketing specialists, organizational behavior specialists, accountants, and others all provide information to management and advise on various phases of the organization's activities. The economist, for example, provides information on contemplated economic conditions. The marketing specialist provides information essential to effective promotion and distribution of goods and services, and the organizational behavior specialist assists in the structure and functioning of the organization itself.

Accounting information

The information provided by accounting is essentially financial in nature, helping the manager to do three things:

1. Plan effectively and focus attention on deviations from plans.
2. Direct day-to-day operations.
3. Arrive at the best solution to the operating problems faced by the organization.

PLAN EFFECTIVELY. The plans of management are expressed formally as *budgets,* and the term *budgeting* is often applied to management planning generally. Budgets are usually prepared on an annual basis, and express the desires and goals of management in specific, quantitative terms. For example, the Discount Furniture Marts, Inc., plans sales by month a full year in advance. These plans are expressed as departmental budgets, which are communicated throughout the organization.

But planning is not enough. Once the budgets have been set, the president and other managers of the Discount Furniture Marts, Inc., will need information inflows that will indicate how well the plans are working out. Accounting assists in this information need, by supplying *performance reports* that help the manager focus in on problems and/or opportunities that otherwise might go unnoticed. If the performance report on a particular department indicates that problems exist, then the manager will need to find the cause of the problems and take corrective action. If the performance reports indicate that things are going well, then the manager's time is free to do other work. In sum, performance reports are a form of feedback to the manager, directing his or her attention toward those parts of the organization where managerial time can be used most effectively.

DIRECT OPERATIONS. The manager has a constant need for accounting information in the routine conduct of day-to-day operations. For example, as departmental managers in the Discount Furniture Marts, Inc., price new items going onto the display floor they will rely on information provided by accounting to ensure that cost/price relationships are in harmony with the marketing strategies adopted by the firm. The company's store managers will rely on other accounting information such as sales volumes and inventory levels as they attempt to prepare advertising programs. And the purchasing department manager will rely on still other accounting information in evaluating the costs of storage and handling. In these and a score of other ways the work of the accountant and the manager are inextricably connected in the conduct of day-to-day operations.

SOLVE PROBLEMS. Accounting information is often a key factor in analyzing alternative methods of solving a problem. The reason is that various alternatives usually have specific costs and benefits that can be measured and used as an input in deciding which alternative is best. Accounting is generally responsible for gathering available cost and benefit data, and for communicating it in a usable form to the appropriate manager. For example, the Discount Furniture Marts, Inc., may discover that competitors are making inroads on the company's business. In deciding between the alternatives of reducing prices, increasing advertising, or doing both in an attempt to maintain its market share, the company will rely heavily on cost/benefit data provided by accounting. It is important to note here that the needed information may not be in readily available form; in fact, accounting may find it necessary to do a large amount of special analytical work, including some forecasting, in order to prepare the needed data.

Information must be in summary form

An essential element of managerial accounting information is that it be in summary form. In your study of financial accounting you learned that an accounting system handles an enormous amount of detail in recording the results of day-to-day transactions. The bulk of this detail is of no interest to the manager, however. The manager's interest is in the *summaries* that are drawn from the accounting records, and it is on these that he or she relies. For this reason, we spend only a minimum of time in this book on the underlying detail in a managerial accounting system. The bulk of our time is spent on learning the *kinds* of summarized data needed by the manager, and learning how these data are *used* in directing the affairs of organizations.

COMPARISON OF FINANCIAL AND MANAGERIAL ACCOUNTING

In our discussion of managerial accounting we have noted that it differs in several ways from financial accounting. To assist the reader in a transition from the study of financial accounting to the study of managerial accounting, it is desirable at this point to summarize these differences, as well as to point out certain similarities between the two fields of study.

Differences between financial and managerial accounting

In all, we can identify eight major differences between financial and managerial accounting:

1. Managerial accounting focuses on providing data for internal uses by the manager.
2. Managerial accounting places much more emphasis on the future.
3. Managerial accounting is not governed by generally accepted accounting principles.
4. Managerial accounting emphasizes relevance and flexibility of data.
5. Managerial accounting places less emphasis on precision, and more emphasis on nonmonetary data.
6 Managerial accounting emphasizes the segments of an organization, rather than just looking at the organization as a whole.
7. Managerial accounting draws heavily from other disciplines.
8. Managerial accounting is not mandatory.

INTERNAL USES BY THE MANAGER.   For internal purposes, the manager does not need the same kinds of information as needed externally by stockholders and others. The manager must direct day-to-day operations, plan for the future, solve problems, and make numerous routine and nonroutine decisions, all of which require their own special information inputs. Much of the information needed by the manager for these purposes would be either confusing or valueless to stockholders and others, because of the form in which the information is prepared and used.

EMPHASIS ON THE FUTURE.   Since a large part of the overall responsibilities of a manager have to do with *planning,* a manager's information needs have a strong future orientation. Summaries of past costs and other historical data are useful in planning, but only to a point. The difficulty with summaries of the past is that the manager can't assume that the future will simply be a reflection of what has happened in the past. Economic conditions, customer needs and desires, competitive conditions, and so on, are constantly changing, all of which demand that the manager's planning framework be built in large part on estimated data that may or may not be reflective of past experience.

By contrast, financial accounting records the *financial history* of an organization. Financial accounting has little to do with estimates and projections of the future. Rather, entries are made in the accounting records only after transactions have already occurred.

GENERALLY ACCEPTED ACCOUNTING PRINCIPLES.   Financial accounting statements must be prepared in accordance with generally accepted accounting principles. The reason is that these statements are relied on by persons outside the organization. These outside persons must have some assurance that the information they are receiving has been prepared in accordance with some common set of ground rules; otherwise, great opportunity could exist for fraud or misrepresentation, and confidence in financial statements would be destroyed. The managers of a company, by contrast, are not governed by generally accepted accounting principles in the information which they receive. Managers can set their own ground rules on the form and content of information which is to be used internally. Whether these ground rules conform to generally accepted accounting principles is immaterial. For example, management might direct that for internal uses fixed assets be stated at appraised value, depreciation be ignored, revenue be recorded before it is realized, and that certain costs be omitted from inventory, even though all of these procedures would be in violation of generally accepted accounting principles. In sum, the managers are free to reshape data as they desire internally in order to obtain information in its most useful form.

RELEVANCE AND FLEXIBILITY OF DATA.   Financial accounting data are expected to be objectively determined, and to be verifiable. For internal uses, the manager is often more concerned about receiving information that is relevant and flexible than about receiving information that is completely objective or even verifiable. By relevant, we mean *pertinent to the problem at hand.* So long as information inflows are relevant to problems which must be solved, the manager may view objectivity and verification as matters of secondary importance. The manager must also have information that is flexible enough to be used in a variety of decision-making situations. For example, the cost information needed for pricing transfers of goods between sister divisions may be far different from the cost information needed for pricing sales to outside customers.

LESS EMPHASIS ON PRECISION.   When information is needed, speed is often more important than precision. The more rapidly information comes to a manager, the more rapidly problems are attended to and resolved. For this reason, the manager is often willing to trade off some accuracy for information that is immediately available. If a decision must be made, waiting a week for information that will be slightly more accurate may be considered less desirable than simply acting on the information that is presently available. Thus, in managerial accounting, estimates and approximations may be more useful than numbers that are accurate to the last penny. In addition, managerial accounting places considerable weight on nonmonetary data. Sales representatives' impressions concerning a new product, information on weather conditions, and even rumors could be helpful to the manager, even though this information is nonmonetary in nature.

SEGMENTS OF AN ORGANIZATION.   Financial accounting is primarily concerned with reporting of business activities for a company as a whole. By contrast, managerial accounting focuses less on the whole, and more on the parts, or segments, of a company. These segments may be the product lines, the sales territories, the divisions, the departments, or any other way that a company can be broken down. In financial accounting, it is true that some companies do report some breakdown of revenues and costs, but this tends to be a secondary emphasis. In managerial accounting, segmented reporting is the primary emphasis.

DRAWS ON OTHER DISCIPLINES.   Managerial accounting extends beyond the boundaries of the traditional accounting system, and draws heavily from other disciplines including economics, finance, statistics, operations research, and organizational behavior. These "outside" sources give managerial accounting a strong interdisciplinary flavor as well as a decidedly pragmatic orientation.

NOT MANDATORY.   Financial accounting is mandatory; that is, it must be done. Financial records must be kept so that sufficient information will be available to satisfy the requirements of various outside parties. Often the financial records that are to be kept are specified by regulatory bodies, such as the Securities and Exchange Commission (SEC). Even if a company is not covered by SEC or other regulations, it must meet certain financial accounting requirements if it is to have its statements examined by professional outside accountants. In addition, *all* companies must keep adequate records to meet the requirements of taxing authorities. By contrast, managerial accounting is not mandatory. A company is completely free to do as much or as little as it wishes. There are no regulatory bodies or other outside agencies that specify what is to be done, or for that matter, whether anything is to be done at all. Since managerial accounting is completely optional, the important question is always "Is the information useful?" rather than "Is the information required?"

Similarities between financial and managerial accounting

Although differences do exist between financial and managerial accounting, they are similar in at least two ways. First, both rely on the accounting information system. It would be a total waste of money to have two *different* data-collecting systems existing side by side. For this reason, managerial accounting makes extensive use of routinely generated financial accounting data, although it both expands on and adds to these data, as discussed earlier. Second, both financial and managerial accounting rely heavily on the concept of *responsibility,* or *stewardship.* Financial accounting is concerned with stewardship over the company *as a whole;* managerial accounting is concerned with stewardship over its *parts,* and this concern extends to the last person in the organization who has any responsibility over cost. In effect, financial accounting may be viewed as being the apex, and managerial accounting as filling in the bulk of the pyramid underneath, from a responsibility accounting point of view.

THE EXPANDING ROLE OF MANAGERIAL ACCOUNTING

Managerial accounting is in its infancy. Historically, it has played a secondary role to financial accounting, and in many organizations it still is little more than a by-product of the financial reporting process. Events of the last two decades have spurred the development of managerial accounting, however, and it is becoming widely recognized as a field of expertise separate from financial accounting.

Increased needs for information

Among the events which have spurred the development of managerial accounting we can note increased business competition, a severe cost-price squeeze, and rapidly developing technology. The changes brought about by these events have intensified the manager's need for information, and particularly for financial information beyond that contained in the traditional income statement and balance sheet. Consider the following:

Over the last two decades products have become obsolete at accelerating rates. Various scientific breakthroughs have resulted in the development of many new basic components, such as the transistor and the electronic "chip," which have literally revolutionized many industries and their products. Scientific researchers report that this "revolution" is only in its beginnings.

Dramatic changes have taken place in production methods over the last two decades. The term "automation" was coined in the early 1950s to describe a process that was new at the time. Today, many products are produced virtually untouched by human hands. Oil refinery operations are controlled by massive computers, machine tools are electronically controlled, and there are even some entire manufacturing plants where workmen do little more than monitor instrument panels.

Modes of management and methods of decision making have been affected by the development of powerful new quantitative tools such as linear programming, probability analysis, and decision theory. These new tools, which have come from the mathematical and statistical sciences, are becoming indispensable in day-to-day decision making.

Whole new industries have emerged as a result of various technological break-throughs. A few short years ago petrochemicals and laser beams were little more than laboratory novelties, and space exploration was little more than a dream. Today the petrochemical industry stands as a powerful competitive force in the business environment, laser beams are used in everything from cutting steel to delicate eye surgery, and students work amazingly complex mathematical computations on tiny electronic calculators that are a direct outgrowth of aerospace exploration.

In some industries, costs have more than doubled over the last ten years. These cost increases have forced the companies involved to make many adjustments, including modification of products, changes in methods of marketing, and the discovery of new sources and means of financing.

The economic impact of these and other factors has been far-reaching. As managers have grappled with the effects of increased competition, escalating costs, and evolving technology, the role of managerial accounting has expanded manyfold from what was common in earlier years. Looking to the future, we can expect this role to expand even further as new concepts and applications are explored and perfected.

The certificate in management accounting (CMA)

Specific recognition is given to the management accountant as a trained professional in the National Association of Accountants' (NAA) *Certificate in Management Accounting* program. The purpose and operation of the program are described in the following excerpts from a brochure issued by the NAA:

More and more people—inside the business world and out—realize the significant changes which have been taking place for years in accounting and in the role of the accountant in business. No longer is he simply a recorder of business history. He now plays a dynamic role in making business decisions, in future planning and in almost every aspect of business operations. This new accountant is called a Management Accountant and he sits with top management because his key responsibility is developing, producing and analyzing information to help management make sound decisions. Many management accountants make their way to top management positions.

In response to the needs of business and at the request of many in the academic community, the National Association of Accountants has established a program to recognize professional competence in this field—a program leading to the Certificate in Management Accounting.

The CMA program requires candidates to pass a series of uniform examinations and meet specific educational and professional standards to qualify for and maintain the Certificate in Management Accounting. NAA has established the Institute of Management Accounting to administer the program, conduct the examinations and grant certificates to those who qualify.

The objectives of the program are threefold: (1) to establish management accounting as a recognized profession by identifying the role of the management accountant and the underlying body of knowledge, and by outlining a course of study by which such knowledge can be acquired; (2) to foster higher educational standards in the field of management accounting; (3) to assist employers, educators and students by establishing objective measurement of an individual's knowledge and competence in the field of management accounting.

SUMMARY

Understanding organizations and the work of those who manage organizations helps us to understand managerial accounting and its functions. All organizations have basic objectives, and a set of strategies for achieving those objectives. The setting of strategy, sometimes called strategic planning, is one of the basic functions of the manager, as well as planning of a more short-term nature. In addition to planning, the work of the manager centers on organizing and directing day-to-day operations, controlling, and decision making.

The managers of an organization choose an organizational structure that will permit a decentralization of responsibility, by placing managers over specific departments and other units. The responsibility relationships between managers are shown by the organizational chart. The organization chart also shows which organizational units are performing line functions and which are performing staff functions. Line functions relate to the specific objectives of the organization, whereas staff functions are supportive in nature, their purpose being to provide specialized services of some type.

A large part of the information needs of management are provided within the structure of the organization itself. Channels of communication exist between various levels of management, through which information flows. Management also calls on various specialists to provide information, including the economist, the engineer, the operations research specialist, the accountant, and others. The information provided internally by the accountant is used by management in three ways: (1) to plan, and to monitor how well plans are working out; (2) to direct day-to-day operations, including setting prices, advertising policy, and so on; and (3) to solve problems confronting the organization.

Since managerial accounting is geared toward the needs of the manager, rather than toward the needs of stockholders and others, it differs substantially from financial accounting. Among other things, it is oriented more toward the future, it is not governed by generally accepted accounting principles, it has less emphasis on precision, it emphasizes segments of an organization (rather than the organization as a whole), it draws heavily on other disciplines, and it is not mandatory. The role of managerial accounting is expanding rapidly, and has become recognized as a field of professional study through which professional certification can be obtained.

KEY TERMS FOR REVIEW

At the end of each chapter a list of *KEY TERMS FOR REVIEW* is given. These terms are drawn from the chapter, and should be studied with care to be sure you understand their meaning. The list for Chapter 1 follows:

Managerial accounting	**Planning and control cycle**
Financial accounting	**Decentralization**
Organization	**Organization chart**
Strategic planning	**Line**
Organizing	**Staff**
Directing	**Controller**
Controlling	**Budget**
Feedback	**Performance report**
Decision making	

QUESTIONS

1–1. Contrast financial and managerial accounting.

1–2. What objectives might be important to the managers of a profit-oriented organization, other than earning a profit?

1–3. Assume that you are about to go into the retail grocery business. Describe some of the operating strategies you might follow.

1–4. A labor union is an organization. Describe a labor union in terms of what might be its objectives, its strategies, its organizational structure, the work of its managers, and its need for information.

1–5. Some persons consider strategic planning to be the most important work a manager does. In what ways might this be true? In what ways might it be false?

1–6. Assume that the central objective of a college basketball team is to win games. What strategies might the team follow to achieve this objective?

1–7. A Little League baseball team is an organization. Describe such a team in terms of its objectives, its strategies, its organizational structure, the work of its manager(s), and its need for information.

1–8. Managerial accounting isn't as important in the government as it is in private industry, since the government doesn't have to worry about earning a profit. Do you agree? Explain.

1–9. What function does *feedback* play in the work of the manager?

1–10. "Essentially, the job of a manager is to make decisions." Do you agree? Explain.

1–11. What is the relationship, if any, between information and decision making?

1–12. Choose an organization with which you are familiar. Prepare an organization chart depicting the structure of the organization you have chosen. (The organization you choose should be sufficiently complex so as to have at least one staff function.) Be prepared to place your organization chart on the board, if your instructor so directs.

1–13. One of the key responsibilities of an Accounting Department is to keep records for the entire organization. Why don't line managers keep their own records?

1–14. Managerial accounting information is sometimes described as a means to an end, whereas financial accounting information is described as an end in itself. In what sense is this true?

1–15. A student planning a career in management commented, "Look, I'm going to be a manager, so why don't we just leave the accounting to the accountants?" Discuss this comment.

1–16. Accountants are sometimes compared to journalists, in that accountants don't just "report" information to the manager, they "editorialize" the information. What implications does this hold for the accountant "managing the news" so to speak?

1–17. "The term controller is a misnomer, because the controller doesn't 'control' anything." Do you agree? Explain.

1–18. A production superintendent once complained, "Accounting is a staff function. Those people have no right to come down here and tell us what to do." Do you agree? Why or why not?

1–19. What are the major differences between financial and managerial accounting? In what ways are the two fields of study similar?

1–20. "If an organization's managerial accounting system functions properly it will provide management with all the information needed to operate with maximum effectiveness." Do you agree? Explain.

PART ONE

MANAGERIAL ACCOUNTING FUNDAMENTALS

Chapter 2

Cost terms, concepts, and classifications

As explained in Chapter 1, the work of management centers on (1) planning, which includes setting objectives and outlining the means of attaining those objectives, and (2) control, which includes the steps taken or means used to ensure that objectives are realized. In order to discharge planning and control responsibilities, the manager needs *information* about the organization. From an accounting point of view, the manager's information needs most often relate to the *costs* of the organization.

In financial accounting, the term cost is defined as the sacrifice made in order to obtain some good or service. The sacrifice may be measured in cash expended, property transferred, service performed, and so on. This definition is easily stated, and widely accepted in financial accounting.

In managerial accounting, the term cost is used in many different ways. The reason is that there are many different types of costs, and these costs are classified differently according to the immediate needs of management. In this chapter we look at some of these different types of costs, and at some of the ways in which managers classify the costs for their own use internally.

GENERAL COST CLASSIFICATIONS

Costs are associated with all types of organizations—business, non-business, service, retail, and manufacturing. Generally, the kinds of costs that are incurred, and the way in which these costs are classified, will depend on the type of organization involved. Cost accounting is as much applicable to one type of organization as to another; for this reason we shall consider the cost characteristics of a variety of organizations—manufacturing, merchandising, and service—in our discussion.

Manufacturing costs

A manufacturing firm is more complex than most other types of organizations. The reason is that the manufacturing firm is broader in its activities, embracing all functions of production, marketing, and administration. An understanding of the cost structure of a manufacturing firm therefore provides a broad, general understanding of costing that can be very helpful in understanding the cost structures of other types of organizations.

Manufacturing involves the transformation of raw materials into finished products, through use of labor and factory facilities. By contrast, *merchandising* is the marketing of products without changing their basic form or content. The cost of a manufactured product is made up of three basic elements:

1. Direct materials.
2. Direct labor.
3. Manufacturing overhead.

DIRECT MATERIALS.   A wide variety of materials can go into the manufacture of a product. These are generally termed raw materials. The term is somewhat misleading in that "raw materials" seems to imply basic, natural resources. Actually, raw materials is inclusive of any materials input into a product, and the finished product of one firm can become the raw materials of another firm. For example, the finished lumber products of a sawmill become the raw material of a construction company.

Direct materials are those materials that become an integral part of a company's finished product, and which can be conveniently traced into it. This would include, for example, the sheet steel in a file cabinet, or the wood in a table. Some items of materials may become an integral part of the finished product, but may be traceable into the product only at great cost and inconvenience. Such items might include the glue used to put a table together, or the welding materials used to bond the sheet metal in a file cabinet. Glue and welding materials would be called *indirect materials,* and would be included as part of manufacturing overhead.

DIRECT LABOR.   The term direct labor is reserved for those labor costs which are directly traceable to the creation of products. The labor costs of assembly line workers, for example, would be direct labor costs, as would the labor costs of carpenters, bricklayers, and machine operators. Labor costs which cannot be traced directly to the creation of products are termed *indirect labor,* and are treated as part of manufacturing overhead, along with indirect materials. Indirect labor would include the labor costs of janitors, supervisors, materials handlers, engineers, and night security guards. Although the efforts of these workers are essential to production, it would be either impractical or impossible to accurately relate the costs to specific units of product. Hence, such labor costs are treated as indirect labor.

MANUFACTURING OVERHEAD.   Manufacturing overhead can be defined very simply as including all costs of manufacturing except direct materials and direct labor. Included within this classification one would expect to find costs such as indirect materials, indirect labor, heat and light, property taxes, insurance, depreciation on factory facilities, repairs, maintenance, and all other costs of operating the manufacturing division of a company.

Manufacturing overhead is known by various names. Sometimes it is called manufacturing expense, factory expense, overhead, factory overhead, or factory burden. All of these terms are synonymous with "manufacturing overhead."

Manufacturing overhead combined with direct labor is known as *conversion cost.* This term stems from the fact that direct labor costs and overhead costs are incurred in the *conversion* of materials into finished products. Direct labor combined with direct materials is known as *prime cost.*

Nonmanufacturing costs

Traditionally, most of the focus of managerial accounting has been on manufacturing costs and activities. The reason is probably traceable to the complexity of manufacturing operations, and to the need for carefully developed costs for pricing and other decisions. However, costing techniques are now coming into use in many nonmanufacturing areas, as firms attempt to get better control over their costs and to provide management with more usable cost data.

Generally, nonmanufacturing costs are subclassified into two categories:

1. Marketing or selling costs.
2. Administrative costs.

Marketing or selling costs would include advertising, shipping, sales travel, sales commissions and salaries, and all other costs necessary to secure customer orders and to get the finished product/service into the hands of the customer. *All* organizations have marketing costs, regardless of whether they are manufacturing, merchandising, or service in nature.

Administrative costs would include all executive, organizational, and clerical costs which cannot logically be included under either production or marketing. Examples of such costs would include executive compensation, general accounting, secretarial, public relations, and similar costs having to do with the overall, general administration of the organization *as a whole.* As in the case of marketing costs, *all* organizations have administrative costs.

As mentioned earlier, the concepts of cost accounting are equally as applicable to nonmanufacturing activities as they are to manufacturing activities, although they have not always been viewed as so. Service organizations particularly are making increased use of cost concepts in analyzing and costing their services. To cite some examples, banks make use of cost analysis in determining the cost of offering various services, such as checking accounts, consumer loans, and credit cards; and insurance companies determine costs of servicing customers by geographical location, age, marital status, and occupation. Cost breakdowns of these types provide data for control over selling and administrative functions in the same way that manufacturing cost data provide for control over manufacturing functions.

Period costs

In addition to manufacturing and nonmanufacturing cost classifications, costs can be classified as being either *period* costs or *product* costs. Period costs are discussed in this section, and product costs are discussed in the following section.

Period costs are those costs which can be identified with measured time intervals, rather than with goods delivered or services provided. Office rent is a good example of a period cost. Assume that office rent is $500 per month. This amount will have to be paid each month without regard to the amount of business activity which occurs during the month. Thus, the office rent is matched against revenues on a *period* basis, and for this reason it is said to be a period cost.

All selling and administrative costs are treated as period costs, and deducted from revenues as incurred. Thus, advertising, executive salaries, secretarial salaries, general accounting, public relations, and other non-manufacturing costs as discussed in the preceding section would all be considered period costs, and will appear on the income statement as expenses on a time-period basis.

Product costs

Some costs are better matched against products produced than they are against periods of time. Such costs should not be treated as expenses in the period they are incurred; rather, they should be treated as expenses in the period in which the related products *are sold.* This means that if costs are incurred during one period, and the related products are not sold until a following period, then the costs should not be treated as expenses until the following period when sale takes place.

Costs of this type—called product costs—consist of those costs which are involved in the manufacture of goods, and include direct materials, direct labor, and manufacturing overhead. These costs are viewed as "attaching" or "clinging" to units of product as the units are produced, and remain attached until sale takes place. At that time, the costs are released as expenses and matched against sales revenues.

Exhibits 2–3 and 2–5 provide graphic and tabular views of product and period costs.

COST CLASSIFICATIONS ON FINANCIAL STATEMENTS

In your prior accounting training you learned that firms prepare periodic reports for creditors, stockholders, and others to show the financial condition of the company and the company's earnings performance over some specified interval. The reports you studied were probably those of merchandising firms, such as retail stores, which simply purchase goods from suppliers for resale to customers.

The financial statements prepared by a *manufacturing* firm are more complex than the statements prepared by a merchandising firm. As stated earlier, manufacturing firms are more complex organizations than merchandising firms, since the manufacturing firm must produce its goods as well as market them. The production process gives rise to many costs that do not exist in a merchandising firm, and somehow these costs must be accounted for on the manufacturing firm's financial statements. In this section we focus our attention on how this accounting is carried out, from a cost classification point of view.

The income statement

Exhibit 2–1 compares the income statement of a merchandising firm to the income statement of a manufacturing firm.

Notice in the case of a merchandising firm that the cost of goods sold simply consists of the purchase cost of the goods from a supplier. By contrast, the cost of goods sold in a manufacturing firm consists of many different costs which have been incurred in the manufacturing process.

Exhibit 2–1
Income statement data: Merchandising firms versus manufacturing firms

	Merchandising Firms		
The cost of goods sold to customers comes from the purchased cost of these goods from an outside supplier.	Sales		$50,000
	Cost of goods sold:		
	Opening inventory	$ 8,000	
	Add purchases	31,000	
	Goods available for sale	$39,000	
	Ending inventory	9,000	30,000
	Gross margin		$20,000
	Less operating expenses:		
	Selling expense	$ 9,000	
	Administrative expense	8,000	17,000
	Net income		$ 3,000

	Manufacturing Firms		
The cost of goods sold to customers comes from the manufacturing costs which have been incurred in the manufacture of the goods. These costs consist of direct materials, direct labor, and manufacturing overhead (see below).	Sales		$80,000
	Cost of goods sold:		
	Opening finished goods inventory	$10,000	
	Add cost of goods manufactured	55,000	
	Goods available for sale	$65,000	
	Ending finished goods inventory	15,000	50,000
	Gross margin		$30,000
	Less operating expenses:		
	Selling expense	$11,000	
	Administrative expense	10,000	21,000
	Net income		$ 9,000

Manufacturing Firms Schedule of Cost of Goods Manufactured		
Direct materials		$16,000
Direct labor		20,000
Manufacturing overhead:		
Indirect materials....................	$ 3,000	
Indirect labor	6,000	
Machine rental	500	
Utilities	1,700	
Insurance	1,300	
Depreciation–Factory	4,000	
Property taxes	2,000	18,500
Total manufacturing costs		$54,500
Add: Beginning work in process		10,000
		$64,500
Deduct: Ending work in process		9,500
Cost of goods manufactured		$55,000

The income statement of a manufacturing firm is supported by a schedule of *cost of goods manufactured* (see Exhibit 2–1). This schedule shows the specific costs which have gone into the goods which have been manufactured during the period. Notice that it contains the three elements of cost—direct materials, direct labor, and manufacturing overhead—which we discussed earlier as being the costs which go into any produced item. Also notice at the bottom of the schedule that one must add the beginning work in process to the production costs of a period, and then deduct the ending work in process, in order to determine the cost of goods manufactured. *Work in process* means goods which are only partially completed at the beginning or end of a period.

The balance sheet

The preparation of the balance sheet, or statement of financial condition, is also more complex in a manufacturing firm than in a merchandising firm. A merchandising firm has only one class of inventory—goods purchased from suppliers which are awaiting resale to customers. By contrast, manufacturing firms have three classes of inventory—goods purchased as raw materials to go into manufactured products (known as "raw materials"), goods only partially complete as to manufacturing at the end of a period (known as "work in process"), and goods completed as to manufacturing but not yet sold to customers (known as "finished goods").

The current asset section of a balance sheet of a manufacturing firm is compared to the current asset section of a balance sheet of a merchandising firm in Exhibit 2–2. The inventory accounts shown in these current asset sections constitute the *only difference* between the balance sheets of the two types of firms.

Exhibit 2–2
Current asset data: Merchandising firms versus manufacturing firms

	Merchandising Firms		
	Current assets:		
	Cash		$ 10,000
	Accounts receivable		60,000
A single inventory account,	Merchandise inventory		150,000
consisting of goods purchased	Prepaid expenses		3,000
from suppliers.	Total		$223,000
	Manufacturing Firms		
	Current assets:		
Three inventory accounts,	Cash		$ 15,000
consisting of materials to be	Accounts receivable		90,000
used in production, goods	Inventories:		
partially manufactured, and	Raw materials	$ 12,000	
goods completely	Work in process	60,000	
manufactured	Finished goods	140,000	212,000
	Prepaid expenses		4,000
	Total		$321,000

Product costs—A closer look

Earlier in the chapter we defined product costs as being the costs which go into the manufacture of goods. We need now to take a closer look at product costs to see more clearly how the costing process affects the income statement and balance sheet of a manufacturing firm.

Product costs are often called *inventoriable* costs. The reason is that partially completed units or unsold units go into inventory, and the costs involved in their manufacture follow them into the inventory accounts. Thus the term inventoriable costs. The concept of an inventoriable or product cost is a key concept in managerial accounting, since these costs can end up on the balance sheet *as assets* (either as work in process or as finished goods) if manufactured products are only partially completed or are unsold at the end of a period.

Exhibit 2–3 illustrates the cost flows in a manufacturing firm. Notice that direct materials, direct labor, and manufacturing overhead are added into work in process. As goods are completed, their cost is transferred from work in process into finished goods. As goods are sold, their cost is then transferred from finished goods into cost of goods sold.

Those costs which are placed in work in process initially are inventoriable or product costs. We indicated earlier that these costs would include

Exhibit 2–3
Cost flows and classifications

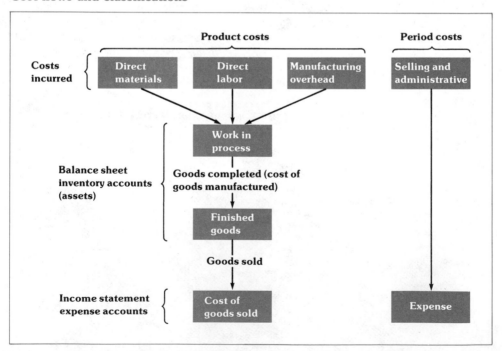

all costs associated with *operating the factory.* By contrast, selling and administrative costs and other costs associated with marketing and administration are not inventoriable costs, since they have nothing to do with the *manufacture* of a product. Rather, they are treated as period costs, and go directly to expense accounts as they are incurred.

AN EXAMPLE OF COST FLOWS.   To illustrate the flow of costs in a manufacturing organization, assume that a company's cost outlay for insurance is $2,000 annually, of which three fourths applies to operation of the factory and one fourth applies to selling and administrative functions. In this case, $1,500 of the insurance cost would be an inventoriable cost, and would be added to the cost of the goods produced during the year. This concept is illustrated in Exhibit 2–4, where $1,500 of insurance cost is added to work in process. As shown in the exhibit, this portion of the year's insurance cost will not become an expense until the goods which are produced during the year are sold (sale may not take place until the following year). Until the goods are sold, the $1,500 will remain as part

Exhibit 2–4
An example of cost flows in a manufacturing company

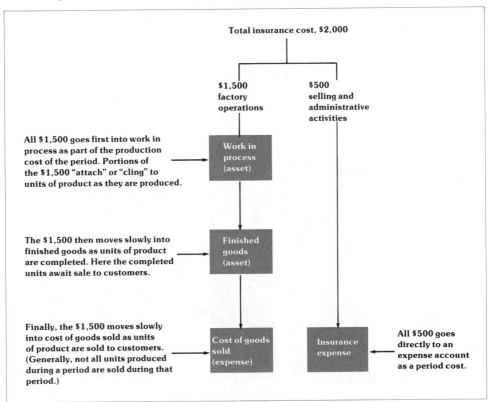

Exhibit 2–5
A summary of product and period costs

Type of firm	Product costs	Period costs	Treatment
Merchandising firm	Cost of purchased inventory from suppliers		Treated as an asset (inventory) until the goods are sold. Then the cost is taken to expense as cost of goods sold.
Manufacturing firm	Direct materials Direct labor Manufacturing overhead (consists of all costs of production other than direct materials and direct labor)		Treated as product costs. These costs go into inventory accounts until the associated goods are completed and sold. Then they are taken (released) to expense as cost of goods sold.

Both merchandising and manufacturing firms		Selling expenses:
		  Salespeople's salaries
		  Depreciation on sales equipment
		  Insurance on sales equipment
		Administration expenses:
		  Secretarial salaries
		  Depreciation on office equipment
		  Insurance on office equipment
			Treated as expenses immediately. Classified as *operating* expenses and deducted *from* gross margin.

of the asset, inventory (either as part of work in process or as part of finished goods), along with the other costs of producing the goods.

By contrast, the $500 of insurance cost which applies to the company's selling and administrative functions will go into an expense account immediately, as a charge against the period.

A SUMMARY OF PRODUCT AND PERIOD COSTS.   The chart in Exhibit 2–5 contains a summary of product and period costs in both manufacturing and merchandising firms.

The reader should study this exhibit with care, noting particularly the treatment of each type of cost as shown in the extreme right column.

FURTHER CLASSIFICATION OF LABOR COSTS

Of all of the costs of production, labor costs often present the most difficult problems of segregation and classification. Although firms vary considerably in their breakdown of labor costs, the following subdivisions represent the most common approach:

1. Direct labor (discussed earlier)
2. Indirect labor (part of manufacturing overhead)
    a. Janitors
    b. Supervisors
    c. Materials handlers
    d. Engineers
    e. Night security guards
    f. Maintenance
    g. Idle time
3. Overtime premium
4. Payroll fringe benefits

The costs under indirect labor should not be viewed as being inclusive, but rather as being representative of the kinds of costs that one might expect to find there. Certain of these costs require further comment.

Idle time

Idle time represents the costs of direct labor workers who are unable to perform their assignments due to machine breakdowns, materials shortages, power failures, and the like. For example, if a press operator earning $4 per hour works 40 hours during a given week but is idle for 3 hours due to breakdowns, labor cost would be allocated as follows:

Direct labor ($4 × 37 hours)	$148
Manufacturing overhead (indirect labor, as idle time) ($4 × 3 hours)	12
Total	$160

Overtime premium

The overtime premium paid to *all* factory workers (direct labor as well as indirect labor) is usually considered to be part of manufacturing overhead, and not assignable to any particular order or batch of production. At first glance this may seem strange; after all, overtime is always spent working on some particular order. Why not charge that order for the overtime cost? The reason is that production is usually scheduled on a random basis. If production is randomly scheduled, then it would be unfair to charge an overtime premium against a particular batch of goods simply because the batch *happened* to fall on the tail end of the daily scheduling sheet.

To illustrate, assume that two batches of goods, order A and order B, each take three hours to complete. The production run on order A is scheduled early in the day, but the production run on order B isn't scheduled until late in the afternoon. By the time the run on order B is completed, two hours of overtime have been logged in. The necessity to work overtime was a result of the fact that *total* production exceeded the regular time available. Order B was no more responsible for the overtime than was order A. Therefore, all production should share in the premium charge that resulted. This method of handling overtime premium is much more equitable as between production runs, and doesn't penalize one run simply because it happens to fall late in the day.

Let us again assume that a press operator in a plant earns $4 per hour. He is paid time-and-a-half for overtime (time in excess of 40 hours a week). During a given week he works 44 hours, and has no idle time. His labor cost for the week would be allocated as follows:

Direct labor ($4 × 44 hours)	$176
Manufacturing overhead (overtime premium) ($2 × 4 hours)	8
Total	$184

Payroll fringe benefits

The proper classification of payroll fringe benefits is not so clearly defined as idle time or overtime. Payroll fringe benefits are made up of employment-related costs paid by the employer, and include the costs of insurance programs, retirement plans, various supplemental unemployment benefits, and hospitalization plans. Many firms treat all such costs as indirect labor, by adding them in total to manufacturing overhead. Other firms draw a distinction between those payroll fringe benefits relating to direct labor costs, and those relating to indirect labor. In the case of direct labor, they are treated as additional direct labor cost; for indirect labor, however, costs of fringe benefits are added to manufacturing overhead.

The cost to the employer for fringe benefits is substantial. A recent nationwide survey by the Chamber of Commerce shows that fringe benefits, on the average, run 32.7 cents for every dollar of gross wages.

COSTS AND CONTROL

The cost classifications which are used to prepare financial statements may not be the same cost classifications which a manager uses to control operations and to plan for the future. For control purposes costs are often classified as variable and fixed, direct and indirect, and controllable and noncontrollable.

Variable and fixed costs

From a planning and control standpoint, perhaps the most useful way to classify costs is by behavior. *Cost behavior* means how a cost will react or respond to changes in the level of business activity. As the activity level rises and falls, a particular cost may rise and fall as well—or it may remain constant. For planning purposes, the manager must be able to anticipate which of these will happen, and if a cost can be expected to change, he or she must know by how much. To provide this information, costs are classified into two categories—variable and fixed.

VARIABLE COSTS. Variable costs are costs which vary, in total, in direct proportion to changes in the level of activity. A good example of a variable cost is direct materials. The cost of direct materials used during a period will vary, in total, in direct proportion to the number of units which are produced. To illustrate this idea, assume that a company produces automobiles, and that each auto produced requires one battery. As the output of autos increases and decreases, the number of batteries used will increase and decrease proportionately. If auto production goes up 10 percent, then the number of batteries used will go up 10 percent as well.

Notice that when we speak of a cost as being variable, we do so in terms of its *total dollar amount*—the total rises and falls as the activity level rises and falls. This idea is presented below, assuming that batteries cost $10 each:

Number of autos produced	Cost per battery	Total variable cost—Batteries
1	$10	$ 10
10	10	100
100	10	1,000
1,000	10	10,000

There are many examples of variable costs. In a manufacturing firm they would include direct materials, direct labor, and some items of manufacturing overhead (such as utilities, supplies, and lubricants). In a merchandising firm they would include cost of goods sold, commissions to salespersons, and billing costs.

FIXED COSTS.   Fixed costs are costs which remain constant, in total, regardless of changes in the level of activity. That is, unlike variable costs, fixed costs are not affected by changes in volume. Consequently, as the activity level rises and falls the fixed costs remain constant in total unless influenced by some external force, such as price changes.

This constancy can create difficulties in costing units of product, since the cost computed on a per unit basis will depend on the number of units being manufactured. As production increases, the average cost per unit will fall as the fixed cost is spread over more units; conversely, as production declines, the average cost per unit will rise since a constant fixed cost figure is being spread over fewer units. This idea is illustrated below, assuming a monthly rental cost of $5,000 for a piece of equipment which is capable of producing up to 1,000 units of product each month. The cost of the equipment expressed on a per unit basis is shown for 10-, 100-, and 1,000-unit levels of output:

Monthly rental cost	Number of units produced	Average cost per unit
$5,000	10	$500
5,000	100	50
5,000	1,000	5

Note that if the company produces only ten units the rental cost will average $500 per unit. But if 1,000 units are produced, the average cost will drop to only $5 per unit. More will be said later on the problems created for both the accountant and the manager by this type of variation in unit costs.

Examples of fixed costs include depreciation, insurance, property taxes, rent, supervisory salaries, and advertising.

Direct and indirect costs

Costs are often classified as being either direct or indirect. However, the terms have no meaning unless one first identifies some organizational segment to which the costs are to be related. The organizational segment might be a product line, a sales territory, a division, or other subpart of a company. A direct cost is a cost which can be obviously and physically traced to the particular segment under consideration. For example, if the segment under consideration is a product line, then the materials and labor involved in the manufacture of the line would both be direct costs. Manufacturing overhead, by contrast, would be an indirect cost of a product line. The reason is that manufacturing overhead is not directly identifiable with any particular product line, but rather is incurred as a consequence of general, overall operating activities. Indirect costs are also known as *common costs.* A key characteristic of all indirect (common) costs is that they must be allocated in order to be assigned to units of product or other segments of a company.

In sum, the following guidelines prevail in distinguishing between direct and indirect (common) costs:

1. If a cost can be obviously and physically traced to a unit of product or other organizational segment, then it is a direct cost with respect to that segment.
2. If a cost must be allocated in order to be assigned to a unit of product or other organizational segment, then it is an indirect (common) cost with respect to that segment.

Controllable and noncontrollable costs

Like direct and indirect costs, whether a cost is controllable or noncontrollable depends on the point of reference. *All* costs are controllable at some level or another in a company. Only at the lower levels of management can some costs be considered to be noncontrollable. Top management has the power to expand or contract facilities, hire, fire, set expenditure policies, and generally exercise control over any cost as it desires. At lower levels of management, however, authority may not exist to control the incurrence of some costs, and these costs will therefore be considered noncontrollable *so far as that level of management is concerned.*

A cost is considered to be controllable at a particular level of management if that level has power to *authorize* the cost. For example, entertainment expense would be controllable by a sales manager if he had power to authorize the amount and type of entertainment for customers. On the other hand, depreciation of warehouse facilities would not be controllable by the sales manager, since he would have no power to authorize warehouse construction.

In some situations there is a time dimension to controllability. Costs which are controllable over the long run may not be controllable over the short run. A good example is advertising. Once an advertising program has been set and a contract signed, management has no power to change the amount of spending. But when the contract expires, advertising costs can be renegotiated, and thus management can exercise control over the long run. Another example is plant acquisition. Management is free to build any size plant it desires, but once a plant is built management is largely powerless to change the attendant costs over the short run.

OTHER COST CONCEPTS

There are three other cost concepts with which we should be familiar as we start our study of managerial accounting. These concepts are differential costs, opportunity costs, and sunk costs.

Differential costs

In making decisions, managers compare the alternatives before them. Each alternative will have certain costs associated with it that must be compared to the costs associated with the other alternatives available. A difference in cost between one alternative and another is known as a *differential* cost. Differential costs are also known as *incremental* costs, although technically an incremental cost should refer only to an increase in cost from one alternative to another; decreases in cost should be referred to as *decremental* costs. Differential cost is a broader term, encompassing both cost increases (incremental costs) and cost decreases (decremental costs) between alternatives.

The accountant's differential cost concept can be compared to the economist's marginal cost concept. In speaking of changes in cost and revenue, the economist employs the terms marginal cost and marginal revenue. The revenue that can be obtained from selling one more unit of product is called marginal revenue, and the cost involved in producing one more unit of product is called marginal cost. The economist's marginal concept is basically the same as the accountant's differential concept.

Differential costs can be either fixed or variable. To illustrate, assume that Cosmetics, Inc. is thinking about changing its marketing method from distribution through retailers to distribution by direct sale. Present cost and revenues are compared to projected costs and revenues below:

	Retailer distribution (present)	Direct sale distribution (proposed)	Differential costs and revenues
Revenues (V)	$700,000	$800,000	$ 100,000
Cost of goods sold (V)	$350,000	$400,000	$ 50,000
Advertising (F)	80,000	45,000	(35,000)
Commissions (V)	0	40,000	40,000
Warehouse depreciation (F)	50,000	80,000	30,000
Other expenses (F)	60,000	60,000	0
Total	$540,000	$625,000	$ 85,000
Net income	$160,000	$175,000	$ 15,000
V = variable; F = fixed.			

The differential revenue is $100,000, and the differential costs total $85,000, leaving a positive differential net income of $15,000 under the proposed marketing plan. As noted earlier, those differential costs representing cost increases could have been referred to more specifically as incremental costs, and those representing cost decreases could have been referred to more specifically as decremental costs. The reader should be acquainted with all of these terms, since they are widely used in day-to-day business practice.

Opportunity costs

An opportunity cost can be defined as the potential benefit that is lost or sacrificed when the choice of one course of action requires the giving up of an alternative course of action. To illustrate, assume that a firm is considering the investment of a large sum of money in land which is to be held for future expansion. Rather than being invested in land, the funds could be invested in high-grade securities. If the land is acquired, the opportunity cost will be the investment income that could have been realized if the securities had been purchased instead.

Opportunity cost is not usually entered on the books of an organization, but it is a cost that must be explicitly considered in every decision that a manager makes. Virtually every alternative has some opportunity cost attached to it. In the example above, if the firm decided to purchase the securities rather than the land, opportunity costs would still be present: the costs associated with trying to obtain suitable land at an acceptable price at some later date.

In short, every alternative course of action facing a manager has a mixture of good and bad features. In rejecting a course of action, the good features must be given up along with the bad. The net good features of a rejected alternative become the opportunity costs of the alternative that is selected.

Sunk costs

A sunk cost is a cost that has already been incurred, and which cannot be changed by any decision made now or in the future. Since sunk costs cannot be changed by any present or future decision, they should not be used in analyzing future courses of action.

To illustrate the notion of a sunk cost, assume that a firm has just paid $50,000 for a special-purpose machine. Since the cost outlay *has been made,* the $50,000 investment in the machine is a sunk cost. What has happened in the past is done; by hindsight the purchase may have been unwise, but no amount of regret can relieve the company of its decision nor can any future decision cause the cost to be avoided. In short, the $50,000 is "out the window" from a decision point of view, and will have to be reckoned with regardless of what future course of action the company may take. For this reason, such costs are said to be sunk.

SUMMARY

Although the term "cost" has a fairly distinctive meaning in financial accounting, it can be used in many different ways in managerial accounting. In this chapter we have looked at some of the ways in which it is used by the manager in order to organize and classify data.

We have learned that costs can be classified as being either period costs or product costs. Period costs are incurred as a function of time, rather than as a function of goods produced. Product costs relate to goods produced, and basically consist of the costs associated with operating the factory. We have found that product costs fall into one of three categories—direct materials, direct labor, and manufacturing overhead. These costs go first into work in process. As goods are completed, the costs come out of work in process and go into finished goods. As goods are sold, the costs come out of finished goods and go into cost of goods sold. The costs of partially completed or unsold goods appear as assets on the balance sheet of a manufacturing company, as work in process inventory or as finished goods inventory.

We have found that costs can also be classified as being either variable or fixed, direct or indirect, and controllable or noncontrollable. In addition, we defined differential costs, opportunity costs, and sunk costs. A differential cost is the difference in cost between two alternatives. An opportunity cost is the benefit that is foregone in rejecting some course of action, and a sunk cost is a cost that has already been incurred.

All of these cost terms and classifications are basic to managerial accounting. We shall use them repeatedly, as well as refine them further, in chapters ahead.

KEY TERMS FOR REVIEW

Manufacturing	**Raw materials**
Merchandising	**Work in process**
Direct material	**Finished goods**
Indirect material	**Inventoriable costs**
Direct labor	**Cost behavior**
Indirect labor	**Variable costs**
Manufacturing overhead	**Fixed costs**
Conversion cost	**Direct costs**
Prime cost	**Indirect costs**
Marketing costs	**Controllable costs**
Administrative costs	**Differential costs**
Period costs	**Incremental costs**
Product costs	**Opportunity costs**
Cost of goods manufactured	**Sunk costs**

QUESTIONS

2–1. What are the three major elements in the cost of a manufactured product?

2–2. Distinguish between merchandising and manufacturing.

2–3. Distinguish between the following: (*a*) direct materials, (*b*) indirect materials, (*c*) direct labor, (*d*) indirect labor, and (*e*) manufacturing overhead.

2–4.   Explain the difference between a product cost and a period cost.

2–5.   Describe how the income statement of a manufacturing firm differs from the income statement of a merchandising firm.

2–6.   Describe how the balance sheet of a manufacturing firm differs from the balance sheet of a merchandising firm, so far as current assets are concerned.

2–7.   Why are product costs sometimes called inventoriable costs? Describe the flow of such costs in a manufacturing firm from point of incurrence until they finally become expenses on the income statement.

2–8.   Is it possible for costs such as salaries or depreciation to end up as assets on the balance sheet? Explain.

2–9.   Of what value is the schedule of cost of goods manufactured? How does it tie into the income statement?

2–10. Give at least three terms that may be substituted for the term "manufacturing overhead."

2–11. Dee Hibbert is employed by Acme Company. Last week she worked 34 hours assembling one of the company's products, and was idle 6 hours due to material shortages. Ms. Hibbert is paid $8 per hour. Allocate her earnings between direct labor and overhead.

2–12. Ronald Jones operates a stamping machine on the assembly line of the Dustin Manufacturing Company. Last week Mr. Jones worked 45 hours. His basic wage rate is $5 per hour, with time-and-a-half for overtime. How should last week's wage cost be allocated as between direct labor and manufacturing overhead?

2–13. Do payroll fringe benefits constitute a significant labor cost? Explain.

2–14. What is meant by the term "cost behavior?"

2–15. "A variable cost is a cost that varies per unit of product, whereas a fixed cost is constant per unit of product." Do you agree? Explain.

2–16. How do fixed costs create difficulties in costing units of product?

2–17. Why is manufacturing overhead considered to be an indirect cost of a unit of product?

2–18. Under what conditions is a cost controllable at a particular level of management?

2–19. Define the following terms: differential cost, opportunity cost, sunk cost.

2–20. Only variable costs can be differential costs. Do you agree? Explain.

EXERCISES

E2–1. The Dana Company plans to lease a barge for hauling freight. Two barges are available from the leasing company:

1. *Type A.* A conventional barge that would require the services of a captain and four helpers. The monthly lease cost would be $1,800, and monthly operating costs would be $650.

2. *Type B.* A largely automated barge that would require the services of a captain and two helpers. The monthly lease cost would be $3,000, and monthly operating costs would be $800.

A captain is paid $1,200 per month, and a helper is paid $800 per month. The company has equipment for loading barges, which is being depreciated at $2,400 per month. Each barge has a capacity of 400,000 tons, and operates at the same speed.

Required:

1. Prepare a schedule showing the differential costs in this decision situation. Which barge should be leased?
2. What sunk costs, if any, are present?

E2–2. Carey Products, Inc. produces automobiles. During March, 19x1, the company purchased 8,000 batteries at a cost of $10 per battery. It withdrew 7,500 batteries from the storeroom during the month. Of these, 200 were used to replace batteries in cars being used by the company's traveling sales staff. The remaining 7,300 batteries were placed in cars being produced by the company; 90 percent of these cars were completed in all respects by the end of March. Of the cars completed during the month, 20 percent were unsold at March 31.

There were no inventories of any type on March 1, 19x1.

Required:

As of March 31, 19x1, determine the cost of batteries that should appear in the following accounts:

a. Raw Materials.
b. Work in Process.
c. Finished Goods.
d. Cost of Goods Sold.
e. Selling Expense.

E2–3. Robert Peterson works on the assembly line of Carter Manufacturing Company. Mr. Peterson is paid $5 per hour. On Friday of last week Mr. Peterson worked ten hours, including two hours of overtime. The first six hours of the day were spent on product X and the last four hours were spent on product Y. The company authorized the overtime in order to be able to start the next week on a fresh batch of orders. Mr. Peterson receives time-and-a-half for overtime.

Required:

1. What portion of Mr. Peterson's labor cost should be allocated to product X? To product Y?
2. Should any portion of Mr. Peterson's labor cost be allocated to manufacturing overhead? Explain.

E2–4. The accounting records of Luxury Binders, Inc., show the following information for 19x7:

Beginning finished goods inventory	$20,000
Ending finished goods inventory	14,000
Beginning work in process inventory	7,000
Ending work in process inventory	9,000
Direct labor	12,000
Indirect labor	8,000

Maintenance of factory equipment	2,000
Insurance on factory equipment	500
Insurance on office equipment	300
Rent on factory facilities	5,000
Depreciation of office equipment	500
Direct materials	10,000
Indirect materials	1,000
Depreciation on factory equipment	1,500

Required:

1. Prepare a schedule of cost of goods manufactured for 19x7.
2. Prepare a schedule of cost of goods sold for 19x7.

E2–5. Classify the following costs as being inventoriable (I) or noninventoriable (N) in a manufacturing company:

1. Depreciation on salespersons' cars.
2. Rent on equipment used in the factory.
3. Lubricants used for maintenance of machines.
4. Salaries of finished goods warehouse personnel.
5. Soap and paper towels used by workers at the end of a shift.
6. Supervisors' salaries.
7. Heat, water, and power consumed in the factory.
8. Materials used in boxing units of finished product for shipment overseas.
9. Advertising outlays.
10. Worker's Compensation Insurance.
11. Depreciation on chairs and tables in the factory lunchroom.
12. The salary of the switchboard operator for the company.
13. Depreciation on a Lear Jet used by the company's executives.
14. Rent on rooms at a Florida resort for holding of the annual sales conference.
15. Replacement of small cutting tools broken on the assembly line.

E2–6. John Hyatt is employed by the Sarver Corporation, and works in the company's assembly plant. He assembles component parts that go into various of the company's products. During a recent week, Mr. Hyatt worked a total of 50 hours. His time was spent as follows:

Assembly of gearboxes (part of a finished product)	46 hours
Idle time	4 hours
Total time reported	50 hours

Mr. Hyatt is paid $8 per hour. The Sarver Corporation has determined that the cost to the company for payroll fringe benefits is $3 per hour. The company treats those payroll fringe benefits relating to direct labor hours as being added direct labor cost. Payroll fringe benefits relating to indirect labor are added to manufacturing overhead. Mr. Hyatt is paid time-and-a-half for time worked in excess of 40 hours per week.

Required:

1. Allocate Mr. Hyatt's wages for the week reported as between direct labor cost and manufacturing overhead.

2. Allocate the payroll fringe benefits for the week reported as between direct labor cost and manufacturing overhead.

E2–7. Selected cost information from the records of Arbor Company is given below for the month of March, 19x5:

Factory utilities	$14,000
Finished goods inventory, March 1	20,000
Finished goods inventory, March 31	22,000
Direct labor cost	18,000
Administrative salaries	6,000
Indirect materials	14,000
Factory insurance	4,000
Sales commissions	5,000
Other factory costs	10,000
Work in process, March 1	17,000
Work in process, March 31	11,000
Direct materials used in production	32,000

Required:

1. Prepare a schedule of cost of goods manufactured for March 19x5.
2. Prepare a schedule of cost of goods sold for March 19x5.

E2–8. The Meriwell Company was organized on May 1, 19x1. On that date the company purchased 7,000 plastic emblems, each with a peel-off adhesive backing. The front of the emblems contained the company's name, accompanied by an attractive logo. Each emblem cost the Meriwell Company $2.

During May, 6,800 emblems were drawn from the raw materials inventory account. Of these, 500 were taken by the sales manager to an important sales meeting with prospective customers, and handed out as a promotional gimmick. The remaining emblems drawn from inventory were affixed to units of the company's product. Of the units of product having emblems affixed during May, 80 percent were fully completed as to production during the month, and were transferred from work in process to finished goods. Of the goods fully completed as to production, 60 percent were sold during the month.

Required:

1. Determine the cost of emblems that would be in each of the following accounts at May 31, 19x1:
   a. Raw Materials.
   b. Work in Process.
   c. Finished Goods.
   d. Promotional Expense.
   e. Cost of Goods Sold.
2. Specify whether each of the above accounts would appear on the balance sheet or on the income statement at May 31.

PROBLEMS

P2–9. *Cost classification.* Various costs associated with the operation of a factory are given below.

1. Electricity for operation of machines.
2. A supervisor's salary.
3. Sand in a cement factory.
4. Lubricants for machines.
5. Direct labor payroll fringe benefits.
6. Property taxes.
7. Janitorial salaries.
8. Factory cafeteria food costs.
9. Laborers assembling a product.
10. Glue in furniture production.
11. Rent on a factory building.
12. Lease cost of equipment to produce units of product.
13. Sugar in soft drinks.
14. Plastic washers in auto production.
15. Peaches in a cannery.
16. Overtime premium, Assembly Department.

Classify each cost as being either variable or fixed with respect to volume or level of activity. Also classify each cost as being either direct or indirect with respect to units of product. Prepare your answer sheet as shown below:

	Cost behavior		To units of product	
Cost item	Variable	Fixed	Direct	Indirect
Example: Factory insurance		X		X

If you are unsure whether a cost would be variable or fixed, consider how it would behave over fairly wide ranges of activity.

P2–10. *Cost identification.* Jerry Genius has invented a new type of mousetrap. After giving the matter much thought, Jerry has decided to quit his $1,200 per month job with a computer firm and produce and sell the mousetraps full-time. Jerry has rented a garage which will be used as a production plant, and the rent has been paid for three months in advance at $150 per month. He has a number of tools and some equipment purchased several years ago at a cost of $4,000 which will be depreciated and used in production.

Jerry has rented a room in the house next door for his sales office. The rent is $75 per month. One month's rent has been paid. He has arranged for the telephone company to attach a recording device to his home phone to get off-hours messages from customers. The device will increase his monthly phone bill by $20. In addition, he is charged $0.50 for each message recorded on the device.

The cost of materials for each mousetrap will be $0.75. Jerry will supervise production, but the actual work will be done by employees who will be paid $0.50 for each completed mousetrap. Jerry has $5,000 in savings at 6 percent interest. The savings will be withdrawn and used to get the business going. Advertising will cost $300 per month.

For the time being, Jerry does not intend to draw any salary from the new company.

Required:

From the foregoing information, identify all of the examples you can of each of the following types of costs. (Note: A single item may be identified as more than one type of cost.)

- *a.* Variable cost.
- *b.* Fixed cost.
- *c.* Product cost.
- *d.* Selling or administrative cost.
- *e.* Opportunity cost.
- *f.* Differential cost (between the alternatives of producing the mouse-traps or staying with the computer firm).
- *g.* Manufacturing overhead cost.
- *h.* Sunk cost.

P2–11. *Cost behavior; Cost of goods manufactured.* The Toronto Company incurred the following costs for the month of April:

Materials used:
Direct materials	$6,600
Indirect materials	1,200

Payroll costs incurred:
Direct labor	6,000
Indirect labor	1,700

Salaries:
Production	2,400
Administration	5,100
Sales	3,200

Other costs:
Building rent (production uses one half of the building space)	1,400
Rent for molding machine	400 per month, plus $0.50 per unit produced.
Royalty paid for use of production patents (calculation based on units produced, $0.80 per unit)	?

Indirect miscellaneous costs:
Production	2,700
Sales and administration	1,800

The opening work in process inventory was $5,000; the closing work in process inventory was $3,000. You may assume that 1,000 units were produced during the month and transferred into finished goods.

Required:

1. Prepare a statement of cost of goods manufactured for the month.
2. Compute the cost to produce one unit of product.

(SMA, adapted)

P2–12. *Schedule of cost of goods manufactured, and cost behavior.* Various sales and cost data for Black Enterprises for 19x6 are given below:

```
Direct labor .....................  $ 18,000
Indirect labor ...................     5,500
Work in process, beginning .........  14,000
Work in process, ending ..........    13,500
Sales ........................       100,000
Selling expenses .................    10,000
Finished goods, beginning .........   10,000
Finished goods, ending ...........     9,000
Depreciation, factory ............    27,000
Administrative expenses ...........    8,000
Utilities, factory ..................   2,000
Direct materials .................    13,000
Maintenance, factory ..............    2,000
Indirect materials ................    4,000
Insurance, factory ...............     1,000
```

Required:

1. Prepare a schedule of cost of goods manufactured for 19x6.
2. Prepare an income statement for 19x6.
3. Assume that the company produced 10,000 units of product during 19x6. What was the unit cost for direct materials? What was the unit cost of factory depreciation? Assume that depreciation is a fixed cost, computed on a straight-line basis.
4. Assume that the company expects to produce 15,000 units of product during the coming year. What total cost and what per unit cost would you expect the company to incur for direct materials at this level of activity? For factory depreciation? Assume no change in cost behavior patterns.
5. As the manager responsible for production costs, explain to the president any difference in unit costs between (3) and (4) above.

P2–13. *Supply missing production and sales data.* Supply the missing data in the cases below. Each case is independent of the others.

	Case 1	Case 2	Case 3	Case 4	Case 5
Sales	$12,500	$18,000	$20,000	$10,000	$15,000
Opening finished goods	3,000	?	6,000	2,000	4,000
Cost of goods manufactured ..	11,000	?	11,000	8,000	?
Ending finished goods	?	4,000	7,000	?	3,000
Cost of goods sold	10,000	13,000	?	7,000	?
Gross margin	?	5,000	?	3,000	5,000
Operating expenses	1,500	2,000	5,000	1,000	1,500
Net income	1,000	3,000	5,000	2,000	3,500
Direct materials	3,000	2,000	5,000	3,000	4,000
Direct labor	4,000	4,000	3,000	?	2,000
Manufacturing overhead	?	3,000	5,000	4,000	2,000
Total manufacturing costs	?	?	?	9,000	?
Beginning work in process ...	2,500	5,000	?	2,000	?
Ending work in process	2,500	2,000	4,000	?	4,000
Cost of goods manufactured ..	11,000	?	?	8,000	9,000

P2–14. *Cost identification.* Mona Goodwin began dabbling in pottery several years ago as a hobby. She has enjoyed the pottery work so much that she has decided to quit her job with an aerospace firm and manufacture pottery products full time. The salary from Ms. Goodwin's aerospace job is $1,500 per month.

Ms. Goodwin has decided to manufacture the pottery in the basement of her home. The basement is now being used as a rental apartment, and is bringing in rental revenues of $200 per month. Ms. Goodwin has some pottery wheels and other equipment which cost $2,000 several years ago. These items will be depreciated and used in the pottery manufacturing operation. Ms. Goodwin has agreed to rent additional equipment from a rental company at a monthly fee of $200. The equipment will be used to manufacture the pottery. Two months' advance rent has been paid, which is not refundable.

Ms. Goodwin figures that the cost of clay and glaze will be about $1 for each finished piece of pottery. She will hire several workers to produce the pottery at a labor rate of $2 per pot. Having the manufacturing operation in her home will cause Ms. Goodwin's insurance to go up $25 per month. In addition, an answering device attached to her home phone for recording after-hours calls for orders will increase her monthly phone bill by $30. She is also charged $0.50 per call recorded on the device.

In order to sell her products, Ms. Goodwin feels she must advertise heavily in the local area. She has signed a contract with an advertising agency that will cost $250 per month for advertising services.

For the time being, Ms. Goodwin does not intend to draw any salary from the new company.

Required:

Prepare an answer sheet with the following column headings:

Name of the Cost	Sunk Cost	Variable Cost	Fixed Cost	Product Cost	Selling & Administrative Cost	Opportunity Cost

Differential Cost*	Manufacturing Overhead Cost

* Between the alternatives of producing the pottery or staying with the aerospace firm.

List the different costs associated with Ms. Goodwin's pottery operation down the extreme left column (under "Name of the Cost"). Then place an X under each heading which helps to describe the type of cost involved. There may be Xs under several column headings for a single cost (that is, a cost may be a sunk cost, a fixed cost, and a product cost; you would place an X under each of these column headings opposite the cost).

P2–15. *Cost identification.* The Crestwood Company specializes in a set of wood patio furniture consisting of a table and four chairs. The set enjoys great popularity, and the company has ample orders to keep production going at its full capacity of 2,000 sets annually. Cost data at full capacity follows:

Depreciation, factory building .... $ 10,000
General office supplies (billing)   3,000
General office salaries   60,000
Materials used (wood, bolts, etc.)   94,000
Advertising   50,000
Utilities, factory   20,000
Factory labor, direct   110,000
Factory supervision   40,000
Property taxes, factory building   5,500
Sales commissions   80,000
Insurance, factory   2,500
Depreciation, office equipment   4,000
Lease cost, factory equipment   12,000
Indirect materials, factory.............   6,000

Required:

1. Prepare an answer sheet with the column headings shown below. Enter each cost item on your answer sheet, placing the dollar amount under the appropriate headings. As examples, this has been done already for the first three items in the list above. Note that each cost item is classified two ways: first, as being either variable or fixed; and second, as being either a selling and administrative cost or a product cost. (If the item is a product cost it should be classified as being either direct or indirect, as shown.)

	Cost behavior		Selling or administrative cost	Product cost	
Cost item	*Variable*	*Fixed*	*cost*	*Direct*	*Indirect**
Depreciation, factory building		$10,000			$10,000
General office supplies (billing)	$3,000		$ 3,000		
General office salaries		60,000	60,000		

* To units of product.

If you are uncertain whether a cost would be variable or fixed, consider how you would expect it to behave over fairly wide ranges of activity.

2. Total the dollar amounts in each of the columns in (1) above. Compute the cost to produce one patio set.
3. Assume that production drops to only 1,000 sets annually. Would you expect the cost per set to increase, decrease, or remain unchanged? Explain. No computations are necessary.
4. Refer to the original data. The president's brother-in-law has considered making himself a patio set, and has priced the necessary materials at a building supply store. The brother-in-law has asked the president if he could purchase a patio set from the Crestwood Company "at cost," and the president has agreed.
   a. Would you expect any disagreement between the two men over the price the brother-in-law should pay? Explain. What price does the president probably have in mind? The brother-in-law?
   b. What cost term used in the chapter might be justification for

the president to charge the full, regular price to the brother-in-law, and still be selling at "cost?"

P2–16. *Statement of cost of goods manufactured, and cost behavior.* For the year ended June 30, 19x5, the following account balances have been taken from the cost records of Romney Products, Ltd.:

Indirect materials	$ 12,000
Indirect labor	65,000
Insurance	23,000
Depreciation, equipment	36,000
Rent, building	60,000
Direct materials	145,000
Utilities	8,600
Finished goods inventory, July 1, 19x4	115,300
Maintenance, equipment	9,000
Property taxes, factory	5,200
Work in process inventory, July 1, 19x4	34,500
Finished goods inventory, June 30, 19x5	?
Work in process inventory, June 30, 19x5	?
Direct labor	?

The cost of goods sold for the year was $466,200, the goods available for sale were $572,400, and total manufacturing costs were $468,800.

Required:

1. A statement of cost of goods manufactured in the form shown in Exhibit 2–1 in the text, and a statement of cost of goods sold.
2. Assume that the dollar amounts above relate to the equivalent of 20,000 units produced during the year. Compute the unit cost for direct materials. Compute the unit cost for rent on the building.
3. Assume that in 19x6 the company produces 32,000 units, and that implied cost behavior patterns persist. What per unit cost would you expect to be incurred for direct materials? For rent on the building?
4. As the manager in charge of production costs, explain to the president the reason for any difference in unit costs between (2) and (3) above.

P2–17. *Cost classification.* Listed below are a number of costs which might typically be found in a merchandising, manufacturing, or service company.

1. Janitorial salaries, factory.
2. Public accounting fees.
3. Fire insurance, factory.
4. Freight-out.
5. Cafeteria food costs, factory.
6. Wood in furniture manufacture.
7. Sandpaper, furniture manufacture.
8. Secretary, office.
9. Material handling labor, Assembly.
10. Idle time, Machining.
11. Salaries, Engineering Department.
12. Overtime premium, Assembly.
13. Depreciation, finished goods warehouses.
14. Lubricants for machines.
15. Rework costs, Machining.
16. Salespersons' entertainment costs.
17. Freight-in on materials used.

18. Billing costs.
19. Aerosol attachment on spray can.
20. Annual company picnic costs.
21. Advertising costs.
22. Packing supplies for shipment overseas.
23. Patterns and dies, auto manufacturer.
24. Glue for labels on bottles.
25. Salespersons' commissions.
26. Bad debts incurred.
27. Fringe benefits, factory labor.
28. Fringe benefits, general office.
29. Workers' compensation insurance.
30. Electricity, machine operation.
31. Training programs, general executive.
32. Sales manager's salary.
33. Samples used by salespersons.
34. Sand used in cement manufacture.
35. Filling compound used by a dentist.

Required:

Prepare an answer sheet with column headings as shown below. For each cost item, indicate whether it would be variable or fixed in behavior, and then whether it would be a selling cost, an administrative cost, or a manufacturing cost. If it is a manufacturing cost, indicate whether it would be direct or indirect to units of product. Three sample answers are provided for illustration. If you are unsure about whether a cost would be variable or fixed, consider whether it would fluctuate substantially over a fairly wide range of volume. There is no need to recopy the account descriptions on your answer sheet—just list the numbers 1–35 down the left side under "Cost item."

Cost item	Variable or fixed	Selling cost	Administrative cost	Manufacturing (product) cost	
				Direct	Indirect
Direct labor	V			X	
Executive salaries	F		X		
Factory rent	F				X

P2–18. *Statement of cost of goods manufactured, and cost behavior.* Selected account balances for the year ended May 31, 19x1 are provided below for Kenwood Company:

Insurance, factory	$ 12,000
Work in process, June 1, 19x0	?
Utilities, factory	24,000
Indirect labor	80,000
Finished goods, June 1, 19x0	85,000
Direct labor	?
Indirect materials	30,000
Work in process, May 31, 19x1	48,000
Rent, factory building	120,000
Finished goods, May 31, 19x1	?
Maintenance, factory	16,000
Direct materials used	160,000

The goods available for sale for the year totaled $659,000, the total manufacturing costs were $582,000, and the cost of goods sold totaled $581,000 for the year.

Required:

1. Prepare a statement of cost of goods manufactured in the form illustrated in Exhibit 2–1 in the text, and a statement of cost of goods sold.
2. Assume that the dollar amounts given above relate to the equivalent of 40,000 units produced during the year. Compute the unit cost for direct materials. Compute the unit cost for rent on the factory building.
3. Assume in 19x2 that the company produces 50,000 units, and that implied cost behavior patterns persist. What would be the per unit and total cost that you would expect to be incurred for direct materials? For rent on the factory building?
4. As the manager in charge of production costs, explain to the president the reason for any difference in unit costs between (2) and (3) above.

P2–19. *Preparing manufacturing statements.* The Carter Company has just completed operations for the year 19x3. The company's assistant accountant (who is very inexperienced) has prepared the following income statement for the year's activities:

CARTER COMPANY
Income Statement
For the Year Ended December 31, 19x3

Sales		$315,000
Operating expenses:		
Insurance expired during the year	$ 4,000	
Utilities paid during the year	10,000	
Direct labor cost	60,000	
Indirect labor cost	12,000	
Depreciation on factory equipment	16,000	
Raw materials purchased during the year	120,000	
Rent paid	40,000	
Selling and administrative salaries	32,000	294,000
Net income		$ 21,000

You have been asked to assist the Carter Company in preparing a corrected income statement for the year 19x3. The following additional information is available:

1. The Carter Company is a manufacturing firm that produces a product for sale to outside customers.
2. 80 percent of the rent paid applies to factory operations; the remainder applies to selling and administrative activities.
3. No raw materials were on hand on January 1. Some $15,000 of the raw materials purchased during 19x3 were still on hand at December 31. The remainder was used in production during the year.
4. 70 percent of the insurance expired, and 90 percent of the utilities paid apply to factory operations; the remainder apply to selling and administrative activities.

5.   Work in process and finished goods inventories were:

	January 1	December 31
Work in process	$42,000	$48,000
Finished goods	54,000	40,000

Required:
1.   Prepare a statement of cost of goods manufactured for 19x3.
2.   Prepare a corrected income statement for 19x3.

P2–20.   *Cost of goods manufactured, and cost of goods sold.*   The information given below was taken from the books of Shaw Manufacturing Company:
Inventories at January 1, 19x2:

Work in process $30,000
Finished goods 60,000

Inventories at December 31, 19x2:

	Work in process	Finished goods
Direct materials	$12,000	$18,000
Direct labor	20,000	40,000
Factory overhead	18,000	?
Total	$50,000	?

Other information for the year ended December 31, 19x2:

Cost of goods manufactured $630,000
Factory overhead (equal to 90%
   of direct labor cost) 225,000

No raw material inventories are maintained. Raw materials are purchased as used in production.

Required:
1.   Prepare a statement of cost of goods manufactured for the year 19x2.
2.   Assume the following additional information for the year 19x2:

Sales $750,000
Selling expenses 70,000
Administrative expenses 30,000

Prepare an income statement for the year.

P2–21.   *Statements from incomplete data.*   Sally Hardluck, the chief accountant of Foremost Enterprises, accidentally tossed the company's cost records into a wastebasket. Realizing her error, she raced to the incinerator but was successful in retrieving only a few scraps from the roaring blaze. From these scraps she has been able to determine the following facts about the current year, 19x4:

1.   Sales totaled $100,000 during 19x4.
2.   The beginning inventories for the year were:

Work in process $12,000
Finished goods 6,000

3. Direct labor is equal to 25 percent of conversion cost.
4. The work in process inventory decreased by $2,000 during 19x4.
5. Gross margin during 19x4 was equal to 55 percent of sales.
6. Manufacturing overhead totaled $24,000 for 19x4.
7. Direct labor is equal to 40 percent of prime cost.
8. Administrative expenses for 19x4 were twice as great as net income, but only 25 percent of selling expenses.

Ms. Hardluck must have an income statement and a schedule of cost of goods manufactured ready for the board of directors in an hour.

Required:

Prepare the income statement and schedule of cost of goods manufactured needed by Ms. Hardluck. The board wants these items in the format shown in Exhibit 2–1 in the text for a manufacturing firm.

P2–22. *Cost behavior; Manufacturing statement; Unit costs.* Polaris Company produces a single product. During the company's most recent year, production, costs, and sales were as follows:

Production in units	10,000
Costs:	
Direct materials used in production	$ 60,000
Direct labor	90,000
Building rent (production uses 80% of the space, administrative and sales offices use the rest)	50,000
Indirect labor	12,000
Royalty paid for use of production patent, $1 per unit produced	?
Utilities, factory	6,000
Rent for special production equipment, $7,000 per year plus $0.10 per unit produced	?
Other selling and administrative costs	40,000
Other factory overhead costs	24,000
Inventories:	
Work in process, January 1	40,000
Work in process, December 31	40,000
Finished goods, January 1	0
Finished goods, December 31	37,500
Direct materials, January 1	0
Direct materials, December 31	3,000 lbs.
Sales in dollars	$272,000

Direct material prices have not changed during the year. Four pounds of direct material are used to make one unit of finished product. The ending inventory of finished goods above is being carried at the average unit cost of production for the year.

Required:

1. Prepare a statement of cost of goods manufactured for the year.
2. Notice that the ending direct materials inventory above is stated in pounds. Determine the cost of this inventory.
3. Determine the number of units in the ending finished goods inventory.
4. Determine the unit selling price used during the year.
5. Prepare an income statement for the year. Show all computations.

Chapter 3

Cost accumulation for product costing

As discussed in Chapter 2, product costing is the process of assigning manufacturing costs to manufactured goods. An understanding of this process is vital to any manager, since the way in which a product is costed can have a substantial impact on reported net income, as well as on the current asset section of the balance sheet.

In this chapter we look at product costing from the *absorption* approach. The approach is so named because it provides for the absorption of all manufacturing costs, fixed and variable, into units of product. It is also known as the "full cost" approach. Later, in Chapter 6, we will look at product costing from another point of view, and then discuss the strengths and weaknesses of the two approaches.

THE NEED FOR FACTORY UNIT COST DATA

In studying product costing, we will focus initially on *unit cost of production,* an item of cost data generally regarded as being highly useful to managers.

Managers need unit cost data for a variety of reasons. First, unit costs are needed in order to cost inventories on financial statements. The units of product remaining on hand at the end of an operating period must have costs attached to them as the units are carried forward on the balance sheet to the next period.

Second, unit costs are needed for determination of a period's net income. The cost of each unit sold during a period must be placed on the income statement as a deduction from total sales revenue. If unit costs are incorrectly computed, then net income will be equally incorrect.

Finally, managers need unit cost data to assist them in a broad range of decision-making situations. Without unit cost data, managers would find it very difficult to set selling prices for factory output.[1] A knowledge of unit costs is also vital in a number of special decision areas, such as whether to add or drop product lines, whether to make or buy production components, whether to expand or contract operations, and whether to accept special orders at special prices. The particular unit costs that are relevant in this variety of decision-making situations will differ, so we need to learn not only how to derive unit costs, but also how to differentiate between those costs that are relevant in a particular situation and those that are not. The matter of relevant costs is reserved until Chapter 11. For the moment we are concerned with gaining an understanding of the concept of unit cost in its broadest sense.

TYPES OF COSTING SYSTEMS

The type of costing system used to measure unit costs will depend heavily on the nature of the manufacturing process involved. Basically,

---

[1] We should note here that unit cost represents only one of many factors involved in pricing decisions. Pricing is discussed in depth in Chapter 12.

two costing systems have emerged in response to variations in how the manufacturing process can be carried out. These two systems are commonly known as *process costing* and *job order costing.*

Process costing

Process costing is employed in those situations where manufacturing involves a single product that is produced for long periods at a time. Examples of industries that would use process costing include cement, flour, brick, and gasoline manufacturing. All of these industries are characterized by a basically homogeneous product that flows evenly through the production process on a more or less continuous basis.

The basic approach to process costing is to accumulate costs in a particular operation or department for an entire period (month, quarter, year), and then to divide this total by the number of units produced during the period. The basic formula for process costing would be:

$$\frac{\text{Total costs of manufacturing}}{\text{Total units produced (gallons, pounds, bottles)}}$$

$$= \text{Unit cost per gallon, pound, bottle}$$

Since one unit of product (gallon, pound, bottle) is completely indistinguishable from any other unit of product, each unit bears the same average cost as any other unit produced during the period. This costing technique results in a broad, average unit cost that applies to many thousands of like units flowing in an almost endless stream off of the assembly or processing line.

Job order costing

Job order costing is used in those manufacturing situations where many *different* products, jobs, or batches of production are being produced each period. Examples of industries that would typically use job order costing include special order printing, furniture manufacturing, and machine tool manufacturing.

These types of industries require a costing system in which costs can be assigned separately to each independent order (such as a special printing job) or batch of goods (such as a production run of ten special-purpose machines), and distinct unit costs determined for each separate item produced. Obviously, a job order costing system will entail problems of record keeping and cost allocation that are not present under the process costing system. Rather than dividing total costs of production by many thousands of like units, under job order costing one must somehow divide total costs of production by a few, basically unlike units.

Regardless of whether one is dealing with process costing or job order costing, the problem of determining unit costs involves a need for *averaging* of some type. The essential difference between the process and job order approaches lies in the way this averaging is carried out. Since the job order approach is the most versatile of the two costing methods, we will focus on it for our initial discussion of product costing.[2]

JOB ORDER COSTING—THE GENERAL OUTLINE

In the preceding chapter the point was made that there are three broad categories of costs involved in the manufacture of any product:

1. Direct materials.
2. Direct labor.
3. Manufacturing overhead.

As we study the operation of a job order costing system, we will look at each of these costs, and at the way in which each is involved in the costing of a unit of product. In studying job order costing, it is our purpose to gain a broad conceptual perspective of a cost accounting system, and of the way in which it provides data for the manager.

Measuring direct materials cost

The production process begins with the transfer of raw materials from the storeroom to the production line. The bulk of these raw materials will be traceable directly to the goods being produced, and will therefore be termed direct materials. Other materials, generally termed indirect materials, will not be charged to a specific job, but rather will be included within the general category of manufacturing overhead. As discussed in Chapter 2, indirect materials would include costs of glue, nails, and miscellaneous supplies.

Raw materials are drawn from the storeroom on presentation of a materials requisition form. A materials requisition form is shown in Exhibit 3–1.

Exhibit 3–1
Materials requisition form

Materials Requisition Number ___14873___		Date ___March 2, 19x2___	
Job Number to be Charged ___2B47___			
Department ___Milling___			

Description	Quantity	Unit Cost	Total Cost
M46 Housing	2	$123	$246
G7 Connector	8	52	416
			$662

---

[2] See Appendix A for a discussion of process costing.

The materials requisition form is a basic, detailed source document that forms the basis for entries in the accounting records.

The job cost sheet

The cost of direct materials is entered on a job cost sheet, similar to the one presented in Exhibit 3–2. A job cost sheet is prepared for each separate job initiated into production. Normally, the job cost sheet is prepared by the accounting department upon notification by the production department that a production order has been issued for a particular job. The production order is issued only on authority of a sales order from the sales department indicating that a firm agreement in terms of quantities, prices, and shipment dates has been reached with the customer.

Exhibit 3–2
The job cost sheet

JOB COST SHEET

Job Number   2B47   Date Initiated   March 2, 19x2
                                Date Completed

Department   Milling
Item   Special order coupling   Units Completed
For Stock

Materials		Direct Labor			Manufacturing Overhead		
Req. No.	Amount	Card	Hours	Amount	Hours	Rate	Amount
14873	$662						

Cost Summary		Units Shipped		
Materials	$	Date	Number	Balance
Direct Labor	$			
Overhead	$			
Total Cost	$			
Unit Cost	$			

As materials are issued, the accounting department makes entries directly on the job cost sheet, thereby charging the specific job noted on the sheet with the cost of direct materials used in production. When the job is completed, the total cost of materials used can be summarized in the "Cost Summary" as one element involved in determining the unit cost characteristics of the order.

Measuring direct labor cost

Direct labor cost is accumulated and measured in much the same way as direct materials cost. Direct labor would include those labor charges that are directly traceable to the particular job in process. By contrast, those labor charges that cannot be traced directly to a particular job, or that can be traced only with the expenditure of great effort, are treated as part of manufacturing overhead. As discussed in Chapter 2, this latter category of labor costs is termed indirect labor, and would include such tasks as maintenance, supervision, and cleanup.

Labor costs are generally accumulated by means of some type of work record prepared each day by each employee. These work records, often termed *time tickets* or *time sheets,* constitute an hour-by-hour summary of the activities and assignments completed during the day by the employee. When working on a specific job, the employee enters the job number on the time sheet and notes the number of hours spent on the particular task involved. When not assigned to a particular job, the employee enters the type of indirect labor tasks to which he or she was assigned (such as cleanup and maintenance), and the number of hours spent on each separate task.

At the end of a day, the time sheets are gathered and the accounting department carefully analyzes each in terms of the number of hours assignable as direct labor to specific jobs, and the number of hours assignable to manufacturing overhead as indirect labor. Those hours assignable as direct labor are entered on individual job cost sheets (such as in Exhibit 3–2), along with the appropriate charges involved. When all direct labor charges associated with a particular job have been accumulated on the job cost sheet, the total can be summarized in the "Cost Summary" section. The daily time sheets, in essence, constitute basic source documents used as a basis for labor cost entries into the accounting records.

Application of manufacturing overhead

Manufacturing overhead must be considered along with direct materials and direct labor in determining unit costs of production. However, the assignment of manufacturing overhead to units of product is often a difficult task. There are several reasons why this is so.

First, as explained in Chapter 2, manufacturing overhead is an *indirect* cost to units of product, and for this reason can't be traced directly to a particular product or job. Second, manufacturing overhead includes a conglomeration of unlike items, involving both variable and fixed costs. It ranges from the grease used in machines to the annual salary of the production superintendent. Finally, firms with strong seasonal variations in production often find that even though output is fluctuating, manufacturing overhead costs tend to remain relatively constant. The reason is that fixed costs generally constitute a large part of manufacturing overhead.

Given these problems, about the only acceptable way to assign overhead costs to units of product is to do so in an *indirect* manner, through an allocation technique. The approach is to choose some base, common to all jobs worked on during a particular period, which measures so far as possible each job's utilization of, or benefits from, the manufacturing overhead incurred. The trick, of course, is to choose the right base so that the overhead application will be equitable as between jobs. Probably the most widely used bases are direct labor-hours (DLH) and machine-hours, although direct labor cost is also used to some extent. Once a base is chosen, it is divided into the *estimated* total manufacturing overhead costs of the period in order to obtain a rate that will be used to apply overhead costs to jobs as they are processed.

THE NEED FOR ESTIMATED DATA. Notice our emphasis above on the use of *estimated* data in computing an overhead application rate. *Actual* overhead costs are rarely, if ever, used in overhead costing. The reason is that actual overhead costs are not available until after a period is over. This is too late for costing purposes, since prices must be set on customer orders, and other decisions involving costs must be made on a day-by-day basis as the year progresses. The postponing of such decisions until after the year is over would obviously destroy an organization's ability to compete effectively.

For this reason, rather than using actual overhead costs, most firms *estimate* total manufacturing overhead costs at the beginning of a year, and *estimate* the direct labor-hours (or whatever base is being used) that will be worked during the year, and develop an overhead rate *in advance* based on these estimates. An overhead rate based on estimated data is known as a *predetermined overhead rate*.

THE PREDETERMINED OVERHEAD RATE. The formula for computing a predetermined overhead rate is:

$$\frac{\text{Estimated total manufacturing overhead costs}}{\text{Estimated total units in the base (direct labor-hours, etc.)}}$$

$$= \text{Predetermined overhead rate}$$

In assigning overhead costs to the job cost sheet (and thereby to units of product), the predetermined overhead rate is multiplied by the number of direct labor-hours (or whatever the base is) worked on the job, and the total amount entered on the job cost sheet. To illustrate, assume that a firm has estimated its total manufacturing overhead costs for the year to be $300,000, and has estimated 100,000 total direct labor-hours for the year. Its predetermined overhead rate for the year would be $3 per direct labor-hour, as shown below:

$$\frac{\$300,000}{100,000 \text{ Direct labor-hours}} = \$3/\text{Direct labor-hour}$$

If a particular job required 54 direct labor-hours to complete, then that job would be allocated $162 (54 × $3) of manufacturing overhead cost. This allocation is shown on the job cost sheet in Exhibit 3–3.

Exhibit 3–3
A completed job cost sheet

JOB COST SHEET

Job Number __2B47__   Date Initiated __March 2, 19x2__
                                           Date Completed __March 8, 19x2__
Department __Milling__
Item __Special order coupling__   Units Completed __150__
For Stock _____

Materials		Direct Labor			Manufacturing Overhead		
Req. No.	Amount	Card	Hours	Amount	Hours	Rate	Amount
14873	$ 662	47	12	$ 36	54	$3/DLH	$162
14875	538	23	30	120			
14912	238	76	8	24			
	$1,438	18	4	20			
			54	$200			

Cost Summary		Units Shipped		
Materials	$ 1,438	Date	Number	Balance
Direct Labor	$ 200	3/8/x2	—	150
Overhead	$ 162			
Total Cost	$ 1,800			
Unit Cost	$ 12*			

* 1,800 ÷ 150 units = $12 per unit.

Exhibit 3–4
The flow of documents in a job order cost system

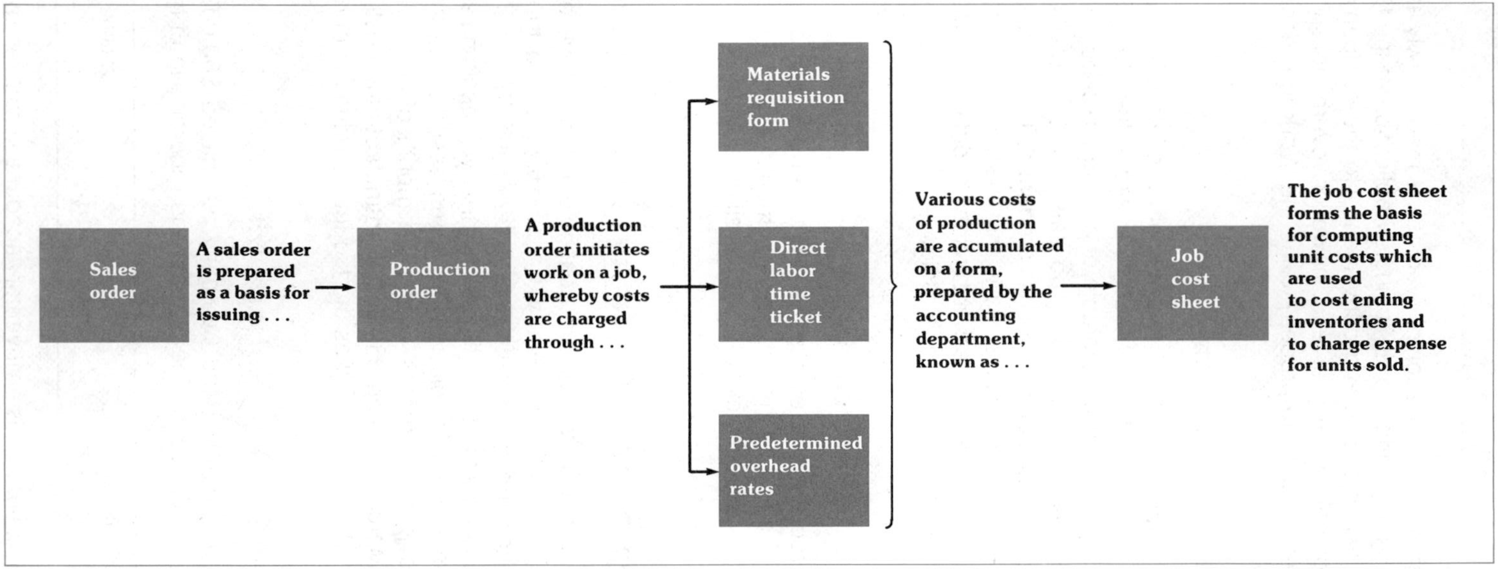

Sales order

A sales order is prepared as a basis for issuing...

Production order

A production order initiates work on a job, whereby costs are charged through...

Materials requisition form

Direct labor time ticket

Predetermined overhead rates

Various costs of production are accumulated on a form, prepared by the accounting department, known as...

Job cost sheet

The job cost sheet forms the basis for computing unit costs which are used to cost ending inventories and to charge expense for units sold.

Whether the application of overhead is made slowly as the job is worked on during the period, or in a single application at the time of completion, is a matter of choice and convenience to the company involved. If a job is not completed at year end, however, overhead should be applied to the extent needed to properly value the Work in Process inventory.

Computation of unit costs

With the application of manufacturing overhead to the job cost sheet, total costs of the job can be summarized in the "Cost Summary" section (see Exhibit 3–3 for an example of a completed job cost sheet). The cost of the individual units in the job can then be obtained by dividing the total costs by the number of units produced. The completed job cost sheet is then ready to be transferred to the finished goods inventory file, where it will serve as a basis for either costing unsold units in the ending inventory, or charging expense for units sold.

A summary of document flows

The sequence of events just discussed is summarized in Exhibit 3–4. A careful study of the flow of documents in this exhibit will provide an excellent visual review of the overall operation of a job order costing system.

JOB ORDER COSTING—THE FLOW OF COSTS

Having obtained a broad, conceptual perspective of the operation of a job order costing system, we are now prepared to take a look at the flow of actual costs through the system itself. We shall consider a single month's activity for a hypothetical company, presenting all data in summary form. As a basis for discussion, let us assume that the Rand Company had two jobs in process during the month of April. Job A was started during March, and had $30,000 in manufacturing costs already accumulated on April 1. Job B was started into production during April.

The purchase and issue of materials

During April, the Rand Company purchased $60,000 in raw materials for use in production. The purchase is recorded in Entry (1) below:

```
Raw Materials ..................................... 60,000
    Accounts Payable ............................         60,000   (1)
```

"Raw Materials" is an inventory account. Whatever raw materials remain in it at the end of a period will appear on the balance sheet under the inventory classification, as explained in Chapter 2.

ISSUE OF DIRECT MATERIALS.   During the month the Rand Company drew $50,000 in raw materials from the storeroom for use in production. Entry (2) records the issue of the materials to the production departments.

| Work in Process | 50,000 | |
| Raw Materials | | 50,000   (2) |

The materials charged to *Work in Process* represent direct materials assignable to specific jobs on the production line. As these materials are entered into the Work in Process account they are also recorded on the separate job cost sheets to which they relate. This point is illustrated in Exhibit 3–5.

Notice from the job cost sheets that Job A contains the $30,000 in manufacturing cost carried forward from the prior month, as does the Work in Process account itself. The reason the $30,000 appears in both places is that the Work in Process account is a control account, and contains a summarized total of all costs appearing on the individual job cost sheets for all jobs in process at any given point in time. (The Rand Company had only Job A in process at the beginning of April.) Of the $50,000 in raw materials added to Work in Process during April, $28,000 was assignable directly to Job A and $22,000 was assignable to Job B, as shown in Exhibit 3–5.

ISSUE OF BOTH DIRECT AND INDIRECT MATERIALS.   In Entry (2) above we have assumed that all of the raw materials drawn from inventory

Exhibit 3–5
Raw materials cost flows

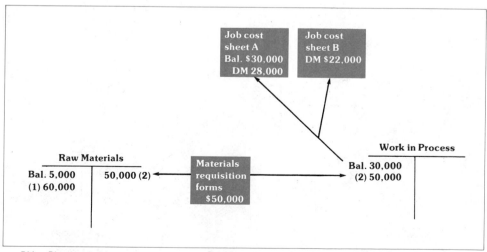

DM = Direct materials.

were assignable to specific jobs, as direct materials. If some of the materials drawn are not assignable to specific jobs, then they must be charged to Manufacturing Overhead, as indirect materials. The entry to record the issue of both direct and indirect materials into production is:

> Work in Process (direct materials) XXX
> Manufacturing Overhead (indirect materials) XXX
>   Raw Materials   XXX

Notice that Manufacturing Overhead is a separate account from Work in Process. The purpose of the Manufacturing Overhead account is to accumulate all manufacturing overhead costs as they are incurred during a period.

Labor costs

As work is performed in various departments of the Rand Company from day to day, employee time tickets are generated, collected, and for-

Exhibit 3–6
Labor cost flows

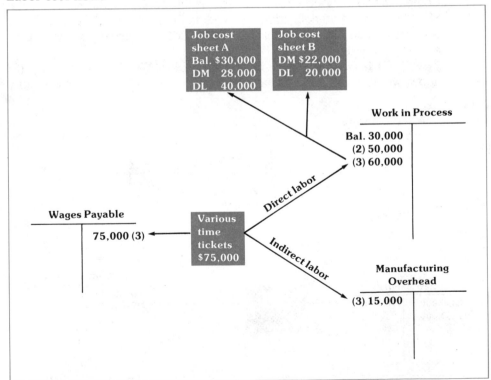

DM = Direct materials.
DL = Direct labor.

warded to the accounting department. There the tickets are costed according to the various rates paid to the employees, and the resulting costs classified in terms of being either direct or indirect labor. This costing and classification for the month of April resulted in the following entry:

Work in Process	60,000	
Manufacturing Overhead	15,000	
Salaries and Wages Payable		75,000 (3)

As with raw materials, the amount charged to Work in Process represents the labor costs chargeable directly to specific jobs. It will equal the total of the direct labor charges on the individual job cost sheets. This concept is illustrated in Exhibit 3–6.

The labor costs charged to Manufacturing Overhead represent the indirect labor costs of the period, such as supervision, janitorial work, and maintenance.

Manufacturing overhead costs

As we learned in Chapter 2, all costs of operating the factory other than direct materials and direct labor are classified as manufacturing overhead costs. These costs are entered directly into the Manufacturing Overhead account as they are incurred. To illustrate, assume that the Rand Company incurred the following general factory costs during the month of April:

Utilities (heat, water, and power)	$18,000
Rent on equipment	12,000
Miscellaneous factory costs	10,000

The entry to record the incurrence of these costs would be:

Manufacturing Overhead	40,000	
Accounts Payable		40,000 (4)

In addition, let us assume that the Rand Company recognized $25,000 in accrued property taxes during April, and recognized $5,000 in insurance expired on factory buildings and equipment. The entry to record these items would be:

Manufacturing Overhead	30,000	
Property Taxes Payable		25,000
Prepaid Insurance		5,000 (5)

Let us further assume that the company recognized $10,000 in depreciation on factory assets during April. The entry to record the accrual of depreciation would be:

```
Manufacturing Overhead .......................... 10,000
     Accumulated Depreciation .....................          10,000   (6)
```

In short, *all* manufacturing overhead costs are recorded directly into the Manufacturing Overhead account as they are incurred day-by-day throughout a period. Notice from the entries above that the recording of *actual* manufacturing overhead costs has no effect on the Work in Process account.

The application of manufacturing overhead

How is the Work in Process account charged for manufacturing overhead cost? The answer is, by means of the predetermined overhead rate. Recall from our discussion earlier in the chapter that a predetermined overhead rate is established at the beginning of each year, by estimating the amount of overhead cost which will be incurred during the year, and by dividing this estimate by some base common to all jobs to be worked on, such as direct labor hours. As the year progresses, overhead is then assigned to each job by multiplying the number of hours it requires for completion by the predetermined overhead rate which has been set. This process of assigning overhead to jobs is known as the *application* or *absorption* of overhead.

To illustrate the cost flows involved, assume that the Rand Company has used direct labor-hours in computing its predetermined overhead rate, and that this rate is $6 per hour. Also assume that during April, 10,000 hours were worked on Job A and 5,000 hours were worked on Job B (a total of 15,000 hours). The entry to record the application of manufacturing overhead would be (15,000 hours $\times$ $6 = $90,000):

```
Work in Process ................................. 90,000
     Manufacturing Overhead ......................          90,000   (7)
```

The flows of costs through Manufacturing Overhead are shown in T-account format in Exhibit 3–7.

The "Actual Overhead Costs" in the Manufacturing Overhead account in Exhibit 3–7 are the costs which were added to the account in Entries (3)–(6). Observe that the incurrence of these actual overhead costs [Entries (3)–(6)] and the application of overhead to Work in Process [Entry (7)] represent two separate and distinct processes.

THE CONCEPT OF A CLEARING ACCOUNT.   The Manufacturing Overhead account operates as a clearing account. As we have noted, actual factory overhead costs are charged to it as they are incurred day by day throughout the year. At certain intervals during the year, usually when a job is completed, overhead cost is relieved from the Manufacturing Over-

Exhibit 3–7
The flow of costs in overhead application

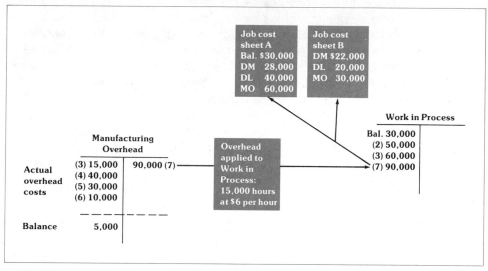

DM = Direct materials.
DL = Direct labor.
MO = Manufacturing overhead.

head account and is applied to Work in Process by means of the predetermined overhead rate. This sequence of events is illustrated below:

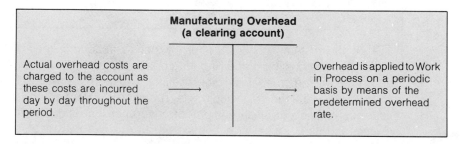

As we emphasized earlier, the predetermined overhead rate is based entirely on estimates of what overhead costs are *expected* to be, and is established before the year begins. As a result, the overhead cost applied during a year may turn out to be more or less than the overhead cost which is actually incurred. For example, notice from Exhibit 3–7 that the Rand Company's actual overhead costs for the period are $5,000 greater than the overhead cost which has been applied to Work in Process, resulting in a $5,000 debit balance in the Manufacturing Overhead account. We will reserve discussion of what to do with this $5,000 balance until a later section, "Problems of Overhead Application."

Nonmanufacturing costs

In addition to incurring costs such as salaries, utilities, and insurance as part of the operation of the factory, manufacturing firms will also incur these same kinds of costs in relation to other parts of their operations. For example, there will be these types of costs arising from activities in the "front office" where secretaries, top management, and others work. There will be identical kinds of costs arising from the operation of the sales staff. The costs of these nonfactory operations should not go into manufacturing overhead since the incurrence of these costs is not related to the manufacture of products. Rather, these costs should be treated as expenses of the period, as explained in Chapter 2, and charged directly to the income statement. To illustrate, assume that the Rand Company incurred the following costs during the month of April:

Top management salaries	$20,000
Other office salaries	12,000
Advertising	30,000
Other selling and administrative expenses	15,000
Total	$77,000

The entry to record incurrence of these costs would be:

Salaries Expense	32,000	
Salaries and Wages Payable	32,000	(8)

Advertising Expense	30,000	
Other Selling and Administrative Expenses	15,000	
Accounts Payable	45,000	(9)

Since these items go directly into expense accounts, they will have no effect on the costing of the Rand Company's production for the month. The same will be true of all other selling and administrative expenses incurred during the month, including depreciation of salesperson's automobiles, depreciation of office equipment, insurance on office facilities, rent on office facilities, and related costs.

Cost of goods finished

When a job has been completed, the finished output is transferred from the production departments to the finished goods warehouse. By this time the accounting department will have charged the job with direct materials and direct labor cost, and the job will have absorbed a portion of manufacturing overhead through the application process discussed earlier. A transfer of these costs must be made within the costing system that *parallels* the physical transfer of the goods to the finished goods warehouse. The transfer within the costing system will be to move the costs of the completed job out of Work in Process, and into the Finished Goods Inventory account.

In the case of the Rand Company, let us assume that Job A was completed during April. The entry to transfer the cost of Job A from Work in Process to Finished Goods would be:

```
Finished Goods ...............................  158,000
     Work in Process  ............................            158,000   (10)
```

The $158,000 represents the completed cost of Job A, as shown on the job cost sheet in Exhibit 3–7.

Since Job B was not completed by month-end, its cost will remain in the Work in Process Inventory account, and carry over to the next month. If a balance sheet is prepared at the end of April, the cost accumulated thus far on Job B will appear under the caption "Work in Process Inventory" in the asset section.

Cost of goods sold

As units of product in Finished Goods are shipped to fill customer orders, the unit cost appearing on the job cost sheets is used as a basis for transferring the cost of the sold items from the Finished Goods Inventory account into the Cost of Goods Sold account. If a complete job is shipped, as in the case where a job has been done to a customer's specifications, then it is a simple matter to transfer the entire cost appearing on the job cost sheet into Cost of Goods Sold. In most cases, however, only a portion of the units involved in a particular job will be sold. In these situations, the unit cost is particularly important in knowing how much product cost should be removed from Finished Goods and charged into Cost of Goods Sold.

For the Rand Company, we will assume that three fourths of the units in Job A were shipped to customers by month-end. The total selling price of these units was $225,000. The entries to record the sales would be:

```
Accounts Receivable  ...........................  225,000
     Sales  .....................................            225,000   (11)
```

```
Cost of Goods Sold  ...........................  118,500
     Finished Goods ...........................            118,500   (12)
     ($158,000 total cost × ¾ = $118,500)
```

With Entry (12) the flow of costs through our job order costing system is completed.

Exhibit 3–8
A summary of cost flows—The Rand Company

Accounts Receivable		Accounts Payable		Capital Stock	
XX			XX		XX
(11) 225,000			(1) 60,000		
			(4) 40,000		
			(9) 45,000		

Prepaid Insurance				Retained Earnings	
XX					XX
	(5) 5,000				

Raw Materials		Salaries and Wages Payable		Sales	
Bal. 5,000	(2) 50,000		XX		(11) 225,000
(1) 60,000			(3) 75,000		
Bal. 15,000			(8) 32,000		

Work in Process		Property Taxes Payable		Cost of Goods Sold	
Bal. 30,000	(10) 158,000		XX	(12) 118,500	
(2) 50,000			(5) 25,000		
(3) 60,000					
(7) 90,000					
Bal. 72,000					

Finished Goods				Salaries Expense	
Bal. 10,000	(12) 118,500			(8) 32,000	
(10) 158,000					
Bal. 49,500					

Accumulated Depreciation				Advertising Expense	
	XX			(9) 30,000	
	(6) 10,000				

Manufacturing Overhead				Other Selling and Administrative Expense	
(3) 15,000	(7) 90,000			(9) 15,000	
(4) 40,000					
(5) 30,000					
(6) 10,000					
Bal. 5,000					

Note: XX = Normal balance in the account (for example, Accounts Receivable normally carries a debit balance).
Explanation of entries:
    (1) The purchase of raw materials.
    (2) The issue of raw materials into production.
    (3) The recording of labor costs.
    (4) The recording of overhead costs.
    (5) The recording of overhead costs.
    (6) The recording of overhead costs.
    (7) The application of overhead costs into Work in Process.
    (8) The recording of salaries and commissions expense.
    (9) The recording of advertising and other selling and administrative expense.
    (10) The transfer of cost of goods manufactured into Finished Goods.
    (11) The sale of goods.
    (12) The recording of cost of goods sold.

A summary of cost flows

To pull the entire Rand Company example together, a summary of cost flows is presented in T-account form in Exhibit 3–8. The flows of costs through the exhibit are keyed to the numbers (1) through (12). These numbers relate to the numbers of the transactions (1) through (12) appearing on the preceding pages.

Exhibit 3–9 presents a schedule of cost of goods manufactured and a schedule of cost of goods sold for the Rand Company.

Exhibit 3–9
Schedules of cost of goods manufactured and cost of goods sold

Cost of Goods Manufactured		
Direct materials:		
Raw materials inventory, April 1	$ 5,000	
Add purchases of raw materials	60,000	
Total raw materials available	$65,000	
Deduct raw materials inventory, April 30	15,000	
Raw materials used in production		$ 50,000
Direct labor		60,000
Manufacturing overhead:		
Indirect labor	$15,000	
Utilities	18,000	
Rent	12,000	
Miscellaneous factory costs	10,000	
Property taxes	25,000	
Insurance	5,000	
Depreciation	10,000	
Actual overhead costs	$95,000	
Less underapplied overhead	5,000*	
Overhead applied to work in process		90,000
Total manufacturing costs		$200,000
Add: Beginning work in process		30,000
		$230,000
Deduct: Ending work in process		72,000
Cost of goods manufactured		$158,000
Cost of Goods Sold		
Opening finished goods inventory		$ 10,000
Add cost of goods manufactured		158,000
Goods available for sale		$168,000
Ending finished goods inventory		49,500
Cost of goods sold		$118,500

* Notice that underapplied overhead must be deducted from actual overhead costs, and only the difference ($90,000 above) added to direct materials and direct labor. The reason is that the schedule of Cost of Goods Manufactured represents a summary of costs flowing through the Work in Process account during a period, and therefore must exclude any overhead costs which were incurred but never applied to production. If a reverse situation had existed and overhead had been overapplied during the period, then the amount of overapplied overhead would have been added to actual overhead costs on the schedule. This would have brought the actual overhead costs up to the amount which had been applied to production.

See Exhibit 3–10 for an illustration of how the $5,000 underapplied overhead above is handled on the income statement.

PROBLEMS OF OVERHEAD APPLICATION

The concept of underapplied and overapplied overhead

Since the predetermined overhead rate is established before a period begins, and is based entirely on estimated data, there generally will be a difference between the amount of overhead cost which is applied to Work in Process and the actual overhead costs which materialize during the period. In the case of the Rand Company, for example, the predetermined overhead rate of $6 per hour resulted in $90,000 of overhead cost being applied to Work in Process, whereas actual overhead costs proved to be $95,000 for the month (see Exhibit 3–7). The difference between the overhead cost applied to Work in Process and the actual overhead costs of a period is termed either *underapplied* or *overapplied* overhead. For the Rand Company, overhead was underapplied, because the applied cost ($90,000) was $5,000 less than the actual cost ($95,000). Had the tables been reversed, and the company applied $95,000 in overhead cost to Work in Process, while incurring actual overhead costs of only $90,000, then a situation of overapplied overhead would have existed.

Since the amount of overhead applied to Work in Process is dependent on the predetermined overhead rate, any difference between applied overhead cost and actual overhead cost must be traceable to the estimates going into its computation. To illustrate, refer again to the formula used in computing the predetermined overhead rate:

$$\frac{\text{Estimated total manufacturing overhead costs}}{\text{Estimated total units in the base (direct labor-hours, etc.)}}$$
$$= \text{Predetermined overhead rate}$$

If either the estimated cost or the estimated level of activity used in this formula differs from the actual cost or the actual level of activity for a period, then the predetermined overhead rate will prove to be inaccurate, and either under- or overapplied overhead will result. Assume, for example, that two firms have prepared the following estimated data for the year 19x1:

	Company A	Company B
Predetermined overhead rate based on	Machine-hours	Direct labor cost
Estimated manufacturing overhead for 19x1 . .	$100,000 (*a*)	$120,000 (*a*)
Estimated machine-hours for 19x1	50,000 (*b*)	—
Estimated direct labor cost for 19x1	—	$ 80,000 (*b*)
Predetermined overhead rate (*a*) ÷ (*b*)	$2 per machine-hour	150% of direct labor cost

Now assume that the *actual* overhead costs and the *actual* level of activity for 19x1 for each firm are as shown below:

	Company A	Company B
Actual manufacturing overhead costs	$99,000	$128,000
Actual machine-hours	48,000	—
Actual direct labor cost	—	$ 88,000

For each company, notice that the actual cost and activity data differ from the estimates used in computing the predetermined overhead rate. The computation of the resulting under- or overapplied overhead for each company is given below:

	Company A	Company B
Actual manufacturing overhead costs	$99,000	$128,000
Manufacturing overhead applied to work in process during 19x1:		
48,000 *actual* machine-hours × $2	96,000	
$88,000 *actual* direct labor cost × 150%		132,000
Underapplied (overapplied) overhead	$ 3,000	($ 4,000)

For Company A, notice that the amount of overhead cost which has been applied to Work in Process ($96,000) is less than the actual overhead cost for the year ($99,000). Therefore, overhead is underapplied. Also notice that the original estimate of overhead in Company A ($100,000) is not directly involved in this computation. Its impact is felt only through the $2 predetermined overhead rate which is used.

For Company B, the amount of overhead cost which has been applied to Work in Process ($132,000) is greater than the actual overhead cost for the year ($128,000), and so a situation of overapplied overhead exists.

Disposition of under- or overapplied overhead balances

What disposition should be made of any under- or overapplied balance remaining in the manufacturing overhead account at the end of a period? Generally any balance in the account is treated in one of two ways:

1. Closed out to Cost of Goods Sold.
2. Allocated between Work in Process, Finished Goods, and Cost of Goods Sold, in proportion to the ending balances in these accounts.

CLOSED OUT TO COST OF GOODS SOLD. Most firms close any under- or overapplied overhead out to Cost of Goods Sold, since this approach is simpler than allocation. Returning to the example of the Rand Company, we see that the entry to close the underapplied overhead to Cost of Goods Sold would be (see Exhibit 3–8 for the $5,000 cost figure):

Cost of Goods Sold	5,000	
Manufacturing Overhead		5,000 (13)

With this entry, the Cost of Goods Sold for the month increases to $123,500:

Original Cost of Goods Sold (from Exhibit 3–8 or Exhibit 3–9)	$118,500
Add underapplied overhead from Entry (13)	5,000
Cost of Goods Sold	$123,500

An income statement for the Rand Company for April would therefore appear as shown in Exhibit 3–10.

Exhibit 3–10

THE RAND COMPANY
Income Statement
For the Month of April, 19xx

Sales		$225,000
Less cost of goods sold ($118,500 + $5,000)		123,500
Gross margin		$101,500
Less selling and administrative expenses:		
Salaries expense	$32,000	
Advertising expense	30,000	
Other expense	15,000	77,000
Net income		$ 24,500

ALLOCATED BETWEEN ACCOUNTS. Allocation of under- or overapplied overhead between Work in Process, Finished Goods, and Cost of Goods Sold is more accurate than closing the entire balance into Cost of Goods Sold, since allocation assigns overhead costs to where they would have gone in the first place had it not been for the errors in the estimates going into the predetermined overhead rate. Although allocation is more accurate than direct write-off, it is used less often in actual practice, because of the time and difficulty involved in the allocation process. Most firms feel that the greater accuracy simply isn't worth the extra effort that allocation requires, particularly when the dollar amounts are small.

A general model of product cost flows

The flow of costs in a product costing system can be presented in general model form, as shown in Exhibit 3–11. This model applies as much to a process costing system as it does to a job order costing system. Visual inspection of the model can be very helpful in gaining a perspective as to how costs enter a system, flow through it, and finally end up as cost of goods sold on the income statement.

Exhibit 3–11
A general model of cost flows

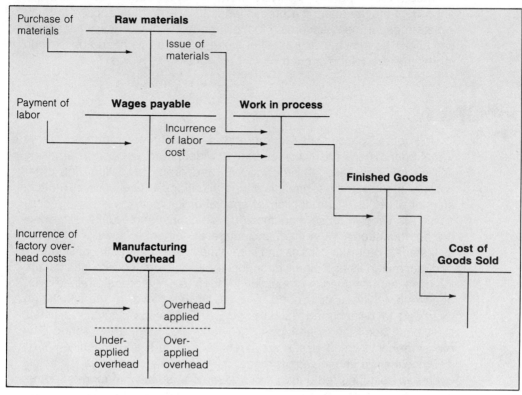

Multiple overhead rates

Our discussion in this chapter has assumed that a single overhead rate was being used throughout an entire factory operation. In small companies, and even in some medium-sized companies, a single overhead rate will be used (called a "plantwide" rate) and is entirely adequate as a means of allocating overhead costs to production jobs. But in larger companies multiple overhead rates are common, for the reason that a single rate may not be capable of equitably handling the overhead costs of all departments. One department may be labor-intensive, for example, and rely almost solely on the efforts of workers in performing needed functions. Allocation of overhead costs in such a department could, perhaps, be done most equitably on a basis of labor-hours or labor cost. Another department in the same factory may be machine-intensive, requiring little in the way of worker effort. Allocation of overhead costs in this department could, perhaps, be done most equitably on a basis of machine-hours.

In short, larger sized organizations will often have many predetermined overhead rates—perhaps a different one for each department. As a unit of product moves along the production line, overhead is applied in each separate department, according to the various overhead rates which have been set. The accumulation of all of these different overhead applications represents the total overhead cost of the job.

SUMMARY

Unit cost of production is one of the most useful items of cost data to a manager. There are two methods in widespread use for determining unit costs. These are job order costing and process costing. Job order costing is used in those manufacturing situations where units of product are not alike, as in production of special-order machine tools. Process costing is used in those manufacturing situations where units of product are homogeneous, as in the manufacture of cement.

Materials requisition forms and labor time tickets control the assignment of direct materials and direct labor cost to production. Indirect manufacturing costs are assigned to production through use of a predetermined overhead rate, which is developed by estimating the level of manufacturing overhead to be incurred during a period and by dividing this estimate by a base common to all jobs to be worked on during the period. The most frequently used bases are direct labor-hours and machine-hours.

Since the predetermined overhead rate is based on estimates, the actual overhead cost incurred during a period may be somewhat more or somewhat less than the amount of overhead applied to production. Such a difference is referred to as underapplied or overapplied overhead. The underapplied or overapplied overhead of a period can be either (1) closed out to Cost of Goods Sold, or (2) allocated between Work in Process, Finished Goods, and Cost of Goods Sold.

The detailed discussion in the chapter has focused on job order costing. A discussion of process costing is contained in Appendix A following, for those who wish to study this costing method in more depth.

KEY TERMS FOR REVIEW

Absorption cost	**Time ticket**
Full cost	**Predetermined overhead rate**
Process costing system	**Overhead application**
Job order costing system	**Underapplied overhead**
Materials requisition form	**Overapplied overhead**
Job cost sheet	**Multiple overhead rates**

APPENDIX A: PROCESS COSTING AND THE CONCEPT OF EQUIVALENT UNITS

In the main body of the chapter we stated that firms which produce basically homogeneous products such as bricks, flour, and cement employ a costing approach known as *process* costing. Process costing is generally used in place of job order costing whenever a firm has units of product that are indistinguishable from each other, and which flow in a constant stream off of an assembly line or out of a processing plant. Our purpose in this section is to look at some of the more important features of process costing systems.

COMPUTING UNIT COSTS

Several basic steps are involved in the structure and operation of a process costing system. These steps can be outlined as follows:

1. Identify individual processing centers.
2. Accumulate the material and processing costs for each separate processing center over some specified period.
3. Measure the output of each separate processing center.
4. Divide the material and processing costs by the period's output to get the unit cost of production for each separate processing center.
5. Add the unit costs of each separate processing center to get the total cost for a fully processed unit of product.

We will now examine each of these steps in some detail.

Identify processing centers

Processing centers are locations in the factory where work is done directly on the goods being produced. For example, a brick factory might have two processing centers—one for mixing and molding clay into brick form, and one for firing the molded brick. There are two critical features to any processing center. First, the activity performed in the processing center must be performed uniformly on all units going through it. And second, the output of the processing center must be homogeneous.

The processing centers for producing a product such as bricks would probably be organized in a *sequential* pattern. Sequential processing centers are illustrated in Exhibit 3–12. The flow of units goes from left to right, with all units undergoing processing in all processing centers.

A different type of processing pattern, known as *parallel* processing, is required in some firms. Parallel processing is used in those situations where all units do not go through all processing centers. For example, the petroleum industry may input crude oil into one processing center

Exhibit 3–12
Sequential processing centers

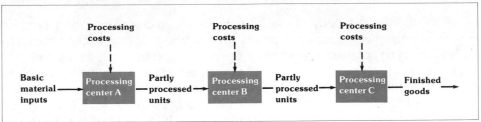

Exhibit 3–13
Parallel processing centers

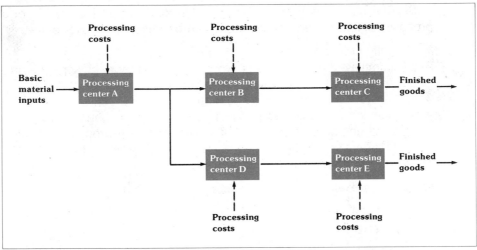

and then use the refined output for further processing into several different end products. Each end product may undergo several steps of further processing after the initial refining, some of which may be shared with other end products and some of which may not. The concept of parallel processing is illustrated in Exhibit 3–13.

Accumulate material and processing costs

Cost accumulation is simpler in a process costing situation than in a job order costing situation. The reason is that costs only need to be identified by processing center—not by separate jobs. This means that costs can be accumulated for longer periods of time, and that just one allocation is needed at the end of a period to assign the accumulated costs to the period's output.

Generally, materials costs and processing costs will be accumulated separately during a period. Materials costs, of course, would be the materials going into the product. These may be raw materials from the warehouse, or they may be the output from the prior process. Processing costs are the labor and overhead costs incurred in the processing center.

Measure the output of the period

After materials and processing costs have been accumulated for a period, the period's *output* must be computed so that appropriate unit costs can be determined. If a processing center has no work in process at the beginning or at the end of a period, this is a simple task. The period's output will simply equal the *completed* units turned out during the period.

If a processing center has work in process at the beginning or at the end of a period, however, *completed* units alone will not accurately measure total output. The reason is that part of the costs of the period will relate to the partially completed units in the ending inventory. These partially completed units will have to be considered along with the fully completed units in measuring the period's output. However, the partially completed units will be measured on an *equivalent units* basis. For example, 100 units 60 percent complete would be equivalent to 60 fully completed units. Therefore, the ending inventory in this case would be said to contain 60 *equivalent units of production.* These equivalent units of production would have to be added to the fully completed units as a step toward computing the total output of the period.

By the same line of reasoning, the *beginning* inventory could also contain equivalent units of production. In this case, however, the equivalent units would relate to work done in the prior period, and the equivalent units would have to be *deducted* from the completed units of the current period. For example, if the beginning inventory contains 200 units 40 percent complete at the start of the period, then the equivalent of 80 units will have already been completed before processing in the current period begins. These 80 equivalent units of production will have to be deducted from the current period's final completed output as a step toward computing the period's *actual* output.

To illustrate the computation of a period's output where equivalent units are involved, assume the following data:

The Regal Company produces a product that goes through three processing centers—Mixing, Molding, and Firing. During 19x1, the following activity took place in the Mixing processing center:

	Materials		Processing	
	Pounds	Percent completed	Pounds	Percent completed
Beginning inventory	500	90%	500	50%
Pounds of raw material entered into the processing center	9,000	—	9,000	—
Ending inventory	200	40	200	10
Completed during the period and transferred to Molding	9,300	—	9,300	—

Required:

Compute the output for 19x1 in the Mixing center.

Since the work in process inventories are at different stages of completion for materials and for processing, two output figures will have to be computed—one for output in terms of materials and one for output in terms of processing. Actually, this is a common practice since material costs and processing costs are normally accumulated and accounted for separately in a processing center, as mentioned earlier. The output computations are shown below:

	Material (pounds)	Processing (pounds)
Completed and transferred to Molding	9,300	9,300
Deduct: Equivalent units in the beginning inventory:		
500 lbs. × 90 percent	450	
500 lbs. × 50 percent		250
	8,850	9,050
Add: Equivalent units in the ending inventory:		
200 lbs. × 40 percent	80	
200 lbs. × 10 percent		20
Output for 19x1 (equivalent units of production)	8,930	9,070

"Output" is always expressed in terms of net equivalent units of production, as we have done above.

Compute unit costs

Once costs have been accumulated by the processing centers, and the period's output has been determined, unit costs can be computed. Generally, this is a fairly simple task involving no more than dividing the accumulated costs by the period's output. One word of caution, however: If the output figure is different for materials than for processing, separate unit cost figures will have to be computed and then added together to obtain a final, total unit cost figure for the department involved. To illustrate, assume that the Regal Company in the preceding section has accumulated the following costs for 19x1 in the Mixing processing center:

Materials	$ 44,650
Processing	81,630
	$126,280

Using the output figures computed in the preceding section, the unit costs for the Mixing processing center for 19x1 would be:

Materials	$\dfrac{\$44,650}{8,930 \text{ lbs.}} =$	$ 5/lb.
Processing	$\dfrac{\$81,630}{9,070 \text{ lbs.}} =$	9/lb.
Total cost		$14/lb.

Since the output of the Mixing center is transferred to the Molding center, the $14 per pound unit cost of the Mixing center becomes the *materials input cost* of the Molding center. In effect, as materials are transferred from processing center to processing center, the *processing* costs of the prior center lose their identity as processing costs, and simply become part of the material input cost of the new processing center.

Add all unit costs to obtain fully processed cost

By the time a unit of product has passed through all processing centers it will have accumulated its total costs of production. That is, the Molding center in the preceding section will add its own processing costs onto the $14 per unit materials cost received from the Mixing center (and perhaps add some more materials costs of its own as well), and then pass the processed units on to the next processing center. By the time a unit of product has passed through all processing centers its costing will be complete.

As an alternative, some firms account for the costs of each processing center separately and don't pass costs on from one center to the other. In these cases, when a unit of product has gone through all processing centers, the costs incurred in the separate centers are totaled individually, and the final unit cost computed.

THE FLOW OF UNITS BETWEEN PROCESSING CENTERS

As mentioned earlier, the units completed in one processing center flow directly into the next processing center. Processing centers are usually required to account for the units on which they work during a period. To illustrate how such an accounting is made, assume the following data:

	Mixing		Engraving		Firing	
	Units	Percent completed	Units	Percent completed	Units	Percent completed
Opening inventory	2,000	40	3,000	60	1,500	70
Units initiated into production	10,000					
Ending inventory	1,000	80	2,000	30	3,000	60

A processing center accounts for the units worked on during a period as one part of its *production report.* A partial production report is shown in Exhibit 3–14, based on the data given above.

Exhibit 3–14
Partial production report—units processed

	Mixing	Engraving	Firing
Units to be accounted for:			
Units in process, beginning	2,000	3,000	1,500
Units initiated into production, or transferred in from the prior center	10,000	11,000	12,000
Total units to account for	12,000	14,000	13,500
Units accounted for as follows:			
Transferred out during the period	11,000	12,000	10,500
Units in process, ending	1,000	2,000	3,000
Total units accounted for	12,000	14,000	13,500
Computation of equivalent units:			
Units transferred out during the period	11,000	12,000	10,500
Deduct: Equivalent units, opening inventory	800	1,800	1,050
	10,200	10,200	9,450
Add: Equivalent units, ending inventory	800	600	1,800
Output (equivalent units)	11,000	10,800	11,250

Transfer costing problems

In those cases where the units in the opening inventory carry the same per unit costs as incurred during the period, no problems exist in transferring costs from one processing center to another. But in those cases where the per unit costs in the opening inventory differ from the per unit costs incurred during the period, a problem arises over the per unit rate to use in transferring the units in the opening inventory to the next processing center when these units are finally completed. Should they be transferred at the per unit rate in the opening inventory, or should they be transferred at the per unit rate incurred during the current period to bring them to a state of full completion? Or should they be transferred at still some other rate? Generally speaking, when the unit costs in the opening inventory differ from the unit costs of the current period, firms will either assume a Fifo cost flow or a moving average cost flow.

Fifo cost flow

Under a Fifo cost flow, the units in the opening inventory are transferred at a figure that includes *both* the prior period and the current period costs. All other units completed during the period are simply transferred at the current period cost. To illustrate, assume the following data:

| | | | Processing | |
	Units (pounds)	Materials cost	Percent completed	Cost
Opening inventory	400	$1,400	60%	$ 1,440
Ending inventory	600	?	80	?
Entered into production	2,000	8,000	—	13,260
Completed and transferred out	1,800	?	—	?

Schedule A below shows the computation of both unit costs and equivalent units for the period.

Schedule A

	Materials	Processing	Total
Cost added by the department (*a*)	$8,000	$13,260	$21,260
Equivalent units (*b*)	2,000 lbs.	2,040 lbs.	—
Unit cost (*a*) ÷ (*b*)	$4	$6.50	$10.50
Computation of equivalent units (pounds):			
Units transferred out	1,800	1,800	
Deduct: Equivalent units, opening inventory	400	240	
	1,400	1,560	
Add: Equivalent units, ending inventory	600	480	
Output (equivalent units)	2,000	2,040	

If a Fifo cost flow is assumed, the 1,800 pounds completed and transferred will be broken into two segments—one segment consisting of the 400 pounds in the opening inventory, and one segment consisting of the remaining 1,400 pounds completed and transferred. The two segments will be costed as follows:

Schedule B

	First 400 lbs.	Remaining 1,400 lbs.	Total Cost
Cost in the opening inventory:			
Materials	$1,400		$ 1,400
Processing	1,440		1,440
Cost required to complete the units in the opening inventory:			
Processing—400 lbs. × 40% × $6.50	1,040		1,040
Cost required to complete all remaining units transferred—1,400 lbs. × $10.50		$14,700	14,700
Total cost transferred	$3,880	$14,700	$18,580

All of the cost and units associated with a period's operations are usually summarized on a production report, such as illustrated in Exhibit 3–15. Notice from the exhibit that the ending inventory is costed at the current period's cost per equivalent unit.

Exhibit 3–15
Production report—Fifo cost method

Units to be accounted for (pounds):	
Units in process, beginning (all materials, 60% processing)	400
Units started into production	2,000
Total units to account for	2,400
Units accounted for as follows (pounds):	
Transferred out during the period	1,800
Units in process, ending (all materials, 80% processing)	600
Total units accounted for	2,400
Cost charged to the department:	
Work in process, opening inventory ($1,400 + $1,440)	$ 2,840
Cost added during the period (Schedule A)	21,260
Total cost to account for	$24,100
Cost accounted for as follows:	
Transferred out: (Schedule B)	$18,580
Work in process, ending inventory:	
Materials: 600 lbs. × $4 . . . . $2,400	
Processing: 600 lbs. × 80% × $6.50 3,120	5,520
Total cost accounted for	$24,100

Moving average cost flow

A much simpler method of costing transfers can be found in the moving average approach. The moving average approach simply adds costs in the opening inventory in with costs incurred currently, making no effort to differentiate between the two. Similarly, in computing the output (equivalent units) for a period, units in the opening inventory are treated *as if they were started and completed during the current period.* That is, they are not deducted out in computing the period's output in equivalent units.

These concepts can be illustrated by referring to the data used in the prior example. The computation of the period's output (equivalent units) and unit costs under the moving average method would be as shown in Schedule C.

Schedule C

	Materials	Processing	Total
Work in process, opening	$1,400	$ 1,440	$ 2,840
Cost added by the department	8,000	13,260	21,260
Total cost (*a*)	$9,400	$14,700	$24,100
Equivalent units (*b*)	2,400 lbs.	2,280 lbs.	—
Unit cost (*a*) ÷ (*b*)	$3.917	$6.447	$10.364
Computation of equivalent units (pounds):			
Units transferred out	1,800	1,800	
Add: Equivalent units, ending inventory	600	480	
Output (equivalent units)	2,400	2,280	

Notice from Schedule C that the formula for computing unit cost by the moving average method can be expressed as:

$$\frac{\text{Cost in the opening inventory} + \text{Cost added during the period}}{\text{Total output (equivalent units)}} = \text{Average unit cost}$$

The production report for the period if the moving average method is used to cost flows of units would be as shown in Exhibit 3–16.

The cost in the ending inventory will be carried forward to the next period and averaged in with that period's costs in order to get a new moving average cost figure. Thus, the term *moving average* cost flow.

Comparison of moving average and Fifo

Any major difference in unit costs as between the moving average and Fifo methods is likely to be traceable to erratic movements in raw materials prices. Processing costs usually will not fluctuate widely from month to month, due to the continuous nature of the flow of goods in process costing situations. In addition, inventory levels in most companies tend to remain quite stable, thereby adding to the general stability of unit costs.

Exhibit 3–16
Production report—moving average method

Units to be accounted for (pounds):	
Units in process, beginning (all materials,	
60% processing)	400
Units started into production	2,000
Total units to account for	2,400
Units accounted for as follows (pounds):	
Transferred out during the period	1,800
Units in process, ending (all materials,	
80% processing)	600
Total units accounted for	2,400
Cost charged to the department:	
Work in process, opening inventory ($1,400 + $1,440)	$ 2,840
Cost added during the period (Schedule C)	21,260
Total cost to account for............................	$24,100
Cost accounted for as follows:	
Transferred out:1,800 lbs. × $10.364	$18,655
Work in process, ending inventory:	
Materials: 600 lbs. × $3.917........................... $2,350	
Processing: 600 lbs. × 80% × $6.447 3,095	5,445
Total cost accounted for	$24,100

From a standpoint of *cost control,* the Fifo method is superior to the moving average method. This is because current performance should be measured in relation to the costs of the *current* period only, and the moving average method inherently mixes these costs with the costs of *prior* periods.

On the other hand, the moving average method is simpler to apply than is the Fifo method. Because of its greater ease of use, some contend that it is more widely used in actual practice. However, specific evidence to support this point is not available.

Other transfer problems

Many other problems can exist in attempting to cost transfers between processing centers. For one thing, it is common to have materials shrink in quantity as processing takes place. For example, processing may cause evaporation resulting in less units (gallons) transferred out than transferred in from the prior process. In other cases, spoilage is common, again resulting in less units transferred out than transferred in. Problems such as these are easily handled in a process costing system, but they are more applicable to advanced managerial accounting courses and will not be considered here.

APPENDIX B: NORMALIZED OVERHEAD RATES

Many firms hesitate to set predetermined overhead rates on the basis of the expected production on a single period if that production is subject to wide variations. The reason is that as production levels fluctuate the predetermined overhead rate also fluctuates, resulting in high per unit costs in periods when production is low and in low per unit costs in periods when production is high. This problem is traceable to the fact that fixed costs often make up a large part of manufacturing overhead, and, as explained in Chapter 2, these costs go on basically unchanged in total regardless of the level of activity. As a result, when production is low, the fixed overhead costs are spread over a small number of units, resulting in a high cost per unit. When production is high, these costs are spread over a large number of units, resulting in a lower cost per unit.

Fluctuating overhead rates

To illustrate the problems caused by fluctuating overhead rates, let us assume the following production, sales, and cost data for a manufacturing firm:

	Year 1	Year 2
Production and sales data:		
Production in units..........................	10,000	6,000
Sales in units	8,000	8,000
Estimated manufacturing overhead:		
Variable overhead ($1 per unit)	$10,000	$ 6,000
Fixed overhead	24,000	24,000
Total overhead	$34,000	$30,000

If the company sets its overhead rates on a basis of the expected production of each year, the rates will be:

$$\text{Year 1:} \frac{\text{Estimated overhead \$34,000}}{\text{Estimated production 10,000 units*}} = \$3.40 \text{ per unit}$$

$$\text{Year 2:} \frac{\text{Estimated overhead \$30,000}}{\text{Estimated production 6,000 units}} = \$5.00 \text{ per unit}$$

* Rather than setting the overhead rate on a basis of number of units produced, the company could have set it on a basis of the number of direct labor-hours needed to produce the units; units of product are being used in this example simply for ease of illustration.

If we further assume that each unit of product requires $2 in direct materials cost, and $3 in direct labor cost, then the total cost of a unit of product manufactured in each separate year will be:

	Year 1	Year 2
Direct materials	$2.00	$ 2.00
Direct labor	3.00	3.00
Manufacturing overhead	3.40	5.00
Total cost per unit	$8.40	$10.00

Notice the wide variation in unit costs between the two years. Looking at the overhead portion of the cost, we can see that the higher production level in Year 1 has caused the overhead to be spread thinner, resulting in a lower cost per unit. Many managers feel that this type of variation in unit costs can lead to distorted financial statements, and can cause confusion on the part of statement users. With unit costs jumping up and down, statements become difficult to interpret and can lead to faulty conclusions and unwise decisions.

This point can be seen clearly by preparing a partial income statement for each of the two years from the data above. (Recall from the original data that sales are planned at 8,000 units annually; we will assume a selling price of $10 per unit.)

	Year 1	Year 2	Total
Sales (8,000 units at $10 each)	$80,000	$80,000	$160,000
Cost of goods sold:			
Year 1: (8,000 units at $8.40 each)	67,200		
Year 2: (2,000 units at $8.40 each)		16,800 ⎫	144,000
(6,000 units at $10.00 each)		60,000 ⎬	
Total cost of goods sold	67,200	76,800	144,000
Gross margin	$12,800	$ 3,200	$ 16,000

Although sales are constant at 8,000 units in each year, the gross margin drops dramatically in Year 2. The reason, of course, is that production dropped off in Year 2, causing a jump in cost per unit and a drop in gross margin per unit. Yet an uninformed manager seeing these data might be misled into thinking that massive inefficiencies were developing, or that a substantial jump in labor or raw materials prices had just taken place. An uninformed stockholder might be led to believe that difficulties were developing in the company that warranted the selling of his or her stock. In reality we can see that none of these conclusions are correct; the variation in gross margin is simply a result of a temporary imbalance between production and sales.

The concept of a normalized overhead rate

The company in our illustration may have had good reasons for producing more than it sold in Year 1. For example, the company may have been building inventories in anticipation of a strike or a supply interruption coming in Year 2, in order to have goods on hand to meet customer needs. In short, the question isn't whether variations in the level of production are desirable—such variations are often unavoidable. The question is whether these variations should be permitted to influence unit costs—pushing costs up in times of low activity and pulling them down in times of high activity. Many managers would argue that the cost of a unit of product should be the same whether it is produced in Year 1, Year 2, or any other year, so long as long-run demand for the product is reasonably stable.

How can uniformity in unit cost be attained if a firm's production is fluctuating from year to year? The answer lies in *normalized* overhead rates. A normalized overhead rate is not based on the expected activity of a single period. Rather, a normalized overhead rate is based on an average activity level that spans many periods—past, present, and future. The approach is to determine what level of activity is *normal* over the long run, and then to set predetermined overhead rates on that figure. Such rates are said to be normalized in the sense that they smooth out the hills and valleys in activity that are largely beyond management's control.

An illustration of normalized overhead rates

To show how normalized overhead rates work, let us return to the data used earlier. On a normalized basis, overhead rates would be set on an average production figure of 8,000 units per year, rather than on a basis of 10,000 units in Year 1 and 6,000 units in Year 2. The computations would be:

	Per unit
Fixed overhead:	
$24,000 ÷ 8,000 units	$3
Variable overhead	1
Total predetermined overhead rate	$4

This overhead rate would be used to cost units of product in both years; therefore, the full cost of a unit produced in either year would be:

Direct materials (as before)	$2
Direct labor (as before)	3
Manufacturing overhead	4
Total cost per unit	$9

With stable unit costs, the erratic behavior that we observed earlier on the company's income statement will be eliminated, as shown below:

	Year 1	Year 2	Total
Sales (8,000 units at $10 each)	$80,000	$80,000	$160,000
Cost of goods sold (8,000 units at $9 each)	72,000	72,000	144,000
Gross margin	$ 8,000	$ 8,000	$ 16,000

As a result of using normalized overhead rates, notice that the gross margin pattern is even over the two-year period. By contrast, recall from our earlier income statement that when fluctuating overhead rates are used to cost production the gross margin pattern is erratic, even though the same number of units is sold in each year. In years when production is high, income is also high; in years when production is low, income is also low.

In short, normalized overhead rates largely eliminate from inventories, from cost of goods sold, and from gross margin any unfavorable impact of having production out of balance with the long-run demand for a company's products.

Overhead variances

When normalized overhead rates are in use, the underapplied or overapplied overhead balances tend to be somewhat larger than when overhead rates are computed on the basis of a single year's activity. For this reason, when normalized overhead rates are in use, rather than closing underapplied or overapplied overhead balances out to Cost of Goods Sold, these amounts are often carried forward on the balance sheet in a permanent account. The thinking is that if the "normal" level of activity on which the predetermined overhead rate is set is carefully chosen, then the net balance in this account will tend to be nominal in amount. The underapplied balance of one period will simply be offset by the overapplied balance of a following period.

KEY TERMS FOR REVIEW (APPENDIXES)

Process costing   **Processing cost**
Processing center   **Production report**
Sequential processing   **Fifo cost flow**
Parallel processing   **Moving average cost flow**
Equivalent units   **Normalized overhead rate**

QUESTIONS

3–1. State the purposes for which it is necessary or desirable to compute per unit manufacturing cost.

3–2. Distinguish between job order costing and process costing.

3–3. What is the essential purpose of any costing system?

3–4. What is the purpose of the job cost sheet in a job order costing system?

3–5. What is a predetermined overhead rate, and how is it computed?

3–6. Explain how a sales order, a production order, a materials requisition form, and a labor time ticket are involved in the production and costing of products.

3–7. Why do firms use predetermined overhead rates rather than using actual manufacturing overhead costs in applying overhead to units of product?

3–8. Explain why some production costs must be assigned to products through an allocation process. Name several such costs. Would such costs be classified as *direct* or as *indirect* costs? Why?

3–9. In computing predetermined overhead rates, why is the estimate of the level of activity an especially important consideration?

3–10. What is meant by the statement that overhead is "absorbed" into units of product? If a company fully absorbs its overhead costs, does this guarantee that a profit will be earned for the period?

3–11. What account is credited when overhead is applied to work in process? Would you expect the amount applied for a period to equal actual overhead costs of the period? Why or why not?

3–12. What is underapplied overhead? Overapplied overhead? What disposition is made of these amounts at period end?

3–13. Enumerate several reasons why overhead might be underabsorbed in a given year.

3–14. What factors should be considered in selecting a base to be used in computing the predetermined overhead rate?

3–15. If overhead rates are set on a basis of each period's activity, then unit costs will rise as the activity level rises, and vice versa. Do you agree? Explain.

3–16. What is the purpose of a normalized overhead rate? Are such rates more or less apt to lead to confusion on the part of statement users than using rates based on the activity of individual periods? Explain.

3–17. Barnaby Company applies overhead to completed jobs on a basis of 80 percent of direct labor cost. If Job 467 shows $10,000 of manufacturing overhead applied, how much was the direct labor cost on the job?

3–18. A company assigns overhead to completed jobs on a basis of 75 percent of direct labor cost. The job cost sheet for Job 313 shows that $4,000 in direct material has been used on the job, and that $8,000 in direct labor time has been incurred. If 1,000 units were produced in Job 313, what is the cost per unit?

3–19. Under what conditions would a process costing system be more appropriate than a job order costing system?

3–20. Distinguish between sequential processing centers and parallel processing centers.

3–21. Why is cost accumulation easier under a process costing system than under a job order costing system?

3–22. What are equivalent units of production? Give an example, showing equivalent units in both the beginning and ending inventory.

3–23. Explain how equivalent units are computed if a company uses the moving average method to cost transfers between processing centers.

3–24. The presence of opening work in process inventories in a department requires the assumption of a particular cost flow, such as Fifo or moving average. Explain why this is so.

EXERCISES

E3–1. The Slater Manufacturing Company produces a product that is subject to wide seasonal variations in demand. Unit costs are computed on a quarterly basis, by dividing each quarter's manufacturing costs (material, labor, and overhead) by the quarter's production in units. The company's estimated costs, by quarter, for the coming year are given below:

	First quarter	Second quarter	Third quarter	Fourth quarter
Direct materials	$16,000	$ 8,000	$ 4,000	$12,000
Direct labor	30,000	15,000	7,500	22,500
Variable manufacturing overhead	12,000	6,000	3,000	9,000
Fixed manufacturing overhead	30,000	30,000	30,000	30,000
Total manufacturing costs	$88,000	$59,000	$44,500	$73,500
Number of units to be produced	20,000	10,000	5,000	15,000
Estimated cost per unit	$4.40	$5.90	$8.90	$4.90

The company is concerned about the variation in unit costs, and wonders if there is a way to more equitably assign the overhead costs to units of product.

Required:

1. The company uses a job order cost system. How would you recommend that overhead be assigned to production? Be specific, and show computations. (Include both variable and fixed overhead in your analysis.)
2. Recompute the company's unit costs in accordance with your recommendations in (1).

E3–2. Estimated cost and operating data for the forthcoming period for three companies are given below:

	Company A	Company B	Company C
Direct labor-hours	12,000	15,000	20,000
Manufacturing overhead	$90,000	$120,000	$150,000
Machine-hours	20,000	20,000	25,000
Direct labor cost	$60,000	$ 75,000	$100,000
Predetermined overhead rates are based on	Direct labor-hours	Direct labor cost	Machine-hours

Required:

1. Compute the predetermined overhead rate to be used in the forthcoming period for each company.

2. Assume for Company B that $80,000 of direct labor cost actually is incurred. How much overhead will be applied to work in process?

3. Assume for Company C that three jobs are worked on during the forthcoming period. Assume the actual machine-hours logged on each job are:

	Machine-hours
Job 417	8,000
Job 469	12,000
Job 511	10,000
Total	30,000

How much overhead will be applied to work in process during the period? If actual overhead costs total $175,000 during the period will overhead be over- or underapplied? By how much?

E3–3. The Diewold Company has two departments: Milling and Assembly. The company uses a job order cost system, and computes a predetermined overhead rate for each department. Milling bases its rate on machine-hours and Assembly bases its rate on direct labor cost. Estimated data for 19x9, the coming year, are given below:

	Milling	Assembly
Machine-hours	60,000	12,000
Direct labor cost	$ 80,000	$120,000
Manufacturing overhead cost	150,000	60,000

Required:

1. Compute the predetermined overhead rate to be used in each department.

2. Assume that Job 174 requires 850 hours of machine time in Milling, and $6,400 of labor cost in Assembly during 19x9. What is the total overhead cost chargeable to the job?

E3–4. The Premier Metal Works produces castings and other metal parts to customer specifications, using a job order cost system. The entire month of March was spent on Job 382, which called for 8,000 machine parts. Cost data for March are given below:

a. Materials requisitioned: 34,000 pounds at $1.20 per pound.

b. Direct labor-hours worked: 4,800 hours at $6.50 per hour.

c. Predetermined overhead rate: $3 per direct labor-hour (based on estimated costs and activity for the full year).

d. Actual overhead costs for the month: $15,500 (credit "Miscellaneous Accounts").

e. The completed job was moved into the finished goods warehouse on March 31, to await delivery to the customer.

Required:

1. Prepare journal entries to record these events.

2. Compute the unit cost that will appear on the job cost sheet.

E3–5. The Greaves Company uses a job order cost system. The table below provides selected data on the three jobs worked on during the company's first month of operations.

	Job number		
	101	102	103
Units of product in the job	2,000	1,800	1,500
Direct labor-hours worked.............	1,200	1,000	600
Direct materials cost	$3,200	$3,980	$1,200
Direct labor cost	6,000	5,000	3,000

Actual overhead costs of $5,880 were incurred during the month. Manufacturing overhead is applied to production on a basis of direct labor-hours, at a predetermined rate of $2 per hour. Jobs 101 and 102 were completed during the month; Job 103 was not completed.

Required:
1. Compute the amount of manufacturing overhead that would have been charged to each job during the month.
2. Compute the unit cost of Jobs 101 and 102.
3. Prepare a journal entry showing the transfer of the completed jobs into the finished goods warehouse.
4. What is the balance in Work in Process at the end of the month?

E3–6. Selected *actual* cost data for four companies for the year just ended (19x5) are given below:

	Company			
	W	X	Y	Z
Direct labor-hours worked	5,000	8,000	15,000	12,000
Machine-hours worked	15,000	25,000	20,000	30,000
Direct labor cost	$25,000	$40,000	$75,000	$60,000
Direct materials cost	12,000	18,000	15,000	20,000
Manufacturing overhead cost	20,000	50,000	72,000	95,000
Predetermined overhead rate	150% of direct material cost	$7 per direct labor-hour	100% of direct labor cost	$3 per machine-hour

Required:
1. For each company, compute the amount of overhead applied to work in process during 19x5.
2. Based on your computations in (1) above, for each company compute the amount of over- or underapplied overhead for 19x5.
3. Assume that Company X worked on only one production order during 19x5. If the order contained 10,000 units, what cost per unit would have appeared on the job cost sheet? (Assume no work in process inventories.)

E3–7. The Beaver Company uses a job order cost system. The following relate to the month of June:

a. Raw materials issued to production, $82,000.
b. Direct labor cost incurred, $61,000.
c. The company applies manufacturing overhead to production on a basis of $3.75 per direct labor-hour. There were 12,000 direct labor-hours recorded for the month.
d. Actual manufacturing overhead costs totaled $43,800 for the month. (Credit "Miscellaneous Accounts.")
e. Production orders costing $185,000 were completed during the month.
f. Production orders that had cost $155,000 to complete were shipped to customers during the month. These goods were invoiced at 25 percent above cost.

Required:

1. Prepare journal entries to record the information above.
2. Compute the ending balance of work in process, assuming the beginning balance was $23,000.

E3–8. Estimated cost and operating data for three companies for 19x5 are given below:

	Company X	Company Y	Company Z
Units to be produced	10,000	8,000	12,000
Machine-hours	50,000	10,000	6,000
Direct labor-hours	12,000	16,000	36,000
Direct labor cost	$ 48,000	$64,000	$144,000
Manufacturing overhead cost	150,000	40,000	60,000

Predetermined overhead rates are computed on the following bases in the three companies:

Company	Overhead rate based on
X	Machine-hours
Y	Direct labor-hours
Z	Units produced

Required:

1. Compute the predetermined overhead rate to be used in each company during 19x5.
2. Assume that during 19x5, 18,000 actual direct labor-hours are worked in Company Y. How much overhead will be applied to work in process?
3. Assume that three jobs are worked on during 19x5 in Company X. Machine-hours recorded by job are: Job 23, 21,000 hours; Job 29, 16,000 hours; and Job 31, 11,000 hours. How much overhead will the company apply to work in process? If actual overhead costs total $149,000 for 19x5, will overhead be over- or underapplied? By how much?

E3–9. The following data relate to the manufacturing activities of Pearl Company for 19x7:

Raw materials inventory, January 1 .... $ 7,000
Raw materials inventory, December 31 4,000
Purchases of raw materials during 19x7 30,000
Work in process inventory, January 1 6,000
Work in process inventory, December 31 7,500
Actual manufacturing overhead cost incurred 48,000
Direct labor cost (10,000 hours) 40,000
Predetermined overhead rate .... $5 per DLH

Required:

1. Compute the amount of under- or overapplied overhead for 19x7.
2. Prepare a schedule of cost of goods manufactured for 19x7.

E3–10. The Carter Company began operations on January 2, 19x5. The following activity took place in the work in process account for the month of January:

Work in Process

Direct materials	10,000	To finished goods	80,000
Direct labor	30,000		
Manufacturing overhead	45,000		

The Carter Company uses a job order costing system, and applies manufacturing overhead to work in process on a basis of direct labor cost. At the end of January, only one job was still in process. This job (Job 15) has been charged with $1,500 in direct labor cost.

Required:

Complete the following job cost sheet for partially completed Job 15:

Job cost sheet—Job 15 (as of January 31, 19x5)

Direct materials .... $_____
Direct labor .... _____
Manufacturing overhead .... _____
        Total cost to January 31 .... ========

E3–11. (Appendix) Mauer Company uses a process costing system. At the end of 19x3, the company's cost records revealed the following information:

	Process A		Process B	
	Units	Percent completed	Units	Percent completed
Opening inventory	4,000	40	6,000	70
Ending inventory	3,000	60	4,000	25
Units entered into production	9,000		10,000	
Units completed and transferred out ...	10,000		12,000	

Required:

Assuming the company uses a Fifo cost flow, compute the equivalent units of production for each process.

E3–12. (Appendix) The cost records associated with Pressboard, Inc.'s process costing system show the following selected data for July 19x5:

	Units	Percent completed
Process A:		
Opening inventory	4,000	80
Closing inventory	3,000	40
Units started into production	30,000	—
Process B:		
Opening inventory	5,000	60
Closing inventory	4,000	70
Units received from Process A	?	—

Units of product are introduced into production at the start of Process A, and flow through both processes on a Fifo basis.

Required:

Prepare a production report dealing with units of product only, including a computation of equivalent units of production.

E3–13. (Appendix) Hill Company has two processes, A and B, through which its single product passes. All materials are added at the beginning of Process A. Data for a recent month for Process A follow:

	Units	Percent completed	Materials	Labor	Overhead
Work in process, opening	4,000	60%	$ 1,800	$ 1,400	$ 2,800
Units started in process	38,000	—			
Units transferred out	36,000	—			
Work in process, ending	6,000	50			
Cost added during the month			19,200	23,950	47,900

The company costs by the moving average method. The "Percent Completed" above relates to labor and overhead only.

Required:

Compute the unit cost of units transferred out during the month.

E3–14. (Appendix) The Superior Pulp Company processes wood pulp for various manufacturers of paper products. The company prepares a monthly production report on its two processes. Cost and other data on these two processes for June 19x8 are presented below:

	Tons of pulp	Percent completed
Process 1:		
Opening inventory, June 1	16,000	60
Ending inventory, June 30	20,000	35
Started into processing during the month	125,000	—
Process 2:		
Opening inventory, June 1	8,000	90
Ending inventory, June 30	15,000	25
Received during the month from Process 1	?	—

The wood which forms the basis for the finished pulp is introduced at the beginning of Process 1, and flows evenly through both processes.

Required:

Prepare a production report dealing with units of product only (tons of pulp), including a computation of equivalent units of production (in tons).

E3–15. (Appendix) The following data are available for one month's activity in a company having a process costing system:

	Amount	Percent completed	Processing cost
Opening inventory	500	40%	$ 1,650
Entered into production	3,800	—	29,541
Completed and transferred out	3,350	—	
Ending inventory	950	30	

The company uses a Fifo cost flow.

Required:

1. Compute the equivalent units of production.
2. Compute the cost per unit for processing during the current month.
3. Prepare a schedule showing the cost of units transferred out during the month.

PROBLEMS

P3–16. *Straightforward job order costing journal entries.* The information given below has been taken from the records of the Pacific Manufacturing Company for the year 19x5. The company's opening finished goods inventory for the year was $40,000.

  a. Raw materials were purchased on account for use in production, $102,000.
  b. Raw materials were requisitioned for use in production, $95,000 (80 percent direct, 20 percent indirect).
  c. Salaries and wages of factory and other employees were incurred:

Direct labor (20,000 hours)	$90,000
Indirect labor	16,000
Selling expense	25,000
Administrative expense	30,000

  d. Heat, light, and power costs were incurred on the factory, $16,000.
  e. Other miscellaneous factory costs were incurred, $34,000.
  f. Miscellaneous administrative expenses were incurred, $12,000.
  g. Depreciation was recorded on factory buildings and equipment, $10,000.
  h. Manufacturing overhead was applied to production at a rate of $4.75 per direct labor-hour.
  i. The cost of goods completed during 19x5 was $260,000.

j. Goods were sold to customers during 19x5 at a total selling price of $400,000. The company's closing finished goods inventory totaled $35,000.

Required:

1. Prepare journal entries to record the information given above.
2. Prepare an income statement for the year. Ignore income taxes.

P3–17. *Unit costs; Journal entries; Overhead analysis.* Randell Company uses a job order cost system. At the start of 19x3, a predetermined overhead rate of $2.10 per direct labor-hour was established, based on estimates of 32,000 direct labor-hours and $67,200 of manufacturing overhead for the year.

Required:

1. During 19x3, Job 316 required $1,400 of raw materials and 310 hours of direct labor time at $7.50 per hour. If Job 316 contained 400 units, what was the cost per unit?
2. Give the journal entries made in charging the costs in (1) to production. Also give the entry showing transfer of the completed job to finished goods.
3. The following selected costs were incurred during 19x3:

Depreciation recorded, factory $32,500
Raw materials purchased (on account) 42,000
Sales commissions accrued 23,400
Indirect labor cost accrued 4,500

Prepare a journal entry to show the incurrence of each cost.
4. During 19x3 the company worked a total of 31,000 direct labor-hours on all jobs, and incurred $66,900 in actual manufacturing overhead costs.
   a. Compute the under- or overapplied overhead for the year, by preparing a T-account titled, "Manufacturing Overhead," and entering the relevant cost data. [Do *not* post data from (1)–(3) to the T-account.]
   b. Prepare a journal entry to close the under- or overapplied overhead to cost of goods sold.

P3–18. *Journal entries for a job order cost system, with T-accounts.* At the beginning of the current year, Maple Products had the following inventory amounts on its balance sheet:

Raw materials $11,500
Work in process 20,000
Finished goods 35,000

Maple Products estimated that it would incur $60,000 in manufacturing overhead during the year, and that it would operate at a level of 15,000 direct labor-hours. During the current year, the following transactions were completed:

a. Purchased raw material on account, $9,500.
b. Raw materials were issued to production, $16,000. 90 percent of these materials were direct, and 10 percent were indirect.

c. Factory payrolls were accrued, $49,000. 80 percent of the factory payroll was direct labor, and 20 percent was indirect labor. 14,000 direct labor-hours were worked.

d. Administrative payrolls were accrued, $12,000. Sales payrolls were accrued, $10,000.

e. Depreciation on factory equipment, $8,250.

f. Factory utilities cost incurred, $7,000.

g. Various administrative expenses incurred, $20,000.

h. Various selling expenses incurred, $15,000.

i. Various manufacturing overhead costs incurred, (other than those indicated above), $30,000.

j. Manufacturing overhead was applied to production.

k. Completed production for the current year, $106,600.

l. Sales to customers for the current year were:

Selling price $160,000
Cost . . . . ?   (Ending finished goods
                                                        inventory, $21,600)

Required:

1. Prepare journal entries to record the above transactions.

2. Prepare T-accounts for Raw Materials, Manufacturing Overhead, Work in Process, Finished Goods, and Cost of Goods Sold. Post the appropriate parts of your journal entries to these T-accounts to determine the ending balance in each account. (Don't forget to enter the opening balances in the inventory accounts.)

3. Prepare the necessary journal entry to close the balance in the manufacturing overhead account to Cost of Goods Sold.

P3–19. *Computation of overhead rates, and costing units of product.* Dorsey Company uses a job order costing system. The company uses predetermined overhead rates in applying manufacturing overhead to individual jobs. The predetermined overhead rate in Department A is based on machine-hours, and the rate in Department B is based on direct labor cost. At the beginning of 19x5, the company's management made the following estimates for the year:

	Dept. A	Dept. B
Direct labor-hours	20,000	45,000
Machine-hours	60,000	12,000
Direct labor cost	$ 80,000	$172,000
Manufacturing overhead	144,000	215,000

Job 237 was initiated into production on August 1, and completed on September 15. The company's cost records show the following information on the job:

	Dept. A	Dept. B
Direct labor-hours	30	40
Machine-hours	85	20
Materials placed into production	$450	$250
Direct labor cost	120	180

Required:

1. Compute the predetermined overhead rate that should be used during 19x5 in Department A. Compute the rate that should be used in Department B.
2. Compute the total overhead cost applied to Job 237.
3. What would be the total cost of Job 237? If the job contained 100 units, what would be the cost per unit?
4. At the end of 19x5, the records of Dorsey Company reveal the following *actual* cost and operating data for all jobs worked on during the year.

	Dept. A	Dept. B
Direct labor-hours	19,500	46,000
Machine-hours	59,000	13,000
Direct labor cost	$ 78,000	$174,000
Manufacturing overhead	142,000	216,000

What was the amount of underapplied or overapplied overhead in each department at the end of 19x5?

P3–20. *Job order entries; Income statement.* The Hudson Company uses a job order cost system. Inventory balances at the beginning of May 19x1 were:

Raw materials	$ 5,800
Work in process	16,500
Finished goods	13,000

During May the following transactions took place:
a. Raw materials purchased on account, $26,000.
b. Direct labor cost incurred, $31,000.
c. Factory utility costs incurred, $6,100.
d. Factory depreciation recorded, $4,000.
e. Administrative expenses incurred, $12,500.
f. Raw materials requisitioned for use in production (all direct), $24,500.
g. Selling expenses incurred, $8,000.
h. Miscellaneous factory overhead costs incurred, $6,000.
i. Manufacturing overhead was applied to production. The company applies overhead on a basis of 50 percent of direct labor cost.
j. Goods costing $65,000 to manufacture were transferred to the finished goods warehouse.
k. Goods were sold on account for $98,000 that had cost $71,000 to manufacture.

Required:

1. Prepare journal entries to record the information given above.
2. Prepare T-accounts for inventories and manufacturing overhead. Post relevant entries to the T-accounts, and determine the ending balance in each account.
3. Prepare a journal entry to close the balance in Manufacturing Overhead to Cost of Goods Sold.
4. Prepare an income statement for May. Ignore income taxes.

P3–21. *Job order costing; Computation of work in process inventory.* Aspen Corporation employs a job order cost system. For 19x5 the company has computed a predetermined overhead rate of $2 per direct labor-hour. On March 1 the company's inventory balances were:

Raw materials $30,000
Work in process 40,000
Finished goods 70,000

During March, the following data were recorded:

Purchases of raw materials on account .... $ 50,000
Issue of direct materials to production 60,000
Direct labor cost incurred (15,000 hours) 75,000
Manufacturing overhead cost incurred 32,000
Cost of goods manufactured 180,000

Required:

1. Prepare journal entries to record the transactions indicated by the March data.
2. Assume that on March 31 the Finished Goods Inventory balance is $60,000. Compute the cost of goods sold for March. Prepare the journal entry to record the cost of goods sold on the company's books.
3. Determine the over- or underapplied overhead for the month by preparing a T-account titled, "Manufacturing Overhead," and posting to it relevant entries from (1).
4. Determine the ending balance in Work in Process by preparing a T-account and entering relevant data.

P3–22. *Overhead rates; Job order cost flows; Pricing.* The Dolby Manufacturing Company's inventory accounts contained the following balances at the beginning and end of 19x6:

	Beginning of year	End of year
Raw materials	$20,000	$22,000
Work in process	35,000	32,000
Finished goods	60,000	68,000

The following costs were incurred during the year:

Purchases of raw materials $140,000
Direct labor cost 80,000
Manufacturing overhead costs:
  Depreciation of equipment.................................... 15,000
  Indirect labor 65,000
  Maintenance 11,500
  Rent, building 30,000

Required:

1. Assume that the company applies overhead on a basis of direct labor cost. At the beginning of 19x6, the following estimates were made: manufacturing overhead, $123,750; direct labor cost, $82,500.
   a. Compute the predetermined overhead rate for 19x6.

    b. Compute the amount of under- or overapplied overhead for the year.

2. Prepare a schedule of cost of goods manufactured for the year.
3. Compute the cost of goods sold for the year. (Do not include any under- or overapplied overhead in your cost of goods sold figure.) What options are available for disposing of under- or overapplied overhead?
4. Job 137 was started and completed during the year. What price would have been charged to the customer if the job required $3,200 in materials and $4,200 in direct labor cost, and the company priced its jobs at 40 percent above cost to manufacture?
5. Direct labor made up $10,000 of the $32,000 ending Work in Process Inventory balance. Supply the information missing below:

Direct materials	$?
Direct labor	10,000
Manufacturing overhead	?
Work in process inventory	$32,000

P3–23. *T-account analysis of cost flows.* Selected ledger accounts of the Barnaby Company are given below for the year 19x8:

Raw Materials Inventory

Jan. 1 Bal.	15,000	19x8 credits	?
19x8 debits	50,000		
Dec. 31 Bal.	12,000		

Manufacturing Overhead

19x8 debits	74,000	19x8 credits	?

Work in Process

Jan. 1 Bal.	35,000	19x8 credits	188,000
Direct materials	48,000		
Direct labor	60,000		
Overhead	75,000		
Dec. 31 Bal.	?		

Factory Wages Payable

19x8 debits	67,000	Jan. 1 Bal.	4,000
		19x8 credits	66,000

Finished Goods

Jan. 1 Bal.	60,000	19x8 credits	?
19x8 debits	?		
Dec. 31 Bal.	48,000		

Cost of Goods Sold

19x8 debits	?		

Required:

1. What was the *actual* manufacturing overhead cost incurred during 19x8?
2. How much of the actual manufacturing overhead in (1) consisted of indirect materials?

3. How much of the actual manufacturing overhead in (1) consisted of indirect labor?
4. What was the cost of goods manufactured for 19x8?
5. What was the cost of goods sold for 19x8?
6. If overhead is applied to production on a basis of direct labor cost, what rate was in effect for 19x8?
7. Was manufacturing overhead over- or underapplied for 19x8? By how much?
8. Compute the ending balance in the Work in Process Inventory account. Assume that this ending balance consists entirely of goods started during the year. If $10,000 of this balance is direct labor cost, how much of it is direct materials cost? Manufacturing overhead cost?

P3–24. *T-Account analysis of job order costs.* Wire Products, Inc., operates under a job order cost system. At the beginning of 19x1 the company showed inventory balances as follows:

Raw materials .... $ 9,500
Work in process 17,900
Finished goods 20,000

During the year, the following transactions were completed:
a. Raw materials were acquired from suppliers on account, $18,500.
b. Raw materials were requisitioned for use in production, $22,000 (80 percent direct, 20 percent indirect).
c. Factory payrolls were accrued, $40,000 (75 percent direct, 25 percent indirect).
d. Cash payments were made:
  To suppliers, $18,000.
  To employees for payrolls, $40,000.
  For factory utilities, $6,000.
  For factory rent, $12,000.
  For miscellaneous factory costs, $3,660.
e. Overhead was applied to jobs on a basis of 115 percent of direct labor cost.
f. The ending Work in Process inventory was determined to be $18,000.
g. The ending Finished Goods inventory was determined to be $12,000.

Required:
1. Enter the above transactions directly into T-accounts.
2. As stated in item (f) above, the ending balance in Work in Process was $18,000. Factory overhead constituted $5,750 of this balance. The management of Wire Products, Inc. would like to know how much of the balance consisted of direct materials and direct labor. Complete the following schedule:

Direct materials .... $?
Direct labor ....   ?
Factory overhead   5,750
Total work in process $18,000

3. What was the underapplied or overapplied factory overhead for the year?
4. Wire Products, Inc. follows the practice of allocating any underapplied or overapplied overhead balance to the pertinent accounts. Prepare a *general journal entry* to show this allocation.

P3–25. *Comprehensive problem: T-accounts, job order cost flows, statements, pricing.* Archer Company uses a job order costing system, and applies overhead to jobs on a basis of $8.50 per direct labor-hour. The following activity occurred during 19x1.

a. Raw materials purchased on account for use in production, $16,500.
b. Raw materials requisitioned from the storeroom for use in production (all direct materials), $18,200.
c. Utility bills received and paid on the factory, $3,400.
d. Wages and salaries cost incurred during the year, $36,000 (60 percent direct labor, 15 percent indirect labor, and 25 percent selling and administrative). A total of 3,600 direct labor-hours were worked during the year.
e. Raw materials costing $1,200 were returned from production to the storeroom.
f. Depreciation was recorded for the year, $10,000 ($8,500 factory and $1,500 selling and administrative).
g. Other overhead costs incurred, $12,000 (credit accounts payable).
h. Other selling and administrative expenses incurred, $4,500 (credit accounts payable).
i. Manufacturing overhead was applied to jobs, _____?_____.
j. Cost of jobs completed during the year, $68,600.
k. Sales for the year totaled $95,000 (all on account).
l. Cost of goods sold for the year totaled _____?_____. (The ending balance in Finished Goods was $9,500.)

The company's inventory accounts showed balances as follows at the beginning of 19x1:

Raw materials .... $ 3,400
Work in process 7,500
Finished goods 10,000

Required:
1. Enter the company's transactions for the year directly into T-accounts. (Don't forget to enter the beginning inventory balances into the T-accounts.) Determine the ending balances in the inventory accounts and in the Manufacturing Overhead account.
2. Prepare a schedule of cost of goods manufactured, and a schedule of cost of goods sold.
3. Prepare a journal entry to close any balance in the Manufacturing Overhead account out to Cost of Goods Sold.
4. Prepare an income statement for 19x1. Ignore income taxes.
5. Job 68 was one of the many jobs started and completed during the year. The job required $1,650 in materials and 204 hours of direct labor time at $6 per hour. If the job contained 300 units and

the company billed the job at 40 percent above cost to manufacture, what price per unit would have been charged to the customer?

P3–26. *Alternative methods of disposing of under- or overapplied overhead.* Alex Company uses a job order cost system. The company uses predetermined overhead rates, based on direct labor-hours, in applying manufacturing overhead to jobs. Estimated cost and operating data for 19x6 are given below:

Estimated direct labor-hours	30,000
Estimated direct labor cost	$ 90,000
Estimated factory overhead	120,000

At the end of 19x6, Alex Company's cost records revealed the following actual cost and operating data:

Direct labor-hours	32,000
Direct labor cost	$ 68,000
Factory overhead	130,000
Raw materials inventory	8,000
Work in process inventory	25,000
Finished goods inventory	50,000
Cost of goods sold	175,000

Required:

1. Compute Alex Company's predetermined overhead rate for 19x6.
2. Compute the underapplied or overapplied overhead for 19x6.
3. Assume that Alex Company closes any underapplied or overapplied overhead directly to cost of goods sold. Prepare the appropriate journal entry.
4. Assume that Alex Company allocates any underapplied or overapplied overhead to the appropriate accounts. Prepare the journal entry to show this allocation.
5. How much higher or lower will net income be for 19x6 if the underapplied or overapplied balance is allocated rather than closed directly to cost of goods sold?

P3–27. *Analysis of job order cost sheets.* The Speedy Print Shop does a wide variety of printing work on a custom basis. For this reason, the company uses a job order cost system. During the month of May, six jobs were worked on. A summary of the job cost sheets on these jobs is given below.

Job no.	Direct materials	Direct labor	Factory overhead applied	Total cost of job
216	$ 410	$ 360	$288	$1,058
217	850	790	632	2,272
218	110	85	68	263
219	1,500	1,140	912	3,552
220	950	850	680	2,480
221	270	115	92	477*

* Ending work in process.

The Speedy Print Shop has used the same overhead rate on all jobs. Job 216 was the only job in process at the beginning of the month. At that time it had incurred direct labor costs of $150, and total costs of $570.

Required:

1. What is the apparent predetermined overhead rate being used by the Speedy Print Shop?
2. Assume that during May factory overhead was overapplied by $600. What was the *actual* factory overhead cost incurred during the month?
3. What was the total amount of direct materials placed into production during May?
4. How much direct labor cost was incurred during May?
5. What was the cost of goods manufactured for May?
6. The beginning finished goods inventory was $2,550. What was the cost of goods sold for the month if the ending finished goods inventory was $3,550?

P3–28. *Comprehensive problem: Job order cost flows; Pricing.* Beacon Products, Inc., uses a job order cost system. The company applies overhead to jobs on a basis of 125 percent of direct labor cost. The following transactions took place during 19x5:

a. Raw materials purchased on account for use in production, $15,000.
b. Raw materials requisitioned for use in production (all direct materials), $17,000.
c. Utility bills received and paid on the factory, $4,000.
d. Wages and salaries cost incurred during the year, $30,000 (70 percent direct labor, 10 percent indirect labor, 5 percent sales salaries, and 15 percent administrative salaries).
e. Depreciation recorded on machinery and equipment used in the factory, $8,000.
f. Depreciation recorded on office equipment, $2,000.
g. Miscellaneous overhead costs incurred (credit Accounts Payable), $12,000.
h. Miscellaneous selling and administrative expenses incurred (credit Accounts Payable):

Selling .... $ 7,000
Administrative 10,000

i. Manufacturing overhead was applied to jobs, ___?___.

j. Cost of jobs completed during the year, ___?___ (the ending balance in the Work in Process Inventory account for 19x5 was $7,000; the beginning balance is given below.)
k. Sales for the year totaled $100,000.
l. Cost of goods sold for the year totaled $60,000.

The balances in the inventory accounts at the beginning of 19x5 were:

Raw materials $4,000
Work in process 5,000
Finished goods 3,000

Required:

1. Prepare journal entries to record the above data.
2. Post your entries to T-accounts. (Don't forget to enter the opening

inventory balances above.) Determine the ending balances in the
inventory accounts and in the Manufacturing Overhead account.

3. Prepare a schedule of cost of goods manufactured and a schedule
of cost of goods sold.

4. Prepare a journal entry to close any balance in Manufacturing Overhead out to Cost of Goods Sold.

5. Prepare an income statement for 19x5. Ignore income taxes.

6. Job 117 was one of many jobs started and completed during the
year. The job required $2,625 in materials and $3,500 in direct labor
cost. If the job contained 500 units and the company billed at 60
percent above cost to manufacture, what price per unit would have
been charged to the customer?

P3–29. *Schedule of cost of goods manufactured.* The Canada Company manufactures a single product. The chief accountant has asked your help in
preparing a schedule of cost of goods manufactured for the month ended
June 30, 19x3. The following information is available:

1. A total of 10,000 units were sold at $20 per unit.

2. A total of 12,000 units were produced. (One unit of raw materials
is required for each finished unit.)

3. The finished goods inventory on June 1 was 3,000 units valued at
$16 each.

4. The raw materials inventory on June 1 was 1,000 units valued at
$5 each.

5. During June two purchases of raw materials were made:

    June 6:   8,000 units at $6 each
    June 22:   5,000 units at $5 each

6. The company uses the first-in, first-out method of determining raw
materials inventories.

7. The work in process inventories were:

    June 1:   2,000 units valued at $16,000
    June 30:   2,000 units valued at $21,000

8. Depreciation is determined on a straight-line basis, at a rate of 10
percent per annum. Fixed assets include:

    Factory machinery: $240,000 original cost
    Office equipment: 6,000 original cost

9. There was no over- or underapplied overhead for the month.

10. Other information provided:

Direct labor	$100,000
Indirect labor	45,000
Salespersons' salaries	10,500
Office salaries	16,000
Sales returns and allowances	5,000
Freight out	2,500
Heat, light, and power	2,000
Factory rent	8,000
Interest expense	2,000
Miscellaneous factory overhead	10,000

Required:

Prepare a schedule of cost of goods manufactured for the month, in good form. Show supporting computations.

(SMA, adapted)

P3–30. *Incomplete data; Review of cost flows.* After a dispute concerning wages, Orville Arson tossed an incendiary device into the Sparkle Company's record vault. Within moments, only a few charred fragments were readable from the company's factory ledger, as shown below:

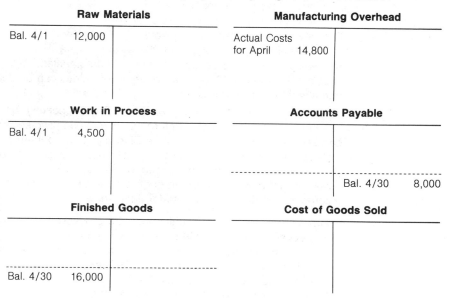

Sifting through ashes and interviewing selected employees has turned up the following additional information:

a. The controller remembers clearly that the predetermined overhead rate was based on an estimated 60,000 direct labor-hours to be worked over the year, and an estimated $180,000 in manufacturing overhead costs.

b. The production superintendent's cost sheets showed only one job in process on April 30. Materials of $2,600 had been added to the job, and 300 direct labor-hours expended at $6 per hour.

c. The accounts payable are for raw material purchases only, according to the accounts payable clerk. He clearly remembers that the balance in the account was $6,000 on April 1. An analysis of canceled checks (kept in the treasurer's office) shows that payments of $40,000 were made to suppliers during the month.

d. A charred piece of the payroll ledger shows that 5,200 direct labor-hours were recorded for the month. The employment department has verified that there are no variations in pay rates among employees (this infuriated Orville, who felt his services were underpaid).

e. Records maintained in the finished goods warehouse indicate that the finished goods inventory totaled $11,000 on April 1.

f. From another charred piece in the vault you are able to discern that the cost of goods manufactured for April was $89,000.

Required:

Determine the following amounts:
1. Work in process inventory, April 30.
2. Raw materials purchased during April.
3. Overhead applied to work in process.
4. Cost of goods sold for April.
5. Over- or underapplied overhead for April.
6. Raw materials usage during April.
7. Raw materials inventory, April 30.

(Hint: A good way to proceed is to bring the fragmented T-accounts up to date through April 30, by posting whatever entries can be developed from the information provided.)

P3–31. *Straightforward process costing problem; Fifo.* (Appendix) Oaks Processing Company produces a detergent compound in two separate processes—Blending and Boxing. In the Blending process three pounds of material are introduced at the start of the process for each unit (consisting of three pounds of blended materials) transferred to Boxing. Processing costs are incurred uniformly throughout the Blending process. Cost records for the Blending process for June show:

In process on June 1, 300 units one third processed.
In process on June 30, 200 units one half processed.
Put into process during June, 2,700 pounds of material.
Transferred to boxing during June, 1,000 units.
Cost of June 1 work in process, $3,700.
Cost of materials added during June, $8,100.
Cost of processing during June, $11,000.

Oaks Processing Company costs units on a first-in, first-out cost flow basis.

Required:

Prepare a production report for the Blending process for the month of June. The report should consist of two parts, one part dealing with units processed, and the other part dealing with cost to be accounted for. Support your report with:
a. A schedule showing computation of unit costs for the month.
b. A schedule showing computation of costs transferred to Boxing during the month.

P3–32. *Cost flows through Work in Process: Average cost method.* (Appendix) Lubricants, Inc., produces a special kind of grease that is widely used by race drivers. The grease is produced in three processes: Refining, Blending, and Packaging. Raw oil products are introduced at the beginning of the Refining process, with processing costs being incurred evenly throughout the operation. The refined output is then transferred to the

Blending operation. The following incomplete Work in Process account is available for the month of March for the Refining operation:

Work in Process—Refining

March 1 inventory (5,000		Completed and transferred	
gal., 1/5 complete)	4,850	to Blending	
March costs added:		(? gal.)	?
Raw oil materials		March 31 inventory	
(30,000 gal.)	15,000	(7,000 gal., 3/5	
Labor	30,000	complete)	?
Overhead	32,400		

The materials cost in the opening inventory is $0.55 a gallon. The company costs units of product by the average cost method.

Required:

1. How many gallons of refined materials were transferred to the Blending Process during March?
2. Compute the units of output (equivalent units of production) in the Refining Process during March for both materials and processing.
3. What average cost of processing should be used for March? What average cost of materials? (Carry answers to three decimal places.)
4. Determine the cost of the units transferred to Blending during March.
5. Determine the cost of the ending Work in Process inventory at March 31.

P3–33. *Production report; Fifo cost flow.* (Appendix)   Production and cost data for one department of a company using a process costing system are presented in the following tabulation:

Production:
Units in process, May 1; 30 percent complete as to processing ...   12,000
Units started into production   90,000
Units completed and transferred out ....   ?
Units in process, May 31; 70 percent complete as to processing ..   8,000
Costs:
Work in process inventory, May 1:
Materials .... $ 28,800
Processing   5,040
Materials used during the month 216,000
Processing costs incurred during the month 139,200

Materials are entered at the beginning of the production process. Processing costs are incurred uniformly throughout the production process. Costing is handled on a Fifo basis.

Required:

Prepare a production report for the month. Support your report with:

a. A schedule showing computation of unit costs for the month.
b. A schedule showing computation of costs transferred out during the month.

P3–34. *Production report: Moving average method.* (Appendix)   Plastering Products, Inc., produces a plastering compound which goes through several processes prior to completion. Data on the first process, Cooking, are given below for August 19x2.

	Units	Processing completed	Materials	Labor	Overhead
Work in process, opening	8,000	3/4	$ 5,150	$ 660	$ 1,320
Units started in process	45,000	—			
Units transferred out	48,000	—	?	?	?
Work in process, ending	?	2/5	?	?	?
Cost added during the month			29,300	9,840	19,680

Materials are added at the beginning of the Cooking process; labor and overhead costs are incurred uniformly throughout the process. The company costs units of product by the moving average method.

Required:

Prepare a production report for the Cooking process for the month of August 19x2. Your production report should contain two parts, one part showing units accounted for, and the other part showing costs accounted for. Support your report with a schedule showing the computation of equivalent units and unit costs.

P3–35. *Unit and cost flows under sequential processing.* (Appendix) Product Specialties, Inc., produces a unique seasoning which is in strong demand by restaurants for seasoning chicken and certain other meats. The seasoning is produced in three consecutive processes: Compounding, Cooking, and Packaging. The following information has been taken from production reports for the month of July:

	Beginning inventory		Units intro- duced for process- ing	Ending inventory	
	Units	Percent com- plete		Units	Percent com- plete
Compounding Process	8,000	20	30,000	6,000	40
Cooking Process	4,000	60	?	5,000	70
Packaging Process	?	80	?	3,000	60

During July, 34,000 units were transferred from the Packaging Process to the finished goods warehouse. All units flow through all three processes. Raw materials are added only at the beginning of the Compounding Process. Processing costs are incurred evenly throughout each process. The company accounts for costs on a Fifo basis.

Required:

1. Determine the number of units introduced for processing in the Cooking and Packaging processes during July.
2. Determine the number of units in the July beginning work in process inventory for the Packaging Process.

3. Compute the total output (equivalent units of production) relating to (*a*) materials and (*b*) processing in the Compounding Process, and relating to processing only in the other two processes.

4. Assume the following cost data relating to the Compounding Process for the month of July:

	Opening inventory	Costs added	Total cost
Materials	$7,200	$28,500	$35,700
Processing	2,320	49,200	51,520
	$9,520	$77,700	$87,220

a. Prepare a schedule showing computation of unit costs in the Compounding Process during July.

b. Prepare a schedule showing a computation of the cost of units transferred to Cooking during July.

P3–36. *Cost flows through Work in Process; Fifo cost method.* (Appendix)   ZAB, Inc., produces a very popular low-calorie soft drink. Two processes, Blending and Bottling, are used to produce the drink. All materials are added at the beginning of the Blending process, with processing costs being incurred evenly throughout the operation. The blended liquid is then transferred to the Bottling operation where it is put into bottles ready for distribution.

The following incomplete Work in Process account for the Blending process is available for the month of June 19x8:

Work in Process—Blending

June 1 inventory (3,500 gal., 40% complete)	1,582	Completed and transferred to Bottling (72,000 gal.)	?
June costs added:			
Materials (? gal.)	22,200	June 30 inventory (5,500 gal., 70% complete)	?
Processing	32,758		

The company costs units of product by the Fifo cost method.

Required:

1. How many gallons of material were put into production during the month?

2. Compute the units of output (equivalent units of production) in the Blending process during June for both materials and processing.

3. What are the per unit (gallon) costs for materials and processing for the work done during June?

4. Compute the cost of the units (gallons) transferred to Bottling during June.

5. Compute the cost of the ending Work in Process inventory.

P3–37. *Production report; Fifo cost flow.* (Appendix)   The Leaky Valve Company produces valves in three separate processes. The company's accountant (who is very inexperienced) has prepared a summary of production and costs for the finishing department for April:

Finishing department costs:
  Beginning work in process inventory, 450 units. All materials
    included, but only 60% complete as to processing costs .... $ 1,860
  Raw materials placed in production during the month, sufficient to
    produce 1,950 units (includes cost transferred in from the pre-
    ceding department) 6,240
  Processing costs incurred during the month 3,420
        Total departmental costs $11,520

Finishing department costs assigned to:
  Units completed and transferred to finished goods, 1,800
    at $6.40 .... $11,520
  Ending work in process inventory, 600 units. All materials included,
    but only 30% complete as to processing costs .... –0–
        Total departmental costs assigned $11,520

The company's inexperienced accountant assigned no cost to the ending Work in Process, since these units were only partially completed. The company computes unit costs on a Fifo cost flow basis. The president of the Leaky Valve Company is confused by the information presented, and would like some new computations made.

Required:

Prepare a production report for the month. Your report should contain two parts, one part dealing with units to be accounted for and the other part dealing with costs to be accounted for. Support your report with:
  a. A schedule showing the computation of equivalent units for the month and showing the computation of unit costs.
  b. A schedule showing the cost of units transferred to finished goods during the month.

P3–38. *Production report: Moving average method.* (Appendix) Playclay, Inc., produces a nontoxic modeling clay for sale through toy stores. The clay goes through three processes before completion: Cooking, Grinding, and Compounding. Selected cost and other data relating to work in the Grinding process during May 19x3, are given below:

	Units	Processing completed	Trans- ferred in	Labor	Overhead
Work in process, opening ...	?	1/2	$ 1,780	$ 1,060	$ 1,325
Transferred in	60,000	—	31,500	—	—
Transferred out	55,000	—	?	?	?
Work in process, ending	9,000	5/9	?	?	?
Cost added during the month				13,340	16,675

No new materials are added in the Grinding process; the labor and overhead costs in the process are incurred evenly throughout the month. The company costs units of product by the moving average method.

Required:

Prepare a production report for the Grinding process for the month, supported by a schedule showing computation of unit costs.

P3–39. *Production report; Average cost method.* (Appendix) The PVC Company produces a high-quality plastic pipe in two processes: Cooking and Molding. Materials are introduced at the start of the Cooking process, and after processing they are moved into the Molding process in which pipe is formed. Materials are accounted for in Cooking on a pounds basis. Labor and overhead costs are incurred evenly during cooking of raw materials.

Selected data relating to the Cooking process during May 19x4, are given below:

Production data:

Pounds in process, May 1; 60% complete as to processing	15,000
Pounds entered into production during May	105,000
Pounds completed and transferred to Molding	?
Pounds in process, May 31; 20% complete as to processing	9,000

Cost data:
Work in Process Inventory, May 1:

Materials costs	$ 15,225
Labor costs	900
Overhead costs	5,320

Cost added during May:

Materials costs	110,775
Labor costs	10,380
Overhead costs	68,000

You may assume that no materials were lost through spoilage or waste during the month. The company accounts for production costs on a moving average basis.

Required:

Prepare a production report for the Cooking process for the month, supported by a schedule showing computation of unit costs.

P3–40. *Production report; Average cost method.* (Appendix) The Patchrite Company produces a product which goes through four processes: Cooking, Grinding, Blending, and Packaging. Information relating to the Blending process for June 19x5, is provided below:

Work in process, June 1:

Units in process	5,000
Processing completed	4/5

Costs in the inventory:

Transferred in from Grinding	$ 8,370
Materials added in Blending	1,000
Labor added in Blending	400
Overhead added in Blending	1,320
Total cost	$11,090

Work in process, June 30:

Units in process	9,000
Processing completed	2/9

Transferred in from Grinding:

Units	32,000
Cost	$51,200
Units completed and transferred to Packaging	28,000

Costs added in Blending:

Materials	$ 4,600
Labor	3,200
Overhead	9,180

Materials are added in the Blending process when processing is one-third completed. Labor and overhead costs are incurred evenly throughout the process. The company uses the moving average method to cost units of product.

Required:

Prepare a production report for June in the Blending process, supported by a schedule showing computation of all unit costs.

P3–41.   *Computation of unit costs of production.* (Appendix)   Kimber Manufacturing Company was organized on January 2 of the current year. The company operates a process costing system. The main product, Throgles, goes through three processes before production is complete. These processes are: Molding, Sanding, and Firing. Selected data from cost and production reports for the current year are given below:

	Molding	Sanding	Firing
Costs added to production:			
Raw materials	$33,000	$ –0–	$ –0–
Processing	6,000	27,000	15,000
Units started into production or			
transferred *in* during the			
current year	44,000	?	?
Ending inventory:			
Number of units	6,000	4,000	5,000
Stage of completion	1/3	1/2	1/5

The raw materials are added at the beginning of the Molding Process. Processing costs are incurred evenly throughout each process.

Required:

1. Determine the number of units transferred out of each process during the current year.
2. Calculate the equivalent units of production in terms of (*a*) materials and (*b*) processing for Molding, and in terms of processing for Sanding and Firing.
3. Compute the unit cost added in each process.
4. Compute the final cost of a complete Throgle.

Chapter 4

Cost behavior patterns — A closer look

In our discussion of cost terms and concepts in Chapter 2, we stated that one way in which costs can be classified is by behavior. We defined cost behavior as meaning how a cost will react or change as changes take place in the level of business activity. An understanding of cost behavior is the key to many decisions in an organization, in that by understanding how costs behave a manager is better able to predict what costs will be under various operating circumstances. Experience has shown that attempts at decision making without a thorough understanding of the costs involved—and how these costs may change with the activity level—can lead to disaster. A decision to double production of a particular product line, for example, might result in the incurrence of far greater additional costs than could be generated in additional revenues. To avoid such problems, a manager must be able to accurately predict what costs will be at various activity levels. In this chapter we shall find that the key to effective cost prediction lies in an understanding of cost behavior patterns.

TYPES OF COST BEHAVIOR PATTERNS

In our brief discussion of cost behavior in Chapter 2 we mentioned only variable and fixed costs. There is a third behavior pattern, generally known as a *mixed* or *semivariable* cost. All three cost behavior patterns—variable, fixed, and mixed—are found in most organizations.

Variable costs

We found in Chapter 2 that a variable cost is so named because it varies in total in direct relationship to changes in the activity level. If the activity level doubles, then one would expect the variable costs to double as well. If the activity level goes up only 10 percent, then one would expect the variable costs to increase by only 10 percent.

In order for variable costs to change in total in direct proportion to changes in the level of activity, they must be constant on a *per unit* basis. Assume, for example, that the Nifty Truck Company produces trucks. There is one radiator to each truck. The radiators cost $25 each. If we look at the cost of radiators on a *per truck* basis, the cost remains constant at $25 per truck. But the total cost of radiators changes in direct proportion to the number of trucks produced as shown below:

Number of trucks produced	Radiator cost per truck	Total radiator cost
250	$25	$ 6,250
500	25	12,500
750	25	18,750
1,000	25	25,000

Exhibit 4–1
Variable cost behavior

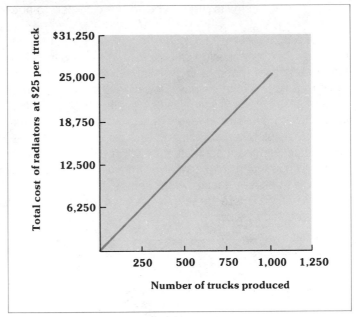

The idea that a variable cost is constant per unit but varies in total with the activity level is crucial to an understanding of cost behavior patterns. We shall rely on this concept again and again in this chapter and in chapters ahead. Exhibit 4–1 contains a graphical illustration of variable cost behavior.

THE ACTIVITY BASE.   In order for a cost to be variable, it must be variable *with something.* That "something" is the activity base. There can be many measures of activity in a firm. Two of the most common activity bases are units produced and units sold. Other activity bases might include the number of miles driven by salespersons, the number of pounds of laundry processed by a hotel, the number of letters typed by a secretary, the number of hours of machine time logged, and the number of beds in a hospital.

In order to plan and control variable costs, a manager must be well acquainted with the various activity bases within the firm. People sometimes get the notion that if a cost doesn't vary with production or with sales, then it is not really a variable cost. This, of course, is not correct. As suggested by the range of bases listed above, costs can be incurred as a function of many different activities within an organization. Whether a cost is variable will depend on whether its incurrence is a function of the activity measure under consideration. For example, if a manager is analyzing the cost of service calls under a product warranty, the relevant activity measure will be the number of service calls made. Those costs which vary in total with the number of service calls made will be variable costs.

EXTENT OF VARIABLE COSTS.   The number and type of variable costs present in an organization will depend in large part on the organization's structure and purpose. A highly capital-intensive organization such as a public utility will tend to have few variable costs. The bulk of its costs will be associated with its plant, and these costs will tend to be quite insensitive to changes in levels of service provided. A manufacturing firm, by contrast, will often have many variable costs. It will have variable costs associated with the manufacture of its products, as well as with their distribution to customers. A service organization or a merchandising firm will tend to fall between these two extremes.

A few of the more frequently encountered variable costs are shown in the tabulation below:

Type of organization	Variable costs
Merchandising firm	Cost of merchandise sold
Manufacturing firm	Manufacturing costs:
	Prime costs:
	Direct materials
	Direct labor
	Variable portion of manufacturing
	overhead:
	Indirect materials
	Lubricants
	Supplies
	Utilities
	Setup time
	Indirect labor
Both merchandising and manufacturing firms	Selling and administrative costs:
	Commissions to salespersons
	Clerical costs, such as invoicing
	Freight out
Service organizations	Supplies, travel, clerical

The costs listed under "variable portion of manufacturing overhead" should not be viewed as being inclusive, but rather as being representative of the kinds of variable costs found in this classification.

True variable versus step-variable costs

Not all variable costs have exactly the same behavior pattern. Some variable costs behave in a *true variable* or *proportionately variable* pattern. Other variable costs behave in a *step-variable* pattern.

TRUE VARIABLE COSTS.   Direct materials would be a true or proportionately variable cost. Direct materials can be purchased in the exact quantity needed, and quantities used will vary directly with output. In addition, any amounts unused can be stored up and carried forward to the next period as inventory.

STEP-VARIABLE COSTS.   Indirect labor is also considered to be a variable cost, but it doesn't behave in quite the same way as direct materials. As an example, let us consider the labor cost of maintenance workers, which would be part of indirect labor.

Unlike direct materials, the time of maintenance workers is obtainable only in large chunks, rather than in exact quantities. Moreover, any maintenance time not utilized cannot be stored up as inventory and carried forward to the next period. Either the time is used effectively as it expires hour by hour, or it is gone forever. Furthermore, the utilization of indirect labor time can be quite flexible, whereas the utilization of direct materials is usually quite set. A maintenance crew, for example, can work at a fairly leisurely pace if pressures are light, but then the crew can intensify its efforts if pressures build up. For this reason, somewhat small changes in the level of production may have no effect on the number of maintenance people needed to properly carry on maintenance work.

A cost (such as the labor cost of maintenance workers) that is obtainable only in large chunks and which increases or decreases only in response to fairly wide changes in activity levels is known as a *step-variable cost.* The behavior of a step-variable cost, contrasted with the behavior of a true variable cost, is illustrated in Exhibit 4–2.

Notice that the need for maintenance help changes only with fairly wide changes in volume, and that when additional maintenance time is obtained it comes in large, indivisible pieces. The strategy of management in dealing

Exhibit 4–2
True variable versus step-variable costs

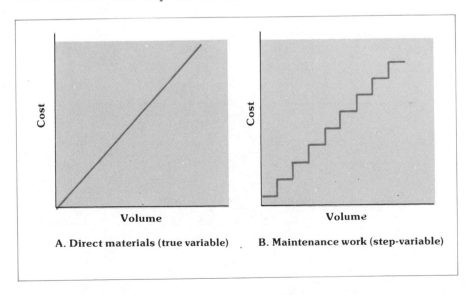

A. Direct materials (true variable)   B. Maintenance work (step-variable)

with step-variable costs must be to obtain the highest level of utilization possible for any given step. Great care must be taken in dealing with these kinds of costs, to prevent "fat" from building up in an organization. There is a tendency to employ additional help more quickly than might be needed, and generally a reluctance to lay people off when volume declines.

The linearity assumption and the relevant range

In dealing with variable costs we have assumed a strictly linear relationship between cost and volume, except in the case of step-variable costs. Economists correctly point out that many costs which the accountant classifies as variable actually behave in a *curvilinear* fashion. The behavior of a curvilinear cost is shown in Exhibit 4–3. Notice that a strictly linear relationship between cost and volume does not exist either at very high or at very low levels of volume.

Although the accountant recognizes that many costs are not linear in their relationship to volume at some points, he or she concentrates on their behavior within narrow bands of activity known as the *relevant range.* The relevant range may be defined as the range over which volume is expected to fluctuate during the period of time under review. Within the

Exhibit 4–3
Curvilinear costs and the relevant range

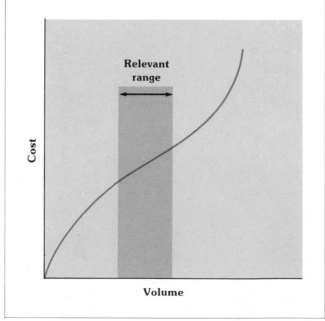

relevant range the relationship of cost to volume is normally stable enough that the assumption of strict linearity can be used with insignificant loss of accuracy. The concept of the relevant range is illustrated in Exhibit 4–3.

Fixed costs

In our discussion of cost behavior patterns in Chapter 2 we stated that fixed costs are costs which remain constant in total regardless of changes in the level of activity. To continue the Nifty Truck Company example, if the company rents a factory building for $50,000 per year the *total* amount of rent paid will not change regardless of the number of trucks produced in a year. This concept is shown graphically in Exhibit 4–4.

Since fixed costs remain constant in total, the amount of cost computed on a *per unit* basis will get progressively smaller the greater the number of units produced. If the Nifty Truck Company produces only 250 trucks in a year the $50,000 fixed rental cost would amount to $200 per truck. If 1,000 trucks are produced it would amount to only $50 per truck. As we noted in Chapter 2, this aspect of fixed costs can be confusing to the manager, although it is necessary in some contexts to express fixed costs on an average per unit basis. We found in Chapter 3, for example, that the manager needs a broad unit cost figure containing both variable and fixed cost elements for purposes of preparing financial statements.

Exhibit 4–4
Fixed cost behavior

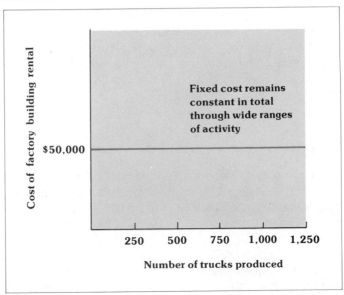

For *internal* uses, however, the manager rarely expresses a fixed cost on a per unit basis, because of the potential confusion involved. Experience has shown that for internal uses fixed costs are most easily (and most safely) dealt with on a total basis, rather than on a per unit basis.

The trend toward fixed costs

The trend in many companies today is toward greater fixed costs relative to variable costs. There are at least two factors responsible for this trend. First, automation is becoming increasingly important in all types of organizations. Although automation has played a significant role in factory operations for well over a century, its role continues to increase. In addition, automation is rapidly becoming a significant factor in some traditionally service-oriented industries as well. Increased automation means increased investment in machinery and equipment, with the attendant fixed depreciation or lease charges.

Second, labor unions have been increasingly successful in stabilizing employment through labor contracts. Labor leaders have set guaranteed annual salaries or guaranteed minimum weeks of work high on their list of goals for the future. Although most people would agree that a stabilization of employment is desirable from a social point of view, guaranteed salaries and work weeks do reduce the response of direct labor costs to changes in production.

This shift away from variable costs toward fixed costs has been so significant in some firms that they have become largely "fixed cost" organizations. The textile industry, for example, can be cited as one in which the bulk of firms have moved heavily toward automation with basically inflexible fixed costs replacing flexible, more responsive variable costs to a considerable extent. These shifts are very significant from a managerial accounting point of view, in that planning in many ways becomes much more crucial when one is dealing with large amounts of fixed costs. The reason is that when dealing with fixed costs the manager is much more "locked in," and generally has fewer options available in day-to-day decisions.

Types of fixed costs

Fixed costs are sometimes referred to as capacity costs, since they result from outlays made for plant facilities, equipment, and so on, needed to provide the basic capacity for sustained operations. For planning purposes, fixed costs can be viewed as being either *committed* or *discretionary*.

COMMITTED FIXED COSTS. Committed fixed costs are those which relate to the investment in plant, equipment, and the basic organization of a firm. Examples of such costs would include depreciation of plant facilities (buildings and equipment), taxes on real estate, insurance, and salaries of key management and operating personnel.

The key factor about committed fixed costs is that they can't be reduced to zero even for a short period of time without impairing either profitability or the long-run goals of a firm. Even if operations are interrupted or cut back, the committed fixed costs will still continue unchanged. During a recessionary period, for example, a firm can't discharge its key executives or sell off part of the plant. Facilities and basic organizational structure must be kept intact at all times. In terms of long-run goals, the costs of any other course of action would be far greater than any short-run savings that might be realized.

Since committed fixed costs are basic to the long-run goals of a firm, their planning horizon usually encompasses many years. The commitments involved in these costs are made only after careful analysis of long-run sales forecasts, and after relating of these forecasts to future capacity needs. Careful control must be exercised by management in the planning stage to ensure that a firm's long-run needs are properly evaluated. Once a decision is made to build a certain size plant, a firm becomes locked into that decision for many years to come.

After a firm becomes committed to a basic plant and organization, how are the associated costs controlled from year to year? Control of committed fixed costs comes through *utilization.* The strategy of management must be to utilize the plant and organization as effectively as possible in bringing about desired goals.

DISCRETIONARY FIXED COSTS.   Discretionary fixed costs (sometimes referred to as *managed* fixed costs) arise from *annual* decisions by management to spend in certain fixed cost areas. Examples of discretionary fixed costs would include advertising, research, and management development programs.

Basically, two key differences exist between discretionary fixed costs and committed fixed costs. First, the planning horizon for a discretionary fixed cost is fairly short-term—usually a single year. By contrast, we indicated earlier that committed fixed costs have a planning horizon that encompasses many years. Second, under dire circumstances it may be possible to cut certain discretionary fixed costs back for short periods of time with minimal damage to the long-run goals of the organization. For example, a firm that has been spending $50,000 annually on management development programs may be forced because of poor economic conditions to reduce its spending in that area during a given year. Although some unfavorable consequences might result from the cutback, it is doubtful that these consequences would be as great as if the company had decided to economize during the year by disposing of a portion of its plant.

The key factor about discretionary fixed costs is that management is not locked into a decision for any more than a single budget period. Each year a fresh look can be taken at the expenditure level in the various discretionary fixed cost areas. A decision can then be made on whether to continue the expenditure, increase it, reduce it, or discontinue it altogether.

TOP MANAGEMENT PHILOSOPHY. In our discussion of fixed costs we have drawn a sharp line between committed fixed costs and discretionary fixed costs. As a practical matter, the line between these two classes of costs should be viewed as being somewhat flexible. The reason is that whether a cost is committed or discretionary will depend in large part on the philosophy of top management.

Some management groups prefer to exercise discretion as often as possible on as many costs as possible. They prefer to review costs frequently, and to adjust costs frequently, as conditions and needs warrant. Management groups who are inclined in this direction tend to view fixed costs as being largely discretionary. Other management groups are slow to make adjustments in costs (especially adjustments downward) as conditions and needs change. They prefer to maintain the status quo, and to leave programs and personnel largely undisturbed even though changing conditions and needs might suggest the desirability of adjustments. Managers inclined in this direction tend to view virtually all fixed costs as being committed.

To cite an example, during recessionary periods when the level of home building is down, many construction companies lay off their workers and virtually disband operations for a period of time. Other construction companies continue large numbers of employees on the payroll, even though the workers have little or no work to do. In the first instance, management is viewing its fixed costs as being largely discretionary in nature. In the second instance, management is viewing its fixed costs as being largely committed. The philosophy of most management groups will fall somewhere between these two extremes.

Fixed costs and the relevant range

The concept of the relevant range also has application in dealing with fixed costs, particularly those of a discretionary nature. At the beginning of a period programs are set and budgets established. The level of discretionary fixed costs will depend on the support needs of the programs which have been planned, which in turn will depend at least in part on the level of activity envisioned in the organization overall. At very high levels of activity, programs are usually broadened or expanded to include many things that might not be pursued at lower levels of activity. In addition, the support needs at high levels of activity are usually much greater than the support needs at lower levels of activity. For example, the advertising needs of a company pushing to increase sales by 25 percent probably would be much greater than if no sales increase was planned.

Fixed costs and the relevant range are shown in Exhibit 4–5.

Exhibit 4–5
Fixed costs and the relevant range

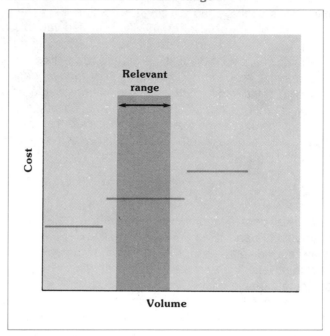

Although discretionary fixed costs are most susceptible to adjustment according to changing needs, Exhibit 4–5 also has application to committed fixed costs. As a company expands its level of activity, it may outgrow its present plant, or the key management core may need to be expanded. The result, of course, will be increased committed fixed costs as a larger plant is built, and as new key management positions are created.

One's first reaction is to say that discretionary and committed fixed costs are really just step-variable costs. To some extent this is true, since *all* costs vary in the long run. There are two major differences, however, between the step-variable costs depicted earlier in Exhibit 4–2 and the fixed costs depicted in Exhibit 4–5.

The first difference is that the step-variable costs can be adjusted very quickly, whereas once fixed costs have been set, even if they are discretionary fixed costs, they often can't be changed in the short run. A step-variable cost such as maintenance labor, for example, can be adjusted upward or downward very quickly by the hiring and firing of maintenance workers. By contrast, once a company has committed itself to a particular program it becomes locked into the attendant fixed costs, at least for the budget period under consideration. Once an advertising contract has been signed, for example, the company is locked into the attendant costs for the contract period.

The second difference is that the *width of the steps* depicted for step-variable costs is much narrower than the width of the steps depicted for fixed costs such as those shown in Exhibit 4–5. The width of the steps relates to volume or level of activity. For step-variable costs the width of a step may be 40 hours of activity or less, if one is dealing, for example, with maintenance labor cost. By contrast, for fixed costs the width of a step may be *thousands* or even *tens of thousands* of hours of activity. In essence, the width of the steps for step-variable costs is generally so narrow that these costs can be treated essentially as variable costs. The width of the steps for fixed costs, on the other hand, is so wide that these costs generally must be treated as being entirely fixed within the relevant range.

Mixed costs

A mixed cost (sometimes called a semivariable cost) is one that contains both variable and fixed cost elements. At certain levels of activity mixed costs may display essentially the same characteristics as a fixed cost; at other levels of activity they may display essentially the same characteristics as a variable cost.

To continue the Nifty Truck Company example, assume that the company leases a large part of the machinery used in its operations. The lease

Exhibit 4–6
Mixed cost behavior

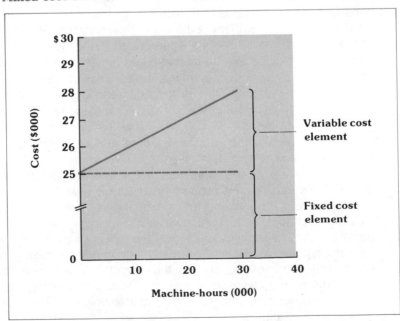

agreement calls for a flat annual lease payment of $25,000, plus $0.10 for each hour that the machines are operated during the year. If during a particular year the machines are operated a cumulative total of 30,000 hours, then the lease cost of the machines will be $28,000, made up of $25,000 in fixed cost, plus $3,000 in variable cost. The concept of a mixed cost is shown graphically in Exhibit 4–6.

Even if the machines leased by the Nifty Truck Company aren't used a single hour during the year, the company will still have to pay the minimum $25,000 charge. This is why the cost line in Exhibit 4–6 intersects the vertical cost axis at the $25,000 point. For each hour the machines are used, the *total* cost of leasing will increase by $0.10. Therefore, the total cost line slopes upward as the variable cost element is added onto the fixed cost element.

THE ANALYSIS OF MIXED COSTS

The concept of a mixed cost is important, since mixed costs are common to a wide range of firms. Examples of mixed costs include electricity, heat, repairs, telephone, and maintenance.

The fixed portion of a mixed cost represents the basic, minimum charge for just having a service *ready and available* for use. The variable portion represents the charge made for *actual consumption* of the service. As one would expect, the variable element varies in proportion to the amount of the service which is consumed.

For planning purposes, how does management handle mixed costs? The ideal approach would be to take each invoice as it comes in and break it down into its fixed and variable elements. As a practical matter, even if this type of minute breakdown were possible the cost of doing so would probably be prohibitive. Analysis of mixed costs is normally done on an *aggregate* basis, concentrating on the *past behavior* of a cost at various levels of activity. If this analysis is done carefully, good approximations of the fixed and variable elements of a cost can be obtained with a minimum of effort.

We will examine three methods of breaking mixed costs down into their fixed and variable elements—the *high-low method,* the *scattergraph method,* and the *least squares method.*

The high-low method

This method of analyzing mixed costs requires that the cost involved (for example, maintenance) be observed both at high and at low levels of activity within the relevant range. The difference in cost observed at the two extremes is divided by the change in activity in order to determine the amount of variable cost involved.

To illustrate, assume that maintenance costs for the Arco Company have been observed as follows within the relevant range of 5,000 to 8,000 direct labor-hours (DLH):

Maintenance cost incurred	Direct labor-hours
$ 700	5,000
800	6,000
900	7,000
1,000	8,000

Since total maintenance cost increases as the activity level increases, it seems obvious that some variable cost is present. To separate the variable cost element from the fixed cost element, we need to relate the change in direct labor-hours between the high and low points to the change which we observe in cost:

	Maintenance cost incurred	Direct labor-hours
High point observed	$1,000	8,000
Low point observed	700	5,000
Change observed	$ 300	3,000

$$\text{Variable rate} = \frac{\text{Change in cost}}{\text{Change in activity}} = \frac{\$300}{3,000} = \$0.10 \text{ per direct labor-hour}$$

Having determined that the variable rate is $0.10 per direct labor-hour, it is now possible to determine the amount of fixed cost present:

$$\begin{aligned} \text{Fixed cost element} &= \text{Total cost} - \text{Variable cost element} \\ &= \$1,000 - (\$0.10 \times 8,000 \text{ hours}) \\ &= \$200 \end{aligned}$$

Both the variable and fixed cost elements have now been isolated. The cost of maintenance within the relevant range analyzed can be expressed as being $200 plus $0.10 per direct labor-hour. This is sometimes referred to as a *cost formula.*

$$\left.\begin{array}{l} \text{Cost formula for maintenance, over} \\ \text{the relevant range of 5,000 to} \\ \text{8,000 direct labor-hours} \end{array}\right\} = \begin{array}{l} \$200 \text{ fixed cost} + \$0.10 \\ \text{per direct labor-hour} \end{array}$$

We can prove the accuracy of the formula, by applying it to any other activity level within the relevant range to obtain total maintenance cost. At an activity level of 6,000 direct labor-hours, for example, total cost would be:

Variable cost ($0.10 × 6,000 DLH)	$600
Fixed cost	200
Total cost	$800

Since the $800 total cost figure agrees with the cost observed earlier at 6,000 direct labor-hours, we can see that the cost formula accurately expresses the incurrence of maintenance cost. The data used in this example are shown graphically in Exhibit 4–7.

Great care must be exercised in applying the high-low method to be sure that the costs being used in the analysis are representative of general business activity, and contain no distortions or unusual charges. Also, it

Exhibit 4–7
High-low method of cost analysis
The Arco Company—maintenance cost

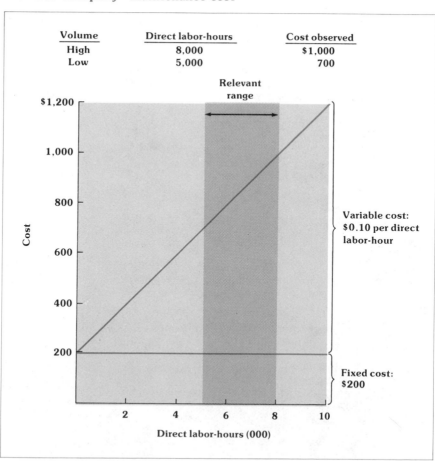

must be kept in mind that the cost formula will not be valid outside of the relevant range.

The scattergraph method

The high-low method works very well in analyzing those cost situations where the variable portion of a mixed cost varies at a constant rate per unit of activity. But many mixed costs are such that the variable portion does not vary at a constant rate, and an *average* rate of variability must be determined.

One approach to determining an average rate of variability is to construct a graph on which cost is shown on the vertical axis, and volume or rate of activity is shown on the horizontal axis. Total costs observed at various levels of activity are then plotted on the graph, and a line is fitted to the plotted points by simple visual inspection. A graph of this type is known as a *scattergraph*, and the line fitted to the plotted points is known as a *regression line.* The regression line, in effect, is a line of averages, with the average variable cost per unit of activity represented by the slope of the line, and the average fixed cost in total represented by the point where the regression line intersects the cost axis.

For purposes of illustration, assume that the Beach Company has recorded costs for water as follows:

Water consumed (000 gallons)	Total cost
10	$230
15	270
12	260
9	220
11	250
13	240
8	220

The total costs of water above have been plotted on the graph in Exhibit 4–8, and a regression line has been fitted to the plotted data by visual inspection.

Since the regression line strikes the cost axis at the $150 point, that amount represents the fixed cost element. The variable cost element would be $8 per 1,000 gallons of water consumed, computed as follows:

Total cost observed at 15,000 gallons of water consumed (a point falling on the regression line in Exhibit 4–8)	$270
Less fixed cost element	150
Variable cost element	$120

$120 ÷ 15,000 gallons = $8 per thousand gallons.

Exhibit 4–8
A completed scattergraph

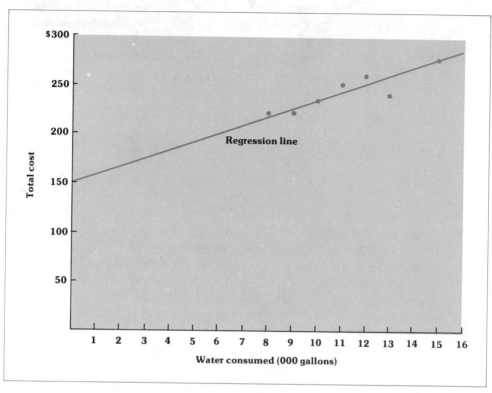

A scattergraph can be an extremely useful tool in the hands of an experienced analyst. Quirks in cost behavior due to strikes, bad weather, breakdowns, and so on, become immediately apparent to the trained observer, and he or she can make appropriate adjustment to the data in fitting the regression line. Many cost analysts would argue that a scattergraph should be the beginning point in all cost analyses, due to the benefits to be gained from having the data visually available in graph form.

The least squares method

The least squares method is a more sophisticated approach to the scattergraph idea. Rather than fitting a regression line through the scattergraph data by simple visual inspection, the least squares method fits the line by statistical analysis.

The least squares method is based on computations which find their foundation in the equation for a straight line. A straight line can be expressed in equation form as:

$$Y = a + bX$$

with a as the fixed element and b as the degree of variability, or the slope of the line. From this basic equation, and given a set of observations, n, two simultaneous linear equations can be developed which will fit a regression line to a linear array of data. The equations are:[1]

$$\Sigma XY = a\Sigma X + b\Sigma X^2 \qquad (1)$$
$$\Sigma Y = na + b\Sigma X \qquad (2)$$

where:

a = Fixed cost.
b = Variable cost.
n = Number of observations.
X = Activity measure (hours, etc.).
Y = Total mixed cost observed.

AN EXAMPLE OF LEAST SQUARES. The application of the least squares method can best be seen through a concrete example. Let us assume that a company is anxious to break its power (electrical) costs down into basic variable and fixed cost elements. Over the past year power costs (Y) have been observed as shown in the tabulation below. The number of hours of machine time logged (X) in incurring these costs is also shown in the tabulation.

Month	Machine-hours (000) (X)	Power costs (Y)	XY	X²
January	9	$ 300	$ 2,700	81
February	8	250	2,000	64
March	9	290	2,610	81
April	10	290	2,900	100
May	12	360	4,320	144
June	13	340	4,420	169
July	11	320	3,520	121
August	11	330	3,630	121
September	10	300	3,000	100
October	8	260	2,080	64
November	7	230	1,610	49
December	8	260	2,080	64
	116	$3,530	$34,870	1,158

Substituting these amounts in the two linear equations given above, we have:

$$\$34,870 = 116a + 1,158b \qquad (1)$$
$$\$ 3,530 = 12a + 116b \qquad (2)$$

In order to solve the equations, it will be necessary to eliminate one of the terms. The "a" term can be eliminated by multiplying Equation

---

[1] The Appendix contains an alternative approach to the least squares method.

(1) by 12, by multiplying Equation (2) by 116, and then by subtracting Equation (2) from Equation (1). These steps are shown below:

Multiply Equation (1) by 12: $418,440 = 1,392a + 13,896b
Multiply Equation (2) by 116: $409,480 = 1,392a + 13,456b

Subtract (2) from (1): $ 8,960 =   440b
                                $ 20.36 = b

Therefore, the variable rate for power cost is $20.36 for each thousand machine-hours of operating time. The fixed cost of power can be obtained by substituting the value for term b in Equation (1):

$$\$34,870 = 116a + 1,158(\$20.36)$$
$$\$34,870 = 116a + \$23,581$$
$$\$11,289 = 116a$$
$$\$ 97.32 = a$$

The fixed rate for power is $97.32 per month. The cost formula for the mixed cost is therefore $97.32 per month plus $20.36 per thousand machine-hours worked.

Cost formula for power over the relevant range of 7,000 to 13,000 machine-hours. } = $97.32 fixed cost + $20.36 per thousand machine-hours.

In terms of the linear equation $Y = a + bX$, the cost formula can be expressed as:

$$Y = \$97.32 + \$20.36X$$

To show how the cost formula is used for planning purposes, if it is expected that 10,500 machine-hours will be worked during the coming month, expected power costs will be:

Variable costs:
    10.5 thousand machine-hours × $20.36 .... $213.78
Fixed costs 97.32
    Total expected power costs $311.10

WHAT DOES "LEAST SQUARES" MEAN?   The term least squares means that the sum of the squares of the deviations from the plotted points to the regression line *is smaller* than would be obtained from any other line fitted to the data. This idea can be illustrated as shown in Exhibit 4–9.

Notice from the exhibit that the deviations from the plotted points to the regression line are measured vertically on the graph. They are not measured perpendicular to the regression line. "Least squares" will have been attained when $\Sigma(Y - Y_1)^2$ is at the lowest possible figure. At the

Exhibit 4–9
The concept of least squares

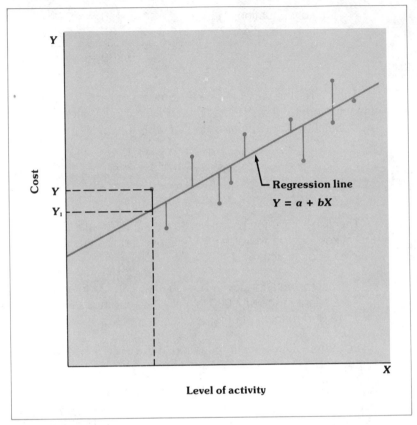

point of "least squares" the best possible fit of a regression line to the
plotted points will have been achieved, in terms of slope and placement
of the line.

The use of judgment in cost analysis

Although a cost formula has the appearance of exactness, the user
should recognize that the breakdown of any mixed cost by any of the
three techniques that we have discussed involves a substantial amount
of estimating. The breakdowns represent *good approximations* of the fixed
and variable elements involved; they should not be construed as being
precise analyses. Managers must be ready to step in at any point in their
analysis of a cost, and to adjust their computations for judgment factors
which in their view are critical to a proper understanding of the mixed
cost involved. However, the fact that computations are not exact, and

involve estimates and judgment factors, does not prevent data from being useful and meaningful in decision making. The managers who wait to make a decision until they have perfect data available will rarely have an opportunity to demonstrate their decision-making ability.

Multiple regression analysis

In all of our computations involving mixed costs, we have assumed a single causive factor as the basis for the behavior of the variable element. That causive factor has been volume or rate of some activity, such as direct labor-hours, machine-hours, production, or sales. This assumption is acceptable for many mixed costs, but in some situations there may be more than one causive factor involved in the behavior of the variable element. For example, in a shipping department the cost of freight-out might depend on both the number of units shipped and the weight of the units, as dual causive factors. In a situation such as this the equation for a simple regression would have to be expanded to include the additional variable:

$$Y = a + bX + cW$$

where W = the weight of a unit, and c = the factor of variability. When dealing with an expanded equation such as this one, the simple regression analysis which we have been doing is no longer adequate. A *multiple regression analysis* is necessary. Although the added variable or variables will make the computations more complex, the principles involved are the same as in a simple regression such as we have been doing. Because of the complexity of the computations involved, multiple regression is generally done with the aid of a computer.

Engineering approach to cost study

Some firms use an engineering approach to the study of cost behavior. Essentially, an engineering approach involves a quantitative analysis of what cost behavior should be, based on the industrial engineer's evaluation of the production methods to be used, the materials specifications, labor needs, equipment needs, efficiency of production, power consumption, and so on. The engineering approach must be used in those situations where no past experience is available on activity and costs. In addition, it is often used in tandem with the methods we have discussed above in order to sharpen the accuracy of cost analysis. An NAA (National Association of Accountants) research report of actual business practices describes the use of the engineering approach as follows:

The industrial engineering approach to determination of how costs should vary with volume proceeds by systematic study of materials, labor, services, and facilities needed at varying volumes. The aim is to find the best way to obtain the desired production. These studies generally make use of past experience, but it is used as a guide or as a check upon the results obtained by direct study of the production methods and facilities. Where no past experience is available, as with a new product, plant, or method, this approach can be applied to estimate the changes in cost that will accompany changes in volume.[2]

THE CONTRIBUTION FORMAT

Once the manager has separated costs into fixed and variable elements what does he or she do with the data? To answer this question will require most of the remainder of this book, since virtually everything the manager does rests in some way on an understanding of cost behavior. One immediate and very significant application of the ideas we have developed, however, is found in a new format to the income statement, known as the *contribution approach*. The unique thing about the contribution approach is that it provides the manager with an income statement geared directly to cost behavior.

Why a new income statement format?

The *traditional* approach to the income statement, such as illustrated in Chapter 2, and such as you studied in financial accounting, is not organized in terms of cost behavior. Rather, it is organized in a "functional" format— emphasizing the functions of production, administration, and sales in the classification and presentation of cost data. No attempt is made to distinguish between the behavior of costs included under each functional heading. Under the heading "Administrative Expense," for example, one can expect to find both variable and fixed costs lumped together.

Although an income statement prepared in the functional format may be useful for external reporting purposes, it has serious limitations so far as usefulness internally to the manager is concerned. Internally, the manager needs cost data organized in a format that will facilitate the carrying out of major responsibilities of planning, control, and decision making. As we shall see in chapters ahead, these responsibilities are discharged most effectively when cost data are available in a fixed and variable format. The contribution approach to the income statement has been developed in response to this need.

The contribution approach

Exhibit 4–10 presents a model of the contribution approach to the income statement, along with the traditional approach with which you are already familiar.

---

[2] National Association of Accountants, *The Analysis of Cost-Volume-Profit Relationships,* Research Report no. 16 (New York: 1960), p. 17.

Exhibit 4–10
Comparison of the contribution income statement with the traditional income statement

Contribution approach (costs organized by behavior)			Traditional approach (costs organized by function)		
Sales		$12,000	Sales		$12,000
Less variable expenses:			Less cost of goods sold ...		6,000*
Variable production	$2,000		Gross margin		$ 6,000
Variable administrative ...	400		Less operating expenses:		
Variable selling	600	3,000	Administrative	$1,900*	
Contribution margin		$ 9,000	Selling	3,100*	5,000
Less fixed expenses:			Net income		$ 1,000
Fixed production	$4,000				
Fixed administrative	1,500				
Fixed selling	2,500	8,000			
Net income		$ 1,000			

* Contains both variable and fixed expenses.

Notice that the contribution approach separates costs into fixed and variable categories, first deducting variable expenses from sales to obtain what is known as the *contribution margin*. The term "contribution margin" means what remains from total sales revenues, after deducting variable expenses, that can be used *to contribute* toward covering of fixed expenses, and then toward profits for the period.

The contribution approach to the income statement is widely used as an internal planning and decision-making tool. Its emphasis on costs by behavior facilitates cost-volume-profit analysis, such as we shall be doing in the following chapter. The approach is also very useful in appraisal of management performance, in segmented reporting of profit data, in budgeting, and in organizing data pertinent to all kinds of special decisions, such as product line analysis, pricing, use of scarce resources, and make or buy analyses. All of these topics are covered in later chapters.

SUMMARY

Managers analyze cost behavior in order to have a basis for predicting how costs will respond to changes in activity levels throughout the organization. We have looked at three types of cost behavior—variable, fixed, and mixed. In the case of mixed costs, we have studied three methods of breaking a mixed cost into its basic variable and fixed elements. The high-low method is the simplest of the three, having as its underlying assumption that the rate of variability is constant per unit of activity. When the rate of variability in a mixed cost is not constant, an average rate of variability must be computed. This can be done by either the scattergraph method or the least squares method. Both methods require the construction of a regression line, the slope of which represents the average rate of variability in the mixed cost being analyzed. The least squares method is the most accurate of the two, in that it uses statistical analysis to fit a regression line to an array of data.

Managers use costs organized by behavior as a basis for many decisions. To facilitate this use, costs are often prepared in a contribution format. The unique thing about the contribution format is that it classifies costs on the income statement by cost behavior, rather than by the functions of production, administration, and sales.

KEY TERMS FOR REVIEW

Activity base
Step-variable costs
Relevant range
Curvilinear costs
Committed costs
Discretionary costs
Mixed costs
Semivariable costs
High-low method

Cost formula
Scattergraph method
Regression line
Least squares method
Multiple regression analysis
Contribution approach
Functional approach
Contribution margin

REVIEW PROBLEM ON COST BEHAVIOR

Consider the following costs of X Company over the relevant range of 2,000 to 6,000 units produced:

	2,000	4,000	6,000
Variable costs	$10,000	$?	$?
Fixed costs	60,000	?	?
Total costs	$70,000	$?	$?
Cost per unit:			
Variable	$?	$?	$?
Fixed	?	?	?
Total	$?	$?	$?

Required:
Compute the missing amounts.

Solution:
The variable cost per unit of product can be computed as:

$$\$10,000 \div 2,000 \text{ units} = \$5 \text{ per unit}$$

Therefore, in accordance with the behavior of variable and fixed costs, the missing amounts are:

	2,000	4,000	6,000
Variable costs	$10,000	$20,000	$30,000
Fixed costs	60,000	60,000	60,000
Total costs	$70,000	$80,000	$90,000
Cost per unit:			
Variable	$ 5	$ 5	$ 5
Fixed	30	15	10
Total	$35	$20	$15

Observe that the variable costs increase in total proportionately with increases in the number of units produced, but remain constant at $5 on a per unit basis. On the other hand, the fixed costs by definition do not change in total with changes in the level of output. They remain constant at $60,000. With increases in production, however, they decrease on a per unit basis, dropping from $30 per unit when 2,000 units are produced to only $10 per unit when 6,000 units are produced. *Because of this troublesome aspect of fixed costs, they are most easily (and most safely) dealt with on a total basis, rather than on a unit basis, in cost analysis work.*

APPENDIX: ALTERNATE APPROACH TO LEAST SQUARES

Some managers prefer an alternate approach to the least squares method, which does not require use of the equations given in the chapter. Assume that a firm wishes to develop a cost formula for its maintenance expense. The company has determined that the variable portion of maintenance is incurred as a function of the number of machine-hours worked. Data on machine-hours and the attendant maintenance expense observed are given below for the first six months of 19x1:

Month	Machine-hours (X)	Maintenance expense (Y)	Variance from average Machine-hours (X')	Variance from average Maintenance expense (Y')	X' Y'	X'²
January	400	$ 180	−100	−$20	+$ 2,000	10,000
February	575	215	+ 75	+ 15	+ 1,125	5,625
March	350	170	−150	− 30	+ 4,500	22,500
April	475	195	− 25	− 5	+ 125	625
May	550	210	+ 50	+ 10	+ 500	2,500
June	650	230	+150	+ 30	+ 4,500	22,500
Total..........	3,000	$1,200			$12,750	63,750
Average	500	$ 200				

Variable rate: $\dfrac{\Sigma X' Y'}{\Sigma X'^2} = \dfrac{\$12,750}{63,750} = \$0.20$ per machine-hour

Total fixed cost: $Y = a + bX$
$\$200 = a + \$0.20(500 \text{ hours})$
$a = \$200 - \$100$
$a = \$100$

Therefore, the cost formula for maintenance expense is $100 fixed cost, plus $0.20 per machine-hour. Or, in equation form it can be expressed as:

$$Y = \$100 + \$0.20X$$

There are six basic steps to computing a cost formula by this method. The reader should trace these six steps back through the example given above.

Step 1: Compute the average activity level (machine-hours, in this case), and the average cost observed (maintenance, in this case).

Step 2: Determine the variance from average for each month for both activity (X') and cost (Y').

Step 3: Multiply the two variances from average by each other for each month ($X' Y'$). (Recall that algebraically a minus times a minus is a plus, but a minus times a plus is a minus, in obtaining the data for the $X' Y'$ column.)

Step 4: Square the activity variance for each month (X'^2).

Step 5: Compute the variable rate by the formula:

$$\frac{\Sigma X' Y'}{\Sigma X'^2} = \text{Variable rate}$$

Step 6: Compute the total fixed cost by substituting in the equation:

$$Y = a + bX$$

where Y = the average cost observed, a = the total fixed cost for which you are seeking, b = the variable rate computed in Step 5, and X = the average activity level observed.

QUESTIONS

4-1. Distinguish between (a) a variable cost, (b) a fixed cost, and (c) a mixed cost.

4-2. Define the following terms: (a) cost behavior, and (b) relevant range.

4-3. What is meant by an "activity base" when dealing with variable costs? Give several examples of activity bases.

4-4. Distinguish between (a) a variable cost, (b) a mixed cost, and (c) a step-variable cost. Chart the three costs on a graph, with activity plotted horizontally and cost plotted vertically.

4-5. The accountant often assumes a strictly linear relationship between cost and volume. How can this practice be defended in face of the fact that many variable costs are curvilinear in form?

4-6. What are discretionary fixed costs? What are committed fixed costs? What impact does management philosophy have on these two classes of costs?

4-7. What factors are contributing to the trend toward increasing numbers of fixed costs, and why is this trend significant from a managerial accounting point of view?

4–8. Does the concept of the relevant range have application to fixed costs? Explain.

4–9. What basic assumption underlies the high-low method of mixed cost analysis?

4–10. What methods are available for determining the average rate of variability in a mixed cost? Which method is most accurate? Why?

4–11. What is meant by a regression line? Give the general formula for a regression line. Which term represents the variable cost? The fixed cost?

4–12. Once a regression line has been drawn, how does one determine the fixed cost element? The variable cost element?

4–13. What is meant by the term "least squares"?

4–14. What is the difference between single regression analysis and multiple regression analysis?

4–15. What is the difference between the contribution approach to the income statement and the traditional approach to the income statement?

4–16. What is meant by contribution margin? How is it computed?

EXERCISES

E4–1. Darby Manufacturing Company has observed that its maintenance cost is $5,000 when operating at a level of 20,000 machine-hours per period. When the operating level drops to 15,000 machine-hours, maintenance cost drops to $4,000.

Required:

1. What is the cost formula for maintenance?
2. What maintenance cost would you expect to be incurred at an operating level of 18,000 machine-hours?

E4–2. Pleasant View Hospital normally takes between 3,000 and 4,000 X rays each year. The hospital has determined by analysis of its costs that the cost formula for X rays within this range is $8,000 plus $3 for each X ray taken.

Required:

1. Plot the cost of X rays on a graph. Make cost the vertical axis and volume the horizontal axis. Clearly show the relevant range on the graph.
2. What total cost would be incurred if 5,000 X rays were taken during a year?

E4–3. Rapid Delivery, Inc., operates a fleet of delivery trucks in a large city. The company has determined that if a truck is driven 105,000 miles during a year the operating cost per mile is 11.4 cents. If a truck is driven only 70,000 miles during a year the operating cost per mile increases to 13.4 cents.

Required:

1. Determine the variable and fixed cost elements of the annual cost of truck operation.
2. Express the variable and fixed costs in the form $Y = a + bX$.
3. If a truck is driven 80,000 miles during a year what total cost would you expect to be incurred?

E4–4. The 19x4 income statement for the Forde Company appeared in the company's annual report as follows:

FORDE COMPANY
Income Statement
For the Year Ending December 31, 19x4

Sales		$500,000
Less cost of goods sold		350,000
Gross margin		150,000
Less operating expenses:		
Administrative	$40,000	
Selling	80,000	120,000
Net income		$ 30,000

Production costs included depreciation, supervisory salaries, and other fixed costs which totaled $220,000. The remainder of the production costs were variable. The administrative expenses were 75 percent fixed and 25 percent variable. A commission of $6 was paid on each unit sold; these commissions were added to selling expense. The remainder of the selling expenses were fixed. The per unit selling price was $50.

Required:

1. Prepare an income statement for the Forde Company for 19x4 using the contribution approach.
2. For every unit sold during 19x4, what was the contribution toward covering fixed expenses and toward earning profits?

E4–5. A Company has observed its selling costs over the last nine months as follows:

Month	Units sold	Selling cost
1........	14	$ 17
2........	10	14
3........	8	13
4........	12	16
5........	19	20
6........	20	22
7........	22	24
	105	$126

Required:

1. Using the least squares method, compute the variable selling cost per unit sold, and the fixed cost in total.
2. Express the cost data in (1) in the form $Y = a + bX$.

3. If 16 units are sold in a period, what selling cost would you expect A Company to incur? Show computations. (Round to two decimal places.)

E4–6. Westmore Hospital contains 450 beds. The average occupancy rate is 90 per cent per month. At this level of occupancy the hospital's operating costs are $16 per occupied bed per day, assuming a 30-day month. This figure contains both fixed and variable cost elements. During June the occupancy rate was only 80 percent. The following costs were incurred during the month:

Fixed operating costs . . . . $ 79,350
Mixed operating costs   105,600

Required:

1. Determine the variable cost per occupied bed on a daily basis.
2. Determine the total fixed operating costs per month.
3. Assume an occupancy rate of 86 percent. What total operating costs would you expect the hospital to incur?

E4–7. The data below have been taken from the cost records of the Atlanta Processing Company. The data relate to the cost of operating one of the company's processing facilities at various levels of activity.

Month	Total cost	Units processed
January	$14,000	8,000
February	16,000	10,000
March	12,500	7,000
April	15,000	9,000
May	12,250	6,500
June	11,700	6,000
July	11,000	5,500

Required:

1. Prepare a scattergraph by plotting the above data on a graph. Plot cost on the vertical axis and activity on the horizontal axis. Fit a line to your plotted points by visual inspection.
2. What is the approximate monthly fixed cost? The approximate variable cost per unit processed?

E4–8. The Alpine House, Inc., is a large retailer of winter sports equipment. An income statement for the company's Ski Department for the most recent quarter is presented below:

THE ALPINE HOUSE, INC.
Income Statement—Ski Dept.
For the Quarter Ended March 31, 19xx

Sales		$100,000
Cost of goods sold		60,000
Gross margin		40,000
Less operating expenses:		
Selling expenses	$15,000	
Administrative expenses	10,000	25,000
Net income		$ 15,000

Skis sell, on the average, for $125 per pair. The administrative expenses are 10 percent variable, and 90 percent fixed. Variable selling expenses are $10 per pair of skis sold. The remainder of the selling expenses are fixed.

Required:

1. Redo the company's income statement in the contribution format.
2. For every dollar of ski sales, how much is available to cover fixed expenses or provide profits for the period?

E4–9. Assume that six monthly observations of shipping expense in a company are to be used as a basis for developing a cost formula. The company has plotted shipping expenses at various levels of activity on a graph, and the plotted points indicate that total shipping expense is a mixed cost in the form $Y = a + bX$. The six monthly observations are:

Month	Pounds shipped .(000)	Total shipping expense (000)
January	25	$45
February	16	36
March	21	40
April	15	35
May	12	32
June	19	40

Required:

Using the least squares technique, determine the cost formula for shipping expense. It is not necessary to prepare a graph.

PROBLEMS

P4–10. *Least squares method of cost analysis; Graphing.* State University operates a large evening school program, and requires its academic departments to report student credit hours and operating costs on a monthly basis. Data reported by the art department over the last five months follow:

Month	Student credit hours	Operating costs
September	750	$13,500
October	850	14,500
November	500	12,750
December	600	12,500
January	400	11,750
	3,100	$65,000

Required:

1. Compute the variable operating cost per student credit hour and the total fixed operating cost per month for the art department. Use the least squares method.

2.   Express the cost data derived in Part 1 in the linear equation form
     $Y = a + bX$. How much cost would you expect the art department
     to incur if 700 student credit hours were reported in a month? (Round
     to the nearest dollar.)
3.   Prepare a scattergraph, and fit a regression line to the plotted points
     using the cost formula derived in (1) above.

P4–11. *High-low method of cost analysis.* Kenton Company has computed its
        total factory overhead costs at high and low levels of activity to be as
        follows:

	Level of activity	
	Low	High
Direct labor-hours	50,000	75,000
Total factory overhead costs	$142,500	$176,250

Assume that the factory overhead costs above consist of indirect materials, rent, and maintenance. The company has analyzed these costs at
the 50,000 direct labor-hours level of activity, and has determined that
at that level these costs exist in the following proportions:

Indirect materials (V)	$ 50,000
Rent (F)	60,000
Maintenance (M)	32,500
Total factory overhead costs	$142,500

V = variable; F = fixed; M = mixed.

For planning purposes, the company wants to break the maintenance
cost down into its variable and fixed elements.

Required:

1.   Determine how much of the $176,250 factory overhead cost at the
     high level of activity above consists of maintenance cost. (Hint: To
     do this, it may be helpful to first determine how much of the $176,250
     consists of indirect materials and rent. Think about the behavior of
     variable and fixed costs within the relevant range!)
2.   By means of the high-low method of cost analysis, determine the
     cost formula for maintenance.
3.   If the Kenton Company works 65,000 direct labor-hours, what should
     be the total factory overhead cost? Show computations.

P4–12. *Scattergraph and least squares.* Argyris Research Corporation has a
        fleet of ten autos which are used by company employees on company
        business. All expenses of operating these autos are entered into an "Auto-
        mobile Expense" account on the company's books. The company also
        keeps a careful record of the number of miles the autos are driven each
        month.
          The president of Arygris Research Corporation wants to know the
        cost of operating the fleet of cars, in terms of the fixed monthly cost
        and the variable cost per mile driven.

The company's records of miles driven and total auto expense by month for the past year are given below:

Month	Total mileage (000)	Total cost
January	8	$ 3,200
February	12	3,400
March	16	3,900
April	10	3,400
May	13	3,700
June	15	3,700
July	11	3,500
August	14	3,700
September	9	3,300
October	14	3,600
November	12	3,600
December	10	3,300
	144	$42,300

Required:

1. By means of a scattergraph, determine the fixed and variable elements in monthly auto expense. Fit your regression line to the plotted data by simple visual inspection. What is the total fixed expense per month? The variable rate per mile?
2. Determine the breakdown of monthly auto expense by the least squares method. (It is not necessary to prepare a graph.)
3. From the data determined in (2) above, prepare an equation that describes the operation of the fleet of cars for one month.

P4–13. *High-low method of cost analysis.* Hurst Company's total overhead costs at various levels of activity are presented below:

Month	Machine-hours	Total overhead costs
January	50,000	$162,000
February	40,000	140,600
March	60,000	183,400
April	70,000	204,800

Assume that the overhead costs above consist of utilities, supervisory salaries, and maintenance. The proportion of these costs at the 40,000 machine-hour level of activity is:

Utilities (V)	$ 42,400
Supervisory salaries (F)	39,300
Maintenance (M)	58,900
Total overhead costs	$140,600

V = variable; F = fixed; M = mixed.

The company wants to break the maintenance cost down into its basic variable and fixed cost elements.

Required:

1. As shown above, overhead costs in April amounted to $204,800. Determine how much of this consisted of maintenance cost. (Hint: To do this, it may be helpful to first determine how much of the $204,800 consisted of utilities and supervisory salaries. Think about the behavior of variable and fixed costs within the relevant range!)
2. By means of the high-low method, determine the cost formula for maintenance.
3. Express the company's total overhead costs in the linear equation form, $Y = a + bX$.
4. What total overhead costs would you expect to be incurred at an operating activity level of 60,000 machine-hours?

P4–14. *Least squares method of cost analysis; Graphing.* The Carter Sales Company has observed its travel expenses and the number of calls made by salespersons over the last several months to be as follows:

Month	Calls made	Travel expense
1	420	$ 3,100
2	450	3,300
3	490	3,400
4	430	3,200
5	470	3,300
6	380	2,900
7	510	3,550
	3,150	$22,750

For planning purposes, management would like the travel expense broken down into basic variable and fixed elements. Management has asked you, as an expert in cost analysis, to assist in this task.

Required:

1. Using the least squares method, make the desired analysis of the travel expense, by determining the variable expense per call made and the total fixed expense per month.
2. Express the cost data derived in (1) in the linear equation form $Y = a + bX$. How much travel expense would you expect the company to incur if 500 calls were made in a month? (Round data to the nearest dollar.)
3. Prepare a scattergraph, with cost on the vertical axis, and plot the data for months 1–7 given above. Using the data in your linear equation from (2), fit a regression line to the plotted points.

P4–15. *Contribution versus traditional income statement.* Marbury, Inc., is a large distributor of pianos. The company purchases its pianos from manufacturers and resells them on a retail basis. Selected information gleaned from the company's records for the month of June is presented below.

1. During June the company sold 40 pianos and delivered them to the purchasers.

2. Pianos cost Marbury, Inc., $805 each on the average, and sell for $1,250 each.
3. The company's selling expenses consist of $40 freight on each piano sold and delivered, $20 insurance on each piano sold, and a 10 percent sales commission, based on selling price. The company also has $700 each month in advertising, $350 in utilities, and $1,200 in depreciation of sales facilities.
4. The company's administrative expenses consist of executive salaries of $2,200 each month, $300 in depreciation of office equipment each month, and monthly clerical expenses of $600 plus $10 for each piano sold.

Required:

1. Prepare an income statement for Marbury, Inc., for the month of June, using the traditional format, with costs organized by function.
2. Redo (1), this time using the contribution format, with costs organized by behavior. Show costs and revenues on both a total and a per unit basis down through contribution margin.
3. Refer to the income statement you prepared in (2). Why might it be misleading to show the fixed costs on a per unit basis?

P4–16. *Identifying cost patterns.* Below are a number of cost behavior patterns that might be found in a company's cost structure. The vertical axis on each graph represents cost, and the horizontal axis on each graph represents level of activity (volume).

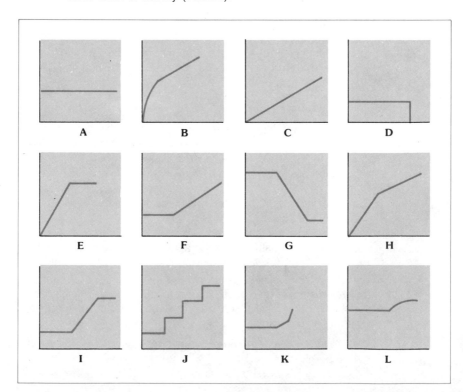

Required:

1. For each of the following situations, identify the graph which illustrates the cost pattern involved. Any graph may be used more than once.

   a. Cost of raw materials, where the cost decreases by $0.05 per unit for each of the first 100 units purchased, after which it remains constant at $2.50 per unit.

   b. Electricity bill—a flat fixed charge, plus a variable cost after a certain number of kilowatt hours are used.

   c. City water bill, which is computed as follows:

First 1,000,000 gallons or less	$1,000 flat fee
Next 10,000 gallons	0.003 per gallon used
Next 10,000 gallons	0.006 per gallon used
Next 10,000 gallons	0.009 per gallon used
Etc.	Etc.

   d. Depreciation of equipment, where the amount is computed by the straight-line method. When the depreciation rate was established, it was anticipated that the obsolescence factor would be greater than the wear and tear factor.

   e. Rent on a factory building donated by the city, where the agreement calls for a fixed fee payment unless 200,000 labor hours are worked, in which case no rent need be paid.

   f. Salaries of repairmen, where one repairman is needed for every 1,000 hours of machine-hours or less (that is, 0 to 1,000 hours requires one repairman, 1,001 to 2,000 hours requires two repairmen, etc.).

   g. Cost of raw material used.

   h. Rent on a factory building donated by the county, where the agreement calls for rent of $100,000 less $1 for each direct labor-hour worked in excess of 200,000 hours, but a minimum rental payment of $20,000 must be paid.

   i. Use of a machine under a lease, where a minimum charge of $1,000 is paid up to 400 hours of machine time. After 400 hours of machine time, an additional charge of $2 per hour is paid up to a maximum charge of $2,000 per period.

2. How would a knowledge of cost behavior patterns such as those above be of help to a manager in analyzing the cost structure of his firm?

(AICPA, adapted)

P4–17. *Scattergraph and least squares.* The Ferrera Company has had great difficulty in the past predicting its costs at various levels of output. The reason is that until now the company has never attempted to study its cost structure by analyzing the underlying cost behavior patterns. The president of the Ferrera Company has now become convinced that such an analysis is necessary if the company is to control its profitability and maintain its competitive position. Accordingly, an analysis of cost behavior patterns has been undertaken. The company has managed to isolate those costs which vary directly with output (variable costs), and those costs which do not vary with output (fixed costs). However, one group of costs has been isolated that does not exhibit either a strictly variable or a strictly fixed pattern. This group of costs in relation to output is shown below:

Level of output in units	Total unexplained costs observed
20	$40
14	33
9	30
16	36
8	27
7	28

The president feels that this group of unexplained costs must contain a mixture of both variable and fixed cost elements. He has assigned you the responsibility of determining whether this is correct.

Required:

1. Prepare a scattergraph, using the output and cost data above. Place cost on the vertical axis and output on the horizontal axis. Fit a regression line to the plotted data, by visual inspection.
2. Is the president correct in assuming that the unexplained costs contain a mixture of fixed and variable costs? If so, what is the approximate total fixed cost, and the approximate variable cost per unit? Determine these amounts by analyzing your scattergraph.
3. Using the least squares technique, determine the approximate fixed cost and variable cost elements in the total cost observed. Notice that the variable cost and fixed cost elements obtained by a least squares analysis differ slightly from the variable cost and fixed cost elements which you worked out in (2) above. How can you account for this difference?

P4–18. *Contribution versus traditional income statement.* The House of Organs, Inc., purchases organs from a well-known manufacturer and distributes them at a retail level, primarily to families for home use. The organs sell, on the average, for $3,500 each. The average cost of an organ from the manufacturer is $2,250.

The House of Organs, Inc., has always kept careful records of its costs. The costs that the company incurs in a typical month are presented below:

Costs	Cost formula
Selling:	
Advertising	$800 per month
Adjustment and tuning of delivered organs	$30 per organ sold
Freight on delivered organs	$75 per organ sold
Insurance on delivered organs	$60 per organ sold
Sales salaries	$2,100 per month, plus 4% of sales dollars
Depreciation	$2,500 per month
Utilities	$280 per month
Administrative:	
Salaries	$2,500 per month
Depreciation	$950 per month
Clerical	$750 per month, plus $15 per organ sold

During the month of December, 19x3, the company sold and delivered 27 organs.

Required:

1. Prepare an income statement for the month of December 19x3, using the traditional format with costs organized by function.
2. Redo (1), this time using the contribution format, with costs organized by behavior. Show costs and revenues on both a total and a per unit basis down through contribution margin.
3. Refer to the income statement you prepared in (2). Why might it be misleading to show the fixed costs on a per unit basis?

P4–19. *Multiple choice on cost analysis.*   Labor-hours and production costs for the last four months of 19x1, which you believe are representative for the year, were as follows:

Month	Labor-hours	Total production costs
September	2,500	$ 20,000
October	3,500	25,000
November	4,500	30,000
December	3,500	25,000
	14,000	$100,000

Based upon the above information, select the best answer for each of Questions 1 through 6.

Let

a = Fixed production costs per month.
b = Variable production costs per labor-hour.
n = Number of months.
x = Labor-hours per month.
y = Total monthly production costs.
Σ = Summation.

1. The equation(s) required for applying the least squares method of computation of fixed and variable production costs could be expressed:
   a. $\Sigma xy = a\Sigma x + b\Sigma x^2$
   b. $\Sigma y = na + b\Sigma x$
   c. $y = a + bx^2$
       $\Sigma y = na + b\Sigma x$
   d. $\Sigma xy = a\Sigma x + b\Sigma x^2$
       $\Sigma y = na + b\Sigma x$

2. The cost function derived by the least squares method:
   a. Would be linear.
   b. Must be tested for minima and maxima.
   c. Would be parabolic.
   d. Would indicate maximum costs at the point of the function's point of inflection.

3. Monthly production costs could be expressed:
   a. $y = ax + b$
   b. $y = a + bx$
   c. $y = b + ax$
   d. $y = \Sigma a + bx$

4. The fixed monthly production cost in total is (use the high-low method):
   a. $10,000
   b. $9,500
   c. $7,500
   d. $5,000

5. The variable production cost per labor-hour is (use the high-low method):
   a. $6
   b. $5
   c. $3
   d. $2

6. The least squares method of cost analysis must be used in those situations where:
   a. The mixed cost being analyzed consists of more than 50 percent fixed cost.
   b. The variable portion of the mixed cost is constant per unit of activity.
   c. The fixed costs being analyzed are discretionary rather than committed.
   d. The variable portion of the mixed cost being analyzed must be determined in terms of some average amount per unit of activity.
   (AICPA, adapted)

P4–20. *Analysis of cost behavior.* Pleasant View Hospital has just hired a new chief administrator. The new chief administrator is anxious to employ sound management and planning techniques in the business affairs of the hospital. She has directed her assistant to summarize the cost structure existing in the various departments of the hospital, in terms of variable, fixed, and mixed cost present. In Department A, the assistant identified the variable and fixed costs fairly easily, but is uncertain how to classify the utilities cost of the department. He has observed utilities cost as follows over the past six months:

Month	Departmental volume in units	Utilities cost observed
January	60	$110
February	80	115
March	40	85
April	70	105
May	90	120
June	50	100

The chief administrator has informed her assistant that the utilities cost is probably a mixed cost, that will have to be broken down into its variable and fixed cost elements by use of a scattergraph. The assistant feels, however, that if an analysis of this type is necessary, then the high-low method should be used, since it is easier and quicker. The chief surgeon of the hospital, standing nearby and hearing the conversation, suggests that statistical least squares (which he heard about from his brother, who is a statistician) is the best approach.

Required:

1. Prepare a cost formula for the utilities expense of Department A, using the high-low method.
2. Repeat (1), this time using a scattergraph and fixing a trend line by visual inspection.
3. Repeat (1) again, this time using least squares analysis.
4. Comment on the accuracy and usefulness of the data derived by each of the methods in (1)–(3) above.

P4–21. *Regression analysis; Graphing.* The Ramon Company manufactures a wide range of products at several different plant locations. The Franklin plant, which manufactures electrical components, has been experiencing difficulties with fluctuating monthly overhead costs. The fluctuations have made it difficult to estimate the level of overhead that will be incurred for any one month.

Management wants to be able to estimate overhead costs accurately in order to better plan its operation and financial needs. A trade association publication to which Ramon Company subscribes indicates that, for companies manufacturing electrical components, overhead tends to vary with direct labor-hours.

One member of the accounting staff has proposed that the cost behavior pattern of the overhead costs be determined. Then overhead costs could be predicted from the budgeted direct labor-hours.

Another member of the accounting staff suggested that a good starting place for determining the cost behavior pattern of overhead costs would be an analysis of historical data. The historical cost behavior pattern would provide a basis for estimating future overhead costs. The methods proposed for determining the cost behavior pattern included the high-low method, the scattergraph method, simple linear regression, multiple regression, and exponential smoothing. Of these methods Ramon Company decided to employ the high-low method, the scattergraph method, and simple linear regression. Data on direct labor-hours and the respective overhead costs incurred were collected for the past two years. The raw data are as follows:

| | 19x1 | | 19x2 | |
Month	Direct labor-hours	Overhead costs	Direct labor-hours	Overhead costs
January	20,000	$84,000	21,000	$86,000
February..........	25,000	99,000	24,000	93,000
March	22,000	89,500	23,000	93,000
April	23,000	90,000	22,000	87,000
May	20,000	81,500	20,000	80,000
June	19,000	75,500	18,000	76,500
July	14,000	70,500	12,000	67,500
August	10,000	64,500	13,000	71,000
September	12,000	69,000	15,000	73,500
October	17,000	75,000	17,000	72,500
November	16,000	71,500	15,000	71,000
December	19,000	78,000	18,000	75,000

All equipment in the Franklin plant is leased, under an arrangement calling for a flat fee up to 19,500 direct labor-hours of activity in the plant, after which rental charges are assessed on a strict hourly basis.

Required:

1. Using the high-low method, determine the cost formula for overhead in the Franklin plant.
2. Repeat (1), this time using the least squares method. Your assistant has computed the following amounts, which may be helpful in your analysis:

    Equation Method:

    $$\Sigma X = 435,000$$
    $$\Sigma Y = \$1,894,000$$
    $$\Sigma XY = \$35,170,500,000$$
    $$\Sigma X^2 = 8,275,000,000$$

    Alternate Method:

    24-month average:
    $$X = 18,125$$
    $$Y = \$78,917$$
    $$\Sigma X' Y' = \$841,750,000$$
    $$\Sigma X'^2 = 390,625,000$$

3. Prepare a scattergraph, including on it all data for the two-year period. Fit a regression line to the plotted points by visual inspection. (It is not necessary to compute variable and fixed cost elements from your regression line.)
4. Assume the Franklin plant works 22,500 direct labor-hours during a month. Compute the expected overhead cost for the month, using the cost formulas developed above with:
    a. The high-low method.
    b. The least squares method.
    c. The scattergraph method [read the expected costs directly off the graph prepared in (3)].

5. Of the three proposed methods, which one should the Ramon Company use to estimate monthly overhead costs in the Franklin plant? Explain fully, indicating the reasons why the other methods are less desirable.
6. Would the relevant range concept probably be more or less important in the Franklin plant than in most companies?

(CMA, adapted)

P4–22. *Manufacturing statements; High-low method of cost analysis.* Selected information on Griffin Company's operations at high and at low levels of activity is given below:

	Level of activity	
	19x4—Low	*19x6—High*
Number of units produced	10,000	15,000
Cost of goods manufactured	$157,000	$225,000
Work in process inventory—beginning	12,000	15,000
Work in process inventory—ending	15,000	10,000
Direct material cost per unit	4	4
Direct labor cost per unit	6	6

The company's manufacturing overhead consists of both variable and fixed costs. In order to have data available for planning, the management of Griffin Company is very anxious to determine how much of the overhead cost is variable with units produced, and to determine how much of it is fixed in total.

Required:

1. For both 19x4 and 19x6, determine how much of the total "Cost of Goods Manufactured" consisted of manufacturing overhead cost. The company had no under- or overapplied overhead in either year. (Hint: A useful way to proceed might be to construct a Cost of Goods Manufactured Statement for each year.)
2. By means of the high-low method of cost analysis, determine the cost formula for manufacturing overhead. Express the variable portion of the cost formula in terms of a variable rate per unit of product.
3. If 12,000 units of product are produced during a period, what would be the cost of goods manufactured, assuming that work in process inventories remain unchanged?

Chapter 5

Cost-volume-profit relationships

Cost-volume-profit analysis involves a study of the interrelationship between the following factors:

1. Prices of products.
2. Volume or level of activity.
3. Per unit variable costs.
4. Total fixed costs.
5. Mix of products sold.

It is a key factor in many decisions, including choice of product lines, pricing of products, marketing strategy, and utilization of productive facilities. The concept is so pervasive in managerial accounting that it touches on virtually everything that a manager does. Although an understanding of cost-volume-profit relationships does not necessarily guarantee profits, it is an indispensable aid in uncovering profit potential in a firm.

THE BASICS OF COST-VOLUME-PROFIT ANALYSIS

Our study of cost-volume-profit analysis begins where our study of cost behavior in the preceding chapter left off—with the contribution income statement. The contribution income statement has a number of interesting characteristics that can be helpful to the manager in trying to judge the impact on profits of changes in cost or volume. To demonstrate these characteristics, we shall use the income statement of the Norton Company, a small manufacturer of microwave ovens:

NORTON COMPANY Contribution Income Statement For the Month of June 19xx		
	Total	Per unit
Sales (400 ovens)	$100,000	$250
Less variable expenses	60,000	150
Contribution margin	$ 40,000	$100
Less fixed expenses	35,000	
Net income	$ 5,000	

For purposes of discussion, we shall assume that the Norton Company produces only one model of oven.

Notice that the company expresses its sales, variable expenses, and contribution margin on a per unit basis, as well as in total. This is commonly done on those income statements prepared for management's own use internally, since, as we shall see, it facilitates profitability analysis.

Contribution margin

As explained in Chapter 4, contribution margin means how much is left from sales revenue, after covering variable expenses, that is contributed toward covering of fixed expenses, and then toward profits for the period. Notice the sequence here—fixed expenses are covered first, and then whatever contribution margin remains goes toward profits for the period. To illustrate this idea, assume that by the middle of a particular month the Norton Company has been able to sell only one oven. At that point the company's income statement will appear as follows:

	Total	Per unit
Sales (1 oven)	$ 250	$250
Less variable expenses	150	150
Contribution margin	$ 100	$100
Less fixed expenses	35,000	
Net loss	$(34,900)	

For each additional oven the company is able to sell during the month, $100 more in contribution margin will become available to help cover the fixed expenses. If a second oven is sold, for example, then the total contribution margin will increase from $100 to $200, and the company will be that much closer to covering its fixed costs for the month. If enough ovens can be sold to generate $35,000 in contribution margin, then all of the fixed costs will be covered, and the company will have managed to at least *break even* for the month—that is, to show neither profit nor loss, but just cover all of its costs. To reach this *break-even point* the company will have to sell 350 ovens in a month, since each oven sold yields $100 in contribution margin:

	Total	Per unit
Sales (350 ovens)	$87,500	$250
Less variable expenses	52,500	150
Contribution margin	$35,000	$100
Less fixed expenses	35,000	
Net income	$ –0–	

Computation of the break-even point is discussed in detail later in the chapter; for the moment we can note that it can be defined equally well as the point where total sales revenue equals total expenses, variable and fixed, or as the point where total contribution margin equals total fixed expenses.

Once the break-even point has been reached, net income will increase by the unit contribution margin for each additional unit sold. If 351 ovens are sold in a month, for example, then we can expect that the net income for the month will be $100, since 1 oven will have been sold beyond that needed to break even:

	Total	Per unit
Sales (351 ovens)	$87,750	$250
Less variable expenses	52,650	150
Contribution margin	$35,100	$100
Less fixed expenses	35,000	
Net income	$ 100	

If two ovens beyond that needed to break even are sold, then we can expect that the net income for the month will be $200, and so forth. To know what the profits will be at various levels of activity, therefore, it is not necessary for a manager to prepare a whole series of income statements. The manager can simply multiply the number of units to be sold beyond the break-even point by the unit contribution margin, and the result will represent the anticipated profits at that activity level. Or, if an increase in sales is planned and the manager wants to know what the impact will be on profits, he or she can simply multiply the increase in units by the unit contribution margin. To illustrate, if the Norton Company is selling 400 ovens per month, and plans to increase sales to 425 ovens per month, the impact on profits will be:

25 ovens × $100 contribution margin per oven

= $2,500 increase in net income

As proof:

	Sales volume		Difference	Per unit
	400 Ovens	425 Ovens	25 ovens	Per unit
Sales	$100,000	$106,250	$6,250	$250
Less variable expenses	60,000	63,750	3,750	150
Contribution margin	$ 40,000	$ 42,500	$2,500	$100
Less fixed expenses	35,000	35,000	–0–	
Net income	$ 5,000	$ 7,500	$2,500	

To summarize the series of examples in this section, we can say that the contribution margin first goes to cover an organization's fixed expenses, and that the potential loss represented by these fixed expenses is reduced successively by the unit contribution margin for each incremental unit sold up to the break-even point. Once the break-even point has been reached, then overall net income is increased by the unit contribution margin for each incremental unit sold from that point forward.

Contribution margin ratio

As well as being expressed on a per unit basis, revenues, variable expenses, and contribution margin for the Norton Company can also be expressed on a percentage basis:

	Total	Per unit	Percentage
Sales (400 ovens)	$100,000	$250	100%
Less variable expenses	60,000	150	60
Contribution margin	$ 40,000	$100	40%
Less fixed expenses	35,000		
Net income	$ 5,000		

The percentage of contribution margin to total sales is referred to either as the *contribution margin ratio* (C/M ratio) or as the *profit/volume ratio* (P/V) ratio). This ratio is extremely useful, in that it shows how contribution margin will be affected by a given dollar change in total sales. To illustrate, notice that the Norton Company has a contribution margin ratio of 40 percent. This means that for each dollar increase in sales, total contribution margin will increase by $0.40 ($1.00 sales × C/M ratio of 40 percent). Net income will also increase by $0.40, assuming that there are no changes in fixed costs. *The impact, therefore, on net income of any given dollar change in total sales can be computed in seconds by simply applying the C/M ratio to the dollar change.* If the Norton Company plans a $30,000 increase in sales during the coming month, for example, management can expect contribution margin to increase by $12,000 ($30,000 increased sales × C/M ratio of 40 percent). As we noted above, net income will increase by a like amount if the fixed costs do not change. As proof:

	Sales volume			
	Present	Expected	Increase	Percentage
Sales	$100,000	$130,000	$30,000	100%
Less variable expenses	60,000	78,000*	18,000	60
Contribution margin	$ 40,000	$ 52,000	$12,000	40%
Less fixed expenses	35,000	35,000	–0–	
Net income	$ 5,000	$ 17,000	$12,000	

* $130,000 × 60% = $78,000.

Many managers find the C/M ratio easier to work with than the unit contribution margin figure, particularly where a company has multiple product lines. This is because the C/M ratio is in ratio form, and therefore makes it easier for the manager to make comparisons between product lines as to relative profitability. Other things equal, the manager will search out those product lines which have the highest C/M ratio figures. The reason, of course, is that for a given dollar increase in sales these product lines will yield the greatest amount of contribution margin toward the covering of fixed costs and toward profits.

Cost structure

We observed in the preceding chapter that a company often has some latitude in trading off between variable and fixed costs. Which cost structure is best, to have high variable costs and low fixed costs, or the opposite? No categorical answer to this question is possible; we can simply note that there may be advantages either way, depending on the specific circumstances involved. To illustrate, the income statements of two companies are given below. Notice that each company has total costs of $90,000 at an activity level of $100,000 in sales.

	Company X		Company Y	
	Amount	Percentage	Amount	Percentage
Sales	$100,000	100%	$100,000	100%
Less variable expenses	60,000	60	30,000	30
Contribution margin	$ 40,000	40%	$ 70,000	70%
Less fixed expenses	30,000		60,000	
Net income	$ 10,000		$ 10,000	

The question as to which company has the best cost structure depends on many factors, including the long-run trend in sales, year-to-year fluctuations in the level of sales, and the attitude of the managers toward risk. If sales are expected to trend above $100,000 in the future, then Company Y probably has the best cost structure, since its C/M ratio is higher and its profits will therefore increase more rapidly as sales increase. For example, assume that each company experiences a 10 percent increase in sales. The new income statements will be:

	Company X		Company Y	
	Amount	Percentage	Amount	Percentage
Sales	$110,000	100%	$110,000	100%
Less variable expenses	66,000	60	33,000	30
Contribution margin	$ 44,000	40%	$ 77,000	70%
Less fixed expenses	30,000		60,000	
Net income	$ 14,000		$ 17,000	

As we would expect, for the same dollar increase in sales Company Y has experienced a greater increase in net income, due to its higher C/M ratio.

On the other hand, if $100,000 represents maximum sales, and sales can be expected to drop below $100,000 from time to time, then Company X probably has the best cost structure. Its fixed costs are lower, and it will not lose contribution margin as rapidly as sales fall off, due to its lower C/M ratio. If sales fluctuate above and below $100,000 it becomes more difficult to tell which company is in a better position.

In sum, Company Y will experience wider movements in net income as changes take place in sales, with greater profits in good years and greater losses in bad years. Company X will enjoy somewhat greater stability in net income, but will do so at the risk of losing substantial profits if sales trend upward in the long run.

Operating leverage

Before leaving the example in the preceding section, one final point should be made. Notice from the two income statements that the 10 percent increase in sales triggered a much larger percentage increase in net income in both companies. In Company X net income increased by 40 percent (from $10,000 to $14,000), and in Company Y net income increased by 70 percent (from $10,000 to $17,000). This is an example of *operating leverage*, which measures the change in net income resulting from a given change in sales volume. Operating leverage is measured by the formula:

$$\frac{\text{Contribution margin}}{\text{Net income}} = \text{Operating leverage}$$

$$\text{Company X leverage:} \frac{\$40,000}{\$10,000} = 4$$

$$\text{Company Y leverage:} \frac{\$70,000}{\$10,000} = 7$$

By interpretation, the operating leverage figures for X and Y tell us that for a given change from the current level of sales we can expect a four times greater change in the net income of Company X, and a seven times greater change in the net income of Company Y, *in percentage terms.* For example, if sales in Company X increase by 10 percent, then we can expect net income in Company X to increase by four times this amount, or by 40 percent:

	(1) Percentage increase in sales	(2) Operating leverage	(1)× (2) Percentage increase in net income
Company X	10%	4	40%
Company Y	10	7	70

The operating leverage concept provides the manager with a tool that can signify quickly what the impact will be on profits of various percentage changes in sales, without the necessity of preparing detailed income statements.

As shown by our example, the effects of operating leverage can be dramatic. These effects are more pronounced the closer a company is to its break-even point, and decrease somewhat in impact as the level of sales and net income rises. To illustrate, assume that Company X in the preceding section increases its total sales from $100,000 per year to $150,000 per year. The operating leverage at each sales level is shown below:

	Amount	Percentage	Amount	Percentage
Sales	$100,000	100%	$150,000	100%
Less variable expenses	60,000	60	90,000	60
Contribution margin	$ 40,000	40%	$ 60,000	40%
Less fixed expenses	30,000		30,000	
Net income	$ 10,000		$ 30,000	
Operating leverage:				
$40,000 ÷ $10,000	4			
$60,000 ÷ $30,000			2	

Notice that the operating leverage is only 2 at the $150,000 per year sales level as compared with 4 at the lower level of sales. The operating leverage figure will continue to decrease the further the company moves from its break-even point.

The operating leverage concept has its basis in a principle discussed earlier: once the break-even point has been reached in a company, net income is increased by the full amount of the contribution margin for each additional unit sold. If this contribution level is very high, and if a company is fairly near its break-even point, then even small increases in sales can yield large increases in profits.

Some applications of CVP concepts

The concepts which we have developed on the preceding pages have many applications in planning and decision making. We will return now to the example of the Norton Company (a manufacturer of microwave ovens) to illustrate some of these applications. Norton Company's basic cost and revenue data are:

	Per unit	Percentage
Sales price	$250	100%
Less variable expenses	150	60
Contribution margin	$100	40%

Recall that fixed expenses are $35,000 per month.

CHANGE IN FIXED COSTS AND SALES VOLUME.   Norton Company's sales manager feels that a $10,000 increase in the monthly advertising budget would increase monthly sales by $30,000. Should the advertising budget be increased?

Solution:

```
Incremental contribution margin:
   $30,000 × 40% C/M ratio ............................ $12,000
Less incremental advertising costs ......................   10,000
Increased net income ...................................  $ 2,000
```

Yes, the advertising budget should be increased.

Notice that the solution does not depend on a knowledge of what sales were previously, nor is it necessary to prepare an income statement. The analysis above is an *incremental analysis,* in that it is based only on those items of cost or revenue that will change if the new program is implemented. Although a new income statement could have been prepared, most managers would prefer the incremental approach. The reason is that it is simpler, more direct, and permits the decision maker to focus attention on the specific items involved in the decision.

CHANGE IN VARIABLE COSTS AND SALES VOLUME.   Refer to the original data. Assume that the Norton Company is currently selling 400 ovens per month. Management is contemplating using less costly components in the manufacture of the ovens, that would reduce variable costs by $25 per oven. However, the sales manager predicts that the lower overall quality would reduce sales to only 350 ovens per month. Should the change be made?

Solution:

The $25 decrease in variable costs will cause the contribution margin per unit to increase from $100 to $125.

```
Proposed total contribution margin:
   350 ovens × $125 ...................................... $43,750
Present total contribution margin:
   400 ovens × $100 ......................................   40,000
Increase in total contribution margin ..........................  $ 3,750
```

Yes, the less costly components should be used in the manufacture of the ovens. Since the fixed costs will not change, net income will increase by the $3,750 increase in contribution margin shown above.

CHANGE IN FIXED COST, SALES PRICE, AND SALES VOLUME.   Refer to the original data. Assume again that the Norton Company is currently selling 400 ovens per month. In order to increase sales, management would like to cut the selling price by $20 per oven and increase the advertising budget by $15,000 per month. If these two steps are taken, management feels that unit sales will increase by 50 percent. Should the changes be made?

Solution:

A decrease of $20 per oven in the selling price will cause the unit contribution margin to decrease from $100 to $80.

Proposed total contribution margin:	
400 ovens × 150% × $80	$48,000
Present total contribution margin:	
400 ovens × $100	40,000
Incremental contribution margin	$ 8,000
Change in fixed costs:	
Less incremental advertising expense	15,000
Reduction in net income	$ (7,000)

No, the changes should not be made. The same solution can be obtained by preparing comparative income statements:

	Present 400 ovens per month		Proposed 600 ovens per month		
	Total	Per unit	Total	Per unit	Difference
Sales	$100,000	$250	$138,000	$230	$38,000
Less variable expenses . .	60,000	150	90,000	150	30,000
Contribution margin	$ 40,000	$100	$ 48,000	$ 80	$ 8,000
Less fixed expenses	35,000		50,000*		15,000
Net income (loss)	$ 5,000		$ (2,000)		$ (7,000)

* $35,000 + $15,000 = $50,000

Notice that the answer is the same as that obtained by the incremental analysis above.

CHANGE IN VARIABLE COST, FIXED COST, AND SALES VOLUME. Refer to the original data. Assume again that the Norton Company is currently selling 400 ovens per month. The sales manager would like to place the sales staff on a commission basis of $15 per oven sold, rather than on flat salaries which presently total $6,000 per month. The sales manager is confident that the change will increase monthly sales by 15 percent. Should the change be made?

Solution:

Changing the sales staff from a salaried basis to a commission basis will affect both fixed and variable costs. Fixed costs will decrease by $6,000, from $35,000 to $29,000. Variable costs will increase by $15, from $150 to $165, and the unit contribution margin will decrease from $100 to $85.

```
Proposed total contribution margin:
  400 ovens × 115% × $85 ............................................  $39,100
Present total contribution margin:
  400 ovens × $100 .................................................   40,000
Decrease in total contribution margin ................................  $  (900)
Change in fixed costs:
  Add salaries avoided if a commission is paid .......................   6,000
Increase in net income .............................................  $ 5,100
```

Yes, the changes should be made. Again, the same answer can be obtained by preparing comparative income statements:

	Present 400 ovens per month		Proposed 460 ovens per month		Difference: increase or (decrease) in net income
	Total	Per unit	Total	Per unit	
Sales	$100,000	$250	$115,000*	$250	$ 15,000
Less variable expenses	60,000	150	75,900	165	(15,900)
Contribution margin	$ 40,000	$100	$ 39,100	$ 85	$(900)
Less fixed expenses	35,000		29,000		6,000
Net income	$ 5,000		$ 10,100		$ 5,100

```
* 400 ovens × 115% = 460 ovens.
  460 ovens × $250 = $115,000.
```

CHANGE IN REGULAR SALES PRICE.   Refer to the original data. Assume again that the Norton Company is currently selling 400 ovens per month. The company has an opportunity to make a bulk sale of 150 ovens to a wholesaler, if an acceptable price can be worked out. This sale would not disturb regular sales currently being made. What price per oven should be quoted to the wholesaler if the Norton Company wants to increase its monthly profits by $3,000?

Solution:

```
Variable cost per oven .......................... $150
Desired profits per oven:
  $3,000 ÷ 150 ovens...........................   20
Quoted price per oven .......................... $170
```

Notice that no element of fixed cost is included in the computation. The reason is the same as that mentioned several times previously: once the break-even point has been reached, any change in contribution margin is reflected directly in net income. Norton Company's regular business puts it beyond the break-even point; therefore, the contribution margin per unit on the special order only needs to be enough to provide the $3,000 desired increase in monthly profits. As shown above, this is $20 per oven, which when added to the variable costs of producing each oven brings the quoted price to $170.

Importance of the contribution margin

As stated in the introduction to the chapter, cost-volume-profit analysis seeks the most profitable combination of variable costs, fixed costs, selling price, and sales volume. The examples which we have just provided show that the effect on the contribution margin is a major consideration in deciding on the most profitable combination of these factors. We have seen that sometimes profits can be improved by reducing the contribution margin, if fixed costs can be reduced by a greater amount. More commonly, however, we have seen that the way to improve profits is to increase the total contribution margin figure. Sometimes this can be done by reducing the selling price and thereby increasing volume. Sometimes it can be done by increasing fixed costs (such as advertising) and thereby increasing volume, and sometimes it can be done by trading off variable and fixed costs with appropriate changes in volume. Many other combinations of factors are possible.

The size of the unit contribution figure (and the size of the C/M ratio) will have a heavy influence on what steps a company is willing to take to improve profits. For example, a company with a $1 unit contribution margin and selling 50,000 units a year will not risk the same advertising outlay to obtain a 10 percent increase in volume as another company selling the same number of units but having a $5 unit contribution margin. In the first case the increase in volume would increase the contribution margin by only $5,000 (50,000 units × 10% × $1), whereas in the second case it would increase it by $25,000 (50,000 units × 10% × $5). This explains in part why companies with high-unit contribution margins (such as auto manufacturers) advertise so heavily, while companies with low-unit contribution margins (such as dishware manufacturers) tend to spend much less for advertising.

In sum, the effect on the contribution margin holds the key to most cost/revenue decisions in a company.

BREAK-EVEN ANALYSIS

Cost-volume-profit analysis is sometimes referred to simply as break-even analysis. This is unfortunate, because break-even analysis is just one part of the entire cost-volume-profit concept. However, it is often a key part, and it can give the manager many insights into the data with which he or she is working.

As a basis for discussion, we will continue with the example of the Norton Company used earlier in the chapter. Recall that the selling price is $250 per oven, the variable expenses are $150 per oven, and the fixed costs total $35,000 per month.

Break-even computations

Earlier in the chapter we stated that the break-even point can be defined equally well as the point where total sales revenue equals total expenses, variable and fixed, or as the point where total contribution margin equals total fixed expenses. As suggested by these two definitions of the break-even point, break-even analysis can be approached in two ways—by what is called the equation technique, or by what is called the unit contribution technique.

THE EQUATION TECHNIQUE. The equation technique centers on the contribution approach to the income statement illustrated earlier in the chapter. The format of this statement can be expressed in equation form as:

Sales = Variable expenses + Fixed expenses + Profits

At the break-even point, profits will be zero. Therefore, the break-even point can be computed by finding that point where sales just equal the total of the variable expenses plus the fixed expenses. For the Norton Company this would be:

Sales = Variable expenses + Fixed expenses + Profits

$$\$250X = \$150X + \$35,000 + 0$$
$$\$100X = \$35,000$$
$$X = 350 \text{ ovens}$$

where:

$X =$ Break-even point in ovens.
$\$250 =$ Unit sales price.
$\$150 =$ Unit variable expenses.
$\$35,000 =$ Total fixed expenses.

After the break-even point in units sold has been computed, the break-even point in sales dollars can be computed by multiplying the break-even level of units by the sales price per unit:

$$350 \text{ ovens} \times \$250 = \$87,500$$

At times, the *dollar* relationship between variable expenses and sales may not be known. In these cases, if one knows the *percentage* relationship between variable expenses and sales, then the break-even point can still be computed, as follows:

$$\text{Sales} = \text{Variable expenses} + \text{Fixed expenses} + \text{Profits}$$

$$X = 0.60X + \$35,000 + 0$$
$$0.40X = \$35,000$$
$$X = \$87,500$$

where:

$X =$ Break-even point in sales dollars.
$0.60 =$ Variable expenses as a percentage of sales.
$\$35,000 =$ Total fixed expenses.

Firms often have data available only in percentage form, and the approach we have just illustrated must be used to find the break-even point. Notice that use of percentages in the equation yields a break-even point in sales dollars, rather than in units sold. The break-even point in units sold would be:

$$\$87,500 \div \$250 = 350 \text{ ovens}$$

THE UNIT CONTRIBUTION TECHNIQUE.   The unit contribution technique is actually just a variation of the equation technique already described. The approach centers on the idea discussed earlier that each unit sold provides a certain amount of contribution margin that goes toward covering of fixed costs. To find how many units must be sold to break even, one must divide the total fixed costs by the contribution margin being generated by each unit sold:

$$\frac{\text{Total fixed expenses}}{\text{Unit contribution margin}} = \text{Break-even point}$$

Each oven which the Norton Company sells generates a contribution margin of $100 ($250 selling price, less $150 variable expenses). Since the total fixed expenses are $35,000, the break-even point is:

$$\frac{\text{Total fixed expenses}}{\text{Unit contribution margin}} = \frac{\$35,000}{\$100} = 350 \text{ ovens}$$

If only the percentage relationship between variable expenses, contribution margin, and sales is known, the computation becomes:

$$\frac{\text{Total fixed expenses}}{\text{C/M ratio}} = \frac{\$35,000}{40\%} = \$87,500$$

This approach to break-even analysis is particularly useful in those situations where a company has multiple product lines and wishes to compute a single break-even point for the company as a whole. More is said on this point in a later section titled, "The Concept of Sales Mix."

Cost-volume-profit relationships in graphical form

The cost data relating to the Norton Company's microwave ovens can be expressed in graphical form. Graphing of data can be very helpful in that it highlights cost-volume-profit relationships over wide ranges of activity, and can give managers a perspective that can be obtained in no other way. Such graphing is sometimes referred to as preparing a "break-even chart." This is correct to the extent that the break-even point is clearly shown on the graph. The reader should be aware, however, that a graphing of cost-volume-profit data highlights cost-volume-profit relationships throughout the *entire* relevant range—not just at the break-even point.

PREPARING THE COST-VOLUME-PROFIT GRAPH. Preparing a cost-volume-profit graph (sometimes called a "break-even chart") involves three steps. These steps are keyed to the graph in Exhibit 5–1.

1. Draw a line parallel to the volume axis, representing total fixed expenses. For the Norton Company, total fixed expenses are $35,000.

Exhibit 5–1
Preparing the cost-volume-profit graph

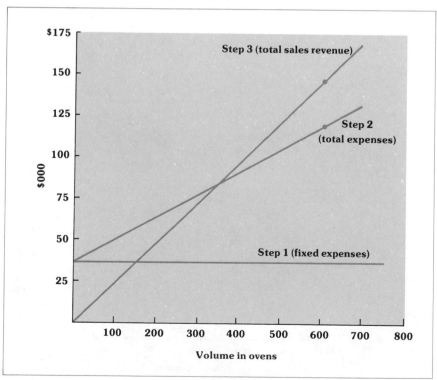

2. Choose some volume of sales above zero and plot the point represent-
    ing total expenses (fixed and variable) at that activity level. In Exhibit
    5–1 we have chosen a sales volume of 600 ovens. Total expenses
    at that activity level would be:

Fixed expenses	$ 35,000
Variable expenses (600 ovens × $150)	90,000
Total expenses	$125,000

After the point is plotted, draw a line through it back to the point
where the fixed expense line intersects the dollars axis.

3. Choose some volume of sales above zero, and plot the point represent-
    ing total sales dollars at that activity level. In Exhibit 5–1 we have
    again chosen a sales volume of 600 ovens. Sales at that activity level
    total $150,000 (600 ovens × $250). Draw a line through this point
    back to the origin.

Exhibit 5–2
The completed cost-volume-profit graph

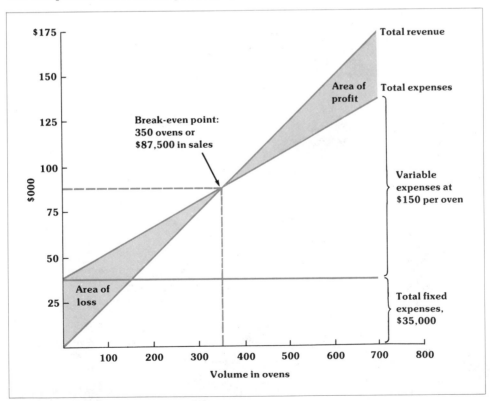

The interpretation of the completed cost-volume-profit graph is given in Exhibit 5–2. The anticipated profit or loss at any given level of sales is measured by the vertical distance between the total revenue line (sales) and the total expense line (variable expense plus fixed expense).

The break-even point is where the total revenue and total expense lines cross. The break-even point of 350 ovens in Exhibit 5–2 agrees with the break-even point obtained for the Norton Company in earlier computations.

AN ALTERNATIVE FORMAT. Some managers prefer an alternative format to the cost-volume-profit graph, as illustrated in Exhibit 5–3.

Note that the "Total Revenue" and "Total Expenses" lines are the same as in Exhibit 5–2. However, the new format in Exhibit 5–3 places the fixed expenses above the variable expenses, thereby allowing the contribution margin to be depicted on the graph. Otherwise, the graphs in the two exhibits are the same.

THE PROFIT-GRAPH. Another approach to the cost-volume-profit graph is presented in Exhibit 5–4. This approach, called a "profit-graph," is preferred by some managers because it focuses more directly on how

Exhibit 5–3
Alternate format to the cost-volume-profit graph

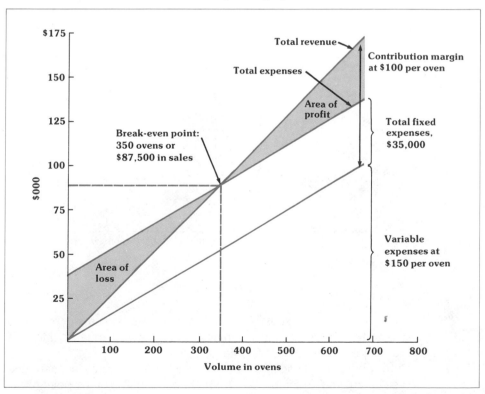

profits vary with changes in volume. It has the added advantage of being easier to interpret than the more traditional approaches illustrated in Exhibits 5–2 and 5–3. It has the disadvantage, however, of not showing as clearly how costs vary with changes in the level of sales.

The "profit-graph" is constructed in two steps. These steps are illustrated in Exhibit 5–4.

Exhibit 5–4
Preparing the "profit-graph"

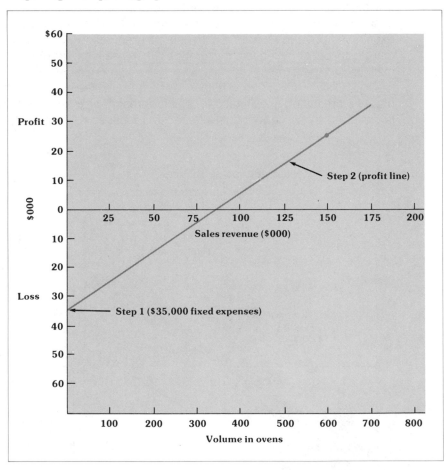

1. Locate total fixed expenses on the vertical axis, assuming zero level of activity. This point will be in the "loss" area, equal to the total fixed expenses expected for the period.
2. Plot a point representing expected profit or loss at any chosen level of sales volume. In Exhibit 5–4 we have chosen to plot the point repre-

senting expected profits at a sales volume of 600 ovens. Expected profits at this activity level are:

Sales (600 ovens × $250)	$150,000
Less variable expenses	
(600 ovens × $150)	90,000
Contribution margin	$ 60,000
Less fixed expenses	35,000
Net income	$ 25,000

After this point is plotted, draw a line through it back to the point on the vertical axis representing total fixed expenses. The interpretation of the completed "profit-graph" is given in Exhibit 5–5. The break-even point is where the profit line crosses the break-even line.

Exhibit 5–5
The completed "profit-graph"

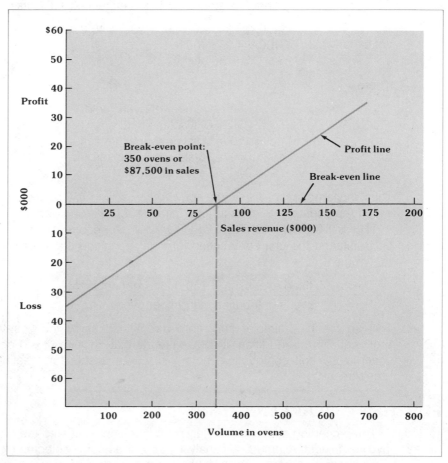

The vertical distance between the two lines represents the expected profit or loss at any given level of sales volume. This vertical distance can be translated directly into dollars by referring to the profit and loss figures on the vertical axis.

Target net profit analysis

Cost-volume-profit formulas can be used to determine the sales volume required to meet a target net profit figure. Suppose that the Norton Company would like to earn a target net profit of $40,000 per month. How many ovens would have to be sold?

THE COST-VOLUME-PROFIT EQUATION.   One approach to the solution would be to use the cost-volume-profit (CVP) equation. The target net profit requirement can be added into the basic equation data, and the solution will then show what level of sales is necessary to cover all expenses, plus yield the target net profit.

$$Sales = Variable\ expenses + Fixed\ expenses + Profits$$

$$\$250X = \$150X + \$35,000 + \$40,000$$
$$\$100X = \$75,000$$
$$X = 750\ ovens$$

where:

$$X = Number\ of\ ovens\ sold.$$
$$\$250 = Unit\ sales\ price.$$
$$\$150 = Unit\ variable\ expenses.$$
$$\$35,000 = Total\ fixed\ expenses.$$
$$\$40,000 = Target\ net\ profit.$$

Thus, the target net profit can be achieved by selling 750 ovens per month, which represents $187,500 in total sales ($250 × 750 ovens).

THE UNIT CONTRIBUTION APPROACH.   A second approach would be to expand the unit contribution formula to include the target net profit requirement:

$$\frac{\$35,000\ fixed\ expenses + \$40,000\ target\ net\ profit}{\$100\ contribution\ margin\ per\ oven} = 750\ ovens$$

This approach is simpler and more direct than using the cost-volume-profit equation. In addition, it shows clearly that once the fixed costs are covered the unit contribution margin is fully available for meeting profit requirements.

FURTHER CVP APPLICATIONS

The preceding sections have given us some insights into the principles involved in cost-volume-profit analysis, as well as some selected examples of how these principles are used by the manager. Before concluding our discussion, it will be helpful to consider two additional applications of the ideas which we have developed: first, the use of CVP concepts in structuring commissions for salespersons; and second, the use of CVP concepts in analyzing sales mix.

Structuring commissions to salespersons

Some firms base salespersons' commissions on contribution margin generated, rather than on sales generated. The reasoning goes like this: Since contribution margin represents the amount of sales revenue available to cover fixed expenses and profits, a firm's well-being will be maximized when contribution margin is maximized. By tying salespersons' commissions to contribution margin the salespersons are automatically encouraged to concentrate on that element which is of most importance to the firm. There is no need to worry about what mix of products the salespersons sell, because they will *automatically* sell that mix of products which will maximize the base on which their commissions are to be paid. That is, if salespersons are aware that their commissions will depend on the amount of contribution margin which they are able to generate, then they will use all of the experience, skill, and expertise which they have at their command to sell that mix of products which will maximize the contribution margin base. In effect, by maximizing their own well-being, they automatically maximize the well-being of the firm.

As a further step, some firms deduct from the total contribution margin generated by a salesperson the amount of the traveling, entertainment, and other expenses which are incurred. This encourages the salespersons to be sensitive to their own costs in the process of making sales.

The concept of sales mix

Sales mix can be defined as the relative proportion of total units sold (or total sales dollars) which is represented by each of a company's several product lines. To illustrate the concept, assume that a company has three product lines—Line A, Line B, and Line C. During 19x1, sales were as follows:

	Line A		Line B		Line C		Total	
	Amount	Per-cent	Amount	Per-cent	Amount	Per-cent	Amount	Per-cent
Sales	$20,000	100%	$50,000	100%	$30,000	100%	$100,000	100%
Sales mix	20%		50%		30%		100%	
Less variable expenses	15,000	75	30,000	60	24,000	80	69,000	69
Contribution margin	$ 5,000	25%	$20,000	40%	$ 6,000	20%	$ 31,000	31%

The company's sales mix would be 20 percent Line A, 50 percent Line B, and 30 percent Line C, since Line A accounts for $20,000 of the total $100,000 in sales, and so on.

Sales mix is an important concept. Most firms have more than one product line and for planning purposes need to know the relative weight of each in total sales. These weights are obtained by analyzing the sales mix. In addition, sales mix has an impact on break-even analysis, as well as on other aspects of cost-volume-profit computations.

SALES MIX AND BREAK-EVEN ANALYSIS. One of the assumptions underlying break-even analysis is that the sales mix will not change. To illustrate, assume that the company represented by the sales data above has fixed costs totaling $15,500. The break-even point for 19x1 would be $50,000 in sales—the total fixed costs of $15,500 divided by the *average* C/M ratio of 31 percent.

$$\frac{\text{Total fixed costs } \$15,500}{\text{C/M ratio } 31\%} = \$50,000 \text{ sales to break even}$$

But $50,000 in sales represents the break-even point for the company only so long as the sales mix does not change. *If the sales mix changes, then the break-even point will also change.* To illustrate, assume that the sales mix shifts away from Line B (a 40 percent C/M ratio), toward Line C (only a 20 percent C/M ratio). Assume that the sales mix in 19x2 is:

	Line A		Line B		Line C		Total	
	Amount	Per-cent	Amount	Per-cent	Amount	Per-cent	Amount	Per-cent
Sales	$20,000	100%	$30,000	100%	$50,000	100%	$100,000	100%
Sales mix...............	20%		30%		50%		100%	
Less variable expenses	15,000	75	18,000	60	40,000	80	73,000	73
Contribution margin	$ 5,000	25%	$12,000	40%	$10,000	20%	$ 27,000	27%

Although total sales remain unchanged at $100,000, the sales mix of Line B and Line C is exactly reversed from what it was in the preceding section. Line B now makes up 30 percent of total sales, whereas it made up 50 percent before, and so on. Notice that this shift in sales mix toward the less profitable Line C has caused the average C/M ratio to drop from 31 percent in 19x1 to only 27 percent in 19x2.

The new break-even point will be:

$$\frac{\text{Total fixed costs } \$15,500}{\text{C/M ratio } 27\%} = \$57,407 \text{ sales to break even}$$

The break-even point has increased from $50,000 in 19x1 to $57,407 in 19x2, as a result of the shift in sales mix toward the less profitable Line C.

In preparing a break-even analysis, some assumption must be made concerning the sales mix. Usually, the assumption is that the sales mix will not change. However, if the manager *knows* that shifts in various factors (consumer tastes, and so on) are causing shifts in the mix of the company's sales, then these factors must be considered in any subsequent cost-volume-profit analyses. Otherwise, the manager may be making decisions on the basis of outmoded or faulty data.

SALES MIX AND PER UNIT CONTRIBUTION MARGIN.   Sometimes the sales mix is measured in terms of the average per unit contribution margin. To illustrate, assume that a company has two products—X and Y. During 19x1 and 19x2 sales of products X and Y were as follows:

	Contri-bution margin per unit	Total units sold		Total contribution margin	
		19x1	19x2	19x1	19x2
Product X	$5.00	1,000	2,000	$ 5,000	$10,000
Product Y	$3.00	3,000	2,000	9,000	6,000
		4,000	4,000	$14,000	$16,000
Average per unit contribution margin ($14,000 ÷ 4,000 units)				$3.50	
Average per unit contribution margin ($16,000 ÷ 4,000 units)					$4.00

Two things should be noted about the schedule above. First, note that the sales mix in 19x1 was 1,000 units of product X and 3,000 units of product Y. This sales mix yielded $3.50 in average per unit contribution margin.

Second, note that the sales mix in 19x2 shifted to 2,000 units for both products, although *total* sales remained unchanged at 4,000 units. This sales mix yielded $4.00 in average per unit contribution margin, an increase of $0.50 per unit over the prior year.

What caused the increase in average per unit contribution margin between the two years? The answer is the shift in sales mix toward the more profitable product X. Although total volume (in units) did not change, total and per unit contribution changed simply because of the change in sales mix.

LIMITING ASSUMPTIONS IN COST-VOLUME-PROFIT ANALYSIS

Several limiting assumptions must be made when using data for cost-volume-profit analysis. These assumptions are:

1. That the behavior of both revenues and expenses is linear throughout the entire relevant range. The economists would differ from this view. They would say that changes in volume will trigger changes in both revenues and expenses in such a way that relationships will not remain linear.

2. That expenses can be accurately divided into variable and fixed categories.
3. That the sales mix is constant.
4. That inventories do not change in break-even computations (this assumption is considered further in Chapter 6).
5. That worker productivity and efficiency do not change throughout the relevant range.

SUMMARY

The analysis of cost-volume-profit relationships is one of management's most significant responsibilities. Basically it involves finding the most favorable combination of variable and fixed costs, in relation to selling price and sales volume. We have found that trade-offs are possible between types of costs, as well as between costs and selling price, and between selling price and sales volume. Sometimes these trade-offs are desirable, and sometimes they are not. Cost-volume-profit analysis provides the manager with a powerful tool for identifying those courses of action which will and which will not improve profitability.

The concepts developed in this chapter represent a *way of thinking,* rather than a mechanical set of procedures. That is, in order to put together the optimum combination of costs, selling price, and sales volume the manager must train himself or herself to think in terms of the unit contribution margin, the break-even point, the C/M ratio, the sales mix, and the other concepts developed in this chapter. These concepts are dynamic, in that a change in one will trigger changes in others—changes which may not be obvious on the surface. Only by learning to *think* in cost-volume-profit terms can the manager move with assurance toward the firm's profit objectives.

KEY TERMS FOR REVIEW

Per unit contribution margin	**The equation technique**
Break-even point	**The unit contribution technique**
Profit/volume ratio	**Cost-volume-profit graph**
Contribution margin ratio	**Break-even chart**
Cost structure	**Profit-graph**
Operating leverage	**Target net profit**
Incremental analysis	**Sales mix**

QUESTIONS

5–1.   What five factors are involved in a study of cost-volume-profit relationships?

5–2.   How is the contribution approach to the income statement useful in break-even analysis?

5-3. Why is the term "break-even analysis" a misnomer?

5-4. What is meant by the term "break-even point"?

5-5. Name three approaches to break-even analysis. Briefly explain how each approach works.

5-6. Beta Company's total contribution margin just equals the company's total fixed costs. Is Beta Company operating at a profit or at a loss? Explain.

5-7. The equation for total expenses in the Carson Company is:

$$Y = \text{total expenses}$$
$$Y = 50,000 + 0.4X$$

If X represents dollars of sales, explain the significance of the 50,000 and the 0.4 items in the equation above.

5-8. What is meant by the term "sales mix"? Explain how a shift in the sales mix could result in a higher break-even point, and at the same time in a lower net income.

5-9. In response to a request from your immediate supervisor, you have prepared a cost-volume-profit graph portraying the cost and revenue characteristics of your company's product and operations. Explain how the lines on the graph would change if (a) the selling price per unit decreased, (b) fixed costs increased throughout the entire range of activity portrayed on the graph, and (c) variable costs per unit increased.

5-10. Al's Auto Wash charges $2 to wash a car. The variable costs of washing a car are 15 percent of sales. Fixed costs total $1,020 monthly. How many cars must be washed each month in order for Al to break even?

5-11. Often the most direct route to a business decision is to make an incremental analysis based on the information available. What is meant by an "incremental analysis"?

5-12. What is meant by a product's "contribution margin ratio"? How is this ratio useful in planning of business operations?

5-13. Able Company and Baker Company are competing firms. Each company sells a single product, widgets, in the same market at a price of $50 per widget. Variable costs are the same in each company—$35 per widget. Able Company has discovered a way to reduce its variable costs by $4 per unit, and has decided to pass half of this cost savings on to its customers in the form of a lower price. Although Baker Company has not been able to reduce its variable costs, it also is thinking about lowering its selling price in order to remain competitive with Able Company. If each company sells 10,000 units each year, what will be the effect of the changes on each company's profits?

5-14. "Changes in fixed costs are much more significant to a company than changes in variable costs." Discuss.

5-15. Explain how the so-called break-even formula can be used as a profit-planning device.

5-16. What is meant by the term "operating leverage?"

5-17. A 10 percent decrease in the selling price of a product will have the same impact on net income as a 10 percent increase in the variable expenses. Do you agree? Why or why not?

5–18. Given the following: S = sales in units; SP = selling price per unit; FC = total fixed costs; VC = variable cost per unit. Using these notations, write out the correct formula for computing the break-even level of sales in units.

EXERCISES

E5–1. The Barker Company manufactures and sells a single product. The selling price per unit is $24, and the variable costs per unit are $18. The fixed costs are $12,000 per month.
1. What is the monthly break-even point in units sold and in sales dollars? Use the equation technique.
2. What is the total contribution margin at the monthly break-even point?
3. How many units would have to be sold each month to earn a target net income of $3,000? Use the unit contribution technique. Prove your answer by preparing a contribution income statement at the target level of sales.
4. What is the company's C/M ratio? If the company is operating above the break-even point and monthly sales increase by $6,000, by how much would you expect monthly net income to increase?

E5–2. The Roberts Company manufactures and sells a single product. The product sells for $40. The contribution margin is 30 percent and fixed expenses are $120,000 per year.

Required:
1. What are the variable expenses per unit?
2. Using the equation technique:
   a. What is the break-even point in units and in dollar sales?
   b. What sales level in units and in dollar sales is required to earn a profit of $24,000?
   c. If the contribution margin is raised to 40 percent, what is the new break-even point in units and in dollar sales?
3. Repeat (2) using the unit contribution approach.

E5–3. Fill in the missing amounts in each of the eight case situations below. Each case is independent of the others.
   a. Assume that only one product is being sold in each of the four following case situations:

Case	Units sold	Sales	Variable expenses	Contribution margin per unit	Fixed expenses	Net income
1	9,000	$81,000	$45,000	$?	$20,000	$?
2	?	50,000	?	4	10,000	10,000
3	8,000	?	40,000	3	?	9,000
4	3,000	45,000	?	?	18,000	(3,000)

b. Assume that more than one product is being sold in each of the four following case situations:

Case	Sales	Variable expenses	Average contri-bution margin (%)	Fixed expenses	Net income
1........	$150,000	$?	35%	$?	$ 8,000
2........	300,000	165,000	?	100,000	?
3........	?	?	30	80,000	(5,000)
4........	350,000	210,000	?	?	30,000

E5–4.   A "break-even" chart, as illustrated below, is a useful technique for showing relationships between costs, volume, and profits.

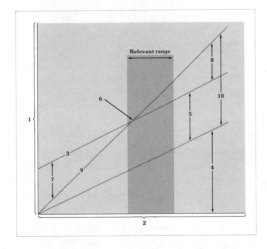

Required:
1. Identify the numbered components of the "break-even" chart.
2. Discuss the significance of the concept of the "relevant range" to break-even analysis.

(AICPA, adapted)

E5–5.   The Valtek Company manufactures and sells prehung doors to home build-ers. The doors are sold for $30 each. Variable costs are $21 per door, and fixed costs total $60,000 per year. The company is presently selling 8,000 doors per year.

Required:
1. Compute the Valtek Company's operating leverage.
2. Management is confident that the company can sell 10,000 doors next year. Using the operating leverage concept, compute the expected net income for next year.

E5–6.   Arbor Company produces and distributes vinegar at the retail level. The company's income statement for the most recent year is given below:

Sales (500,000 gal. at $2.50)	$1,250,000
Variable expenses	800,000
Contribution margin.................	$ 450,000
Less fixed expenses	475,000
Net loss	$ (25,000)

Another manufacturing company that uses vinegar as an ingredient in its product has offered to buy 100,000 gallons of vinegar a year "if the price is right." Arbor Company would not have to pay the regular sales commission of 25 cents per gallon on this business. Regular business would be undisturbed by the manufacturing company sales.

Required:

What price per gallon should be quoted to the manufacturing company in order for Arbor Company to earn a net income of $15,000 per year on *total* vinegar sales?

E5–7.   Spaceage Toys, Inc. sells a toy rocket at a price of $12. The variable costs of producing and selling the rocket are $8 per unit. Fixed costs associated with the rocket total $24,000 annually.

Required:

1.   Assume that next year sales are projected to total 7,000 rockets nationally. Prepare an income statement, using the contribution format.
2.   Prepare a cost-volume-profit graph, with units ranging from a volume of 1,000 to 10,000 units.
3.   Prepare a "profit-graph" using the same volume range of 1,000 to 10,000 units.

E5–8.   Carrier Company is one of several producers of a part used in the small appliance industry. The company is presently producing and selling 120,000 parts a year. The selling price is $4 per part; variable expenses are $2.50 per part, and fixed expenses are $150,000 per year.

Required:

1.   Compute the break-even point in units and in sales dollars.
2.   After a study of the market, the president is convinced that a 5 percent reduction in the unit selling price will result in a 20 percent increase in the number of parts sold. Prepare two contribution income statements, one under present operating conditions, and one as operations would appear after the proposed changes. Show two column headings on each statement, one for "Total" and one for "Per Unit" data.
3.   Refer to the data in (2) above. Show the effect of the proposed changes on net income, using the incremental approach illustrated in the text.
4.   Refer to the data in (2) above. How many units would have to be sold at the new selling price to yield the net income presently being earned?

E5–9.   ABC Company's most recent income statement is shown below:

	Total	Per unit
Sales (30,000 units)	$150,000	$5
Less variable expenses	90,000	3
Contribution margin	$ 60,000	$2
Less fixed expenses	50,000	
Net income	$ 10,000	

Required:

Prepare a new income statement under each of the following conditions (consider each case independently):

1. Sales volume increases by 15 percent.
2. The selling price decreases by 50 cents per unit, and the sales volume increases by 20 percent.
3. The selling price increases by 50 cents per unit, fixed expenses increase by $10,000, and the sales volume decreases by 5 percent.
4. Variable expenses increase by 20 cents per unit, the selling price increases by 12 percent, and the sales volume decreases by 10 percent.

PROBLEMS

P5–10. *Straightforward break-even computation, graphing of data, and incremental analysis.* Mr. Egon, president of the Tic-Tok Clock Company, recently completed a course in managerial accounting at the state university. He believes he can apply certain aspects of the course to his business. He is particularly interested in adopting the cost-volume-profit approach to decision making. Thus, he has prepared the following analysis:

Sales price per clock		$8.00	100%
Variable expenses per clock:			
Materials	$2.00		
Labor	1.80		
Variable overhead	1.00	4.80	60
Contribution margin		$3.20	40%
Fixed expenses (per year):			
Depreciation–equipment	$10,000		
Rental of building	20,000		
Selling	16,000		
Administrative	18,000		
	$64,000		

Required:

1. What is the break-even point in units and in dollar sales?
2. What is the appearance of the cost-volume-profit data in graphical form?
3. If net income was $18,000 last year, how many clocks were sold?
4. Mr. Egon presently has one full-time and one part-time salesperson working for him. It will cost Mr. Egon an additional $8,000 per year to convert the part-time position to a full-time position. He believes

the move will bring in an additional $24,000 in sales each year. Should Mr. Egon convert the position? Show all calculations.

P5–11. *Break even; Sensitivity analysis; Operating leverage.* The Royal Company owns and operates a luxurious motel in a famous resort area. The motel presently rents rooms to singles and groups of two or more people. The following data are representative of the last two years:

	Per night
Average room rate	$50
Average variable expense	22
Average contribution margin	$28

Fixed costs average $2,100 per night. The motel has 150 rooms, with an average occupancy rate of 60 percent.

Required:

1. Prepare a contribution-type income statement, showing the average net income per night.
2. What is the motel's break-even point in rooms per night? In total rental revenues?
3. Present the motel's cost-volume-profit data in graphical form.
4. The Royal Company is considering not renting rooms to singles. If this is done, it is believed that the average room rate will be $60 per night, average variable expenses will be $26 per night, and fixed costs will remain the same. It is expected that the occupancy rate will decline to 48 percent. Should the change be made? Show computations.
5. Refer to the original data. Compute the motel's operating leverage. Suppose that the motel industry trade journal predicts that tourism will be up 5 percent next year. Assuming no change in cost relationships, by what percentage should the motel's profits increase? Use the operating leverage concept to determine your answer.

P5–12. *Sales mix assumptions; Break-even analysis.* The Clark Company sells three products—X, Y, and Z. Budgeted sales by product and in total for the coming month are shown below:

		Product		
	X	Y	Z	Total
Percentage of total sales	25%	40%	35%	100%
Sales	$20,000	$32,000	$28,000	$80,000
Less variable expenses	12,000	20,800	11,200	44,000
Contribution margin	$ 8,000	$11,200	$16,800	$36,000
C/M ratio	40%	35%	60%	45%
Less fixed expenses				25,350
Net income				$10,650

Break-even sales: $\dfrac{\$25,350}{0.45} = \$56,333$

As shown by these data, net income is budgeted at $10,650, and break-even sales at $56,333. Assume that actual sales for the month are: X—$24,000; Y—$48,000; and Z—$8,000.

Required:

1. Prepare a contribution income statement for the month based on actual sales data. Present the statement in the format shown above.
2. Compute the break-even sales for the month, based on your actual data.
3. Considering the fact that the company met its $80,000 sales budget for the month, prepare a brief memo for the president explaining why the net income and break-even sales are different from what was budgeted.

P5–13. *Impact of cost-volume changes on net income.* The following data pertain to the budget of Yama Company for the next year:

```
Sales ..................... 200,000 units
Sales price ............... $1.50 per unit
Variable expenses ......... $1.00 per unit
Fixed expenses ............ $50,000
```

Required:

1. What is the projected net income?
2. What would be the net income under each of the following independent cases?
   a. Sales volume increases by 10 percent.
   b. Sales volume decreases by 10 percent.
   c. Sales price increases by 10 percent.
   d. Sales price decreases by 10 percent.
   e. Variable expenses increase by 10 percent.
   f. Variable expenses decrease by 10 percent.
   g. Fixed expenses increase by 10 percent.
   h. Fixed expenses decrease by 10 percent.
   i. Sales volume increases by 15 percent, and sales price decreases by 5 percent.
   j. Variable expenses decrease by 12 percent, and fixed expenses increase by $20,000.

P5–14. *Break-even analysis; Operating leverage.* The Thayer Aspirin Company manufactures a high-quality aspirin product which is distributed throughout the western part of the United States. The company sells an average of 250,000 bottles of aspirin each month, with the following cost relationships:

	Per bottle
Selling price	$0.50
Variable expense	0.15
Contribution margin	$0.35
Fixed monthly cost:	
Building rental	$12,250
Equipment depreciation	8,000
Salaries	20,000
Advertising	25,000
Other fixed cost	15,250
Total	$80,500

Required:

1. Prepare a contribution-type income statement, showing the company's monthly profits. Include "Total," "Per Unit," and "Percentage" columns.
2. What is the monthly break-even point in bottles of aspirin? In total sales dollars?
3. Suppose that the company would like to earn a monthly profit of $10,500. How many bottles of aspirin would have to be sold?
4. If the building rental were doubled, what would be the monthly break-even point in bottles of aspirin? In total sales dollars?
5. Refer to the original data. If salespersons are given a 2 cent bonus commission for each bottle sold, what is the new monthly break-even point in bottles of aspirin? In total sales dollars?
6. Refer to the original data. If salespersons are given a 2 cent bonus commission for each bottle sold over the break-even point, what would the Thayer Aspirin Company's net income be if 260,000 bottles were sold? (Use the incremental approach.)
7. Refer to the original data. The president is confident that an additional $5,000 in advertising each month would generate a 10 percent increase in sales. Would you recommend the increased advertising? (Use the incremental approach.) Would your answer be the same if the contribution margin was $0.15 per bottle, rather than $0.35? Explain.
8. Refer to (1) above. Compute the Thayer Aspirin Company's operating leverage. Suppose that monthly sales increase by 7,500 bottles. What percentage increase would you expect to see in the company's net income? Use the operating leverage concept in obtaining your answer.

P5–15. *Basics of CVP analysis.* The Dyer Company has been experiencing difficulty for some time. The company's income statement for the most recent year is given below:

Sales (6,000 units at $12)	$72,000
Less variable expenses	54,000
Contribution margin	$18,000
Less fixed expenses	21,000
Net loss	$ (3,000)

Required:

1. Compute the company's C/M ratio, and its break-even point in both units and dollars.
2. The president is certain that a $4,000 increase in the advertising budget, combined with an intensified effort by the salespersons, will result in a $30,000 increase in sales. If the president is right, what will be the effect on the company's overall net income or loss? (Use the incremental approach.)
3. The sales manager is convinced that a $1 reduction in the selling price, combined with an increase of $5,000 in the advertising budget, will cause unit sales to double. What will the new income statement look like if these changes are adopted?

4. Refer to the original data. The president's wife thinks that a fancy new package for the Dyer Company's product would help sales. The new package would increase packaging costs by 25 cents per unit. Assuming no other changes in cost behavior, how many units would have to be sold each year to earn a profit of $2,000?

5. Refer to the original data. By automating certain operations the company could reduce variable expenses by $1 per unit; however, fixed costs would increase by $8,000 annually.

   a. Compute the new C/M ratio, and break-even point in both units and dollars.

   b. If sales are expected to be 9,000 units next year would this change seem advisable? Explain.

   c. What risks are involved if the change is made?

6. Refer to the original data. Another company has offered to purchase 2,000 units on a special price basis. Variable selling expenses of $2 per unit could be avoided on these sales. What price per unit should be quoted by the Dyer Company if it desires to make an overall net income of $4,000 for the company as a whole? (Present sales would not be disturbed by this order.)

P5–16. *Break even; Sensitivity analysis; Operating leverage.* The management of Audio, Inc., is pleased with the company's performance for 19x6, the year just ended. The company earned a record profit of $100,000 on sales of 30,000 cassette recorders (its only product line):

Sales		$1,500,000
Less cost of goods sold:		
Direct materials	$450,000	
Direct labor	240,000	
Factory overhead	310,000	1,000,000
Gross margin		$ 500,000
Less operating expenses:		
Selling expense	$250,000	
Administrative expense	150,000	400,000
Net income		$ 100,000

Concern has been expressed by the sales manager about increased competition, and about whether the company will be able to retain its market share during the coming year. In order to retain its market share, the company is considering three alternatives: (1) reducing the selling price; (2) improving the overall quality of the product by using more costly inputs; and (3) increasing advertising.

A breakdown of variable costs for 19x6 shows:

Variable costs	Per unit
Direct materials	$15
Direct labor	8
Variable factory overhead	2
Variable selling expense	5
Total	$30

Required:

1. Redo the company's income statement for 19x6 in the contribution format. (Include "Per unit" figures for sales, total variable expenses, and contribution margin.)
2. Compute the break-even point in units.
3. Redo the income statement and recompute the break-even point under *each* of the three following alternatives:
   a. The unit selling price is reduced by 8 percent in order for the company to retain its present market share in units sold.
   b. The total variable expenses (per unit) are increased by 8 percent as a result of the use of more costly inputs (market share remains constant).
   c. The fixed expenses are increased by 8 percent as a result of more advertising (market share remains constant).
4. Suppose that the company does not want its profits to drop below $100,000 per year. How many units would have to be sold under each of the alternatives in (3) above in order to earn this level of profits? In each case, what increase does this represent over present sales in units? Which course of action would you advise management to follow?
5. Refer to the original data. Compute the company's operating leverage. Suppose that management has decided to maintain present selling prices and costs, but to intensify the efforts of its salespersons. If by doing this the company is able to increase its market share by 8 percent, what will be the effect on profits? Use the operating leverage concept to obtain your answer.

P5–17. *Impact of a manager's salary on contribution margin and net income.* The Ross Lamp Shop sells lamps to retail customers. The shopowner, Mr. Ross, purchases the lamps from various sources and sells the lamps at a 60 percent markup over the purchase price. The lamps cost, on the average, $18 each. In addition to the cost of the lamps, other variable expenses are $2.80 per lamp. Fixed expenses are $360 per month.

Required:

1. What is the break-even point in units and in dollar sales?
2. What level of sales is required (in units and in dollars) in order to make a profit of $1,000 per month?
3. Mr. Ross is going to hire a manager to run the shop. The manager will be paid $500 per month, plus a commission of $1 per lamp for the first 150 lamps sold each month, and $2 for each additional lamp sold. How many lamps must be sold each month for the shop to show a monthly profit of $400?
4. What possible problems might arise with the compensation plan for the manager? How can these problems be solved?

P5–18. *Basics of CVP analysis.* Harlow Company produces a product which sells for $12 per unit. Variable costs are $9 per unit, and fixed costs total $24,000 annually.

Required:

Answer the following independent questions:
1. What is the C/M ratio for the product?
2. Use the C/M ratio to determine the break-even point in sales dollars.
3. The company estimates that sales will increase by $25,000 during the coming year. By how much should net income increase?
4. Assume that operating results for last year were:

Sales	$120,000
Less variable expenses	90,000
Contribution margin	$ 30,000
Less fixed expenses	24,000
Net income	$ 6,000

Compute the company's operating leverage. Draft a brief memo for the president, explaining what operating leverage means.
5. Refer to the original data. Assume that the company sold 12,000 units last year. The sales manager is convinced that a 5 percent reduction in the selling price, combined with an $8,000 increase in promotional expenditures, would cause annual sales in units to increase by 50 percent. Prepare two contribution income statements, one showing the results of last year's operations, and one showing the results of operations if these changes are made. Would you recommend that the Harlow Company do as the sales manager suggests?
6. Refer to the original data. Assume again that the company sold 12,000 units last year. The president does not want to tinker with the selling price. Instead, he wants to increase the sales commission by 50 cents per unit. He thinks that this move, combined with some increase in advertising, would increase annual sales by 30 percent. By how much could advertising be increased with profits remaining unchanged? Do not prepare an income statement; use the incremental analysis approach.
7. Refer to the original data. Assume that the company presently is selling 8,800 units per year. An order has been received from a wholesale distributor who wants to purchase 2,000 units on a special price basis. What unit price would have to be quoted to the distributor if the Harlow Company wants to double its current profits? (Present sales would not be disturbed by this special order.)

P5–19. *Sales mix.* Alpine, Inc., is a producer of recreational equipment. The company's sleeping bag division produces three types of sleeping bags—the Backpacker, the Regular, and the Economy. Selected information on the bags is given below:

	Backpacker	Regular	Economy
Selling price per bag	$60.00	$45.00	$32.00
Variable expenses per bag:			
Production	23.00	19.00	16.50
Selling	2.40	2.10	1.80
Administrative	1.10	1.10	1.10

The company operates on a regional basis, with sales restricted to the western United States. All sales are made through the company's own retail outlets. The cost records show that the following fixed costs are assignable to the sleeping bag division:

	Per month
Fixed production costs	$43,250
Fixed selling costs	24,600
Fixed administrative costs	16,500
Total	$84,350

Sales, in units, over the past two months have been:

	Backpacker	Regular	Economy	Total
May	1,650	1,220	1,540	4,410
June	1,050	950	3,280	5,280
Total	2,700	2,170	4,820	9,690

Required:

1. Prepare an income statement for May, and an income statement for June. Use the contribution approach, with the following headings:

Total		Backpacker		Regular		Economy	
Amount	Percent	Amount	Percent	Amount	Percent	Amount	Percent

Sales
Etc.

Place the fixed expenses only in the "Total" column. Do not show percentages for the fixed expenses.

2. Upon seeing the May and June income statements, one of the stockholders exclaimed, "The company needs a new manager in that sleeping bag division. Just look at these income statements. June sales are up, but net income is down. That manager just can't control costs." What other explanation can you give for the drop in net income?

3. Compute the division's break-even point in dollars for the month of May.

4. Has June's break-even point in dollars gone up or down from May's break-even point? Explain without computing a break-even point for June.

5. Assume that sales of the Backpacker bag increase by $10,000. What would be the effect on net income? What would be the effect if Regular bag sales increased by $10,000? Economy bag sales increased by $10,000? Do not prepare income statements.

P5–20. *CVP analysis.* (This problem requires a maximum of thought and a minimum of pencil pushing.) The most recent income statement for Deseret Company is given below:

```
Sales ............................  $96,000
Less variable expenses ............   60,000
Contribution margin ...............  $36,000
Less fixed expenses ...............   30,000
Net income .......................  $ 6,000
```

The Deseret Company has ample unused capacity, and is studying various ways of improving profits.

Required:

Each of the situations below is independent of the others. Provide the information requested.

1. New equipment has come onto the market that would allow the Deseret Company to automate a portion of its operations. Unit variable costs could be reduced by 10 percent. However, total fixed costs would increase by 20 percent.

    a. Prepare two contribution-type income statements, one showing present operations and one showing how operations would appear if the new equipment was purchased. On each statement show an "Amount" and a "Percentage" column. Do not show percentages for the fixed costs.

    b. As a manager, what factor would be paramount in your mind in deciding whether to purchase the new equipment? (You may assume that plenty of funds are available to make the purchase.)

2. The company is thinking about changing its marketing method. Under the new method sales would increase by 15 percent, and net income would increase by one third. Fixed costs could be slashed to only $25,120 each period. Compute the break-even point for the company before and after the change in marketing method.

3. Due to a sudden and unprecedented surge in demand, the company's sales increased by 25 percent during one period. During that period net income doubled. Would you congratulate management for an outstanding performance, or would you chastise management for not doing its job well during the period? Explain.

P5–21. *Changing sales mix, commission structure, and the break-even point.* The Calvin Pipe Company produces quality pipes out of carbon in a revolutionary manner. The company makes a standard model pipe and a deluxe model pipe, and sells them to retail tobacco shops throughout the country. The standard model pipes are sold to retailers for $10 each. The deluxe model pipes are sold to retailers for $12 each. The variable costs associated with each model of pipe are given below (in cost per pipe):

	Standard	Deluxe
Materials	$1.25	$1.25
Labor	2.40	3.80
Variable factory overhead	1.20	1.90
Sales commissions (10% of sales price)	1.00	1.20
Total	$5.85	$8.15

The Calvin Pipe Company's fixed expenses for each month are:

Depreciation–equipment	$ 3,600
Depreciation–building	3,200
Selling	2,000
Administrative	3,200
Total	$12,000

Sales, in units, for the previous two months are as follows:

	Standard	Deluxe	Total
September	4,000	2,000	6,000
October	3,000	3,000	6,000

Required:

1. *a.* Prepare an income statement for September, and an income statement for October. Use the contribution format, with the following headings:

	Standard		Deluxe		Total	
	Amount	Percent	Amount	Percent	Amount	Percent
Sales						
Etc.						

   Place the fixed expenses only in the "Total" column. Do not show percentages for the fixed expenses.

   b. Explain why there was a difference in net income between the two months, even though the same *total* number of pipes was sold in each month.

2. What can be done to the sales commissions to optimize the sales mix?

3. *a.* Using October's figures, what was the break-even point for the month in sales dollars?

   b. Has October's break-even point gone up or down from that of September? Explain your answer without resorting to calculating the break-even point for September.

P5–22. *Changing levels of fixed and variable costs.* The Edman Company is considering a new product line which will require a fixed cost of $20,000 per month in order to manufacture 18,000 units. To manufacture over 18,000 units, the firm will have to spend an additional $12,000 in fixed costs per month. The product will sell for $2.50 per unit. Variable costs will be $1.60 per unit for the first 18,000 units, and $1.70 per unit for anything over 18,000 units.

Required:

1. What is the monthly break-even point in units and in dollar sales?
2. How many units must be sold in order to make a profit of $11,200 each month?

3. If the sales manager receives a bonus of $0.10 per unit sold in excess of the break-even point, how many units must be sold in order to make a profit of $11,200 per month?

P5–23. *Detailed income statement; CVP sensitivity analysis.* The most recent income statement for Wesco, Inc. appears below.

WESCO, INC.
Income Statement
For the Year Ended June 30, 19x1

Sales (35,000 units at $5)		$175,000
Less cost of goods sold:		
Direct materials	$35,000	
Direct labor	26,250	
Factory overhead	53,100	114,350
Gross margin		$ 60,650
Less operating expenses:		
Selling expense:		
Variable:		
Sales commissions $14,000		
Shipping 3,500	$17,500	
Fixed (advertising, salaries)	30,000	
Administrative expense:		
Variable	1,750	
Fixed	18,000	67,250
Net loss		$ (6,600)

All variable expenses vary in terms of units sold except for sales commissions, which are based on sales dollars. Variable factory overhead is $0.50 per unit. Wesco, Inc.'s plant has a capacity of 60,000 units.

Management is very disappointed with 19x1's operating results. Several possible courses of action are being studied to determine what should be done to make 19x2 profitable.

Required:

1. Redo Wesco, Inc.'s 19x1 income statement in the contribution format. Show a "Total" and a "Per Unit" column. Allow adjacent space to enter the solution to (2).

2. *a.* For 19x2 the sales manager would like to reduce the unit selling price by 10 percent. He is certain that this would fill the plant to capacity.

   b. For 19x2 the executive vice president would like to increase the unit selling price by 10 percent, increase the sales commission to 12 percent of sales, and increase advertising by $25,000. She thinks that this would trigger a 60 percent increase in volume. Prepare two contribution income statements, one showing what profits would be under the sales manager's proposal, and one showing what profits would be under the executive vice president's proposal. On each statement include both "Total" and "Per Unit" columns.

3. Refer to the original data. The president thinks it would be unwise to change the unit selling price. Instead, he wants to use less costly

materials in manufacturing units of product, thereby reducing unit costs by 25 cents. How many units would have to be sold in 19x2 to earn a target profit of $12,000?

4. Refer to the original data. Wesco, Inc.'s advertising agency thinks that the problem lies in inadequate promotion. How much may advertising be increased and still allow the company to earn a target return of 5 percent on sales of 50,000 units?

5. Refer to the original data. The company has been approached by an overseas distributor who wants to purchase 15,000 units on a special price basis. There would be no sales commission on these units; however, shipping costs would be doubled. In addition, a foreign import duty of $4,500 would have to be paid by Wesco, Inc., on behalf of the overseas distributor. What unit price would have to be quoted on the 15,000 units by Wesco, Inc., to allow the company to earn a profit of $10,500 on total operations? Regular business would not be disturbed by the special order.

P5–24. *CVP and sales mix variations.* The officers of the Bradshaw Company reviewed the profitability of the company's four products and the potential effect of several proposals for varying the product mix. An excerpt from the income statement for 19x1 and other data follows:

		Product			
	Total	P	Q	R	S
Sales	$62,600	$10,000	$18,000	$12,600	$22,000
Cost of goods sold	44,274	4,750	7,056	13,968	18,500
Gross profit	18,326	5,250	10,944	(1,368)	3,500
Operating expenses	12,012	1,990	2,976	2,826	4,220
Net income before taxes ..	$ 6,314	$ 3,260	$ 7,968	$ (4,194)	$ (720)
Units sold		1,000	1,200	1,800	2,000
Sales price per unit		$10.00	$15.00	$7.00	$11.00
Variable cost of goods sold per unit		$2.50	$3.00	$6.50	$6.00
Variable operating expenses per unit........		$1.17	$1.25	$1.00	$1.20

Total fixed costs are not expected to fluctuate as a result of changes under consideration.

Required:

1. The effect on net income if Product R is discontinued.

2. The effect on net income if Product R is discontinued and if a consequent loss of customers causes a decrease of 200 units in sales of Product Q.

3. The effect on net income if Product R's sale price is increased to $8 with a decrease in the number of units sold to 1,500 with no effect on the other products.

4. The effect on net income if a new Product T is introduced and Product R is discontinued with no effect on the other products. The total vari-

able costs per unit of Product T would be $8.05, and 1,600 units can be sold at $9.50 each. The plant in which Product R is produced can be used to produce Product T.

5. The effect on net income if production of Product P is reduced to 500 units (to be sold at $12 each), and if production of Product S is increased to 2,500 units (to be sold at $10.50 each). (Part of the plant in which Product P is produced can easily be adapted to produce Product S, but changes in quantities make changes in the sales price advisable.)

6. The effect on net income if production of Product P is increased by 1,000 units to be sold at $10 each by adding a second shift. Higher wages must be paid, thus increasing the variable cost of goods sold per unit to $3.50 for each additional unit.

(AICPA, adapted)

P5–25. *Case on plant expansion; Break-even analysis.* "In my opinion, it will be a mistake if that new plant is built," said John Buttars, controller and financial vice president of Tanka Toys. "Why, if that plant was in existence right now we would be reporting a loss of $37,800 for the year [1980], rather than a profit, and 1980 sales have been the best in the history of the company."

Mr. Buttars was speaking of a new, highly automated production plant which Tanka Toys is considering building. The company was organized only eight years ago, but has become one of the leaders in the industry due to the innovative toys which it has designed and marketed. Annual sales since inception of the company, along with net income as a percentage of sales, are presented below:

1973	$ 699,000	6.9%
1974	857,000	6.7
1975	1,071,000	6.8
1976	1,360,000	5.5
1977	1,845,000	5.7
1978	1,476,000	1.7
1979	2,860,000	3.2
1980	3,892,000	3.4

Although the company has always been profitable, in recent years rising costs have cut into its profit margins. The main production plant was constructed in 1975, but growth has been greater than anyone anticipated, making it necessary to rent additional production and storage space in various locations around the country. This spreading out of production facilities has caused costs to rise, particularly since the company is somewhat limited in the amount of automated equipment which it can use and thereby must rely on training a large number of new workers each year during peak production seasons.

Tanka Toys produces about 75 percent of its toys between April and September, and only about 25 percent during the remainder of the year. This seasonal production pattern is followed by many toy manufacturers, since it saves on storage costs and reduces the chances of toy obsolescence due to style changes. Other toy manufacturers produce evenly throughout the year, thereby maintaining a stable work force. Jana Hardy, manufacturing vice president of Tanka Toys, is pushing the new plant very hard, since it would permit Tanka Toys to produce on a more even basis, as well as to automate many hand operations and thereby dramatically reduce variable costs.

Although total toy sales are quite stable, individual toy manufacturers can experience wide fluctuations from year to year according to how well their toys are received by the market. For example, Tanka Toys "missed the market" on one of its toy lines in 1978, causing a sharp drop in sales and profits, as shown above. Other manufacturers have experienced even sharper drops in sales, some on a prolonged basis, and Tanka Toys feels fortunate in the sales stability which it has enjoyed.

Mr. Buttars points out that although variable costs will be reduced by the new plant, fixed costs will rise steeply to $1,400,000 per year. On the other hand, fixed costs presently are only $450,000 per year. Mr. Buttars is confident (and Ms. Hardy agrees) that with stringent cost control variable costs can be held at 82 percent of sales if the company continues with its present production setup. Variable expenses will be 65 percent of sales if the new plant is built.

Ms. Hardy points out that marketing projections predict only a 10 percent annual growth rate in sales if the company continues with its present production setup, whereas sales growth is expected to be as much as 20 percent annually if the new plant is built. The new plant would provide ample capacity to meet projected sales needs for many years into the future. Economies of expansion dictate, however, that any expansion undertaken be made in one step, since expansion by stages is too costly to be a feasible alternative.

Required:

1. Assuming that the company continues with its present production setup:
   a. Compute the break-even point in sales dollars.
   b. Express the break-even point as a percentage of estimated 1981 sales. In a managerial sense, what is the significance of this percentage figure?
   c. Compute the expected profits for 1981, and the operating leverage.
2. Assuming that the company builds the new plant, redo the computations in (1) above.
3. Prepare a cost-volume-profit graph for Tanka Toys, showing on the graph the cost/revenue data for both the present plant and the proposed new plant.
4. Compute the level of sales at which profits would be equal with either the old or the new plant. Show this point on the graph which you prepared in (3) above.
5. Refer to the original data. Assume that Tanka Toys "misses the market" in 1981, and that sales fall by the same rate that sales fell in 1978. Compute the net profit or loss for 1981 with and without the new plant.

6. Refer to the original data. Assume that sales growth is as expected.
   a. Prepare a table showing gross sales at both a 10 percent and a 20 percent annual growth for each of the years 1981–84. [You already have 1981 gross sales from (1) and (2) above.]
   b. Disregarding the computations made in (a), assume that gross sales in 1984 will be $5,698,277 if the company keeps its present plant, and $8,070,451 if the new plant is built. Prepare an income statement for each alternative, and compute the operating leverage.
7. Refer to the original data. Suppose that the company is anxious to again earn a profit of at least 6 percent of sales. At what sales level will this be achieved if the new plant is built?
8. Based on the data in (1)–(7) above, evaluate the risks and merits of building the new plant, and recommend to management which course of action you think should be taken. Be prepared to defend your recommendation in class.

P5–26. *Break-even and sales mix.* Hewtex Electronics manufactures two products—tape recorders and electronic calculators—and sells them nationally to wholesalers and retailers. The Hewtex management is very pleased with the company's performance for the current fiscal year. Projected sales through December 31, 19x7, indicate that 70,000 tape recorders and 140,000 electronic calculators will be sold this year. The projected earnings statement, which appears below, shows that Hewtex will exceed its earnings goal of 9 percent on sales after taxes.

HEWTEX ELECTRONICS
Projected Earnings Statement
For the Year Ended December 31, 19x7

	Tape recorders		Electronic calculators		
	Total amount (000)	Per unit	Total amount (000)	Per unit	Total (000)
Sales	$1,050	$15.00	$3,150	$22.50	$4,200.0
Production costs:					
Materials	$ 280	$ 4.00	$ 630	$ 4.50	$ 910.0
Direct labor	140	2.00	420	3.00	560.0
Variable overhead	140	2.00	280	2.00	420.0
Fixed overhead	70	1.00	210	1.50	280.0
Total production costs	$ 630	$ 9.00	$1,540	$11.00	$2,170.0
Gross margin	$ 420	$ 6.00	$1,610	$11.50	$2,030.0
Fixed selling and administrative expenses					1,040.0
Net income before income taxes					$ 990.0
Income taxes (55%)					544.5
Net income					$ 445.5

The tape recorder business has been fairly stable the last few years, and the company does not intend to change the tape recorder price. However, the competition among manufacturers of electronic calculators has been increasing. Hewtex's calculators have been very popular with consumers. In order to sustain this interest in their calculators and to meet the price reductions expected from competitors, management has decided to reduce the wholesale price of its calculator from $22.50 to $20.00 per unit effective January 1, 19x8. At the same time the company plans to spend an additional $57,000 on advertising during fiscal year 19x8. As a consequence of these actions, management estimates that 80 percent of its total revenue will be derived from calculator sales as compared to 75 percent in 19x7. As in prior years, the sales mix is assumed to be the same at all volume levels.

The total fixed overhead costs will not change in 19x8, nor will the variable overhead cost rates (applied on a direct labor-hour base). However, the cost of materials and direct labor is expected to change. The cost of solid state electronic components will be cheaper in 19x8. Hewtex estimates that material costs will drop 10 percent for the tape recorders and 20 percent for the calculators in 19x8. However, direct labor costs for both products will increase 10 percent in the coming year.

Required:

1. How many tape recorder and electronic calculator units did Hewtex Electronics have to sell in 19x7 to break even?
2. What volume of sales is required if Hewtex Electronics is to earn a profit in 19x8 equal to 9 percent on sales after taxes?
3. How many tape recorder and electronic calculator units will Hewtex have to sell in 19x8 to break even?

(CMA, adapted)

PART TWO

USES OF MANAGERIAL ACCOUNTING DATA

Chapter 6

Segmented reporting, and the contribution approach to costing

One aspect of the accountant's work centers on the problem of allocating costs to various parts of an organization. Cost allocation is necessary to provide useful and relevant data for three purposes:

1. For product costing and for pricing.
2. For appraisal of managerial performance.
3. For making special decisions.

There are two basic approaches to costing in use today. One is known as the absorption approach, and the other is known as the contribution approach. The absorption approach to costing was discussed at length in Chapter 3. The contribution approach was discussed briefly in Chapters 4 and 5. We shall now look more closely at the contribution approach to costing, to see what benefits it may have to offer in meeting the data needs listed above. Since the contribution approach emphasizes costs by behavior, many persons feel that it provides insights into cost data that may be obscured by the absorption approach.

SEGMENTED REPORTING

To operate effectively, managers must have a great deal more information available to them than that provided by a single income statement. Some product lines may be profitable, and some may be unprofitable; some salespersons may be more effective than others; some sales territories may have a poor sales mix, or may be overlooking sales opportunities; or some producing divisions may be ineffectively using their capacity and/or resources. To uncover problems such as these, the manager needs reports that focus on the *segments* of the company. A segment can be defined as any part or activity of an organization about which a manager seeks cost data. Examples of segments would include sales territories, manufacturing divisions, producing departments and operations, and groups or lines of products. One of the most valuable uses of the contribution approach to costing is for preparation of segmented reports that can be used for profitability analysis of various segments of an organization.

Differing levels of segmented reports

Segmented reports can be prepared for activity at many different levels of an organization, and in differing formats. Exhibit 6–1 illustrates three levels of segmented reports, presented in a format that is widely used. Observe from the exhibit that the total company is first segmented in terms of divisions. Then one of these segments, Division 2, is further segmented in terms of the product lines sold within the division. In turn, one of these segments, the Regular Model of Division 2, is further segmented in terms of the territories in which it is sold. Notice that as we go from one segmented report to another we are looking at smaller and smaller pieces of the

Exhibit 6–1
Cost allocation through the contribution approach—An illustration of segmented reports

Segments Defined as Divisions

			Segments	
		Total company	Division 1	Division 2
Sales		$90,000	$50,000	$40,000
Less variable expenses:				
Cost of goods sold		$40,000	$27,000	$13,000
Other variable expenses		10,000	7,000	3,000
Total variable expenses		$50,000	$34,000	$16,000
Contribution margin		$40,000	$16,000	$24,000
Less direct fixed expenses		15,000	8,000	7,000*
Divisional segment margin		$25,000	$ 8,000	$17,000
Less common fixed expenses		16,000		
Net income		$ 9,000		

Segments Defined as Product Lines of Division 2

			Segments	
		Division 2	Deluxe model	Regular model
Sales		$40,000	$15,000	$25,000
Less variable expenses:				
Cost of goods sold		$13,000	$ 5,000	$ 8,000
Other variable expenses		3,000	2,000	1,000
Total variable expenses		$16,000	$ 7,000	$ 9,000
Contribution margin		$24,000	$ 8,000	$16,000
Less direct fixed expenses		3,000	1,000	2,000
Product line segment margin		$21,000	$ 7,000	$14,000
Less common fixed expenses		4,000		
Divisional segment margin		$17,000		

Segments Defined as Sales Territories for One Product Line of Division 2

			Segments	
		Regular model	Home sales	Foreign sales
Sales		$25,000	$18,000	$ 7,000
Less variable expenses:				
Cost of goods sold		$ 8,000	$ 6,000	$ 2,000
Other variable expenses		1,000	300	700
Total variable expenses		$ 9,000	$ 6,300	$ 2,700
Contribution margin		$16,000	$11,700	$ 4,300
Less direct fixed expenses		1,000	700	300
Territorial segment margin		$15,000	$11,000	$ 4,000
Less common fixed expenses		1,000		
Product line segment margin		$14,000		

* Notice that this $7,000 in direct fixed expense is divided into two parts—$3,000 direct and $4,000 common—when Division 2 is broken down into product lines. The reasons for this are discussed in a later section, "Classifications Are Not Static."

company. This is a widely used approach to segmented reporting. If management desired, Division 1 could also be segmented into smaller pieces the same way as we have segmented Division 2, thereby providing a detailed look at all aspects and levels of the company's operations.

The benefits accruing to the manager from a series of reports such as contained in Exhibit 6–1 are obvious. By carefully examining trends and results the manager will be able to gain insight into performance at many levels, and perhaps will be able to discover courses of action that otherwise would have remained hidden from view.

Basic allocation concepts

As shown in Exhibit 6–1, the contribution approach to costing assigns costs to the various segments of an organization according to two general guidelines:

1. First, according to cost behavior patterns (that is, variable and fixed).
2. Second, according to whether the costs are *directly traceable* to the various segments.

Under the contribution approach, costs are never arbitrarily assigned to a segment. If a cost cannot be traced directly to some segment, then it is treated as a *common* cost and kept separate from the segments themselves. We will now consider various parts of the exhibit in greater depth.

Variable expenses and contribution margin

To obtain the contribution margin by segments, sales revenues and variable expenses must be allocated to the segments responsible for them. This is normally a simple task, since records are generally kept by segment showing sales and other activity.

Variable expenses deducted from sales revenue yields contribution margin. The concept of contribution margin is unique to the contribution approach to costing. No such concept exists in absorption costing. The reader will recall that the absorption approach to costing is based on a *functional* classification of costs, as illustrated earlier in Exhibit 4–10, rather than on a classification by cost behavior.

The contribution margin yielded by the contribution approach to costing is an extremely useful piece of data. It is particularly useful for determining the effect on net income of short-run changes in sales volume, as discussed in Chapter 5. If sales volume goes up or down, the impact on net income can be quickly computed by simply multiplying the per unit contribution margin by the change in units sold, or by multiplying the change in sales dollars by the C/M ratio. Segmented statements give the manager the ability to make such analyses on a product-by-product, division-by-division, or territory-by-territory basis, thereby providing the information needed to shore up areas of weakness and capitalize on areas of strength.

The contribution margin is basically a short-run planning tool. As such, it is especially valuable in decisions relating to temporary uses of capacity, to special orders, to short-term product line promotion, and to related kinds of activities. Decisions relating to the short run usually involve only variable costs and revenues, which of course are the very elements involved in contribution margin. Thus, the contribution margin provides the manager with the exact tool needed to make those decisions relating to the various segments which will maximize short-run benefits.

The importance of fixed costs

The emphasis which we place on the usefulness of the contribution margin should not be taken as a suggestion that fixed costs are not important. *Fixed costs are very important in any organization.* What the contribution approach does imply is that *different costs are needed for different purposes.* For one purpose, variable costs and revenues alone may be adequate for a manager's needs; for another purpose his or her needs may encompass the fixed costs as well.

The breaking apart of fixed and variable costs also emphasizes to management that the costs are controlled differently, and that these differences must be kept clearly in mind for both short-run and long-run planning. Moreover, the grouping of fixed costs together under the contribution approach highlights the fact that net income emerges only after the fixed costs have been covered. It also highlights the fact that after the fixed costs have been covered, net income will increase to the extent of the contribution margin generated on each additional unit sold. All of these concepts are useful to the manager *internally,* for planning purposes.

Direct and common costs

Direct costs can be defined as those costs which can be identified directly with a particular segment, and which arise either because of the existence of the segment, or because of the activity within it. As stated in Chapter 2, direct costs can be *obviously* and *physically* traced to the unit (segment) under consideration.

Common costs can be defined as those costs which cannot be identified directly with a particular segment, but rather are identified in common with all segments existing at a particular level of an organization. Common costs are costs which cannot be allocated to the segments at a particular level except on some highly arbitrary basis, such as sales dollars. They are also known as *indirect costs.*

In Chapter 2 the following guidelines were given in distinguishing between direct and indirect (common) costs:

1. If a cost can be obviously and physically traced to a unit of product or other organizational segment, then it is a direct cost with respect to that segment.
2. If a cost must be allocated in order to be assigned to a unit of product or other organizational segment, then it is an indirect (common) cost with respect to that segment.

Examples of direct costs would include individual segment advertising and promotional outlays, salaries of segment supervisors, and depreciation of segment fixed assets. Examples of common costs would include salaries of top corporate administrative officers, corporate image advertising, and depreciation of facilities *shared by several* segments.

CLASSIFICATION GUIDELINES.   As the reader may suppose, the distinction between direct and common costs is not always easy to maintain. One widely used rule of thumb is to treat as direct costs *only those costs that would disappear if the segment itself disappeared.* For example, if Division 1 in Exhibit 6–1 was discontinued, then it is unlikely that the division manager would be retained either. Since she would disappear with her division, then her salary should be classified as a direct fixed cost of Division 1. On the other hand, the president of the company very likely would continue even if Division 1 was dropped. Therefore, the cost of his salary is common to both divisions. The same idea can be expressed another way: treat as *direct costs* only those costs that are *added* as a result of the creation of a segment.

There will always be some costs that fall between the direct and common categories, which will require considerable care and good judgment for proper classification. The important point is to resist the temptation to allocate arbitrarily. *Any arbitrary allocation of common costs would simply destroy the value of the segment margin as a guide to long-run individual segment profitability.*

CLASSIFICATIONS ARE NOT STATIC.   The reader should take particular note from Exhibit 6–1 that fixed costs which are direct at one level of segmented reporting may become common costs at a lower level of segmented reporting. This is due to the fact that there are limits to how finely a cost may be separated without resorting to arbitrary allocation. The more finely segments are defined, the more costs there are that become common.

To illustrate, notice from Exhibit 6–1 that when segments are defined as divisions, Division 2 has $7,000 in direct fixed costs. Only $3,000 of this amount *remains* direct, however, when we narrow our definition of a segment from divisions to that of product lines in Division 2 alone. Notice that the other $4,000 then becomes a *common* cost of Division 2 product lines.

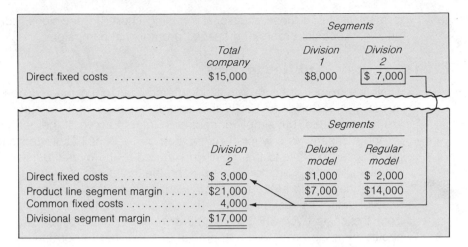

	Total company	Segments	
		Division 1	Division 2
Direct fixed costs	$15,000	$8,000	$ 7,000

	Division 2	Segments	
		Deluxe model	Regular model
Direct fixed costs	$ 3,000	$1,000	$ 2,000
Product line segment margin	$21,000	$7,000	$14,000
Common fixed costs	4,000		
Divisional segment margin	$17,000		

Why would $4,000 of direct fixed costs become common costs when the division is broken down into product line segments? The $4,000 could be the monthly salary of the manager of Division 2. His salary would be a *direct* cost when we are speaking of the division as a whole. But his salary would be *common* to the separate product lines within the division, since charging it to the product lines would require some type of arbitrary allocation (such as on a basis of sales dollars).

The $3,000 that remains a direct fixed cost even after the division is broken down into product line segments would consist of amounts that could be identified with the lines on a nonarbitrary basis. It might consist of advertising, for example, expended for product line promotion, of which one third ($1,000) was expended for promotion of the Deluxe Model and two thirds ($2,000) was expended for promotion of the Regular Model. Product line advertising would be a direct cost of the division as a whole, and it would still be a direct cost when looking only at the product lines within the division, since it could be assigned to the lines without the necessity of making an arbitrary allocation.

Segment margin

The divisional segment margin, the product line segment margin, and the territorial segment margin in Exhibit 6–1 were all obtained by deducting the direct fixed costs from the contribution margin of the segment. *The segment margin is viewed as being the best gauge of the long-run profitability of a segment.* It represents what remains after a segment has covered all of its own direct costs, that may be applied toward covering of common costs, and then toward net income for the firm as a whole.

From a decision-making point of view, the segment margin is most useful in those decisions relating to long-run needs and performance, such as capacity changes, long-run pricing policy, and segment return on investment. As we noted earlier, the contribution margin by contrast is most useful in those situations involving short-run decisions, such as pricing of special orders and special promotional campaigns.

Common costs and net income

Notice from Exhibit 6–1 that no attempt has been made to allocate any of the costs falling below the segment margin line. Common costs are not allocated, but simply deducted in total to arrive at the net income for the company as a whole.[1] Advocates of the contribution approach to cost allocation contend that nothing is added to the overall usefulness of data by allocating common costs among the segments of an organization. Rather, they would argue that such allocations tend to *reduce* the usefulness of data. The reason is that arbitrary allocations draw attention away from the costs over which a segment manager has control, and which should form the basis for an appraisal of his or her performance.

In addition, it is argued that any attempt to allocate common fixed costs among segments of an organization may result in misleading data, or may obscure important relationships between segment revenues and segment earnings. Backer and McFarland state the problem as follows:

A characteristic of all arbitrary allocations is that they lack universality. Sooner or later circumstances arise in which allocation procedures break down and yield misleading or even absurd results.[2]

Backer and McFarland point out that arbitrary allocations of common fixed costs often result in a segment *appearing* to be unprofitable, whereas it may be contributing substantially above its own direct costs toward the overall profitability of the firm. In such cases, the arbitrary allocation of common fixed costs may lead to the unwise elimination of a segment, and to a *decrease* in total profits for the firm.

Varying breakdowns of total sales

In order to obtain more detailed information, a company may show total sales broken down into several different segment arrangements. For example, a company may show total sales segmented in three different ways: first, segmented according to divisions; second, segmented according to product lines, without regard to the divisions in which the products are sold; and third, segmented according to the sales territories in which the sales were made. In each case, the sum of the sales by segments would add up to total company sales; the variation in segment arrangements would simply give management the power to look at the total company from several different directions. This type of segmented reporting

[1] For external reporting purposes, the Financial Accounting Standards Board requires that all common costs be allocated among segments on a "reasonable" basis. *Statement of Financial Accounting Standards No. 14—Financial Reporting for Segments of a Business Enterprise* (Stamford, Conn.: Financial Accounting Standards Board, 1976), par. 10(d).

[2] Morton Backer and Walter B. McFarland, *External Reporting for Segments of a Business* (New York: National Association of Accountants, 1968), p. 23.

provides much the same perspective as looking at a beautiful landscape from several different directions—from every angle you see something you didn't see before.

After this type of segmentation of total sales has been made, many companies then go ahead and break each segment down more finely, such as we illustrated earlier in Exhibit 6–1, and such as is illustrated graphically in Exhibit 6–2. With the availability of the computer, the type of segmentation which we describe here is well within the reach of most companies today.

To illustrate how total sales can be divided into more than one segment arrangement, assume that the Fairfield Company sells two products, X and Y, in two sales territories, the East and the West. Cost and revenue data on the products and the sales territories follow:

1. Selling price, variable expenses, and contribution margin per unit:

	X	Y
Selling price per unit	$10	$6
Variable expense per unit	6	4
Contribution margin per unit	$ 4	$2

Exhibit 6–2
Graphical presentation of segmented reporting—The Detroit Motor Company

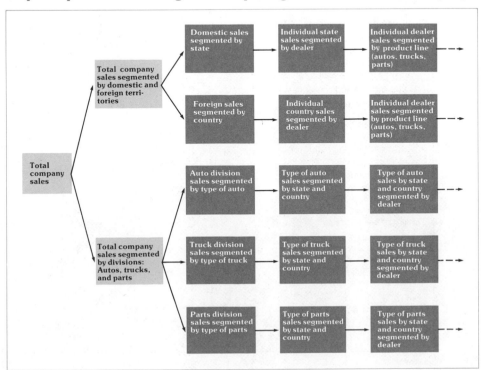

Exhibit 6–3
Cost allocation through the contribution approach—varying breakdowns of total sales

Total Sales Presented by Product Lines

	Total firm	Product X	Product Y
Sales	$190,000	$100,000	$90,000
Less variable expenses	120,000	60,000	60,000
Contribution margin	$ 70,000	$ 40,000	$30,000
Less direct fixed expenses:			
Production	$ 14,000	$ 8,000	$ 6,000
Administration—Product lines	3,500	2,000	1,500
Total direct fixed expenses	$ 17,500	$ 10,000	$ 7,500
Product line segment margin	$ 52,500	$ 30,000	$22,500
Less common fixed expenses:			
Selling—Sales territories	$ 22,000		
Administration—Sales territories	4,500		
General administration	9,000		
Total common fixed expenses	$ 35,500		
Net income	$ 17,000		

Total Sales Presented by Sales Territories

	Total firm	Sales territory East	Sales territory West
Sales	$190,000	$66,000*	$124,000*
Less variable expenses	120,000	42,000†	78,000†
Contribution margin	$ 70,000	$24,000	$ 46,000
Less direct fixed expenses:			
Selling—Sales territories	$ 22,000	$12,000	$ 10,000
Administration—Sales territories	4,500	2,200	2,300
Total direct fixed expenses	$ 26,500	$14,200	$ 12,300
Territorial segment margin	$ 43,500	$ 9,800	$ 33,700
Less common fixed expenses:			
Production	$ 14,000		
Administration—product lines	3,500		
General administration	9,000		
Total common fixed expenses	$ 26,500		
Net income	$ 17,000		

* Sales by sales territory:

	East	West
Product X at $10 per unit sold	$30,000	$ 70,000
Product Y at $ 6 per unit sold	36,000	54,000
Total sales, as above	$66,000	$124,000

† Variable expenses by sales territory:

	East	West
Product X at $6 per unit sold	$18,000	$ 42,000
Product Y at $4 per unit sold	24,000	36,000
Total variable expenses, as above	$42,000	$ 78,000

2. Sales in units during 19x1 were:

	Sales territory		Total sales
	East	West	
Product X sales	3,000	7,000	10,000
Product Y sales	6,000	9,000	15,000

3. Fixed costs incurred during 19x1 were:

	Product line		Sales territory	
	X	Y	East	West
Fixed production costs	$8,000	$6,000	—	—
Fixed selling costs	—	—	$12,000	$10,000
Fixed administrative costs . .	2,000	1,500	2,200	2,300

In addition, the company had $9,000 in fixed general administrative costs during 19x1 that cannot be charged directly to any segment.

Exhibit 6–3 presents total sales for the company for 19x1, broken down first between product lines and second between sales territories. Notice from the exhibit that although the product lines are about equally profitable, this equality does not carry over to the sales territories. The West is much more profitable than the East. Thus, the segmented statements point out to management areas that may be in need of attention.

In summary, segmented reporting gives a company the ability to look at itself from many different directions. Some of the ways in which cost and profitability data can be generated include:

1. By division.
2. By product lines.
3. By sales territory.
4. By region of the country.
5. By domestic and foreign operations.

As we have noted, each of these segments in turn can be broken down into many parts. Indeed, the number of possible directions in which segments can be defined is limited only by one's imagination or by the needs of the firm.

INVENTORY VALUATION UNDER THE CONTRIBUTION APPROACH—DIRECT COSTING

As discussed in Chapter 3, absorption costing allocates a portion of fixed manufacturing overhead to each unit produced during a period, along with variable manufacturing costs. Since absorption costing mingles variable and fixed costs together, units of product costed by that method are not well suited for inclusion in a contribution-type income statement. This has led to the development of an alternative unit costing method that has come to be known as *direct costing.*

Direct costing

Under direct costing, only variable manufacturing costs are included as part of the cost of a unit of product. Fixed manufacturing overhead is not viewed to be an inventoriable item; that is, it is not included as part of a product's cost of production. Rather, fixed manufacturing overhead is charged off against income each period in total as a *period cost,* much as are selling and administrative expenses.

To illustrate, assume the following data:

The Boley Company produces a single product. The cost characteristics of the product and of the manufacturing plant are given below:

Direct materials cost per unit	$3
Direct labor cost per unit........................	$2
Variable manufacturing overhead cost per unit.......	$3
Fixed manufacturing overhead (total)..............	$15,000
Number of units produced each year	3,000

Required:

1. Compute the cost of a unit of product under absorption costing.
2. Compute the cost of a unit of product under direct costing.

Absorption Costing	
Direct materials	$ 3
Direct labor	2
Variable overhead	3
Total variable production cost	8
Fixed overhead ($15,000 ÷ 3,000 units of product)	5
Total cost per unit	$13
Direct Costing	
Direct materials	$ 3
Direct labor	2
Variable overhead	3
Total cost per unit	$ 8
(The $15,000 fixed overhead will be charged off in total against income as a period expense.)	

If the Boley Company sells a unit of product, and absorption costing is being used, then $13 will be deducted on the income statement as cost of goods sold. If the company sells a unit of product, and direct costing is being used, then only $8 will be deducted as cost of goods sold. In a similar manner, under absorption costing, units of inventory on the balance sheet will be valued at $13 each. Under direct costing, units of inventory on the balance sheet will be valued at only $8 each.

The controversy over fixed costs

The term "direct costing" is really a misnomer. Direct costing could more accurately be called variable or marginal costing, since it centers on the notion that only variable production costs should be added to the cost of goods produced. The term direct costing is so firmly imbedded in the literature, however, that it seems unlikely that any change in terminology will be made.

Probably no subject in all of managerial accounting has created as much controversy among accountants as direct costing. The controversy isn't over whether costs should be separated as between variable and fixed in matters relating to planning and control. Rather, the controversy is over the theoretical justification of excluding fixed production costs from inventory.

Advocates of direct costing take the position that fixed costs of production relate to the *capacity* to produce rather than to the production of specific units of product in any given year. That is, fixed costs of production such as depreciation and supervisory salaries are viewed as being costs that will be incurred regardless of whether any actual production takes place. For this reason, it is felt that they should be charged against the *period,* rather than against the *product.*

Advocates of absorption costing view the matter differently. They feel that the distinction between variable and fixed costs is immaterial so far as product costing is concerned. Since both fixed and variable costs are required in the production of goods, it is argued that both should be included in costing individual units of product.

Comparison of absorption and direct costing

Income statements prepared under the absorption and direct costing approaches are shown in Exhibit 6–4. In preparing these statements the following data have been assumed:

Beginning inventory	–0–	Cost of producing one unit of product:	
Units produced	5,000	Under direct costing:	
Units sold	4,000	Variable cost of production only (all $10,000 of fixed production cost is charged against the period)	$4
Sales price per unit	$ 10		
Selling and administrative expense:		Under absorption costing:	
Variable per unit	$ 1	Variable cost of production	$4
Fixed (total)	$ 2,000	Fixed cost of production ($10,000 ÷ 5,000 units produced)	2
Costs of production:			
Variable (direct materials, direct labor, and variable overhead) per unit	$ 4	Total	$6
Fixed (total)	$10,000		

Exhibit 6–4
Comparison of direct and absorption costing

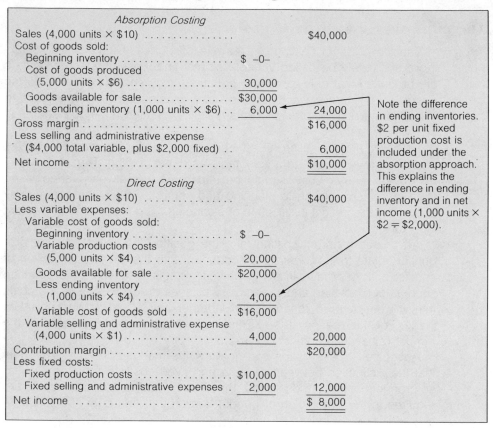

Absorption Costing		
Sales (4,000 units × $10)		$40,000
Cost of goods sold:		
Beginning inventory	$ –0–	
Cost of goods produced		
(5,000 units × $6)	30,000	
Goods available for sale	$30,000	
Less ending inventory (1,000 units × $6) . .	6,000	24,000
Gross margin		$16,000
Less selling and administrative expense		
($4,000 total variable, plus $2,000 fixed) . .		6,000
Net income		$10,000
Direct Costing		
Sales (4,000 units × $10)		$40,000
Less variable expenses:		
Variable cost of goods sold:		
Beginning inventory	$ –0–	
Variable production costs		
(5,000 units × $4)	20,000	
Goods available for sale	$20,000	
Less ending inventory		
(1,000 units × $4)	4,000	
Variable cost of goods sold	$16,000	
Variable selling and administrative expense		
(4,000 units × $1)	4,000	20,000
Contribution margin		$20,000
Less fixed costs:		
Fixed production costs	$10,000	
Fixed selling and administrative expenses .	2,000	12,000
Net income		$ 8,000

Note the difference in ending inventories. $2 per unit fixed production cost is included under the absorption approach. This explains the difference in ending inventory and in net income (1,000 units × $2 = $2,000).

Several points should be noted from the statements in this exhibit:

1. Under absorption costing, the fixed costs of production are unitized (at $2 per unit) and added to the cost of the units produced. As units of product are sold, these fixed costs of production are released to expense as part of cost of goods sold. Units remaining unsold at the end of a period carry a portion of these fixed costs of production *forward with them* to the next period. In Exhibit 6–4, 1,000 units remain unsold at the end of the period. The $6,000 inventory value of these units is computed as follows:

Variable costs of production: 1,000 units × $4	$4,000
Fixed costs of production: 1,000 units × $2	2,000
Total inventory value	$6,000

The $2,000 in fixed production costs carried forward in inventory to the next period will become an expense in that period as the units of product making up the inventory are sold. In summary, of the $10,000 total fixed costs of production incurred for the year, only $8,000 is charged against revenues as part of cost of goods sold. The remaining $2,000 has been *deferred* in inventory as part of the cost of unsold units of product.

2. Under direct costing, fixed costs of production are not included as part of the cost of units produced, but rather are expensed in total ($10,000) as a period cost, along with selling and administrative expenses. The expensing of all fixed costs of production explains the reason for the ending inventory value under direct costing being $2,000 lower than it is under absorption costing. Under direct costing, only the variable production costs have been inventoried:

> Variable costs of production: 1,000 units × $4 . . . . $4,000

The difference in ending inventories also explains the difference in net income reported under the two costing approaches. Since under absorption costing we have *deferred* $2,000 of fixed costs in inventory, net income is $2,000 *higher* under that approach than it is under direct costing.

3. Since the absorption costing income statement makes no distinction between fixed and variable costs it is not well suited for cost-volume-profit computations, which we have emphasized as being important to good planning and control. In order to generate data for cost-volume-profit analysis, it would be necessary to spend considerable time reworking and reclassifying the absorption statement.

4. The direct costing approach to costing units of product blends very well with the contribution approach to the income statement, since both concepts are based on the idea of classifying costs by behavior. The direct costing data in Exhibit 6–4 could be used immediately in cost-volume-profit computations.

The definition of an asset

Essentially, the difference between the absorption and the direct costing approaches centers on the matter of timing. Direct costing advocates say that fixed manufacturing costs should be released against revenues immediately in total, whereas absorption costing advocates say that fixed manufacturing costs should be released against revenues bit by bit as units of product are sold. Any units of product not sold under absorption costing result in fixed costs being inventoried and carried forward *as assets* to the next period. The solution to the controversy as to which costing method is "right" should therefore rest in large part on whether fixed costs added to inventory fall within the definition of an asset as this concept is generally viewed in accounting theory.

WHAT IS AN ASSET?   A cost is normally viewed as being an asset if it can be shown that it has revenue producing powers, or if it can be shown that it will be beneficial in some way to operations in future periods. In short, a cost is an asset if it can be shown that it has *future service potential* that can be identified. For example, insurance prepayments are viewed as being assets, since they have future service potential. The prepayments acquire protection that can be used in future periods to guard against losses that might otherwise hinder operations. If fixed production costs added to inventory under absorption costing are indeed properly called assets, then they, too, must meet this test of service potential.

THE ABSORPTION COSTING VIEW.   Advocates of absorption costing argue that fixed production costs added to inventory do, indeed, have future service potential. They take the position that if production exceeds sales then a benefit to future periods is created in the form of an inventory that can be carried forward and sold, resulting in a future inflow of revenue. They argue that *all costs* that are involved in the creation of inventory should be carried forward as assets—not just the variable costs. The fixed costs of depreciation, taxes, insurance, supervisory salaries, and so on, are just as essential to the creation of units of product as are the variable costs. It would be just as impossible to create units of product in the absence of equipment as it would be to create them in the absence of raw materials, or in the absence of workers to operate the machines. In sum, until the fixed production costs have been recognized and attached, units of product have not been fully costed. Both variable and fixed costs become inseparably attached as units are produced, and *remain* insepararbly attached regardless of whether the units are sold immediately, or carried forward as inventory to generate revenue in future periods.

THE DIRECT COSTING VIEW.   Direct costing advocates argue that a cost has service potential and is therefore an asset *only if its incurrence now will make it unnecessary to incur the same cost again in the future.* Service potential, therefore, is said to hinge on the matter of *future cost avoidance.* If the incurrence of a cost now will have no effect on whether or not the same cost will be incurred again in the future, then that cost is viewed as having no relevance to future events. It is argued that such a cost can in no way represent a future benefit or service.

For example, the prepayment of insurance is viewed as being an asset because the cash outlays made when the insurance is acquired make it unnecessary to sustain the same outlays again in the future periods for which insurance protection has been purchased. In short, by making insurance payments now, a company *avoids* having to make payments in the future. Since prepayments of insurance result in *future cost avoidance,* the prepayments qualify as assets.

This type of cost avoidance does not exist in the case of fixed production costs. The incurring of fixed production costs in one year in no way reduces the necessity to incur the same costs again in the following year. Since the incurring of fixed production costs does not result in *future cost avoid-ance,* the costs of one year can have no relevance to future events, and therefore cannot possibly represent a future benefit or service. Direct cost-ers argue, therefore, that no part of the fixed production costs of one year should ever be carried forward as an asset to the following year. Such costs do not result in future cost avoidance—the key test for any asset.[3]

Extended comparison of income data

Having gained some insights into the conceptual differences between absorption and direct costing, we are now prepared to take a more detailed look at the differences in income data generated by these two approaches to cost allocation. Exhibit 6–5 presents data covering a span of three years. In the first year, production and sales are exactly equal. In the second year production exceeds sales. In the third year the tables are reversed, with sales exceeding production.

Certain generalizations can be drawn from the data in this exhibit:

1. When production and sales are equal, the same net income will be produced regardless of whether absorption or direct costing is being used (see Year 1 in Exhibit 6–5). The reason is that when production and sales are equal there is no chance for fixed costs to be deferred in inventory or released from inventory under absorption costing.

2. When production exceeds sales, the net income reported under absorption costing will be greater than the net income reported under direct costing (see Year 2 in Exhibit 6–5). The reason is that when more is produced than is sold, a portion of the fixed production costs are deferred in inventory under absorption costing. For example, in Year 2, $3,000 of fixed costs (1,000 units $\times$ $3 per unit) have been deferred in inventory under the absorption approach. Only that portion of fixed production costs not deferred in inventory has been charged against income.

By contrast, under direct costing all of the fixed production costs have been charged against income. The result is that net income is $3,000 lower under direct costing than it is under absorption costing. Exhibit 6–6 contains a reconciliation of the direct costing and absorption costing net income figures.

3. When sales exceed production, the net income reported under the absorption costing approach will be less than the net income reported under the direct costing approach (see Year 3 in Exhibit 6–5).

The reason is that when more is sold than is produced, inventories are drawn down, and fixed costs that were previously deferred in inventory under absorption costing are released and charged against income. For

---

[3] For further discussion, see David Green, Jr., "A Moral to the Direct Costing Contro-versy?" *Journal of Business,* vol. 33, no. 3 (July 1960), pp. 218–26; and Charles T. Horngren and George H. Sorter, "Direct Costing for External Reporting," *Accounting Review,* vol. 36, no. 1 (January 1961), pp. 88–93.

Exhibit 6–5
Absorption costing versus direct costing—extended income data

Basic Data

Sales price per unit .... $ 12
Variable production costs per unit (direct materials, direct labor,
  and variable overhead) .... $ 5
Fixed production costs (total) $24,000

Cost of producing one unit of product:
  Under direct costing:
    Variable production costs .... $ 5

  Under absorption costing:
    Variable production costs .... $ 5
    Fixed production costs (based on a normal production volume of
      8,000 units per year—$24,000 ÷ 8,000) 3
        Total absorption costs .... $ 8

Selling and administrative expenses are assumed, for simplicity,
to be all fixed at $25,000 per year.

	Year 1	Year 2	Year 3	Three years together
Opening inventory in units	–0–	–0–	1,000	–0–
Units produced during the year	8,000	8,000	8,000	24,000
Units sold during the year	8,000	7,000	9,000	24,000
Ending inventory in units	–0–	1,000	–0–	–0–

Direct Costing

	Year 1	Year 2	Year 3	Three years together
Sales	$96,000	$84,000	$108,000	$288,000
Less variable expenses	40,000*	35,000*	45,000*	120,000
Contribution margin	$56,000	$49,000	$ 63,000	$168,000
Less fixed expenses:				
Production	$24,000	$24,000	$ 24,000	$ 72,000
Selling and administrative	25,000	25,000	25,000	75,000
Total fixed expenses	$49,000	$49,000	$ 49,000	$147,000
Net income	$ 7,000	$ –0–	$ 14,000	$ 21,000

Absorption Costing

	Year 1	Year 2	Year 3	Three years together
Sales	$96,000	$84,000	$108,000	$288,000
Opening inventory	$ –0–	$ –0–	$ 8,000	$ 8,000
Cost of goods produced	64,000	64,000	64,000	192,000
Goods available for sale	$64,000	$64,000	$ 72,000	$200,000
Ending inventory	–0–	8,000	–0–	8,000
Cost of goods sold	$64,000	$56,000	$ 72,000	$192,000
Gross margin	$32,000	$28,000	$ 36,000	$ 96,000
Selling and administrative expenses	25,000	25,000	25,000	75,000
Net income	$ 7,000	$ 3,000	$ 11,000	$ 21,000

    * Variable expenses: Year 1: 8,000 units sold × $5 = $40,000
                Year 2: 7,000 units sold × $5 = $35,000
                Year 3: 9,000 units sold × $5 = $45,000

Exhibit 6–6
Reconciliation of direct costing and absorption costing—net income data from Exhibit 6–5

	Year 1	Year 2	Year 3
Direct costing net income	$7,000	$ –0–	$14,000
Add: Fixed production costs deferred in inventory under absorption costing (1,000 units × $3 per unit)	—	3,000	—
Deduct: Fixed production costs released from inventory under absorption costing (1,000 units × $3 per unit)	—	—	(3,000)
Absorption costing net income	$7,000	$3,000	$11,000

example, in Year 3 the $3,000 fixed costs deferred in inventory under the absorption approach in the prior years are released from inventory through the sales process and charged against income. As a result, cost of goods sold for Year 3 contains not only all of the fixed production costs for Year 3 (since all that was produced in Year 3 was sold in Year 3), but also $3,000 of the fixed production costs of Year 2 as well.

By contrast, under direct costing only the fixed production costs of Year 3 have been charged against Year 3. The result is that net income under direct costing is $3,000 higher than it is under absorption costing. Exhibit 6–6 contains a reconciliation of the direct costing and the absorption costing net income figures.

4. Over an *extended* period of time the net income figures reported under absorption costing and direct costing will tend to be the same. The reason is that over the long run sales can't exceed production, nor can production much exceed sales. The shorter the time period, the more the net income figures will tend to vary.

Sales constant, production fluctuates

Exhibit 6–7 presents a reverse situation from that depicted in Exhibit 6–5. In Exhibit 6–5 we made production constant, and allowed sales to fluctuate from period to period. In Exhibit 6–7, sales are constant, and production fluctuates. Our purpose in Exhibit 6–7 is to observe the effect of changes in production on net income under both absorption and direct costing.

DIRECT COSTING. Net income is not affected by changes in production under direct costing. Notice from Exhibit 6–7 that net income is the same for all three years under the direct costing approach, although production exceeds sales in one year, and is less than sales in another year. In short, the only thing that can affect net income under direct costing

Exhibit 6–7
Sensitivity to changes in production and sales

Basic Data			
Sales price per unit			$ 10
Variable production costs per unit			$ 4
Fixed production costs (total)			$24,000
Selling and administrative expenses (all assumed, for simplicity, to be fixed) .			$ 5,000

	Year 1	Year 2	Year 3
Number of units produced	6,000	8,000	4,000
Number of units sold	6,000	6,000	6,000
Cost of producing one unit:			
Under direct costing (variable production			
costs only)	$4	$4	$4
Under absorption costing:			
Variable production costs	$4	$4	$4
Fixed production costs ($24,000 total spread			
in each year over the number of units			
produced)	4	3	6
Total cost per unit	$8	$7	$10

Direct Costing			
Sales (6,000 units)	$60,000	$60,000	$60,000
Less variable expenses (6,000 units)	24,000	24,000	24,000
Contribution margin	$36,000	$36,000	$36,000
Less fixed expenses:			
Fixed production expenses	$24,000	$24,000	$24,000
Fixed selling and administrative expenses	5,000	5,000	5,000
Total fixed expenses	$29,000	$29,000	$29,000
Net income	$ 7,000	$ 7,000	$ 7,000

Absorption Costing			
Sales (6,000 units)	$60,000	$60,000	$60,000
Opening inventory	$ -0-	$ -0-	$14,000
Cost of goods produced	48,000	56,000	40,000
Goods available for sale	$48,000	$56,000	$54,000
Ending inventory	-0-	14,000	-0-
Cost of goods sold (6,000 units)	$48,000	$42,000	$54,000·
Gross margin	$12,000	$18,000	$ 6,000
Less selling and administrative expenses	5,000	5,000	5,000
Net income	$ 7,000	$13,000	$ 1,000

is a change in sales—a change in production has no impact when direct costing is in use.

ABSORPTION COSTING. Net income *is* affected by changes in production when absorption costing is in use. Notice from Exhibit 6–7 that net income goes up in Year 2, in response to the increase in production for that year, and goes down in Year 3, in response to the drop in production for that year. The reason for this effect can be traced to the shifting of fixed overhead between periods through the inventory account under absorption costing.

When production exceeds sales, then units of product are carried forward as inventory to the next period. These units of product take a portion of the current period's fixed costs forward to the next period with them, thereby relieving the current period of costs, and causing its income to rise in comparison with past periods. This effect can be observed in Year 2 in Exhibit 6–7. Even though Year 2 sold the same number of units as Year 1, its net income was substantially higher, due to the shifting of part of its fixed costs into Year 3.

The reverse effect occurs in Year 3. Since sales exceed production in Year 3, that year is forced to cover all of its own fixed overhead costs as well as the fixed overhead costs carried forward in inventory from Year 2. The result is a substantial drop in net income during Year 3, as shown in Exhibit 6–7.

Opponents of absorption costing argue that this shifting of fixed overhead between periods can be confusing to a manager, and can cause him or her either to misinterpret data or to make faulty decisions. The reader may recall from Chapter 3 that one way to overcome problems of this type is to use *normalized* overhead rates. Even if normalized overhead rates are used, the same problems can arise if the under- or overapplied overhead resulting from production being out of balance with sales is taken to cost of goods sold. The only way to avoid the problems entirely is to use normalized overhead rates, and to place any under- or overabsorbed overhead in a balance sheet clearing account of some type.

Cost-volume-profit analysis and absorption costing

Absorption costing is widely regarded as a product costing method. Many firms use the absorption approach exclusively because of its focus on "full" costing of units of product. If the approach has a weakness, it is to be found in its inability to dovetail well with cost-volume-profit analysis under certain conditions.

To illustrate, refer again to Exhibit 6–5. Let us compute the break-even point for the firm represented by the data in this exhibit. To obtain the break-even point, we divide total fixed costs by the contribution margin per unit:

Sales price per unit	$12
Variable costs per unit	5
Contribution margin per unit	$ 7
Fixed production costs	$24,000
Fixed selling and administrative costs	25,000
Total fixed costs	$49,000

$$\frac{\text{Total fixed costs}}{\text{Contribution margin per unit}} = \frac{\$49,000}{\$7} = 7,000 \text{ units}$$

We have computed the break-even point to be 7,000 units sold. Notice from Exhibit 6–5 that in Year 2 the firm sold exactly 7,000 units, the break-even volume. Under the contribution approach, using direct costing, the firm does exactly break even in Year 2, showing zero net income or loss. *Under absorption costing, however, the firm shows a positive net income of $3,000 for Year 2.* How can this be so? How can absorption costing produce a positive net income when the firm sold exactly the break-even volume of units?

The answer lies in the fact that in Year 2 under absorption costing $3,000 in fixed costs were deferred in inventory and did not appear as charges against income. By deferring these fixed costs in inventory, the firm was able to show a profit even though it sold exactly the break-even volume of units. This leads us to a general observation about absorption costing. The only way that absorption costing data can be used in a break-even analysis is to assume that inventories will not change. Unfortunately, such an assumption often falls far short of reality.

Absorption costing runs into similar kinds of difficulty in other areas of cost-volume-profit analysis, and often requires considerable manipulation of data before figures are available that are usable for decision-making purposes.

External reporting and income taxes

For external reporting on financial statements, a company is required to cost units of product by the absorption costing method. In like manner, the absorption costing method must be used in preparing tax returns. In short, the contribution approach is limited to *internal* use, by the managers of a company.

The majority of accountants would agree that absorption costing *should* be used in external reporting. That is, most accountants feel that for *external reporting* purposes, units of product *should* contain a portion of fixed manufacturing overhead, along with variable manufacturing costs. The absorption costing argument that a unit of product is not fully costed until it reflects a portion of the fixed costs of production is difficult to refute, particularly as it applies to the preparing of information to be reported to stockholders and others.

The contribution approach finds its greatest application internally, as an assist to the manager in those situations where the absorption costing data are not well suited for cost-volume-profit analysis, or are not well suited for a segment-type analysis, such as covered earlier in the chapter. No particular problems are created by using *both* costing methods—the contribution method internally, and the absorption method externally. As we demonstrated earlier in Exhibit 6–6, the adjustment from direct costing net income to absorption costing net income is a simple one, and can be made in a few hours' time at year end, in order to produce an absorption costing net income figure for use on financial statements.

ADVANTAGES OF THE CONTRIBUTION APPROACH

As stated in the preceding section, many accountants feel that under the appropriate circumstances there are certain advantages to be gained from using the contribution approach (with direct costing) internally, even if the absorption approach is used externally for reporting purposes. These advantages have been summarized by the National Association of Accountants as follows:[4]

1. Cost-volume-profit relationship data wanted for profit planning purposes is readily obtained from the regular accounting statements. Hence management does not have to work with two separate sets of data to relate one to the other.
2. The profit for a period is not affected by changes in absorption of fixed expenses resulting from building, or reducing inventory. Other things remaining equal (for example, selling prices, costs, sales mix) profits move in the same direction as sales when direct costing is in use.
3. Manufacturing cost and income statements in the direct cost form follow management's thinking more closely than does the absorption cost form for these statements. For this reason, management finds it easier to understand and to use direct cost reports.
4. The impact of fixed costs on profits is emphasized because the total amount of such cost for the period appears in the income statement.
5. Marginal income figures facilitate relative appraisal of products, territories, classes of customers, and other segments of the business without having the results obscured by allocation of joint fixed costs.
6. Direct costing ties in with such effective plans for cost control as standard costs and flexible budgets.[5] In fact, the flexible budget is an aspect of direct costing and many companies thus use direct costing methods for this purpose without recognizing them as such.
7. Direct cost constitutes a concept of inventory cost which corresponds closely with the current out-of-pocket expenditure necessary to manufacture the goods.

SUMMARY

Cost allocation problems exist in every company. The contribution approach attempts to handle these problems by defining segments of an organization, and by classifying costs as being either direct or common to the segments. Only those costs that are direct to the segments are allocated. Costs that are not direct to the segments are treated as common costs, and are not allocated.

The contribution approach also classifies costs by behavior. For this

---

[4] National Association of Accountants, *Direct Costing,* Research Series No. 23 (New York: National Association of Accountants, 1953), p. 55.

[5] Standard costs and flexible budgets are covered in Chapters 8 and 9.

reason those costs traceable *directly* to a segment are classified as be-tween variable and fixed. Total variable costs deducted from sales yields a contribution margin, which is highly useful in short-run planning and decision making. The direct fixed costs of a segment are then deducted from the contribution margin, yielding a segment margin. The segment margin is highly useful in long-run planning and decision making. Segments can be arranged in many ways, including by sales territory, by division, by product line, by salesperson, and so on.

In costing units of product in a manufacturing firm, the contribution method with direct costing adds only the variable manufacturing costs to units of product. The fixed manufacturing costs are taken directly to the income statement as expenses of the period.

Although the contribution approach cannot be used externally either for financial reporting or for tax purposes, it is often used internally by management. Its popularity internally can be traced in large part to the fact that it dovetails well with cost-volume-profit concepts that are often indispensable in profit planning and decision making.

KEY TERMS FOR REVIEW

Organizational segment   **Segment margin**
Segmented reporting   **Variable costing**
Direct costs   **Direct costing**
Common costs   **Marginal costing**

QUESTIONS

6–1. Define a segment of an organization. Give several examples of segments.

6–2. How does the contribution approach attempt to assign costs to segments of an organization?

6–3. Distinguish between a direct and a common cost. Give several examples of each.

6–4. Explain why the concept of a contribution margin is important to man-agement.

6–5. Explain how the segment margin differs from the contribution margin. Which concept is most useful to the manager? Why?

6–6. Why aren't common costs allocated to segments under the contribution approach?

6–7. How does the manager benefit from segmented reporting?

6–8. How is it possible for a direct cost under one segment arrangement to become a common cost under another segment arrangement?

6–9. In what way does absorption costing differ from direct costing?

6–10. Explain how fixed overhead costs are shifted from one period to another under absorption costing.

6–11. If production exceeds sales, which method would you expect to show the highest net income, direct costing, or absorption costing? Why?

6–12. If sales and production are equal, which method would you expect to show the highest net income, direct costing, or absorption costing? Why?

6–13. What arguments can be advanced in favor of adding fixed overhead to the cost of production?

6–14. What arguments can be advanced in favor of treating fixed overhead as a period cost, rather than as a cost of production?

6–15. What special assumption must be made in order to compute a break-even point under absorption costing?

6–16. What limitations are there to the use of the contribution approach (with direct costing)?

6–17. "One of the main objections to the contribution approach to costing is that it ignores fixed costs." Do you agree? Explain.

EXERCISES

E6–1. The Fitz Company has two divisions, Division A and Division B. Operating data for a recent period are given below:

	Total company	Segments Division A	Segments Division B
Sales	$150,000	$60,000	$90,000
Less variable expenses	107,500	40,000	67,500
Contribution margin	$ 42,500	$20,000	$22,500
Less direct fixed expenses	17,000	8,000	9,000
Divisional segment margin	$ 25,500	$12,000	$13,500
Less common fixed expenses	10,000		
Net income	$ 15,500		

Required:

1. How much would net income increase if Division A increased sales by $12,000?
2. How much would net income increase if Division B increased sales by $12,000?
3. How much would net income increase if Division A increased sales by $12,000 and increased fixed expenses by $1,500?

E6–2. Refer to Exercise 6–1. Assume that Division A's sales by product are:

	Division A	Segments Product X	Segments Product Y
Sales	$60,000	$40,000	$20,000
Less variable expenses	40,000	30,000	10,000
Contribution margin	$20,000	$10,000	$10,000
Less direct fixed expenses	5,000	2,000	3,000
Product line segment margin	$15,000	$ 8,000	$ 7,000
Less common fixed expenses	3,000		
Divisional segment margin	$12,000		

The Fitz Company plans to spend $1,000 in direct advertising in Division A on either Product X or Product Y. If spent on Product X, sales of Product X will increase by $4,000. If spent on Product Y, sales of Product Y will increase by $3,500.

Required:

1. On which product line should the company spend the advertising funds? Show your calculations.
2. In Exercise 6–1, Division A shows $8,000 in direct fixed expenses. What happened to the $8,000 in this exercise?

E6–3. The Moore Company produces and sells a single product. The following cost data are available:

Direct materials cost per unit	$6
Direct labor cost per unit	$3
Variable manufacturing overhead cost per unit	$2
Fixed manufacturing overhead (total)	$20,000
Number of units produced each year	5,000

The selling price is $20 per unit. Selling and administrative expenses are $10,000 per year, and are all fixed.

Required:

1. Compute the cost of a unit of product under absorption costing.
2. Compute the cost of a unit of product under direct costing.
3. If 4,000 units are sold during a particular year, what is the net income under absorption costing? Assume there is no beginning inventory.
4. If 4,000 units are sold during a particular year, what is the net income under direct costing? Assume there is no beginning inventory.

E6–4. Selected information on the operations of Wood Company for 19x4 is given below:

Units produced	4,000
Units sold	3,500
Units in beginning inventory	0
Contribution margin ratio	50%
Direct materials used	$20,000
Direct labor	32,000
Selling and administrative expenses:	
Variable	16,000
Fixed	21,000
Manufacturing overhead:	
Variable	24,000
Fixed	28,000

The company maintains no work in process inventories.

Required:

1. Assume the company uses absorption costing. What is the ending finished goods inventory?
2. Assume the company uses direct costing. What is the ending finished goods inventory?
3. Which costing method would show the highest net income for 19x4? By how much?

E6–5. The Porter Company sells Trinkets and Gadgets. An income statement for a recent period is given below:

PORTER COMPANY
Income Statement

	Total sales	Trinkets	Percent	Gadgets	Percent
		Product lines			
Sales	$500	$200	100%	$300	100%
Less variable expenses	240	90	45	150	50
Contribution margin	$260	$110	55%	$150	50%
Less direct fixed expenses	150	80		70	
Segment margin	$110	$ 30		$ 80	
Less common fixed expenses	60				
Net income	$ 50				

The Trinkets and Gadgets are sold in a home market and in a foreign market, as follows:

	Home	Foreign
Trinket sales	$120	$ 80
Gadget sales	190	110
Total sales	$310	$190

The common fixed expenses above are partly traceable to the home market, partly traceable to the foreign market, and partly traceable to general administration:

Home market fixed expenses	$20
Foreign market fixed expenses	25
General administration fixed expenses	15
Total common fixed expenses (above).........	$60

Required:

Prepare a segmented income statement, as above, but this time with the segments defined as the home and foreign markets. (It is *not* necessary to state segment sales, variable expenses, and so on, in percentage terms.) The direct fixed expenses of the product lines should not be allocated to the markets; treat these as common fixed expenses on this segmented statement.

E6–6.   The Bemis Company was organized just one year ago. The results of the company's first year of operations are shown below (absorption costing basis):

BEMIS COMPANY
Income Statement

Sales (6,000 units at $15)		$90,000
Less cost of goods sold:		
Opening inventory	$ 0	
Cost of goods produced (8,000 units at $11)	88,000	
Goods available for sale..........................	$88,000	
Ending inventory (2,000 units at $11)	22,000	66,000
Gross margin.....................................		$24,000
Less selling and administrative expenses.............		18,000
Net income		$ 6,000

The selling and administrative expenses are all fixed. The company's $11 unit cost is computed as follows:

Direct materials .... $ 3
Direct labor 2
Variable factory overhead 2
Fixed factory overhead ($32,000 ÷ 8,000) 4
Total unit cost $11

Required:

1. Redo the company's income statement in the contribution format, using direct costing.
2. Explain any difference in net income between the direct costing statement you have prepared and the absorption costing statement above.

E6–7. Mr. Taylor, president of the Martin Company, wants a contribution-type income statement prepared by products. The following data are available for the firm:

Sales $140,000
Less variable expenses 93,000
Contribution margin .... $ 47,000
Less fixed expenses 25,000
Net income .... $ 22,000

The firm produces three products. Sales, contribution margin ratios, and direct fixed expenses for the three products are as follows:

	Product A	Product B	Product C
Sales	$60,000	$50,000	$30,000
Contribution margin ratio	30%	40%	30%
Direct fixed expenses	$ 8,000	$ 7,000	$ 5,000

Required:

1. Prepare a contribution-type income statement by products, as desired by Mr. Taylor. Include the net income for the entire firm in your statement.
2. The firm has an opportunity to increase sales of Product B by 50 percent. However, this would require an additional outlay for fixed expenses of $8,000 per period. Prepare an analysis to determine whether the firm should undertake this expansion program.

E6–8. You have a client who operates a large retail self-service grocery store that has a full range of departments. The management has encountered difficulty in using accounting data as a basis for decisions as to possible changes in departments operated, products, marketing methods, and so forth. List several overhead costs, or costs not applicable to a particular department, and explain how the existence of such costs (sometimes called *common costs* or *joint costs*) complicates and limits the use of accounting data in making decisions in such a store.

(AICPA)

E6–9. Milex, Inc., uses absorption costing for external reporting purposes. The company's income statements for the last three years are given below:

MILEX, INC.
Income Statement
For Years 19x3, 19x4, and 19x5

	19x3	19x4	19x5
Sales	$80,000	$48,000	$96,000
Cost of goods sold	50,000	30,000	60,000
Gross margin	$30,000	$18,000	$36,000
Selling and administrative expenses	15,000	15,000	15,000
Net income	$15,000	$ 3,000	$21,000

Sales and production data for these three years are:

Units produced	10,000	10,000	10,000
Units sold	10,000	6,000	12,000

Variable manufacturing costs total $3 per unit. Fixed overhead is applied to units of product on a basis of $2 per unit. Assume a Fifo inventory flow.

Required:

1. Prepare income statements for the three years, using direct costing.
2. Reconcile the absorption costing and direct costing net income figures for each year.

PROBLEMS

Problems 6–10 through 6–16 deal primarily with segmented reporting issues; problems 6–17 through 6–24 deal primarily with absorption versus direct costing issues.

P6–10. *Segmented reporting.* The most recent monthly income statement for the Ashland Company is given below:

ASHLAND COMPANY
Income Statement

Sales	$100,000
Less variable expenses	55,000
Contribution margin	$ 45,000
Less fixed expenses	41,000
Net income	$ 4,000

Management is very disappointed with the company's performance, and is wondering what can be done to improve overall profits. By examining sales and cost records, you have determined the following:

1. The company is divided into two sales territories—City and State. Sixty percent of monthly sales come from the city, and $30,000 of the variable expenses are traceable to the city. Fixed expenses of $14,000 and $12,000 are traceable to the city and state territories, respectively.
2. The company sells two products—Awls and Pows—in each sales territory. Sales of Awls and Pows totaled $10,000 and $30,000, respectively, in the state last month. Variable expenses are 40 percent

of the selling price for Awls, and 70 percent for Pows. Cost records show that $4,000 of the state's fixed expenses are assignable directly to Awls, and $5,000 to Pows.

Required:

1. Prepare segmented income statements such as illustrated in Exhibit 6–1, first showing the total company broken down between sales territories, and then showing the state territory broken down by product line.
2. Looking at the data contained in the segmented statements, what seems to be a major problem in the state territory?

P6–11. *Cost allocation by product line and by sales territory.* Selected information relating to the operations of Stratford Company for a recent period is given below:

	Product line			
	A	B	C	Total
Sales in units	10,000	20,000	15,000	45,000
Selling price per unit	$ 15	$ 12	$ 7	$ —
Variable cost per unit for production, administration, and sales	9	9	5	—
Depreciation of production equipment	3,000	4,000	2,000	9,000
Product line supervisor	12,000	14,000	10,000	36,000
General factory overhead— fixed	—	—	—	10,000
Administrative expense— fixed	—	—	—	25,000
Selling expense—fixed	—	—	—	60,000

Stratford Company products are sold throughout the United States, in three sales territories—the East, the Midwest, and the West. $20,000 of the $25,000 administrative expense above, and all of the $60,000 selling expense above is traceable to these three sales territories, as shown below. The remainder of the administrative expense represents general company expense that cannot be allocated to the sales territories. The percentage of product line sales made in each of the three sales territories is also shown below.

	Sales territory			
	East	Midwest	West	Total
Administrative expense	$ 5,000	$ 5,000	$10,000	$20,000
Selling expense	14,000	16,000	30,000	60,000
Product line A	40%	50%	10%	100%
Product line B	40	40	20	100
Product line C	20	20	60	100

Required:

1. Prepare a segmented income statement for the period, showing the total company segmented by product line.

2. Prepare another segmented income statement for the period, this time showing the total company segmented by sales territory. (Do not allocate the direct fixed expenses of the product lines to the sales territories; treat these as common costs.)

3. Comment on the profitability of the various sales territories. What factors would you be particularly anxious to bring to the attention of management?

P6–12. *Segmented reporting and analysis.* Valcor Corporation manufactures and sells three products, A, B, and C in two regional markets, X and Y. For the fiscal year 19x1, the following absorption costing income statement was prepared:

VALCOR CORPORATION
Income Statement
For the Year 19x1

	Total	Region X	Region Y
Sales	$2,600,000	$2,100,000	$500,000
Cost of goods sold	1,940,000	1,550,000	390,000
Gross margin	$ 660,000	$ 550,000	$110,000
Selling and administrative			
expenses	500,000	403,000	97,000
Net income	$ 160,000	$ 147,000	$ 13,000
Ratio of net income to sales	6.2%	7.0%	2.6%

After reviewing the above results, Ms. Samuels, the president of Valcor Corporation, requested additional information on Region Y, because of the region's poor ratio of net income to sales. Ms. Samuels has suggested that it may be necessary to eliminate Region Y. In response to the president's request, the following additional information has been assembled for the current year:

1. Sales by product, and selected variable expense data:

	Products		
	A	B	C
Sales	$1,000,000	$1,000,000	$600,000
Variable manufacturing expenses as a			
percentage of sales	50%	50%	70%
Variable selling expenses	$40,000	$40,000	$30,000
Variable selling expenses as a			
percentage of sales	4%	4%	5%

2. Sales of product by region:

Product	Region X	Region Y	Total
A...............	$ 800,000	$200,000	$1,000,000
B...............	900,000	100,000	1,000,000
C...............	400,000	200,000	600,000
	$2,100,000	$500,000	$2,600,000

3. Fixed selling expenses total $260,000 per year. $210,000 of this amount is incurred in Region X and $50,000 is incurred in Region Y.
4. Fixed administrative expenses total $130,000 per year. These expenses are common to the two sales regions. However, in the income statement above the fixed administrative expenses were allocated to the two regions on a basis of sales dollars. This allocation resulted in $105,000 being allocated to Region X and $25,000 being allocated to Region Y.
5. Fixed manufacturing overhead is common to the two regions.

Required:

1. Prepare a contribution-type income statement by region and in total for the company, for the current year.
2. Based on the data available, would you recommend elimination of Region Y? Explain.

P6–13. *Preparing segmented income statements.* The Atwood Company's income statement for 19x5, using the contribution approach, is as follows:

ATWOOD COMPANY
Income Statement
For the Year 19x5

	Total company	Division A	Division B
Sales	$190,000	$80,000	$110,000
Less variable expenses:			
Manufacturing	$ 87,000	$32,000	$ 55,000
Other	9,500	4,000	5,500
Total	$ 96,500	$36,000	$ 60,500
Contribution margin	$ 93,500	$44,000	$ 49,500
Less direct fixed expenses	35,000	15,000	20,000
Divisional segment margin	$ 58,500	$29,000	$ 29,500
Less common fixed expenses	25,000		
Net income	$ 33,500		

Selected additional information on Division B is presented below:

	Product X	Product Y	Product Z
Sales	$40,000	$40,000	$30,000
Variable manufacturing expenses as a percentage of sales	60%	40%	50%
Other variable expenses as a percentage of sales	5%	5%	5%
Direct fixed expenses	$5,000	$5,000	$5,000

Product X is sold in a local market and in a regional market. Sales and other data on Product X are given below:

	Product	Sales market	
	X	Local	Regional
Sales	$40,000	$30,000	$10,000
Variable manufacturing expenses as a percentage of sales	60%	60%	60%
Other variable expenses as a percentage of sales	5%	2%	14%

Direct fixed expenses of $4,000 are divided equally between the Local and Regional markets. Common fixed expenses total $1,000 for the two markets.

Required:

1. Prepare a segmented income statement for Division B using the contribution approach, with segments defined by product.
2. Prepare a segmented income statement for Product X using the contribution approach, with segments defined by markets.
3. Mr. Reed, president of the company, wants to spend $1,000 on advertising of Product X in Division B. If he spends it in the local market, sales of Product X in the local market will increase by $5,000. If he spends it in the regional market, sales of Product X in that market will increase by $6,000. In which market should he spend the $1,000? Explain.

P6–14. *Segmented reporting; Expansion analysis.* Meredith Company produces and sells three products (A, B, and C), which are sold in a local market and a regional market. At the end of the first quarter of the current year, the following absorption basis income statement has been prepared:

MEREDITH COMPANY
Income Statement
For the First Quarter

	Total	Local	Regional
Sales	$1,300,000	$1,000,000	$300,000
Cost of goods sold	1,010,000	777,000	233,000
Gross margin	$ 290,000	$ 223,000	$ 67,000
Selling expenses	$ 105,000	$ 60,000	$ 45,000
Administrative expenses	52,000	40,000	12,000
Total	$ 157,000	$ 100,000	$ 57,000
Net income	$ 133,000	$ 123,000	$ 10,000

Management has expressed special concern with the regional market because of the extremely poor return on sales. This market was entered a year ago because of excess capacity. It originally was believed that the return on sales would improve with time, but after a year no noticeable improvement can be seen from the results in the above quarterly statement.

In attempting to decide whether to eliminate the regional market, the following information has been gathered:

	Products		
	A	B	C
Sales	$500,000	$400,000	$400,000
Variable manufacturing expenses as a percentage of sales	40%	35%	30%
Variable selling expenses as a percentage of sales	3%	2%	2%
Fixed manufacturing expenses traceable directly to the product lines	$190,000	$150,000	$210,000

	Sales by markets	
Product	Local	Regional
A	$ 400,000	$100,000
B	300,000	100,000
C	300,000	100,000
Total sales	$1,000,000	$300,000

The administrative expenses shown on the income statement above are common to both the markets and the product lines. They have been allocated to the markets above on a basis of sales dollars. The selling expenses shown on the income statement above are all direct to the markets, as shown. Inventory levels are nominal, and can be ignored.

Required:

1. Prepare a segmented income statement for the quarter, using the contribution approach, segmented into local and regional markets.
2. Assuming there are no alternative uses for the company's present capacity, would you recommend dropping the regional market? Why or why not?
3. Prepare another segmented income statement for the quarter, again using the contribution approach, but this time segmented by product line. (Do not allocate the fixed selling expenses to the product lines; treat these as common costs.)
4. Assume that product lines B and C are both at full capacity. The company would like to add sufficient additional capacity to double the output of one of these two product lines. Overall cost relationships for the added capacity would follow the same cost behavior patterns as with present capacity for each product line. The company's executive committee has decided to double the capacity of Product C, because of its higher C/M ratio. Explain why you do or do not agree with this decision.

(CMA, adapted)

P6–15. *Segmented statements; Product line analysis.* "The situation is slowly turning around," declared Bill Aiken, president of Datex, Inc. "This $42,500 loss for June is our smallest yet. If we can just strengthen lines A and C somehow, we'll soon be making a profit." Mr. Aiken was referring to the company's latest monthly income statement, presented below (absorption costing basis):

DATEX, INC.
Income Statement

	Total	Line A	Line B	Line C
Sales	$1,000,000	$400,000	$250,000	$350,000
Cost of goods sold	742,500	300,000	180,000	262,500
Gross margin	$ 257,500	$100,000	$ 70,000	$ 87,500
Less operating expenses:				
Selling	$ 150,000	$ 60,000	$ 22,500	$ 67,500
Administrative	150,000	60,000	37,500	52,500
Total	$ 300,000	$120,000	$ 60,000	$120,000
Net income (loss)	$ (42,500)	$ (20,000)	$ 10,000	$ (32,500)

"How's that new business graduate doing that we just hired?" asked Mr. Aiken. "He's supposed to be well trained in internal reporting; can he help us pinpoint what's wrong with lines A and C?" "He claims it's partly the way we make up our segmented statements," declared Margie Nelson, the controller. "Here are a lot of data he's prepared on what he calls direct and common costs that he thinks we ought to be isolating in our reports." The data to which Ms. Nelson was referring are shown below:

	Line A	Line B	Line C
Variable costs:*			
Production (materials, labor, and variable overhead)	20%	30%	25%
Selling	5%	5%	5%
Direct fixed costs:			
Production	$100,000	$30,000	$70,000
Selling†	40,000	10,000	50,000

    * As a percentage of sales.
    † Salaries and advertising. Advertising contracts are signed annually.

1. All fixed production costs over the $100,000, $30,000, and $70,000 amounts shown above should be considered as common to the three product lines.
2. All administrative costs are common to the three product lines.
3. Work in process and finished goods inventories are nominal and can be ignored.

"I don't get it," said Mr. Aiken, "our CPAs assure us that we're following good absorption costing methods in our cost allocations, and we're segmenting our statements like they want us to do. So what could be wrong?"

At that moment John Young, the production superintendent, came bursting into the room. "Word has just come that Fairchild Company, the supplier of our type B4 chips, has just gone out on strike. The trade says that they'll be out for at least a month, and our inventory of B4 chips is low. We'll have to cut back production of either line A or line B, since that chip is used in both products." (A single B4 chip is used per unit of each product.) Mr. Aiken looked at the latest monthly statement and declared, "Thank goodness for these segmented statements. It's pretty obvious that we should cut back production of line A. Pass the word, and concentrate all of our B4 chip inventory on production of line B."

Required:

1. Prepare a new segmented income statement, segmented by product line, using the contribution approach. Show both "amount" and "percentage" columns for each of the product lines.
2. Do you agree with Mr. Aiken's decision to cut back production of line A? Why or why not?
3. Assume that the company's executive committee is considering the elimination of line C, due to its poor showing. If you were serving on this committee, what points would you make for or against elimination of the line?
4. Line C is sold in both a home and a foreign market, with sales and cost data as follows:

	Home market	Foreign market
Sales	$300,000	$50,000
Direct fixed costs:		
Selling	10,000	40,000

The fixed production costs of line C are considered to be common to the markets in which the product is sold. Variable expense relationships in the markets are the same as those shown in the main body of the problem for line C.

a. Prepare a segmented income statement, showing line C segmented by markets.
b. What points revealed by this statement would you be particularly anxious to bring to the attention of management?

P6–16. *Preparing various segmented reports; Segment profitability analysis.* "We're clearly one of the industry leaders," declared Roxanne Richie, president of Kitchen Specialities, Inc., as she looked at the company's most recent monthly operating statement. "Our 5.5 percent ratio of income to sales is well above the 4.25 percent industry average."

Kitchen Specialities, Inc., produces and distributes three product lines throughout the United States. To facilitate distribution, the country is divided into three sales regions—the East, the Midwest, and the West. The operating statement to which Ms. Richie was referring is shown below:

Sales		$500,000	100.0%
Less production and packaging expenses		336,500	67.3
Gross margin		$163,500	32.7%
Less operating expenses:			
Marketing	$88,000		
Administration	48,000	136,000	27.2
Net income		$ 27,500	5.5%

"If we're going to maintain our profit position, we'll need to keep things moving smoothly," said Ms. Richie to the controller. "How's that new business school graduate doing that is supposed to be well trained in internal reporting?" "He's trying," replied the controller, "but I'm afraid they aren't too practical in those business schools. He wants us to break our operating statement down two or three different ways. I know he means well, but as you've pointed out, we're already one of the most profitable firms in the industry, so why go to a lot of unnecessary book-keeping expense? Besides, we already know that Line A is our best line, and that the East is our best sales region. He's worked up a lot of figures showing what he calls direct costs and common costs that he thinks we ought to be using in our statements." The data to which the controller was referring are shown below:

	Total sales	Production and packaging	Marketing	Adminis-tration
Sales and variable expenses:				
Line A	$250,000	55%	5%	—
Line B	100,000	47	5	—
Line C	150,000	35	5	—
Direct fixed expenses:				
Line A		$10,000	$15,000	—
Line B		45,000	9,000	—
Line C		44,500	5,000	—
West Region		—	10,000	$ 9,500
Midwest Region		—	13,500	7,000
East Region		—	10,500	16,500
Common fixed expenses:				
General administration		—	—	15,000

The percentage figures above are in terms of total sales. Corporate head-quarters does some advertising directly for each product line on a national basis, which is supplemented by each sales region doing whatever additional advertising it deems necessary. The sales by region (which have been constant in terms of mix for some time) are shown below:

	Percentage of product line sales		
	Line A	Line B	Line C
West Region	15%	50%	60%
Midwest Region	25	20	30
East Region	60	30	10
	100%	100%	100%

Required:

1. Prepare segmented income statements, as follows:
   a. For the company as a whole, broken down into product line segments. Use the contribution format. Show both "Amount"

and "Percentage" columns, with the percentages rounded to one decimal place.

b. For the company as a whole, broken down into regional markets. Use the contribution format. Show both "Amount" and "Percentage" columns, with the percentages rounded to one decimal place. (Do not allocate the direct fixed expenses of the product lines to the regions; treat these as common costs.)

2. Refer to the statement you prepared in (1a) above.

a. Analyze the statement, and indicate the points you would be particularly anxious to bring to the attention of management.

b. The company is about to launch a national promotional campaign for one of the product lines. Assuming that ample capacity exists, and that none of the product lines has reached market saturation, which product line would you recommend to management? Explain the reason for your choice.

3. Refer to the statement you prepared in (1b) above. Analyze the statement and indicate the points you would be particularly anxious to bring to the attention of management.

4. Upon seeing the statement prepared in (1a) above, the president is anxious to get more data on product line B. Assume that the product line consists of Bullion Powder, which is sold through vending machine, home, and institutional markets. The relevant cost data are:

	Total sales	Production and packaging	Marketing
Sales and variable expenses:			
Home market	$30,000	50%	5%
Institutional market	60,000	44	5
Vending machine market	10,000	56	5
Direct fixed expenses:			
Home market		$6,750	$2,500
Institutional market		6,250	3,000
Vending machine market		8,500	1,500

a. Prepare a segmented income statement for product line B, with the product line in total broken down into home, institutional, and vending machine segments. Use the contribution format. Show both "Amount" and "Percentage" columns, with the percentages rounded to one decimal place. (That portion of product line B fixed expenses which are not shown as direct to the markets should be deducted as common costs.)

b. Analyze the statement which you have just prepared. What points would you be particularly anxious to bring to the attention of management?

P6–17. *Prepare and reconcile direct costing statements.* Income statements for Hal Company for 19x1 and 19x2 are given below (absorption costing basis):

HAL COMPANY
Income Statement
For Years 19x1 and 19x2

	19x2	19x1
Sales	$120,000	$120,000
Cost of goods sold	83,200	88,000
Gross margin	$ 36,800	$ 32,000
Selling and administrative expense....	20,000	20,000
Net income	$ 16,800	$ 12,000

Sales and production data are:

	19x2	19x1
Sales in units	8,000	8,000
Production in units...............	10,000	8,000
Variable production cost per unit ... $	8	$ 8
Fixed overhead cost	$24,000	$24,000

Fixed overhead costs are applied to units of product on a basis of each year's production. Variable selling and administrative expenses are $1 per unit sold.

Required:

1. Compute the cost of producing one unit of product in 19x1 and in 19x2 by the absorption approach.
2. Explain why the net income for 19x2 was higher than the net income for 19x1, when the same number of units was sold in each year. No computations are necessary.
3. Prepare income statements for 19x1 and 19x2 by the contribution approach, using direct costing.
4. Reconcile the 19x2 absorption costing and direct costing net income figures.

P6–18. *A comparison of costing methods.* The Staub Company manufactures and sells bus token boxes to a number of bus manufacturing companies. The Staub Company has used absorption costing for both financial and managerial purposes in the past, but now wants to use direct costing internally. The following data are available for the month of October:

Beginning inventory	–0–
Units produced	5,000
Units sold	4,500
Sales price per unit	$ 300
Selling and administrative expenses (all fixed)	50,000
Costs of production:	
Direct materials cost per unit	50
Direct labor cost per unit	60
Variable manufacturing overhead per unit	30
Fixed manufacturing overhead (total)	50,000

Required:

1. Compute the cost of a unit of product under absorption costing.
2. Compute the cost of a unit of product under direct costing.

3. What is the net income for the month under absorption costing?
4. What is the net income for the month under direct costing?
5. Explain the reason for the difference in net income under absorption costing and direct costing.

P6–19. *A comparison of costing methods.* The Donell Company is a major manufacturer of slot machines in Nevada. The firm's accounting department is preparing an income statement for 19x4, and has gathered the following data:

Beginning inventory	–0–
Units produced	10,000
Units sold	9,600
Sales price per unit	$ 1,300
Selling and administrative expenses:	
Variable per unit	60
Fixed (total)	700,000
Costs of production:	
Direct materials cost per unit	65
Direct labor cost per unit	140
Variable manufacturing overhead per unit	25
Fixed manufacturing overhead (total)	3,800,000

Required:

1. Prepare an income statement for the year, using absorption costing.
2. Prepare an income statement for the year, using direct costing.
3. *a.* What is the value of the ending inventory under absorption costing?
   b. What is the value of the ending inventory under direct costing?
   c. Explain the reason for the difference in ending inventory under absorption costing and direct costing.

P6–20. *Absorption versus direct costing: Production constant, sales fluctuate.* Tami Tyler opened Tami Products, Inc., a small manufacturing company, at the beginning of last month. In order to get the company through its first month of operations, it has been necessary for Ms. Tyler to place a considerable strain on her own personal finances. An income statement for the month is shown below. The statement was prepared by a friend who has just completed a course in managerial accounting at State University.

TAMI PRODUCTS, INC.
Income Statement

Sales (50,000 units)		$125,000
Less variable expenses:		
Variable cost of goods sold*	$60,000	
Selling and administrative expenses	20,000	80,000
Contribution margin		$ 45,000
Less fixed expenses:		
Fixed manufacturing overhead	$41,250	
Selling and administrative expenses	8,750	50,000
Net loss		$ (5,000)

* Consists of direct materials, direct labor, and variable overhead.

Ms. Tyler is very discouraged over the loss shown for the month, particularly since she had planned to use the statement as support for a bank loan. Another friend, a CPA, insists that the company should be using absorption costing, rather than direct costing, and argues that if absorption costing had been used the company probably would have reported a nice profit for the month. Production during the month was 75,000 units.

Required:

1. *a.* Redo the company's income statement, using absorption costing.
   b. Reconcile the direct costing and absorption costing net income figures.
2. *a.* Was the CPA correct in suggesting that the company really earned a "profit" for the month? Explain.
   b. Suppose that instead of producing 75,000 units during the month, the company had produced only 50,000 units. Under this assumption, prepare an income statement, using absorption costing. Do you still feel the same about your answer to (*a*) above?
3. Refer to the original data. During the second month of operations, the company again produced 75,000 units, but sold 100,000 units. (Assume no change in total fixed expenses.)
   a. Prepare an income statement for the month, using direct costing.
   b. Prepare an income statement for the month, using absorption costing.
   c. Reconcile the direct costing and absorption costing net income figures.

P6–21. *Contribution income statement prepared from absorption costing data.* The income statement (using absorption costing) for the Swinson Company for the year ending December 31, 19x7, is presented below:

THE SWINSON COMPANY
Income Statement
For the Year Ending December 31, 19x7

Sales (14,000 units × $30 selling price)		$420,000
Less cost of goods sold:		
Beginning inventory	$ –0–	
Cost of goods produced (15,000 units × $20) .	300,000	
Goods available for sale	$300,000	
Less ending inventory (1,000 units × $20)	20,000	280,000
Gross margin		$140,000
Less selling and administrative expenses		90,000
Net income		$ 50,000

Total fixed manufacturing expenses are $75,000 per year. The firm's contribution margin ratio is 40 percent. Some of the selling and administrative expenses are variable, and some are fixed.

Required:

1. Prepare an income statement for 19x7 using direct costing.
2. Mr. Calvin, president of the firm, has an opportunity to sell the remaining 1,000 units of the year's output at a price of $20 per unit. Assuming

that the Swinson Company will not encounter any legal problems or loss of customer goodwill, should Mr. Calvin accept this offer? Show your calculations.

P6–22. *Absorption costing, direct costing, and shifting of fixed overhead.* Rayco, Inc., was organized on January 2, 19x1. Operating results for the first three years of activity were as follows:

	19x3	19x2	19x1
Sales	$75,000	$60,000	$75,000
Cost of goods sold:			
Opening inventory	$20,000	$ 0	$ 0
Cost of goods produced	52,000	60,000	56,000
Goods available for sale	$72,000	$60,000	$56,000
Less ending inventory	13,000	20,000	0
Cost of goods sold	$59,000	$40,000	$56,000
Gross margin	$16,000	$20,000	$19,000
Selling and administrative expenses	15,000	13,000	15,000
Net income	$ 1,000	$ 7,000	$ 4,000

Additional information on the operations of these three years is given below:

a. Sales and production data for the three years:

	19x3	19x2	19x1
Sales in units	10,000	8,000	10,000
Production in units	8,000	12,000	10,000

b. Variable manufacturing costs were $2 per unit in each year. Fixed manufacturing costs totaled $36,000 in each year.

c. Variable selling and administrative expenses were $1 per unit in each year. The remainder of the selling and administrative expenses are fixed.

d. The company applies fixed manufacturing costs to units of product on a basis of each year's actual production.

e. Assume a Fifo inventory flow.

Required:

1. Explain why net income is higher in 19x2 than it is in 19x1, in light of the fact that fewer units were sold in 19x2 than in 19x1.

2. Explain why net income is lower in 19x3 than it is in 19x1, in light of the fact that the same number of units was sold in each year.

3. Prepare income statements for each year, using the contribution approach with direct costing.

4. Reconcile the absorption costing and direct costing net income figures for each year.

P6–23. *The case of the perplexed president.* Budgeted sales for Advance Products, Inc., for the four quarters of 19x3 are given below, along with actual sales for the first two quarters of the year:

	First	Second	Third	Fourth
Budgeted sales in units	10,000	12,000	12,000	14,000
Actual sales in units	10,000	12,000	—	—

The income statements for the first two quarters are presented below:

ADVANCE PRODUCTS, INC.
Income Statement
For the First Two Quarters

	First quarter		Second quarter	
Sales		$200,000		$240,000
Cost of goods sold:				
Opening inventory	$ 40,000		$ 60,000	
Cost of goods produced . . .	120,000		80,000	
Goods available for				
sale	$160,000		$140,000	
Less ending inventory	60,000		20,000	
Cost of goods sold	$100,000		$120,000	
Add underapplied				
overhead	—	100,000	24,000	144,000
Gross margin		$100,000		$ 96,000
Less selling and adminis-				
trative expenses		80,000		90,000
Net income		$ 20,000		$ 6,000

Mr. Walter Ovard, the president of Advance Products, Inc., was looking forward to receiving the second quarter income statement. He knew that the sales budget of 12,000 units sold had been met during the second quarter, and that this represented a substantial increase in sales over the first quarter. Mr. Ovard was especially happy about the increase in sales, since Advance Products, Inc., was about to approach its bank for additional loan money for expansion purposes. Mr. Ovard anticipated that the strong second-quarter showing would be a real plus in persuading the bank to extend the additional credit.

For this reason, Mr. Ovard was shocked when he received the second-quarter income statement above, which showed a substantial drop in net income from the first quarter. Mr. Ovard was sure that there had to be an error somewhere, and immediately called the controller into his office to find the problem. The controller stated, "That net income figure is correct, Chief. I agree that sales went up during the quarter, but the problem is in production. You see, we budgeted to produce 12,000 units each quarter, but a strike in one of our supplier's plants forced us to cut production back to only 8,000 units in the second quarter. That's what caused the drop in net income."

Mr. Ovard was angered by the controller's explanation. "I call you in here to find out why income dropped when sales went up, and you talk about production! So what if production was off? What does that have to do with the sales that we made? If sales go up, then income ought to go up. If your statements can't show a simple thing like that, then we're spending too much money in your area!"

Fixed manufacturing overhead amounts to $72,000 each quarter. Variable manufacturing costs are $4 per unit. The fixed overhead is applied to units of product at a rate of $6 per unit, based on budgeted production of 12,000 units each quarter. Any under- or overapplied overhead is taken to cost of goods sold. Variable selling and administrative expenses are $5 per unit sold.

Required:

1. How would you have explained the drop in net income to Mr. Ovard?
2. Prepare income statements for each quarter using the contribution approach with direct costing.
3. Reconcile the absorption costing and direct costing net income figures for each quarter.

P6–24. *Absorption and direct costing; Uneven production; Break-even.* As vice president of sales for Keller Company, Flora Fisher would like to be able to predict how profits will change with changes in sales volume. She is confused by the monthly income statements for the last quarter, which show decreasing profits even though sales increased from 50,000 units in April to 55,000 units in May and 60,000 units in June. Ms. Fisher is particularly disturbed by the $45,000 loss shown for June. Monthly income statements for the quarter are shown below:

KELLER COMPANY
Monthly Income Statements

	April	May	June
Sales	$500,000	$550,000	$600,000
Less cost of goods sold:			
Opening inventory	$ 25,000	$100,000	$125,000
Cost applied to production:			
Variable production cost	130,000	120,000	80,000
Fixed production cost	195,000	180,000	120,000
Goods available for sale	$350,000	$400,000	$325,000
Less ending inventory	100,000	125,000	25,000
Cost of goods sold	$250,000	$275,000	$300,000
Under- or (overapplied) fixed overhead cost	(15,000)	—	60,000
Cost of goods sold at actual	$235,000	$275,000	$360,000
Gross margin	$265,000	$275,000	$240,000
Less selling and administrative expenses*	245,000	265,000	285,000
Net income (loss)	$ 20,000	$ 10,000	$ (45,000)

* Contains both variable and fixed expenses.

Ms. Fisher is convinced that there must be a better way to report profit data to management, so that changes in profits are more correlated with changes in sales volume. Sales and production data for the quarter follow:

	April	May	June
Sales in units	50,000	55,000	60,000
Production in units	65,000	60,000	40,000

Five thousand units were in inventory at the beginning of April. Fixed overhead cost is applied to production based on a budgeted production volume of 60,000 units each month. Actual fixed production costs totaled $540,000 for the quarter, and were incurred evenly throughout the quarter.

Required:

1. Prepare an income statement for each month, using direct costing.
2. Compute the break-even point under:
   a. Direct costing.
   b. Absorption costing.
   Be prepared to defend your computations.
3. Explain to Ms. Fisher why profits have moved erratically over the three-month period, and why they have not been more closely correlated with changes in sales volume.
4. Reconcile the direct costing and absorption costing net income figures for each month.

Chapter 7

Profit planning

In this chapter we are interested in looking at the planning that businesses do for profits—generally called *profit planning*. We shall see that profit planning is accomplished through the preparation of a number of *budgets*, which combined together form an integrated business plan known as the *master budget*. We shall find that the data going into the preparation of the master budget focus heavily on the *future*, rather than on the past.

THE BASIC FRAMEWORK OF BUDGETING

Definition of budgeting

A budget is a detailed plan showing how resources will be acquired and used over some specific time interval. It represents a plan for the future expressed in formal quantitative terms. The act of preparing a budget is called *budgeting*. The use of budgets to control a firm's activities is known as *budgetary control*.

The *master budget* is a summary of all phases of a company's plans and goals for the future. It sets specific targets for sales, production, distribution, and financing activities, and generally culminates in a projected statement of net income and a projected statement of cash position. In short, it represents a comprehensive expression of management's plans for the future, and how these plans are to be accomplished.

Nearly everyone budgets

Nearly everyone prepares and uses budgets of some sort, even though they may not recognize what they are doing as budgeting. For example, most people make estimates of the income to be realized over some future time period, and plan expenditures for food, clothing, housing, and so on, accordingly. As a result of this planning, spending will usually be restricted by limiting it to some predetermined, allowable amount. This type of action is using a budget as a control device. At other times, individuals will use estimates of income and expenditures to predict what their financial condition will be at some specific future time. The budgets involved here may exist only in the mind of the individual, but they are budgets nonetheless in that they involve plans of how resources will be acquired and used over some specific time period.

The budgets of a business firm serve much the same functions as the budgets prepared informally by individuals. Business budgets tend to be much more detailed and involve much more work in preparation (mostly because they are formal, rather than informal), but are similar in most other respects. As in the case of the individual, they assist in planning and controlling expenditures, and they assist in predicting operating results and financial condition in future periods.

Difference between planning and control

The terms planning and control are often confused, and occasionally used in such a way as to suggest that they mean the same thing. Actually they are two quite distinct concepts. Planning involves the development of future objectives, and the formulation of steps to achieve these objectives. Control involves the means by which management assures that all parts of the organization function properly, and attain the objectives set down in the planning stage. To be completely effective, a good budgeting system must provide for *both* planning and control. Good planning without effective control is time wasted. On the other hand, unless plans are laid down in advance, there are no objectives toward which control can be directed.

Advantages of budgeting

There is an old saying to the effect that "A man is usually down on what he isn't up on." Managers who have never tried budgeting or attempted to find what benefits might be available through the budget process are usually quick to state that budgeting is a waste of time. These managers may argue that even though budgeting may work well in *some* situations, it would never work well in their companies because of the complexities and uncertainties involved. Yet these managers invariably will be constantly planning (albeit on an informal basis). Most managers will have well-defined thoughts about what they want to accomplish, and when they want it accomplished. The difficulty is that unless they have some way of communicating their thoughts and plans to others, the only way the company will ever attain the desired objectives will be through accident. Even though such companies may attain a certain degree of success, they never attain the heights that could have been reached had the efforts of the entire organization been coordinated by means of a detailed system of budgets.

One of the great values of budgeting is that it requires managers to bring planning to the forefront of their minds. Moreover, it provides a vehicle for communicating these plans in an orderly way throughout an entire organization. No one has any doubt about what the managers want to accomplish, or how they want it done. Other benefits of budgeting are:

1. It forces managers to *think ahead* by requiring them to *formalize* their planning efforts.
2. It provides definite goals and objectives which serve as *benchmarks* for evaluating subsequent performance.
3. It uncovers potential *bottlenecks* before they occur.
4. It *coordinates* the activities of the entire organization by *integrating* the plans and objectives of the various parts. By so doing, the budget ensures that the plans and objectives of the parts are consistent with the broad goals of the entire organization.

Consider the following situation encountered by the author:

Company X is a mortgage banking firm. For years the company operated with virtually no system of budgets whatever. Management contended that budgeting wasn't well suited to their type of operation. Moreover, management pointed out that the firm was already profitable. Indeed, outwardly the company gave every appearance of being a well-managed, smoothly operating organization. If one took a careful look within, however, he or she found that day-to-day operations were far from smooth, and often approached chaos. The average day was nothing more than an exercise in putting out one brush fire after another. The cash account was always at crisis levels. At the end of a day no one ever knew if enough cash would be available the next day to cover required loan closings. Departments were uncoordinated, and it was not uncommon to find that one department was pursuing a course that conflicted with the course of another department. Employee morale was low and turnover was high. Employees complained bitterly that when a job was well done, nobody ever knew about it.

Company X was bought out by a new group of stockholders who required that the company establish an integrated budgeting system to control operations. Within one year's time, significant changes were evident. Brush fires were rare. Careful planning virtually eliminated the problems that had been experienced with cash, and departmental efforts were coordinated and directed toward predetermined overall company goals. Although they were very wary of the new budgeting program initially, employees became "converted" when they saw the positive effects that it brought about. The more efficient operations caused profits to jump dramatically. Communication increased throughout the organization. When a job was well done, everybody knew about it. As one employee stated, "For the first time we know what the company expects of us."

Responsibility accounting

Most of what we say in the remainder of this chapter and in Chapters 8 through 10 centers on the concept of *responsibility accounting*. The basic idea behind responsibility accounting is that each manager's performance should be judged by how well he manages those items directly under his control. To judge a manager's performance in this way, the costs (and revenues) of an organization must be carefully scrutinized, and classified according to the various levels of management under whose control the costs rest. Each level of management is then charged with those costs under its care, and the managers held responsible for variations between budgeted goals and actual results. In effect, responsibility accounting *personalizes* the accounting system by looking at costs from a *personal control* standpoint, rather than from an *institutional* standpoint. This concept is central to any effective profit planning and control system.

We will look at responsibility accounting in more detail in Chapters 8, 9, and 10. For the moment we can summarize the overall idea by noting that it rests on three basic premises. The first is that costs can be organized in terms of levels of management responsibility. The second is that the costs charged to a particular level are controllable at that level by its managers. And the third premise is that effective budget data can be generated as a basis for evaluating actual performance. The purpose of the present chapter is to show the steps involved in budget preparation.

Choosing a budget period

Budgets covering acquisition of capital equipment (often called *capital budgets*) generally have quite long time horizons, and may extend 30 years or more into the future. The later years covered by such budgets may be quite indefinite, but at least management is kept planning ahead sufficiently to ensure that funds will be available when purchases of equipment become necessary. As time passes, capital equipment plans that were once somewhat indefinite come more sharply into focus, and the capital budget is updated accordingly. Without such long-term planning, an organization can suddenly come to the realization that substantial purchases of capital equipment are needed, but find that no funds are available to make the acquisitions.

Operating budgets are ordinarily set to cover a one-year period. This one-year period should correspond to whatever fiscal year the company is following so that comparisons of budget to actual results can be made. Many companies divide their budget year into four quarters. The first quarter is then subdivided into months, and monthly budget figures are established. These near-term figures can usually be established with considerable accuracy. The last three quarters are carried in the budget at quarterly totals only. As the year progresses, the figures for the second quarter are broken down into monthly amounts, then the third quarter figures are broken down, and so forth. This approach has the advantage of requiring a constant review and reappraisal of budget data.

Continuous or perpetual budgets are becoming very popular. A continuous or perpetual budget is one which covers a 12-month period, but which is constantly adding a new month on the end as the current month is completed. Advocates of continuous budgets state that this approach to budgeting is superior to other approaches in that it keeps management thinking and planning a full 12 months ahead. Thus, it stabilizes the planning horizon. Under other budget approaches, the planning horizon becomes shorter as the year progresses.

The self-imposed budget

The success of any budget program will be determined in large part by the way in which the budget itself is developed. Generally, the most

successful budget programs are those that permit managers with responsibility over cost control to prepare their own budget estimates, as illustrated
in Exhibit 7–1. This approach to preparing budget data is particularly important if the budget is to be used in controlling a manager's activities after
it has been developed. If a budget is forced on a manager from above,
it likely will generate resentment and ill will rather than cooperation and
increased productivity.

Exhibit 7–1
The initial flow of budget data

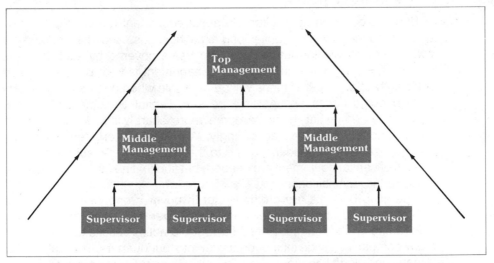

The initial flow of budget data is from lower levels of responsibility to higher levels
of responsibility. Each person with responsibility for cost control will prepare his
or her own budget estimates and submit them to the superior. These estimates
are consolidated as they move upward in the organization.

When managers prepare their own budget estimates, the budgets which
they prepare become *self-imposed* in nature. Certain distinct advantages
arise from the self-imposed budget:

1. Individuals on all levels of the organization are recognized as members
   of the team, whose views and judgments are valued by top management.
2. The person in direct contact with an activity is in the best position to
   make budget estimates. Therefore, budget estimates tend to be more
   accurate and reliable.
3. A person is much more apt to work at fulfilling a budget which he
   has set himself than he is to work at fulfilling a budget imposed on
   him from above.
4. A self-imposed budget contains its own unique system of control, in
   that if people are not able to meet budget specifications they only

have themselves to blame. On the other hand, if a budget is imposed on them from above, they can always say that the budget was unreasonable or unrealistic to start with, and therefore was impossible to meet.

Once self-imposed budgets are prepared, are they subject to any kind of review? The answer is yes. Even though individual preparation of budget estimates is critical to a successful budgeting program, such budget estimates cannot necessarily be accepted without question by higher levels of management. If no system of checks and balances is present, the danger exists that self-imposed budgets will be too loose, and allow too much freedom in activities. The result will be inefficiency and waste. Therefore, before budgets are accepted, they must be carefully reviewed by immediate superiors. If changes from the original budget seem desirable, the items in question are discussed, and compromises reached that are acceptable to all concerned.

In essence, all levels of an organization work together to produce the budget. Since top management is generally unfamiliar with detailed, day-to-day cost matters, they will rely on subordinates to provide detailed budget information. On the other hand, top management has a perspective on the company as a whole that is vital in making broad policy decisions in budget preparation. Each level of responsibility in an organization contributes in the way that it best can in a *cooperative* effort to develop an integrated budget document.

The matter of human relations

The attitudes of lower management personnel toward the budget program will in large part be a reflection of the attitude of top management, and a reflection of the way in which top management *uses* budgeted data.

If a budget program is to be successful, it must have the wholehearted support of top management. Moreover, the budget should never be used as an excuse to conduct "witch hunts" or to find someone to "blame" for a particular problem. Employees are rarely excited about any technique that makes it possible for a superior to "check up" on their performance. If the technique is used as a device to beat them over the head, or to hold them up in shame to their peers, then it becomes all but intolerable, and will be destined for almost certain failure.

The budget should never be used in any way as a tool for harassing an employee. Rather, it should be used as a positive instrument to aid the company in setting standards of performance, in measuring results, in working toward short- and long-range goals, and in isolating areas that are in need of extra effort or attention. Any misgivings that employees have about a budget program can be overcome by careful salesmanship from the top management level, and by proper use of the program over a period of time. Administration of a budget program is a sensitive and delicate task. The ultimate objective must be to develop the realization that the budget is designed to be a positive aid in achieving both individual and company goals.

The paramount importance of the human relations dimension in budgeting cannot be overemphasized. Too often managers have become preoccupied with the technical aspects of the budget program to the exclusion of the human aspects. Accountants particularly are open to criticism in this regard. Unfortunately, preoccupation with the dollars and cents in the budget can lead to insensitivity to the purposes which the budget program is designed to accomplish, in terms of human motivation and coordination of efforts.

The budget committee

A standing budget committee will usually be responsible for overall policy matters relating to the budget program and for coordination in preparation of the budget itself. This committee generally consists of the president; vice presidents in charge of various functions such as sales, production, and purchasing; and the controller. Difficulties and disputes between segments of the organization in matters relating to the budget are resolved by the budget committee. In addition, the budget committee approves the final budget, and receives periodic reports on the progress of the company in attaining budgeted goals.

The master budget—A network of interrelationships

The master budget is a network consisting of many separate budgets that are interdependent. This network is illustrated in Exhibit 7–2.

THE SALES BUDGET. Nearly all other parts of the master budget are dependent in some way on the sales budget. Once the sales budget has been set, a decision can be made on the level of production that will be needed to support sales, and the production budget can be set as well. The production budget then becomes a key factor in the determination of other budgets, including the direct materials budget, the direct labor budget, and the manufacturing overhead budget. These budgets, in turn, are needed to assist in formulating a cash budget for the budget period. In essence, the sales budget triggers a chain reaction that leads to the development of many other budget figures in an organization.

As shown in the exhibit, the selling and administrative expense budget is both dependent on and a determinant of the sales budget. This reciprocal relationship arises from the fact that sales will in part be determined by the funds available for advertising and sales promotion.

THE CASH BUDGET. Once the operating budgets (sales, production, and so on) have been established, the cash budget and other financial budgets can be prepared. Notice from Exhibit 7–2 that all of the operating

Exhibit 7–2
The master budget interrelationships

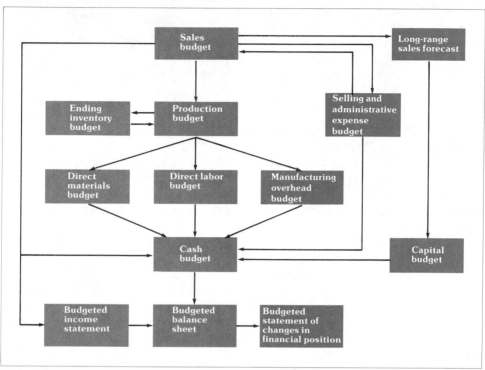

budgets, including the sales budget, have an impact of some type on the cash budget. In the case of the sales budget, the impact comes from the planned cash receipts to be received on sales. In the case of the other budgets, the impact comes from the planned cash expenditures within the budgets themselves.

Sales forecasting—A critical step

Since nearly all budgets are derived from it in some way, the sales budget is the key to the entire budgeting process. If the sales budget is sloppily done, then the entire master budget will be worthless, and a waste of time and effort.

The sales budget is prepared from the *sales forecast*. A sales forecast is broader than a sales budget, generally encompassing potential sales for the entire industry, as well as potential sales for the firm preparing the forecast. Factors which are considered in making a sales forecast include:

1. Past experience in terms of sales volume.
2. Prospective pricing policy.

3. Unfilled order backlogs.
4. Market research studies.
5. General economic conditions.
6. Industry economic conditions.
7. Movements of economic indicators such as gross national product, employment, prices, and personal income.
8. Advertising and product promotion.
9. Industry competition.
10. Market share.

Previous sales volume is usually the starting point in preparing a sales forecast. Forecasters examine sales data in relation to various factors, including prices, competitive conditions, availability of supplies, general economic conditions, and so on. Projections are then made into the future, based on those factors which the forecasters feel will be significant over the budget period. In-depth discussions generally characterize the gathering and interpretation of all data going into the sales forecast. These discussions, held on all levels of the organization, develop perspective, and assist in assessing the significance and usefulness of data.

Statistical tools such as regression analysis, trend and cycle projection, and correlation analysis are widely used in sales forecasting. In addition, some firms have found it useful to build econometric models of their industry or of the nation to assist in forecasting problems. Such models hold great promise for improving the overall quality of budget data.

PREPARING THE MASTER BUDGET

To show how the separate budgets making up the master budget are developed and integrated, we focus now on The Able Company. The Able Company produces and sells a single product, which we will call Product A. Each year the company prepares the following budget documents:

1. A sales budget, including a computation of expected cash receipts.
2. A production budget.
3. A direct materials budget, including a computation of expected cash payments for raw materials.
4. A direct labor budget.
5. A manufacturing overhead budget.
6. An ending finished goods inventory budget.
7. A selling and administrative expense budget.
8. A cash budget.
9. A budgeted income statement.
10. A budgeted balance sheet.

These budgets for the year 19x1 are illustrated in schedules 1 through 10 following.

The sales budget

The sales budget is the starting point in preparing the master budget. As shown earlier in Exhibit 7–2, nearly all other items in the master budget, including production, purchases, inventories, and expenses, depend on it in some way.

The sales budget is constructed by multiplying the expected sales in units by the sales price. Schedule 1 following contains the sales budget for The Able Company for 19x1, by quarters.

Generally the sales budget is accompanied by a computation of expected cash receipts for the forthcoming budget period. This computation is needed to assist in preparing the cash budget for the year. Expected cash receipts are composed of collections on sales made to customers in prior periods, plus collections on sales made in the current budget period. Schedule 1 below contains a computation of expected cash collections for The Able Company.

Schedule 1

THE ABLE COMPANY
Sales Budget
For the Year Ended December 31, 19x1

	Quarter				
	1	2	3	4	Year
Expected sales in units	1,000	1,500	2,000	1,500	6,000
Selling price per unit	× $75	× $75	× $75	× $75	× $75
Total sales	$75,000	$112,500	$150,000	$112,500	$450,000

Schedule of Expected Cash Collections

	1	2	3	4	Year
Accounts receivable, 12/31/x0	$24,000				$ 24,000
1st quarter sales ($75,000)	30,000	$ 45,000			75,000
2d quarter sales ($112,500)		45,000	$ 67,500		112,500
3d quarter sales ($150,000)			60,000	$ 90,000	150,000
4th quarter sales ($112,500)				45,000	45,000
Total cash collections	$54,000	$ 90,000	$127,500	$135,000	$406,500

Note: 40 percent of a quarter's sales are collected in the quarter of sale; the remaining 60 percent is collected in the quarter following.

The production budget

After the sales budget has been prepared, the production requirements for the forthcoming budget period can be determined. Sufficient goods will have to be available to meet sales needs, plus provide for the desired ending inventory. A portion of these goods will already exist in the form of a beginning inventory. The remainder will have to be produced. Therefore, production needs can be determined by adding budgeted sales (in units or in dollars) to the desired ending inventory (in units or in dollars), and deducting the beginning inventory (in units or in dollars) from this total. Schedule 2 below contains a production budget for The Able Company.

Schedule 2

THE ABLE COMPANY
Production Budget
For the Year Ended December 31, 19x1
(in units)

| | Quarter | | | | |
	1	2	3	4	Year
Expected sales (Schedule 1)	1,000	1,500	2,000	1,500	6,000
Add: Desired ending inventory of finished goods*	150	200	150	110‡	110
Total needs	1,150	1,700	2,150	1,610	6,110
Less: Beginning inventory of finished goods†	100	150	200	150	100
Units to be produced	1,050	1,550	1,950	1,460	6,010

* Ten percent of the next quarter's sales.
† The same as the prior quarter's *ending* inventory.
‡ Estimated.

Students are often surprised to learn that firms budget the level of their ending inventories. Budgeting of inventories is a common practice, however. If inventories are not carefully planned, the levels remaining at the end of a period may be excessive, causing an unnecessary tie-up of funds and an unneeded expense of carrying the unwanted goods. On the other hand, without proper planning, inventory levels may be too small, thereby requiring crash production efforts in following periods, and perhaps loss of sales due to inability to meet shipping schedules.

The direct materials budget

After production needs have been computed, a direct materials budget should be prepared to show the materials that will be required in the production process. Sufficient raw materials will have to be available to meet production needs, plus to provide for the desired ending raw materials inventory for the budget period. Part of this raw materials requirement will already exist in the form of a beginning raw materials inventory. The remainder will have to be purchased from suppliers. In sum, the format for computing raw materials needs is:

Raw materials needed to meet the production schedule	XXXXX
Plus desired ending inventory of raw materials	XXXXX
Total raw materials needs	XXXXX
Less beginning inventory of raw materials	XXXXX
Raw materials to be purchased	XXXXX

Schedule 3 contains a direct materials purchases budget for The Able Company. Notice that materials requirements are first determined in units (pounds, gallons, and so on), and then translated into dollars by multiplying by the appropriate unit cost.

Schedule 3

THE ABLE COMPANY
Direct Materials Budget
For the Year Ended December 31, 19x1

	Quarter				
	1	2	3	4	Year
Units to be produced (Schedule 2)	1,050	1,550	1,950	1,460	6,010
Raw material needs per unit (lbs.)	× 2	× 2	× 2	× 2	× 2
Production needs (lbs.)	2,100	3,100	3,900	2,920	12,020
Desired ending inventory of raw materials* (lbs.)	620	780	584	460	460
Total needs (lbs.)	2,720	3,880	4,484	3,380	12,480
Beginning inventory of raw materials (lbs.)	420	620	780	584	420
Raw materials to be purchased (lbs.)	2,300	3,260	3,704	2,796	12,060
Raw materials cost per pound	× $5	× $5	× $5	× $5	× $5
Cost of raw materials to be purchased	$11,500	$16,300	$18,520	$13,980	$60,300

Schedule of Expected Cash Disbursements

Accounts payable 12/31/x0	$ 6,000				$ 6,000
1st quarter purchases ($11,500)	5,750	$ 5,750			11,500
2d quarter purchases ($16,300)		8,150	$ 8,150		16,300
3d quarter purchases ($18,520)			9,260	$ 9,260	18,520
4th quarter purchases ($13,980)				6,990	6,990
Total cash disbursements	$11,750	$13,900	$17,410	$16,250	$59,310

Note: Fifty percent of a quarter's purchases are paid for in the quarter of purchase; the remaining 50 percent are paid for in the quarter following.

* Twenty percent of the next quarter's production needs. For example, the second quarter production needs are 3,100 lbs. Therefore, the desired ending inventory for the first quarter would be 20 percent × 3,100 lbs. = 620 lbs. The ending inventory of 460 lbs. for the fourth quarter is estimated.

The direct materials budget is usually accompanied by a computation of expected cash disbursements for raw materials. This computation is needed to assist in developing a cash budget. Disbursements for raw materials will consist of payments for prior periods, plus payments for current budget-period purchases. Schedule 3 contains a computation of expected cash disbursements for The Able Company.

The direct labor budget

The direct labor budget is also developed from the production budget. Direct labor requirements must be computed so that the company will know if sufficient labor time is available to meet production needs. By knowing in advance just what will be needed in the way of labor time throughout the budget year, plans can be developed to adjust the labor force as the situation may require. Firms that neglect to budget run the risk of facing labor shortages or having to hire and fire at awkward times. Erratic labor policies lead to insecurity and inefficiency on the part of employees.

To compute direct labor requirements, the number of units of finished product to be produced each period (month, quarter, and so on) is multiplied by the number of direct labor-hours required to produce a single unit. Many different types of labor may be involved. If so, then computations should be by type of labor needed. The hours of direct labor time resulting from these computations can then be multiplied by the direct labor cost per hour to obtain budgeted total direct labor costs. Schedule 4 following contains such computations for The Able Company.

Schedule 4

THE ABLE COMPANY
Direct Labor Budget
For the Year Ended December 31, 19x1

	Quarter				
	1	2	3	4	Year
Units to be produced (Schedule 2)	1,050	1,550	1,950	1,460	6,010
Direct labor time per unit (hrs.)	× 5	× 5	× 5	× 5	× 5
Total hours of direct labor time needed	5,250	7,750	9,750	7,300	30,050
Direct labor cost per hour	× $4	× $4	× $4	× $4	× $4
Total direct labor cost	$21,000	$31,000	$39,000	$29,200	$120,200

The manufacturing overhead budget

The manufacturing overhead budget should provide a schedule of all costs of production other than direct materials and direct labor. These costs should be broken down by cost behavior for budgeting purposes, and a predetermined overhead rate developed. This rate will be used to apply manufacturing overhead to units of product throughout the budget period. In the case of The Able Company, the contribution approach to costing is being used internally for planning purposes, and so only variable overhead is included in the predetermined overhead rate.

A computation showing budgeted cash disbursements for manufacturing overhead should be made for use in developing the cash budget. The critical thing to remember in making this computation is that depreciation is a noncash charge. Therefore, any depreciation charges included in manufacturing overhead must be deducted from the total in computing expected cash payments.

We will assume that the variable overhead rate is $2 per direct labor-hour, and that fixed overhead costs are budgeted at $15,000 per quarter, of which $3,750 represents depreciation. All overhead costs involving cash disbursements are paid for in the quarter incurred. The manufacturing overhead budget, by quarters, and the expected cash disbursements, by quarters, are both shown in Schedule 5.

Schedule 5

THE ABLE COMPANY Manufacturing Overhead Budget For the Year Ended December 31, 19x1					
	1	*2*	*3*	*4*	*Year*
Budgeted direct labor-hours	5,250	7,750	9,750	7,300	30,050
Variable overhead rate	× $2	× $2	× $2	× $2	× $2
Budgeted variable overhead	$10,500	$15,500	$19,500	$14,600	$ 60,100
Budgeted fixed overhead	15,000	15,000	15,000	15,000	60,000
Total budgeted overhead	$25,500	$30,500	$34,500	$29,600	$120,100
Less depreciation	3,750	3,750	3,750	3,750	15,000
Cash disbursements for overhead	$21,750	$26,750	$30,750	$25,850	$105,100

Cost of a unit of product

After completing Schedules 1–5, sufficient data will have been generated to compute the cost of a unit of finished product. This computation is needed for two reasons. First, to know how much to charge as cost of goods sold on the budgeted income statement. And second, to know what value to place on the balance sheet for the ending finished goods inventory.

For The Able Company, the cost of a unit of finished product is $40, consisting of $10 of direct materials, $20 of direct labor, and $10 of variable manufacturing overhead. The computations behind these figures are shown below in Schedule 6.

Schedule 6

```
                        THE ABLE COMPANY
                Ending Finished Goods Inventory Budget
                 For the Year Ended December 31, 19x1
```

Item	Quantity	Cost	Total
Variable production cost per unit:			
Raw materials	2 lbs.	$5/lb.	$10
Direct labor	5 hrs.	$4/hr.	20
Variable manufacturing overhead	5 hrs.	$2/hr.	10
			$40
Budgeted finished goods inventory:			
Ending finished goods inventory in units (Schedule 2)			110
Total variable production cost per unit (see above)			× $40
Ending finished goods inventory in dollars			$4,400

The selling and administrative expense budget

The selling and administrative expense budget contains a listing of anticipated expenses for the budget period that will be incurred in areas other
than manufacturing. The budget will be made up of many smaller, individual
budgets submitted by various persons having responsibility for cost control
in selling and administrative matters. If the number of expense items is
very large, separate budgets may be needed for the selling and administrative functions.

Schedule 7

```
                        THE ABLE COMPANY
              Selling and Administrative Expense Budget
                 For the Year Ended December 31, 19x1
```

	Quarter				
	1	2	3	4	Total
Budgeted sales in units	1,000	1,500	2,000	1,500	6,000
Variable selling and administrative expense per unit*	× $5	× $5	× $5	× $5	× $5
Budgeted variable expense	$ 5,000	$ 7,500	$10,000	$ 7,500	$30,000
Fixed selling and administrative expense:					
Advertising	2,250	2,250	2,250	2,250	9,000
Executive salaries	6,250	6,250	6,250	6,250	25,000
Insurance	—	6,000	—	—	6,000
Property taxes	—	—	—	2,000	2,000
Total budgeted selling and administrative expenses	$13,500	$22,000	$18,500	$18,000	$72,000

* Commissions, clerical, and freight-out.

Schedule 7 contains the selling and administrative expense budget for The Able Company for 19x1.

The cash budget

The cash budget pulls together much of the data developed in the preceding steps, as illustrated earlier in Exhibit 7–2. The reader should restudy this exhibit before reading on.

The cash budget is composed of four major sections:

1. The receipts section.
2. The disbursements section.
3. The cash excess or deficiency section.
4. The financing section.

The receipts section consists of the opening cash balance added to whatever is expected in the way of cash receipts during the budget period. Generally the major source of receipts will be from sales, as discussed earlier.

The disbursements section consists of all cash payments that are planned for the budget period. These payments will include raw materials purchases, direct labor payments, manufacturing overhead costs, and so on, as contained in their respective budgets. In addition, other cash disbursements such as income taxes, capital equipment purchases, and dividend payments will also be included.

The cash excess or deficiency section consists of the difference between the cash receipts section totals and the cash disbursements section totals. If a deficiency exists, the company will need to arrange for borrowed funds from its bank. If an excess exists, funds borrowed in previous periods can be repaid, or the idle funds can be placed in short-term investments.

The financing section provides a detailed account of the borrowings and repayments projected to take place during the budget period. It also includes a detail of interest payments that will be due on money borrowed. Banks are becoming increasingly insistent that firms in need of borrowed money give long advance notice of the amounts and times that funds will be needed. This permits the banks to plan, and helps to assure that funds will be ready when needed. Moreover, careful planning of cash needs via the budgeting process avoids unpleasant surprises for companies as well. Few things are more disquieting to an organization than to run into unexpected difficulties in the cash account. A well-coordinated budgeting program eliminates the uncertainty as to what the cash situation will be two months, six months, or a year from now.

The cash budget should be broken down into time periods that are as short as feasible. Many firms budget cash on a weekly basis, and some larger firms go so far as to plan daily cash needs. The more common planning horizons are geared to monthly or quarterly figures. The cash

Schedule 8

THE ABLE COMPANY
Cash Budget
For the Year Ended December 31, 19x1

	Schedule	1	2	Quarter 3	4	Total year
Cash balance, beginning		$12,000	$ 10,000	$ 10,350	$ 10,065	$ 12,000
Add receipts:						
Collections from customers	1	54,000	90,000	127,500	135,000	406,500
Total cash available before current financing		$66,000	$100,000	$137,850	$145,065	$418,500
Less disbursements:						
Direct materials	3	$11,750	$ 13,900	$ 17,410	$ 16,250	$ 59,310
Direct labor	4	21,000	31,000	39,000	29,200	120,200
Manufacturing overhead	5	21,750	26,750	30,750	25,850	105,100
Selling and administrative	7	13,500	22,000	18,500	18,000	72,000
Income taxes	9	4,000	4,000	4,000	4,000	16,000
Equipment purchases			16,000			16,000
Dividends		2,000	2,000	2,000	2,000	8,000
Total disbursements		$74,000	$115,650	$111,660	$ 95,300	$396,610
Excess (deficiency) of cash available over disbursements		$ (8,000)	$ (15,650)	$ 26,190	$ 49,765	$ 21,890
Financing:						
Borrowings (at beginning)		$18,000*	$ 26,000	$ —	$ —	$ 44,000
Repayments (at ending)		—	—	$ (15,000)	$ (29,000)	(44,000)
Interest (at 10% per annum)		—	—	(1,125)†	(2,250)	(3,375)
Total financing		$18,000	$ 26,000	$ (16,125)	$ (31,250)	$ (3,375)
Cash balance, ending		$10,000	$ 10,350	$ 10,065	$ 18,515	$ 18,515

* The company requires a minimum cash balance of $10,000. Therefore, borrowing must be sufficient to cover the cash deficiency of $8,000 plus provide for the minimum cash balance of $10,000.

† The interest payments relate only to the principal being repaid at the time it is repaid. For example, the interest in quarter 3 relates only to the $15,000 principal being repaid at that point in time ($15,000 × 10% × 9 months = $1,125 interest).

budget for The Able Company for 19x1 is shown on a quarterly basis in Schedule 8.[1]

The budgeted income statement

A budgeted income statement can be prepared from the data developed in Schedules 1–8. *The budgeted income statement is one of the key schedules in the budget process.* It is the document that tells how profitable operations are anticipated to be in the forthcoming period. After it is developed it stands as a benchmark against which subsequent company performance can be measured.

Schedule 9 below contains a budgeted income statement for The Able Company for 19x1.

Schedule 9

THE ABLE COMPANY
Budgeted Income Statement
For the Year Ended December 31, 19x1

	Schedule		
Sales (6,000 units at $75)	1		$450,000
Less variable expenses:			
Variable cost of goods sold (6,000 units at $40)	6	$240,000	
Variable selling and administrative	7	30,000	270,000
Contribution margin			$180,000
Less fixed expenses:			
Manufacturing overhead	5	$ 60,000	
Selling and administrative	7	42,000	102,000
Net operating income			$ 78,000
Less interest expense	8		3,375
Net income before taxes			$ 74,625
Less income taxes	*		16,000
Net income			$ 58,625

* Estimated.

The budgeted balance sheet

The budgeted balance sheet is developed by beginning with the current balance sheet and adjusting it for the data contained in the other budgets. A budgeted balance sheet for The Able Company for 19x1 is presented in Schedule 10. The company's beginning-of-year balance sheet, from

[1] The Able Company has an open line of credit with its bank, which can be used as needed to bolster the cash position. Borrowings must be in round $1,000 amounts, and interest is 10 percent per annum. Interest is computed and paid on principal as the principal is repaid. All borrowings take place at the beginning of a quarter, and all repayments are made at the end of a quarter.

which the budgeted balance sheet in Schedule 10 has been derived in part, is presented below:

THE ABLE COMPANY
Balance Sheet
December 31, 19x0

Assets

Current Assets:

Cash	$12,000	
Accounts receivable	24,000	
Raw materials inventory (420 lbs.)	2,100	
Finished goods inventory (100 units)	4,000	
		$ 42,100

Fixed Assets:

Land	$40,000	
Buildings and equipment..................	60,000	
Accumulated depreciation	(40,000)	
		60,000
Total Assets		$102,100

Liabilities and Stockholders' Equity

Current Liabilities:

Accounts payable (raw materials)...........		$ 6,000
Stockholders' Equity:		
Common stock, no par	$40,000	
Retained earnings	56,100	
		96,100
Total Equities		$102,100

ZERO-BASE BUDGETING

Zero-base budgeting has received great attention recently as a new approach to the budgeting process. The method gets its name because managers are required to start at zero budget levels every year and justify all costs as if the programs involved were being initiated for the first time. By this we mean that no costs are viewed as being ongoing in nature; the manager must start at the ground level each year and present justification for all costs in the proposed budget, regardless of the type of cost involved. This is done in a series of "decision packages" in which the manager ranks all of the activities in the department according to relative importance, going from those that he or she considers essential to those that he or she considers of least importance. Presumably this allows top management to evaluate each decision package independently, and to pare back in those areas that appear less critical or which do not appear to be justified in terms of the cost involved.

This process differs from traditional budgeting in which budgets are generally initiated on an incremental basis; that is, the manager starts with last year's budget and simply adds to it (or subtracts from it) according

Schedule 10

THE ABLE COMPANY
Budgeted Balance Sheet
December 31, 19x1

Assets

Current Assets:

Cash	$ 18,515	(*a*)
Accounts receivable	67,500	(*b*)
Raw materials inventory	2,300	(*c*)
Finished goods inventory	4,400	(*d*)
		$ 92,715

Fixed Assets:

Land	$ 40,000	(*e*)
Buildings and equipment	76,000	(*f*)
Accumulated depreciation	(55,000)	(*g*)
		61,000
Total Assets		$153,715

Liabilities and Stockholders' Equity

Current Liabilities:

Accounts payable (raw materials)		$ 6,990 (*h*)

Stockholders' Equity:

Common stock, no par	$ 40,000	(*i*)
Retained earnings	106,725	(*j*)
		146,725
Total Equities		$153,715

Explanation of December 31, 19x1, balance sheet figures:

a. The ending cash balance, as projected by the cash budget in Schedule 8.

b. 60 percent of fourth-quarter sales, from Schedule 1 ($112,500 × 60 percent = $67,500).

c. From Schedule 3, the ending raw materials inventory will be 460 lbs. This material costs $5 per lb. Therefore, the ending inventory in dollars will be 460 lbs. × $5 = $2,300.

d. From Schedule 6.

e. From the December 31, 19x0, balance sheet (no change).

f. The December 31, 19x0, balance sheet indicated a balance of $60,000. During 19x1, $16,000 additional equipment will be purchased (see Schedule 8), bringing the December 31, 19x1, balance to $76,000.

g. The December 31, 19x0, balance sheet indicated a balance of $40,000. During 19x1 $15,000 of depreciation will be taken (see Schedule 5), bringing the December 31, 19x1, balance to $55,000.

h. One half of the fourth-quarter raw materials purchases, from Schedule 3.

i. From the December 31, 19x0, balance sheet (no change).

j.

December 31, 19x0, balance	$ 56,100	
Add net income, from Schedule 9	58,625	
	114,725	
Deduct dividends paid, from Schedule 8	8,000	
December 31, 19x1, balance	$106,725	

to anticipated needs. The manager doesn't have to start at the ground each year and justify ongoing costs (such as salaries) for existing programs.

In a broader sense, zero-base budgeting isn't really a new concept at all. Managers have always advocated in-depth reviews of departmental costs. The only difference is the frequency with which this review is carried out. Zero-base budgeting says that it should be done annually; critics of the zero-base idea say that this is too often, and that such reviews should be made only every five years or so. These critics say that annual in-depth reviews are too time-consuming and too costly to be really feasible, and in the long run probably cannot be justified in terms of the cost savings involved. In addition, it is argued that annual reviews soon become mechanical, and the whole purpose of the zero-base idea is then lost.

The question of frequency of zero-base reviews must be left to the judgment of the individual manager. In some situations annual zero-base reviews may be justified; in other situations they may not because of the time and cost involved. Whatever the time period chosen, however, there is no question but that zero-base reviews can be helpful, and should be an integral part of the overall budgeting process.

THE NEED FOR FURTHER BUDGETING MATERIAL

The material covered in this chapter represents no more than an introduction into the vast area of budgeting and profit planning. Our purpose has been to present an overview of the budgeting process, and to show how the various operating budgets build on each other in guiding a firm toward its profit objectives. However, the matter of budgeting and profit planning is so critical to the intelligent management of a firm in today's business environment that we can't stop with simply an overview of the budgeting process. We need to look more closely at budgeting to see how it helps managers in the day-to-day conduct of business affairs. We will do this by studying standard costs and flexible budgets in the following two chapters, and by introducing the concept of performance reporting. In Chapter 10 we will expand on these ideas by looking at budgeting and profit planning as tools for control of decentralized operations, and as facilitating factors in judging managerial performance.

In sum, the materials in the following two chapters build on the budgeting and profit planning foundation which has been laid in this chapter, by expanding on certain concepts which have been introduced, and by refining others. The essential thing to keep in mind at this point is that the material covered in the current chapter does not conclude our study of budgeting and profit planning, but rather just introduces the ideas.

KEY TERMS FOR REVIEW

Budgeting   **Self-imposed budgets**
Planning   **Budget committee**
Control   **Master budget**
Responsibility accounting   **Sales forecast**
Capital budgets   **Sales budget**
Continuous budgets   **Production budget**

Direct materials budget   **Cash budget**
Direct labor budget   **Zero-base budget**
Manufacturing overhead budget

APPENDIX: ECONOMIC ORDER QUANTITY AND THE REORDER POINT

As stated in the main body of the chapter, inventory planning and control is an essential part of a budgeting system. We have seen that inventory levels are not left to chance, but rather are carefully planned for, both in terms of opening and closing balances. Major questions which we have left unanswered are, "How does the manager know what inventory level is 'right' for the firm?" and, "Won't the level that is 'right' vary from organization to organization?" The purpose of this section is to examine methods available to the manager for answering these questions.

Costs associated with inventory

There are three groups of costs associated with inventory. The first group represents the costs of ordering inventory. The second group represents the costs of carrying inventory. The third group represents the costs of not carrying *sufficient* inventory. Examples of costs associated with each group are given below:

Cost of ordering inventory:

1.   Clerical costs.
2.   Transportation costs.

Costs of carrying inventory:

1.   Storage space costs.
2.   Handling costs.
3.   Property taxes.
4.   Insurance.
5.   Obsolescence losses.
6.   Interest on capital invested in inventory.

Costs of not carrying sufficient inventory:

1.   Customer ill will.
2.   Quantity discounts foregone.
3.   Erratic production (expediting of goods, extra setup, etc.).
4.   Inefficiency of production runs.
5.   Added transportation charges.
6.   Lost sales.

In a broad conceptual sense, the "right" level of inventory to carry is that which will minimize the total of these three classes of costs. This is not easily done, however, since certain of these costs are in direct conflict with each other. Notice, for example, that as inventory levels increase the costs of carrying inventory will also increase, but the costs of not carrying sufficient inventory will decrease. In working toward total cost minimization, therefore, the manager must balance the three groups of costs off against each other: The problem really has two dimensions— how much to order (or how much to produce in a production run), and how often to do it.

Computing the economic order quantity

The "how much to order" is commonly referred to as the *economic order quantity.* It is the order size which will result in a minimization of the first two classes of costs above. We will consider two approaches to computing the economic order quantity—the tabular approach and the formula approach.

The tabular approach

Given a certain annual consumption of an item, a firm might place a few orders each year of a large quantity each, or it might place many orders of a small quantity each. Placing only a few orders would result in few ordering costs, but high inventory carrying costs since the average inventory level would be very large. On the other hand, placing many orders would result in high ordering costs, but low inventory carrying costs since in this case the average inventory level would be quite small. As stated above, the economic order quantity seeks that order size which will balance off these two classes of costs. To show how it is computed, assume that a manufacturer uses 3,000 subassemblies in the manufacturing process each year. The subassemblies are purchased from a supplier at a cost of $20 each. Other cost data are given below:

Inventory carrying costs, per unit, per year $0.80
Cost of placing a purchase order $10

Exhibit 7–3 contains a tabulation of total costs associated with various order sizes for the subassemblies. Notice that total annual cost is lowest (and is equal) at the 250- and 300-unit order sizes. The economic order quantity will lie somewhere between these two points. We could locate it precisely by adding more columns to the tabulation, and we would in time zero in on 274 units as being the exact economic order quantity.

The cost relationships from this tabulation are shown graphically in Exhibit 7–4. Notice from the graph that total annual cost is minimized at that point where annual carrying costs and annual purchase order costs are equal. The same point identifies the economic order quantity, since

Exhibit 7–3
Tabulation of costs associated with various order sizes

				Order size in units					
Symbol*	25	50	100	200	250	300	400	1,000	3,000
O/2 Average inventory in units	12.5	25	50	100	125	150	200	500	1,500
Q/O Number of purchase orders	120	60	30	15	12	10	7.5	3	1
C(O/2) Annual carrying cost at $0.80 per unit	$ 10	$ 20	$ 40	$ 80	$100	$120	$160	$400	$1,200
P(Q/O) Annual purchase order cost at $10 per order	1,200	600	300	150	120	100	75	30	10
T Total annual cost	$1,210	$620	$340	$230	$220	$220	$235	$430	$1,210

* Symbols: O = Order size in units (see headings above).
  Q = Annual quantity used, in units (3,000 in this example).
  C = Annual cost of carrying one unit in stock.
  P = Cost of placing one order.
  T = Total annual cost.

Exhibit 7–4
Graphical solution to economic order size

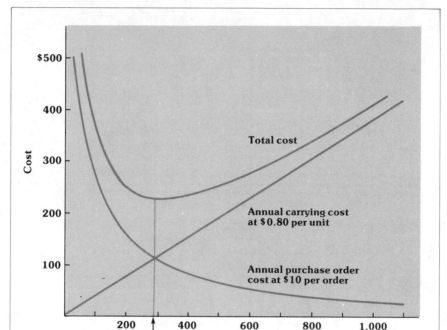

the purpose of the computation is to find the point of exact trade-off between these two classes of costs.

Observe from the graph that total cost shows a tendency to flatten out between 200 and 400 units. Most firms look for this minimum cost range, and choose an order size that falls within it, rather than choosing the exact economic order quantity. The primary reason is that suppliers often will ship goods only in round lot sizes.

The formula approach

The economic order quantity can also be found by means of a formula. The formula is (derived by calculus):

$$0 = \sqrt{\frac{2QP}{C}}$$

where $0 =$ the order size in units, $Q =$ the annual quantity used in units, $P =$ the cost of placing one order, and $C =$ the annual cost of carrying one unit in stock.

Substituting with the data used in our preceding example, we have:

Q= 3,000 subassemblies used per year.
P= $10 cost to place one order.
C= $0.80 cost to carry one subassembly in stock for one year.

$$0 = \sqrt{\frac{2(3,000)(\$10)}{\$0.80}} = \sqrt{\frac{\$60,000}{\$0.80}} = \sqrt{75,000}$$

$0 = 274$ (the economic order quantity)

Although data can be obtained very quickly using the formula approach, it has the drawback of not providing as great a range of information as the methods discussed above.

Production runs

The economic order quantity concept can also be applied to the problem of determining the optimal size of production runs. Deciding when to start and when to stop production runs is a problem that has plagued manufacturers for years. The problem can be solved quite easily by inserting the *setup cost* for a new production run into the economic order quantity formula in place of the purchase order cost. The setup cost includes the labor and other costs involved in getting facilities ready for a run of a different production item.

To illustrate, assume that the Chittenden Company has determined the following costs associated with one of its product lines:

Q= 15,000 units produced each year.
P= $150 setup costs to change a production run.
C= $2 to carry one unit in stock for one year.

What is the optimal production-run size for this product line? It can be determined by using the same formula as used to compute the economic order quantity:

$$0 = \sqrt{\frac{2(15,000)(\$150)}{\$2.00}} = \sqrt{\frac{\$4,500,000}{\$2.00}} = \sqrt{2,250,000}$$

$0 = 1,500$ (economic production-run size in units)

The Chittenden Company will minimize its overall costs by producing in runs of 1,500 units each.

Reorder point and safety stock

We stated earlier that the inventory problem has two dimensions—how much to order and how often to do it. The "how often to do it" involves what is commonly termed the *reorder point* and the *safety stock,* and seeks to find the optimal trade-off between the second two classes of inventory costs outlined earlier (the costs of carrying inventory and the costs of not carrying sufficient inventory).

The reorder point tells the manager when to place an order or when to initiate production to replenish depleted stocks. It is dependent on three factors—the economic order quantity (or economic production-run size), the *lead time,* and the rate of usage during the lead time. The lead time can be defined as the interval between when an order is placed and when the order is finally received from the supplier or from the production line.

Constant usage during the lead time

If the rate of usage during the lead time is known with certainty, the reorder point can be determined by the following formula:

Reorder point = Lead time × Average daily or weekly usage

To illustrate the formula's use, assume that a company's economic order quantity is 500 units, the lead time is 3 weeks, and the average weekly usage is 50 units.

Reorder point = 3 weeks × 50 units per week = 150 units

The reorder point would be 150 units. That is, the company will automatically place a new order for 500 units when inventory stocks drop to a level of 150 units, or three weeks' supply, left on hand.

Variable usage during the lead time

The previous example assumed that the 50 units per week usage rate was constant, and known with certainty. Although some firms enjoy the luxury of certainty, the more common situation is to find considerable variation in the rate of usage of inventory items from period to period. If usage varies from period to period, the firm that reorders in the way computed above may soon find itself out of stock. A sudden spurt in demand, a delay in delivery, or a snag in processing an order may cause inventory levels to be depleted before a new shipment arrives.

Companies that experience problems in demand, delivery, or processing of orders have found that they need some type of buffer to guard against stockouts. Such buffers are usually called *safety stocks.* Safety stocks serve as a kind of insurance against greater than usual demand, and against problems in ordering and delivery of goods. Their size is determined by deducting *average usage* from the *maximum usage* that can be reasonably expected during a period. For example, if the firm in the preceding example was faced with a situation of variable demand for its product, it would compute a safety stock as follows:

Maximum expected usage per week	65 units
Average usage per week	50 units
Excess	15 units
Lead time	×3 weeks
Safety stock	45 units

The reorder point is then determined by *adding the safety stock to the average usage during the lead time.* In formula form, the reorder point would be:

Reorder point
$$= (\text{Lead time} \times \text{Average daily or weekly usage}) + \text{Safety stock}$$

Computation of the reorder point by this approach is shown both numerically and graphically in Exhibit 7–5.

Exhibit 7–5
Determining the reorder point—variable usage

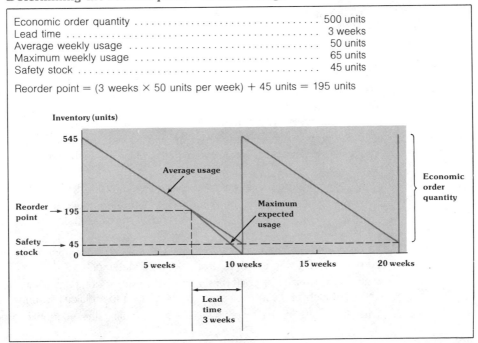

Economic order quantity	500 units
Lead time	3 weeks
Average weekly usage	50 units
Maximum weekly usage	65 units
Safety stock	45 units

Reorder point = (3 weeks × 50 units per week) + 45 units = 195 units

Thus, the company will place a new order for 500 units when inventory stocks drop to a level of 195 units left on hand.

KEY TERMS FOR REVIEW (APPENDIX)

Economic order quantity   **Economic production-run size**
Inventory carrying costs   **Safety stock**
Reorder point   **Lead time**

QUESTIONS

7–1.   What is a budget? What is budgetary control?

7–2.   Discuss some of the major benefits to be gained from budgeting.

7–3.   What is meant by the term "responsibility accounting?"

7–4.   "Budgeting is designed primarily for organizations that have few complexities and uncertainties in their day-to-day operations." Do you agree? Why or why not?

7–5.   What is a master budget? Briefly describe its contents.

7–6.   Which is a better basis for judging actual results, budgeted performance or past performance? Why?

7–7.   Why is the sales forecast always the starting point in budgeting?

7–8.   Is there any difference between a sales forecast and a sales budget? Explain.

7–9.   "As a practical matter, planning and control mean exactly the same thing." Do you agree? Explain.

7–10. Describe the flow of budget data in an organization. Who participates in the budgeting process, and how do they participate?

7–11. "To a large extent, the success of a budget program hinges on education and good salesmanship." Do you agree? Explain.

7–12. What is a self-imposed budget? What are the major advantages of self-imposed budgets? What caution must be exercised in their use?

7–13. In structuring a cash budget, what important factors must be considered in planning cash collections from sales? In planning cash disbursements to suppliers?

7–14. How can budgeting assist a firm in its employment policies?

7–15. "The principal purpose of the cash budget is to see how much cash the company will have in the bank at the end of the year." Do you agree? Explain.

7–16. List at least three costs associated with a company's inventory policy that do not appear as an expense on the income statement.

7–17. What three classes of costs are associated with a company's inventory policy? Which of these classes of costs is the most difficult to quantify?

7–18. What trade-offs in costs are involved in computing the economic order quantity?

7–19. "Managers are more interested in a minimum cost *range* than they are in a minimum cost point." Explain.

7–20. Define "lead time" and "safety stock."

7–21. How does zero base budgeting differ from traditional budgeting?

EXERCISES

E7–1. Clovis Products, Ltd., has budgeted sales for the next four months as follows:

	Sales in units
April	40,000
May	65,000
June	80,000
July	70,000

The company is now in the process of preparing a production budget for the second quarter. Past experience has shown that end-of-month inventory levels must equal 15 percent of the following month's sales. The inventory at the end of March was 6,000 units.

Required:

How many units must be produced during each month of the second quarter, and for the quarter in total?

E7–2. The sales budget for Briggs Sales Company for the first quarter of 19x4 is given below:

	January	February	March	Total
Budgeted sales	$55,000	$75,000	$90,000	$220,000

In order to have data available for preparing a cash budget, the company is anxious to determine the budgeted cash collections from sales. To this end, the following information has been assembled:

Collections on sales
{
60% in month of sale
30% in month following sale
8% in second month following sale
2% uncollectible
}

Briggs Sales Company gives a 2 percent cash discount for payments made by customers during the month of sale. The accounts receivable balance to start the year is $22,000, of which $4,000 represents uncollected November sales, and $18,000 represents uncollected December sales.

Required:

1. What were the total sales for November? For December?
2. Prepare a schedule showing the budgeted cash collections from sales, by month and in total, for the three-month period.

E7–3. Three ounces of musk oil are required for each bottle of "Allure," a very popular perfume. The cost of the musk oil is $3 per ounce. Scheduled production of "Allure" for 19x5 is given below, by quarters:

	First	Second	Third	Fourth
Production in bottles	7,500	10,000	18,000	6,000

Musk oil has become so popular as a perfume base that it has become necessary to carry large inventories as a precaution against stockouts. For this reason, the inventory of musk oil at the end of any quarter must not be less than 25 percent of the following quarter's production needs.

Required:

Compute the budgeted purchases of musk oil for the second and third quarters, in both ounces and dollars.

E7–4. A cash budget, by quarters, is given below. Fill in the missing amounts (000 omitted). The company requires a minimum cash balance of at least $5,000 to start each quarter.

	1	2	3	4	Year
Cash balance, beginning	$ 6	$?	$?	$?	$?
Add collections from customers	?	?	96	?	323
Total cash available	71	?	?	?	?
Less disbursements:					
Purchase of inventory	35	45	?	35	?
Operating expenses	?	30	30	?	113
Equipment purchases	8	8	10	?	36
Dividends	2	2	2	2	?
Total disbursements	?	85	?	?	?
Excess (deficiency) of cash available over disbursements	(2)	?	11	?	?
Financing:					
Borrowings	?	15	—	—	?
Repayments (with interest)	—	—	(?)	(17)	(?)
Total financing	?	?	?	?	?
Cash balance, ending	$?	$?	$?	$?	$?

E7–5. Tronac Company needs a cash budget for the month of September 19x4. The following information is available.
1. The cash balance on September 1 is $7,500.
2. Actual sales for July and August, and expected sales for September, are:

	July	August	September
Cash sales	$ 4,500	$ 4,800	$ 5,500
Credit sales	20,000	30,000	35,000
Total sales	$24,500	$34,800	$40,500

Credit sales are collected over a three-month period, in the ratio 60 percent, 30 percent, 9 percent, with 1 percent uncollectible.
3. Purchases of inventory will total $18,000 for September. Seventy percent of a month's purchases are paid during the month of purchase. Accounts payable for August purchases total $5,700, which will be paid in September.
4. Selling and administrative expenses are budgeted at $14,000 for September. Of this amount $5,000 is for depreciation.

5. Dividends of $4,000 will be paid during September, and equipment costing $12,000 will be purchased.
6. The company must maintain a minimum cash balance of $5,000. An open line of credit is available from the company's bank to bolster the cash position as needed.

Required:

Prepare a cash budget for the month of September. Indicate in the financing section any borrowing that will be necessary during the month.

E7–6. (Appendix) Classify the following either as (*a*) costs of carrying inventory, or (*b*) costs of not carrying sufficient inventory:
1. Air freight on a rush order of a critical part needed in production.
2. Interest paid on investment funds.
3. State and local taxes on personal property.
4. Spoilage of perishable goods.
5. Excessive setup costs.
6. Customers lost through inability of the company to make prompt delivery.
7. Quantity discounts lost as a result of purchasing in small lots.
8. Fire insurance on inventory.
9. Loss sustained when a competitor comes out with a less expensive, more efficient product.
10. A general feeling of ill will among customers, due to broken delivery promises.

E7–7. (Appendix) The Hurd Company uses 8,000 units of a certain part each year.
1. The company has determined it costs $40 to place an order for the part from the supplier, and $4 to carry one part in inventory each year. Compute the economic order quantity for the part.
2. Assume that the Hurd Company's ordering costs increase to $50 per order. What will be the effect on the economic order quantity? Show computations.
3. Assume that the Hurd Company's carrying costs increase to $5 per part. (Ordering costs remain unchanged at $40.) What will be the effect on the economic order quantity? Show computations.
4. In (2) and (3) above, why does an increase in cost increase the economic order quantity in one case, and reduce it in the other?

E7–8. (Appendix) Selected information relating to an inventory item carried by the Sikes Company is given below:

Economic order quantity	700 units
Maximum weekly usage	60 units
Lead time	4 weeks
Average weekly usage	50 units

Sikes Company is trying to determine the proper safety stock to carry on this inventory item, and the proper reorder point.

Required:

1. Assume that no safety stock is to be carried. What is the reorder point?

2. Assume that a full safety stock is to be carried.
   a. What would be the size of the safety stock in units?
   b. What would be the reorder point?

E7–9. (Appendix) Aspen Products manufactures a variety of decorative furniture pieces. About 10,000 units of one item, a small table, are sold each year. The company has been producing the table in production runs of 1,000 tables each, but this has made it necessary to have a production run every five weeks, and setup costs for a run are very high. On the other hand, if production runs are too large, then the company is "eaten up" with insurance and other inventory carrying costs.

The company's cost analyst estimates that it costs $500 to set up a run of the tables. Variable production costs total $50 per table, and the tables sell for $80 each. Insurance and other inventory carrying costs total about 2 percent of variable production costs per table per year.

Required:

Compute the economic production-run size. Round your solution to the nearest whole table.

PROBLEMS

P7–10. *Production and purchases budgets.* Barker Products manufactures and distributes a number of products to retailers. One of these products, Playclay, requires 3 pounds of Material A in its manufacture. In order to keep production moving smoothly, the company wants raw materials on hand at the beginning of each month equal to one half of the month's production needs. This requirement was met on July 1, the start of the third quarter, 19x5. The company maintains no work in process inventories. A sales budget for Playclay for the last six months of 19x5 is given below:

	Budgeted sales in units
July	15,000
August	18,000
September	24,000
October	26,000
November	19,000
December	16,000

Barker Products has found that the finished goods inventory at the end of each month must be equal to 5,000 units plus 10 percent of the next month's sales. On June 30, the finished goods inventory totaled 6,500 units.

Required:

Prepare a budget showing the quantity of Material A to be purchased for July, August, and September 19x5. (Hint: In order to prepare a materials purchases budget, it will be necessary first to prepare a production budget for each of the months July–October.)

P7–11. *Cash budget.* Mary Roberts, president of Crestline Products, has just approached the company's bank with a request for a short-term loan of $16,000. The purpose of the loan is to assist the company in building inventories in support of peak April sales. Although Crestline Products has borrowed from the bank before for this purpose, the amount of the present loan is considerably more than has been needed in prior years. For this reason, the bank's loan officer is somewhat concerned over Crestline Products' ability to repay the loan as planned. The company's plan is to borrow the money on March 1, repayable at 10 percent interest three months later, on May 31.

The loan officer has asked Ms. Roberts to submit a cash budget covering the loan period, to see what Crestline Products' cash balance will be on May 31, assuming the loan is made as planned. Accordingly, Ms. Robert's staff has assembled the following budgeted information for the next three months:

	March	April	May
Sales	$30,000	$40,000	$20,000
Merchandise purchases	24,000	12,000	8,000
Payroll	4,000	4,500	3,000
Lease payments	3,000	3,000	3,000
Other cash payments	4,000	6,000	3,000
Depreciation expense	1,000	1,000	1,000
Net income	3,000	6,000	1,000
Equipment purchases	2,000	—	—

On March 1, the company plans to have a cash balance of $4,000. Accounts receivable on that date are planned at $16,800, of which $15,600 will be collected during March, and $800 will be collected during April. The remainder probably will be uncollectible. The company's collection pattern for sales is 20 percent during the month of sale, 75 percent in the month following sale, and 4 percent in the second month following sale. On March 1, the accounts payable balance will be $18,000, representing February purchases of merchandise inventory. All purchases are paid for in the month following purchase.

Required:

1. Prepare a schedule of budgeted cash collections on sales and accounts receivable.
2. Prepare a cash budget, by month and in total, for the loan period assuming that the loan is made and repaid as planned.
3. If the company needs a minimum cash balance of $4,000 at the beginning of each month, can the loan be repaid as planned? Explain.

P7–12. *Direct materials budget.* A sales budget for the first five months of 19x3 is given for a particular product line manufactured by Arthur Frank Co. Ltd.

Month	Sales budget in units
January	10,800
February	15,600
March	12,200
April	10,400
May	9,800

The inventory of finished products at the end of each month is to be equal to 25 percent of the sales estimate for the next month. On January 1, there were 2,700 units of product on hand. No work is in process at the end of any month.

Each unit of product requires two types of materials in the following quantities:

Material A: 4 units
Material B: 5 units

Materials equal to one half of the next month's production needs are to be on hand at the end of each month. This requirement was met on January 1, 19x3.

Required:

Prepare a budget showing the quantities of each type of material to be purchased each month for the first quarter of 19x3. (Hint: Remember that a production budget must be prepared before a materials purchases budget can be prepared.)

(SMA, adapted)

P7–13. *Master budget.* The balance sheet of Darby Sales Company as of May 31, 19x4, is given below:

DARBY SALES COMPANY
Balance Sheet
May 31, 19x4

Assets

Cash	$ 8,000
Accounts receivable, customers	26,500
Inventory	47,000
Plant and equipment, net of depreciation	140,000
Total assets	$221,500

Liabilities and Equity

Accounts payable, suppliers	$ 38,000
Note payable	8,000
Capital stock, no pàr	120,000
Retained earnings	55,500
Total liabilities and equity	$221,500

Darby Sales Company has never budgeted before, and for this reason is limiting its master budget planning horizon to just one month—June 19x4. The company has assembled the following budgeted information relating to the month of June:

a. Sales are budgeted at $130,000. Of these sales, $30,000 will be for cash; the remainder will be credit sales. Fifty percent of credit sales are collected in the month the sales are made, and the remainder is collected in the following month. All of the May 31 accounts receivable will be collected during June.

b. Purchases of inventory are expected to total $80,000 during the month, all on account. Forty percent of all purchases are paid for in the month of purchase; the remainder is paid in the following month.

All of the May 31 accounts payable to suppliers will be paid during June.

c. The June 30 inventory balance is budgeted at $36,000.

d. Operating expenses for June are budgeted at $29,000, exclusive of depreciation. These expenses will all be paid in cash. Depreciation is budgeted at $2,000 for the month.

e. Equipment costing $15,000 will be acquired on June 30. The company will give a note payable to its bank in order to obtain funds to cover the equipment cost. The note will be due in one year.

f. The note payable at May 31 will be paid in June, with $500 interest.

Required:

1. Prepare a cash budget for the month of June 19x4.
2. Prepare a budgeted income statement for the month of June 19x4. Use the traditional income statement format. Ignore income taxes.
3. Prepare a budgeted balance sheet as of June 30, 19x4.

P7–14. *Planning bank financing by means of a cash budget.* When the treasurer of Besner Company approached the company's bank late in 19x1 seeking short-term financing, he was told that money was very tight, and that any borrowing over the next year would have to be supported by a detailed statement of cash receipts and disbursements. The treasurer also was told that it would be very helpful to the bank if borrowers would indicate the quarters in which they would be needing funds, as well as the amounts that would be needed and the quarters in which repayments could be made.

Since the treasurer is unsure as to the particular quarters in which the bank financing will be needed, he has assembled the following budgeted data for 19x2, as well as selected actual data for the last quarter of 19x1:

	Sales	Merchandise purchases
19x1–Fourth quarter actual	$200,000	$126,000
19x2–First quarter estimated	300,000	186,000
Second quarter estimated	400,000	246,000
Third quarter estimated	500,000	282,000
Fourth quarter estimated	200,000	126,000

Operating expenses for 19x2 are budgeted quarterly at $50,000 plus 15 percent of sales. Of the fixed amount, $20,000 each quarter is depreciation. Besner Company plans to pay $10,000 in dividends each quarter. The company also plans to make equipment purchases of $75,000 in the second quarter and $67,000 in the third quarter.

The company normally collects 65 percent of a quarter's sales before the quarter ends, and another 33 percent in the following quarter. The remainder is uncollectible. Eighty percent of a quarter's merchandise purchases are paid for within the quarter. The remainder is paid in the quarter following. This pattern of collections and payments is now being experienced in the 19x1 fourth quarter actual data.

The cash account at the end of 19x1 contains $10,000. The treasurer of Besner Company feels that this represents a minimum cash balance that must be maintained. Any borrowing will take place at the beginning of a quarter, and any repayments will be made at the end of a quarter at an annual interest rate of 10 percent. All borrowings and all repayments of principal must be in round $1,000 amounts.

Required:
1. Prepare schedules of budgeted cash collections on sales and budgeted cash payments for merchandise purchases.
2. Prepare a cash budget for 19x2, by quarter and in total for the year. Show clearly in your budget the quarter(s) in which borrowing will be necessary, and the quarter(s) in which repayments can be made, as requested by Besner Company's bank.

P7–15. *Master budget completion.* Following is selected information relating to the operations of Paradise Company:

Current assets as of March 31, 19x4:

Cash	$ 8,000
Accounts receivable	20,000
Inventory	36,000
Fixed assets, net	120,000
Accounts payable	21,750
Capital stock	150,000
Retained earnings	12,250

a. Gross profit is 25 percent of sales.
b. Actual and budgeted sales data:

March (actual)	$50,000
April	60,000
May	72,000
June	90,000
July	48,000

c. Sales are 60 percent for cash, and 40 percent on credit. Credit sale terms are n/30, and therefore accounts are collected in the month following sale. The accounts receivable at March 31 are a result of March credit sales.
d. Inventory is to be on hand at the end of each month equal to 80 percent of the following month's sales needs, stated at cost.
e. All inventory purchases are on terms of 2/15, n/30; therefore, half of a month's purchases are paid for in the month of purchase, and half in the following month. All purchase discounts are taken, and treated as "Other Income" on the income statement. (Purchase discounts are not recorded until payment is made.) The accounts payable at March 31 are a result of March purchases of inventory.
f. Monthly expenses are as follows: salaries and wages, 12 percent of sales; rent, $2,500 per month; other expenses (excluding depreciation), 6 percent of sales. Assume that these expenses are paid monthly. Depreciation is $900 per month (includes depreciation on new assets).
g. Fixed assets costing $2,500 will be purchased in April, and fixed assets costing $1,000 will be purchased in May.

h. The company must maintain a minimum cash balance of $6,000. An open line of credit is available at a local bank. All borrowing is made at the beginning of a month, and all repayments at the end of a month. Interest is paid only at the time of repayment of principal. The interest rate is 12 percent per annum. All borrowing must be in multiples of $1,000.

Required:

Using the data above:

1. Complete the following schedule:

Schedule of Expected Cash Collections

	April	May	June	Total
Cash sales	$36,000			
Credit sales	20,000			
Total collections	$56,000			

2. Complete the following:

Inventory Purchases Budget

	April	May	June	Total
Purchases for current sale	$ 9,000*			
Purchases for inventory	43,200†			
Total purchases	$52,200			

Schedule of Expected Cash Disbursements—Purchases

	April	May	June	Total
March purchases	$21,750			
April purchases	26,100			
May purchases				
June purchases				
Total	$47,850			
Less 2% discount	957			
Net disbursements	$46,893			

* For April sales: $60,000 × 75% cost ratio = $45,000 × 20% = $9,000.
† For May sales: $72,000 × 75% cost ratio = $54,000 × 80% = $43,200.

3. Complete the following:

Schedule of Expected Cash Disbursements—Expenses

	April	May	June	Total
Salaries and wages	$ 7,200			
Rent	2,500			
Other expenses	3,600			
Total disbursements	$13,300			

4. Complete the following cash budget:

Cash Budget

	April	May	June	Quarter
Cash balance, beginning	$ 8,000			
Add cash collections	56,000			
Total cash available	$64,000			
Less cash disbursements:				
For inventory	$46,893			
For expenses	13,300			
For fixed assets	2,500			
Total	$62,693			
Excess (deficiency) of cash	$ 1,307			
Financing:				
Etc.				

5. Prepare an income statement for the quarter ended June 30.

6. Prepare a balance sheet as of June 30.

P7–16. *Defending a budget proposal.* Kendall Corporation is a medium-sized manufacturer of a number of consumer products. You have been working for the company for only a few months. In order for you to become familiar with the company's operations, the president assigned you to do a general study of its manufacturing and financing activities. You were instructed to prepare a memo for the president outlining any new programs or changes that seemed desirable for the company to consider.

In your study, you have found that the company is experiencing certain operating difficulties, particularly in controlling costs and coordinating operations. You have recommended to the president in your memo that the company give serious consideration to implementing a comprehensive budgeting program as one step toward overcoming these difficulties. The president is very much interested in your suggestion, and has brought the matter before the company's executive committee, with you present for the purpose of answering any questions. Upon hearing the president's comments, one of the senior members of the committee replies, "I just can't see trying to budget in our size of operation. I don't doubt that it works well in the giants, like General Motors, but we're just a drop in the bucket compared to them. Besides, we have special problems, like reliance on a couple of foreign suppliers, and concentration of sales on the coast. If we were nationwide, it might be different. And I seriously question whether the accounting people would ever be able to guess our expenses in advance—there are just too many variables involved. Besides, when would Bill (the controller) find time to make up a lot of budgets? It's all he can do to get out the monthly statements as it is. Even if Bill did get the time to make budgets, who would follow them?"

As you glance around the table, you notice that several heads are nodding affirmatively to the committee member's comments. The president turns to you for a reply.

Required:

Write your reply out in narrative form, keeping in mind that all eyes are on you as you speak.

P7–17. *Quarterly cash budget.* As part of the company's overall planning program, the controller of the So Good Blueberry Packing Co., Ltd., prepares a cash budget by quarters each year.

The company's operations consist solely of processing and canning the yearly crop of blueberries. As this is a seasonal commodity, all manufacturing operations take place in the quarter of October through December. Sales are made throughout the year and the company's fiscal year ends on June 30.

The sales forecast for the coming year indicates (all figures in thousands):

1st quarter (July–September 19x1)	$ 780
2d quarter (October–December 19x1)	1,500
3d quarter (January–March 19x2)................	780
4th quarter (April–June 19x2)	780

All sales are on account. The beginning balance of receivables is expected to be collected during the first quarter. It is anticipated that subsequent collections will follow the pattern of two-thirds collected in the quarter of sales, the remaining one-third in the quarter following.

Purchases of blueberries are scheduled as follows: $240,000 in the first quarter and $720,000 in the second quarter. Payment is made in the quarter of purchase.

Direct labor of $700,000 is incurred and paid in the second quarter.

Factory overhead cost (paid in cash during quarter it is incurred) is $860,000 in the second quarter. The standby (fixed) amount in each of the other three quarters is $200,000.

Selling and administrative expenses, incurred and paid, amount to $100,000 per quarter during the year.

To finance its seasonal working capital needs, the company has obtained a line of short-term credit with the Royal Toronto Bank. The company maintains a minimum cash balance of $8,000 and borrows and repays only in multiples of $5,000. It repays as soon as it is able without impairing the minimum cash balance. Interest is at 8 percent and is paid at time of loan repayment. It is assumed that all borrowing is made at the beginning of a quarter, and the repayments are made at the end of a quarter. (Round interest calculations to nearest $1,000.)

The company plans to spend the following amounts on fixed assets:

3d quarter	$150,000
4th quarter	50,000

Account balances as of July 1, 19x1 were:

Cash	$ 8,000
Accounts receivable	25,000

Required:

1. Prepare a schedule of budgeted cash collections on sales.
2. Prepare a cash budget by quarter and for the year in total ending June 30, 19x2.
3. Comment briefly on the nature and purpose of cash budgets for management.

(SMA, adapted)

P7–18. *Production budget, purchases budget, and income statement.* The sales budget of Marvel Glue Products calls for sales of 200,000 bottles of Formula 7, one of the company's glue products, during the second quarter of 19x8. The sales budget calls for a selling price of $5 per bottle. Since sales of this product tend to fall off during the summer months, the finished goods inventory at the end of the second quarter is planned to be down by 20 percent from its present level of 20,000 bottles.

Only six minutes of direct labor time is required to produce each bottle of Formula 7. The direct labor rate is $4 per hour. Two different raw materials ingredients go into the production of Formula 7. Material X costs 15 cents per ounce, and four ounces are required per bottle of Formula 7. Material Y costs 80 cents per ounce, but only two ounces are required per bottle. The following inventory levels are existing or planned for the second quarter:

	Actual beginning	Planned ending
Material X	80,000 ozs.	60,000 ozs.
Material Y	45,000 ozs.	60,000 ozs.

Material Y is sometimes hard to find; therefore, inventory levels of Material Y are being increased. Other variable costs include manufacturing overhead of 25 cents per bottle of Formula 7, and selling and administrative expenses of 20 cents per bottle. Fixed costs are given below per quarter:

Manufacturing overhead $90,000
Selling and administrative 60,000

Required:

1. Prepare a production budget for Formula 7 for the second quarter.
2. Prepare a raw materials purchases budget for both Material X and Material Y for the second quarter. Show the budgeted purchases in both ounces and dollars.
3. Prepare a budgeted income statement for the second quarter. Show sales revenue and variable expense data per unit and in total.

P7–19. *Cash budget.* Home Sales, Inc., is planning its cash needs for the second quarter of 19x2. The company usually has to borrow money during this quarter to support peak sales of lawn care equipment, which occur during May. The following information has been assembled to assist in preparing a cash budget for the quarter:

a. Budgeted monthly income statements for April–July 19x2 are:

	April	May	June	July
Sales	$17,000	$24,000	$18,000	$16,000
Cost of goods sold	10,200	14,400	10,800	9,600
Gross margin	$ 6,800	$ 9,600	$ 7,200	$ 6,400
Less operating expenses:				
Selling expense	$ 2,300	$ 3,000	$ 2,400	$ 2,200
Administrative expense*	2,660	3,080	2,720	2,600
Total	$ 4,960	$ 6,080	$ 5,120	$ 4,800
Net income	$ 1,840	$ 3,520	$ 2,080	$ 1,600

* Includes $1,200 depreciation each month.

b. Sales are 20 percent for cash and 80 percent on credit.

c. Credit sales are collected over a three-month period, in the ratio 10 percent, 70 percent, 20 percent. February's sales totaled $14,000 and March's sales totaled $15,000.

d. Inventory purchases are paid for within 15 days. Therefore, approximately 50 percent of a month's inventory purchases are paid for in the month of purchase. The remaining 50 percent is paid in the following month. Accounts payable for inventory purchases at March 31 total $4,650.

e. The company maintains its ending inventory levels at $5,000 plus 25 percent of the cost of the merchandise to be sold in the following month. The merchandise inventory at March 31 is $7,550.

f. Dividends of $2,000, declared in March, will be paid in April.

g. Equipment costing $5,000, received in April, is being paid in two equal payments, starting in April.

h. The company must maintain a cash balance of at least $5,000. The cash balance on March 31 is $5,155.

i. The company can borrow from its bank as needed to bolster the cash account. Borrowings must be in multiples of $500. All borrowings take place at the beginning of a month, and all repayments are made at the end of a month. The interest rate is 12 percent per annum. Compute interest on whole months (e.g., 1/12, 2/12, and so on).

Required:

1. Prepare a schedule of budgeted cash collections from sales for each of the months April, May, and June.

2. Prepare a schedule of budgeted cash payments for inventory purchases for each of the months April, May, and June.

3. Prepare a cash budget for the second quarter, 19x2. Show figures by month as well as for the quarter in total. Show borrowings from the company's bank and repayments to the bank as needed to maintain the minimum cash balance.

P7–20. *Master budget preparation.* Actual sales for June, and budgeted sales for July–October 19x2 are presented below for the Portland Company:

June (actual)	$40,000
July	50,000
August	64,000
September	80,000
October	36,000

The company is preparing its master budget for the third quarter. The following information is available:

a. Sales are 40 percent for cash, and 60 percent on credit. All credit sale terms are n/30; therefore, accounts are collected in the month following sale. The accounts receivable at June 30 are a result of June credit sales..

b. The gross profit rate is 30 percent of sales.

c. Monthly expenses are as follows: salaries and wages, 15 percent of sales; rent, $2,200 per month; other expenses (excluding depreciation), 5 percent of sales. Depreciation is $1,000 per month.

d. Inventory is to be on hand at the end of each month equal to 75 percent of the following month's sales needs, stated at cost. In addition, inventory is purchased each month sufficient to provide for the month's sales needs beyond what is available in the opening inventory.

e. All inventory purchases are on terms of 2/15, n/30; therefore, half of a month's purchases are paid for in the month of purchase, and half in the following month. All purchase discounts are taken, and treated as "Other Income" on the income statement. (Purchase discounts are not recorded until payment is made.) The accounts payable at June 30 are a result of June purchases of inventory.

f. Fixed assets costing $2,500 will be purchased in August.

g. The company must maintain a minimum cash balance of $5,000. An open line of credit is available at a local bank. All borrowing is made at the beginning of a month, and all repayments at the end of a month. Borrowings and repayments of principal must be in multiples of $1,000. Loan repayments are on a Fifo basis. Interest is paid only at the time of repayment of principal; however, any interest on unpaid loans should be properly accrued when statements are prepared. The interest rate is 12 percent per annum.

h. Dividends of $1,500 will be declared and paid in September.

i. Balances in various balance sheet accounts at June 30 follow:

Cash	$ 6,000
Accounts receivable	24,000
Inventory	26,250
Fixed assets, net	150,000
Accounts payable	16,625
Capital stock..........................	175,000
Retained earnings	14,625

Required:

Using the data above, complete the following statements and schedules:

1.   Schedule of expected cash collections:

	July	August	September	Total
Cash sales	$20,000			
Credit sales	24,000			
Total collections	$44,000			

2.   *a.*   Purchases budget:

	July	August	September	Total
Purchases for current sale	$ 8,750*			
Purchases for inventory	33,600†			
Total purchases........	$42,350			

* For July sales: $50,000 × 70% cost ratio = $35,000 × 25% = $8,750.
† For August sales: $64,000 × 70% cost ratio = $44,800 × 75% = $33,600.

b. Schedule of cash disbursements for purchases:

	July	August	September	Total
For June purchases	$16,625			
For July purchases	21,175			
For August purchases				
For September purchases				
Total	$37,800			
Less 2% discount	756			
Net cash disbursements	$37,044			

3. Schedule of cash disbursements for expenses:

	July	August	September	Total
Salaries and wages	$ 7,500			
Rent	2,200			
Other expenses	2,500			
Total cash disbursements ...	$12,200			

4. Cash budget:

	July	August	September	Total
Cash balance, beginning	$ 6,000			
Add cash collections	44,000			
Total cash available	$50,000			
Less disbursements:				
For inventory purchases	$37,044			
For expenses	12,200			
For equipment purchases	—			
For dividends	—			
Total disbursements	$49,244			
Excess (deficiency) of cash	756			
Financing:				
Etc.				

5. Prepare an income statement for the quarter ending September 30.
6. Prepare a balance sheet as of September 30.

P7–21. *Monthly cash budget.* The directors of Royal Company, Ltd., of which you are accountant, decide that in the future a short-term cash budget should be prepared for each quarter. Your company sells directly to the public for cash and through trade outlets on credit terms of 2/10, n/30. The accounts receivable have been analyzed and show the following record of collection:

70 percent of credit sales collected within the discount period.
20 percent collected at the end of the 30-day period.
Balance collected at the end of a 60-day period.

At the end of any month, 25 percent of sales on which the cash discounts will be taken are still uncollected. Estimated sales for your first quarterly cash budget are as follows:

	19x1		
	January	February	March
Cash sales	$31,000	$38,000	$45,500
Credit sales	74,000	79,000	85,000

Royal Company, Ltd., makes purchases of goods for resale by paying for goods as delivered. By so doing they obtain a cash discount of 3 percent.

The markup presently in effect provides a gross margin of 33 percent on sales (before cash discounts).

Sufficient inventory is to be on hand at the end of each month to provide for the sales needs of the following month. Sales at retail for April are budgeted at $135,000. Sales peak in April, and then trend downward.

Expenses are estimated as follows:

	Selling	General
Fixed expenses............	$6,000 per month	$10,000 per month
Variable expenses	10% of sales	5% of sales

Expenses are paid monthly as they arise.

Ten percent of fixed expenses represents depreciation and amortization of deferred charges.

A piece of land priced at $30,000 is under option. Your cash budget will indicate to the directors whether or not they can purchase the land for cash on March 31, 19x1. Cash must be available to pay a quarterly dividend of $7,500 on preferred shares on March 31. The purchase of land must not affect the general current position of the company.

The following information is from the December 31, 19x0, balance sheet:

Cash $29,000
Accounts receivable 20,000*
Inventory at gross cost 70,000

* Credit sales for December were $31,580, of which $15,000 is still outstanding. November sales still outstanding are $4,000. $1,000 is uncollectible.

Required:

1. Prepare a schedule of expected cash collections for each of the months January–March. (Round all amounts to the nearest dollar.)
2. Prepare a schedule showing expected disbursements for inventory purchases for each of the months January–March.
3. Prepare a cash budget for each of the months January–March, and for the quarter in total. Will the company be able to purchase the land, as desired? Explain.

(SMA, adapted)

P7–22. *Master budget, with supporting budgets.* You have just been hired as a new management trainee by Super Sales Company, a nationwide distributor of a revolutionary new cigarette lighter. The company has an exclusive franchise on distribution of the lighter, and sales have grown so rapidly over the last few years that it has become necessary to add new members to the management team. You have been given direct responsibility for all planning and budgeting. Your first assignment is to prepare a master budget for the next three months, starting April 1. You are anxious to make a favorable impression on the president, and have assembled the information below.

The company desires a minimum ending cash balance each month of $10,000. The lighters are forecasted to sell for $8 each. Recent and forecasted sales in units are:

January (actual) 20,000	April 35,000	July 40,000
February (actual) 24,000	May 45,000	August 36,000
March (actual) 28,000	June 60,000	September 32,000

The large buildup in sales before and during the month of June is due to Father's Day. Ending inventories are supposed to equal 90 percent of the next month's sales in units. The lighters cost the company $5 each.

Purchases are paid for as follows: 50 percent in the month of purchase, the remaining 50 percent in the following month. All sales are on credit, with no discount, and payable within 15 days. The company has found, however, that only 25 percent of a month's sales are collected by month-end. An additional 50 percent is collected in the month following, and the remaining 25 percent collected in the second month following. Bad debts have been negligible.

The company's monthly operating expenses are given below:

Variable:
  Sales commissions . . . . . $1 per
                                lighter
Fixed:
  Wages and salaries $36,000
  Utilities   1,000
  Insurance expired   1,200
  Depreciation   1,500
  Miscellaneous   2,000

All operating expenses are paid during the month, in cash, with the exception of depreciation and insurance expired. New fixed assets will be purchased during May, for $25,000 cash. The company declares dividends of $12,000 each quarter, payable in the first month of the following quarter. Super Sales Company's balance sheet at March 31 is given below:

Assets

Cash	$ 14,000
Accounts receivable ($48,000 February sales; $168,000 March	
sales)...	216,000
Inventory (31,500 units).....................................	157,500
Unexpired insurance	14,400
Fixed assets, net of depreciation	172,700
Total assets	$574,600

Liabilities and Equity

Accounts payable, purchases	$ 85,750
Dividends payable	12,000
Capital stock, no par	300,000
Retained earnings	176,850
Total liabilities and equity	$574,600

Super Sales Company can borrow money from its bank at 10 percent annual interest. All borrowing must be made at the beginning of a month, and repayments must be made at the end of a month. Interest is computed and paid only when the principal is repaid. Repayments of principal must be in round $1,000 amounts. Borrowing can be in any amount.

Required:

Prepare a master budget for the three-month period ending June 30. Include the following detailed budgets:

1. *a.* A sales budget, by month and in total.
    b. A schedule of budgeted cash collections from sales and accounts receivable, by month and in total.
    c. A purchases budget in units and in dollars. Show the budget by month and in total.
    d. A schedule of budgeted cash payments for purchases, by month and in total.
2. A cash budget. Show the budget by month and in total.
3. A budgeted income statement for the three-month period ending June 30. Use the contribution approach.
4. A budgeted balance sheet as of June 30.

P7–23. *Tabulation approach to EOQ.* (Appendix) Yales Jewelers, Inc., purchases 30,000 one-quarter carat diamonds each year for various mountings. Pertinent information relating to the diamonds is given below:

Purchase cost per diamond	$30
Cost to carry one diamond in inventory	
for one year	5
Cost of placing one order to the	
company's supplier	40

The maximum order which the insurance company will permit is 1,500 diamonds. The minimum order which the supplier will permit is 300 diamonds, with all orders required to be in multiples of 300 diamonds. The company has been purchasing in the maximum allowable volume of 1,500 diamonds per order.

Required:

1. By use of the tabulation approach to EOQ, determine the volume in which the company should be placing its diamond orders.
2. Compute the annual cost savings that will be realized if the company purchases in the volume you have determined in (1) above, as compared to its present purchase policy.

P7–24. *Safety stocks.* (Appendix)   Marcy's, Inc., a large department store, has made a study of the sales of one of its most popular lines. The study covered a period of 100 weeks, and revealed the following sales of the line, in units:

(1) Number of weeks	(2) Sales in units	Weighted sales in units (1) × (2)
2 100		200
6 200		1,200
12 250		3,000
20 300		6,000
24 350		8,400
16 400		6,400
10 450		4,500
6 500		3,000
4 600		2,400
100		35,100

Weighted average sales = 351 units per week.

The lead time required to receive an order of this line from the supplier is one week. The following additional data are available:

Economic order quantity .... 684 units
Cost to place one order $20
Annual carrying cost per unit 3

Required:

1. Assume that no safety stock is to be provided. What is the reorder point? What percentage of the weeks will stockouts occur?
2. Assume that the store can tolerate no stockouts. What size safety stock in units would be required?
3. Assume that a 96 percent protection against stockouts is adequate. What size safety stock in units would be required? What would be the cost of maintaining this safety stock?
4. As a manager, how would you use the cost data computed in (3) in determining whether the safety stock is justified?

P7–25. *Economic order quantity and safety stock.* (Appendix)   Dexter Manufacturing Company uses 100,000 units of Material A each year. The material is used evenly throughout the year in the company's production process. A recent cost study indicates that it costs $0.60 to carry one unit of Material A in stock for a year. The company estimates that the cost of placing an order for Material A is $75.

On the average, it takes six days to receive an order from the supplier. Occasionally, orders do not arrive for 9 days, and at rare intervals (about 1 percent of the time) orders do not arrive for 11 days. Each unit of Material A costs the Dexter Manufacturing Company $4. The company works an average of 360 days per year. Round all figures to the nearest whole unit.

Required:

1. Compute the economic order quantity.
2. What size safety stock would you recommend for Material A? Why?
3. What is the reorder point for Material A in units?
4. Compute the *total cost* associated with ordering and carrying Material A for a year.

P7–26. *Inventory control systems.* (Appendix) You have been engaged to install an accounting system for the Kaufman Corporation. Among the inventory control features Kaufman desires in the system are indicators of "how much" to order "when." The following information is furnished for one item, called a "komtronic," which is carried in inventory:

a. Komtronics are sold by the gross (12 dozen) at a list price of $800 per gross, f.o.b. shipper. Kaufman receives a 40 percent trade discount off list price on purchases in gross lots.

b. Freight cost is $20 per gross from the shipping point to Kaufman's plant.

c. Kaufman uses about 5,000 komtronics during a 259-day production year but must purchase a total of 36 gross per year to allow for normal breakage. Minimum and maximum usages are 12 and 28 komtronics per day, respectively.

d. Normal delivery time to receive an order is 20 working days from the date a purchase request is initiated. A stockout (complete exhaustion of the inventory) of komtronics would stop production, and Kaufman would purchase komtronics locally at list price rather than shut down.

e. The cost of placing an order is $30.

f. Space storage cost is $24 per year per average gross in storage.

g. Insurance and taxes are approximately 12 percent of the net delivered cost of average inventory, and Kaufman expects a return of at least 8 percent on its average investment (ignore ordering costs and carrying costs in making these computations.)

Required:

1. Prepare a schedule computing the total annual cost of komtronics based on uniform order lot sizes of one, two, three, four, five, and six gross of komtronics. (The schedule should show the total annual cost according to each lot size.) Indicate the economic order quantity.

2. Prepare a schedule computing the minimum stock reorder point for komtronics. This is the point below which reordering is necessary to guard against a stockout. Factors to be considered include average lead period usage and safety stock requirements.

(AICPA, adapted)

P7–27. *Integration of purchases budget, reorder point, and safety stock.* (Appendix) The Press Company manufactures and sells industrial components. The Whitmore Plant is responsible for producing two components referred to as AD-5 and FX-3. Plastic, brass, and aluminum are used in the production of these two products.

Press Company has adopted a 13-period reporting cycle in all of its plants for budgeting purposes. Each period is four weeks long and has 20 working days. The projected inventory levels for AD-5 and FX-3 at the end of the current (seventh) period and the projected sales for these two products for the next three four-week periods are presented below.

Component	Projected inventory level (in units) end of seventh period	Projected sales (in units) Eighth period	Ninth period	Tenth period
AD-5	3,000	7,500	8,750	9,500
FX-3	2,800	7,000	4,500	4,000

Past experience has shown that adequate inventory levels for AD-5 and FX-3 can be maintained if 40 percent of the next period's projected sales are on hand at the end of a reporting period. Based on this experience and the projected sales, the Whitmore Plant has budgeted production of 8,000 AD-5 and 6,000 of FX-3 in the eighth period. Production is assumed to be uniform for both products within each four-week period.

The raw material specifications for AD-5 and FX-3 are as follows:

	AD-5 (lbs.)	FX-3 (lbs.)
Plastic	2.0	1.0
Brass	0.5	—
Aluminum	—	1.5

Data relating to the purchase of raw materials are presented below.

	Purchase price per pound	Standard purchase lot (lbs.)	Reorder point (lbs.)	Projected inventory status at the end of the seventh period (lbs.) On hand	On order	Lead time in working days
Plastic	$0.40	15,000	12,000	16,000	15,000	10
Brass	0.95	5,000	7,500	9,000	—	30
Aluminum	0.55	10,000	10,000	14,000	10,000	20

The sales of AD-5 and FX-3 do not vary significantly from month to month. Consequently, the safety stock incorporated into the reorder point for each of the raw materials is adequate to compensate for variations in the sales of the finished products.

Raw material orders are placed the day the quantity on hand falls below the reorder point. Whitmore Plant's suppliers are very dependable so that the given lead times are reliable. The outstanding orders for plastic and aluminum are due to arrive on the tenth and fourth working days of the eighth period respectively. Payments for all raw material orders are remitted in the month of delivery.

Required:

Whitmore Plant is required to submit a report to corporate headquarters of Press Company summarizing the projected raw material activities before each period commences. The data for the eighth period report are being assembled. Determine the following items for plastic, brass, and aluminum for inclusion in the eighth period report:

1. Projected quantities (in pounds) of each raw material to be issued to production.
2. Projected quantities (in pounds) of each raw material ordered and the date (in terms of working days) the order is to be placed.
3. The projected inventory balance (in pounds) of each raw material at the end of the period.
4. The payments for purchases of each raw material.

(CMA)

Chapter 8

Control through standard costs

In attempting to control costs, managers have two types of decisions to make—decisions relating to prices paid, and to quantities used. Managers are expected to pay the lowest possible prices, consistent with the quality of output desired, in attaining the objectives of their firms. In attaining these objectives the managers are also expected to consume the minimum quantity of whatever resources they have at their command, again consistent with the quality of output desired. Breakdowns in control over either price or quantity will lead to excessive costs and to deteriorating profit margins.

How do managers attempt to control price paid and quantity used? Managers could personally examine every transaction that takes place, but this obviously would be an inefficient use of management time. The answer to the control problem lies in *standard costs*.

STANDARD COSTS—MANAGEMENT BY EXCEPTION

A standard can be defined as a benchmark for measuring performance. Standards are found in many facets of day-to-day life. Students entering a college or university often are required to perform at a certain level on a standard achievement exam as a condition for admittance, the autos we drive are built under exacting engineering standards, and the food we eat is generally prepared under standards of both cleanliness and nutritional content. Standards are also widely used in managerial accounting. Here the standards relate to the *cost* and *quantity* of inputs used in the manufacture of goods or in the providing of services.

Cost and quantity standards are set by managers for all three elements of cost input—materials, labor, and overhead—which we have discussed in preceding chapters. Quantity standards say how much of a cost element, such as labor time, should be used in producing a single unit of product, or in providing a unit of service. Cost standards say what the cost of this amount of time should be. Actual quantities and actual costs of inputs are measured against these standards to see if operations are proceeding within the limits that management has set. If either quantity or cost of inputs exceeds the bounds which management has set, attention is directed to the difference, thereby permitting the manager to focus his or her efforts where they will do the most good. This process is called *management by exception*.

Who uses standard costs?

Manufacturing, service, food, and not-for-profit organizations all make use of standards (either in terms of costs or quantities) to some extent. Auto service centers, for example, often set specific labor time standards for the completion of certain work tasks, such as installing a carburetor, or doing a valve job, and then measure actual performance against these standards. Fast-food outlets such as McDonalds have exacting standards as to the quantity of meat going into a sandwich, as well as standards for the cost of the meat. Hospitals have standard costs (such as for food and laundry) for each occupied bed per day, as well as standard time allowances for the performing of certain routine activities, such as laboratory tests. In short, the business student is likely to run into standard cost concepts in virtually any line of business that she or he may enter.

The broadest application of the standard cost idea is probably found in manufacturing firms, where standards relating to materials, labor, and overhead are developed in detail for each separate product line. These standards are then organized into a *standard cost card* which tells the manager what the final, manufactured cost should be for a single unit of product. In the following section we provide a detailed example of the setting of standard costs and the preparation of a standard cost card.

SETTING STANDARD COSTS

The setting of standard costs is more of an art than a science. It requires the combined thinking and expertise of all persons who have responsibility over prices and quantities of inputs. In a manufacturing setting, this would include the managerial accountant, the purchasing agent, the industrial engineer, production supervisors, and line managers.

The beginning point in setting standard costs is a rigorous look at past experience. The managerial accountant can be of great help in this task by preparing data on the cost characteristics of prior years' activities at various levels of operations. A standard for the future must be more than simply a projection of the past, however. Data must be adjusted and modified in terms of changing economic patterns, demand and supply characteristics, and changing technology. Past experience in certain costs may be distorted due to inefficiencies. To the extent that such inefficiencies can be identified, the data must be appropriately adjusted. The manager must realize that the past is of value only insofar as it helps to predict the future. Standards must be reflective of what costs *should be,* not just what they *have been.*

Ideal versus practical standards

Should standards be attainable all of the time, only part of the time, or should they be so tight that they become, in effect, "the impossible dream"? Opinions among managers vary, but standards tend to fall into one of two categories—either ideal or practical.

Ideal standards are those that can be attained only under the best circumstances. They allow for no machine breakdowns or work interruptions, and call for a level of effort that can be attained only by the most skilled and efficient employee working at peak effort 100 percent of the time. Some managers feel that such standards have a motivational value. These managers argue that even though an employee knows he will never stay within the standard set, it is a constant reminder to him of the need for ever-increasing efficiency and effort. Few firms use ideal standards. Most managers are of the opinion that ideal standards tend to discourage even the most diligent workers. Moreover, when ideal standards are used, variances from standards have little meaning. The reason is that they contain elements of "normal" inefficiency, not just the abnormal inefficiencies that managers would like to have isolated and brought to their attention.

Practical standards can be defined as standards that are "tight, but attainable." They allow for normal machine breakdown time and employee rest periods, and are such that they can be attained through reasonable, though highly efficient, efforts by the average worker at a task. Variances from such a standard are very useful to management in that they represent deviations that fall outside of normal, recurring inefficiencies, and signal a need for management attention. Furthermore, practical standards can serve multiple purposes. In addition to signaling abnormal deviations in costs, they can also be used in forecasting cash flows and in inventory planning. By contrast, ideal standards cannot be used in forecasting and planning; they do not allow for normal inefficiencies, and therefore result in unrealistic planning and forecasting figures.

Throughout the remainder of this chapter we will assume the use of practical, rather than ideal, standards.

Setting direct materials standards

As stated earlier, managers prepare separate standards for price and quantity of inputs. Direct material price standards should reflect the final, delivered cost of materials, net of any discounts taken. For example, the standard price of a pound of Material A might be determined as follows:

Purchase price, top grade, in 500–lb. quantities	$4.00
Freight, by truck, from the supplier's plant	0.28
Receiving and handling	0.05
Less: purchase discount	(0.08)
Standard price per pound	$4.25

Notice that the standard price reflects a particular grade of material (top grade), purchased in particular lot-sizes (500 pounds), and delivered by a particular type of carrier (truck). Allowances have also been made for handling and discounts. If all proceeds according to plans, the net standard price of a pound of Material A should therefore be $4.25.

Direct material quantity standards should reflect the amount of material going into each unit of finished product, as well as an allowance for unavoidable waste, spoilage, and other normal inefficiencies. To illustrate, the standard quantity of Material A going into a unit of product might be determined as follows:

```
Per bill of materials, in pounds ........................ 2.7
Allowance for waste and spoilage, in pounds ............ 0.2
Allowance for rejects, in pounds ....................... 0.1
                                                        ────
Standard quantity per unit of product, in pounds ........ 3.0
                                                        ════
```

A bill of materials is simply a list which shows the quantity of each item of material going into a unit of finished product. It is a handy source for determining the basic material input per unit, but it must be adjusted for waste and other factors, as shown above, in determining the full standard quantity per unit of product. "Rejects" represents the direct material contained in units of product that are rejected at final inspection. The cost of this material must be added back to good units.

Once the price and quantity standards have been set, the standard cost of Material A per unit of finished product can be computed, as follows:

$$3.0 \text{ lbs.} \times \$4.25 = \$12.75 \text{ per unit}$$

This $12.75 cost figure will appear as one item on the standard cost card of the product under consideration.

Setting direct labor standards

Direct labor price and quantity standards are usually expressed in terms of labor rate and labor-hours. The standard direct labor rate would include not only wages earned but also an allowance for fringe benefits and other labor-related costs. The computation might be as follows:

```
Basic wage rate per hour ........................... $7.00
Employment taxes, at 10% of the basic rate ..........  0.70
Fringe benefits, at 25% of the basic rate ...........  1.75
                                                      ─────
Standard rate per direct labor-hour ................ $9.45
                                                      ═════
```

Many companies prepare a single standard rate for all employees in a department, even though the actual wage rates may vary somewhat between employees due to seniority or other reasons. This simplifies the use of standard costs and also permits the manager to monitor the use of employees within departments. More is said on this point a little later. If all proceeds according to plans, the direct labor rate for our mythical company should average $9.45 per hour.

The standard direct labor time required to complete a unit of product is perhaps the single most difficult standard to determine. One approach is to divide each operation performed on the product into elemental body movements (such as reaching, pushing, turning over). Published tables of standard times for such movements are available. These times can be applied to the movements, and then added together to determine the total standard time allowed per operation. Another approach is for an industrial engineer to do a time and motion study, actually clocking the time required for certain tasks. As stated earlier, the standard time developed must include allowances for coffee breaks, personal needs of employees, cleanup, and machine downtime. The resulting standard time might appear as follows:

```
Basic labor time per unit, in hours ..................... 2.0
Allowance for breaks and personal needs .............. 0.1
Allowance for cleanup and machine downtime .......... 0.2
Allowance for rejects ................................... 0.1
Standard hours per unit of product ................... 2.4
```

Once the rate and time standards have been set, the standard labor cost per unit of product can be computed as follows:

$$2.4 \text{ hrs.} \times \$9.45 = \$22.68 \text{ per unit}$$

This $22.68 cost figure will appear along with direct materials as one item on the standard cost card of the product under consideration.

Setting variable overhead standards

As in the case with direct labor, the price and quantity standards for variable overhead are generally expressed in terms of rate and hours. The rate represents *the variable portion of the predetermined overhead rate,* discussed in Chapter 3; the hours represent whatever hours-base is used to apply overhead to units of product (often direct labor-hours, as we learned in Chapter 3). To illustrate, if the variable portion of the predetermined overhead rate was $5 and overhead was applied to units of product on a basis of direct labor-hours, the standard variable overhead cost per unit of product in our example would be:

$$2.4 \text{ hrs.} \times \$5.00 = \$12.00 \text{ per unit}$$

A more detailed look at the setting of overhead standards is reserved until Chapter 9.

To summarize our example on the setting of standard costs, the completed standard cost card for one unit of product in our mythical company is presented in Exhibit 8–1.

Are standards the same as budgets?

Essentially standards and budgets are the same thing. The only distinction between the two terms is that a standard is a *unit* concept, whereas a budget is a *total* concept. That is, the standard cost for materials in a unit of product may be $5. If 1,000 units of the product are to be produced

Exhibit 8–1
Standard cost card—variable production cost

Inputs	(1) Standard quantity or hours	(2) Standard price or rate	Standard cost (1) × (2)
Direct materials	3.0 lbs.	$4.25	$12.75
Direct labor	2.4 hrs.	$9.45	22.68
Variable overhead	2.4 hrs.	$5.00	12.00
Total standard cost per unit			$47.43

during a period, then the budgeted cost of materials is $5,000. In effect, a standard may be viewed as being the *budget for a single unit of product.*

Advantages of standard costs

A number of distinct advantages can be cited in favor of using standard costs in an organization.

1.   As stated earlier, the use of standard costs makes possible the concept of "management by exception." So long as costs remain within the standards set, no attention by management is needed. When costs fall outside of the standards set, then the matter is brought to the attention of management at once as an "exception." "Management by exception" makes possible more productive use of management time.

2.   Standard costs facilitate cash planning and inventory planning.

3.   So long as standards are set on a "practical" basis, they promote economy and efficiency in that employees normally become very cost and time conscious. In addition, wage incentive systems can be tied to a system of standard costs once the standards have been set.

4.   In income determination, a system of standard costs may be more economical and simpler to operate than a historical cost system. Standard cost cards can be kept for each product or operation, and costs for material, labor, and manufacturing overhead charged out according to the standards set. This greatly simplifies the bookkeeping process.

5.   Standard costs can assist in the implementation of "responsibility accounting," in which responsibility over cost control is assigned, and the extent to which that responsibility has been discharged can be evaluated through performance reports.

A GENERAL MODEL FOR VARIANCE ANALYSIS

One reason for separating standards into two categories— price and quantity—is that control decisions relating to price paid and quantity used will generally fall at different points in time. In the case of raw materials, for example, control over price paid comes at the time of purchase. By contrast, control over quantity used does not come until the raw materials are used in production, which may be many weeks or months after the purchase date. In addition, control over price paid and quantity used will generally be the responsibility of two different managers, and will therefore need to be assessed independently. As we have stressed earlier, no manager should be held responsible for a cost over which he or she has no control. It is important, therefore, that we separate price considerations from quantity considerations in our approach to the control of costs.

The general model

A general model exists that is very useful in variance analysis. A *variance* is the difference between *standard* prices and quantities and *actual* prices and quantities. This model, which deals with variable costs,[1] helps to distinguish between *price* variances and *quantity* variances, as well as showing how each of these variances is computed. The model is presented in Exhibit 8–2.

Three things should be noted from the exhibit. First, that a price variance and a quantity variance can be computed for all three variable cost elements—direct materials, direct labor, and variable manufacturing overhead—even though the variance is not called by the same name in all cases. For example, a price variance is called a "materials price variance" in the case of direct materials, but a "labor rate variance" in the case of direct labor and an "overhead spending variance" in the case of variable manufacturing overhead.

Second, even though a price variance may be called by different names, it is computed in exactly the same way regardless of whether one is dealing

Exhibit 8–2
A general model for variance analysis—variable production costs

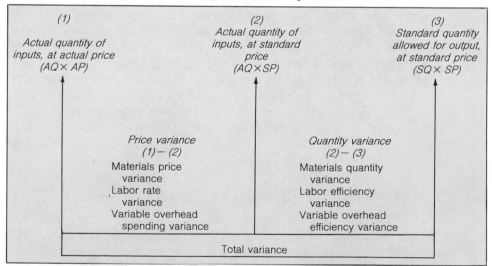

[1] Variance analysis of fixed costs is reserved until Chapter 9.

with direct materials, direct labor, or variable manufacturing overhead. The same is true with the quantity variance.

And third, variance analysis is actually a matter of input/output analysis. The inputs represent the actual quantity of direct materials, direct labor, and variable manufacturing overhead used; the output represents the good production of the period, expressed in terms of the *standard quantity of inputs allowed* in its manufacture (see column 3 in Exhibit 8–2). By standard quantity we mean the amount of direct material, direct labor, or variable manufacturing overhead *that should have been used* to produce what was produced during the period. This might be more or less than what was *actually* used, depending on the efficiency or inefficiency of operations.

With this general model as a foundation, we will now examine the price and quantity variances in more detail.

USING STANDARD COSTS—DIRECT MATERIAL VARIANCES

To illustrate the computation and use of direct material variances we will return to the standard cost data for direct materials contained in Exhibit 8–1. This exhibit shows the standard cost of direct materials per unit of product in our mythical company to be:

$$3.0 \text{ lbs.} \times \$4.25 = \$12.75$$

We will assume that during June the company purchased 2,100 pounds of material at a cost of $4.10 per pound. All of the material was used in the manufacture of 600 units of product. The computation of the price and quantity variances for the month is shown in Exhibit 8–3.

Exhibit 8–3
Variance analysis—direct materials

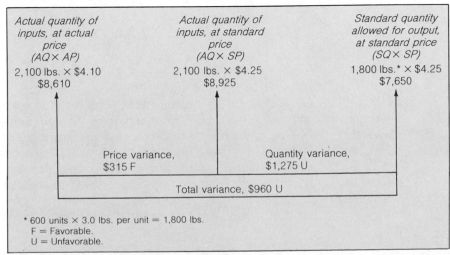

Actual quantity of inputs, at actual price (AQ× AP)	Actual quantity of inputs, at standard price (AQ× SP)	Standard quantity allowed for output, at standard price (SQ× SP)
2,100 lbs. × $4.10 $8,610	2,100 lbs. × $4.25 $8,925	1,800 lbs.* × $4.25 $7,650

Price variance, $315 F   Quantity variance, $1,275 U

Total variance, $960 U

* 600 units × 3.0 lbs. per unit = 1,800 lbs.
F = Favorable.
U = Unfavorable.

A variance is unfavorable if the actual price or quantity exceeds the standard price or quantity; a variance is favorable if the actual price or quantity is less than the standard.

Materials price variance—A closer look

A materials price variance measures the difference between what is paid for a given quantity of materials and what should have been paid according to the standard that has been set. From Exhibit 8–3 this difference can be expressed by the following formula:

$$(AQ \times AP) - (AQ \times SP) = \text{Price variance}$$

The formula can be factored into simpler form as:

$$AQ(AP - SP) = \text{Price variance}$$

Some managers prefer this simpler formula, since it permits variance computations to be made very quickly. Using the data from Exhibit 8–3 in this formula, we have:

$$2,100 \text{ lbs. } (\$4.10 - \$4.25) = \$315 \text{ F}$$

Notice that the answer is the same as that yielded in the exhibit. If the company wanted to put these data into a performance report, it would appear as follows:

MYTHICAL COMPANY
Performance Report–Purchasing Department

	(1)	(2)	(3)	(4)		
				Difference	Total price	
Item	Quantity	Actual	Standard	in price	variance	
purchased	purchased	price	price	(2) − (3)	(1) × (4)	Explanation
Material A	2,100 lbs.	$4.10	$4.25	$.15	$315 F	Second-grade materials purchased, rather than top grade

F = Favorable.
U = Unfavorable.

ISOLATION OF VARIANCES. At what point should variances be isolated and brought to the attention of management? The answer is, the earlier the better. One of the basic reasons for utilizing standard costs is to facilitate cost control. Therefore, the sooner deviations from standard are brought to the attention of management, the sooner problems can be evaluated and corrected. If long periods are allowed to elapse before variances are computed, costs that otherwise could have been controlled may accumulate to the point that significant damage may be done to profits. Most firms compute the materials price variance, for example, when materials are purchased, rather than when the materials are placed into production. This permits earlier isolation of the variance, since materials may lay in the warehouse for many months before being used in production. Isolating the price variance when materials are purchased also permits the company to carry its raw materials in the inventory accounts at standard cost. This greatly simplifies the process of costing materials as they are later placed into production.[2]

Once a performance report has been prepared, what does management do with the price variance data? The variances should be viewed as "red flags," calling attention to the fact that an exception has occurred which will require some follow-up effort. Normally the performance report itself will contain some explanation of the reason for the variance, as shown above.

RESPONSIBILITY FOR THE VARIANCE.   Who is responsible for the materials price variance? Generally speaking, the purchasing agent has control over the price to be paid for goods, and therefore is responsible for any price variances. Many factors control the price paid for goods, including size of lots purchased, delivery method used, quantity discounts available, rush orders, and the quality of materials purchased. To the extent that the purchasing agent can control these factors, he or she is responsible for seeing that they are kept in agreement with the factors anticipated when the standard costs were initially set. A deviation in any factor from what was intended in the initial setting of a standard cost can result in a price variance. For example, purchase of second-grade materials, rather than top grade, would result in a favorable price variance since the lower grade materials would generally be less costly (but perhaps less suitable for production).

There may be times, however, when someone other than the purchasing agent is responsible for a materials price variance. Production may be scheduled in such a way, for example, that the purchasing agent is required to obtain delivery by air freight, rather than by truck, or he or she may be forced to buy in uneconomical quantities. In these cases, the production manager would bear responsibility for variances that develop.

A word of caution is in order. Variance analysis should not be used as an excuse to conduct witch hunts, or as a means of beating line managers over the head. The emphasis must be on the control function in the sense of *supporting* the line managers, and *assisting* them in meeting the goals they have participated in setting for the company. In short, the emphasis must be positive, rather than negative. Excessive dwelling on what has already happened, particularly in terms of trying to find someone to "blame," can often be destructive to the goals of an organization.

---

[2] See the Appendix for an illustration of journal entries in a standard cost system.

Materials quantity variance—A closer look

Although the materials quantity variance is concerned with the physical usage of materials, the variance is generally stated in dollar terms, as shown in Exhibit 8–3. The formula for the materials quantity variance is:

$$(AQ \times SP) - (SQ \times SP) = \text{Quantity variance}$$

Again, the formula can be factored into simpler terms:

$$SP(AQ - SQ) = \text{Quantity variance}$$

Using the data from Exhibit 8–3 in the formula, we have:

$$\$4.25(2,100 \text{ lbs.} - 1,800 \text{ lbs.}^*) = \$1,275 \text{ U}$$

* 600 units $\times$ 3.0 lbs. per unit = 1,800 lbs.

The answer, of course, is the same as that yielded in Exhibit 8–3. The data would appear as follows if a formal performance report was prepared:

MYTHICAL COMPANY
Performance Report—Production Department

Type of materials	(1) Standard price	(2) Actual quantity	(3) Standard quantity allowed	(4) Difference in quantity (2) – (3)	Total quantity variance (1) × (4)	Explanation
Material A	$4.25	2,100 lbs.	1,800 lbs.	300 lbs.	$1,275 U	Second-grade materials, unsuitable for production

U = Unfavorable.
F = Favorable.

The materials quantity variance is best isolated at the time that materials are placed into production. Materials are drawn for the number of units to be produced, according to the standard bill of materials for each unit. Any additional materials are usually drawn on an excess materials requisition slip, which is different in color from the normal requisition slips. This procedure calls attention to the excessive usage of materials *while production is still in process,* and permits opportunity for early control of any developing problem.

Excessive usage of materials can result from many factors, including faulty machines, inferior quality of materials, untrained workers, and poor supervision. Generally speaking, it is the responsibility of the production department to see that material usage is kept in line with standards. There may be times, however, when the *purchasing* department may be responsible for an unfavorable material quantity variance. If the purchasing department obtains materials of inferior quality in an effort to economize on price, the materials may prove to be unsuitable for use on the production line and may result in excessive waste. Thus, purchasing rather than production would be responsible for the quantity variance.

USING STANDARD COSTS—DIRECT LABOR VARIANCES

To illustrate the computation and use of direct labor variances we will use the standard cost data for direct labor contained in Exhibit 8–1. This exhibit shows the standard cost of direct labor per unit of product in our mythical company to be:

$$2.4 \text{ hrs.} \times \$9.45 = \$22.68$$

We will assume that during June the company recorded 1,360 hours of direct labor time. The actual cost of this labor time was $13,260, or an average of $9.75 per hour. Recall that the company produced 600 units of product during June. The computation of the labor rate and efficiency variances for the month is shown in Exhibit 8–4.

Exhibit 8–4
Variance analysis—direct labor

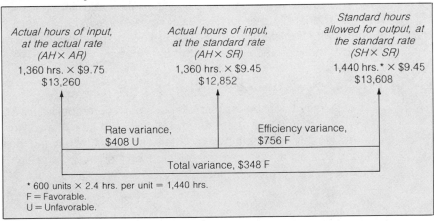

Actual hours of input, at the actual rate (AH× AR)	Actual hours of input, at the standard rate (AH× SR)	Standard hours allowed for output, at the standard rate (SH× SR)
1,360 hrs. × $9.75 $13,260	1,360 hrs. × $9.45 $12,852	1,440 hrs.* × $9.45 $13,608

Rate variance, $408 U — Efficiency variance, $756 F

Total variance, $348 F

* 600 units × 2.4 hrs. per unit = 1,440 hrs.
F = Favorable.
U = Unfavorable.

Notice that the column headings in Exhibit 8–4 are the same as those used in the prior two exhibits, except that in Exhibit 8–4 the terms "hours" and "rate" are used in place of the terms "quantity" and "price."

Labor rate variance—A closer look

As explained earlier, the price variance for direct labor is commonly termed a *rate* variance. This variance measures any deviation from standard in the average hourly rate paid to direct labor workers. From Exhibit 8–4, the formula for the labor rate variance is:

$$(AH \times AR) - (AH \times SR) = \text{Rate variance}$$

It can be factored into simpler form as:

$$AH(AR - SR) = \text{Rate variance}$$

Using the data from Exhibit 8–4 in the formula, we have:

$$1,360 \text{ hrs.}(\$9.75 - \$9.45) = \$408 \text{ U}$$

In many firms the rates paid workers are set by union contract; therefore, rate variances, in terms of amounts paid to workers, tend to be almost nonexistent. Rate variances can arise, though, through the way labor is used. Skilled workers with high hourly rates of pay can be given duties that require little skill and call for low hourly rates of pay. This type of misallocation of the work force will result in unfavorable labor rate variances since the actual hourly rate of pay will exceed the standard rate authorized for the particular task being performed. A reverse situation exists when unskilled or untrained workers are paid hourly rates rather than piecework rates. The low productivity of the unskilled workers will result in unfavorable rate variances. Unfavorable rate variances can also arise from overtime work at premium rates.

Who is responsible for controlling the labor rate variance? Since rate variances generally arise as a result of how labor is used, those supervisors in charge of effective utilization of labor time bear responsibility for seeing that labor rate variances are kept under control.

Labor efficiency variance—A closer look

The quantity variance for direct labor, more commonly called the labor *efficiency* variance, measures the productivity of labor time. No variance is more closely watched by management since increasing productivity of labor time is a vital key to reducing unit costs of production. From Exhibit 8–4, the formula for the labor efficiency variance is:

$$(AH \times SR) - (SH \times SR) = \text{Efficiency variance}$$

Factored into simpler terms, the formula is:

$$SR(AH - SH) = \text{Efficiency variance}$$

Using the data from Exhibit 8–4 in the formula, we have:

$$\$9.45(1,360 \text{ hrs.} - 1,440 \text{ hrs.}) = \$756 \text{ F}$$

where

$$600 \text{ units} \times 2.4 \text{ hrs. per unit} = 1,440 \text{ hrs.}$$

Causes of the labor efficiency variance include poorly trained workers; poor quality materials, requiring more labor time in processing; faulty equipment, causing breakdowns and work interruptions; and poor supervision of workers. Those managers in charge of production would generally be responsible for control of the labor efficiency variance. However, the variance might be chargeable to purchasing if the acquisition of poor quality materials resulted in excessive labor processing time.

USING STANDARD COSTS—VARIABLE OVERHEAD VARIANCES

The variable portion of manufacturing overhead can be analyzed and controlled using the same basic variance formulas as in analyzing direct materials and direct labor. In order to lay a foundation for the following chapter, where we discuss overhead control at length, it will be helpful at this time to illustrate the analysis of variable overhead using these basic formulas. As a basis for discussion, we will again use the cost data found in Exhibit 8–1. The exhibit shows the standard variable overhead cost per unit of product in our mythical company to be:

$$2.4 \text{ hrs.} \times \$5.00 = \$12.00$$

We will assume that the total actual variable overhead cost for the month of June was $7,480. Recall from our earlier discussion that 1,360 hours of direct labor time were recorded during the month, and that the company produced 600 units of product. Exhibit 8–5 contains an analysis of the variable overhead variances.

Notice the similarities between Exhibits 8–4 and 8–5. These similarities arise from the fact that direct labor-hours are being used as a base for allocating overhead to units of product; thus, the same hours figures appear in Exhibit 8–5 for variable overhead as in Exhibit 8–4 for direct labor. The main difference between the two exhibits is in the standard hourly rate being used, which is much lower for variable overhead.

Exhibit 8–5
Variance analysis—variable overhead

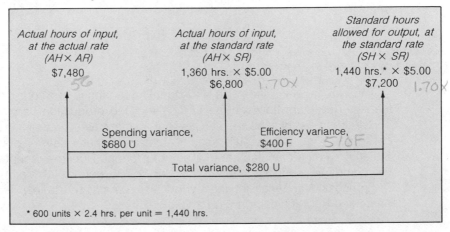

Actual hours of input, at the actual rate (AH × AR)	Actual hours of input, at the standard rate (AH × SR)	Standard hours allowed for output, at the standard rate (SH × SR)
$7,480	1,360 hrs. × $5.00 $6,800	1,440 hrs.* × $5.00 $7,200

Spending variance, $680 U | Efficiency variance, $400 F

Total variance, $280 U

* 600 units × 2.4 hrs. per unit = 1,440 hrs.

Overhead variances—A closer look

The variable overhead spending and efficiency variances can be expressed in formula format, the same as the direct materials and direct labor variances. For the spending variance, the formula is:

$$(AH \times AR) - (AH \times SR) = \text{Spending variance}$$

or, factored into simpler terms:

$$AH(AR - SR) = \text{Spending variance}$$

For the efficiency variance, the formula is:

$$(AH \times SR) - (SH \times SR) = \text{Efficiency variance}$$

or, factored into simpler terms:

$$SR(AH - SH) = \text{Efficiency variance}$$

Using the data from Exhibit 8–5, we see that the computation of the variances using these formulas would be:

Spending variance: 1,360 hrs. ($5.50* − $5.00) = $680 U
Efficiency variance: $5.00(1,360 hrs. − 1,440 hrs.†) = $400 F

* 7,480 ÷ 1,360 hrs. = $5.50
† 600 units × 2.4 hrs. per unit = 1,440 hrs.

We will reserve further discussion of the variable overhead spending and efficiency variances until Chapter 9, where overhead analysis is discussed in depth.

Before proceeding on, it will be helpful for the reader to pause at this point and go back and review the data contained in Exhibits 8–1 through 8–5. These exhibits and the accompanying text discussion represent a comprehensive, integrated illustration of standard setting and variance analysis.

GRAPHICAL ANALYSIS OF THE PRICE AND QUANTITY VARIANCES

The way in which the price and quantity variances are computed can lead to a problem between the purchasing and production departments. The problem can best be seen by presenting these two variances in graphical form. To do this, we will assume that a company uses 4 pounds of Material X in the manufacture of a unit of product. During a recent period, the company produced 450 units, using 2,000 pounds of Material X in the process. Variances for the period are summarized below, and then presented in graphical form in Exhibit 8–6.

Summary of data—Material X

Standard price per pound	$2.00
Actual price per pound	$2.20
Standard quantity for production of 450 units of product (4 lbs. per unit ×	
450 units)...	1,800 lbs.
Actual quantity used in production of 450 units of product	2,000 lbs.

SUMMARY OF VARIANCES—MATERIAL X:

$$AQ(AP- SP) = \text{Price variance}$$
$$2{,}000 \text{ lbs. } (\$2.20 - \$2.00) = \$400 \text{ U}$$
$$SP(AQ- SQ) = \text{Quantity variance}$$
$$\$2.00 \ (2{,}000 \text{ lbs.} - 1{,}800 \text{ lbs.}) = \$400 \text{ U}$$

The problem referred to can arise from the upper right corner of the graph in Exhibit 8–6. This corner represents a *mutual price-quantity variance,* although we have shown it to be part of the price variance in our computations above. The purchasing agent may contend that it is unfair

Exhibit 8–6
Graphical analysis of price and quantity variances

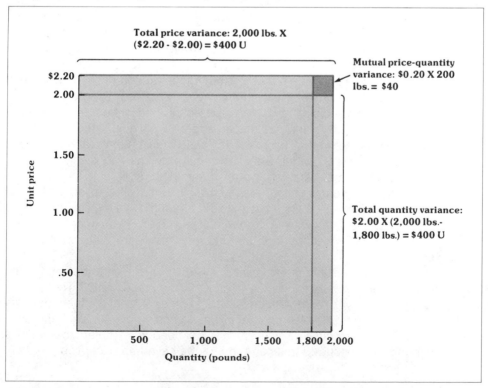

to charge her for the $40 mutual price-quantity variance represented in this corner since it has arisen only because of the inefficient use of materials by the production department. If the production department had produced at standard and used only the 1,800 pounds of materials called for, then the extra 200 pounds of materials wouldn't have been purchased in the first place, and the extra $40 of variance would not have arisen. The purchasing agent may argue, therefore, that the $40 mutual price-quantity variance should be charged to production, not to purchasing.

Whether the mutual price-quantity variance is computed as part of the price variance, as we have done, or as part of the quantity variance, will depend on which variance management feels is most important. Generally speaking, the quantity variance is viewed as being the most important of the two since quantity used tends to be more controllable than price paid. For this reason, most firms will consider the mutual price-quantity variance to be part of the price variance in an effort to keep the quantity variance as "clean" as possible.

VARIANCE ANALYSIS AND MANAGEMENT BY EXCEPTION

Variance analysis and performance reports provide a vehicle for implementation of the concept of management by exception. Simply put, management by exception means that the manager's attention must be directed toward those parts of the organization where things are not proceeding according to plans. Since a manager's time is limited, every hour must be used as effectively as possible, and time and effort not wasted looking after those parts of the organization where things are going smoothly.

The budgets and standards discussed in this and in the preceding chapter represent the "plans" of management. If all goes smoothly then it would be expected that costs will fall within the budgets and standards that have been set. To the extent that this happens, the manager is free to spend time elsewhere with the assurance that, at least in the budgeted areas, all is proceeding according to expectations. To the extent that actual costs and revenues do not conform to the budget, however, a signal comes to the manager that an "exception" has occurred. This exception comes in the form of a variance from the budget or standard that was originally set.

The major question at this point is, "Are *all* variances to be considered exceptions that will require the attention of management?" The answer is no. If every variance was considered to be an exception, then management would get little else done other than chasing down nickel-and-dime differences. Obviously, some criteria are needed to determine when a variance has occurred that can properly be called an exception. We consider some of these criteria below.

Criteria for determining "exceptions"

It is probably safe to say that only by the rarest of coincidences will actual costs and revenues ever conform exactly to the budgeted pattern. The reason is that even though budgets may be prepared with the greatest of care, it will never be possible to develop budgeted data that contain the precise allowances necessary for each of the multitude of variables that can affect actual costs and revenues. For this reason, one can expect that in every period virtually every budgeted figure will produce a variance of some type when compared to actual cost data. How do managers decide which of all of these variances are worthy of their attention? We can identify at least four criteria that are used in actual practice: materiality, consistency of occurrence, ability to control, and nature of the item.

MATERIALITY. Ordinarily, management will be interested only in those variances that are material in amount. To separate the material variances from the immaterial variances, firms often set guidelines, such as stating that any variance that differs from the budget by 10 percent or more will be considered a material variance. Notice that we said "differs" from the budget, not "exceeds" the budget. We say "differs" because management will be just as interested in those material variances that are *under* the budget as they are in those that exceed it. The reason is that a level of spending that is under the budget can be just as critical to profitability as a level of spending that exceeds the budget. For example, if advertising is budgeted to be $100,000 during a period and only $80,000 is spent, this favorable spending variance could be damaging to profits because of insufficient promotion of the firm's products.

Generally, a guideline such as a 10 percent deviation from budget will not be sufficient to judge whether a variance is material. The reason is that a 5 percent variance in some costs could be far more critical to profits than a 20 percent variance in other costs. For this reason, a firm will often supplement the percentage guideline with some minimum absolute dollar figure, stating that even if a variance doesn't exceed the percentage guideline it will still be considered material if it exceeds the minimum dollar figure. To illustrate, a firm might state that any variance will be considered material if it differs from the budget by 10 percent or more, or $1,000.

CONSISTENCY OF OCCURRENCE. Even if a variance never exceeds the minimum stated percentage or the minimum dollar amount, many firms want it brought to the attention of management if it comes *close* to these limits period after period. The thinking here is that the budget or standard could be out of date, and adjustment to more current levels might improve overall profit planning. Or, that some laxness in cost control may be present, warranting an occasional check by the relevant supervisor.

ABILITY TO CONTROL. Some costs are largely out of the control of management, and in such cases even though variances may occur that are material in amount, no follow-up action on management's part is necessary. For example, utility rates and local tax rates are generally not controllable internally, and large variances resulting from rate increases will require little or no follow-up effort, even though they may be presented on the variance report for information purposes.

NATURE OF THE ITEM. By their very nature, some costs are much more critical to long-run profitability than others. One such cost is advertising. As mentioned above, underutilization of the advertising budget can have a severe adverse impact on sales, with a resulting loss of revenue that greatly outweighs any saving in advertising dollars. Another such cost is maintenance. Although inadequate maintenance may produce short-run savings in costs, these savings will likely be more than offset by future breakdowns, repairs, and loss of revenue from reduced productivity and efficiency.

Because of the critical nature of costs such as advertising and maintenance, the guidelines for determining whether a variance is material are usually much more stringent than for other costs. That is, these variances are generally watched more closely by management than those in other, less critical, areas. It may be that management will want to see *any* variance in certain key areas such as advertising and promotion. In addition, the normal guidelines may be reduced by half in other key areas such as maintenance and certain critical component parts.

Statistical analysis of random variances

The purpose of establishing criteria for separating material from immaterial variances is to isolate those variances which are *not* due to random causes, and which can and should be controlled by the company. The "10 percent of budget, or $1,000" approach described in the preceding section is a somewhat crude way of accomplishing this objective, although it is used widely in practice. The approach is crude because it really is based on rough guessing and on rules of thumb rather than on precise analysis.

A much more dependable way of separating random variances from those variances which are controllable can be found in statistical analysis. This approach to segregating random variances has its basis in the idea that a budget or standard represents a *range* of acceptability, rather than a single point. Any variance falling within this range is considered to be due solely to random causes which either are not within the ability of management to control or which would be impractical to control. One author puts the idea this way:

Measured quality of manufactured product is always subject to a certain amount of variation as a result of chance. Some stable "system of chance causes" is inherent in any particular scheme of production and inspection. Variation within this stable pattern is inevitable. The reasons for variation outside this stable pattern [should] be discovered and corrected.[3]

How does a firm isolate the range within which variances from budget will be due to chance or random causes? This is done by means of statistical sampling of the population represented by the budgeted data. Random samples of the population are drawn, and the variances found in these samples are plotted on a *control chart,* such as illustrated in Exhibit 8–7. In effect, the upper and lower limits on the chart represent the normal distribution (bell-shaped curve), with the upper and lower limits generally being three standard deviations from the grand mean. Any variances falling within the upper and lower control limits will be due simply to chance occurrences and, therefore, will not be within the ability of management

Exhibit 8–7
A statistical control chart

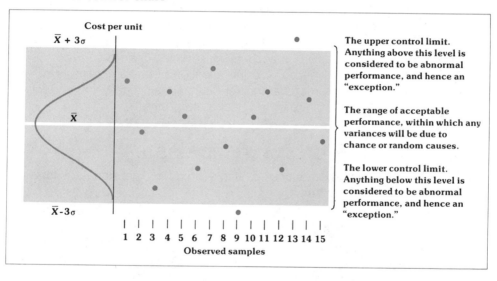

to control. Any variances falling outside of these limits will not be due to random or chance causes, and will be considered "exceptions" toward which management attention will need to be directed.

The value of a budgeting system is greatly increased if variances are analyzed by a statistical approach such as that described above, rather than by the "10 percent or $1,000" approach described earlier. The reason, of course, is that the statistical approach eliminates guesswork and

[3] Eugene L. Grant and Richard L. Leavenworth, *Statistical Quality Control,* 4th ed. (New York: McGraw-Hill Book Company, 1972), p. 3. Used with permission of McGraw-Hill Book Company.

zeros management in on those cost variations that are indeed within its ability to control.[4]

SUMMARY

Cost control centers in two areas—price paid, and quantity used. The best way to effect control in these two areas is through use of standard costs. A standard can be viewed as being the budget for a single unit of product expressed in terms of either price or quantity.

Generally, standards are set by the cooperative effort of many people in an organization, including the accountant, the industrial engineer, and various levels of management. Standards are normally "practical" in nature, meaning that they can be attained by reasonable, though highly efficient, efforts. Such standards are generally felt to have a favorable motivational impact on employees.

Comparing standards against actual performance results in variances. If a variance falls outside of the limits set by management, it is considered to be an exception toward which management time and attention must be directed. Ordinarily, the accounting system will be organized in such a way as to bring exceptions to the attention of management as early in time as possible in order that control may be maintained, and corrections made before significant damage is done to profits.

REVIEW PROBLEM ON STANDARD COSTS

Xavier Company produces a single product. The standard costs for one unit of product are:

Direct material: 6 oz. at $0.50 per oz.	$ 3.00
Direct labor: 2 hrs. at $5.00 per hr.	10.00
Variable overhead: 2 hrs. at $2.00 per hr.	4.00
Total standard variable cost per unit	$17.00

During June, 400 units were produced. The costs associated with the month were:

Material purchased: 4,000 oz. at $0.55	$2,200
Material used in production: 2,800 oz.	—
Direct labor: 890 hrs. at $4.70	4,183
Variable overhead costs incurred	2,047

---

[4] For further discussion of this and other statistical uses in cost analysis, see Joel S. Demski, *Information Analysis* (Reading, Mass: Addison-Wesley Publishing Company, Inc., 1972), chap. 6.

Materials variances

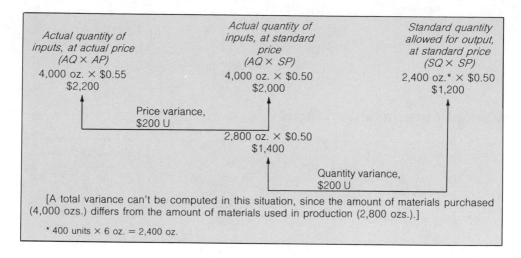

Actual quantity of inputs, at actual price (AQ × AP)	Actual quantity of inputs, at standard price (AQ × SP)	Standard quantity allowed for output, at standard price (SQ × SP)
4,000 oz. × $0.55 $2,200	4,000 oz. × $0.50 $2,000	2,400 oz.* × $0.50 $1,200

Price variance, $200 U

2,800 oz. × $0.50 $1,400

Quantity variance, $200 U

[A total variance can't be computed in this situation, since the amount of materials purchased (4,000 ozs.) differs from the amount of materials used in production (2,800 ozs.).]

* 400 units × 6 oz. = 2,400 oz.

The same variances in shortcut format would be:

$$AQ(AP - SP) = \text{Price variance}$$
$$4,000 \text{ oz. } (\$0.55 - \$0.50) = \$200 \text{ U}$$

$$SP(AQ - SQ) = \text{Quantity variance}$$
$$\$0.50 \ (2,800 \text{ oz. } - 2,400 \text{ oz.}) = \$200 \text{ U}$$

· Notice that the price variance is computed on the entire amount of material purchased (4,000 ounces), whereas the quantity variance is computed only on the portion of this material used in production during the period (2,800 ounces). This is a common situation. The price variance is always computed on whatever materials have been purchased. The quantity variance, however, can only be computed on that portion of the purchased materials *actually used* during the period.

Labor variances

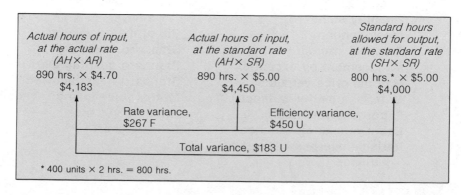

Actual hours of input, at the actual rate (AH × AR)	Actual hours of input, at the standard rate (AH × SR)	Standard hours allowed for output, at the standard rate (SH × SR)
890 hrs. × $4.70 $4,183	890 hrs. × $5.00 $4,450	800 hrs.* × $5.00 $4,000

Rate variance, $267 F   Efficiency variance, $450 U

Total variance, $183 U

* 400 units × 2 hrs. = 800 hrs.

The same variances in shortcut format would be:

$$AH(AR - SR) = \text{Rate variance}$$
$$890 \text{ hrs. } (\$4.70 - \$5.00) = \$267 \text{ F}$$

$$SR(AH - SH) = \text{Efficiency variance}$$
$$\$5.00 (890 \text{ hrs. } - 800 \text{ hrs.}) = \$450 \text{ U}$$

Variable overhead variances

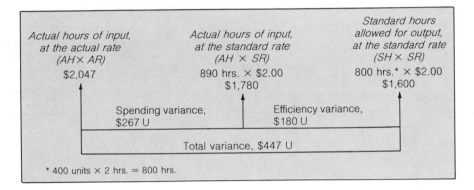

Actual hours of input, at the actual rate $(AH \times AR)$	Actual hours of input, at the standard rate $(AH \times SR)$	Standard hours allowed for output, at the standard rate $(SH \times SR)$
$2,047	890 hrs. × $2.00 $1,780	800 hrs.* × $2.00 $1,600
	Spending variance, $267 U	Efficiency variance, $180 U
	Total variance, $447 U	

* 400 units × 2 hrs. = 800 hrs.

The same variances in shortcut format would be:

$$AH(AR - SR) = \text{Spending variance}$$
$$890 \text{ hrs. } (\$2.30^* - \$2.00) = \$267 \text{ U}$$

$$SR(AH - SH) = \text{Efficiency variance}$$
$$\$2.00 (890 \text{ hrs. } - 800 \text{ hrs.}) = \$180 \text{ U}$$

* $2,047 ÷ 890 hrs. = $2.30.

KEY TERMS FOR REVIEW

Price standard
Quantity standard
Ideal standard
Practical standard
Management by exception
Material price variance
Material quantity variance
Labor rate variance
Labor efficiency variance
Variable overhead spending variance

Variable overhead efficiency variance
Bill of materials
Standard cost card
Standard quantity allowed
Standard hours allowed
Mutual price-quantity variance
Random variance
Control chart

APPENDIX: GENERAL LEDGER ENTRIES TO RECORD VARIANCES

Although standard costs and variances can be computed and used by management without being formally entered into the accounting records, most organizations prefer to make formal entries, for three reasons. First, entry into the accounting records encourages early recognition of variances. As mentioned in the main body of the chapter, the earlier that variances can be recognized, the greater their value to management in the control of costs. Second, formal entry tends to give variances a greater emphasis than generally is possible through informal, out-of-record computations, thus communicating throughout the organization management's keen interest in keeping cost flows within the limits that have been set. And third, formal use of standard costs simplifies the bookkeeping process. By using standard costs within the accounting system itself, management eliminates the need to keep track of troublesome variations in actual costs and quantities, thereby providing for a flow of costs that is smoother, simpler, and more easily accounted for.

Direct materials variances

To illustrate the general ledger entries needed to record standard cost variances, we will return to the data contained in the review problem at the end of the chapter. The entry to record the purchase of direct materials would be:

```
Raw Materials (4,000 ozs. at $0.50) . . . . . . . . . . . . . 2,000
Materials Price Variance (4,000 ozs. at $0.05 U) . . .   200
    Accounts Payable (4,000 ozs. at $0.55) . . . . . . .            2,200
```

Notice that the price variance is recognized at the time purchases are made, rather than later when materials are actually used in production. This permits the price variance to be isolated early, and also permits the materials to be carried in the inventory account at standard cost. As direct materials are later drawn from inventory and used in production, the quantity variance is isolated, as follows:

```
Work in Process (2,400 ozs. at $0.50) . . . . . . . . . . . 1,200
Materials Quantity Variance (400 ozs. U at $0.50) . .   200
    Raw Materials (2,800 ozs. at $0.50) . . . . . . . . . .            1,400
```

Thus, direct materials enter into the Work in Process account at standard cost, both in terms of price and quantity.

Notice that both the price variance and the quantity variance above are unfavorable, thereby showing up as debit (or additional cost) balances.

If these variances had been favorable, they would have appeared as credit (or reduction in cost) balances, as in the case of the direct labor rate variance below.

Direct labor variances

Referring again to the cost data in the review problem at the end of the chapter, the general ledger entry to record the incurrence of direct labor cost would be:

```
Work in Process (800 hrs. at $5) ............... 4,000
Labor Efficiency Variance (90 hrs. U at $5) ........   450
     Labor Rate Variance (890 hrs. at $0.30 F) .....            267
     Wages Payable (890 hrs. at $4.70)  .........           4,183
```

Thus, as in the case with direct materials, direct labor costs enter into the Work in Process account at standard, both in terms of the rate and the hours allowed for the production of the period.

Variable overhead variances

Variable overhead variances generally aren't recorded in the accounts separately, but rather determined as part of the general analysis of overhead, which is discussed in Chapter 9.

QUESTIONS

8–1. What is a quantity standard? What is a price standard?

8–2. What is the beginning point in setting a standard? Where should final responsibility for standard setting fall?

8–3. Why must a standard for the future be more than simply a projection of the past?

8–4. What types of organizations make use of standard costs?

8–5. Distinguish between ideal and practical standards.

8–6. If employees are unable to meet a standard, what effect would you expect this to have on their productivity?

8–7. What is the difference between a standard and a budget?

8–8. What is meant by the term "variance"?

8–9. What is meant by the term "management by exception"?

8–10. Why are variances generally segregated in terms of a price variance and a quantity variance?

8–11. Who generally is responsible for the materials price variance? The materials quantity variance? The labor efficiency variance?

8–12. An examination of the cost records of the Chittenden Furniture Company indicates that the materials price variance is favorable, but that the materials quantity variance is unfavorable by a substantial amount. What might this indicate?

8–13. What dangers lie in using standards as punitive tools?

8–14. "Our workers are all under labor contracts; therefore, our labor rate variance is bound to be zero." Discuss.

8–15. Why is the mutual price-quantity variance generally buried in the price variance, rather than in the quantity variance?

8–16. If variable manufacturing overhead is applied to production on a basis of direct labor-hours and the direct labor efficiency variance is unfavorable, will the variable overhead efficiency variance be favorable, be unfavorable, or could it be either? Explain.

8–17. What factors are considered by management in determining whether a variance is properly called an exception?

8–18. What is a statistical control chart, and how is it used?

EXERCISES

E8–1. The direct materials and direct labor standards for one bottle of Product 412 are given below:

	Standard quantity	Price or rate	Standard cost
Direct materials	7.5 ounces	$1.50 per ounce	$11.25
Direct labor	0.5 hours	$6 per hour	3.00

During a recent period, the following activity took place:
a. 15,000 ozs. of material were purchased at a cost of $1.25 per oz.
b. All of the material purchased was used to produce 1,760 bottles of Product 412.
c. 835 hours of direct labor time were recorded during the period at a total labor cost of $5,177.

Required:

1. Compute materials price and quantity variances for the period.
2. Compute labor rate and efficiency variances for the period.

E8–2. Harmon Household Products, Inc., manufactures a number of consumer items for general household use. One of these products, a chopping board, requires an expensive hardwood in its manufacture. During a recent month, the company manufactured 4,000 chopping boards, using 11,200 board feet of hardwood in the process. The hardwood cost the company $13,552.

The company's standards for one chopping board are 2.5 board feet of hardwood, at a cost of $1.30 per board foot.

Required:

1. What cost should have been incurred in the manufacture of the 4,000 chopping blocks? How much greater or less is this than the cost that was incurred?

2. Break the difference computed in (1) down in terms of a material price variance and a material quantity variance.

E8–3. Vincent Corporation produces machine tools for industry. The company uses standards to control its costs. The labor standards which have been set for one very popular machine tool are:

Direct labor time per tool .... 15 minutes
Direct labor rate per hour $5.20

During 19x5, the company worked 7,750 hours in order to produce 30,000 of these tools. The direct labor cost amounted to $39,525.

Required:

1. What direct labor cost should have been incurred in the manufacture of the 30,000 machine tools? By how much does this cost differ from the cost that was incurred?
2. Break the difference in cost from (1) down in terms of a labor rate variance and a labor efficiency variance.
3. For each direct labor-hour worked, the company expects to incur $5 in variable overhead cost. This rate was experienced in 19x5. What effect did the efficiency (or inefficiency) of labor have on variable overhead cost in 19x5?

E8–4. The auto repair shop of Divan Motor Sales uses standards to control labor time and labor cost in the shop. The standard time for a motor tune-up is 2.5 hours. The record showing time spent in the shop last week on tune-ups has been misplaced; however, the shop supervisor recalls that 50 tune-ups were completed during the week and the controller recalls that the labor rate variance on tune-ups was $87, favorable. The shop has set a standard labor rate of $9 per hour for tune-up work. The total labor variance for the week on tune-up work was $93, unfavorable.

Required:

1. Determine the number of actual hours spent on tune-up work last week.
2. Determine the actual hourly rate of pay for tune-up work last week.

E8–5. The direct material and direct labor standards per unit of Product A are given below:

	Standard quantity	Price or rate	Standard cost
Direct material	8 feet	$0.50 per foot	$4
Direct labor	2 hours	$4 per hour	8

During the month of June, the following activity occurred:
a. 6,000 feet of material were purchased at a cost of $0.48 per foot.
b. 5,400 feet of material were used to produce 650 units of Product A.
c. 1,365 hours of direct labor time were worked to produce the 650 units of Product A. The cost of labor time averaged $3.90 per hour.

Required:

1. Compute the material price and quantity variances that would have resulted from the June activities.

2. Compute the labor rate and efficiency variances that would have resulted from the June activities.
3. Prepare journal entries to record all activity relating to direct materials and direct labor for the month of June.

E8–6. Zonka Toys, Ltd., produces toys for national distribution. The management has recently established a standard cost system to control costs. The standards on a particular toy are:

Materials: 12 pieces per toy at $0.56 per piece.
Labor: 2 hours per toy at $3.75 per hour.

During the month of August 19x1 the company produced 1,000 toys. Production data for the month follow:

Materials: 17,500 pieces were purchased for use in production, at a total cost of $8,925, of which 3,500 pieces were still in inventory at the end of the month.
Labor: 2,500 hours were worked, at a cost of $10,500.

Required:

1. Compute the materials price and quantity variances and the labor rate and efficiency variances for the month.
2. Prepare a brief memo for management, giving the significance and possible explanation of each variance.

(SMA, adapted)

E8–7. Diehl Company produces a powerful cleaning solvent. Each quart of solvent requires an input of 1.2 quarts of material X and 1.5 pounds of material Y. (A portion of material X is lost in evaporation during production.)

Material X is purchased in 15-gallon containers, at a cost of $45 per container. Discount terms of 2/10, n/30 are offered by the supplier. Diehl Company takes all discounts available. Freight is paid by the supplier.

Material Y is purchased in 100-pound cartons, at a cost of $40 per carton. No discount terms are available. Diehl Company must pay all freight charges, which amount to $58 for an average shipment of 50 cartons.

About 2 percent of material Y is wasted in shipment.

Required:

Compute the standard material cost for one quart of cleaning solvent. (Carry all computations to three decimal places.)

E8–8. The following data are available on the single product produced by the Cates Company:

	Direct materials	Direct labor
Standard quantity per unit............	3 feet	? hours
Standard price or rate	$5 per foot	? per hour
Standard cost per unit	$15	?

During the most recent period the company paid $55,650 for direct materials, all of which was used in the production of 3,200 units of the product, and worked 4,900 direct labor-hours at a cost of $36,750. The following variance data are available:

Materials quantity variance .... $4,500 U
Total labor variance .... 1,650 F
Labor efficiency variance .... 800 U

Required:

1. Compute the actual cost paid per foot for direct materials.
2. Compute the materials price variance.
3. Compute the standard direct labor rate per direct labor-hour.
4. Compute the standard hours allowed for the production of the period and per unit.

(Hint: In completing the exercise, it may be helpful to move from known to unknown data in the variance formulas.)

PROBLEMS

P8–9. *Setting labor standards.* The Mason Company is going to expand its punch press department. The company is about to purchase several new punch presses from Equipment Manufacturers, Inc. Equipment Manufacturers' engineers report that their mechanical studies indicate that for Mason's intended use, the output rate for one press should be 1,000 pieces per hour. Mason Company has similar presses now in operation. At the present time, production from these presses averages 600 pieces per hour.

A detailed study of the Mason Company's experience shows that the average is derived from the following individual outputs:

Worker	Output per hour (pieces)
J. Smith	750
H. Brown	750
R. Jones	600
J. Hardy	550
P. Clark.............................	500
B. Randall	450
Total........................	3,600
Average	600

Mason's management also plans to institute a standard cost accounting system in the near future. The company's engineers are supporting a standard based upon 1,000 pieces per hour, the accounting department is arguing for a standard of 750 pieces per hour, and the department supervisor is arguing for a standard of 600 pieces per hour.

Required:

1. What arguments would each proponent be likely to use to support his or her case?
2. Which alternative best reconciles the needs of cost control and motivation for improved performance? Explain the reasons for your choice.

(CMA, adapted)

P8–10. *Straightforward variance analysis.* The standard cost sheet for one of the products produced by Advance Template Design, Inc., is presented below:

Direct materials	8 feet at $3	$24
Direct labor	2 hours at $4.50	9
Variable overhead	2 hours at $4	8
Total standard cost per unit		$41

During a recent month, the following activity occurred:

a. Actual production, 800 units.
b. Materials purchased, 8,000 feet at $3.12.
c. There was no beginning inventory of materials on hand at the start of the month; at the end of the month 1,200 feet of the materials purchased during the month were still on hand unused.
d. Direct labor cost incurred (1,550 hours), $7,285.
e. Variable overhead cost incurred, $6,045.

Required:

1. Compute the direct materials price and quantity variances.
2. Compute three variances each (one of the variances will be a total variance) for direct labor and variable overhead. The variable overhead rate is based on direct labor-hours.
3. If overhead is applied to production on a basis of direct labor-hours, is it possible to have a favorable direct labor efficiency variance and an unfavorable variable overhead efficiency variance? Explain.

P8–11. *Variances; Unit costs; Journal entries.* Wickingham Mills, Inc., is a large producer of men and women's clothing. The company uses standard costs for all of its products. The standard costs and actual costs for a recent period are given below for one of the company's product lines (per unit of product):

	Standard cost	Actual cost
Materials:		
Standard: 4.0 yards at $2.10 per yard	$ 8.40	
Actual: 4.4 yards at $2.00 per yard		$ 8.80
Labor:		
Standard: 1.6 hours at $4.50 per hour	7.20	
Actual: 1.4 hours at $4.85 per hour		6.79
Variable overhead:		
Standard: 1.6 hours at $1.80 per hour	2.88	
Actual: 1.4 hours at $2.15 per hour		3.01
Total cost	$18.48	$18.60

During this period the company produced 4,800 units of product. A comparison of standard and actual costs for the period on a total cost basis is given below:

Actual costs: 4,800 units at $18.60		$89,280
Standard costs: 4,800 units at $18.48		88,704
Difference in cost		$ 576

There was no inventory of materials on hand to start the period. During the period, 21,120 yards of materials were purchased, all of which was used in production.

Required:

1. For direct materials:
   a. Compute the price and quantity variances for the period.
   b. Prepare journal entries to record all activity relating to direct materials for the period.
2. For direct labor:
   a. Compute the rate and efficiency variances.
   b. Prepare a journal entry to record the incurrence of direct labor cost for the period.
3. Compute the variable overhead spending and efficiency variances.
4. On seeing the $576 total cost variance, the company's president stated, "This variance of $576 is only 0.6 percent of the $88,704 standard cost for the period. It's obvious that our costs are well under control." Do you agree? Explain.
5. State the possible causes of each variance which you have computed.

P8–12. *The impact of variances on unit costs; Variance analysis.* Metal Specialties, Inc., produces a number of products. The standards relating to one of these products are shown below, along with actual cost data for the month of May (per unit):

	Standard cost	Actual cost
Direct materials:		
Standard: 1.5 pounds at $1.40 per pound	$2.10	
Actual: 1.48 pounds at $1.50 per pound		$2.22
Direct labor:		
Standard: 0.40 hours at $4.50 per hour	1.80	
Actual: 0.45 hours at $4.40 per hour..........		1.98
Variable overhead:		
Budget: 0.40 hours at $3.00 per hour	1.20	
Actual: 0.45 hours at $2.80 per hour..........		1.26
Total per unit cost	$5.10	$5.46
Increase in per unit cost over standard		$0.36

When the production superintendent saw these unit cost figures, he stated, "This is no good. We sell these units for only $5.50 each. If they are costing us $5.46 each to produce, that leaves a contribution margin of only $0.04. We've got to isolate and correct the cost problem. We can't stay in business with a four-cent contribution margin."

Actual production for the month was 11,000 units.

Required:

1. Compute the following variances for the month of May:
   a. Material price and quantity.

    b. Labor rate and efficiency.

    c. Overhead spending and efficiency.

  2. Show how much of the $0.36 excessive unit cost is traceable to each of the variances computed in (1) above.

  3. Show how much of the $0.36 excessive unit cost is traceable to the inefficient use of labor time.

P8–13. *Setting materials and labor standards.* The Scera Company manufactures trivets. The company is just starting to use standard costs. From accounting records, industrial engineering studies, and other sources the following information has been developed:

    a. The clocked labor time to produce one trivet (good or defective) is 1.5 hours.

    b. Ten percent of all completed trivets are scrapped as defective. The scrapped trivets have no monetary value.

    c. The materials required in the production of one trivet (good or defective) are:

Material	Quantity required per trivet	Invoice cost	Freight
H–4	3.6 qts.*	$3 per qt.	$0.10 per qt.
H–11	2.7 lbs.	$4 per lb.	$0.20 per lb.

    * After spillage or evaporation loss.

    d. All materials are purchased subject to a 2 percent cash discount if paid within ten days. All discounts are taken.

    e. Only 80 percent of Material H-4 finds its way into a trivet. The remainder is lost through spillage or evaporation.

    f. The labor rate is $6 per hour.

    g. Coffee breaks, clean-up, and so on, consumes about 0.8 hours of labor time each eight-hour day. The company works a 40-hour week.

Required:

  1. Compute the standard quantity of Material H-4 and the standard quantity of Material H-11 for each acceptable trivet, allowing for the normal loss factors mentioned above.

  2. Compute the standard cost of each type of material per acceptable trivet.

  3. Compute the standard amount of labor time per acceptable trivet, again allowing for normal loss factors.

  4. Compute the standard labor cost per acceptable trivet.

P8–14. *Variance analysis; Incomplete data; Journal entries.* Super Surf Boards manufactures a single product. The standard cost of one unit of this product is:

Direct materials: 6 feet at $1.00	$ 6.00
Direct labor: 1 hour at $4.50	4.50
Variable overhead: 1 hour at $3.00	3.00
Total standard variable cost per unit	$13.50

During the month of October, 6,000 units were produced. Selected cost data relating to the month's production follow:

Material purchased: 60,000 feet at $0.95 . . . . $57,000
Material used in production: 38,000 feet . . . . —
Direct labor: ? hours at $? per hour 27,950
Variable overhead cost incurred 20,475
Variable overhead efficiency variance . . . . 1,500 U

There was no beginning inventory of raw materials. The variable overhead rate is based on direct labor-hours.

Required:

1. For direct materials:
   a. Compute the price and quantity variances for the month.
   b. Prepare journal entries to record activity for the month.
2. For direct labor:
   a. Compute the rate and efficiency variances for the month.
   b. Prepare a journal entry to record labor activity for the month.
3. For variable overhead:
   a. Compute the spending variance for the month, and prove the efficiency variance given above.
   b. If overhead is applied to production on a basis of direct labor-hours, is it possible to have a favorable direct labor efficiency variance and an unfavorable overhead efficiency variance? Explain.
4. State the possible causes of each variance which you have computed.

P8–15. *Reports for management; Preparation of a variance report.* Quality Plastic Products uses a standard cost system for planning and control purposes. Management has been unhappy with the system in that great difficulty has been experienced in trying to interpret the reports coming from the accounting department, and in trying to determine how to control the variances being reported. A typical report is shown below. This report contains cost variance data for the month of July on one of the company's products.

	Total	Per unit
Excess plastic used in production	$ 370	$0.74
Excess direct labor cost incurred	600	1.20
Excess variable overhead cost incurred	240	0.48
Total excess cost incurred	$1,210	$2.42

During July, 500 units of this product were produced. The per unit actual costs of production were:

Plastic: 3.8 pounds at $4.30 per pound $16.34
Direct labor: 0.8 hour at $5.25 per hour 4.20
Variable overhead: 0.8 hour at $3.60 . . . . 2.88
Total actual cost per unit $23.42

The standard cost of one unit of product is given below:

Plastic: 3.9 pounds at $4.00 per pound $15.60
Direct labor: 0.6 hour at $5.00 per hour 3.00
Variable overhead: 0.6 hour at $4.00 per hour 2.40
Total standard cost per unit $21.00

Quality Plastic Products has hired you, as an expert in cost analysis, to help management clarify the reports coming from accounting.

Required:

1. What criticisms can be made of the cost variance reports presently being prepared by accounting?
2. Prepare a report which will give management better insight into the causes of the $1,210 excess cost incurred during July. This report should include detailed variances for materials, labor, and overhead, on both a total and a per unit basis.

P8-16. *Standards and variances from incomplete data.* The following information is available on the single product produced by Carbo-Weld, Inc., for the month of March:

	Materials used	Direct labor	Variable overhead
Total standard cost*	$260	$1,900	$950
Actual costs incurred	276	?	985
Materials price variance	?		
Materials quantity variance	20F		
Labor rate variance		?	
Labor efficiency variance		?	
Overhead spending variance			?
Overhead efficiency variance			?

* For the month's production.

The following additional information is available for March production:

Number of units produced 100
Actual direct labor-hours 410
Standard overhead rate per hour $2.50
Standard price of one pound of materials $0.40
Overhead is based on .... Direct labor-hours
Difference between standard and actual cost per unit
  produced during March $1.19U

Required:

1. What is the standard cost of a single unit of product?
2. What was the actual cost of a unit of product produced during March?
3. How many pounds of material are required at standard per unit of product?
4. What was the materials price variance for March?
5. What was the labor rate variance? The labor efficiency variance?
6. What was the overhead spending variance? The overhead efficiency variance?

7. Devise a method to prove the accuracy of the variances for the month. [Hint: In devising a method, it may be helpful to use certain data from (1) and (2) above.]

P8–17. *Multiple products; Standard costs; Variance analysis.* Frank Company produces two products, both of which pass through two operations. The company uses a standard cost system, with standard usage of materials and labor as follows for each product (on a per unit basis):

	Raw materials (pounds)		Standard labor time (hours)	
Product	A	B	Operation 1	Operation 2
Awls	1.5	3.0	2	3
Pows	2.0	3.4	1	4

Selected information relating to materials purchased and materials used in production last month follows:

Material	Purchases (pounds)	Purchase cost	Standard price per pound	Usage (pounds)
A	2,400	$11,760	$4.50	1,800
B	4,100	24,190	6.25	3,900

The following additional information is available:

a. The standard labor rate is $6.50 per hour in Operation 1, and $8.00 per hour in Operation 2.
b. Last month 1,700 direct labor-hours were worked in Operation 1, and 4,450 direct labor-hours were worked in Operation 2. The labor cost was $12,070 and $33,820 in the two operations, respectively.
c. Last month 600 awls were completed, and 550 pows were completed. There was no work in process inventory at either the beginning or the end of the month.

Required:

1. In terms of materials and labor, compute the standard cost of one unit of each product.
2. a. Compute the price variance for each material.
   b. Compute the quantity variance for each material, in terms of both pounds and dollars.
3. a. Compute the labor rate variance for each operation.
   b. Compute the labor efficiency variance for each operation, in terms of both hours and dollars.
4. When might it be better to express variances in units (pounds, hours) rather than in dollars? In dollars rather than in units?

P8–18. *Multiple products; Incomplete data; Journal entries.* Cutter Pharmaceutical Company produces two products, Milex and Silex, in Department 4. Materials and other inputs into each product are shown below:

	Per batch		Standard price or rate
	Milex	Silex	
Direct materials:			
Material A	2 lbs.	1 lb.	$4 per lb.
Material B	—	3 lbs.	$3 per lb.
Material C	1 gal.	1 gal.	$5 per gal.
Direct labor	0.8 hrs.	1.5 hrs.	$8 per hr.
Variable overhead	0.8 hrs.	1.5 hrs.	$3 per hr.

During the month of March, the company produced 900 batches of Milex and 1,200 batches of Silex. The following additional information is available:

a. Materials purchased during the month:

	Amount (pounds)	Purchase cost
Material A	3,600	$14,940
Material B	3,800	10,830
Material C	—	—

b. Inventories on hand at the start of the month:

	Amount	Inventory cost
Material A	500 lbs.	$ 2,000
Material B	400 lbs.	1,200
Material C	2,500 gal.	12,500

c. Materials issued into production during the month:

	Amount	Cost
Material A	3,450 lbs.	?
Material B	3,500 lbs.	?
Material C	2,400 gal.	?

d. Total actual direct labor cost for the month was $20,250.
e. Total actual variable overhead cost for the month was $8,775. Variable overhead is allocated to production on a basis of direct labor-hours.
f. The variable overhead efficiency variance was $540, unfavorable.
g. There was no work in process at the beginning or end of the month.

Required:

1. Determine the standard variable cost of one batch of each product.
2. Determine the actual number of direct labor-hours worked during the month.
3. For direct materials:
    a. Compute the price variance for each material purchased. Prepare a journal entry to record each purchase.

       b. Compute the quantity variance for the month for each material. Prepare journal entries to record the placing of materials into production.

4. For direct labor:
    a. Compute the rate and efficiency variances for the month.
    b. Prepare a journal entry to record the incurrence of direct labor cost for the month.

5. State the possible causes of each variance which you have computed.

P8–19. *Standard costs and variance analysis.* Arnett Company produces a single product in its factory, and uses a standard cost system. According to the standards which have been set, the factory should work 145 direct labor-hours each week, and produce 2,900 units of product. The standard costs associated with this level of production activity are:

	Total	Per unit of product
Direct materials	$3,770	$1.30
Direct labor	696	0.24
Variable overhead (based on direct labor-hours)	435	0.15
		$1.69

During the first week of June, the factory worked 140 direct labor-hours, and produced 2,940 units of product. The following actual costs were recorded during the week:

	Total	Per unit of product
Direct materials (1,500 yds.)	$3,969	$1.35
Direct labor	735	0.25
Variable overhead	294	0.10
		$1.70

Each unit of product should require only 0.5 yards of material.

Required:

For the first week of June, compute:

1. The materials price and quantity variances.
2. The labor rate and efficiency variances.
3. The variable overhead spending and efficiency variances.

(Hint: Take care that you don't try to mix apples and oranges in your variance analysis!!)

P8–20. *Variance analysis; Multiple lots.* Ricardo Shirts, Inc., manufactures short- and long-sleeved men's shirts for large stores. Ricardo produces a single-quality shirt in lots to each customer's order and attaches the store's label to each. The standard direct costs for a dozen long-sleeved shirts include:

Direct materials: 24 yards at $0.65 . . . . $15.60
Direct labor: 3 hours at $7.25 . . . .   21.75

During April, Ricardo worked on three orders for long-sleeved shirts. Job cost records for the month disclose the following:

Lot	Units in lot (dozens)	Materials used (yards)	Hours worked
30	1,000	24,100	2,980
31	1,700	40,440	5,130
32	1,200	28,825	2,890

The following additional information is available:

a. Ricardo purchased 95,000 yards of material during the month at a cost of $66,500.
b. Direct labor cost incurred amounted to $80,740 during April.
c. There was no work in process at April 1. During April, lots 30 and 31 were completed, and all material was issued to lot 32, which was 80 percent completed as to labor.

Required:

1. Compute the materials price variance for April, and show whether the variance was favorable or unfavorable.
2. Determine the materials quantity variance for the month in both yards and dollars:
   a. For the company in total.
   b. For each lot worked on during the month.
3. Compute the labor rate variance for April, and show whether the variance was favorable or unfavorable.
4. Determine the labor efficiency variance for the month in both hours and dollars:
   a. For the company in total.
   b. For each lot worked on during the month.
5. In what situations might it be better to express variances in units (e.g., hours, yards, and so on) rather than in dollars? In dollars rather than in units?

(AICPA, adapted)

P8–21. *Fragmentary data; Journal entries; Unit costs.* You have just been hired by Barfex Company, which manufactures cough syrup. The syrup requires two materials, A and B, in its manufacture, and is produced in batches. The company uses a standard cost system, with the controller preparing variances on a weekly basis. These variances are discussed in a meeting attended by all relevant managers. The meeting to discuss last week's variances is tomorrow, and since you will be working initially in the planning and control area the president thinks this would be a good chance for you to get acquainted with the company's control system, and has asked that you attend and be prepared to participate fully in the discussion. Accordingly, you have taken home the controller's figure sheet containing last week's variances, as well as the ledger pages from which these variances were derived. You are sure that with a little study you'll be able to make a sterling impression, and be launched into a bright and successful career.

After completing your study that night, the weather being warm and humid you leave your windows open upon retiring, only to arise the next morning horrified to discover that a sudden shower has obliterated most of the controller's figures (left laying on a table by an open window). Only the following fragments are readable:

Raw Materials—A		**Wages Payable**	
Bal. 6/1 600			1,725
- - - - - - - - - -	- - - - - - - -		
Bal. 6/7 1,380			

Raw Materials—B		**Material A—Price Variance**	
Bal. 6/1 0	600	220	
- - - - - - - - - -	- - - - - - - -		
Bal. 6/7 200			

Work in Process		**Material B—Quantity Variance**	
Bal. 6/1 0			40
Material A 2,400			
- - - - - - - - - -	- - - - - - - -		
Bal. 6/7 0			

Accounts Payable		**Labor Efficiency Variance**	
	4,240	240	

Not wanting to admit your carelessness to either the president or the controller, you have decided that your only alternative is to reproduce the obliterated data. From your study last night you recall the following:

a. The wages payable are only for direct labor.

b. The accounts payable are for purchases of both Material A and B.

c. The standard cost of Material A is $6 per gallon, and the standard quantity is 5 gallons per batch of syrup.

d. Purchases last week were: Material A: 550 gallons; Material B: 200 pounds.

e. The standard rate for direct labor is $8 per hour; a total of 230 actual hours were worked last week.

Required:

1. How many batches of syrup were produced last week? (Double check this figure before going on!)

2. For Material A:
   a. How many gallons were used in production last week?
   b. What was the quantity variance?
   c. What was the cost of Material A purchased during the week?
   d. Prepare journal entries to record all activity relating to Material A during the week.
3. For Material B:
   a. What is the standard cost per pound of Material B?
   b. How many pounds of Material B were used in production last week? How many pounds should have been used at standard?
   c. What is the standard quantity of Material B per batch?
   d. What was the price variance for Material B?
   e. Prepare journal entries to record all activity relating to Material B during the week.
4. For direct labor:
   a. What were the standard hours allowed for last week's production?
   b. What are the standard hours per batch?
   c. What was the direct labor rate variance?
   d. Prepare a journal entry to record all activity relating to direct labor during the week.
5. In terms of materials and labor, compute the standard cost of one batch of syrup.

Chapter 9

Flexible budgets and overhead analysis

There are four problems involved in overhead cost control. First, manufacturing overhead is usually made up of many (perhaps scores) of separate costs. Second, these separate costs are often very small in dollar amount, making it highly impractical to control the costs the same way that direct materials and direct labor costs are controlled. Third, these small, separate costs are often the responsibility of different managers. And fourth, manufacturing overhead costs vary in behavior, some being variable, some fixed, and some mixed in nature.

Most of these problems can be overcome by use of a *flexible budget.* In this chapter we study flexible budgets, and their use in overhead cost control. We also expand the study of overhead variances which we started in Chapter 8.

FLEXIBLE BUDGETS

Characteristics of a flexible budget

The budgets we studied in Chapter 7, including the sales budget, the production budget, and the cash budget all have two points in common:

1. They are geared toward a single level of activity.
2. They are *static* in nature. Comparison of actual results is made against the original single level of activity.

The flexible budget is different from other budgets on both of these points. It does not confine itself to a single level of activity, but rather is geared toward a *range* of activity. Also, the flexible budget is *not* static in nature. A budget can be constructed, *even after the fact,* to compare against any level of actual activity and costs within the relevant range. Hence, the term "flexible" budget. In sum, the characteristics of a flexible budget are:

1. It is geared toward a *range* of activity rather than toward a single level of activity.
2. It is *dynamic* in nature rather than static. A budget can be tailored for any level of activity, even after the period's activity is over. That is, a manager can look at what activity level *was attained* during a period, and then turn to the flexible budget to determine what costs *should have been* at that activity level.

Deficiencies of the static budget

To illustrate the difference between a static budget and a flexible budget, let us assume that the Assembly Operation of Rocco Company has budgeted to produce 10,000 units during March. The variable overhead budget which has been set is shown in Exhibit 9–1.

Exhibit 9-1

ROCCO COMPANY
Static Budget
Assembly Operation
For the Month of March 19x1

Budgeted production in units	10,000
Budgeted variable overhead costs:	
Indirect materials	$1,000
Lubricants	800
Power	500
Total	$2,300

Let us assume that the production goal of 10,000 units is not met. The company is able to produce only 9,000 units during the month. *If a static budget approach is used,* the performance report for the month will appear as shown in Exhibit 9–2.

What's wrong with this report? The deficiencies of the static budget can be explained as follows. A production manager has two prime responsibilities to discharge in the performance of his or her duties—*production control* and *cost control.* Production control is involved with seeing that production goals in terms of output are met. Cost control is involved with seeing that output is produced at the least possible cost, consistent with quality standards. These are different responsibilities, and must be kept separate in attempting to assess how well the production manager is doing his or her job. The main difficulty with the static budget is that it fails completely to distinguish between the production control and the cost control dimensions of a manager's performance.

Of the two, the static budget does a good job of measuring only whether

Exhibit 9-2

ROCCO COMPANY
Static Budget Performance Report
Assembly Operation
For the Month of March 19x1

	Budget	Actual	Variance
Production in units	10,000	9,000	1,000 U
Variable overhead costs:			
Indirect materials	$1,000	$ 910	$ 90 F*
Lubricants	800	730	70 F*
Power	500	475	25 F*
Total	$2,300	$2,115	$185 F*

* These cost variances are useless, since they have been derived by comparing actual costs at one level of activity against budgeted costs at a *different* level of activity.

production control is being maintained. Look again at the data in Exhibit 9–2. The data on the top line relate to the production superintendent's responsibility for production control. These data for Rocco Company properly reflect the fact that production control was not maintained during the month. The company failed to meet its production goal by 1,000 units.

The remainder of the data on the report deal with cost control. These data are useless in that they are comparing apples to oranges. Although the production manager may be very proud of the favorable cost variances, they tell nothing about how well costs were controlled during the month. The problem is that the budget costs are based on an activity level of 10,000 units, whereas actual costs were incurred at an activity level substantially below this (only 9,000 units). From a cost control point of view, it is total nonsense to try to compare costs at one activity level to costs at a different activity level. Such comparisons will always make a production manager look good so long as the actual production is less than the budgeted production.

How the flexible budget works

The basic idea of the flexible budget approach is that, through a study of cost behavior patterns, a budget can be prepared that is geared to a *range* of activity rather than to a single level. The basic steps in preparing a flexible budget are:

1. Determine the relevant range over which activity is expected to fluctuate during the coming period.
2. Analyze costs that will be incurred over the relevant range in terms of determining cost behavior patterns (variable, fixed, mixed).
3. Separate costs by behavior, determining the formula for variable and mixed costs, as discussed in Chapter 4.
4. Using the formula for the variable portion of the costs, prepare a budget showing what costs will be incurred at various points throughout the relevant range.

To illustrate, let us assume that Rocco Company's production normally fluctuates between 8,000 and 11,000 units each month. A study of cost behavior patterns over this relevant range has revealed the following formulas for the variable portion of overhead:

Cost	Variable cost formula (per unit)
Indirect materials	$0.10
Lubricants	$0.08
Power	$0.05

Based on these cost formulas, a flexible budget for Rocco Company would appear as follows:

Exhibit 9-3

```
ROCCO COMPANY
Flexible Budget
Assembly Operation
For the Month of March 19x1
```

Budgeted production in units 10,000

	Cost formula (per unit)	Range of production in units			
		8,000	9,000	10,000	11,000
Variable overhead costs:					
Indirect materials	$0.10	$ 800	$ 900	$1,000	$1,100
Lubricants	0.08	640	720	800	880
Power	0.05	400	450	500	550
Total	$0.23	$1,840	$2,070	$2,300	$2,530

USING THE FLEXIBLE BUDGET. Once the flexible budget is prepared, the manager is ready to compare actual results for a period against the comparable budget level anywhere within the relevant range. The manager isn't limited to a single budget level as with the static budget. To illustrate, let us again assume that Rocco Company is unable to meet its production goal of 10,000 units during the month of March. As before, we will assume that only 9,000 units are produced. Under the flexible budget approach, the performance report would appear as follows:

Exhibit 9-4

```
ROCCO COMPANY
Performance Report
Assembly Operation
For the Month of March 19x1
```

Budgeted production in units 10,000
Actual production in units 9,000

	Budget 9,000 units	Actual 9,000 units	Spending variance
Variable overhead costs:			
Indirect materials	$ 900	$ 910	$10 U*
Lubricants	720	730	10 U*
Power	450	475	25 U*
Total	$2,070	$2,115	$45 U*

* These cost variances are usable in evaluating cost control, since they have been derived by comparing actual costs and budgeted costs at the *same* level of activity.

In contrast to the performance report prepared earlier under the static budget approach (Exhibit 9-2), this performance report distinguishes clearly between production control and cost control. The production data at the top of the report indicate whether the production goal was met. The cost data at the bottom of the report tell how well costs were controlled for the 9,000 units that actually were produced.

Notice that all cost variances are *unfavorable,* as contrasted to the *favorable* cost variances on the performance report prepared earlier under the static budget approach. The reason for the change in variances is that by means of the flexible budget approach we are able to compare budgeted and actual costs at *the same activity level* (9,000 units produced), rather than being forced to compare budgeted costs at one activity level against actual costs at a different activity level. In effect, using a flexible budget makes it possible for us to compare apples to apples, rather than forcing us to compare apples to oranges. The result shows up in more usable variances.

A DYNAMIC TOOL. Even if actual activity results in some odd figure that does not appear in the flexible budget, such as 9,200 units, budgeted costs can still be prepared to compare against actual costs. One simply develops a budget at the 9,200-unit level by using the cost formulas contained in the flexible budget. Herein lies the strength and dynamic nature of the flexible budget approach. It is possible to develop a budget, *after the fact,* for *any* activity level within the relevant range by simply applying the cost formulas.

The measure of activity—A critical choice

In the Rocco Company example we chose to use units of production as the activity base for developing a flexible budget. Rather than units of production we could have used some other base such as direct labor-hours or machine-hours. What is "best" in terms of an activity base will vary from firm to firm. At least three factors should be considered in the activity base decision:

1. The existence of a causal relationship between the activity base and overhead costs.
2. The avoidance of dollars in the activity base itself.
3. The selection of an activity base that is simple and easily understood.

CAUSAL RELATIONSHIP. There should be a direct causal relationship between the activity base and a company's variable overhead costs. That is, the variable overhead costs should vary as a result of changes in the activity base. In a machine shop, for example, one would expect that power usage and other variable overhead costs would vary in relationship to the number of machine-hours worked. Machine-hours would therefore be the proper base to use in the flexible budget.

Other common activity bases include direct labor-hours, miles driven by salespersons, contacts made by salespersons, number of invoices processed, number of beds in a hospital, and number of X rays given. Any one of these could be used as the base for preparing a flexible budget in the proper situation.

DO NOT USE DOLLARS. The activity base should be expressed in units rather than in dollars, whenever possible. If dollars are used, they should be standard dollars rather than actual dollars.

The problem with dollars is that they are subject to price-level changes, which can cause a distortion in the activity base if it is expressed in dollar terms. A similar problem arises when wage-rate changes take place, if direct labor cost is being used as the activity base in a flexible budget. The change in wage rates will cause the activity base to change, even though no change will have taken place in the overhead costs themselves. These types of fluctuations generally make dollars difficult to work with, and argue strongly for units rather than dollars in the activity base. The use of *standard* dollar costs, rather than *actual* dollar costs, overcomes the problem to some degree, but standard costs still have to be adjusted from time to time as changes in actual costs take place. On the other hand, *units* as a measure of activity (beds, hours, miles, and so on) are subject to few distorting influences, and are less likely to cause problems in preparing and using a flexible budget.

KEEP THE BASE SIMPLE. The activity base should be simple and easily understood. A base that is not easily understood by the manager who works with it day by day will probably result in confusion and misunderstanding rather than serve as a positive means of cost control.

THE OVERHEAD PERFORMANCE REPORT— A CLOSER LOOK

A special problem arises in preparing overhead performance reports when the flexible budget is based on *hours* of activity such as direct labor-hours, rather than on units of product. The problem relates to what hour base to use in constructing budget allowances on the performance report.

The problem of budget allowances

The nature of the problem can best be seen through a specific example. Assume that the Packaging Operation of the Condor Corporation is budgeting its activities for the month of June. The flexible budget which has been prepared is shown in Exhibit 9–5.

As shown in Exhibit 9–5, the company uses machine-hours as an activity base in its flexible budget, and has budgeted to operate at an activity level of 6,500 machine-hours during the month. Let us assume that two machine-hours are required to produce one unit of output. Under this assumption, budgeted production for the month is 3,250 units (6,500 budgeted machine-hours ÷ 2 hours per unit = 3,250 units). After the month

Exhibit 9–5

	CONDOR CORPORATION Flexible Budget Packaging Operation				

Budgeted machine-hours 6,500

	Cost formula (per machine- hour)	Machine-hours			
		5,000	5,500	6,000	6,500
Variable overhead costs:					
Indirect labor	$0.12	$ 600	$ 660	$ 720	$ 780
Lubricants	0.08	400	440	480	520
Maintenance	0.02	100	110	120	130
Total variable	$0.22	$1,100	$1,210	$1,320	$1,430

is over, suppose the company finds that actual production for the month was 2,900 units, and that it required 6,000 hours of machine time to produce these units. A summary of actual activity and costs for the month follows:

Number of machine-hours worked	6,000	
Number of units produced	2,900	
		Actual costs incurred
Indirect labor		$ 780
Lubricants		360
Maintenance		300
Total actual costs		$1,440

In preparing a performance report for the month, what hour base should the Condor Corporation use in computing budget allowances to compare against actual results? There are two possibilities. The company could use:

1. The 6,000 hours *actually worked* during the month.
2. The 5,800 hours that *should have been worked* during the month to produce 2,900 units of output (since it should take 2 hours to produce one unit).

Which base the company chooses will depend on how much detailed variance information it wants. As we learned in the preceding chapter, variable overhead can be analyzed in terms of a *spending* variance and an *efficiency* variance. The two bases provide different variance output.

Spending variance alone

If the Condor Corporation chooses alternative 1, and bases its performance report on the 6,000 hours actually worked during the period, then the performance report will show only a spending variance for overhead. A performance report prepared this way is shown in Exhibit 9–6.

The formula behind the spending variance was introduced in the preceding chapter. For review, that formula is:

$$(AH \times AR) - (AH \times SR) = \text{Spending variance}$$

or, in factored form:

$$AH(AR - SR) = \text{Spending variance}$$

The report in Exhibit 9–6 is prepared around the first, or unfactored, format.

Exhibit 9–6

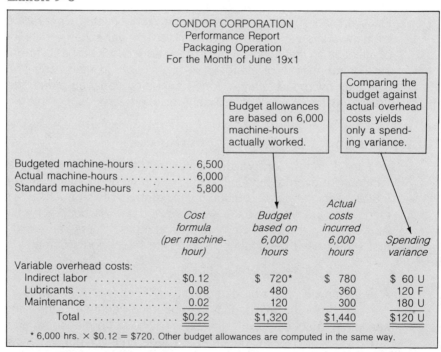

CONDOR CORPORATION
Performance Report
Packaging Operation
For the Month of June 19x1

Budget allowances are based on 6,000 machine-hours actually worked.

Comparing the budget against actual overhead costs yields only a spending variance.

Budgeted machine-hours 6,500
Actual machine-hours 6,000
Standard machine-hours 5,800

	Cost formula (per machine-hour)	Budget based on 6,000 hours	Actual costs incurred 6,000 hours	Spending variance
Variable overhead costs:				
Indirect labor	$0.12	$ 720*	$ 780	$ 60 U
Lubricants	0.08	480	360	120 F
Maintenance	0.02	120	300	180 U
Total	$0.22	$1,320	$1,440	$120 U

* 6,000 hrs. × $0.12 = $720. Other budget allowances are computed in the same way.

INTERPRETING THE SPENDING VARIANCE.   The overhead spending variance is affected by two things. First, a spending variance may occur simply because of price increases over what is shown in the flexible budget. For the Condor Corporation this means that prices paid for overhead items may have gone up during the month, resulting in unfavorable spending variances. This portion of the overhead spending variance is just like the price variance for raw materials.

Second, the overhead spending variance is affected by waste or excessive usage of overhead materials. A first reaction is to say that waste or excessive usage of materials ought to show up as part of the efficiency variance. But this isn't true so far as overhead is concerned. Waste or excessive usage will show up as part of the spending variance. The reason is that the overhead spending variance measures more than just deviations in price paid; it measures deviations in the amount *spent* for overhead items. Total spending can be affected as much by waste as it can by higher than expected prices.

In sum, the overhead spending variance contains both price and quantity (waste) elements. These two elements could be broken out and shown separately on the performance report, but this is rarely done in actual practice.

USEFULNESS OF THE SPENDING VARIANCE. Most firms consider the overhead spending variance to be highly useful. Generally the price element in this variance will be small, so the variance permits a focusing of attention on that thing over which the supervisor probably has the greatest control—usage of overhead in production. In many cases, firms will limit their overhead analysis to the spending variance alone, feeling that the information it yields is sufficient for overhead cost control.

Both spending and efficiency variances

If the Condor Corporation wants both a spending and an efficiency variance for overhead, then it should compute budget allowances for *both* 5,800 machine-hour and 6,000 machine-hour levels of activity. The 5,800 machine-hours would be the *standard hours of production* for the month. As defined in the preceding chapter, standard hours represent the time that should have been taken to complete the period's output:

2,900 units × 2 standard hours per unit = 5,800 standard hours

A performance report prepared this way is shown in Exhibit 9–7.

Notice from the exhibit that the spending variance is the same as the spending variance shown in Exhibit 9–6. The performance report in Exhibit 9–7 has simply been expanded to include an efficiency variance as well. Together, the spending and efficiency variances make up the total variance, as explained in the preceding chapter.

INTERPRETING THE EFFICIENCY VARIANCE. The term "overhead efficiency variance" is a misnomer, since this variance has nothing to do with efficiency in the use of overhead. What the variance really measures is how efficiently the *base* underlying the flexible budget is being utilized in production. Recall from the preceding chapter that the variable overhead efficiency variance is a function of the difference between the actual hours

Exhibit 9–7

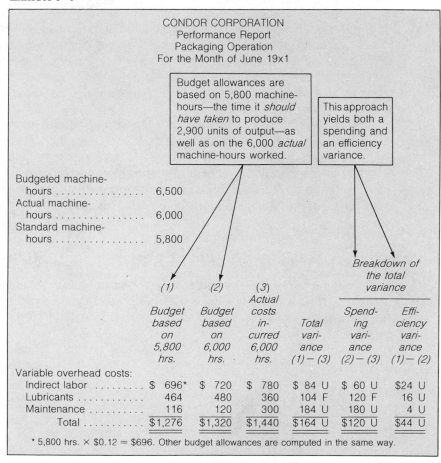

CONDOR CORPORATION
Performance Report
Packaging Operation
For the Month of June 19x1

Budget allowances are based on 5,800 machine-hours—the time it *should have taken* to produce 2,900 units of output—as well as on the 6,000 *actual* machine-hours worked.

This approach yields both a spending and an efficiency variance.

Budgeted machine-hours 6,500
Actual machine-hours 6,000
Standard machine-hours 5,800

Breakdown of the total variance

	(1) Budget based on 5,800 hrs.	(2) Budget based on 6,000 hrs.	(3) Actual costs in-curred 6,000 hrs.	Total vari-ance (1) − (3)	Spend-ing vari-ance (2) − (3)	Effi-ciency vari-ance (1) − (2)
Variable overhead costs:						
Indirect labor	$ 696*	$ 720	$ 780	$ 84 U	$ 60 U	$24 U
Lubricants	464	480	360	104 F	120 F	16 U
Maintenance	116	120	300	184 U	180 U	4 U
Total	$1,276	$1,320	$1,440	$164 U	$120 U	$44 U

* 5,800 hrs. × $0.12 = $696. Other budget allowances are computed in the same way.

utilized in production, and the hours that should have been taken to produce the period's output:

$$(AH \times SR) - (SH \times SR) = \text{Efficiency variance}$$

or, in factored form:

$$SR(AH - SH) = \text{Efficiency variance}$$

If more hours are worked than allowed at standard, then the overhead efficiency variance will be unfavorable to reflect this inefficiency. As a practical matter, however, the inefficiency isn't in the use of overhead, *but rather in the use of the base itself.*

This point can be illustrated by looking again at Exhibit 9–7. Two hundred more machine-hours were used during the period than should have been used to produce the period's output. Each of these hours required the incurrence of $0.22 of variable overhead, resulting in an unfavorable variance of $44 (200 hours × $0.22). Although this $44 variance is called an overhead efficiency variance, it could better be called a "machine-hours efficiency variance," since it measures the efficiency of utilization of machine time. The term "overhead efficiency variance" is so firmly engrained in day-to-day use that a change is unlikely, however. Even so, the user must be careful to interpret the variance with a clear understanding of what it really measures.

CONTROL OF THE EFFICIENCY VARIANCE. Who is responsible for control of the overhead efficiency variance? Since the variance really measures efficiency in the utilization of the base underlying the flexible budget, whoever is responsible for control of this base is responsible for control of the variance. If the base is direct labor-hours, then the supervisor responsible for the use of labor time will be chargeable for any overhead efficiency variance.

FIXED COSTS AND THE FLEXIBLE BUDGET

Should the flexible budget contain fixed costs as well as variable costs? The term "flexible budget" implies variable costs only. As a practical matter, however, most firms include fixed overhead costs in the budget as well.

Exhibit 9–8 illustrates a flexible budget that contains fixed overhead costs as well as variable overhead costs. Actually, the fixed cost portion

Exhibit 9–8

	Cost formula (per machine-hour)	Machine-hours			
		3,000	4,000	5,000	6,000

DONNER COMPANY
Flexible Budget
Stamping Department

Budgeted Machine-Hours 5,000

	Cost formula (per machine-hour)	3,000	4,000	5,000	6,000
Variable overhead costs:					
Indirect labor	$0.10	$ 300	$ 400	$ 500	$ 600
Lubricants	0.20	600	800	1,000	1,200
Total	$0.30	$ 900	$1,200	$1,500	$1,800
Fixed overhead costs:					
Depreciation		$4,000	$4,000	$4,000	$4,000
Supervisory salaries		3,000	3,000	3,000	3,000
Insurance		350	350	350	350
Total		$7,350	$7,350	$7,350	$7,350
Total overhead costs, variable and fixed		$8,250	$8,550	$8,850	$9,150

of the budget is a *static budget* in that the amounts remain unchanged throughout the relevant range.

Fixed costs are often included in the flexible budget for at least two reasons. First, to the extent that a fixed cost is controllable by a manager, it should be included in the evaluation of his or her performance. Such costs should be placed on the manager's performance report, along with the variable costs for which he is responsible. And second, fixed costs are needed in the flexible budget for product costing purposes. Recall from Chapter 3 that overhead costs are added to units of product by means of the predetermined overhead rate. *The flexible budget provides the manager with the information needed to compute this rate.* In the remainder of this chapter we discuss the use of the flexible budget for this purpose, and demonstrate the preparation and use of fixed overhead variances.

FIXED OVERHEAD ANALYSIS

The analysis of fixed overhead differs considerably from the analysis of variable overhead, simply because of the difference in the nature of the costs involved. To provide a background for our discussion, we will first review briefly the need for, and computation of, predetermined overhead rates. This review will be helpful since the predetermined overhead rate plays a role in fixed overhead analysis. We will then show how fixed overhead variances are computed, and make certain observations as to their usefulness to the manager.

Flexible budgets and overhead rates

Fixed costs come in large indivisible chunks that by definition do not change with changes in the level of activity. As we learned in Chapter 3, this creates a problem in product costing, since a given level of fixed overhead cost spread over a small number of units produced will result in a higher cost per unit than if the same amount of cost is spread over a large number of units. Consider the data in the table below:

Month	(1) Fixed overhead cost	(2) Number of units produced	Unit cost (1) ÷ (2)
January	$6,000	1,000	$6.00
February	6,000	1,500	4.00
March	6,000	800	7.50

Notice that the large number of units produced in February results in a low unit cost ($4.00), whereas the small number of units produced in March results in a high unit cost ($7.50). This problem arises only in connection with the fixed portion of overhead, since by definition the variable portion of overhead remains constant on a per unit basis, rising and falling in total proportionately with changes in the activity level. For product costing purposes, managers need to stabilize the fixed portion of unit cost, so that a single unit cost figure can be used throughout the year without regard to month-by-month changes in activity levels. As we learned in Chapter 3, this stability can be accomplished through use of the predetermined overhead rate.

DENOMINATOR ACTIVITY.   The formula which we used in Chapter 3 to compute the predetermined overhead rate is given below, with one added feature. We have titled the estimated activity portion of the formula as being the *denominator activity:*

$$\frac{\text{Estimated total manufacturing overhead costs}}{\substack{\text{Estimated direct labor-hours or machine-hours}\\ \text{(denominator activity)}}} = \text{Predetermined overhead rate}$$

Recall from our discussion in Chapter 3 that once an estimated activity level (denominator activity) has been chosen, it remains unchanged throughout the year, even if actual activity later proves the estimate (denominator) to be somewhat in error. The reason for not changing the denominator, of course, is to maintain stability in the amount of overhead applied to each unit of product regardless of when it is produced during the year.

COMPUTING THE OVERHEAD RATE.   When predetermined overhead rates were discussed in Chapter 3 we did so without elaboration as to the source of the estimated data going into the formula. These data are normally derived from the flexible budget, with the denominator activity being the budgeted activity level for the forthcoming period, as shown in the budget. To illustrate, turn back to the flexible budget for the Donner Company contained in Exhibit 9–8. Notice that the budgeted activity level for the forthcoming period is 5,000 machine-hours. As explained, this becomes the denominator activity in the formula, with the overhead cost (variable and fixed) at this activity level becoming the estimated overhead cost in the formula ($8,850 from Exhibit 9–8). In sum, the predetermined overhead rate for the Donner Company will be:

$$\frac{\$8,850}{5,000 \text{ MH}} = \$1.77 \text{ per machine-hour}$$

Or, the company can break its predetermined overhead rate down into variable and fixed elements rather than using a single combined figure:

$$\text{Variable element} \frac{\$1,500}{5,000 \text{ MH}} = \$0.30 \text{ per machine-hour}$$

$$\text{Fixed element} \quad \frac{\$7,350}{5,000 \text{ MH}} = \$1.47 \text{ per machine-hour}$$

For every standard machine-hour of operation, work in process will be charged with $1.77 of overhead, of which $0.30 will be variable overhead and $1.47 will be fixed overhead. If a unit of product takes five machine-hours to complete, then its cost will include $1.50 variable overhead and $7.35 fixed overhead, as shown on the *standard cost card* below:

Standard Cost Card—Per Unit	
Direct materials (assumed)	$ 5.00
Direct labor (assumed)	10.00
Variable overhead (5 hrs. at $0.30)	1.50
Fixed overhead (5 hrs. at $1.47)	7.35
Total standard cost per unit	$23.85

Thus the flexible budget provides the manager with the data needed for determining the amount of overhead cost that will be charged to units of product; at the same time, it provides the manager with the denominator activity figure by which he or she is able to artificially stabilize the fixed overhead element of unit cost.

Overhead application in a standard cost system

To understand the fixed overhead variances, it is necessary first to understand how overhead is applied to work in process in a standard cost system. In Chapter 3, recall that we applied overhead to work in process on a basis of actual hours of activity (multiplied times the predetermined overhead rate). This procedure was correct, since at the time we were dealing with an actual cost system. However, we are now dealing with a standard cost system, and when standards are in operation, overhead is applied to work in process on a basis of the *standard hours allowed for the output of the period,* rather than on a basis of the actual number of hours worked. This point is illustrated in Exhibit 9–9.

Exhibit 9–9
Applied overhead costs: Actual cost system versus standard cost system

Actual cost system Manufacturing Overhead		Standard cost system Manufacturing Overhead	
Actual overhead costs incurred.	Applied overhead costs: actual hours × predetermined overhead rate.	Actual overhead costs incurred.	Applied overhead costs: standard hours allowed for output × predetermined overhead rate.
Under- or overapplied overhead		Under- or overapplied overhead	

The reason for using standard hours to apply overhead to production is to assure that every unit of product moving through the system bears the same overhead cost, regardless of any time variations that may be involved in its manufacture.

The fixed overhead variances

To illustrate the computation of fixed overhead variances, we will refer again to the flexible budget data for the Donner Company contained in Exhibit 9–8.

Denominator activity in hours 5,000
Budgeted fixed overhead cost $7,350
Fixed portion of the predetermined
   overhead rate (computed earlier) .... $ 1.47

Let us assume that the following actual operating results were recorded for the period:

Actual machine-hours 4,200
Standard machine-hours allowed* 4,000
Actual fixed overhead costs $7,540

  * For the actual production of the period.

From these data two variances can be computed for fixed overhead—a budget variance and a volume variance. The variances are shown in Exhibit 9–10.

Notice from the exhibit that overhead has been applied to work in process on a basis of 4,000 standard hours allowed for the output of the period, rather than on a basis of 4,200 actual hours worked. As stated earlier, this keeps unit costs from being affected by any efficiency variations.

Exhibit 9–10
Computation of the fixed overhead variances

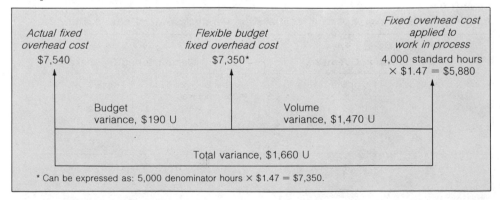

Actual fixed overhead cost	Flexible budget fixed overhead cost	Fixed overhead cost applied to work in process
$7,540	$7,350*	4,000 standard hours × $1.47 = $5,880

Budget variance, $190 U   Volume variance, $1,470 U

Total variance, $1,660 U

 * Can be expressed as: 5,000 denominator hours × $1.47 = $7,350.

The budget variance—A closer look

As shown in Exhibit 9–10, the budget variance represents the difference between actual fixed overhead costs, and budgeted fixed overhead costs as shown on the flexible budget. The variance can also be shown in the following format:

Actual fixed overhead costs	$7,540
Budgeted fixed overhead costs (from the flexible budget in Exhibit 9–8)	7,350
Budget variance	$ 190 U

Although the budget variance is somewhat similar to the variable overhead spending variance, care must be exercised in how it is used. One must keep in mind that fixed costs are often beyond immediate managerial control. Therefore, the use of the budget variance in many cases will be largely informational, and simply serve to call the manager's attention to changes in price factors rather than serve as a measure of managerial performance.

The volume variance—A closer look

The volume variance is a measure of utilization of plant facilities. It is computed by comparing the denominator activity figure to the standard hours allowed for the output of the period, and multiplying any difference by the fixed portion of the predetermined overhead rate:

$$\begin{array}{c}\text{Fixed portion of}\\\text{the predetermined}\\\text{overhead rate}\end{array} \times \left(\begin{array}{c}\text{Denominator}\\\text{hours}\end{array} - \begin{array}{c}\text{Standard hours}\\\text{allowed}\end{array}\right) = \begin{array}{c}\text{Volume}\\\text{variance}\end{array}$$

Applying this formula to the Donner Company, the volume variance would be:

$$\$1.47 \ (5,000 \ \text{MH} - 4,000 \ \text{MH}) = \$1,470 \ \text{unfavorable}$$

The reason for the unfavorable volume variance can be explained as follows: If the company's activity level for the period had been 5,000 hours as planned, then work in process would have been charged with the full $7,350 in fixed costs contained in the flexible budget:

$$5,000 \ \text{machine-hours} \times \$1.47 = \$7,350$$

But the activity level for the period (at standard) was only 4,000 hours, *so even though the full $7,350 in fixed costs would have been incurred, less than this amount would have been charged to work in process:*

$$4,000 \ \text{machine-hours} \times \$1.47 = \$5,880$$

The difference between these two figures is the volume variance:

$$\$7,350 - \$5,880 = \$1,470 \text{ U}$$

The volume variance does not measure over- or underspending. A company would normally incur the *same* dollar amount of fixed overhead cost regardless of whether actual activity was above or below the denominator level. The variance is a measure of *utilization* of plant facilities. It is explainable only by activity, and is controllable only through activity. In the case of the Donner Company, management should seek an explanation as to why the denominator activity of 5,000 machine-hours was not reached during the period, since the result was an underutilization of available plant facilities.

To summarize:

1. If the denominator activity and the standard hours allowed for the output of the period are the same, then there is no volume variance.
2. If the denominator activity is greater than the standard hours allowed for the output of the period, then the volume variance is unfavorable, signifying an underutilization of available facilities.
3. If the denominator activity is less than the standard hours allowed for the output of the period, then the volume variance is favorable, signifying an overutilization of available facilities.

Graphical analysis of fixed overhead variances

Some insights into the budget and volume variances can be gained through graphical analysis. The needed graph is presented in Exhibit 9–11.

As shown in the graph, fixed overhead is applied to work in process at $1.47 per standard hour of activity. Notice that the applied line crosses the budgeted fixed cost line at the denominator level of activity (5,000 machine-hours). Therefore, as we stated earlier, if the denominator hours from the flexible budget and the standard hours allowed for actual output achieved are the same, then there can be no volume variance. The budgeted fixed overhead and applied fixed overhead lines will exactly meet on the graph. It is only when the standard hours are less than or greater than the denominator hours that a volume variance can arise.

Cautions in fixed overhead analysis

There can be no volume variance for variable overhead, since budgeted costs and applied costs are *both* dependent on activity and will always coincide. The reason we get a volume variance for fixed overhead is that budgeted costs *do not* depend on activity, but yet when applying

Exhibit 9–11
Graphical analysis of fixed overhead variances

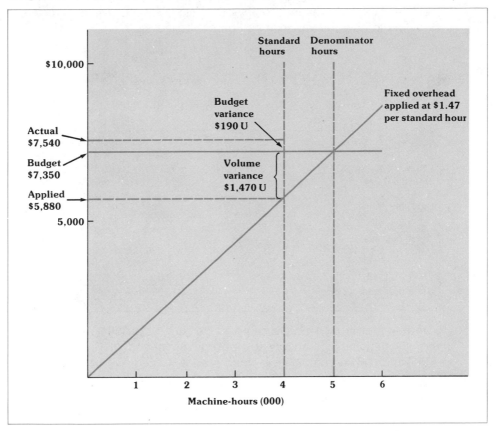

the costs we treat them *as if* they were variable. This point can be seen from the graph in Exhibit 9–11. Notice from the exhibit that fixed overhead is applied to work in process at $1.47 per hour *as if* it indeed was variable at this rate. This *as if* treatment is necessary for product costing purposes, as explained earlier, but there are some real dangers here. The manager can easily become misled, and start thinking of the fixed overhead costs as if they were in fact variable. The manager must keep clearly in mind that fixed overhead costs come in *large, indivisible chunks* that cannot be broken down. Any breakdown of such costs, though necessary for product costing purposes, is *artificial* in nature. That is why the volume variance is not a controllable variance from a spending point of view. The per hour dollar figure used to compute the variance is simply a derived figure needed for product costing purposes, but which has no significance from a cost control viewpoint.

Because of these factors, some companies present the volume variance in terms of physical units (hours), rather than in dollars. These companies feel that stating the variance in physical units gives management a clearer signal as to how the variance can be controlled.

SUMMARY PROBLEM ON OVERHEAD ANALYSIS

A flexible budget for Carey Company is given below:

	Cost formula (per DLH)	Direct labor-hours		
Overhead costs		4,000	6,000	8,000
Variable costs:				
Supplies	$0.20	$ 800	$ 1,200	$ 1,600
Indirect labor	0.30	1,200	1,800	2,400
Total	$0.50	$ 2,000	$ 3,000	$ 4,000
Fixed costs:				
Depreciation		$ 4,000	$ 4,000	$ 4,000
Supervision		5,000	5,000	5,000
Total		$ 9,000	$ 9,000	$ 9,000
Total overhead costs		$11,000	$12,000	$13,000

Five hours of labor time are required per unit of product. The company has set denominator activity for the coming period at 6,000 hours (or 1,200 units). The computation of the predetermined overhead rate would be:

$$\text{Total } \frac{\$12,000}{6,000 \text{ DLH}} = \$2.00 \text{ per DLH}$$

$$\text{Variable element } \frac{\$3,000}{6,000 \text{ DLH}} = \$0.50 \text{ per DLH}$$

$$\text{Fixed element } \frac{\$9,000}{6,000 \text{ DLH}} = \$1.50 \text{ per DLH}$$

Assume the following actual results for the period:

Number of units produced	1,300
Actual direct labor-hours	6,800
Standard direct labor-hours allowed*	6,500
Actual variable overhead cost	$ 4,080
Actual fixed overhead cost	$ 9,450
Overhead applied to production (6,500 standard hours × $2.00)	$13,000
* For 1,300 units of product.	

Therefore, the company's manufacturing overhead account would appear as follows at the end of the period:

Manufacturing Overhead			
Actual overhead costs	13,530	13,000	Overhead costs applied
Underapplied overhead	530		

Required:

Analyze the $530 underapplied overhead in terms of:
1. A variable overhead spending variance.
2. A variable overhead efficiency variance.
3. A fixed overhead budget variance.
4. A fixed overhead volume variance.

Variable overhead spending variance:

Actual variable overhead cost	$4,080
Actual inputs at the standard rate:	
6,800 hrs. × $0.50	3,400
Spending variance	$ 680 U

Variable overhead efficiency variance:

$$SR(AH - SH) = \text{Efficiency variance}$$
$$\$0.50\,(6,800 \text{ hrs.} - 6,500 \text{ hrs.}) = \$150 \text{ U}$$

Fixed overhead budget variance:

Actual fixed overhead	$9,450
Budgeted fixed overhead	9,000
Budget variance	$ 450 U

Fixed overhead volume variance:

$$\text{Fixed portion of the predetermined overhead rate} \times \left(\text{Denominator hours} - \text{Standard hours} \right) = \text{Volume variance}$$

$$\$1.50\,(6,000 \text{ hrs.} - 6,500 \text{ hrs.}) = \$750 \text{ F}$$

Alternate format for the fixed overhead budget and volume variances:

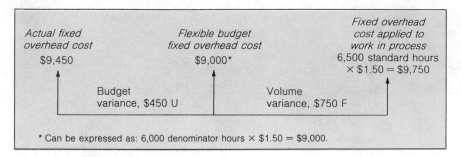

* Can be expressed as: 6,000 denominator hours × $1.50 = $9,000.

Summary of variances:

Variable overhead:	
Spending variance	$680 U
Efficiency variance	150 U
Fixed overhead:	
Budget variance	450 U
Volume variance	750 F
Underapplied overhead	$530

Notice that the $530 summary variance figure agrees with the underapplied balance in the company's manufacturing overhead account. This agreement stands as proof of the accuracy of our variance analysis. *Each period* the under- or overapplied overhead balance should be analyzed as we have done above. These variances will help the manager to see where his or her time and the time of the subordinates should be directed for better control of costs and operations.

KEY TERMS FOR REVIEW

Static budget   **Denominator activity**
Flexible budget   **Budget variance**
Cost control   **Volume variance**
Production control   **Standard cost card**

QUESTIONS

9–1. What is a static budget?

9–2. What is a flexible budget, and how does it differ from a static budget? What is the main deficiency of the static budget?

9–3. What are the two prime responsibilities of the production manager? How do these two responsibilities differ?

9–4. Name three criteria that should be considered in choosing an activity base on which to construct a flexible budget.

9–5. In comparing budgeted data to actual data in a performance report for variable manufacturing overhead, what variance(s) will be produced if the budgeted data are based on actual hours worked? On both actual hours and standard hours allowed?

9–6. What is meant by the term "standard hours of production?"

9–7. How does the variable manufacturing overhead spending variance differ from the materials price variance?

9–8. Why is the term "overhead efficiency variance" a misnomer?

9–9. "Fixed costs have no place in a flexible budget." Discuss.

9–10. In what way is the flexible budget involved in product costing?

9–11. What problem is created by the fact that fixed overhead costs come in large indivisible chunks?

9–12. What is meant by the term "denominator level of activity?"

9–13. The text states that the denominator activity concept serves to artificially stabilize the fixed element of unit cost in product costing. In what way is this stability "artificial"?

9–14. What does the fixed overhead budget variance measure? Is the variance controllable by management? Explain.

9–15. Why do we apply overhead to work in process on a basis of standard hours allowed in Chapter 9, when we applied it on a basis of actual hours in Chapter 3? What is the difference in costing systems between the two chapters?

9–16. Under what circumstances would you expect the volume variance to be favorable? Unfavorable? Does the variance measure deviations in spending for fixed overhead items? Explain.

9–17. How might the volume variance be measured, other than in dollars?

9–18. What dangers are there in expressing fixed costs on a per unit basis?

9–19. In Chapter 3 you became acquainted with the concept of under- or overapplied overhead. What four variances can be computed from the under- or overapplied overhead total?

9–20. If factory overhead is overapplied for the month of August, would you expect the total of the overhead variances to be favorable or unfavorable? Why?

EXERCISES

E9–1. The cost formulas for Rider Company's overhead costs are given below. The costs cover a range of 4,000 to 6,000 direct labor-hours.

Cost	Cost formula
Indirect labor	$1,800 plus $0.25 per direct labor-hour
Supplies	$0.15 per direct labor-hour
Maintenance	$1,500 plus $0.10 per direct labor-hour
Depreciation	$2,000
Utilities	$0.12 per direct labor-hour

Required:

Prepare a flexible budget in increments of 1,000 direct labor-hours. Include the fixed costs in your flexible budget.

E9–2. Flexible budget and actual overhead cost data for 19x5 are presented below for the Harper Company:

	Cost formula (per direct labor-hour)	Flexible budget costs*	Actual costs
Variable overhead	$1.15	$17,250	$15,904
Fixed overhead		30,000	30,850
Total cost		$47,250	$46,754

* At a denominator activity level of 15,000 direct labor-hours per year.

During 19x5 the company produced 6,850 units of product, and worked 14,200 actual hours. The standard direct labor time per unit is two hours.

Required:

1. Compute the predetermined overhead rate used during 19x5. Divide it into fixed and variable elements.
2. Compute the standard hours allowed for the output of 19x5.
3. Compute the fixed overhead budget and volume variances for 19x5.

E9–3. Selected operating information on four different companies for the year 19x8 is given below:

	A	B	C	D
Full capacity direct labor-hours	11,500	14,000	9,000	16,000
Budgeted direct labor-hours*	9,000	14,000	6,000	15,000
Actual direct labor-hours	9,250	13,500	6,000	15,500
Standard direct labor-hours for actual production	8,600	14,000	6,500	14,000

* Denominator activity.

Required:

In each case, state whether the company would have:
a. No volume variance.
b. A favorable volume variance.
c. An unfavorable volume variance.
Also state in each case why you chose (*a*), (*b*) or (*c*).

E9–4. An incomplete flexible budget is given below:

		Direct labor-hours			
Overhead costs	Cost formula	2,000	4,000	6,000	8,000
Variable:					
Maintenance			$ 720		
Supplies			440		
Rework time			320		
Total					
Fixed:					
Depreciation			1,400		
Taxes			800		
Supervision			3,500		
Total					
Total overhead costs					

Required:

Provide the missing information in the budget.

E9–5. Brandon Machine Company's flexible budget is given below.

BRANDON MACHINE COMPANY
Flexible Budget

Overhead costs	Cost formula (per unit)	Number of units		
		10,000	*11,000*	*12,000*
Maintenance	$1.15	$11,500	$12,650	$13,800
Indirect materials	0.80	8,000	8,800	9,600
Rework time	0.50	5,000	5,500	6,000
Total	$2.45	$24,500	$26,950	$29,400

During a recent period the company produced 11,400 units. The overhead costs incurred were:

Maintenance	$11,172
Indirect materials	9,804
Rework time	7,068

The production budgeted for the period had been 11,500 units.

Required:

1. Prepare a performance report for the period. Indicate whether variances are favorable (F) or unfavorable (U).
2. Discuss the significance of the variances. Might some variances be the result of others? Explain.

E9–6. Maravich Company's flexible budget allowances and predetermined overhead rate at an activity level of 8,000 direct labor-hours are given below:

Variable overhead	$ 8,400
Fixed overhead	24,800
Total overhead	$33,200

$$\frac{\$33,200}{8,000 \text{ DLH}} = \$4.15 \text{ per DLH}$$

In working 8,000 standard direct labor-hours, the company should produce 3,200 units of product. During 19x1, the company produced 3,500 units of product. Actual operating results were:

Actual direct labor-hours	8,500
Actual variable overhead costs	$ 9,860
Actual fixed overhead costs	$25,100

Required:

1. What were the standard hours allowed for the output of 19x1?
2. Compute the variable overhead spending and efficiency variances for 19x1, and the fixed overhead budget and volume variances.

E9–7.　Operating at a normal level of 24,000 direct labor-hours, the ABC Company produces 8,000 units of product. The direct labor wage rate is $6.30 per hour. Two pounds of raw materials go into each unit of product, at a cost of $4.20 per pound. A flexible budget is used to plan and control overhead costs:

Flexible Budget Data

Budgeted activity level	24,000 DLH
Variable overhead	$ 38,400
Fixed overhead	84,000
Total overhead costs	$122,400

Required:

1.　Compute the predetermined overhead rate, and break it down into fixed and variable elements.
2.　Complete the standard cost card below for one unit of product:

Direct materials, 2 lbs. at $4.20	$8.40
Direct labor,　　　?	?
Variable overhead, ?	?
Fixed overhead,　　?	?
Total standard cost per unit	$?

E9–8.　Below is the standard cost card for the single product produced by Stanco, Inc.:

Standard Cost Card—Per Unit

Direct materials, 4 yds. at $2.50	$10.00
Direct labor, 1.5 hrs. at $6.00	9.00
Variable overhead, 1.5 hrs. at $0.50	0.75
Fixed overhead, 1.5 hrs. at $2.00	3.00
Total standard cost per unit	$22.75

Overhead is applied to production on a basis of direct labor-hours. During a recent period, the company worked 7,000 hours, and produced 4,500 units of product. The following additional information is available:

Actual fixed overhead cost incurred	$15,525
Volume variance (unfavorable)	$ 1,500

Required:

1.　What denominator activity level does the company use in setting predetermined overhead rates? (Hint: It may be helpful to work from known to unknown data in the variance formulas.)
2.　What is the total fixed overhead cost contained in the flexible budget?
3.　Compute the fixed overhead budget variance for the period.

E9–9.　Brinson Company's budgeted and actual fixed overhead costs for 19x6 are given below:

	Flexible budget	*Actual*
Fixed overhead costs	$90,000	$91,300

Other information on the company is given below:

	Direct labor-hours
Full capacity	40,000
Budgeted for 19x6	30,000
Actual hours worked during 19x6	35,000
Standard hours for work completed during 19x6	32,000

Required:

1. Assume that the company uses budgeted hours as the denominator activity. Compute the fixed overhead budget and volume variances.
2. Assume that the company uses full capacity hours as the denominator activity. Compute the fixed overhead budget and volume variances.
3. Explain why the budget variances computed in (1) and (2) are the same, and why the volume variances are different.

PROBLEMS

P9–10. *Overhead analysis.* The FAB Company operates with a standard cost system, and produces a single product. Selected information from the company's flexible budget for 19x4 follows:

Budgeted direct labor-hours	15,000*
Budgeted variable overhead	$24,750
Budgeted fixed overhead	$52,500

* Denominator activity level.

During 19x4, the following operating results were recorded:

Actual direct labor-hours worked	13,600
Standard direct labor-hours allowed	14,000
Actual variable overhead	$24,480
Actual fixed overhead	$52,000

Overhead rates in the FAB Company are based on direct labor-hours. At the end of 19x4, the company's manufacturing overhead account contained the following items:

Manufacturing Overhead

Actual 76,480	72,100 Applied
4,380	

Required:

1. Compute the predetermined overhead rate that would have been used during 19x4. Break it down into variable and fixed cost elements.
2. How was the $72,100 "applied" figure in the manufacturing overhead account computed?
3. Analyze the $4,380 underapplied overhead figure in terms of variable

overhead spending and efficiency variances, and fixed overhead budget and volume variances.

4. Explain the meaning of each variance which you computed in (3), and indicate how each variance is controlled.

P9–11. *Overhead analysis.* According to the Archer Company's flexible budget, the company should incur the following overhead costs at a denominator activity level of 15,000 machine-hours per month:

Variable overhead costs	$24,000
Fixed overhead costs	52,500
Total overhead costs	$76,500

During 19x5, the company recorded the following actual operating results:

Actual machine-hours worked	16,200
Standard machine-hours allowed	15,800
Actual variable overhead costs	$23,490
Actual fixed overhead costs	$52,950

Required:

1. Compute the predetermined overhead rate that the company would have used during 19x5. Break it down into fixed and variable elements.
2. Prepare a T-account for manufacturing overhead.
   a. Enter the actual overhead costs for 19x5 into the T-account.
   b. Compute the applied overhead for 19x5, and enter the amount into the T-account.
   c. Compute the under- or overapplied overhead for 19x5, and enter the amount into the T-account.
3. Analyze the under- or overapplied overhead figure in terms of variable overhead spending and efficiency variances, and fixed overhead budget and volume variances.
4. Explain the meaning of each variance which you computed in (3).

P9–12. *Flexible budgets and overhead analysis.* The Billings Company assembles all of its products in the assembly department. The budgeted costs for the operation of this department during 19x7 have been established as follows:

Variable costs:		
Direct materials	$	850,000
Direct labor		500,000
Indirect labor		100,000
Indirect materials		60,000
Other variable overhead		40,000
		$1,550,000

Fixed costs:		
Maintenance	$	35,000
Heat, light, and power		75,000
Taxes and insurance		25,000
Depreciation		140,000
	$	275,000
Total budgeted costs		$1,825,000

Operating activity in the assembly department is best measured in direct labor-hours. Direct labor cost is budgeted at $4 per direct labor-hour. The cost formulas used to develop the budgeted costs above are valid over a relevant range of 100,000 to 150,000 direct labor-hours per year.

Required:

1. Prepare a flexible overhead budget in good form for the assembly department, in increments of 25,000 hours. (The company does not include direct material and direct labor costs in the flexible budget.)
2. Assume that the company computes predetermined overhead rates by department. Compute the rates, variable and fixed, that will be used by the assembly department during 19x7 to apply overhead costs to production.
3. Suppose during 19x7 that the following actual activity and costs are recorded:

Actual direct labor-hours worked 122,000
Standard direct labor-hours allowed
  for the output of the year 120,000
Actual variable overhead cost (total) $189,100
Actual fixed overhead cost (total) $273,600

   a. A T-account for manufacturing overhead costs for 19x7 in the assembly department is given below. Show how the underapplied overhead figure was computed.

Manufacturing Overhead

?	?
Underapplied overhead 6,700	

   b. Analyze the underapplied overhead figure in terms of variable overhead spending and efficiency variances, and fixed overhead budget and volume variances.

P9–13. *Overhead analysis, with graphing.* A condensed flexible budget for the Eaton Company is given below:

Overhead costs	Cost formula (per direct labor-hour)	8,000	10,000	12,000
		Direct labor-hours		
Variable costs	$1.40	$11,200	$14,000	$16,800
Fixed costs		42,000	42,000	42,000
Total overhead costs		$53,200	$56,000	$58,800

The company produces a single product, which requires 2.5 hours of direct labor time to complete, at a rate of $5 per hour. Each unit of product requires 2 yards of material at $5.60 per yard. Overhead is applied to units of product on a basis of direct labor-hours. During the most recent period, the following actual costs and output were recorded:

Number of units produced 3,400
Actual direct labor-hours 8,800
Actual fixed overhead cost $42,650

Required:

1. Assume that the company computes predetermined overhead rates by using a denominator activity of 8,000 direct labor-hours.
   a. Compute the predetermined overhead rate, and break it down into variable and fixed cost elements.
   b. Prepare a standard cost card, showing the cost to produce one unit of product.
2. Refer to the original data. Assume that the company computes predetermined overhead rates by using a denominator activity of 12,000 direct labor-hours.
   a. Compute the predetermined overhead rate under this assumption, and break it down into variable and fixed cost elements.
   b. Prepare a standard cost card, showing the cost to produce one unit of product.
3. Refer to your computations in (1).
   a. Using these data, compute the budget and volume variances for the most recent period.
   b. Prepare a graph showing budgeted fixed costs throughout the relevant range, and showing an applied overhead line for fixed costs from a zero level of activity through the denominator level of activity. Indicate on your graph the volume variance you have just computed. In your own words explain why a volume variance arises.
4. Refer to your computations in (2).
   a. Using these data, compute the budget and volume variances for the most recent period.
   b. Prepare another graph showing budgeted fixed overhead and applied fixed overhead, as well as the volume variance you have just computed.
5. What are the implications of this problem regarding the setting of fixed overhead rates for product costing purposes? Are such rates useful control tools? Explain.

P9–14. *Materials, labor, and overhead variances.* The Bateman Company uses a standard cost system, and sets predetermined overhead rates on a denominator activity of 10,000 standard direct labor-hours per month. At this activity level, the company's flexible budget shows that variable overhead costs are $0.50 per standard direct labor-hour. The standard cost card for the company's single product is given below:

Direct materials, 3 yards at $4.40 .... $13.20
Direct labor, 2 hrs. at $6.00 .... 12.00
Overhead, 40% of direct labor cost 4.80
       Total standard cost per unit $30.00

Production data for the month of August 19x1 follow:

Number of units produced 6,000
Materials purchased, 24,000 yds. at $4.80 .... $115,200
Materials used in production (in yards) 18,500
Variable overhead cost incurred .... $ 6,380
Direct labor cost incurred, 11,600
    hrs. at $6.50 .... $ 75,400
Fixed overhead cost incurred .... $ 20,400

Required:

1. Redo the standard cost card in a clearer, more usable format, by detailing the variable and fixed overhead cost elements.
2. Prepare a complete analysis of variances for materials, labor, variable overhead, and fixed overhead.
3. What additional information would you need to tell whether costs are under control?

P9–15. *Overhead analysis, with graphing.* For 19x5, the York Company has planned a denominator activity level of 16,000 direct labor-hours. At this level of activity, the following overhead costs are budgeted:

Variable overhead $19,200
Fixed overhead 44,800

The company produces a single product that requires 2.5 hours to complete. The direct labor rate is $6.50 per hour. The product requires 4 pounds of raw materials, at $3.20 per pound.

Required:

1. Compute the predetermined overhead rate that the company will use during 19x5. Break the rate down into fixed and variable cost elements.
2. Prepare a standard cost card for one unit of product, using the following format:

Direct materials, 4 lbs. at $3.20 .... $12.80
Direct labor,   ? .... ?
Variable overhead, ? .... ?
Fixed overhead,   ? .... ?
    Total standard cost per unit .... $?

3. Graph the following costs from an activity level of zero to 18,000 direct labor-hours:
    a. Budgeted fixed overhead (in total).
    b. Applied fixed overhead [applied at the hourly rate computed in (1)].
4. Assume that during 19x5 the company works 15,500 actual direct labor-hours and produces 6,000 units of product. Actual fixed overhead costs are $45,100.
    a. Compute the fixed overhead budget and volume variances.
    b. Show the volume variance on the graph which you prepared in (3).

5. Assume that during 19x5 the company works 16,400 actual direct labor-hours and produces 6,600 units of product. Actual fixed overhead costs are again $45,100.
    a. Compute the fixed overhead budget and volume variances.
    b. Show the volume variance on the chart which you prepared in (3).

P9-16. *Materials, labor, and overhead variances.* The Molina Company uses a standard cost system, and sets predetermined overhead rates on a denominator activity of 12,000 standard direct labor-hours per month. The company's flexible budget shows that fixed overhead costs are budgeted at $18,000 per month. A standard cost card showing the standard cost to produce one unit of product is given below:

Direct materials, 4 lbs. at $1.80 . . . . $ 7.20
Direct labor, 3 hrs. at $7.00 . . . .   21.00
Overhead, 30% of direct labor cost 6.30*
　　Standard cost per unit $34.50

* Includes both variable and fixed overhead cost.

Production data for the month of March 19x2 follow:

Number of units produced   3,500
Materials purchased, 20,000 lbs. at $1.55 . . . . $31,000
Materials used in production (in pounds)   14,700
Direct labor cost incurred, 10,000 hrs. at $7.50 . . . . $75,000

At the end of the month, the manufacturing overhead account contained the following figures:

Manufacturing Overhead

Actual costs	25,700*	22,050	Applied costs

* Variable costs: $7,300; fixed costs: $18,400.

Required:

1. Redo the standard cost card in a clearer, more usable format, by detailing the variable and fixed overhead cost elements.
2. Prepare a complete analysis of variances for materials and labor.
3. How was the $22,050 "applied" figure in the manufacturing overhead account computed?
4. Determine the under- or overapplied overhead for the month, and analyze it in terms of the variable overhead spending and efficiency variances, and the fixed overhead budget and volume variances.

P9-17. *Comprehensive overhead analysis, with graphing.* The Orton Company produces a product that requires direct material and direct labor inputs as follows:

Direct materials, 4 yds. at $3.50
Direct labor, 2 hrs. at $4.75

The company uses a flexible budget to plan and control overhead costs, and for product costing purposes. Overhead rates are based on a normal activity level of 30,000 standard direct labor-hours each month. At this activity level, the flexible budget shows variable overhead costs of $39,000 and fixed overhead costs of $67,500.

Required:

1. Compute the predetermined overhead rate used by the Orton Company, and divide it into fixed and variable elements. Compute the standard cost to produce one unit of product.
2. Assume the following results for the month of June:

Standard hours allowed for the output of the month 28,000
Actual hours worked during the month 29,200
Actual variable overhead cost $35,040
Actual fixed overhead cost $68,200

 a. Prepare a T-account for manufacturing overhead, and enter the actual overhead costs shown above. Determine the amount of overhead cost that would have been applied to production during the month and enter this amount into the T-account. Compute the under- or overapplied overhead.
 b. Analyze the under- or overapplied overhead in terms of variable overhead spending and efficiency variances, and fixed overhead budget and volume variances.
 c. Prepare a graph showing the budgeted fixed overhead per month, and showing applied fixed overhead from zero activity through 30,000 direct labor-hours of activity each month. Show where the volume variance for June would appear on the graph.
3. Assume the following results for the month of July:

Standard hours allowed for the output of the month 34,000
Actual hours worked during the month 32,500
Actual variable overhead cost $45,500
Actual fixed overhead cost $66,800

 a. Again prepare a T-account for manufacturing overhead (do *not* carry over any figures in the account from the month of June), and enter the actual overhead costs shown above. Determine the amount of overhead that would have been applied to production during the month and enter this amount into the T-account. Again compute the under- or overapplied overhead.
 b. Analyze the under- or overapplied overhead in terms of variable overhead spending and efficiency variances, and fixed overhead budget and volume variances.
 c. Refer to the graph prepared in (2c) above. Show where the volume variance for the month of July would appear on the graph.
4. What effect, if any, does the choice of a denominator activity level have on unit costs? Is the volume variance controllable from a spending point-of-view? Explain.

P9–18. *Comprehensive problem—Overhead costing and analysis.* The condensed flexible budget of the Hoover Company is given below for 19x2:

Overhead costs	Cost formula (per direct labor-hour)	Direct labor-hours		
		4,000	6,000	8,000
Variable costs	$2.30	$ 9,200	$13,800	$18,400
Fixed costs		36,000	36,000	36,000
Total overhead costs		$45,200	$49,800	$54,400

The company produces a single product that requires 3.5 direct labor-hours to complete. The direct labor wage rate is $5.80 per hour. Three yards of raw material are required for each unit of product at a cost of $4.50 per yard.

Required:

1. Assume that the company chooses 6,000 direct labor-hours as the denominator level of activity. Compute the predetermined overhead rate, breaking it down into fixed and variable cost elements.
2. Assume that the company chooses 8,000 direct labor-hours as the denominator level of activity. Repeat the computations in (1).
3. Complete two standard cost cards, as outlined below. Each card should relate to a single unit of product.

Denominator Activity: 6,000 DLH

Direct materials, 3 yds. at $4.50	$13.50
Direct labor, ?	?
Variable overhead, ?	?
Fixed overhead, ?	?
Total standard cost per unit	$?

Denominator Activity: 8,000 DLH

Direct materials, 3 yds. at $4.50	$13.50
Direct labor, ?	?
Variable overhead, ?	?
Fixed overhead, ?	?
Total standard cost per unit	$?

4. Assume that 6,400 actual hours are worked during 19x2, and that 1,900 units are produced. Actual overhead costs for the year are:

Variable overhead	$15,960
Fixed overhead	36,875
Total	$52,835

  a. Compute the standard hours allowed for 19x2 production.
  b. Compute the missing items from the manufacturing overhead account below. Assume that denominator activity is 6,000 direct labor-hours, as used in (1).

Manufacturing Overhead

Actual costs	52,835	?	Applied costs
Under-applied overhead	?	?	Over-applied overhead

    c. Analyze your under- or overapplied overhead balance in terms of variable overhead spending and efficiency variances and fixed overhead budget and volume variances.

P9–19. *Comprehensive overhead analysis.* The Clemson Company produces a single product which requires 2 pounds of raw materials in its manufacture at a cost of $1.85 per pound, and 3 hours of direct labor time at a rate of $5.00 per hour. Overhead costs are planned and controlled through a flexible budget, which is shown in condensed form below:

| | Cost formula (per DLH) | Direct labor-hours | | |
		5,000	10,000	15,000
Variable overhead	$1.60	$ 8,000	$16,000	$24,000
Fixed overhead		30,000	30,000	30,000
Total overhead cost		$38,000	$46,000	$54,000

Actual operating results for the most recent period are shown below:

Number of units produced	2,000
Actual direct labor-hours worked	5,600
Standard hours allowed for the output of the period	?
Actual variable overhead cost	$10,080
Actual fixed overhead cost	$31,500

Required:

1. Assume that the company normally operates at an activity level of 10,000 standard direct labor-hours each period, and that this figure is used as the denominator activity in computing predetermined overhead rates.

    a. Compute the predetermined overhead rate, and break it down into fixed and variable cost elements.

    b. Prepare a standard cost card, showing the standard cost to produce one unit of product.

2. Refer to the original data. Assume that the company decides to use 5,000 standard direct labor-hours as the denominator activity in computing predetermined overhead rates.

    a. Under this assumption, compute the predetermined overhead rate, and break it down into fixed and variable cost elements.

    b. Prepare another standard cost card, showing the standard cost to produce one unit of product.

3. Refer to the computations you made in (1).

   a. Prepare a T-account for manufacturing overhead, and enter the actual overhead costs for the most recent period, as shown in the original data to the problem. Determine the amount of overhead that would have been applied to production during the period, and enter this amount into the T-account.

   b. Compute the amount of under- or overapplied overhead for the period, and then analyze it in terms of the variable overhead spending and efficiency variances and the fixed overhead budget and volume variances.

4. Refer to the computations you made in (2).

   a. Prepare another T-account for manufacturing overhead, and again enter the actual overhead costs for the most recent period. Determine the amount of overhead that would have been applied to production during the period, and enter this amount into the T-account.

   b. Compute the amount of under- or overapplied overhead for the period, and then analyze it in terms of the variable overhead spending and efficiency variances and the fixed overhead budget and volume variances.

5. Firms are sometimes accused by competitors and others of selling products "below cost." What implications does this problem have regarding the "cost" of a unit of product, so far as the setting of fixed overhead rates is concerned?

P9–20. *Incomplete data.* Each of the cases below is independent. You may assume that each company uses a standard cost system, and that each company's flexible budget is based on standard direct labor-hours.

Item	Company A	Company B
1. Denominator activity in hours	?	6,500
2. Standard hours allowed for units produced	5,250	?
3. Actual hours worked	5,600	?
4. Flexible budget variable overhead per direct labor-hour . . . . $	?	$ 1.70
5. Flexible budget fixed overhead (total)	?	?
6. Actual variable overhead	8,000	12,960
7. Actual fixed overhead	20,500	24,000
8. Variable overhead applied to production*	?	11,730
9. Fixed overhead applied to production*	21,000	?
10. Variable overhead spending variance	?	?
11. Variable overhead efficiency variance	525 U	510 F
12. Fixed overhead budget variance	?	1,250 U
13. Fixed overhead volume variance	1,000 F	?
14. Variable portion of predetermined overhead rate	?	?
15. Fixed portion of predetermined overhead rate	?	?
16. Underapplied or (overapplied) overhead	?	?

* Based on standard hours allowed for units produced.

Required:

Compute the unknown amounts.

P9–21. *Flexible budget and performance report.* You have just been hired by Hannis Company, the manufacturer of a revolutionary new garage door opening device. Ms. Kathy Smith, the president, has asked that you review the company's costing system, and "do what you can to help us get better control over overhead costs." You find that the company has never used a flexible budget, and suggest that this would be an excellent first step in overhead planning and control. After much effort and cost analysis, you are able to determine the following overhead cost formulas for the company's normal operating range of 4,000 to 6,000 units of product monthly:

Cost	*Cost formula*
Utilities	$500 plus $0.40 per unit
Supplies	$0.80 per unit
Indirect labor	$6,000 plus $1.75 per unit
Depreciation	$14,000
Maintenance	$12,000 plus $0.30 per unit

To show the president how the flexible budget concept works, you have gathered the following actual cost data for the most recent month (March 19x1), in which the company produced 4,800 units of product:

Utilities	$ 2,660
Supplies	3,600
Indirect labor	15,840
Depreciation	14,000
Maintenance	12,960

During March the company had originally budgeted to produce 5,000 units of product. There were no variances in the fixed overhead costs for the month. You view the fixed utilities cost as being largely beyond the control of anyone within the company.

Required:

1. Prepare a flexible budget for the company in increments of 1,000 units. Make the flexible budget inclusive enough to be used for both control and product costing purposes.
2. Prepare a performance report for the company for the month of March 19x1. Show only a spending variance on your report.
3. Some managers contend that fixed costs do not belong on a performance report. Give arguments for and against their inclusion.
4. Explain to the president how the flexible budget can be used for product costing purposes.

P9–22. *Flexible budget and performance report.* The Durrant Company has had great difficulty controlling overhead costs. At a recent convention, the president heard about a control device for overhead costs known as a flexible budget, and has hired you to implement this budgeting program in the Durrant Company. After some effort, you develop the following cost formulas for the company's machining department. These costs are based on a normal operating range of 8,000 to 10,000 machine-hours per month:

Cost	Cost formula
Machine setup	$0.20 per machine-hour
Lubricants	$500 plus $0.10 per machine-hour
Utilities	$300 plus $0.08 per machine-hour
Supplies	$0.30 per machine-hour
Indirect labor	$2,000 plus $0.80 per machine-hour

The manager of the machining department has no control over the fixed utilities cost; however, he has control over the other fixed costs incurred in his department.

During March, the first month after your preparation of the above data, the machining department worked 9,400 machine-hours and produced 18,000 units of product. The actual costs of this production were:

Machine setup	$ 2,068
Lubricants	1,346
Utilities	1,052
Supplies	3,290
Indirect labor	9,050
Total costs	$16,806

There were no variances in the fixed costs. The department had originally budgeted to work 10,000 machine-hours during March.

Required:

1. Prepare a flexible budget for the machining department in increments of 1,000 hours. Make the flexible budget inclusive enough to be used for both control and product costing purposes.
2. Prepare a performance report for the machining department for the month of March. Show only a spending variance on the report.
3. What additional information would you need to have in order to compute an overhead efficiency variance for the department?
4. Explain to the president how the flexible budget might be used for product costing purposes as well as for cost control purposes.

P9–23. *Evaluating and interpreting a performance report.* Several years ago Rolex Company developed a comprehensive budgeting system for profit planning and control purposes. The line supervisors have been very happy with the budgeting system, but considerable dissatisfaction has been expressed on the part of middle and upper management. A typical performance report for a recent period is shown below:

ROLEX COMPANY
Performance Report
Assembly Operation
For the Month of August

	Budget	Actual	Variance
Units produced	15,000	12,000	
Variable overhead:			
Indirect materials	$15,000	$13,800	$1,200 F
Rework time	3,000	2,880	120 F
Machine setup	1,500	1,380	120 F
Utilities	6,000	5,400	600 F
Total variable costs..........	$25,500	$23,460	$2,040 F
Fixed overhead:			
Maintenance	$12,000	$11,800	$ 200 F
Inspection	15,000	15,000	—
Total fixed costs	$27,000	$26,800	$ 200 F
Total overhead costs	$52,500	$50,260	$2,240 F

Upon receiving a copy of this performance report, the supervisor of the assembly operation stated, "These reports are great. It makes me feel really good to see how well things are going in my part of the shop. I can't understand why those guys upstairs complain so much."

Required:

1. If you were the immediate superior of the supervisor of the assembly operation, how would you feel about the performance report above?
2. What changes, if any, would you recommend be made in the performance report, in order to give you better insight into how well the supervisor is doing her job?
3. Prepare a new performance report for the month of August, incorporating any changes you suggested in (2) above.

P9–24. *Spending and efficiency variances; Evaluating a performance report.* Ronald Davis, superintendent of the milling department of Mason Company, is very happy with his performance report for the past month. The report is shown below:

MASON COMPANY
Performance Report—Milling Department

	Budget	Actual	Vari-ance
Direct labor hours	12,000	10,000	
Variable overhead:			
Indirect materials	$13,200	$12,500	$ 700 F
Utilities	1,800	1,200	600 F
Machine set up	3,000	2,900	100 F
Maintenance	4,800	4,700	100 F
Total variable costs	$22,800	$21,300	$1,500 F
Fixed overhead:			
Supervision	$ 9,000	$ 9,000	—
Maintenance	6,500	6,800	$ 300 U
Depreciation	12,000	12,000	—
Total fixed costs	$27,500	$27,800	$ 300 U
Total overhead costs	$50,300	$49,100	$1,200 F

Upon receiving a copy of this report, John Arnold, the production manager, commented, "I've been getting these reports for months now, and I still can't see how they help me assess efficiency and cost control in that department. I agree that the budget for the month was 12,000 direct labor-hours, but that represents 6,000 units of product. The department produced only 4,600 units during the month, and took 10,000 hours of direct labor time to do it. Why do all the variances turn up favorable?"

Required:

1. In answer to Mr. Arnold's question, why do all the variances turn up favorable? Evaluate the performance report.
2. Prepare a new performance report that will help Mr. Arnold assess efficiency and cost control in the milling department. (Hint: Exhibit 9–7 may be helpful in structuring your report; include both variable and fixed costs in the report.)

P9–25. *Detailed performance report.* The Barr Company produced 4,500 units of product during May 19x2. The standard cost card shows that the standard direct labor time is 2 hours per unit, or a total of 9,000 direct labor-hours for May. The company actually worked 9,400 direct labor-hours during the month. The company's actual variable overhead costs for the month are given below, along with the standard cost per direct labor-hour, as shown in the flexible budget:

Variable overhead item	Flexible budget cost formula (per direct labor-hour)	Actual costs incurred
Supplies	$0.15	$1,128
Power	0.08	940
Maintenance	0.12	846
Setup time	0.20	1,692
Total variable overhead	$0.55	$4,606

Required:

Prepare a performance report for the month, using the following column headings in your report:

Overhead item	Budget based on 9,000 hours	Budget based on 9,400 hours	Actual costs in-curred 9,400 hours	Total variance	Breakdown of the total variance — Spend-ing variance	Effi-ciency variance

P9–26. *Comprehensive problem, flexible budget and performance reports.* Pacific States Fabricating, Inc., has recently introduced budgeting as an integral part of its corporate planning process. The company's first effort at constructing a flexible budget for overhead is shown below.

Percentage of capacity	80%	100%
Direct labor-hours	4,800	6,000
Maintenance	$1,480	$ 1,600
Supplies	1,920	2,400
Utilities	1,940	2,300
Supervision	3,000	3,000
Machine setup	960	1,200
Total overhead cost	$9,300	$10,500

The budgets above are for costs over a relevant range of 80 percent to 100 percent of capacity on a monthly basis. The managers who will be working under these budgets have control over both fixed and variable costs.

Required:

1. Redo the company's flexible budget, presenting it in better format. Show the budget at 80 percent, 90 percent, and 100 percent levels of capacity. (Use the High-Low Method to separate fixed and variable costs.)
2. Express the budget prepared in (1) in cost formula form, using a single cost formula to express all overhead costs.
3. The company operated at 95 percent of capacity during April in terms of actual hours of direct labor time recorded in the factory. Five thousand six hundred standard direct labor-hours were allowed for the output of the month. Actual overhead costs incurred were:

Maintenance	$ 2,083
Supplies	3,420
Utilities	2,666
Supervision	3,000
Machine setup	855
Total costs	$12,024

There were no variances in the fixed costs. Prepare a performance report for the month of April. Structure your report so that it shows only a spending variance for overhead. You may assume that the original budget for April called for an activity level during the month of 6,000 direct labor-hours.

4. Upon receiving the performance report you have prepared, the production manager commented, "I have two observations to make. First, I think there's an error on your report. You show an unfavorable spending variance for supplies, yet I know that we paid exactly the budgeted price for all the supplies we used last month. Shonna Adams, the purchasing agent, made a comment to me that our supplies prices haven't changed in over a year. Second, I wish you would modify your report to include an efficiency variance for overhead. The reason is that waste has been a problem in the factory for years, and the efficiency variance would help us get overhead waste under control."

   a. Explain the probable cause of the unfavorable spending variance for supplies.

   b. Compute an efficiency variance for *total* variable overhead, and explain to the production manager why it would or would not contain elements of overhead waste.

Chapter 10

Control of decentralized operations

In this chapter we expand our knowledge of performance reports by looking more closely at responsibility accounting. This concept was first introduced in Chapter 7, and has been the "why" behind most of our work with budgets and performance reports in preceding chapters. We shall now use the responsibility accounting concept to show how the reports developed in these chapters fit together into an integrated reporting system. In the process we will extend the technique of performance reporting to the company as a whole, and demonstrate methods of evaluating the performance of top management.

RESPONSIBILITY ACCOUNTING

Responsibility accounting centers on the idea that an organization is simply a group of individuals working toward common goals. The more each individual can be assisted in the performance of his or her tasks, then the better chance the organization has of reaching the goals it has set. As we have seen in preceding chapters, responsibility accounting recognizes each person in an organization who has any control over cost or revenue to be a *separate responsibility center,* whose stewardship must be defined, measured, and reported upward in the organization. One author expresses the idea this way:

In effect, the system personalizes the accounting statements by saying, "Joe, this is what you originally budgeted and this is how you performed for the period with actual operations as compared against your budget." By definition it [responsibility accounting] is a system of accounting which is tailored to an organization so that costs are accumulated and reported by levels of responsibility within the organization. Each supervisory area in the organization is charged *only* with the cost for which it is responsible and over which it has control.[1]

Although the idea behind responsibility accounting is not new, the implementation of the idea on a widespread basis is quite recent, and has come about in response to the manager's need for better and more efficient ways to control operations.

The functioning of the system

In order to broaden our perspective of how a responsibility accounting system functions, we will consider selected data relating to the Potter Company. Potter Company is part of the Western Division of National Corporation. A partial organization chart for Potter Company is shown in Exhibit 10–1. The data in this chart form the basis for exhibits found on the following pages.

---

[1] John A. Higgins, "Responsibility Accounting," *The Arthur Andersen Chronicle* (April 1952), p. 94.

Exhibit 10–1
Organization chart

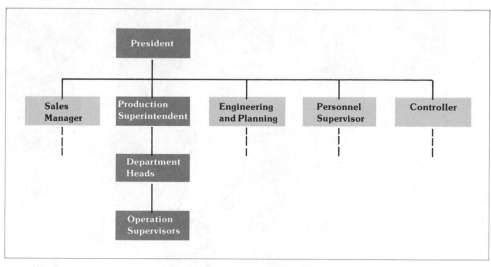

Although the concepts underlying responsibility accounting apply equally well to all parts of an organization, we will concentrate our discussion on the shaded area of Potter Company's organization chart. It depicts the line of responsibility for the production activities of the firm. This line of responsibility begins with the operation supervisors, and moves upward in the organization, with each successive level having greater overall responsibility than the level which preceded it. To see how this concept of an upward flowing, broadening line of responsibility can be integrated into the accounting statements, refer to Exhibit 10–2.

Exhibit 10–2 provides us with a bird's eye view of the structuring of reports in a responsibility accounting system. Notice that the performance reports *start at the bottom and build upward* with each manager receiving information on his own performance as well as on the performance of each manager under him in the chain of responsibility. We will now start at the bottom of this chain and follow it upward to show how the reports are used by the various levels of management.

The flow of information

The responsibility accounting system depicted in Exhibit 10–2 is structured around four levels of responsibility. The number of levels of responsibility will vary from company to company, according to organizational structure and needs.

FOURTH LEVEL OF RESPONSIBILITY. The fourth, or lowest, level of responsibility is that of the Wiring Operation Supervisor. The performance

Exhibit 10–2

POTTER COMPANY
An Overview of Responsibility Accounting*

President's Report

The president's performance report summarizes all company data. Since variances are given, the president can trace the variances downward through the company as needed to determine where his and his subordinates' time can best be spent.

Responsibility Center:	Budget	Actual	Variance
Sales manager	X	X	X
Production superintendent	$26,000	$29,000	$3,000 U
Engineering and planning	X	X	X
Personnel supervisor	X	X	X
Controller	X	X	X
	$54,000	$61,000	$7,000 U

Production Superintendent

The performance of each department head is summarized for the Production Superintendent. The totals on the Superintendent's performance report are then passed upward to the next level of responsibility.

Responsibility Center:	Budget	Actual	Variance
Cutting Department	X	X	X
Machining Department	X	X	X
Finishing Department	$11,000	$12,500	$1,500 U
Packaging Department	X	X	X
	$26,000	$29,000	$3,000 U

Finishing Department Head

The performance report of each supervisor is summarized on the performance report of the department head. The department totals are then summarized upward to the Production Superintendent.

Responsibility Center:	Budget	Actual	Variance
Sanding Operation	X	X	X
Wiring Operation	$ 5,000	$ 5,800	$ 800 U
Assembly Operation	X	X	X
	$11,000	$12,500	$1,500 U

Wiring Operation Supervisor

The supervisor of each operation receives a performance report on his or her center of responsibility. The totals on these reports are then communicated upward to the next higher level of responsibility.

Variable costs:	Budget	Actual	Variance
Direct materials	X	X	X
Direct labor	X	X	X
Manufacturing overhead	X	X	X
	$ 5,000	$ 5,800	$ 800 U

* Adapted from an illustration prepared by John A. Higgins, "Responsibility Accounting," *The Arthur Andersen Chronicle* (April 1952), p. 105.

report prepared for the supervisor will be similar to the performance reports discussed in the preceding chapter. This report will show budgeted data, actual data, and variances in terms of materials, labor, and overhead. This information will be communicated upward to the department head, along with detailed variance analyses.

THIRD LEVEL OF RESPONSIBILITY.   The third level of responsibility is the Finishing Department Head, who oversees the work of the Wiring Operation Supervisor as well as the work of the other supervisors in this department. Notice from Exhibit 10–2 that the department head will receive summarized data from each of the operations within the department. If the department head desires to know the reasons behind the variances reported in these summaries (such as the $800 variance in the Wiring Operation), he or she can look at the detailed, individual performance reports prepared on the separate operations.

SECOND LEVEL OF RESPONSIBILITY.   The second level of responsibility is the Production Superintendent who has responsibility for all producing department activities. Notice from Exhibit 10–2 that the summarized totals from the Finishing Department Head's performance report are reported upward to the Production Superintendent, along with summarized totals from the performance reports of other departments. In addition to the summarized totals, the Production Superintendent undoubtedly will also require that detailed copies of the performance reports themselves be furnished to him, as well as detailed copies of the performance reports from all separate operations within the departments. Availability of these reports will permit the Production Superintendent to go right to the heart of any problem in cost control. This, of course, is the implementation of the "management by exception" principle discussed in earlier chapters. By having variances from budget highlighted on each performance report, the Production Superintendent is able to see where his or her time and the time of the department heads and supervisors can best be spent.

FIRST LEVEL OF RESPONSIBILITY.   The president of a company has ultimate responsibility for all costs and revenues. On his or her performance report, therefore, the activities of all phases of the business must be summarized for review.

The president may require that the detailed copies of the performance reports from *all* levels of responsibility be supplied to him. On the other hand, he may concern himself only with broad results, leaving the more detailed data for the scrutiny of the managers of the lower responsibility centers such as the Production Superintendent. Thus, the system provides a great deal of flexibility, and can be expanded or contracted in terms of data provided to suit the needs and interests of the particular manager involved.

In the absence of a responsibility accounting system, managers are left with little more than a "seat-of-the-pants" feel for what is going on in their own areas of responsibility, as well as that of their subordinates.

Exhibit 10–3
The National Company organization—An expansion of the responsibility accounting concept

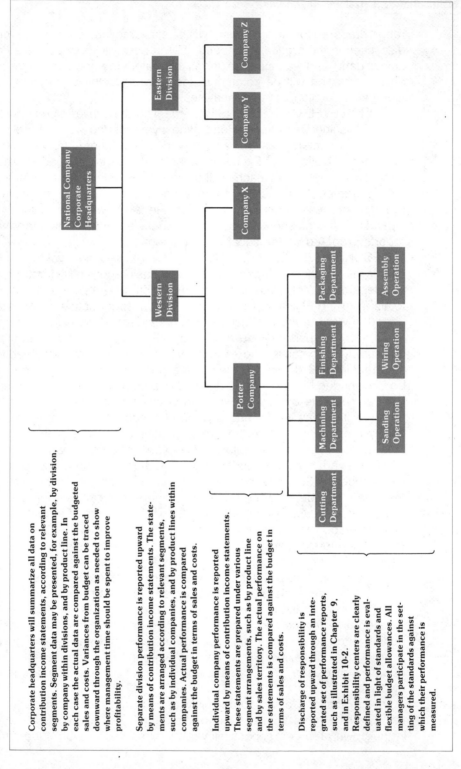

Corporate headquarters will summarize all data on contribution income statements, according to relevant segments. Segment data may be presented, for example, by division, by company within divisions, and by product line. In each case the actual data are compared against the budgeted sales and costs. Variances from budget can be traced downward through the organization as needed to show where management time should be spent to improve profitability.

Separate division performance is reported upward by means of contribution income statements. The statements are arranged according to relevant segments, such as by individual companies, and by product lines within companies. Actual performance is compared against the budget in terms of sales and costs.

Individual company performance is reported upward by means of contribution income statements. These statements are prepared under various segment arrangements, such as by product line and by sales territory. The actual performance on the statements is compared against the budget in terms of sales and costs.

Discharge of responsibility is reported upward through an integrated set of performance reports, such as illustrated in Chapter 9, and in Exhibit 10-2. Responsibility centers are clearly defined and performance is evaluated in light of standards and flexible budget allowances. All managers participate in the setting of the standards against which their performance is measured.

In today's highly competitive business environment, a "seat-of-the-pants" feel for how well costs are being controlled is rarely sufficient to sustain profitable operations.

Expanding the responsibility accounting idea

We have indicated earlier that the Potter Company is a part of the Western Division of National Company. Exhibit 10–3 shows more clearly just how Potter Company fits into the structure of the National Company organization.

This exhibit illustrates a further expansion of the responsibility accounting idea. Notice from the exhibit that contribution income statements are used to report company level performance to the division manager, and to report divisional performance to corporate headquarters.

On a corporate headquarters level, all data are summarized into various segment arrangements for an overall performance evaluation of the entire corporate structure. (See Exhibit 10–3.) Since variances from budgeted sales and costs are shown on the contribution income statements, managers at the various levels of responsibility can see clearly where profit objectives are not being met. An illustration of a contribution income statement with variances is presented in Exhibit 10–4. Income statements of this type are prepared at both the company and division levels, and then consolidated on a corporate level.

Exhibit 10–4

NATIONAL COMPANY
Contribution Income Statement Comparing
Budgeted Data to Actual Data
(000)

	Budget	Actual	Variance
Sales	$100,000	$97,000	$3,000 U
Variable expenses:			
Variable cost of sales	$ 45,000	$46,000	$1,000 U
Other variable expenses	15,000	14,500	500 F
Total variable expenses	$ 60,000	$60,500	$ 500 U
Contribution margin	$ 40,000	$36,500	$3,500 U
Less fixed expenses:			
Selling	$ 13,000	$13,000	—
Administrative	4,000	4,300	$ 300 U
Manufacturing	13,000	13,700	700 U
Total fixed expenses	$ 30,000	31,000	$1,000 U
Net income	$ 10,000	$ 5,500	$4,500 U

Exhibit 10–5
The National Company organization

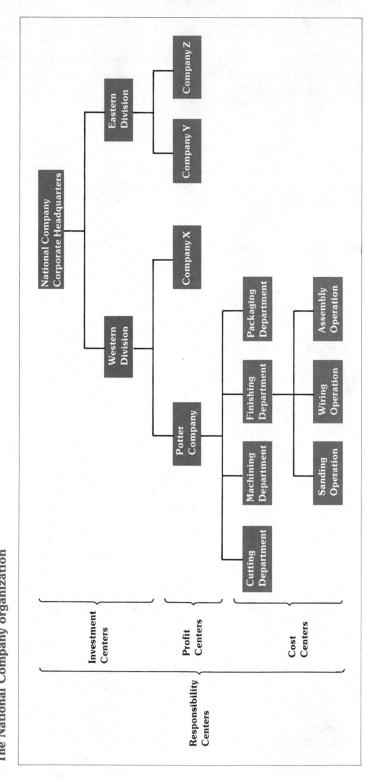

Investment, profit, and cost centers

In a responsibility accounting system, the structure of an organization such as National Company is visualized as consisting of various centers, such as shown in Exhibit 10–5.

RESPONSIBILITY CENTER. A *responsibility center* is any point within an organization where control over incurrence of cost or generating of revenue is found. Such a point could be an individual, an operation, a department, a company, a division, or the entire organization itself.

COST CENTER. A *cost center* is any responsibility center that has control over the incurrence of cost. A cost center has no control over sales or over the generating of revenue.

PROFIT CENTER. By contrast to a cost center, a *profit center* has control over both cost and revenue. Potter Company, for example, would be a profit center in the National Company organization since it would be concerned with marketing its goods as well as producing them.

INVESTMENT CENTER. An *investment center* is any responsibility center within an organization that has control over cost and revenue, and also has control over investment funds. The corporate headquarters of National Company would clearly be an example of an investment center. Corporate officers have ultimate responsibility for seeing that production and marketing goals are met. In addition, they have responsibility for seeing that adequate facilities are available to carry out the production and marketing functions, and for seeing that adequate working capital is available for operating needs. Whenever a segment of an organization has control over the making of investment in such areas as physical plant and equipment, receivables, inventory, and entry into new markets, then it is termed an investment center. Potter Company itself could be an investment center if it were given control over investment funds for some of these purposes. In the more usual situation, however, Potter Company would be a profit center within the larger organization, with most (or all) investment decisions being made at the divisional or central headquarters levels.

Measuring management performance

These concepts of responsibility accounting are very important, since they assist in defining a manager's sphere of responsibility and also in determining how performance will be evaluated.

Cost centers are evaluated by means of performance reports, in terms of meeting cost standards that have been set. Profit centers are evaluated by means of contribution income statements, in terms of meeting sales and cost objectives. Investment centers are also evaluated by means of contribution income statements, but normally in terms of the *rate of return* they are able to generate on *invested funds*. In the following section we discuss rate of return as a tool for measuring managerial performance in an investment center.

RATE OF RETURN FOR MEASURING MANAGERIAL PERFORMANCE

The development of concepts such as investment centers, profit centers, and cost centers is largely a result of the rapid growth of decentralization in corporate structures. Managers of investment centers and profit centers are generally given large amounts of autonomy in directing the affairs in their areas of responsibility. So great is this autonomy that the various profit and investment centers are often viewed as being virtually independent businesses, with their managers having about the same control over decisions as if they were in fact running their own independent firms. With this autonomy, fierce competition often develops between managers, with each striving to make his or her operation the "best" in the company.

Competition is particularly keen when it comes to passing out funds for expansion of product lines, or for introduction of new product lines. How do top managers in corporate headquarters go about deciding who gets new investment funds as they become available, and how do these managers decide which investment centers are most profitably using the funds which have already been entrusted to their care? One of the most popular ways of making these judgments is to measure the rate of return which investment center managers are able to generate on their assets. This can be done through the *return on investment (ROI)* formula.

The ROI formula

To understand the concepts behind the ROI formula, refer to the funds flow model illustrated in Exhibit 10–6.

Exhibit 10–6
The funds flow model

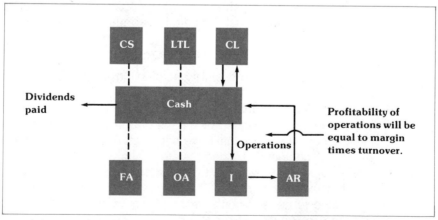

CS = Capital stock; LTL = long-term liabilities; CL = current liabilities; FA = fixed assets; OA = other assets; I = inventory; AR — accounts receivable.

As a dollar leaves the central pool of cash in Exhibit 10–6, it is invested in inventory. The inventory is then sold, and an account receivable is created, which is subsequently collected from the customer. Upon collection from the customer, the dollar which was started through the system is returned back into the central pool of cash from which it began its journey. This dollar will bring back with it whatever additional pennies the customer has been willing to pay above the cost of the goods which he or she purchased. Thus, the seller's profitability will at least in part be measured by the number of these additional pennies, which we may call the *margin* earned.

But a moment's reflection will indicate that a firm's profitability is also dependent on another factor. Realizing that a dollar going through the system will bring back a certain number of additional pennies with it, we will be anxious to send that dollar through the system as many times during the period as we possibly can. The number of trips a dollar makes through the system during a period is known as the *turnover*. Thus, we can see that a firm's profitability will be a product of the margin (number of pennies brought back by a dollar in one trip through the system), multiplied by the turnover (number of times a dollar makes the trip through the system during the period). This line of reasoning gives rise to the ROI formula:

$$\text{Margin} \times \text{Turnover} = \text{Profitability, or return on investment}$$

Factors underlying rate of return

Armed with a conceptual perspective of the ROI formula, we can now examine the detailed factors making up the margin and the turnover elements:

$$\text{Margin} \times \text{Turnover} = \text{Return on investment}$$

$$\text{Margin} = \frac{\text{Net operating income}}{\text{Sales}} \qquad \text{Turnover} = \frac{\text{Sales}}{\text{Operating assets}}$$

therefore,

$$\frac{\text{Net operating income}}{\text{Sales}} \times \frac{\text{Sales}}{\text{Operating assets}} = \text{Return on investment}$$

In the past, managers have tended to focus only on the margin earned and have ignored the turnover of assets. To some degree, at least, the margin earned can be a valuable measure of a manager's performance. But standing alone it overlooks one very crucial area of a manager's responsibility—the control of investment in operating assets. Excessive funds tied up in operating assets can be just as much of a drag on profitability as excessive operating expenses. One of the real advantages of the ROI formula is that it forces the manager to control his or her investment in operating assets as well as to control expenses, the gross profit rate, and sales volume.

The Du Pont Company was the first major corporation to recognize the importance of looking at both margin *and* turnover in assessing the performance of a manager. To them must go the credit for pioneering the ROI concept. Monsanto Chemical Company and other major corporations have followed the Du Pont lead, and the ROI formula is now recognized as one of the best single measures of a manager's performance when that manager has control of an investment center. It blends together many aspects of the manager's responsibilities into a single figure that can be compared against competing investment centers, as well as against other firms in the industry.

Operating income and the asset base

The reader may have noticed in the ROI formula above that net *operating* income was used rather than simply net income. The reason is that the definition of income used in the formula should be consistent with the asset base to which it is related. When dealing with *operating* assets as a base, it is common practice to use *net operating* income. Net operating income is income before interest and taxes. In business jargon it is sometimes referred to as EBIT (earnings before interest and taxes). The reader should become familiar with this term.

The operating asset base used in the formula is computed as the *average* between the beginning and the end of the year. "Operating assets" would include cash, accounts receivable, inventory, fixed assets and all other assets held for productive use in the organization.

CONTROLLING THE RATE OF RETURN

When being measured by the ROI formula, a manager can improve profitability in three ways:

1. By increasing sales.
2. By reducing expenses.
3. By reducing assets.

To illustrate how the rate of return can be controlled by each of these three actions, let us assume the following data for an investment center:

Net operating income	$ 10,000
Sales	100,000
Operating assets	50,000

The rate of return generated by the investment center would be:

$$\frac{\text{Net operating income}}{\text{Sales}} \times \frac{\text{Sales}}{\text{Operating assets}} = \text{Return on investment}$$

$$\frac{\$10,000}{\$100,000} \times \frac{\$100,000}{\$50,000} = \text{Return on investment}$$

$$10\% \times 2 = 20\%$$

Approach 1: Increase sales. Assume that the center above is able to increase sales from $100,000 to $110,000. Assume that net operating income increases from $10,000 to $12,000. The operating assets remain constant.

$$\frac{\$12,000}{\$110,000} \times \frac{\$110,000}{\$50,000} = \text{Return on investment}$$

$$10.9\% \times 2.2 = 23.98\%$$

Approach 2: Reduce expenses. Assume that the center above is able to reduce expenses by $1,000, so that net operating income increases from $10,000 to $11,000. Both sales and operating assets remain constant.

$$\frac{\$11,000}{\$100,000} \times \frac{\$100,000}{\$50,000} = \text{Return on investment}$$

$$11\% \times 2 = 22\%$$

Approach 3: Reduce assets. Assume that operating assets can be reduced from $50,000 to $45,000. Sales and net operating income remain unchanged.

$$\frac{\$10,000}{\$100,000} \times \frac{\$100,000}{\$45,000} = \text{Return on investment}$$

$$10\% \times 2.22 = 22.2\%$$

Increase sales

In first looking at the ROI formula one is inclined to think that the sales figure is neutral, since it appears as the denominator in the margin computation and as the numerator in the turnover computation. The sales figure *could* be canceled out, but we don't do so for two reasons. First, it would tend to draw attention away from the fact that the rate of return is a function of two variables, margin and turnover. And second, it would tend to conceal the fact that control of sales is one way in which to control profitability. If a manager can either (1) increase sales proportionately faster than expenses, or (2) increase sales while holding the investment in assets relatively constant, he or she can increase the rate of return.

How can sales be increased proportionately faster than expenses? This is often possible in those situations where fixed expenses are high relative to variable expenses. Once the break-even point is reached, net operating income will increase very rapidly for each additional unit sold, as explained in our discussion of operating leverage in Chapter 5. This explains how the net operating income could increase so much more rapidly than sales in Approach 1 above.

Reduce expenses

Often the easiest route to increased profitability is simply to cut the ''fat'' out of an organization through a concerted effort to control expenses. When profit margins begin to be squeezed, this is generally the first line of attack by a manager. The discretionary fixed costs usually come under scrutiny first, with various programs either curtailed or eliminated in an effort to cut costs. Firms under extreme pressures to reduce expenses have gone so far as to eliminate coffee breaks, under the reasoning that nothing could more emphatically impress the staff with the need to be cost conscious.

One of the most common ways to reduce variable expenses is to use less costly inputs of materials. Another way is to automate processes as much as possible, particularly where large volumes of units are involved.

Reduce operating assets

Managers have always been sensitive to the need to control operating expenses and operating margins. They have not always been equally as sensitive, however, to the need to control investment in operating assets. Firms that have adopted the ROI approach to measuring managerial performance report that one of the first reactions on the part of investment center managers is to trim down their investment in operating assets. The reason, of course, is that these managers quickly realize that an excessive investment in operating assets will reduce the asset turnover, and hurt the rate of return. As these managers pare down their investment in operating assets, funds are released that can be used elsewhere in the organization. Consider the following actual situation:

X Company, a firm located in a western state, is a manufacturer of high-quality cast iron pipe. A few years ago, a large conglomerate acquired a controlling interest in the stock of X Company. X Company became an investment center of the larger organization. The parent company measured the performance of the investment center managers by the ROI formula. X Company managers quickly found that their performance was below that of other investment centers within the organization. With their mediocre performance, X Company managers realized that they were in a poor position to compete for new investment funds. As one step in an effort to improve the rate of return, the company took a hard look at its investment in operating assets. As a result, it was able to reduce inventory alone by nearly 40 percent. This resulted in several million dollars becoming available for productive use elsewhere in the company. Within two years's time, the rate of return being generated by X Company improved dramatically. The controller of X Company, speaking at a management development conference, stated that the company had always been profitable in terms of net income to sales, so there really had been no incentive to watch the investment in operating assets prior to being put under the ROI microscope.

What avenues are open to an investment center manager in attempts to control the investment in operating assets? One approach is to pare out obsolete and redundant inventory. The computer has been extremely helpful in this regard, making perpetual inventory methods more feasible as well as facilitating the use of statistical methods of inventory control, such as discussed in Chapter 7. Another approach is to devise various methods of speeding up the collection of receivables. For example, many firms now employ the lock box technique by which customers in distant states remit directly to local post office boxes. The funds are received and deposited by a local banking institution in behalf of the payee firm. This can greatly speed up the collection process, thereby reducing the total investment required to carry accounts receivable. As the level of investment in receivables is reduced, the asset turnover is increased.

The problem of allocated expenses and assets

In decentralized organizations such as National Company it is common practice to allocate the expenses of operating corporate headquarters out to the separate divisions. When such allocations are made, a very thorny question arises as to whether these expenses should be considered in rate of return computations.

It can be argued on the one hand that allocated expenses should be included in rate of return computations, since they represent the value of services rendered to the divisions by central headquarters. On the other hand, it can be argued that they should not be included, since the divisional managers have no control over the incurrence of the expenses, and since the "services" involved are often of questionable value, or are hard to pin down.

At the very least, *arbitrary* allocations should be avoided in rate of return computations. If arbitrary allocations are made, great danger exists of creating a bias for or against a particular division. Expense allocations should be limited to the cost of those *actual* services provided by central headquarters which the divisions *otherwise* would have had to provide for themselves. The amount of expense allocated to a division should not exceed the cost which the division would have incurred if it had provided the service for itself.

The same guidelines apply to asset allocations from central corporate headquarters to the separate divisions.

THE CONCEPT OF RESIDUAL INCOME

Up to this point we have assumed that the purpose of an investment center should be to maximize the rate of return which it is able to generate on operating assets. There is another approach to measuring performance in an investment center which focuses on a concept known as *residual income*. Residual income is the net operating income which an investment center is able to earn *above* some minimum rate of return on operating assets. When residual income is used to measure performance, the purpose is to maximize the total amount of residual income, *not* to maximize the overall ROI figure.

Consider the following data for two comparable divisions:

	Performance measured by	
	Rate of return (Division A)	Residual income (Division B)
Average operating assets	$100,000 (a)	$100,000
Net operating income	$ 20,000 (b)	$ 20,000
ROI (b) ÷ (a)	20%	
Minimum required rate of return is assumed to be 15%. 15% × $100,000		15,000
Residual income		$ 5,000

Many companies view residual income as being a better measure of performance than rate of return. They argue that the residual income approach encourages managers to make profitable investments that would be rejected by managers being measured by the ROI formula. To illustrate, assume that each of the divisions above is presented with an opportunity to make an investment of $25,000 in a new project that would generate a return of 18 percent on invested assets. The manager of Division A would probably reject this opportunity. Note from the tabulation above that his division is already earning a return of 20 percent on its assets. If he takes on a new project that provides a return of only 18 percent, then his overall ROI will be reduced, as shown below:

	Present	New project	Overall
Average operating assets (a)	$100,000	$25,000	$125,000
Net operating income (b)	$ 20,000	$ 4,500*	$ 24,500
ROI (b) ÷ (a)	20%	18%	19.6%

* $25,000 × 18% = $4,500.

Since the performance of the manager of this division is being measured according to the *maximum* rate of return which he is able to generate on invested assets, he will be unenthused about any investment opportunity which reduces his current ROI figure. He will tend to think and act along these lines, even though the opportunity he rejects may have benefited the company *as a whole.*

On the other hand, the manager of Division B will be very anxious to accept the new investment opportunity. The reason is that she isn't concerned about maximizing her rate of return. She is concerned about maximizing her residual income. Any project that provides a return greater than the minimum required 15 percent will be attractive since it will add to the *total amount* of the residual income figure. Under these circumstances the new investment opportunity with its 18 percent return will clearly be attractive, as shown below:

	Present	New project	Overall
Average operating assets	$100,000	$25,000	$125,000
Net operating income	$ 20,000	$ 4,500*	$ 24,500
Minimum required rate of return is again assumed to be 15%	15,000	3,750†	18,750
Residual income	$ 5,000	$ 750	$ 5,750

* $25,000 × 18% = $4,500.
† $25,000 × 15% = $3,750.

Thus, by accepting the new investment project, the manager of Division B will increase her division's overall residual income figure, and thereby show an improved performance as a manager. The fact that her division's overall ROI might be lower as a result of accepting the project is immaterial, since performance is being evaluated by residual income, not ROI. The well-being of both the manager and the company as a whole will be maximized by accepting all investment opportunities down to the 15 percent cutoff rate.

The residual income approach has one major disadvantage. It can't be used to compare the performance of divisions of different sizes, since by its very nature it creates a bias in favor of larger divisions. That is, one would expect the larger divisions to have more residual income than the smaller divisions, not necessarily because they are better managed but simply because of the bigger numbers involved.

TRANSFER PRICING

Special problems arise in applying the rate of return or residual income approaches to performance evaluation whenever one segment of a company supplies goods or services to another. The problems revolve around the question of what *transfer price* to charge for the transfer of goods or for the exchange of services.

The need for transfer prices

Assume that a vertically integrated firm has four divisions. The four divisions are:

Mining Division.
Processing Division.
Fabricating Division.
Manufacturing Division.

The Mining Division mines raw materials that are transferred to the Processing Division. After processing, the Processing Division transfers the processed materials to the Fabricating Division which makes fabricated parts and then transfers them to the Manufacturing Division. The Manufacturing Division then includes the fabricated parts as part of its finished product.

In this example we have three transfers of goods between divisions within the same company. What price should control these transfers? The choice of a transfer price can be complicated by the fact that each division may be supplying portions of its output to outside customers, as well as to sister divisions.

The price charged to outside customers will be dictated largely by the competitive conditions of the market. But should this same price be used in pricing transfers *between* divisions? This is a key question since the price charged by one division becomes a cost to the other division. The higher this cost, the lower will be the purchasing division's net operating income and overall rate of return (or residual income).

As the reader may guess, the problem of what transfer price to set between segments of a company has no easy solution, and often leads to protracted and heated disputes between investment center managers. Yet some transfer price *must* be set if data are to be available for performance evaluation of the various parts or divisions of a company. In practice, four general approaches are used in setting transfer prices:

1. Setting transfer prices at cost.
2. Setting transfer prices at variable cost.
3. Setting transfer prices at market price.
4. Setting transfer prices at negotiated market price.

Transfer prices at cost

Many firms make transfers between divisions on the basis of the accumulated cost of the goods being transferred. One problem with this approach is that the only division that will show any profits is the one that makes the final sale to an outside party. Other divisions will show no returns for their efforts, and evaluation by the rate of return formula, or by the residual income approach, will not be possible. A further problem arises in defining just what should be included in "cost," and whether this figure should be allowed to fluctuate from period to period according to changes in production levels, and so forth. Arguments pro and con can be almost endless, and the source of considerable friction and ill-feeling.

The most serious criticism of cost-based transfer prices lies in their general inability to provide incentive for control of costs. If the costs of one division are simply passed on to the next, then there is little incentive for anyone to control costs. The final selling division is simply burdened with the accumulated waste and inefficiency of intermediate processors, and will be penalized with a rate of return that is deficient in comparison to competitors. Experience has shown that unless costs are subject to some type of competitive pressures at transfer points, waste and inefficiency almost invariably develop.

Despite these shortcomings, cost-based transfer prices are in fairly common use. Advocates argue that they are easily understood and highly convenient to use. If transfer prices are to be based on cost, then the costs should be standard costs, rather than actual costs. This will at least avoid the passing on of inefficiency from one division to another.

Transfer prices at variable cost

Basically the same comments can be made about pricing transfers at variable cost as those made above about pricing transfers at full cost. Variable costs do have one advantage, however, in that *so far as the short run is concerned* their use may tend to insure the best utilization of total corporate facilities. The reason is that, in the short run, fixed costs don't change. Any use of facilities, therefore, that brings in revenues in excess of variable costs will increase short-run profitability. The danger lies in becoming locked into what was intended to be a short-run arrangement but which proves to be unprofitable over the longer term when full costs are considered.

Transfer prices at market price

Some form of competitive market price is generally regarded as the best approach to the transfer pricing problem. The reason is that it dovetails very well with the profit center concept, and makes profit-based performance evaluation feasible at many levels of an organization. This approach also tends to lead to the best decisions involving transfer questions that may arise on a day-to-day basis, as we shall illustrate.

The market price approach is designed for use in highly decentralized organizations; that is, in those organizations where divisional managers have sufficient autonomy in decision making that the various divisions can be viewed as being virtually independent businesses, with independent profit responsibility. The idea in using market prices to control transfers is to create the competitive market conditions that would exist if the various divisions were *indeed* separate firms, and engaged in arm's length, open-market bargaining. To the extent that the resulting transfer prices reflect actual market conditions, divisional operating results provide an excellent basis for evaluating managerial performance.

The National Association of Accountants describes other advantages and the overall operation of the market price approach as follows:

> Internal procurement is expected where the company's products and services are superior or equal in design, quality, performance, and price, and when acceptable delivery schedules can be met. So long as these conditions are met, the receiving unit suffers no loss and the supplier unit's profit accrues to the company. Often the receiving division gains advantages such as better control over quality, assurance of continued supply, and prompt delivery.[2]

The guidelines that should be followed in using market prices to control transfers between divisions are:

1. The buying division must purchase internally so long as the selling division meets all bona fide outside prices, and wants to sell internally.
2. If the selling division does not meet all bona fide outside prices, then the buying division is free to purchase outside.
3. The selling division must have the option of not selling internally if it prefers to sell outside.[3]
4. An impartial board must be established to arbitrate disputes over prices.

Illustrating the market price approach

To illustrate the operation of the market price approach, let us assume that the Processing Division of International Company has a product that can be sold either to the Fabricating Division or to outside customers. The cost structures of the Processing and Fabricating Divisions are given below:

Processing Division		*Fabricating Division*	
Intermediate market price if		Final market price outside	$10
sold outside	$5	Transfer price from Processing	
Variable costs	$3	Division	$ 5
		Variable costs added in	
		Fabricating Division	$ 2

The choices facing the Processing and Fabricating Divisions are shown graphically in Exhibit 10–7.

---

[2] *Accounting for Intra-Company Transfers,* Research Series No. 30 (New York: National Association of Accountants, June 1956), pp. 13–14.

[3] The reason for this guideline is that the selling division may have opportunities for using its facilities to produce and sell other, more profitable, products.

Exhibit 10–7
Illustration of transfers at market price

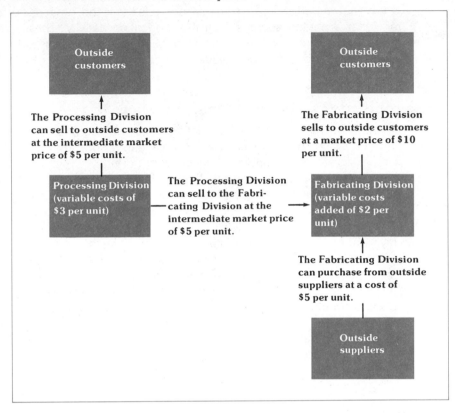

So long as the Processing Division can get a transfer price of $5 per unit out of the Fabricating Division, it will be completely willing to sell all of its output internally. In selling to the Fabricating Division, the Processing Division will be just as well off as if it had sold its product outside at the $5 price. In like manner, so long as the price charged by outside suppliers is not less than $5 per unit, the Fabricating Division will be willing to pay that price to the Processing Division. The $5 per unit intermediate market price, therefore, serves as an acceptable transfer price between the two divisions. The results of transfers at this price can be summarized as follows:

	Processing Division	Fabricating Division	Entire company
Sales price per unit	$5	$10	$10
Variable costs added per unit	3	2	5
Transfer cost per unit	—	5	—
Contribution margin per unit	$2	$ 3	$ 5

The contribution margin realized for the entire company is $5 per unit. By using market prices for intracompany transfers, the firm is able to show that a portion of this margin accrues from the processing activity and that a portion accrues from the fabricating activity. These data will then serve as an excellent basis for evaluating managerial performance using the rate of return or residual income approaches.

The problem of a change in market price

But what happens if the Fabricating Division finds an outside supplier who is willing to supply units at only $4 each? The answer is that the Processing Division should be given an opportunity to meet this price. If it meets the $4 price, then the Fabricating Division should continue to purchase from the Processing Division, as indicated in the guidelines given earlier. But is the Processing Division *required* to meet the $4 price? The answer is no. The guidelines given earlier indicate that the selling division is not required to sell internally. In this case, the Processing Division would *not* cut its price to $4 to retain the internal sales, so long as sufficient sales could be made to outside customers at $5.[4]

If the Processing Division decided not to reduce its price to $4 to meet outside competition, should the Fabricating Division be forced to continue to pay $5 and to buy internally? The answer again is no. The guidelines given earlier state that if the selling division is not willing to meet all bona fide outside prices, then the buying division is free to go outside to get the best price it can.

Transfers at negotiated market prices

The market price at transfer points represents an *upper limit* on the charge that can be made on transfers between divisions. In many situations a lesser price can be justified. For example, selling and administrative expenses may be less when intracompany sales are involved, or the *volume* of units may be sufficiently large to justify quantity discounts. In other cases, the selling division may have substantial excess capacity, which may justify a price below the prevailing market.

Situations such as those just described can probably best be served by some type of *negotiated* market price. A negotiated market price is one agreed upon between the selling and buying divisions that reflects unusual or mitigating circumstances. Negotiated market prices are also required in those situations where no independent market prices are available. For example, one division may produce an item that is not available

---

[4] If sufficient business could not be obtained outside at the $5 price, then the Processing Division might want to turn its facilities over to other, more profitable products.

from any other source. Some type of negotiated market price would be required to establish the price to be paid by the buying division.

The matter of opportunity cost

The use of market price in transfer pricing helps to guard against setting transfer prices below the selling division's opportunity costs. (Recall from Chapter 2 that opportunity cost can be defined as the potential benefit that is lost or sacrificed when the choice of one course of action requires the giving up of an alternative course of action.) The opportunity costs of the selling division may differ, depending on whether it is operating at full or at partial capacity.

SELLING DIVISION AT FULL CAPACITY. If the selling division is already selling all that it can produce to outside customers, then the division's opportunity cost is the purchase price which these outside customers are willing to pay. The reason is that in accepting inside business, the selling division would have to give up outside business, and sacrifice the revenues that could have been received on the outside sales. *Thus, the transfer price inside should never be less than this opportunity cost (reduced by any costs that are avoided as a result of inside sales, as discussed earlier), or the selling division will suffer, and the company as a whole may suffer as well.*

SELLING DIVISION WITH EXCESS CAPACITY. If the selling division has substantial excess capacity, then a different situation exists. Under these conditions opportunity costs *may* be zero (depending on what alternative uses the seller has for his or her excess capacity). Even if opportunity costs are zero, many managers would argue that the transfer price should still be based on prevailing market prices, to the extent that they can be determined accurately and fairly. Other managers would argue that excess capacity combined with zero, or near zero, opportunity costs calls for a negotiation of the transfer price downward from prevailing market rates, so that both the buyer and the seller can profit from the intracompany business.

Under excess capacity conditions, so long as the selling division can receive a price greater than its variable costs (at least in the short run) all parties will benefit by keeping business inside rather than having the buying division go outside. If the selling division has excess capacity and the buying division purchases from an outside supplier then suboptimization[5] will result for the selling division, possibly for the buying division, and certainly for the company as a whole. In short, if excess capacity exists every effort should be made to negotiate a price acceptable

---

[5] By *suboptimization* we mean that overall profitability will be less than it could have been.

to both the buyer and the seller that will keep business within the company as a whole.

Divisional autonomy and suboptimization

A question often arises as to how much autonomy should be granted to divisions in setting their own transfer prices, and in making decisions concerning whether to sell internally or to sell outside. Should the divisional heads have complete authority to make these decisions, or should top corporate management step in if it appears that a decision is about to be made that would result in suboptimization? For example, if excess capacity exists in the selling division and divisional managers are unable to agree on a transfer price, should top corporate management step in and *force* settlement of a dispute?

Effort should always be made, of course, to bring disputing managers together. But the almost unanimous feeling among top corporate executives is that divisional heads should not be forced into an agreement over a transfer price. That is, if a particular divisional head flatly refuses to change his or her position in a dispute, *then this decision should be respected,* even if it results in suboptimization. This is simply the price that is paid for the concept of divisional autonomy. If top corporate management steps in and forces the decisions in difficult situations, then the concepts which we have been developing in this chapter largely evaporate and the company simply becomes a centralized operation, with decentralization of only minor decisions and responsibilities. In short, if a division is to be viewed as an autonomous unit with independent profit responsibility, then it must have control over its own destiny—even to the extent of the right to make bad decisions.

We should note, however, that if a division consistently makes bad decisions, the results will soon have an impact on its rate of return, and the divisional manager may find himself having to defend the division's performance. Even so, his right to get himself into an embarrassing situation must be respected if the divisional concept is to operate successfully. The overwhelming experience of multidivisional companies is that divisional autonomy and independent profit responsibility leads to much greater success and profitability than closely controlled, centrally administered operations. Part of the price of this success and profitability is an occasional situation of suboptimization, due to pettiness, bickering, or just plain managerial cussedness.

SUMMARY

Responsibility accounting centers on the notion that any point within an organization having control over cost or revenue is a responsibility center. The way in which the various responsibility centers discharge their control over cost or revenue is communicated upward in an organization, from lower levels of responsibility to higher levels of responsibility, through a system of integrated performance reports.

Those responsibility centers having control over cost are known as cost centers. Those having control over both cost and revenue are known as profit centers, and those having control over cost, revenue and investment funds are known as investment centers. The ROI formula is widely regarded as a method of evaluating performance in an investment center because it summarizes into one figure many aspects of an investment center manager's responsibilities. As an alternative to the ROI formula, some companies use residual income as a measure of investment center performance. These companies argue that the residual income approach encourages profitable investment in many situations where the ROI approach might discourage investment.

Transfer pricing relates to the price to be charged in a transfer of goods or an exchange of services between two units (such as divisions) within an organization. The predominant feeling is that the best transfer price is some version of the market price, to the extent that a market price exists for the good or service involved. The use of market price in transfers between units facilitates performance evaluation by permitting both the buyer and the seller to be treated as independent, autonomous units.

KEY TERMS FOR REVIEW

Responsibility centers
Cost centers
Profit centers
Investment centers
Return on investment (ROI)
Margin
Turnover

Net operating income
Residual income
Transfer pricing
Market price approach
Negotiated market price
Suboptimization

QUESTIONS

10–1. In what way does the concept of responsibility accounting give emphasis to a firm's organizational structure?

10–2. Describe the general flow of information in a responsibility accounting system.

10–3. What is meant by the term responsibility center? Could a responsibility center be a person as well as a department, and so on? Does the concept apply to nonmanufacturing as well as to manufacturing activities?

10–4. Distinguish between a cost center, a profit center, and an investment center.

10–5. How is performance in a cost center generally measured? Performance in a profit center? Performance in an investment center?

10–6. What is meant by the terms margin and turnover?

10–7. In what way is rate of return a more exacting measure of performance than the ratio of net income to sales?

10–8. When the rate of return formula is being used to measure performance, what three avenues are open to the manager in improving the overall profitability?

10–9. The sales figure could be canceled out in the ROI formula, leaving simply net operating income over operating assets. Since this abbreviated formula would yield the same ROI figure, why leave sales in?

10–10. A student once commented to the author, "It simply is not possible for a decrease in operating assets to result in an increase in profitability. The way to increase profits is to *increase* the operating assets." Discuss.

10–11. X Company has high fixed expenses and is presently operating somewhat above the break-even point. From this point on, will percentage increases in net income tend to be greater than, about equal to, or less than percentage increases in total sales? Why? Ignore income taxes.

10–12. What is meant by residual income?

10–13. In what way can ROI lead to dysfunctional decisions on the part of the investment center manager? How does the residual income approach overcome this problem?

10–14. Division A has operating assets of $100,000 and Division B has operating assets of $1,000,000. Can residual income be used to compare performance in the two divisions? Explain.

10–15. What is meant by the term transfer price, and why are transfer pricing systems needed?

10–16. Why are cost-based transfer prices in widespread use? What are the disadvantages of cost-based transfer prices?

10–17. If a market price for a product can be determined, why is it generally considered to be the best transfer price?

10–18. Under what circumstances might a negotiated market price be a better approach to pricing transfers between divisions than actual market price?

10–19. In what ways can suboptimization result if divisional managers are given full autonomy in setting, accepting, and rejecting transfer prices?

EXERCISES

E10–1. Selected operating data for two divisions of Arco Company are given below:

	East division	West division
Sales	$60,000	$75,000
Operating assets	30,000	25,000
Net operating income	5,100	5,625
Long-term debt	5,000	6,000

Required:

1. Compute the rate of return for each division, using the return on investment formula.
2. So far as you can tell from the data available, which divisional manager seems to be doing the best job? Why?

E10–2. Listed below are three charges found on the monthly report of a division which manufactures and sells products primarily to outside customers. Divisional performance is evaluated by the use of return on investment (ROI). You are to state which, if any, of the following charges are consistent with the "responsibility accounting" concept, and support each answer with a brief explanation:

1. A charge for the cost of operating general corporate headquarters, at 10 percent of division sales.
2. A charge for goods purchased from another division. The charge is based upon the competitive market price for the goods.
3. A charge for the use of the corporate computer facility. The charge is determined by taking actual annual computer department costs and allocating an amount to each division on the ratio of its use to total corporate use.

(CMA, adapted)

E10–3. Division A produces a product that can be sold either to Division B or to outside customers. During 19x1, the following activity occurred in Division A:

```
Units produced  ......................... 500
Units sold to Division B  ................. 100
Units sold to outside customers  ........... 400
Unit selling price  ........................ $10
Unit cost of production  ................... $ 6
```

The units purchased by Division B were processed further at a cost of $4 per unit, and sold to outside customers for $15 each. All transfers between divisions are made at market price.

Required:

1. Prepare income statements for 19x1 for Division A, Division B, and the company as a whole.
2. Assume that Division A's manufacturing capacity is 500 units. In 19x2, Division B wants to purchase 200 units from Division A, rather than only 100 units as in 19x1. Should Division A sell the extra units to Division B, or continue selling the units to outside customers? Explain.

E10–4. Provide the missing data in the following tabulation:

	Division A	Division B	Division C	Division D
Sales	$450,000	$?	$500,000	$?
Net operating income	22,500	10,000	20,000	?
Operating assets	90,000	?	?	100,000
Margin	?	4%	?	8%
Turnover	?	?	?	3
Return on investment	?	16%	10%	?

E10–5. The Transistor Division of Consumer Products, Inc., produces transistors which are sold to the Company's Radio Division, as well as to outside customers. Operating data for the Transistor Division for last year are given below:

	To the Radio Division	To outside customers
Sales:		
100,000 units at $4*	$400,000	
200,000 units at $5		$1,000,000
Variable expenses at $2 and $3	200,000	600,000
Contribution margin	$200,000	$ 400,000
Fixed expenses	125,000	250,000
Net income	$ 75,000	$ 150,000

*$5 outside selling price less expenses applicable to outside sales.

The manager of the Radio Division has just received an offer from an outside supplier to supply the transistors at $3.25 each. The manager of the Transistor Division is not willing to meet the $3.25 price. He argues that it costs him $3.25 to produce and sell a transistor to the Radio Division, so he would show no profit on the Radio Division sales. No additional sales can be made to outside customers.

Required:

1. Show how the Transistor Division manager computed the $3.25 unit cost figure.
2. Should the Transistor Division manager be *required* to meet the outside price of $3.25 for Radio Division sales? Explain.
3. If you were the Transistor Division manager, would *you* meet the $3.25 outside price? Explain.

E10–6. Cordell Enterprises has just purchased a large amount of high-speed data processing equipment, and has placed it in a newly organized Computer Division. The Computer Division is to provide computer services for all other divisions within the Cordell Enterprises organization. Computer usage is very significant in all divisions.

The Computer Division charges $300 per hour for computer services, which represents depreciation plus annual operating costs, divided by expected annual usage in hours. Some divisional managers have complained that the charge is too high, and that they can do better outside. The executive committee of the company has decided, however, that the $300 figure will stand as it is, and that divisional managers will not be free to go outside for computer services. As one member of the committee explained, "We know the charge is high, but that equipment represents a major investment, and we need to recover the investment as fast as we can."

Required:

1. Does the $300 figure represent a transfer price?
2. Evaluate the executive committee's decision.

E10–7.   Selected sales and operating data for three companies are given below:

	Company X	Company Y	Company Z
Sales	$150,000	$120,000	$200,000
Net operating income	6,000	3,600	7,500
Operating assets	50,000	30,000	100,000
Stockholders' equity	35,000	20,000	75,000
Minimum required rate			
of return	10%	12%	8%

Required:
1. Compute the residual income for each company.
2. Assume that each company is presented with an investment opportunity that would yield a rate of return of 11 percent. Which companies will accept? Reject? Why?

E10–8.   Supply the missing data in the tabulation below.

	Division			
	A	B	C	D
Sales	$50,000	$45,000	$90,000	$75,000
Net operating income	5,000	?	4,500	?
Operating assets	20,000	15,000	?	50,000
Return on investment	?	20%	7.5%	?
Minimum required rate of				
return:				
Percentage...................	20%	?	?	6%
Dollar amount	$?	$?	$ 6,000	$?
Residual income	?	750	?	-0-

PROBLEMS

P10–9.   *ROI and residual income.*   Right-Way Products, Inc., is a decentralized organization with six autonomous divisions. Divisions are evaluated on a basis of the return which they are able to generate on invested assets, with year-end bonuses given to divisional managers who have the highest ROI figures. Operating results in the Cosmetics Division for the most recent year are given below:

Sales.....................................	$5,000,000
Less variable expenses	3,000,000
Contribution margin	$2,000,000
Less fixed expenses	1,600,000
Net operating income	$ 400,000
Divisional operating assets	$2,000,000

The company had an overall ROI last year of 15 percent (considering all divisions). The Cosmetics Division has an opportunity to add a new product line which would require an additional investment in operating assets of $500,000. Cost and revenue characteristics of the new product line would be:

```
Sales ......................... $1,000,000
Variable expenses ............. 60% of sales
Fixed expenses ................ $320,000
```

Required:

1. As manager of the Cosmetics Division, would you accept or reject the new product line? Explain, providing appropriate computations.
2. As the president of Right-Way Products, Inc., would you want the Cosmetics Division to accept or reject the new product line? Explain.
3. Suppose that the company views a return of 12 percent on invested assets as being the minimum that should be earned by any division, and evaluates performance by the residual income approach. Under these circumstances, as manager of the Cosmetics Division would you accept or reject the new product line? Explain, and provide supporting computations.

P10–10. *ROI; Comparison of company performance.* Comparative data on three companies in the same industry are given below:

	A	B	C
Sales	$800,000	$300,000	$?
Net operating income	80,000	30,000	?
Operating assets	400,000	?	3,000,000
Margin	?	?	0.5%
Turnover	?	?	2
Return on investment	?	1%	?

Required:

1. What advantages can you see in breaking the ROI computation down into two separate elements, margin and turnover?
2. Fill in the missing information above, and comment on the relative performance of the three companies in as much detail as the data permit. Make specific recommendations on steps to be taken to improve the return on investment, where needed.

(Adapted from NAA Research Report No. 35, p. 34.)

P10–11. *The appropriate transfer price.* Management Consultants, Inc., is organized into three independent groups:

Engineering Group.
Systems Group.
Personnel Planning Group.

Each group performs consulting services for outside clients, as well as for other groups within the company. The normal pricing and cost structure for each group is:

	Per consulting hour		Monthly	
			Total fixed	Consulting hours
	Fee	Variable cost	cost	available
Engineering Group	$25	$10	$60,000	5,000
Systems Group	30	12	90,000	6,000
Personnel Planning Group	25	10	55,000	4,500

The company desires to evaluate each group as if it were an autonomous company.

Required:

1. Assume that the Systems Group has need for consulting services from the Engineering Group. The Engineering Group has ample opportunity to utilize its consulting time with outside clients. What transfer price should be charged to the Systems Group? Why?

2. Assume that the going rate for engineering consulting services is $25 per hour. Under the conditions posed in (1) is there any reason why the Engineering Group should provide services to the Systems Group for less than this figure? Explain.

3. Again assume the conditions posed in (1). Also assume that the Systems Group has found an engineering firm that will provide the desired consulting services for only $23 per hour. Should the Engineering Group meet this figure in order to keep the business within the company? Explain.

4. Assume again that the going rate for engineering consulting time is $25 per hour. However, the Engineering Group has decided to raise its rate to $30 per hour, and wants to do consulting work for the Systems Group. Should the Systems Group be required to pay the higher price in order to keep the business within the firm? Explain.

5. Assume again that the going rate for engineering consulting time is $25 per hour. The Engineering Group has unused time available, which it is willing to supply to the Systems Group at the going rate. Should the Systems Group accept the Engineering Group's offer? Explain.

6. Assume again that the Engineering Group has unused time available. The Systems Group has found an outside engineering firm that is willing to do the needed consulting for only $18 per hour. Should the Engineering Group meet this price? Explain.

7. Under the conditions posed in Part (6), if the Engineering Group refuses to meet the $18 hourly rate, should the Systems Group be permitted to go outside for its consulting services? Why or why not?

8. Under the conditions posed in Part (6), what is the lowest price that the Engineering Group could accept and still be better off profit-wise than if it did no consulting work for the Systems Group?

P10–12. *Straightforward rate of return computation.* The accounting records
of Design Services, Inc., reveal the following information for the prior
two years:

	Last year	This year
Sales	$60,000	$64,000
Net income	4,500	5,120
Net operating income	6,000	6,720
Stockholders' equity	15,000	20,000
Average operating assets	20,000	25,000

Required:

1. Compute the ratio of net income to sales for each year.
2. Compute the ratio of net operating income to sales for each year.
3. Compute the rate of return for each year, using the rate of return
    formula.
4. Using the data computed in (1) to (3) above, explain why the rate
    of return is the better measure of managerial performance.

P10–13. *Integrating cost-volume-profit analysis, ROI, and transfer pricing.* The
Valve Division of Wesco, Inc., produces a small valve that is used by
various companies as a component part in the manufacture of their
products. The Valve Division's fixed costs total $105,000 per period,
and variable costs are $3 per valve. The division has a target return
on investment (ROI) of 10 percent. Its asset structure is:

Cash	$ 10,000
Accounts receivable	20,000
Inventory	70,000
Fixed assets (net)	50,000
Total assets	$150,000

The selling price is $5 per valve.

Required:

1. How many valves must the division sell in order to obtain the desired
    rate of return on its assets?
    a. What is the margin earned at this sales level?
    b. What is the turnover of assets at this sales level?
2. The divisional manager is thinking about dropping the sales price
    to $4.75 per unit. She thinks this would increase the volume of
    sales to 70,000 units each period. Compute the margin, turnover,
    and ROI if these changes are made.
3. Refer to the original data. Rather than dropping the sales price,
    the manager could increase the price to $5.25 per unit, but this
    would cause the volume of units sold to drop to only 50,000 units
    each period. Compute the margin, turnover, and ROI if these
    changes are made.
4. Refer to the original data. Assume that the normal volume of sales
    is 60,000 units each period at a price of $5 each. The division
    has a capacity to produce 70,000 units. Another division in the

company is now buying 10,000 valves each period from an outside source, at a price of $4.50 per valve. The manager of the Valve Division has adamantly refused to meet this price, pointing out that it allows for no profit for her division's efforts:

Selling price per valve		$4.50
Cost per valve:		
Variable	$3.00	
Fixed ($105,000 ÷ 70,000)	1.50	4.50
Net income per valve		$ 0

The manager of the Valve Division also points out that the normal $5 selling price barely allows her division the desired 10 percent rate of return. "If we take on more business at only $4.50 per unit, then our ROI is obviously going to suffer," she reasons, "and maintaining that ROI figure is the key to my future. Besides, taking on these extra units would require us to increase our assets by at least $20,000 due to the larger inventories and receivables that we would be carrying." Would you recommend that she sell to the other division at $4.50? Show ROI computations to support your answer.

P10–14. *Transfer pricing.* The Detroit Motor Company has just acquired a new Battery Division. The Battery Division produces a standard 12-volt battery which it sells to retail outlets at a competitive price of $15. The retail outlets purchase about 1,200,000 batteries a year. Since the Battery Division has a capacity of 2,000,000 batteries a year, top management is thinking that it might be wise for the company's Automotive Division to start purchasing from the newly acquired Battery Division.

The Automotive Division now purchases 600,000 batteries a year from an outside supplier, at a price of $14 per battery. The discount from the competitive $15 price is a result of the large quantity purchased.

The Battery Division's cost per battery is shown below:

Direct materials	$ 6
Direct labor	2
Variable overhead	1
Fixed overhead	2*
Total cost	$11

* Based on 1,200,000 batteries.

Both divisions are to be treated as investment centers, and their performance evaluated by the ROI formula.

Required:

1. *a.* What transfer price would you recommend? Why?
   b. If the transfer price you recommend is accepted, what will be the effect on the profits of the company as a whole? Show computations.
   c. If the transfer price you recommend is accepted, would you expect the ROI in the Battery Division to increase, decrease, or remain unchanged? Why? (No computations are necessary.)

What would be the effect on the ROI of the Automotive Division? Explain.

2. Assume that the Battery Division is now selling 2,000,000 batteries a year to retail outlets.

   a. What transfer price would you recommend? Why? Will any transfers take place between the two divisions?

   b. If the Battery Division decides to sell to the Automotive Division for $14 per battery, what will be the effect on the profits of the company as a whole? Show computations.

P10–15. *Choosing an appropriate transfer price.* Worldwide Enterprises has just acquired a small company which produces condenser units for refrigerators. The company will operate as a division of Worldwide Enterprises, under the name of the Condenser Division. The newly acquired Condenser Division produces and sells condenser units to various refrigerator manufacturers across the country. The price is $50 per condenser. The president of Worldwide Enterprises feels that the company's own Refrigerator Division should begin to purchase its condenser units from the newly acquired Condenser Division.

Worldwide Enterprises' Refrigerator Division is presently purchasing 400,000 condenser units each year from an outside supplier. The price is $48 per condenser, which represents the normal $50 price less a quantity discount due to the large number of units being purchased.

The Condenser Division's cost per condenser unit is presented below:

Direct materials	$18
Direct labor	14
Variable overhead	6
Fixed overhead	4*
Total cost	$42

* Operating at 2,000,000 units capacity.

The president of Worldwide Enterprises is trying to decide what transfer price should control the sales between the two divisions.

Required:

1. Assume that the newly acquired Condenser Division has sufficient excess capacity to supply all the Refrigerator Division's condenser needs. Explain why each of the following transfer prices would or would not be an appropriate price to charge the Refrigerator Division on the intracompany sales.

   a. $50
   b. $48
   c. $43
   d. $42
   e. $38

2. Assume that the newly acquired Condenser Division is presently selling all it can produce to outside customers. Under these circumstances, explain why each of the transfer prices given in (1a) through (1e) above would or would not be an appropriate price to charge the Refrigerator Division on the intracompany sales.

P10–16. *Transfer pricing dispute.* The Timer Division of Household Appliances, Inc., produces an electronic timing device that is used by the company's Range Division in producing ovens and cooktops, as well as by other appliance manufacturers in the industry. The Timer Division is now operating at its capacity of 800,000 timing devices per year, 25 percent of which is purchased by the Range Division. The Timer Division's income statement for the most recent year is given below:

TIMER DIVISION
Income Statement
For the Year 19x1

	Sales breakdown		
	Range Division	Other companies	Total
Sales	$2,300,000	$7,200,000	$9,500,000
Less variable expenses at $9	1,800,000	5,400,000	7,200,000
Contribution margin	$ 500,000	$1,800,000	$2,300,000
Less fixed expenses.............	360,000	1,080,000	1,440,000
Net operating income	$ 140,000	$ 720,000	$ 860,000

Sales to other companies are at $12 per timing device. Sales to the Range Division are at $11.50, due to a quantity discount.

The rapid growth of the electronics industry has created intense competition for the Timer Division. Another manufacturer of timing devices has offered a firm contract to the Range Division to supply all of its timing device needs for only $10 per unit.

The manager of the Timer Division will not lower his price to the Range Division. He argues that if he does lower his price, it will result in a loss of $0.80 per unit, or $160,000 in total ($0.80 × 200,000 units), on Range Division sales. The fixed costs of the Timer Division will not be affected by the decision.

Required:

1. What will be the impact on the operating income of the Timer Division if the Range Division accepts the contract offered by the outside manufacturer?
2. What will be the impact on the operating income of Household Appliances, Inc., *as a company* if the Range Division accepts the contract?
3. What decision do you expect the manager of the Range Division to make regarding the contract offered? Explain.
4. Assume that the capacity now being used to produce timing devices for the Range Division could be used to produce an electronic sensing device that could be sold in a new market. The sensing devices would require an additional $100,000 in fixed expenses each period, and variable costs would be $15 per unit. At a selling price of $18, the Timer Division could sell 150,000 of the sensing devices each period. Would you recommend that the new sensing devices be produced, or that the Timer Division continue producing only timing

devices and meet the $10 price being offered to the Range Division? Show computations.

P10–17. *The appropriate transfer price.* Electronic Products, Inc., has just purchased a small company that specializes in the manufacture of electronic tuners that are used in the TV industry as a component part in TV sets. Electronic Products, Inc. is a decentralized organization, and will treat the newly acquired company as an autonomous division with full profit responsibility. The new Tuner Division's fixed costs total $60,000 per month; production capacity is 10,000 tuners per month; and variable costs per tuner are $11. The selling price per tuner is $20.

Electronic Products, Inc. has an Assembly Division that assembles TV sets. This division currently is purchasing 3,000 tuners per month from an overseas supplier. The president of Electronic Products, Inc. is anxious for the Assembly Division to begin purchasing its tuners from the newly acquired Tuner Division in order to "keep the profits within the corporate family."

Required:

For (1)–(4), assume that demand for tuners is strong enough that the Tuner Division can sell all of its output to outside TV manufacturers at its quoted prices. *Each question is independent.*

1. If the Assembly Division purchases 3,000 tuners per month from the Tuner Division, what price should control the transfers? Why?
2. If the market price for tuners is $20, is there any reason why the Tuner Division should sell to the Assembly Division for less than this figure? Explain.
3. Suppose that the Assembly Division is now purchasing from the overseas supplier at a price of $18 per tuner. Should the Tuner Division meet this price in order to keep the profits within the corporate family? Explain. If the $18 price is met, what will be the effect on the profits of the company as a whole? Show computations.
4. Suppose that the Tuner Division has just raised its price to $21 per tuner, even though the Assembly Division can buy tuners overseas at $18. Should the Assembly Division be required to meet the $21 price in order to keep the profits on its purchases within the corporate family? Explain. If the $21 price is met, what will be the effect on the profits of the company as a whole? Show computations.

For (5)–(8), assume that the Tuner Division is presently selling only 7,000 tuners to outside TV manufacturers at the stated $20 price.

5. Suppose that the Assembly Division is presently paying a price of $18 per tuner to its overseas supplier. What price should control transfers between the Tuner and Assembly Divisions? Explain.
6. Suppose that the overseas supplier drops its price to only $16 per tuner. Should the Tuner Division meet this price? Explain. If the Tuner Division does not meet the $16 price, what will be the effect on the profits of the company as a whole?
7. Refer to Question 6. If the Tuner Division refuses to meet the $16

price, should the Assembly Division be required to purchase from the Tuner Division at a higher price, for the good of the company as a whole? Explain.

8. What is the lowest price that the Tuner Division could accept from the Assembly Division and still be better off profitwise?

P10–18. *Cost-volume profit analysis, ROI, and transfer pricing.* The Bearing Division of Timkin Company produces a small bearing that is used by a number of companies as a component part in the manufacture of their products. The Timkin Company operates its divisions as autonomous units, giving its divisional managers great discretion in pricing and other decisions. Each division is expected to generate a return on its assets of at least 12 percent. The Bearing Division has operating assets as follows:

Cash	$ 10,000
Accounts receivable	60,000
Inventories..................................	105,000
Fixed assets (net)	125,000
Total assets	$300,000

The bearings are sold for $4 each. Variable costs are $2.50 per bearing, and fixed costs total $234,000 each period. The division's capacity is 200,000 bearings each period.

Required:

1. How many bearings must be sold each period in order for the division to obtain the desired rate of return on its assets?
   a. What is the margin earned at this sales level?
   b. What is the turnover of assets at this sales level?

2. The divisional manager is considering two ways of increasing the ROI figure:
   a. Market studies suggest that an increase in price to $4.25 per bearing would result in sales of 160,000 units each period. The decrease in units sold would allow the division to reduce its investment in assets by $10,000, due to the lower level of inventories and receivables needed to support sales. Compute the margin, turnover, and ROI if these changes are made.
   b. Other market studies suggest that a reduction in price to $3.75 per bearing would result in sales of 200,000 units each period. However, this would require an increase in total assets of $10,000 due to the somewhat larger inventories and receivables that would be carried. Compute the margin, turnover, and ROI if these changes are made.

3. Refer to the original data. Assume that the normal volume of sales is 180,000 bearings each period at a price of $4 per bearing. Another division of the Timkin Company is presently purchasing 20,000 bearings each period from an overseas supplier at $3.25 per bearing. The manager of the Bearing Division says that this price is "ridiculous," and refuses to meet it, since it would result in a loss of $0.42 per bearing for her division:

Selling price $3.25
Cost per bearing:
  Variable cost $2.50
  Fixed cost ($234,000 ÷ 200,000 bearings) 1.17   3.67
Loss per bearing . . . .   ($ .42)

You may assume that sales to the other division would require an increase of $25,000 in the total assets carried by the Bearing Division. Would you recommend that the Bearing Division meet the $3.25 price, and start selling 20,000 bearings per period to the other division? Support your answer with ROI computations.

P10–19. *Transfer pricing and marketing decisions.* Neutron Division, a division of Diversified Enterprises, Inc., produces a component part which is used in the manufacture of hi-fi sets. The cost per part is:

Variable cost per part . . . . $ 70
Fixed cost per part 30*
    Total cost per part $100

  * Based on a capacity of 1,000 parts per month.

Part of the Neutron Division's output is sold to outside manufacturers of hi-fi sets, and part is sold to Diversified Enterprises' Quark Division, which produces a hi-fi set under its own name. The price per part is $150.

The Quark Division's cost and revenue structure is:

Selling price per set $500
Less variable costs per set:
  Cost of parts from the Neutron Division $150
  Variable costs added   200
    Total variable costs   350
Contribution margin per set $150
  Less fixed costs per set 50*
Net income per set $100

  * Based on a capacity of 100 sets per month.

The Quark Division has an order from an overseas source for ten hi-fi sets. The overseas source wants to pay only $340 per set.

Required:

1. Is the Quark Division likely to accept the $340 price offered, or to reject it? Explain.
2. If both the Neutron Division and the Quark Division have excess capacity, would the Quark Division's action benefit or be a disadvantage to the company as a whole? Explain, showing computations.
3. Assume that the Quark Division has excess capacity, but that the Neutron Division is operating at full capacity and could sell all of its parts to outside manufacturers. Compute the dollar advantage or disadvantage of the Quark Division accepting the ten set order at the $340 price.
4. What kind of transfer pricing information is needed by the Quark Division in making decisions such as these?

P10–20. *Transfer pricing dispute; Behavioral problems.* The Lorax Electric Company manufactures a large variety of systems and individual components for the electronics industry. The firm is organized into several divisions with division managers given the authority to make virtually all operating decisions. Management control over divisional operations is maintained by a system of divisional profit and return on investment measures which are reviewed regularly by top management. The top management of Lorax has been quite pleased with the effectiveness of the system they have been using and believe that it is responsible for the company's improved profitability over the last few years.

The Devices Division manufactures solid-state devices and is operating at capacity. The Systems Division has asked the Devices Division to supply a large quantity of integrated circuit IC378. The Devices Division currently is selling this component to its regular customers at $40 per hundred.

The Systems Division, which is operating at about 60 percent capacity, wants this particular component for a digital clock system. It has an opportunity to supply large quantities of these digital clock systems to Centonic Electric, a major producer of clock radios and other popular electronic home entertainment equipment. This is the first opportunity any of the Lorax divisions have had to do business with Centonic Electric. Centonic Electric has offered to pay $7.50 per clock system.

The Systems Division prepared an analysis of the probable costs to produce the clock systems. The amount that could be paid to the Devices Division for the integrated circuits was determined by working backward from the selling price. The cost estimates employed by the division reflected the highest per unit cost the Systems Division could incur for each cost component and still leave a sufficient margin so that the division's income statement could show reasonable improvement. The cost estimates are summarized below.

Proposed selling price		$7.50
Costs excluding required integrated circuits (IC378):		
Components purchased from outside suppliers	$2.75	
Circuit board etching—labor and		
variable overhead	0.40	
Assembly, testing, packaging—labor and		
variable overhead	1.35	
Fixed overhead allocations	1.50	
Profit margin	0.50	6.50
Amount which can be paid for integrated		
circuits IC378 (5 at $20 per hundred)		$1.00

As a result of this analysis, the Systems Division offered the Devices Divison a price of $20 per hundred for the integrated circuit. This bid was refused by the manager of the Devices Division because he felt the Systems Division should at least meet the price of $40 per hundred which regular customers pay. When the Systems Division found that it could not obtain a comparable integrated circuit from outside vendors, the situation was brought to an arbitration committee which had been set up to review such problems.

The arbitration committee prepared an analysis which showed that $0.15 would cover variable costs of producing the integrated circuit, $0.28 would cover the full cost including fixed overhead, and $0.35 would provide a gross margin equal to the average gross margin on all of the products sold by the Devices Division. The manager of the Systems Division reacted by stating, "They could sell us that integrated circuit for $0.20 and still earn a positive contribution toward profit. In fact, they should be required to sell at their variable cost—$0.15 and not be allowed to take advantage of us."

Lou Belcher, manager of Devices, countered by arguing that, "It doesn't make sense to sell to the Systems Division at $20 per hundred when we can get $40 per hundred outside on all we can produce. In fact, Systems could pay us up to almost $60 per hundred and they would still have a positive contribution to profit."

The recommendation of the committee, to set the price at $0.35 per unit ($35 per hundred), so that Devices could earn a "fair" gross margin, was rejected by both division managers. Consequently, the problem was brought to the attention of the vice president of operations and his staff.

Required:

1. What is the immediate economic effect on the Lorax Company as a whole if the Devices Division were required to supply IC378 to the Systems Division at $0.35 per unit—the price recommended by the arbitration committee. Explain your answer.
2. Discuss the advisability of intervention by top management as a solution to transfer pricing disputes between division managers such as the one experienced by Lorax Electric Company.
3. Suppose that Lorax adopted a policy of requiring that the price to be paid in all internal transfers by the buying division would be equal to the variable costs per unit of the selling division for that product and that the supplying division would be required to sell if the buying division decided to buy the item. Discuss the consequences of adopting such a policy as a way of avoiding the need for the arbitration committee or for intervention by the vice president.

(CMA, adapted)

P10–21. *Transfer pricing and divisional performance.* Wexpro Company is a decentralized organization containing six divisions. The Brake Division has asked the Electrical Division (which is operating at capacity) to supply it with a large quantity of electrical fitting No. 1726. The Electrical Division sells this fitting to its regular customers for $7.50 each. The Brake Division, which is operating at 50 percent of capacity, wants to pay $5 each for the fittings. The Brake Division will put the fittings into a brake unit which it is manufacturing and will sell on essentially a cost basis to a large commerical airplane manufacturer.

The Electrical Division has a variable cost of producing fitting No. 1726 of $4.25. The cost of the brake unit being built by the Brake Division follows:

Purchased parts (from outside vendors)	$22.50
Electrical fitting No. 1726	5.00
Other variable costs.................................	14.00
Fixed overhead and administration	8.00
Total cost per brake unit	$49.50

The manager of the Brake Division believes that the price concession from the Electrical Division is necessary if his division is to get the airplane manufacturer job.

The company uses return on investment and dollar profits in the measurement of division and division-manager performance.

Required:

1. Assume that you are the division controller of the Electrical Division. Would you recommend that the Electrical Division supply fitting No. 1726 to the Brake Division, as requested? Why or why not? (Ignore any tax issues.)
2. Would it be to the short-run economic advantage of the Wexpro Company for the Electrical Division to supply the Brake Division with the fittings at $5 each? Explain your answer. (Ignore any tax issues.)
3. Discuss the organizational and manager behavior difficulties, if any, inherent in this situation. As the Wexpro Company controller, what would you advise the Wexpro Company president to do in this situation?

(CMA, adapted)

P10–22. *Transfer pricing.* This problem is more difficult than the preceding problems. Division A produces a component part which can be sold either to outside customers or to Division B. Selected operating data on the two divisions are given below:

Division A

Unit selling price to outside customers	$	75
Variable production cost per unit		45
Variable selling and administrative		
expense per unit		2
Fixed production cost in total		300,000*

Division B

Outside purchase price per unit		
(net of quantity discount)	$	72

   * Capacity 20,000 units per year.

Division B has always purchased its component parts from outside suppliers, but now consideration is being given to purchasing component parts from Division A. As the company's president stated, "It's just plain smart to buy and sell within the corporate family when you can."

A study has determined that the variable selling and administrative expenses of Division A would be cut in half for any sales to Division B. Top management wants to treat each division as an autonomous unit with independent profit responsibility.

Required:

1. Assume that Division A has ample excess capacity to handle all of Division B's needs.
   a. What is the highest transfer price that can be justified between the two divisions? Explain.
   b. What is the lowest transfer price that can be justified between the two divisions? Explain.
   c. Assume that Division B finds an outside supplier who will sell the needed component parts for only $65 per unit. Should Division A be required to meet this price? Explain.
   d. Refer to the original data. Assume that Division A decides to raise its price to outside customers to $80 per unit. If Division B is forced to pay this price, and to start purchasing from Division A, will it result in greater or less total corporate profits? How much per unit?
   e. Under the circumstances posed in (*d*) above, should Division B be forced to purchase from Division A? Explain.
2. Assume that Division A can sell all that it can produce to outside customers. Repeat (*a*) through (*e*) above.

Chapter 11

Relevant costs in nonroutine decisions

The making of decisions is one of the basic functions of a manager. The manager is constantly faced with problems of deciding what products to sell, what production methods to use, whether to make or buy component parts, what prices to charge, what channels of distribution to use, whether to accept special orders at special prices, and so forth. At best, decision making is a difficult and complex task. This difficulty is usually increased by the existence of not just one or two, but numerous courses of action that might be taken in any given situation facing a firm.

In decision making, *cost* is always a key factor. The costs of one alternative must be compared against the costs of other alternatives as one step in the decision-making process. The problem is that some costs associated with an alternative may not be *relevant* to the decision to be made. To be successful in decision making, managers must have tools at their disposal to assist them in identifying relevant and irrelevant costs, so that the latter can be eliminated from the decision framework. The purpose of this chapter is to acquire these tools, and to show their application in a wide range of decision-making situations.

COST CONCEPTS FOR DECISION MAKING

Three cost terms discussed in Chapter 2 are particularly applicable to this chapter. These terms are differential costs, opportunity costs, and sunk costs. The reader may find it helpful to turn back to Chapter 2 and refresh his or her memory of these terms before reading on.

Identifying relevant costs

What costs are relevant in decision making? The answer is easy. All costs are relevant in decision making, except those costs which are not avoidable. Unavoidable costs fall into two categories, as follows:

1.   Sunk costs.
2.   Future costs that *do not differ* between the alternatives at hand.

As we learned in Chapter 2, a sunk cost is a cost which has already been incurred and which cannot be avoided regardless of which course of action a manager may decide to take. As such, these costs have no relevance to future events and must be ignored in decision making. Similarly, if a future cost will be incurred regardless of which course of action a manager may take, then the cost cannot possibly be of any help in deciding which course of action is best. Such a cost is not avoidable, and hence is not relevant to the manager's decision.

Stated another way, *the relevant costs in a decision are those costs (and revenues) which are differential as between the alternatives being considered.* To identify those costs which are differential and therefore relevant, the manager's approach to cost analysis should include the following steps:

1. Assemble *all* costs associated with *each* alternative being considered.
2. Eliminate those costs which are sunk.
3. Eliminate those costs which do not differ between alternatives.
4. Make a decision based on the remaining cost data. These costs will be the differential costs, and hence the costs relevant to the decision to be made.

Cost relevance versus cost precision

There is a difference between cost relevance and cost precision. Managers sometimes confuse relevance with precision, thinking that they mean the same thing. Actually, they are very different ideas. A cost can be very precise, but yet totally irrelevant to the decision at hand. For example, the salary of a company's purchasing agent may be precisely $30,000 per year, but this figure probably would have no relevance to whether the company should acquire Machine A or Machine B for use on the assembly line.

SUNK COSTS ARE NOT RELEVANT COSTS

One of the most difficult conceptual lessons that managers have to learn is that sunk costs are never relevant in decisions. The tendency to want to include sunk costs within the decision framework is especially strong in the case of book value of old equipment. We focus on book value of old equipment below, and then consider other kinds of sunk costs in other parts of the chapter. We shall see that regardless of the kind of sunk cost involved, the conclusion is always the same—sunk costs are not avoidable and must be eliminated from the manager's decision framework.

Book value of old equipment

Assume the following data:

Old machine		Proposed new machine	
Original cost	$10,000	List price new	$12,000
Remaining book value	$ 8,000	Expected life	4 years
Remaining life	4 years	Disposal value in 4 years	–0–
Disposal value now	$ 3,000	Annual variable expenses	
Disposal value in 4 years	–0–	to operate	$15,500
Annual variable expenses		Annual revenue from sales	$50,000
to operate	$20,000		
Annual revenue from sales	$50,000		

Should the old machine be disposed of and the new machine purchased? Many accountants and managers alike would say no, since disposal of the old machine would result in a "loss from disposal" of $5,000:

Remaining book value	$8,000
Disposal value now	3,000
Loss if disposed of now . . . . :	$5,000

Even though the new machine is more efficient than the old machine, there is a general inclination to reason that "we have already made an investment in the old machine, so now we have no choice but to use the machine until we get our money out of it." Although it may be appealing to think that an error of the past can be corrected by simply *using* the item involved, this, unfortunately, is not correct. The investment that has been made in the old machine is a sunk cost. The portion of this investment that remains on the company's books (the book value of $8,000) should not be considered in a decision about whether to buy the new machine. We can prove this assertion by the following analysis:

	All four years together		
	Keep old machine	Differential costs	Purchase new machine
Sales	$200,000	$ –0–	$200,000
Variable expenses	(80,000)	18,000	(62,000)
Depreciation on the new machine	–0–	(12,000)	(12,000)
Depreciation on the old machine, or lump-sum write-off	(8,000)	–0–	(8,000)*
Disposal value of the old machine	–0–	3,000	3,000*
Total net income over the four years	$112,000	$ 9,000	$121,000

* These two items would be combined and deducted as a single $5,000 "loss from disposal" figure if a formal income statement was being prepared.

Looking at all four years together, notice that the firm will be $9,000 better off by purchasing the new machine. Also notice that the $8,000 book value of the old machine had *no effect* on the outcome of the analysis. Since this book value is a sunk cost, it must be absorbed by the firm regardless of whether the old machine is kept and used or whether it is sold. If the old machine is kept and used, then the $8,000 book value is deducted in the form of depreciation. If the old machine is sold, then the $8,000 book value is deducted in the form of a lump-sum write-off. Either way, the company bears the same $8,000 deduction.

FOCUSING ON RELEVANT COSTS. What costs in the example above are relevant in the decision concerning the new machine? Following the steps outlined earlier, we should eliminate (1) the sunk costs, and (2) the future costs that do not differ between the alternatives at hand:

1. The sunk costs:
   a. The remaining book value of the old machine ($8,000).
2. The future costs that do not differ:
   a. The annual sales revenue ($50,000).
   b. The annual variable expenses (to the extent of $15,500).

The costs that remain will form the basis for a decision. The analysis is:

	All four years together
Reduction in variable expense promised by the new machine ($4,500* per year × 4 years)	$18,000
Cost of the new machine	(12,000)
Disposal value of the old machine	3,000
Net advantage of the new machine	$ 9,000

* $20,000 − $15,500 = $4,500.

Note that the items above are the same as those in the middle column of the earlier analysis, and represent those costs and revenues which are differential as between the two alternatives.

DEPRECIATION AND RELEVANT COSTS. Since the book value of old equipment is not a relevant cost, there is a tendency to assume that depreciation of *any* kind is irrelevant in the decision-making process. This is not a correct assumption. Depreciation is irrelevant in decisions only if it relates to a sunk cost. Notice from the comparative income statements in the preceding section that the $12,000 depreciation on the new machine appears in the middle column as a relevant item in trying to assess the desirability of the new machine's purchase, while depreciation on the old machine does not. The difference is that the investment in the new machine has *not yet been made,* and therefore it does not represent depreciation of a sunk cost.

FUTURE COSTS THAT DO NOT DIFFER ARE NOT RELEVANT COSTS

Any future cost that does not differ between the alternatives under consideration is not a relevant cost. As stated earlier, if a company is going to sustain a cost regardless of what decision it makes, then that cost can in no way tell the company which decision is best. The only way a future cost can help in the decision-making process is by being different as between the alternatives under consideration.

An illustration

To illustrate the irrelevance of future costs that do not differ, let us assume that a firm is contemplating the purchase of a new laborsaving machine. The machine will cost $10,000 and have a ten-year useful life. The company's sales and cost structure on an annual basis with and without the new machine are shown below:

	Present costs	Expected costs with the new machine
Units produced	5,000	5,000
Sales price per unit	$ 10	$ 10
Direct materials cost per unit	4	4
Direct labor cost per unit	3	2
Variable overhead cost per unit	1	1
Fixed costs, other	4,000	4,000
Fixed costs, new machine	–0–	1,000

The new machine promises a saving of $1 per unit in direct labor costs, but will increase fixed costs by $1,000 per period. All other costs, as well as the total number of units produced, will remain the same. Following the steps outlined earlier, the analysis is:

1. Eliminate the sunk costs. (No sunk costs are identified in this example.)
2. Eliminate the future costs (and revenues) that do not differ:
    a. The sales price per unit does not differ.
    b. The direct materials cost per unit does not differ.
    c. The variable overhead cost per unit does not differ.
    d. The total fixed costs, other, do not differ.

This leaves just the per unit labor costs, and the fixed costs associated with the new machine as being differential costs:

Savings in direct labor costs (5,000 units at a cost saving of $1 per unit)	$5,000
Less increase in fixed costs	1,000
Net annual cost savings promised by the new machine	$4,000

The accuracy of this solution can be proved by looking at *all* items of cost data (both those that are relevant and those that are not) under the two alternatives for a period, and comparing the net income results.

	5,000 units produced and sold		
	Present method	Differential costs	New machine
Sales	$50,000	$ –0–	$50,000
Variable expenses:			
Direct materials	$20,000	–0–	$20,000
Direct labor	15,000	5,000	10,000
Variable overhead	5,000	–0–	5,000
Total variable expenses	$40,000		$35,000
Contribution margin	$10,000		$15,000
Less fixed expenses:			
Other	$ 4,000	–0–	$ 4,000
New machine	–0–	(1,000)	1,000
Total fixed expenses	$ 4,000		$ 5,000
Net income	$ 6,000	$4,000	$10,000

Why isolate relevant costs?

In the preceding example we used two different methods to show that the purchase of the new machine was desirable. First, we considered only the relevant costs; and second, we considered all costs, both those that were relevant and those that were not. We obtained the same answer under both approaches. When students see that the same answer can be obtained under either approach, they often ask the question, "Why bother to isolate relevant costs when total costs will do the job just as well?" The isolation of relevant costs is desirable for at least two reasons.

First, only rarely will enough information be available to prepare a detailed income statement such as we have done in the preceding examples. Since only limited data normally are available, the decision maker *must* know how to recognize which costs are relevant and which are not. Assume, for example, that you are called upon to make a decision relating to a matter in a *single operation* of a multidepartmental, multiproduct firm. Under these circumstances it would be virtually impossible to prepare an income statement of any type. You would have to rely on your ability to recognize which costs were relevant and which were not in order to assemble the necessary data to make a decision.

Second, the use of irrelevant costs intermingled with relevant costs may confuse the picture, and draw the decision maker's attention away from the matters that are really critical to the problem at hand. Furthermore, the danger always exists that an irrelevant piece of data may be used improperly, resulting in an incorrect decision. The best approach is to isolate the relevant items, and to focus all attention directly on them, and on their impact on the decision to be made.

Relevant cost analysis, combined with the contribution approach to the income statement, provides a powerful tool for making decisions in special, nonroutine situations. We will investigate various uses of this tool in the remaining sections of this chapter.

ADDING AND DROPPING PRODUCT LINES

The decisions relating to when to drop old product lines and when to add new product lines are among the stickiest that a manager has to make. In such decisions, many factors must be considered that are both qualitative and quantitative in nature. Ultimately, however, any final decision to drop an old product line, or to add a new product line, is going to hinge primarily on the impact the decision will have on net income. In order to assess this impact, it is necessary to make a careful analysis of the costs involved.

An illustration of cost analysis

As a basis for discussion, let us consider the product lines of the Discount Drug Company. The company has three major product lines—drugs, cosmetics, and housewares. Sales and cost information for the preceding month for the store in total and for each separate product line is given in Exhibit 11–1.

Exhibit 11–1
Discount Drug Company product lines

	Total	Drugs	Cosmetics	Housewares
Sales	$250,000	$125,000	$75,000	$50,000
Less variable expenses	105,000	50,000	25,000	30,000
Contribution margin	$145,000	$ 75,000	$50,000	$20,000
Less fixed expenses:				
Salaries	$ 50,000	$ 29,500	$12,500	$ 8,000
Advertising	15,000	1,000	7,500	6,500
Utilities	2,000	500	500	1,000
Depreciation—fixtures	5,000	1,000	2,000	2,000
Rent	20,000	10,000	6,000	4,000
Insurance	3,000	2,000	500	500
General administrative	30,000	15,000	9,000	6,000
Total fixed expenses	$125,000	$ 59,000	$38,000	$28,000
Net income (loss)	$ 20,000	$ 16,000	$12,000	$ (8,000)

What can be done to improve the company's overall performance? One product line—housewares— shows a net loss for the month. Perhaps dropping this line would cause profits in the company as a whole to improve. In deciding whether the line should be dropped, management will need to reason as follows:

If the housewares line is dropped, then the company will lose $20,000 per month in contribution margin that presently is available to help cover the fixed costs. By dropping the line, however, it may be possible to avoid certain of these fixed costs. It may be possible, for example, to discharge certain employees, or it may be possible to reduce advertising costs. If by dropping the housewares line the company is able to avoid more in fixed costs than it loses in contribution margin, then it will be better off if the line is eliminated, since overall net income should improve. On the other hand, if the company is not able to avoid as much in fixed costs as it loses in contribution margin, then the housewares line should be retained. In short, in order to identify the differential costs in decisions of this type the manager must ask, "What costs can I avoid to offset my loss of revenue if I drop this product line?"

As we have seen from our earlier discussion, not all costs are avoidable. Some costs associated with a product line may be sunk costs, for example; other costs may be allocated common costs which will not differ in total regardless of whether the product line is dropped or retained. To show how the manager should proceed in a product line analysis, suppose that the management of the Discount Drug Company has analyzed the costs being charged to the three product lines, and has determined the following:

1. The salaries represent salaries paid to employees working directly in each product line area. All of the employees working in housewares can be discharged if the line is dropped.
2. The advertising represents direct advertising of each product line, and is avoidable if the line is dropped.
3. The utilities represent utilities costs for the entire company. The amount charged to each product line represents an allocation based on space occupied.
4. The depreciation represents depreciation on fixtures used for display of the various product lines. Although the fixtures are nearly new, they are custom-built and will have little resale value if the housewares line is dropped.
5. The rent represents rent on the entire building housing the company, and is allocated to the product lines on a basis of sales dollars. The monthly rent of $20,000 is fixed under a long-term lease agreement.
6. The insurance represents insurance carried on inventories maintained within each of the three product line areas.
7. The general administrative expense represents the costs of accounting, purchasing, and general management, which are allocated to the product lines on a basis of sales dollars. Total administrative costs will not change if the housewares line is dropped.

With this information, management can identify those costs which can and which cannot be avoided if the product line is dropped:

	Total cost	Not avoidable*	Avoidable
Salaries	$ 8,000		$ 8,000
Advertising	6,500		6,500
Utilities	1,000	$ 1,000	
Depreciation—fixtures	2,000	2,000	
Rent	4,000	4,000	
Insurance	500		500
General administrative	6,000	6,000	
Total fixed expenses	$28,000	$13,000	$15,000

* These costs represent either (1) sunk costs, or (2) costs which will not change regardless of whether the housewares line is retained or discontinued.

The costs which can be avoided by dropping the housewares line can be compared against the contribution margin which will be lost, to determine how dropping the line will affect the overall profits of the company:

Contribution margin lost if the housewares line is discontinued (see Exhibit 11–1)	$(20,000)
Less fixed costs which can be avoided if the housewares line is discontinued	15,000
Decrease in overall company net income	$(5,000)

In this case, the fixed costs which can be avoided by dropping the product line are less than the contribution margin which will be lost; therefore, the housewares line should not be discontinued unless a more profitable use can be found for the floor and counter space which it is occupying.

A comparative format

Some managers prefer to approach decisions of this type by preparing comparative income statements showing the effects on the company as a whole with and without the product line in question. A comparative analysis of this type for the Discount Drug Company is shown in Exhibit 11–2.

As shown by column 3 in the exhibit, overall company net income will decrease by $5,000 each period if the housewares line is dropped. This is the same answer, of course, as we obtained in our earlier analysis.

Beware of allocated fixed costs

Our conclusion to not drop the housewares line seems to conflict with the data shown in Exhibit 11–1. Notice from the exhibit that the housewares line is showing a net loss rather than a profit. The explanation for this apparent inconsistency lies at least in part with the common fixed costs which are being allocated to the product lines.

Exhibit 11–2
A comparative format for product line analysis

	Keep housewares	Drop housewares	Difference: Net income increase or (decrease)
Sales	$50,000	$ –0–	$(50,000)
Less variable expenses	30,000	–0–	30,000
Contribution margin	$20,000	$ –0–	$(20,000)
Less fixed expenses:			
Salaries	$ 8,000	$ –0–	$ 8,000
Advertising	6,500	–0–	6,500
Utilities	1,000	1,000	–0–
Depreciation—fixtures	2,000	2,000	–0–
Rent	4,000	4,000	–0–
Insurance	500	–0–	500
General administrative	6,000	6,000	–0–
Total fixed expenses	$28,000	$ 13,000	$ 15,000
Net income (loss)	$ (8,000)	$(13,000)	$(5,000)

As we observed in Chapter 6, one of the great dangers in allocating common fixed costs is that such allocations can make a product line (or other segment of a business) *look* less profitable than it really is. Consider the following example:

A bakery distributed its products through route salesmen, each of whom loaded a truck with an assortment of products in the morning and spent the day calling on customers in an assigned territory. Believing that some items were more profitable than others, management asked for an analysis of product costs and sales. The accountants to whom the task was assigned allocated all manufacturing and marketing costs to products to obtain a net profit for each product. The resulting figures indicated that some of the products were being sold at a loss, and management discontinued these products. However, when this change was put into effect, the company's overall profit declined. It was then seen that, by dropping some products, sales revenues had been reduced without commensurate reduction in costs because the joint manufacturing costs and route sales costs had to be continued in order to make and sell remaining products.[1]

The same thing has happened in the Discount Drug Company as described in the bakery company example above. That is, by allocating the common fixed costs among all product lines, the Discount Drug Company has made the housewares line *look* as if it is unprofitable, whereas, in fact, dropping the line would result in a decrease in overall company net income. This point can be seen clearly if we recast the data in Exhibit 11–1, and eliminate the allocation of the common fixed costs. This recasting of data is shown in Exhibit 11–3.

---

[1] Walter B. McFarland, *Concepts for Management Accounting* (New York: National Association of Accountants, 1966), p. 46.

Exhibit 11–3
Discount Drug Company product lines—recast in contribution format
(from Exhibit 11–1)

	Total	Drugs	Cosmetics	Housewares
Sales	$250,000	$125,000	$75,000	$50,000
Less variable expenses	105,000	50,000	25,000	30,000
Contribution margin	$145,000	$ 75,000	$50,000	$20,000
Less direct fixed expenses:				
Salaries.........................	$ 50,000	$ 29,500	$12,500	$ 8,000
Advertising	15,000	1,000	7,500	6,500
Depreciation—fixtures	5,000	1,000	2,000	2,000
Insurance	3,000	2,000	500	500
Total	$ 73,000	$ 33,500	$22,500	$17,000
Product line segment margin	$ 72,000	$ 41,500	$27,500	$ 3,000*
Less common fixed expenses:				
Utilities	$ 2,000			
Rent............................	20,000			
General administrative	30,000			
Total	$ 52,000			
Net income	$ 20,000			

* If the housewares line is dropped, this $3,000 in segment margin will be lost to the company. In addition, we have seen that the $2,000 depreciation on the fixtures is a sunk cost which cannot be avoided. The sum of these two figures ($3,000 + $2,000 = $5,000) represents another way of obtaining the $5,000 figure which we found earlier will be the decrease in the company's overall profits if the housewares line is discontinued.

Exhibit 11–3 gives us a much different perspective of the housewares line than does Exhibit 11–1. As shown in Exhibit 11–3, the housewares line is covering all of its own direct fixed costs, and is generating a $3,000 segment margin toward covering of the common fixed costs of the company. Unless another product line can be found which will generate a greater segment margin than this, then, as we have noted, the company will be better off to keep the housewares line and at least get some contribution toward the common fixed costs of the organization from the space it is occupying.

Finally, we should note that even in those situations where the contribution of a particular product line is small in comparison with other product lines, managers will often retain the line, rather than replace it, if it is necessary to the sale of other products, or if it serves as a "magnet" to attract customers. Bread, for example, is not an especially profitable line in food stores, but customers expect it to be available and many undoutedly would shift their buying elsewhere if a particular store decided to stop carrying it.

THE MAKE OR BUY DECISION

Many steps are involved in getting a finished product into the hands of a consumer. First, raw materials must be obtained through mining, drilling, growing of crops, raising of animals, and so forth. Second, these raw materials must be processed to remove impurities, or to extract the desirable and usable materials from the bulk of materials available. Third, the usable materials must be fabricated into desired form, to serve as basic inputs for manufactured products. Fourth, the actual manufacturing of the finished product must take place, with several products perhaps coming from the same basic raw material input (as, for example, several different items of clothing coming from the same basic cloth input). And finally, the finished product must be distributed to the ultimate consumer.

When a company is involved in more than one of these steps, it is said to be *vertically integrated.* Vertical integration is very common. Some firms go so far as to control *all* activities relating to their products, from the mining of raw materials or the raising of crops right up to the final distribution of finished goods. Other firms are content to integrate on a less grand scale, and perhaps will do no more than produce the fabricated parts which go into their finished products.

A decision to produce a fabricated part internally, rather than to buy the part externally from a supplier, is often called a "make or buy" decision. Actually, any decision relating to vertical integration is a "make or buy" decision, since the company is deciding whether to meet its own needs internally, rather than to buy externally.

The advantages of integration

Certain advantages arise from integration. The integrated firm is less dependent on its suppliers, and may be able to ensure a smoother flow of parts and materials for production than the nonintegrated firm. For example, a strike against a major parts supplier might cause the operations of a nonintegrated firm to be interrupted for many months, whereas the integrated firm that is producing its own parts may be able to continue operations. Also, many firms feel that they can control quality better by producing their own parts and materials, rather than by relying on the quality control standards of outside suppliers. In addition, the integrated firm realizes profits from the parts and materials that it is "making," rather than "buying," as well as profits from its regular operations.

The advantages of integration are counterbalanced by a number of hazards. A firm that produces all of its own parts runs the risk of destroying long-run relationships with suppliers, that may prove to be harmful and disruptive to the firm. Once relationships with suppliers are severed, they are often difficult to reestablish. If product demand becomes heavy, a firm may not have sufficient capacity to continue producing all of its own parts internally, but then may experience great difficulty in trying to secure assistance from a severed supplier. In addition, changing technology often makes continued production of one's own parts more costly than purchasing from the outside, but this change in cost may not be obvious to the firm. In sum, these factors suggest that although certain advantages may accrue to the integrated firm, the "make or buy" decision should be weighed very carefully before any move is undertaken that may prove to be costly in the long run.

An example of make or buy

How does a firm approach the make or buy decision? Basically, the matters that must be considered fall into two broad categories—qualitative and quantitative. Qualitative matters deal with issues such as those raised in the preceding section. Quantitative matters deal with cost—what is the cost of producing as compared to the cost of buying? Several kinds of costs may be involved here, including opportunity costs.

To illustrate, assume that The Bonner Company is now producing a subassembly that goes into its final product. The Bonner Company reports the following costs of producing the subassembly:

	Per unit	8,000 units
Direct materials	$ 3	$ 24,000
Direct labor	4	32,000
Variable overhead	4	32,000
Fixed overhead, direct	5	40,000
Fixed overhead, common, but allocated	8	64,000
Total cost	$24	$192,000

The Bonner Company has received an offer from a supplier who will provide 8,000 subassemblies a year at a firm price of $21 each. Should The Bonner Company stop producing the subassemblies, and start purchasing them from the supplier? To make this decision, the manager must again focus on the differential costs. As we have seen before, the differential costs can be obtained by eliminating from the cost data those costs which are not avoidable (the sunk costs, and the future costs that will continue regardless of the decision). If the costs that remain after making this elimination are less than the outside purchase price, then the company should continue to make its subassemblies, rather than to purchase them from the outside.

Note first that The Bonner Company is allocating a portion of its common fixed costs to the subassemblies. Since these costs are common to all items produced in the factory, they will continue unchanged even if the subassemblies are purchased from the outside. The allocated costs, therefore, are not differential costs (since they will not differ between the make or buy alternatives), and must be eliminated from the decision framework.

The variable costs of producing the subassemblies (materials, labor, and variable overhead) are differential costs, since they can be avoided by buying the subassemblies from the outside. If the direct fixed costs can also be avoided by buying from the outside, then they, too, will be differential costs, and relevant to the decision. Assuming that *both* the variable costs and the direct fixed costs can be avoided by buying from the outside, the analysis takes the following form:

	Per unit differential costs		8,000 units	
	Make	Buy	Make	Buy
Cost of purchasing		$21		$168,000
Direct materials .... $ 3			$ 24,000	
Direct labor.............................	4		32,000	
Variable overhead	4		32,000	
Fixed overhead, direct (can be avoided by buying)	5		40,000	
Total costs	$16	$21	$128,000	$168,000
Difference in favor of continuing to make	$5		$40,000	

According to these data, The Bonner Company should reject the supplier's offer, and should continue to make its own subassemblies. Before coming to any final decision, however, The Bonner Company should consider one more factor—the opportunity cost of the space now being used to produce subassemblies.

The matter of opportunity cost

If the space now being used to produce subassemblies *would otherwise be idle,* then The Bonner Company should continue to produce its own subassemblies, and the supplier's offer should be rejected, as we stated above. Idle space that has no alternative use has an opportunity cost of zero.

But what if the space now being used to produce subassemblies would not sit idle, but rather could be used for some other purpose? In that case, the space would have an opportunity cost that would have to be considered in assessing the desirability of the supplier's offer. What would this opportunity cost be? It would be the segment margin that could be derived from the best alternative use of the space.

To illustrate, assume that the space now being used to produce subassemblies could be used to produce a new product line that would generate a segment margin of $50,000 per year. Under these conditions, The Bonner Company would be better off to accept the supplier's offer and to use the available space to produce the new product line:

	Make	Buy
Cost of purchasing (see prior example)		$168,000
Cost of making (see prior example)	$128,000	
Opportunity cost—segment margin foregone on a potential new product line	50,000	
Total cost	$178,000	$168,000
Difference in favor of purchasing from the outside supplier	$10,000

Perhaps we should again emphasize that opportunity costs are not recorded in the accounts of an organization. They do not represent actual dollar outlays. Rather, they represent those economic benefits that are *foregone* as a result of pursuing some course of action. The opportunity costs of The Bonner Company are sufficiently large in this case to make continued production of the subassemblies very costly from an economic point of view.

UTILIZATION OF SCARCE RESOURCES

Firms are often faced with the problem of deciding how scarce resources are going to be utilized. A department store, for example, has a limited amount of floor space, and therefore cannot stock every product line that may be available. A manufacturing firm has a limited number of machine-hours, and a limited number of direct labor-hours at its disposal. When capacity becomes pressed, the firm must decide which orders it will accept and which orders it will reject. In making these decisions, the contribution approach is necessary, since the firm will want to select that course of action that will maximize its *total* contribution margin.

Contribution in relation to scarce resources

To maximize total contribution margin, a firm may not necessarily want to promote those products that have the highest *individual* contribution margins. Rather, total contribution margin will be maximized by promoting those products or accepting those orders that promise the highest contribution margin *in relation to the scarce resources of the firm*. This concept can be demonstrated by assuming that a firm has two product lines, A and B. Cost and revenue characteristics of the two product lines are given below:

	A	B
Sales price per unit	$10	$12
Variable cost per unit	5	8
Contribution margin	$ 5	$ 4
C/M ratio	50%	33%

Product line A appears to be much more profitable than product line B. It has a $5 per unit contribution margin, as compared to only $4 per unit for product line B, and it has a 50 percent C/M ratio as compared to only 33 percent for B.

But now let us add one more piece of information—it takes two machine-hours to produce one unit of A, and only one machine-hour to produce one unit of B. The firm has only 2,000 machine-hours of capacity available in the plant per period. If demand becomes strong, which orders should the firm accept, those for product line A or those for product line B? The firm should accept orders for product line B. Even though product line A has the highest *per unit* contribution margin, product line B provides the highest contribution margin in relation to the scarce resource of the firm, which in this case is machine-hours available.

	A	B
Contribution margin per unit (above) (*a*)	$5	$4
Machine-hours required to produce one unit (*b*)	2	1
Contribution margin per machine-hour (*a*) ÷ (*b*)	$2.50	$4
Total contribution margin promised:		
Total machine-hours available	2,000	2,000
Contribution margin per machine-hour	× $2.50	× $4
Total contribution margin	$5,000	$8,000

This example shows clearly that looking at unit contribution margins alone is not enough; the contribution margin promised by a product line must be viewed in relation to whatever resource constraints a firm may be working under.

One of the most common resource constraints is advertising dollars available. Firms typically concentrate their efforts on those product lines that promise the greatest contribution margin per dollar of advertising expended. Another common resource constraint is floor space. The discount department stores and discount food chains have utilized the concept of maximum contribution margin per square foot by concentrating on those product lines that have a rapid turnover, thereby generating large amounts of contribution in small amounts of space available.

The problem of multiple constraints

What does a firm do if it is operating under *several* scarce resource constraints? For example, a firm may have limited raw materials available, limited direct labor-hours available, limited floor space, and limited advertising dollars to spend on product promotion. How would it proceed to find the right combination of products to produce under such a variety of constraints? The proper combination, or "mix" of products, can be found by use of a quantitative method known as *linear programming*. Linear programming is a very powerful analytical tool that is illustrated in the Appendix to this chapter.

JOINT PRODUCT COSTS AND THE CONTRIBUTION APPROACH

The manufacturing processes of some firms are such that several end products are produced from a single raw material input. The meat-packing industry, for example, inputs a pig into the manufacturing process and comes out with a great variety of end products, including bacon, ham, spare ribs, pork roasts, and so on. Firms that produce several end products from a common input (e.g., a pig) are faced with the problem of deciding how the cost of that input is going to be divided up among the products (bacon, ham, pork roast, and so on) that result. Before we address ourselves to this problem, it will be helpful to define three terms—joint products, joint product costs, and split-off point.

Two or more products that are produced from a common input are known as *joint products*. The term *joint product costs* is used to describe those manufacturing costs that are incurred in producing joint products up to the *split-off point*. The *split-off point* is that point in the manufacturing process at which the joint products (bacon, ham, spare ribs, and so on) can be recognized as individual units of output. At this point some of the joint products will be in final form, ready to be marketed to the consumer. Others will still need further processing on their own before they are in marketable form. These concepts can be shown graphically as follows:

Exhibit 11–4
Joint products

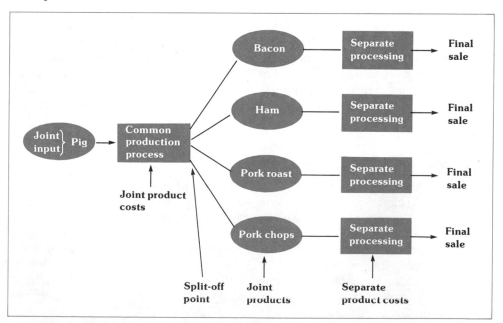

The pitfalls of allocation

Joint product costs are really common costs incurred to simultaneously produce a variety of end products. Traditional cost accounting books are full of elaborate approaches to allocating these common costs among the different products at the split-off point. The most usual approach is to allocate the joint product costs according to the relative sales value of the end products.

Although allocation of joint product costs is needed for some purposes, such as balance sheet inventory valuation, such allocations should be used with great caution *internally* in the decision-making process. Unless a manager proceeds with care, he or she may be led into incorrect decisions as a result of relying on allocated common costs. Consider the following situation which occurred in a firm several years ago:

A company located on the Gulf of Mexico is a producer of soap products. It has six main soap product lines which are produced from common inputs. Joint product costs up to the split-off point constitute the bulk of the production costs for all six product lines. These joint product costs are allocated to the six product lines on a basis of the relative market value of each line at the split-off point.

The company has a waste product that results from the production of the six main product lines. Up until a few years ago, the company loaded the waste onto barges, and dumped it into the Gulf of Mexico, since the waste was thought to have no commercial value. The dumping was stopped, however, when the company's research division discovered that with some further processing the waste could be made commercially saleable as a fertilizer ingredient. The further processing was initiated at a cost of $175,000 per year. The waste was then sold to fertilizer manufacturers at a total price of $300,000 per year.

The accountants responsible for allocating manufacturing costs included the sales value of the waste product along with the sales value of the six main product lines in their allocation of the joint product costs at the split-off point. This allocation resulted in the waste product being allocated $150,000 in joint product cost. This $150,000 allocation, when added to the further processing costs of $175,000 for the waste, caused the waste product to show a net loss:

Sales value of the waste product after further processing	$300,000
Less costs assignable to the waste product ..	325,000
Net loss	($ 25,000)

When presented with this analysis, the company's management decided that further processing of the waste was not desirable after all. The company went back to dumping the waste in the Gulf.

The contribution approach to the problem

Joint product costs are irrelevant in decisions regarding what to do with a product from the split-off point forward. The reason is that by the time one arrives at the split-off point, the joint product costs have already been incurred, and therefore are sunk costs. In the case of the soap company example above, the $150,000 in allocated joint product costs should not have been permitted to influence what was done with the waste product from the split-off point forward. The analysis should have been:

	Dump in Gulf	Process further
Sales value	-0-	$300,000
Additional processing costs	-0-	175,000
Contribution margin	-0-	$125,000
Advantage of processing further	$125,000	

By continuing to dump the waste in the Gulf, the company is losing the opportunity to enjoy an additional $125,000 in net income each year.

As a general guide, it will always be profitable to continue processing joint products after the split-off point *so long as the incremental revenue from such processing exceeds the incremental processing costs.* Joint product costs that have *already been incurred* up to the split-off point are sunk costs, and are always irrelevant in decisions concerning what to do from the split-off point forward.

SUMMARY

The accountant is responsible for seeing that relevant, timely data are available for guiding management in its decisions, particularly those decisions relating to special, nonroutine situations. Reliance by management on irrelevant data can lead to incorrect decisions, reduced profitability, and inability to meet stated objectives. *All* costs are relevant in decision making, *except:*

1. Sunk costs.
2. Future costs that will not differ between the alternatives under consideration.

The concept of cost relevance has wide application. In this chapter we have observed its use in equipment replacement decisions, in make or buy decisions, in discontinuance of product line decisions, in joint product decisions, and in decisions relating to the effective use of scarce resources. This list is not inclusive of the possible applications of the relevant cost concept. Indeed, *any* decision involving costs hinges upon the proper identification and use of those costs which are relevant, if the decision is to be made properly. For this reason, we shall continue to focus upon the concept of cost relevance in the next chapter, where we deal with the matter of pricing, and in the two chapters following, where we consider long-run investment decisions.

KEY TERMS FOR REVIEW

Sunk costs	**Make or buy**
Differential costs	**Vertical integration**
Opportunity costs	**Joint product costs**
Relevant costs	**Joint products**
Avoidable costs	**Split-off point**

APPENDIX: LINEAR PROGRAMMING

Linear programming is a mathematical tool designed to assist management in making decisions in those situations where constraining or limiting factors are present. Limiting factors might include, for example, a scarcity of raw materials needed in the production of a company's products, or a plant with inadequate machine time to produce all of the products being demanded by a firm's customers. Linear programming is designed to assist the manager in putting together the "right" mix of products in situations such as these, so that the scarce resources of the firm (e.g., raw materials, machine time) can be utilized in a way that will maximize profits.

A graphical approach to linear programming

To demonstrate a linear programming analysis, let us assume the following data:

A firm produces two products, X and Y. The contribution margin per unit of X is $8, and the contribution margin per unit Y is $10. The firm has 36 hours of production time available each period. It takes 6 hours of production time to produce one unit of X and 9 hours of production time to produce one unit of Y.

The firm has only 24 pounds of raw material available for use in production each period. It takes 6 pounds of raw material to produce one unit of X and 3 pounds of raw material to produce one unit of Y.

Management estimates that no more than three units of Y can be sold each period. The firm is interested in maximizing contribution margin. What combination of X and Y should be produced and sold?

There are four basic steps in a linear programming analysis:

1. Determine the objective function and express it in algebraic terms.
2. Determine the constraints under which the firm must operate, and express them in algebraic terms.
3. Determine the area of feasible product combinations on a graph. This area will be bounded by the constraint equations derived in (2) above, after the constraint equations have been expressed on the graph in linear form.
4. Determine from the area of feasible product combinations that mix of products which will maximize (or minimize) the objective function.

We shall now examine each of these steps in order, by relating them to the data in the example above.

1. *Determine the objective function and express it in algebraic terms.*

The objective function simply represents the goal which is to be achieved, expressed in terms of the variables involved. The goal might be to maximize total contribution margin, as in our example; alternatively, it might be to minimize total cost.

In our example, for each unit of X that is sold $8 in contribution margin will be realized. For each unit of Y that is sold $10 in contribution margin will be realized. Therefore, total contribution margin for the firm can be expressed by the following objective function equation:

$$Z = 8X + 10Y \qquad (1)$$

where Z = the total contribution margin that will be realized with an optimal mix of X and Y; X = the number of units of product X that should be produced and sold to yield the optimal mix; and Y = the number of units of product Y that should be produced and sold to yield the optimal mix.

2. *Determine the constraints under which the firm must operate, and express them in algebraic terms.*

From the data in our example we can identify three constraints. First, only 36 hours of production time is available. Since it requires 6 hours to produce one unit of X and 9 hours to produce one unit of Y, this constraint can be expressed in the following form:

$$6X + 9Y \leq 36 \qquad (2)$$

Notice the inequality sign ($\leq$) in the equation. This signifies that the total production of both X and Y taken together cannot *exceed* the 36 hours available, but that this production *could* require *less* than the 36 hours available.

The second constraint deals with raw material usage. Only 24 pounds are available each period. It takes 6 pounds of raw material to produce one unit of X and 3 pounds to produce one unit of Y. This constraint can be expressed in the following algebraic terms:

$$6X + 3Y \leq 24 \qquad (3)$$

The third constraint deals with market acceptance of product Y. The market can absorb only 3 units of Y each period. This constraint can be expressed as follows:

$$Y \leq 3 \qquad (4)$$

3. *Determine the area of feasible product combinations on a graph.*

A graph containing the constraint equations [Equations (2)–(4) above] is presented in Exhibit 11–5. In placing these three equations on the graph, we have asked the questions, "How much product X could be produced if all resources were allocated to it, and none were allocated to product

Y?"; and "How much product Y could be produced if all resources were allocated to it, and none were allocated to product X?" For example, consider Equation (2), dealing with production capacity. A total of 36 hours of production time is available. If all 36 hours are allocated to product X, 6 units can be produced each period (since it takes 6 hours to produce one unit of X, and 36 hours are available). On the other hand, if all 36 hours are allocated to product Y, then 4 units of Y can be produced each period (since it takes 9 hours to produce one unit of Y, and 36 hours are available).

If all production capacity is allocated to Product X	If all production capacity is allocated to Product Y
$6X + \text{-0-} \leq 36$	$\text{-0-} + 9Y \leq 36$
$X = 6$	$Y = 4$

Therefore, the line on the graph in Exhibit 11–5 expressing the production constraint equation [Equation (2)] extends from the six-unit point on the X axis to the four-unit point on the Y axis. Of course production

Exhibit 11–5
A linear programming graphical solution

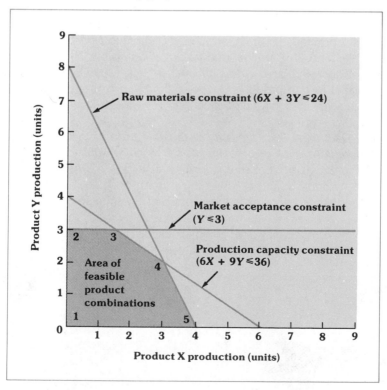

could fall anywhere on this constraint line; the points on the axes (6,4) simply represent the extremes that would be possible.

The equation associated with the raw materials constraint [Equation (3)] has been placed on the graph through a similar line of reasoning. Since 24 pounds of raw materials are available, the firm could produce either 4 units of X or 8 units of Y, if all of the raw materials were allocated to one or the other (since it takes 6 pounds to produce a unit of X, and 3 pounds to produce a unit of Y). Therefore, the line expressing the equation extends from the 4-unit point on the X axis to the 8-unit point on the Y axis. Again, production could fall anywhere on this constraint line; the points on the axes (4,8) simply represent the extremes that would be possible.

Since the third constraint equation [Equation (4)] concerns only product Y, the line expressing the equation on the graph does not touch the X axis at all. It extends from the 3-unit point on the Y axis and runs horizontal to the X axis, thereby signifying that regardless of the number of units of X that are produced, there can never be more than 3 units of Y produced.

Having now plotted on the graph the lines representing the three constraint equations, we have isolated the area of feasible product combinations. This area has been shaded on the graph. Notice that the area of feasible product combinations is formed by the lines of the constraint equations. Each line has served to limit the size of the area to some extent. The reason, of course, is that these lines represent constraints under which the firm must operate, and thereby serve to limit the range of choices available. The firm could operate anywhere within the area of feasible product combinations. One point within this area, however, represents an optimal mix of products X and Y that will result in a maximization of the objective function (contribution margin). Our task now is to find precisely where that point lies.

4. Determine from the area of feasible product combinations that mix of production which will maximize the objective function.

The optimal product mix will always fall on a corner of the area of feasible product combinations. If we scan the graph in Exhibit 11–5 we can see that the area of feasible product combinations has five corners. The five corners will yield the following product mixes between X and Y (starting at the origin, and going clockwise around the area of feasible product combinations):

| | Units produced | |
Corner	X	Y
1...........	0	0
2...........	0	3
3...........	1½	3
4...........	3	2
5...........	4	0

Which production mix is optimal? To answer this question we will need to calculate the total contribution margin promised at each corner. We can do this by referring to the unit contribution margin data given in the objective function equation.

$$Z = 8X + 10Y \qquad (1)$$

This equation tells us that each unit of X promises $8 of contribution margin, and that each unit of Y promises $10 of contribution margin. Relating these figures to the production mixes at the five corners, we find that the following total contribution margins are possible:

X		Y		Total contri-bution margin
$8(0)	+	$10(0)	=	$ 0
8(0)	+	10(3)	=	30
8(1½)	+	10(3)	=	42
8(3)	+	10(2)	=	44
8(4)	+	10(0)	=	32

The firm should produce 3 units of X and 2 units of Y. This production mix will yield a maximum contribution margin of $44. Given the constraints under which the firm must operate, it is not possible to obtain a greater total contribution margin than this amount. Any production mix different from 3 units of X and 2 units of Y will result in *less* total contribution margin.

Why always on a corner?

It was stated earlier that we will always find the optimal product mix on a *corner* of the area of feasible product combinations. Why does the optimal mix always fall on a corner? Look at the objective function equation again for a moment [Equation (1)]. This equation expresses a straight line with a −⅘ slope. Place a ruler on the graph in Exhibit 11–5 extending from the 8 point on the Y axis to the 10 point on the X axis (a −⅘ slope). Now bring your ruler down toward the origin of the graph, taking care to keep it parallel to the line from which you started. Note that the first point which your ruler touches is the corner of the area of feasible product combinations showing a production mix of 3 units of X and 2 units of Y. Your ruler touches this point first because it is the farthest point from the origin in relation to the objective function line. Therefore, that point must yield the greatest total contribution margin for the firm. Any point closer to the origin would result in less total contribution margin.[2]

___

[2] The objective function line could coincide with one of the lines bounding the area of feasible product combinations. In this case, a number of different product combinations would be possible, each resulting in the same total contribution margin. However, our state-

Direction of the constraint

Exhibit 11–5 shows the direction of all the constraints to be *inward* toward the origin of the graph. The direction of the constraint will always be inward, so long as the constraint equation is stated in terms of less than or equal to ($\leq$).

The direction of the constraint will be *outward,* away from the origin of the graph, whenever the constraint equation is stated in terms of greater than or equal to ($\geq$). To illustrate, assume the following constraint:

X weighs 4 oz. and *Y* weighs 9 ozs. *X* and *Y* must be mixed in such a way that their total weights is at least 72 ozs.

Constraint equation: $4X + 9Y \geq 72$ ozs.

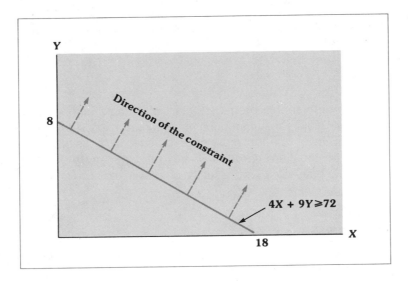

Since the direction of this constraint line is upward rather than downward, the area of feasible product combinations will be found *above* it, rather than below it. Constraints expressed in terms of *greater than or equal to,* as illustrated above, can be found in any linear programming problem, but are most common in *minimization* problems.

The simplex method

In our examples we have dealt with only two products, X and Y. When more than two products are involved in a linear programming problem, the graphical method no longer is adequate to provide a solution. In these

---

ment that the solution will always be found on a corner is still true even under these conditions, since the product mix at the corners of the line would yield the same total contribution margin as any point on the line.

cases, a more powerful version of linear programming is needed. This more powerful version is commonly called the *simplex* method.

The simplex method is considerably more complex in operation than the graphical method, even though the principles underlying its operation are identical to those already discussed in connection with the graphical method. Generally, linear programming simplex solutions are carried out on the digital computer. The mechanics of the method are covered in most advanced managerial accounting texts.

Applications of linear programming

Linear programming has been applied to an extremely wide range of problems in many different fields. Decision makers have found that it is by far the best tool available for combining manpower, materials, and facilities together to the best advantage of a firm. Although the use of linear programming has been most extensive in the industrial, agricultural, and military sectors, it has also been applied to problems in economics, engineering, and the sciences. Problems to which linear programming has been successfully applied include gasoline blending, production scheduling to optimize use of total facilities, livestock feed blending to obtain a desired nutritional mix at the least cost, routing of boxcars to desired points at the least cost, selecting sites for electrical transformers, forestry maintenance, and choosing flight paths for space satellites.

KEY TERMS FOR REVIEW (APPENDIX)

Linear programming
Objective function equation
Constraint equation

Area of feasible product combinations
Simplex method

QUESTIONS

11-1. Define the following terms: incremental cost; opportunity cost; sunk cost.

11-2. Distinguish between cost relevance and cost precision.

11-3. Are variable costs always relevant costs? Explain.

11-4. The book value of a machine on the balance sheet is an asset to a company, but this same book value is irrelevant in decision making. Explain why this is so.

11-5. "Sunk costs are easy to spot—they're simply the fixed costs associated with a decision." Do you agree? Explain.

11-6. "Sometimes depreciation on equipment is a relevant cost in a decision, and sometimes it isn't." Do you agree? Explain.

11-7. "My neighbor offered me $25 for the use of my boat over the weekend, but I decided that renting it out is just too risky." What cost term would you use to describe the $25? Explain.

11–8. "Variable costs and differential costs mean the same thing." Do you agree? Explain.

11–9. "All future costs are relevant." Do you agree? Why?

11–10. Prentice Company is considering dropping one of its product lines. What costs of the product line would be relevant to this decision? Irrelevant?

11–11. Why is the term "avoidable cost" used in connection with product line and make or buy decisions?

11–12. "If a product line is generating a loss, then that's pretty good evidence that the product line should be discontinued." Do you agree? Explain.

11–13. What is the danger in allocating common fixed costs among product lines or other segments of an organization?

11–14. What is meant by the term "make or buy?"

11–15. How does opportunity cost enter into the make or buy decision?

11–16. Give four examples of limiting or scarce factors that might be present in an organization.

11–17. How will the relating of product line contribution margins to scarce resources help a company ensure that profits will be maximized?

11–18. Define the following terms: joint products; joint product costs; split-off point.

11–19. What pitfalls are there in allocating common costs among joint products, from a decision-making point of view?

11–20. What guideline can be used in determining whether a joint product should be sold at the split-off point or processed further?

11–21. Airlines often offer reduced rates during certain times of the week to members of a businessperson's family if they accompany him or her on trips. How does the concept of relevant costs enter into the decision to offer reduced rates of this type?

11–22. Schloss Company has decided to use linear programming as a planning tool. The company can't decide whether to use marginal contribution per unit or gross profit per unit in its linear programming computations. Which would you suggest? Why?

11–23. Define "objective function" and "constraint" as these concepts relate to linear programming.

11–24. Sever Company produces two products. Product A has a contribution margin per unit of $10. Product B has a contribution margin per unit of $8. Explain why a linear programming analysis might suggest that the company produce more of product B than product A. (Ample market exists for either product.)

11–25. What is meant by an "area of feasible product combinations?"

EXERCISES

E11–1. The costs associated with the acquisition and annual operation of a truck are given on the following page:

Insurance $1,600
Licenses   250
Taxes (vehicle)   150
Garage rent for parking   1,200
Depreciation ($9,000 ÷ 5 yrs) 1,800*
Gasoline, oil, tires, and repairs 07/mile

* Based on obsolescence, rather than on wear and tear.

Required:

1. Assume that the Dandy Company has purchased one truck, and the truck has been driven 50,000 miles during the first year. Compute the average cost per mile of owning and operating the truck.

2. At the beginning of the second year, the Dandy Company is unsure whether to use the truck, or leave it parked in the garage and have all hauling done commercially. (The state requires the payment of vehicle taxes, even if the vehicle isn't used.) What costs above are relevant to this decision?

3. Assume that the company decides to use the truck during the second year. Near year-end an order is received from a customer over 1,000 miles away. What costs above are relevant in a decision between using the truck to make the delivery and having the delivery done commercially?

4. Occasionally the company could use two trucks at the same time. For this reason some thought is being given to purchasing a second truck. The total miles driven would be the same as if only one truck was owned. What costs above are relevant in a decision over whether to purchase the second truck?

E11–2. Listed below are a number of "costs" for the Darby Company:

1. Direct labor
2. Direct materials
3. Variable production overhead
4. Fixed production overhead (general)
5. Variable selling and administrative expense
6. Fixed selling and administrative expense
7. Book value of Machine A
8. Market value of Machine A (current resale)
9. Market value of Machine B (cost)
10. Rate of return available from outside investments

Using the above list, indicate which "costs" are relevant for the following independent cases:

a. The Darby Company wants to purchase Machine B to replace Machine A. Both machines have the same capacity, and a remaining life of five years. Machine B will reduce direct materials costs by 15 percent, due to less waste. Other production costs will not change.

b. The Darby Company wants to purchase Machine B to increase production and sales. Machine A will continue to be used.

E11–3. Clark Company produces three products, A, B, and C, from a joint process. Each product may be sold at the split-off point or processed further.

Additional processing requires no special facilities, and all additional processing costs are variable. Joint processing costs to the split-off point total $100,000 annually. The additional processing costs and sales value after further processing for each product line (on an annual basis) are:

Product	Additional processing costs	Sales value
A	$20,000	$60,000
B	30,000	90,000
C	25,000	80,000

The sales values of the three products at the split-off point are: A—$35,000; B—$70,000; C—$55,000.

Required:

1. Which products should be sold at the split-off point, and which should be processed further? Show computations. (The products are produced in equal amounts.)
2. What general statement can be made with respect to joint costs and the decision to process further?

E11–4. The Dorsey Print Shop prints and distributes weekly, monthly, and yearly date books. These date books are printed with various company letterheads, and are used by these companies for advertising purposes. Data for the past six months follow:

	Total	Weekly date books	Monthly date books	Yearly date books
Sales	$200,000	$50,000	$70,000	$80,000
Less variable expenses	85,000	25,000	28,000	32,000
Contribution margin	$115,000	$25,000	$42,000	$48,000
Less fixed expenses:				
Depreciation of special equipment	$ 11,000	$ 3,000	$ 3,500	$ 4,500
Salary of line supervisor	25,000	8,000	8,000	9,000
Common, but allocated*	70,000	17,500	24,500	28,000
Total fixed expenses	$106,000	$28,500	$36,000	$41,500
Net income (loss)	$ 9,000	$ (3,500)	$ 6,000	$ 6,500

* Allocation based on sales dollars.

The data above are representative of the long-run trend of sales and costs. The special equipment used to print weekly date books has no resale value.

Required:

1. Should the Dorsey Print Shop stop the printing of Weekly Date Books? Prepare computations to support your answer.
2. Recast the above data in a format that would be more usable to management in assessing the long-run profitability of the various product lines.

E11–5.   The Cummins Manufacturing Company manufactures a variety of engines for use in heavy equipment. The company has always produced all of the necessary parts for its engines, including all of the subassemblies. An outside supplier has offered to produce and sell one subassembly to the Cummins Manufacturing Company at a cost of $18 per unit. In order to evaluate this offer, the Cummins Manufacturing Company has gathered the following information relating to its own "cost" of producing the subassembly internally:

	Per unit	10,000 units per year
Direct materials	$ 6	$ 60,000
Direct labor	5	50,000
Variable production overhead	3	30,000
Fixed production overhead, direct	3	30,000*
Fixed production overhead, common, but allocated	5	50,000
Total cost	$22	$220,000

* One third supervisory salaries; two thirds depreciation of special equipment (no resale value).

a.   Assuming there are no alternative uses for the facilities, should the offer be accepted?

b.   Assuming that a new product that will generate a segment margin of $50,000 per year could be produced if the subassembly were purchased, should the offer be accepted?

E11–6.   Martin Metal Products is considering replacing Machine A with Machine B. Selected information on the two machines is given below:

	Machine A	Machine B
Original cost new	$28,000	$20,000
Accumulated depreciation to date	10,000	—
Current salvage value	2,000	—
Estimated cost savings each year over Machine A	—	5,000
Remaining years of useful life	6 years	6 years

Required:

Prepare a computation covering the six-year period which will show the net advantage or disadvantage of purchasing Machine B. Ignore income taxes.

E11–7.   Electro Controls, Inc., produces and sells 300,000 units of Product X each year, at a selling price of $16 per unit. The company's cost to manufacture one unit of Product X at a 300,000-unit level of activity is:

Direct materials	$ 3
Direct labor	6
Factory overhead	5*
Total cost per unit	$14

* Contains both variable and fixed overhead cost.

Fixed factory overhead totals $900,000 per year. The company has received an order from a foreign distributor for 50,000 units of Product X, to be delivered over the next year. The distributor has offered to pay $13 per unit for the 50,000 units ordered. Shipping costs overseas would be $1 per unit, which would be paid by Electro Controls, Inc. The sales to the foreign distributor would not disturb regular sales of Product X. The company has sufficient excess capacity to handle the additional units, with no increase in fixed overhead costs.

Required:

Prepare an analysis showing whether the foreign distributor's offer should be accepted. Ignore income taxes.

E11–8.   The Moore Equipment Company has been experiencing losses on Product Line 4 for several years. The most recent income statement on Product Line 4 is given below:

MOORE EQUIPMENT COMPANY
Income Statement
For Product Line 4

Sales		$75,000
Less costs, direct and allocated:		
Manufacturing costs:		
Variable manufacturing costs	$16,000	
Depreciation of equipment (no resale value)	8,000	
Salary of line manager	12,000	
General factory costs—fixed	10,000	
Total manufacturing costs	$46,000	
Selling costs:		
Commissions	$ 4,000	
Freight-out	3,000	
Advertising—direct	10,000	
Total selling costs	$17,000	
Other costs:		
General office (allocated on a basis of sales		
dollars)	$15,000	
Purchasing (allocated on a basis of sales		
dollars)	6,000	
Total other costs	$21,000	
Total costs		84,000
Net loss		$ (9,000)

The total costs of the General Factory, General Office, and Purchasing will not change if Product Line 4 is discontinued. The discontinuance of Product Line 4 would not affect sales of other product lines.

Required:

Would you recommend that Product Line 4 be discontinued? Show computations.

E11–9.   Bill has just returned from a duck hunting trip. He has brought home 10 ducks. Bill's wife detests cleaning ducks, and to discourage him from further duck hunting has presented him with the following cost estimate per duck:

Camper and equipment:
   Cost $4,000. Usable for 8 seasons, 10 hunting trips per season . . . . . . $ 50
Travel expense (pickup truck):
   100 miles at $0.12 per mile (gas, oil, and tires—$0.07 per mile;
   depreciation and insurance—$0.05 per mile) 12
Shotgun shells (2 boxes) 10
Boat:
   Cost $240. Usable for 8 seasons, 10 hunting trips per season 3
Fine paid for speeding on the way to the river 16
Hunting license:
   Cost $30 for the season, 10 hunting trips per season 3
Money lost playing poker:
   Loss $18. (Bill plays poker every weekend.) 18
1 fifth of "Old Grandad":
   Cost $8. (Used to ward off the cold.) . . . . _8_
Total cost $120

Cost per duck ($120 ÷ 10 ducks) . . . . $ 12

Required:

1. Assuming that the duck hunting trip Bill has just completed is typical, what costs are relevant to a decision as to whether Bill should go duck hunting again this season?
2. Discuss the wife's computation of the cost per duck.

E11–10. The MJG Company produces three product lines, A, B, and C. The cost and revenue characteristics of the product lines are (per unit):

	A	B	C
Selling price	$32	$25	$40
Less variable expenses:			
Direct materials	$14	$15	$ 8
Direct labor	8	4	16
Variable overhead	2	1	4
Total	$24	$20	$28
Contribution margin	$ 8	$ 5	$12
Contribution margin ratio	25%	20%	30%

At the moment, demand for the company's products far exceeds its capacity to produce. Management is trying to determine which product line(s) to concentrate on next week in filling its backlog of orders. The direct labor rate is $4 per hour, and only 1,000 hours of labor time are available each week.

Required:

1. Compute the amount of contribution margin which will be obtained per hour of labor time spent on each product.
2. Which orders would you recommend that the company work on next week—those orders for A, for B, or for C? Show computations.

E11–11. (Appendix).   Murl Company produces two products, Awls and Pows. Two types of material, A and B, are used in the production of each product. The quantities required by product are:

	Material A (pounds)	Material B (pounds)
Awls	3	2
Pows	1	2
Total available	10	12

Market conditions are such that no more than five Pows can be sold. Contribution margin of the Awls and Pows is $3 and $2 per unit, respectively.

Required:

1. Prepare an objective function equation, and constraint equations for the Awls and Pows.
2. Determine how much of each product should be produced, by means of the linear programming graphical method.

E11–12. (Appendix).   Stoner Products, Inc., uses 2 pounds of Material A in the manufacture of both its large and small mugs. The large mugs also require 3 ounces of Material B. The small mugs do not use Material B. Both size mugs use Material C. The large mugs use 3 ounces, and the small mugs use 1 ounce. The contribution margin of the large and small mugs is $3 and $2, respectively. The amount of materials available each period is:

    Material A . . . . 8 lbs.
    Material B . . . . 9 ozs.
    Material C . . . . 6 ozs.

Required:

1. Assume that the company wishes to maximize contribution margin. Prepare an objective function equation, and constraint equations.
2. Determine how much of each product should be produced each period by means of the linear programming graphical method.

PROBLEMS

P11–13. *Relevant cost analysis; Book value.*   The Matz Machine Shop purchased a new milling machine one year ago at a cost of $28,000. The machine has been working very satisfactorily, but the shop manager has just received information on an electronically controlled milling machine that is vastly superior to the machine which has already been purchased. Comparative data on the two machines are given on the following page:

	Present machine	Proposed new machine
Purchase cost new	$28,000	$36,000
Estimated useful life new	7 years	6 years
Salvage value now	$ 8,000	—
Annual straight-line depreciation	4,000	$ 6,000
Remaining book value	24,000	—
Annual costs to operate	40,000	32,000

The shop manager makes the following quick computation, and exclaims, "There's no way I could buy that new machine. If the boss found out that I took a loss on the old machine, he'd crucify me."

Remaining book value of the old machine	$24,000
Salvage value now of the old machine	8,000
Net loss from disposal	$16,000

Sales from the milling operation are expected to remain unchanged at $90,000 per year indefinitely. Other costs associated with the milling operation total $30,000 annually.

Required:

1. Prepare a summary income statement covering six years, assuming:
    a. That the new machine is not purchased.
    b. That the new machine is purchased.
    Would you recommend that the new machine be purchased?
2. Prepare an analysis of the desirability of purchasing the new machine, using only relevant costs.

P11–14. *Sell or process further.* From a particular joint process, Morrell Company produces three products—X, Y, and Z. Each product may be sold at the split-off point or processed further. Additional processing requires no special facilities, and production costs of further processing are entirely variable and traceable to the products involved. In 19x1 all three products were processed beyond split-off. Joint production costs for the year were $60,000. Sales values and costs needed to evaluate Morrell Company's production policy during 19x1 follow:

Product	Units produced	Sales values at split-off	Additional costs and sales values if processed further	
			Sales values	Added costs
X	6,000	$25,000	$42,000	$9,000
Y	4,000	41,000	45,000	7,000
Z	2,000	24,000	32,000	8,000

Joint costs are allocated to the products in proportion to the relative physical volume of output (50 percent to X, 33 percent to Y, and 17 percent to Z).

Required:

1. For Product X, what unit production cost figure is relevant to a sell at split-off, or process further, decision?
2. Evaluate the company's 19x1 production policy. Did the company maximize its profits by processing all products further? Show computations.

(CPA, adapted)

P11–15. *Opportunity costs; Special order.* The Sparks Battery Company produces batteries for sale under its own name to the public. The batteries sell for $18 each; annual sales are 240,000 batteries. The cost per battery is given below:

Variable production costs	$10
Fixed overhead ($1,200,000 total, divided by	
240,000 batteries)	5
Total cost per battery	$15

Fixed selling and administrative expenses total $200,000 annually. Variable selling and administrative expenses total $1 per battery.

Faststart Company, which operates a chain of auto supply stores, has offered the Sparks Battery Company $14 per battery on an order of 100,000 batteries. The batteries would be produced carrying the Faststart Company name, and sold through the Faststart stores. The Faststart stores are located in a different part of the country from where the Sparks Battery Company normally sells its batteries.

Because of the bulk order, there would be no variable selling and administrative expenses associated with the sale to the Faststart Company. A machine used to imprint the Faststart Company name on batteries would cost $5,000 and would be usable almost indefinitely.

The Sparks Battery Company has a capacity of 300,000 batteries per year. Faststart Company has made it clear that it will not accept less than 100,000 batteries; therefore, if the Faststart Company offer is accepted it will be necessary for the Sparks Battery Company to give up regular sales of 40,000 batteries per year.

Required:

1. Compute the opportunity cost to the Sparks Battery Company of accepting the Faststart Company offer.
2. Would you recommend that the offer be accepted? Show all computations.

P11–16. *Shutdown versus continue to operate decision.* Tanner Company normally produces and sells 40,000 units of Component A each quarter, at a selling price of $12 per unit. Variable costs total $7 per unit, and fixed overhead costs total $160,000 each quarter.

Employment-contract strikes in the companies which purchase Component A have caused Tanner Company's sales to drop to only 5,000 units per month. Tanner Company estimates that the strikes will last for about three months, after which time sales of Component A should return to normal. During the months that the strikes are on, however,

Tanner Company is thinking about closing its own plant, due to the low level of sales. If Tanner Company does close its plant, the fixed overhead costs will drop to only $90,000 per quarter. Start-up costs at the end of the shutdown period would total $15,000. Since Tanner Company normally produces strictly for customer orders, no inventories are on hand.

Required:

1. Assuming that the strikes continue for three months, as estimated, would you recommend that Tanner Company close its own plant? Show computations.
2. At what level of quarterly sales (in units) would the company be indifferent as to closing the plant or keeping it open? Show computations.

P11–17. *Discontinuance of a department.* Sales have never been good in Department C of Stacey's Department Store. For this reason, management is considering eliminating the department. A summarized income statement for the store, by departments, for the most recent quarter is given below:

STACEY'S DEPARTMENT STORE
Summary Income Statement
For the Latest Quarter

	A	B	C	Total
Sales	$175,000	$195,000	$110,000	$480,000
Cost of goods sold	70,000	77,600	45,800	193,400
Gross margin	$105,000	$117,400	$ 64,200	$286,600
Operating expenses:				
Salaries	$ 18,000	$ 16,000	$ 15,000	$ 49,000
Utilities	2,500	1,900	1,600	6,000
Direct advertising	8,400	6,500	5,000	19,900
General advertising	4,000	4,000	4,000	12,000
Rent on building	15,000	12,000	10,000	37,000
Employment taxes*	1,800	1,600	1,500	4,900
Depreciation of fixtures and				
equipment	12,000	15,000	8,000	35,000
Insurance on inventories, fixtures,				
and equipment	1,800	2,200	1,200	5,200
Property taxes on inventories,				
fixtures, and equipment	600	700	400	1,700
Service department expenses	24,000	31,000	26,000	81,000
Total operating expenses	$ 88,100	$ 90,900	$ 72,700	$251,700
Net income or (loss)	$ 16,900	$ 26,500	$ (8,500)	$ 34,900

* Based on salaries paid directly in each department.

The following additional information is available:

1. All departments are housed in the same building. The store leases the entire building at a fixed annual rental rate.
2. If Department C is eliminated, the utilities bill will be reduced by about $500 per quarter.
3. One of the employees in Department C is the president's dim-witted

son-in-law. The son-in-law will be transferred to another department if Department C is eliminated. The son-in-law's salary is $2,500 per quarter.

4. The fixtures and equipment in Department C would be transferred to the other departments. One fourth of the insurance and property taxes in Department C relates to the fixtures and equipment in the department.

5. Stacey's Department Store has three service departments—Purchasing, Warehouse, and General Office. One employee in Purchasing and one employee in Warehouse could be discharged if Department C is dropped. The combined salaries and other employment costs of these two employees is $4,500 per quarter.

Required:

1. Assume that Stacey's Department Store has no alternative use for the space now being occupied by Department C. Should the department be eliminated? You may assume that eliminating Department C would have no effect on sales in the other departments.

2. Assume that Stacey's Department Store has an opportunity to sublease the space now being occupied by Department C, at a monthly rental rate $20,000. Would you advise the store to eliminate Department C, and sublease the space? Show computations.

P11–18. *Relevant costs; Purchase of a new machine.* The Ross Company purchased a machine two years ago at a cost of $48,000. The machine is being depreciated on a straight-line basis. When purchased, the machine was given an estimated life of 12 years, and assigned a zero scrap value.

A computer-controlled machine which performs the same work as the machine purchased by the Ross Company has just come on the market. The new machine sells for $60,000. Although the new machine is more costly to purchase than the old machine, it would slash annual operating costs by $8,000. The new machine would last about ten years, and have a zero scrap value. The old machine can be sold now for only $16,000, due to the presence of the new machine on the market.

The president of the Ross Company has prepared the following cost analysis:

Savings promised by the new machine ($8,000 per year × 10 years)		$80,000
Cost of the new machine:		
Purchase price	$60,000	
Loss on the old machine	24,000	84,000
Net disadvantage of purchasing the new machine		($ 4,000)

The president handed her analysis to the controller and stated, "The loss that we would sustain on the old machine would more than wipe out any savings that the new machine might give us. We can't think about getting rid of that old machine if it means taking a loss on it."

Operating costs of the old machine are $18,000 per year. Sales are expected to remain unchanged at $40,000 per year. Selling and administrative expenses will be $12,000 per year.

Required:

1. Comment on the president's cost analysis.
2. Prepare a summary income statement covering the next ten years, assuming:
   a. That the new machine is not purchased.
   b. That the new machine is purchased.
3. Analyze the desirability of purchasing the new machine, using only relevant costs in your analysis.

P11–19. *Product mix shift; Scarce resources.* The Joanna Company manufactures a line of dolls and a doll dress sewing kit. The management requests assistance from you in determining an economical sales and production mix for the coming year. The sales department provides the following data:

Product	Estimated demand for next year (units)	Selling price per unit
Joanna	50,000	$6.00
Trish	42,000	2.90
Sarah	35,000	9.90
Mike	40,000	5.00
Sewing kit	325,000	3.00

The following additional information is available:

a. Material and labor standard costs per unit are:

Product	Direct materials	Direct labor
Joanna	$1.40	$1.60
Trish	0.70	1.00
Sarah	2.69	2.80
Mike	1.00	2.00
Sewing kit	0.60	0.80

b. The labor rate of $4 per hour is expected to continue without change in the next year. The plant has an effective capacity of 130,000 labor-hours per year on a single-shift basis. Present equipment can produce all of the products.

c. Next year's total fixed costs will be $520,000. Variable overhead costs will be equivalent to 25 percent of direct labor cost.

d. The company's present inventory of finished products is small and can be ignored.

e. You may assume that all nonmanufacturing costs are fixed.

Required:

1. Determine the contribution margin for a unit of each product.
2. For each product, determine the contribution margin which will be realized per labor-hour expended on the product.

3. Prepare a schedule showing the total labor-hours which will be required to produce the units estimated to be sold next year.
4. Examine the data which you have computed in (1)–(3) above. Indicate the product and number of units to be increased or decreased so that total production time is equal to the 130,000 production hours available.
5. Assume that the company does not want to reduce sales of any product. Identify the ways the company could obtain the additional output, and any problems which might be encountered.

(CPA, adapted)

P11–20. *Relevant costs; Special order.* Integrated Circuits, Inc. (ICI) is presently operating at 50 percent of capacity producing 50,000 units annually of a patented electronic component. ICI has received an offer from a company in Yokohama, Japan, to purchase 30,000 components at $6 per unit, f.o.b. ICI's plant. ICI has not previously sold components in Japan. Budgeted production costs for 50,000 and 80,000 units of output follow:

Units	50,000	80,000
Costs:		
Direct materials	$ 75,000	$120,000
Direct labor	75,000	120,000
Factory overhead	200,000	260,000
Total costs	$350,000	$500,000
Cost per unit	$7.00	$6.25

The sales manager thinks the order should be accepted, even if it results in a loss of $1 per unit, because the sale may build up future markets. The production manager does not wish to have the order accepted primarily because the order would show a loss of $0.25 per unit when computed on the new average unit cost.

Required:

1. Show the breakdown of the unit costs at the 50,000 and 80,000 unit levels of activity, in terms of direct materials, direct labor, variable overhead, and fixed overhead.
2. On the basis of the information given in the problem, and the information which you have computed above, should the order be accepted or rejected? Show computations to support your answer.
3. In addition to revenue and costs, what additional factors should be considered before making a final decision?

(CPA, adapted)

P11–21. *Relevant cost potpourri.* Unless otherwise indicated, each of the following parts is independent. In all cases, show computations to support your answer.
1. Haskins Company produces several products from processing of one ton of krypton, a rare mineral. Material and processing costs total $60,000 per ton, one sixth of which is allocable to Product

A. Product A can either be sold at the split-off point or processed further at a cost of $15,000 and then sold for $48,000. The sales value of Product A at the split-off point is $30,000. Should Product A be processed further or sold at the split-off point?

2. Sells Company produces three products, X, Y, and Z. Cost and revenue characteristics of the three products follow (per unit):

	X	Y	Z
Selling price	$10	$8	$15
Less variable expenses:			
Direct materials	$ 4	$2	$ 6
Labor and overhead	4	4	4
Total variable expenses	$ 8	$6	$10
Contribution margin	$ 2	$2	$ 5
Contribution margin ratio	20%	25%	33%

Demand for the company's products is very strong, with far more orders on hand each month than the company has raw materials available to produce. The same material is used in each product. The material costs $2 per pound, with a maximum of 6,000 pounds available each month. Which orders would you advise the company to accept first, those for X, for Y, or Z? Which orders second? Third?

3. For many years Condor Company has produced a small electrical part which it uses in the production of its standard line of diesel tractors. The company's cost of producing one part, based on a production level of 10,000 parts per year, is:

	Per part	Total
Direct materials	$ 4.00	
Direct labor	2.50	
Variable overhead	2.50	
Fixed overhead, direct	1.50	$15,000
Fixed overhead, common (allocated on a basis of labor-hours)	2.00	20,000
Total cost per part	$12.50	

An outside supplier has offered to supply the electrical parts to the Condor Company for only $10.25 per part. The company has determined that one third of the direct fixed costs represent supervisory salaries and other costs which can be eliminated if the parts are purchased. The other two thirds of the direct fixed costs represent depreciation of special equipment which has no resale value. The decision will have no effect on the common fixed costs of the company, and the space being used to produce the parts will otherwise be idle. Show the dollar advantage or disadvantage of accepting the supplier's offer.

4. Glade Company produces a single product. The cost of producing and selling a single unit of this product at the company's normal activity level of 6,000 units per month is:

Direct materials	$3.00
Direct labor	1.25
Variable overhead	1.25
Fixed overhead	2.00
Variable selling and administrative expense	1.50
Fixed selling and administrative expense	1.00

The normal selling price is $12 per unit. The company's capacity is 8,000 units per month. An order has been received from an overseas source for 2,000 units at a price of $9.50 per unit. This order would not disturb regular sales. If the order is accepted, by how much will monthly profits be increased or decreased? (The order will not change the company's total fixed costs.)

5. Refer to the data in Question 4. Assume that the company has 500 units of this product left over from last year, which are inferior to the current model. The units must be sold through regular channels at reduced prices. What unit cost figure is relevant for establishing a minimum selling price for these units? Explain.

P11–22. *Make or buy.* The Landy Company manufactures a variety of ball-point pens. The company has just received an offer from an outside supplier to provide the ink cartridge for the company's Zippo pen line, at a price of $0.48 per dozen cartridges. The company is interested in this offer, since its own production of cartridges is at capacity.

The Landy Company estimates that if the supplier's offer is accepted, the direct labor and variable overhead costs of the Zippo pen line would be reduced by 10 percent, and that the direct materials cost would be reduced by 20 percent.

Under present operations the Landy Company manufactures all of its own pens from start to finish. The Zippo pens are sold through wholesalers at $4 per box. Each box contains one dozen pens. Fixed overhead costs charged to the Zippo pen line total $50,000 each period. These fixed overhead costs are common, since the same equipment and facilities are used to produce several pen lines. The present cost of producing one dozen Zippo pens (one box) is given below:

Direct materials	$1.50
Direct labor	1.00
Manufacturing overhead	0.80*
Total cost	$3.30

* Includes both variable and fixed overhead, based on capacity production of 100,000 boxes of pens each period.

Required:

1. Should the Landy Company accept the outside supplier's offer? Show computations.
2. What is the maximum price that the Landy Company would be willing to pay to the outside supplier per dozen cartridges?
3. Assume that sales of the Zippo pen line increase to 125,000 boxes each period. In order to produce the 25,000 extra cartridges, the Landy Company would incur added fixed expenses of $12,500.

Under these conditions, should the supplier's offer be accepted? For how many boxes of Zippo cartridges?

P11–23. *Relevant cost potpourri.* Unless otherwise indicated, each of the following parts is independent. In all cases, show computations to support your answer.

1. A merchandising company has two departments, A and B. A recent monthly income statement for the company follows:

	Total	A	B
Sales	$100,000	$60,000	$40,000
Less variable expenses	40,000	22,000	18,000
Contribution margin	$ 60,000	$38,000	$22,000
Less fixed expenses	50,000	20,000	30,000
Net income (loss)	$ 10,000	$18,000	$ (8,000)

A study indicates that $14,000 of the fixed expenses being charged to Department B are sunk costs and allocated costs which will continue even if B is dropped. In addition, the elimination of Department B will result in a 10 percent decrease in the sales of Department A. If Department B is dropped, what will be the effect on the income of the company as a whole?

2. For many years Futura Company has purchased the starters which it installs in its standard line of farm tractors. Due to a reduction in output of certain of its products, the company has idle capacity which could be used to produce the starters. The chief engineer has recommended against this move, however, pointing out that the cost to produce the starters would be greater than the current $8.40 per unit purchase price:

	Per unit	Total
Direct materials	$3.40	
Direct labor	2.50	
Supervision	1.50	$18,000
Depreciation	1.00	12,000
Variable overhead	0.50	
Rent	0.30	3,600
Total cost	$9.20	

A supervisor would have to be hired to oversee production of the starters. However, the company has sufficient idle tools and machinery that no new equipment would have to be purchased. The rent charge above is based on space utilized in the plant. The total rent on the plant is $60,000 per period. Prepare computations to show the dollar advantage or disadvantage per period of making the starters.

3. Wexpro, Inc., produces several products from processing of one ton of clypton, a rare mineral. Material and processing costs total $12,000 per ton, one fourth of which is allocable to Product X. Five hundred units of Product X are produced from each ton of clypton. The units can either be sold at the split-off point for $9

each, or processed further at a total cost of $1,000 and then sold for $12 each. Should Product X be processed further or sold at the split-off point?

4. Delta Company produces a single product. The cost of producing and selling a single unit of this product at the company's normal activity level of 40,000 units per year is:

Direct materials	$2.50
Direct labor	4.00
Variable overhead	2.00
Fixed overhead	1.75
Variable selling and administrative expense	1.50
Fixed selling and administrative expense	2.25

The normal selling price is $15 per unit. The company's capacity is 50,000 units per year. An order has been received from a mail-order house for 10,000 units at a special price of $12 per unit. This order would not disturb regular sales. If the order is accepted, by how much will annual profits be increased or decreased? (The order will not change the company's total fixed costs.)

5. Refer to the data in Question 4. Assume that the company has 1,000 units of this product left over from last year, which are vastly inferior to the current model. The units must be sold through regular channels at reduced prices. What unit cost figure is relevant for establishing a minimum selling price for these units? Explain.

P11-24. *Discontinuance of a store.* Superior Markets, Inc., operates three stores in a large metropolitan area. A condensed income statement for the most recent year is presented below:

SUPERIOR MARKETS, INC.
Condensed Income Statement
For the Latest Year

	Store A	Store B	Store C	Total
Sales	$434,750	$740,000	$675,250	$1,850,000
Cost of goods sold	265,250	392,200	351,130	1,008,580
Gross margin	$169,500	$347,800	$324,120	$ 841,420
Operating expenses:				
Selling	$121,000	$150,000	$142,500	$ 413,500
Administrative	69,970	103,940	95,610	269,520
Total	$190,970	$253,940	$238,110	$ 683,020
Net income (loss)	$ (21,470)	$ 93,860	$ 86,010	$ 158,400

The company is very concerned about Store A's inability to show a profit, and consideration is being given to discontinuing the store. The company has retained you to make a recommendation concerning what to do with Store A. The following additional information is available:

1. The breakdown of the selling expenses and the administrative expenses is:

	Store A	Store B	Store C	Total
Selling expenses:				
Sales salaries	$ 70,000	$ 90,000	$ 85,000	$245,000
Direct advertising	12,000	15,000	10,000	37,000
General advertising	3,000	3,000	3,000	9,000
Store rent	25,000	30,000	34,000	89,000
Depreciation of store				
fixtures	3,500	4,500	3,000	11,000
Delivery salaries	6,000	6,000	6,000	18,000
Depreciation of delivery				
equipment	1,500	1,500	1,500	4,500
Total selling expenses	$121,000	$150,000	$142,500	$413,500
Administrative expenses:				
Store management				
salaries	$ 15,000	$ 18,000	$ 16,000	$ 49,000
General office salaries	23,500	40,000	36,500	100,000
Insurance expense on				
fixtures and				
inventory	6,000	8,000	8,000	22,000
Utilities	4,500	4,700	4,600	13,800
Employment taxes	6,870	9,240	8,610	24,720
General office	14,100	24,000	21,900	60,000
Total administrative				
expenses	$ 69,970	$103,940	$ 95,610	$269,520

2. The lease on the building housing Store A can be broken, with no penalty.
3. The fixtures being used in Store A would be transferred to the other two stores.
4. One of the sales personnel in Store A is a long-time employee, who will be retained even if Store A is closed. This employee would be transferred to one of the other stores. His salary is $6,000 per year. All other employees in Store A would be discharged.
5. One delivery crew serves all three stores. Since Store A has relatively few deliveries, there would be no reduction in this crew if the store is discontinued.
6. Employment taxes are 6 percent of salaries.
7. One third of the insurance in Store A is on the store's fixtures.
8. The general office salaries and expenses relate to the general management of Superior Markets, Inc. These expenses are allocated to the stores on a basis of sales dollars.
9. No change in general office salaries and expenses is expected if Store A is dropped.

Required:

1. Prepare a schedule showing the change in revenues and expenses if Store A is discontinued.
2. What recommendation would you make to the management of Superior Markets, Inc.?
3. Assume that because of the close location of Store C to Store A, if Store A is closed sales in Store C will increase by at least $150,000

per year. Store C's gross margin rate is 48 percent. Store C has ample capacity to handle the increased sales. What effect would these factors have on your recommendation concerning Store A? Show computations.

P11–25. *Make or buy.* The Vernom Corporation, which produces and sells to wholesalers a highly successful line of summer lotions and insect repellents, has decided to diversify in order to stabilize sales throughout the year. A natural area for the company to consider is the production of winter lotions and creams to prevent dry and chapped skin.

After considerable research, a winter products line has been developed. However, because of the conservative nature of the company management, Vernom's president has decided to introduce only one of the new products for this coming winter. If the product is a success, further expansion in future years will be initiated.

The product selected (called Chap-Off) is a lip balm that will be sold in a lipstick-type tube. The product will be sold to wholesalers in boxes of 24 tubes for $8 per box. Because of available capacity, no additional fixed charges will be incurred to produce the product. However, a $100,000 fixed charge will be absorbed by the product to allocate a fair share of the company's present fixed costs to the new product.

Using the estimated sales and production of 100,000 boxes of Chap-Off as the expected volume, the accounting department has developed the following costs per box:

```
Direct material  . . . . . . . . . . . . . . . . . . . . . . . . .  $3.00
Direct labor  . . . . . . . . . . . . . . . . . . . . . . . . .      2.00
Total overhead . . . . . . . . . . . . . . . . . . . . . . . .      1.50
        Total cost  . . . . . . . . . . . . . . . . . . . . . .  $6.50
```

The costs above include costs for producing both the lip balm and the tube into which the lip balm is to be placed. As an alternative to making the tubes, Vernom has approached a cosmetics manufacturer to discuss the possibility of purchasing the tubes for Chap-Off. The purchase price of the empty tubes from the cosmetics manufacturer would be $0.90 per 24 tubes. If the Vernom Corporation accepts the purchase proposal, it is predicted that direct labor and variable overhead costs would be reduced by 10 percent and direct materials costs would be reduced by 20 percent.

Required:

1. Should the Vernom Corporation make or buy the tubes? Show calculations to support your answer.
2. What would be the maximum purchase price acceptable to the Vernom Corporation? Support your answer with an appropriate explanation.
3. Instead of sales of 100,000 boxes, revised estimates show sales volume at 125,000 boxes. At this new volume, additional equipment, at an annual rental of $10,000, must be acquired to manufacture the tubes. However, this incremental cost would be the only additional fixed cost required even if sales increased to 300,000 boxes.

(The 300,000 level is the goal for the third year of production.) Under these circumstances, should the Vernom Corporation make or buy the tubes? Show calculations to support your answer.
4. The company has the option of making and buying tubes at the same time. What would be your answer to (3) if this alternative was considered? Show calculations to support your answer.
5. What nonquantifiable factors should the Vernom Corporation consider in determining whether they should make or buy the tubes?

(CMA, adapted)

P11–26. *Special order; Relevant costs.* Miles Hanson operates a small machine shop. He manufactures one standard product available from many similar businesses, and he also manufactures products to customer order. His accountant prepared the annual income statement shown below:

	Custom sales	Standard sales	Total
Sales	$50,000	$25,000	$75,000
Materials used	9,100	8,400	17,500
Labor	20,000	9,000	29,000
Depreciation	6,300	3,600	9,900
Power used	2,000	900	2,900
Rent	6,000	1,000	7,000
Heat and light	600	100	700
Total costs	44,000	23,000	67,000
Net profit	$ 6,000	$ 2,000	$ 8,000

The depreciation charges are for machines used in the respective product lines. Mr. Hanson has found that power used consistently equals 10 percent of labor cost. The rent is for the building space which has been leased for ten years at $7,000 per year. The rent and heat and light are apportioned to the product lines based on amount of floor space occupied. All other costs are current expenses identified with the product line causing them.

A valued custom-parts customer has asked Mr. Hanson if he would manufacture 5,000 special units for her. Mr. Hanson is working at capacity and would have to give up some other business in order to take this business. He can't renege on custom orders already agreed to, but he could reduce the output of his standard product about one half for one year while producing the specially requested custom part. The customer is willing to pay $7.25 for each part. The material cost will be about $2.00 per unit and the labor will be $3.60 per unit. Mr. Hanson will have to spend $2,000 for a special device which will be discarded when the job is done.

Required:
1. Calculate the opportunity cost of taking the special order.
2. Would you advise Mr. Hanson to take the order? Show appropriate computations to support your answer.
3. What nonquantitative factors should Mr. Hanson consider before taking the special order?

(CMA, adapted)

P11–27. *Break even; Eliminating an unprofitable line.* Marla Adams, president of the Eastern Company, wants guidance on the advisability of eliminating Product C, one of the company's three similar products, in hope of improving the company's overall operating performance. The company's three products are manufactured in a single plant, and occupy roughly equal amounts of floor space. Below is a condensed statement of operating income for the company and for Product C for the quarter ended October 31, 19x6:

	All three products	Product C
Sales	$2,800,150	$350,000
Cost of sales:		
Raw materials	$ 515,000	$ 68,500
Direct labor	1,305,000	168,000
Fringe benefits (15% of labor)	195,750	25,200
Royalties (1% of Product C sales)	3,500	3,500
Building rent and maintenance	6,000	2,000
Factory supplies	15,000	2,100
Depreciation (straight line)	75,200	21,100
Electrical power—machines	29,300	3,600
Total cost of sales	$2,144,750	$294,000
Gross margin	$ 655,400	$ 56,000
Selling and administrative expense:		
Sales commissions	$ 120,000	$ 15,000
Officers' salaries	31,500	10,500
Product line managers' salaries	14,000	5,300
Fringe benefits (15% of salaries and commissions)	24,900	4,620
Shipping expense	79,500	9,350
Advertising expense	227,000	37,300
Total selling and administrative	$ 496,900	$ 82,070
Net operating income (loss)	$ 158,500	$ (26,070)

Inventories carried by the company are small, and can be ignored. Each element of cost is entirely fixed or variable within the relevant range. The dropping of Product C would have little (if any) effect on sales of the other two product lines.

Required:

1. Before a decision is made on whether Product C should be dropped, Ms. Adams would first like to know the overall break-even point for Product C (in sales dollars), given the cost and revenue data shown above.

2. Would you recommend to Ms. Adams that Product C be dropped? Prepare appropriate computations to support your answer. You may assume that the plant space now being used to produce Product C would otherwise be idle. The equipment being used to produce Product C has no resale value.

(CPA, adapted)

P11–28. *Discussion questions on relevant costs.* The Hayes Company normally produces and sells 30,000 units of Product X each month. The company's unit costs at this level of activity are given below:

Direct materials	$4
Direct labor	3
Variable overhead	4
Fixed overhead	5
Variable selling	3
Fixed selling	1

Below are a number of questions relating to production and sales of Product X. Unless otherwise stated, *each question is independent of the others.* Assume a normal selling price of $22 per unit, unless a different selling price is given.

Question 1. Assume that the Hayes Company has sufficient capacity to produce 40,000 units each month. The company has an opportunity to sell 10,000 units in a foreign market. The only selling costs that would be associated with the foreign order would be $2 per unit in shipping. Legal fees, foreign permits, and other costs of getting the order would be $6,000. What would be the per unit break-even price on the order?

Question 2. Assume again that the Hayes Company has sufficient capacity to produce 40,000 units each month. The company could increase sales by 20 percent above the present 30,000 units each month, if it were willing to increase its fixed advertising by $35,000 monthly. Would the increased advertising expenditure be justified?

Question 3. Five hundred units of Product X produced last month have small blemishes, and it will be impossible to sell these units at regular prices. If the company wishes to sell the blemished units through regular distribution channels, what unit cost figure is relevant for setting a minimum selling price?

Question 4. The U.S. Army would like to make a one-time-only purchase of 5,000 units of Product X. The contract would call for a fixed fee of $.30 per unit, plus reimbursement for Hayes Company's costs of production. Assume that regular sales of Product X have temporarily slumped to only 25,000 units per month. If the Hayes Company accepts the army contract, by how much will profits be increased or decreased from what they would be if only 25,000 units were sold? There would be no variable selling expenses associated with the army's order.

Question 5. Assume the same situation as described in Question 4, except that the company is presently selling 30,000 units through regular channels. Accepting the army order would require giving up regular sales of 5,000 units. If the army contract is accepted, by how much will profits be increased or decreased from what they would be if the 5,000 units were sold through regular channels?

Question 6. An outside manufacturer has offered to produce Product X for the Hayes Company, and to ship it directly to the Hayes Company's customers. This arrangement would permit the Hayes Company to reduce its variable selling expenses by one third. The Hayes Company's plant would be completely idle but fixed overhead would continue at 60 percent of its present level. What unit cost figure is relevant for comparison against the quotation received from the outside manufacturer?

P11–29.   *Straightforward maximization problem.* (Appendix)   The Haag Company can produce two different products, A and B. The company has four manufacturing operations—Cutting, Sanding, Assembly, and Packing. Product B goes through all four operations. Product A goes through all operations except Assembly. The manufacturing requirements in terms of hours per unit are given below for A and B for each of the company's operations:

	Product A	Product B
Cutting Operation	2	3
Sanding Operation	3	1
Assembly Operation	–	4
Packing Operation	1	1

Each operation is limited in terms of number of hours available. The available hours by operation are: Cutting—30 hours; Sanding—15 hours; Assembly—24 hours; and Packing—8 hours.

   Each unit of product A which is sold yields $3 in contribution margin, and each unit of product B which is sold yields $4 in contribution margin. The company wishes to maximize contribution margin.

Required:

1.   Prepare equations to express the objective function, and each of the constraints.
2.   Determine the optimum mix of products A and B, using the graphical method of linear programming.

P11–30.   *Optimum production mix to maximize profits.* (Appendix)   Bill Sagers has just retired, and is anxious to open a small pottery business to occupy his time. Mr. Sagers has decided to produce just two items initially—pots and bowls. The local pottery supply house has indicated that because of shortages in supplies, Mr. Sagers can be allowed only 80 pounds of high-quality clay each week, and only 11¼ gallons of glazing material.

   Mr. Sagers has purchased a used kiln, which he feels can be operated about 60 hours per week. His wife will package all finished products, and will have a maximum of about 11 hours per week to work for the pottery business. Mr. Sagers has determined the following additional information:

		Per batch	
Operation	Item needed	Pots	Bowls
Molding	Clay	8 lbs.	5 lbs.
Glazing	Glaze	5 qts.	3 qts.
Firing	—	4 hrs.	6 hrs.
Packaging	—	1 hr.	1 hr.

Mr. Sagers feels that no more than nine batches of bowls can be sold each week. The pots yield $50 in profits per batch, and the bowls $40 per batch. Mr. Sagers wishes to maximize his profits.

Required:

1. Prepare equations to express the objective function, and each of the constraints. Identify pots as *X* and bowls as *Y*.
2. Determine how many batches of pots and how many batches of bowls should be produced each week. Identify pots as *X* and bowls as *Y* on your linear programming graph.

P11–31. *Optimum candy mixture; Cost minimization.* (Appendix) (Based on a situation described by Miller and Starr, *Executive Decisions and Operations Research*, pp. 217–22.) The Happy Valley Candy Company produces and sells a box of candy made up of caramels and creams. The company would like to find the optimal mixture of the two kinds of candy, in order to meet the specifications per box as outlined in the following table:

	Caramels	Creams	Per box
Weight per piece	1.2 ozs.	0.6 ozs.	18.0 ozs. or more
Number of pieces	?	?	25 or more
Cost per piece	$.03	$.02	$0.66 maximum cost

The company wants at least six caramels in each box of candy. The company can produce either caramels or creams in unlimited numbers, so the objective is to minimize the cost of candy going into each box. The mixture will not affect the selling price per box.

Required:

1. Prepare equations expressing the objective function, and the constraints under which the company must operate.
2. Determine the optimal mix of caramels and creams in order to minimize the total cost per box of candy. Use a linear programming graph, with caramels on the horizontal axis (*X*), and creams on the vertical axis (*Y*).

P11–32. *Cost minimization.* (Appendix) [Prepared from a situation described by Naylor and Byrne, *Linear Programming* (Wadsworth Publishing Company, p. 45)] Recycled Metals, Inc., has received an order from a customer who wants to purchase a minimum of 2,500 pounds of scrap metal. The customer requires that the scrap metal contain at least 1,200 pounds of high-quality aluminum that can be melted down and used in fabrication. The customer also requires that the scrap delivered to him contain no more than 480 pounds of unfit metal. By "unfit" the customer means metal that contains so many impurities that it can't be melted down and used at all.

Recycled Metals, Inc., can purchase aluminum scrap metal from either of two suppliers. The scrap being sold by the two suppliers contains the following proportions of high-quality aluminum and unfit scrap:

	Supplier A	Supplier B
High-quality aluminum	80%	30%
Unfit scrap	20%	15%

Either supplier has unlimited quantities of scrap metal available. Supplier A charges $0.25 per pound, and Supplier B charges $0.12 per pound. Recycled Metals, Inc., would like to minimize the total cost it will have to pay to acquire the needed scrap metal to fill the customer's order.

Required:

1. Prepare equations to express the objective function and the constraints under which Recycled Metals, Inc., must make its purchase.
2. Determine the amount of scrap metal which should be purchased from each supplier, by using the linear programming graphical method.

P11–33. *Pricing and joint products.* (Note to the instructor: Problem 12–18 at the end of Chapter 12 can be assigned very effectively in conjuction with Chapter 11. The problem contains a number of concepts covered in Chapter 11, as well as touching on the problem of pricing.)

Required:

Turn to and solve Problem 12–18 at the end of Chapter 12.

Chapter 12

The pricing decision

Many firms have no pricing problems at all. They produce a product that is in competition with other, similar, products for which a market price already exists. Customers will not pay more than this price, and there is no reason for any firm to charge less. Under these circumstances, no price calculations are necessary. Any firm entering the market simply charges the price the market directs it to accept. To a large extent, farm products follow this type of pattern. In these situations, the question isn't what price to charge; the question is simply how much to produce.

In this chapter we are concerned with the more common situation in which a firm is faced with the problem of setting its own prices, as well as deciding how much to produce. The pricing decision is considered by many to be the single most important decision that a manager has to make. The reason is that the pricing of products isn't just a marketing decision or a financial decision; rather, it is a decision touching on *all* aspects of a firm's activities, and as such affects the entire enterprise. Since the prices charged for a firm's products largely determine the quantities customers are willing to purchase, the setting of prices dictates the inflows of revenues into a firm. If these revenues consistently fail to cover all of the costs of the firm, then in the long run the firm cannot survive. This is true regardless of how carefully costs may be controlled, or how innovative the managers of the firm may be in the discharge of their other responsibilities.

Cost is a key factor in the pricing decision. As we have already seen, however, "cost" is a somewhat fluid concept, and sometimes hard to pin down. Our purpose in this chapter is to look at some of the cost concepts developed in earlier chapters and to see how these concepts can be applied in the pricing decision. This chapter is not intended to be a comprehensive guide to pricing; rather, its purpose is to integrate those cost concepts with which we are already familiar into a general pricing framework.

THE ECONOMIC FRAMEWORK FOR PRICING

A large part of microeconomic theory (theory of the firm) is devoted to the matter of pricing. In order to establish a framework for the pricing decision, it will be helpful to review certain of these economic theory concepts. This review will also assist us in showing the relationship between the models involved in microeconomic theory and the concept of incremental analysis discussed in preceding chapters.

Total revenue and total cost curves

Microeconomic theory states that the best price for a product is that price which maximizes the difference between total revenue and total costs.

The economist illustrates this concept by constructing a model such as that shown in Exhibit 12–1.

This model is based on a number of assumptions. The economist assumes, first, that it is not possible to sell an unlimited number of units at the same price. If an unlimited number of units could be sold at the same price, then the total revenue (*TR*) curve would appear as a straight line, beginning at the origin of the graph. Since the economist assumes that at some point price reductions will be necessary to sell more units, the *TR* curve is shown increasing at a decreasing rate as quantity sold in-

Exhibit 12–1
Total revenue and total cost curves

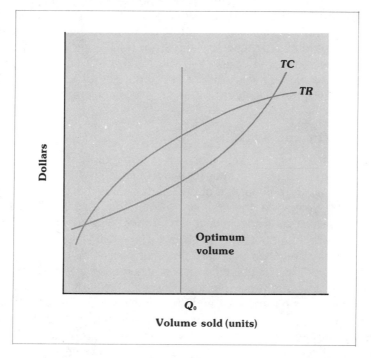

creases. That is, as price is reduced to stimulate more sales, total revenue will continue to increase for each unit sold, but the *rate* of this increase will begin to decline. As price is reduced more and more, the increase in total revenue will continue to decline, as depicted by the flattening tendency in the *TR* curve in the exhibit.

The total cost (*TC*) curve in Exhibit 12–1 assumes that the cost of producing additional units of product is not constant, but rather increases as attempts are made to squeeze more and more production out of a given set of productive facilities. So long as the rate of this increase is less than the rate of increase in total revenue, the company can profit by producing and selling more units of product. At some point, however, the rate of increase in total cost will become equal to the rate of increase in total revenue—that is, at some point the two lines will become parallel to each other. At this point the increase to total cost from producing and selling one more unit of product is exactly equal to the increase to total revenue from that unit of product, and its production and sale yields zero increase in total profits in the firm. This point is shown in the graph in Exhibit 12–1 as quantity Q_0, representing the optimum volume of production and sales for the firm.

At Q_0 volume of units the difference between total revenue and total cost is maximized. If we move to the right of Q_0 volume, total cost is increasing more rapidly than total revenue, and therefore total profits would be decreased. If we move to the left of Q_0 volume, then total revenue is increasing more rapidly than total cost, and the company can profit by further expanding output up to Q_0 level of activity. In sum, Q_0 represents the optimum volume of sales for the firm, and the correct price to charge is the price which will allow the firm to sell this volume of units.

Marginal revenue and marginal cost curves

These same concepts can be shown in terms of marginal revenue and marginal cost. Marginal revenue can be defined as the addition to total revenue resulting from the sale of one additional unit of product. Marginal cost can be defined as the addition to total cost resulting from the production and sale of one additional unit of product. The economist expresses these concepts in model form as shown in Exhibit 12–2.

The marginal revenue (MR) and marginal cost (MC) curves in Exhibit 12–2 have their basis in the economist's assumption that the total revenue and total cost curves behave in the way depicted earlier in Exhibit 12–1. That is, the marginal revenue and marginal cost curves are derived by measuring the rate of *change* in total revenue and total cost at various levels of activity, and by plotting this change in graph form. Since the total revenue curve in Exhibit 12–1 depicts a declining rate of increase in total revenue, the marginal revenue curve in Exhibit 12–2 slopes downward to the right. And since the total cost curve in Exhibit 12–1 depicts total cost as increasing with volume, the marginal cost curve slopes upward to the right in Exhibit 12–2. As discussed in Chapter 2, the economist's marginal concept is basically the same as the accountant's incremental concept.

Notice that Exhibit 12–2 depicts average revenue, which represents the *average price* obtained for each unit sold, as being greater than marginal revenue. Why is this so? The reason can be shown by means of a simple example. Assume that at a price of $5 per unit ten units of product X can be sold. If the price is dropped to $4.75, then 1 additional unit, or

Exhibit 12–2
Marginal revenue and marginal cost curves

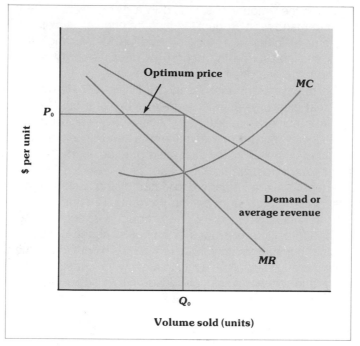

11 units in total, can be sold. The *marginal* revenue from the 11th unit will therefore be $4.75 (the unit's selling price). But the *average* revenue per unit sold will be $4.98 ($50.00 + $4.75 = $54.75 ÷ 11 units = $4.98 per unit). By this line of reasoning, average revenue will always be greater than marginal revenue, so long as prices must be reduced to sell more units.

The optimum price to charge is determined by the intersection of the marginal revenue and the marginal cost curves. The intersection of these two curves occurs at volume Q_0. This is the same volume as shown earlier in Exhibit 12–1, depicting the point of maximum difference between total revenues and total costs. At volume Q_0 price P_0 should be charged for each unit sold.

Elasticity of demand

A product's price elasticity is a key concept in any pricing decision. Price elasticity measures the degree to which volume of sales is affected by a change in price per unit. Demand for a product is price inelastic if a change in price has little or no effect on the volume of units sold. Demand is price elastic if a change in price has a substantial effect on the volume of units sold. Salt is a good example of a product that tends to be price inelastic. Raising or lowering the price of salt probably would have little or no effect on the amount of salt sold in a given year.

Whether demand for a product tends to be price elastic or price inelastic can be a crucial factor in a decision relating to a change in price. The problem is that measuring the degree of price elasticity is an extremely difficult thing to do. It's one thing to observe generally that a given product tends to be price elastic, and it's another thing to determine exactly the *degree* of that elasticity—that is, to determine what change in volume of sales will take place as a result of specific changes in price. Yet this is exactly the kind of information that managers need in their pricing decisions, and the kind of information that they attempt to obtain by carefully planned marketing research programs.

Pricing decisions are further complicated by the fact that cross-elasticity often exists in the demand for certain products. Cross-elasticity measures the degree to which demand for one product is affected by a change in the price of a substitute product. For example, as the price of galvanized pipe goes up, consumers may switch to plastic pipe. One of the problems of measuring cross-elasticity is trying to identify the substitutes for a particular product, and the willingness of consumers to accept those substitutes in place of the product itself. Although problems of this type are often difficult to quantify, the concept of cross-elasticity of demand is an important concept, and cannot be disregarded in the pricing decision.

Limitations to the general models

Although the models in Exhibits 12–1 and 12–2 do a good job of showing the general outlines of the incremental profit approach to pricing, they must be viewed as being only broad, conceptual guides in pricing decisions. There are several reasons why. First, cost and revenue data available to managers generally are sufficient to provide only rough approximations of the shape of the various cost and revenue curves depicted in the models. As our methods of measurement are improved and refined in years to come this situation may change, but at present managers usually have only a general idea of the shape of the demand curve which they are facing.

Second, the models are directly applicable only in conditions of *monopoly* (no directly competing product in the market) and *monopolistic competition* (many sellers of similar products, with no one seller having a large enough share of the market for other sellers to be able to discern the effect of his or her pricing decision on their sales). The models are not applicable between these two extremes, where the market is characterized by situations of *oligopoly* (a few large sellers, competing directly with each other). The reason is that the models make no allowance for retaliatory pricing decisions by competing firms, and retaliatory pricing is a prime characteristic of oligopolistic industries.

Where oligopoly exists, the marginal revenue curve of a firm will depend on how the firm's competitors react to price changes. If one firm reduces its prices, then the other firms in the industry probably will retaliate by reducing their prices as well. On the other hand, if one firm increases its prices, its competitors may not follow suit. In such situations, the firm increasing its prices will see its sales drop off sharply, as consumers turn to the firm's competitors. These effects can be seen in a variation of the general pricing model, which is characterized by a *kinked* demand curve, as shown in Exhibit 12–3.

Exhibit 12–3
Kinked demand curve faced by oligopolistic firms

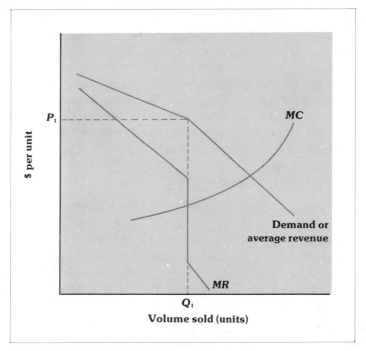

Notice from Exhibit 12–3 that both the demand curve and the marginal revenue curve are kinked at price P_1. Price P_1 is the prevailing price in the industry. Any attempt to expand volume by reducing price below P_1 will result in a severe drop in marginal revenue, since marginal revenue falls off sharply to the right of Q_1, the present volume of sales.

As a practical matter, a kink of this type is likely to appear only if competitor firms are *not* operating at full capacity. If they are operating at full capacity, then they will be unable to absorb extra sales and one firm may be able to raise its prices with little loss of business. If so, then its competitors probably will quickly follow suit and raise their prices as well.

A third limitation to the general models arises from the fact that price is just one element in the marketing of a product. Many other factors must also be considered, which can have a significant impact on the number of units of a product that can be sold at a given price. Among these factors one can find promotional strategy, product design, intensity of selling effort, and the selection of distribution channels.

A final limitation to the general models is that even if business firms had a precise knowledge of the shape of their demand curves, we cannot automatically assume that they would price in such a way as to maximize profits. The reason is that this might bring charges from the public of "profiteering" and "charging all that the traffic will bear." Rather than attempting to maximize profits, many firms seek only to earn a "satisfactory" profit for the company. They think in terms of a reasonable return on the investment which has been made in the company, and strive to set prices in such a way as to earn that return. The concept of a "satisfactory" profit underlies the actions of a great many business firms today.

Although the limitations discussed above preclude the *direct* use of the economic pricing models in pricing decisions, these models nonetheless are highly useful in providing the general framework within which the price setter must work. They state the pricing problem in *conceptual* terms, and as such constitute the starting point in any pricing decision.

PRICING STANDARD PRODUCTS

Not all pricing decisions are approached in the same way. Some pricing decisions relate to the pricing of standard products which are sold to customers in the routine day-to-day conduct of business activities. Other pricing decisions relate to special orders of standard or near-standard products, and still others relate to pricing of special products taken on in an effort to fill out unused productive capacity. In this section we consider the pricing of standard products. The pricing of special orders of various types is reserved to a later section.

Cost-plus pricing formulas

In pricing standard products the key concept is to recognize that selling prices must be sufficient in the long run to cover *all* costs of production, administration, and sales, both fixed and variable, as well as to provide for a reasonable return on the stockholders' investment, if a firm is to survive and grow. This point is often missed by some pricing enthusiasts who seem to imply in their writings that any price above variable or incremental costs is an acceptable price for any product under any circumstances.[1]

In setting normal long-run prices on standard products *all costs* are

---

[1] For a discussion of the circumstances under which variable or incremental costs are useful as a pricing guide, see the section, "Special Pricing Decisions."

relevant in the pricing decision, and must be explicitly considered by the price setter if long-run profit goals are to be met. This means that a portion of the fixed costs (even if the fixed costs are sunk) must be considered along with the variable costs, and that the costs of administration and sales must be weighted in along with the costs of production, as prices are set.

The most common approach to the pricing of standard products is to employ some type of *cost-plus* pricing formula. The approach is to compute a "cost" base, and then to add to this base some predetermined markup to arrive at a target selling price. The "cost" in cost-plus is defined according to the method being used to cost units of product. In Chapters 3 and 6 we found that units of product can be costed in two different ways— by the absorption approach or by the contribution approach (with direct costing). We consider both costing methods below, and the approach each takes to cost-plus pricing of standard products.

The absorption approach

The absorption approach to cost-plus pricing defines the cost base as the cost to produce one unit of product. Other costs, such as administration and sales, are provided for through the markup that is added to this base. The markup is also structured in such a way as to provide for some desired profit margin above all costs.

To illustrate, let us assume that the Ritter Company is in the process of setting a selling price on one of its standard products, which has just undergone some slight modifications in design. The accounting department has accumulated the following cost data on the redesigned product:

	Per unit	Total
Direct materials	$5	
Direct labor	4	
Variable overhead	4	
Fixed overhead (based on 10,000 units)	7	$70,000
Variable selling and administrative expenses	2	
Fixed selling and administrative expenses (based on 10,000 units)	1	10,000

The first step is to compute the full cost to produce one unit of product. Once this cost has been determined, it becomes the base in the cost-plus pricing formula, to which the desired markup can be added. For the Ritter Company, the cost to produce one unit of product is $20, computed as follows:

Direct materials	$ 5
Direct labor	4
Overhead ($4 variable, plus $7 fixed, or 275% of direct labor cost)	11
Total absorption cost to manufacture one unit	$20

Let us assume that the Ritter Company has a general policy of adding a markup equal to 50 percent of cost to manufacture, in order to obtain its target selling prices. A price quotation sheet for the company prepared under this assumption is presented in Exhibit 12–4.

Exhibit 12–4
Price quotation sheet—absorption basis

Direct materials	$ 5
Direct labor	4
Overhead at 275% of direct labor cost	11
Total cost to manufacture	$20
Markup to cover selling and administrative expenses, and desired profit—50% of cost to manufacture	10
Target selling price	$30

As shown in Exhibit 12–4, even though this pricing approach is termed cost-plus, part of the costs involved are buried in the *plus,* or markup part of the formula. The buried costs are those associated with the selling and administrative activities. These costs could be broken out separately and added to the cost base along with the cost to manufacture, but this is rarely done in actual practice. The reason centers on the difficulty that would be involved in making the necessary allocations among the various products of the firm. For example, the salary of the company president would be a common cost among all products. It would be a difficult task to try to allocate the president's salary in any meaningful way to these products. The great majority of firms feel that selling and administrative costs can be provided for adequately in final, target selling prices by simply expanding the markup over cost to manufacture to include them as well as the desired profit. This means, of course, that the markup must be structured with great care in order to ensure that it is sufficient to cover all that it is supposed to cover. More will be said on this point a little later.

If the Ritter Company produces and sells 10,000 units of its product at a selling price of $30 each, the income statement will appear as shown in Exhibit 12–5.

Exhibit 12–5

RITTER COMPANY Income Statement Absorption Basis	
Sales (10,000 units at $30)	$300,000
Cost of goods sold (10,000 units at $20)	200,000
Gross margin	$100,000
Selling and administrative expenses (10,000 units at $2 variable and $1 fixed)	30,000
Net income	$ 70,000

The contribution approach

The contribution approach to preparing price quotation sheets is similar to the absorption approach in that it is structured around the need to cover *all* costs in setting long-run prices. It differs from the absorption approach in that it emphasizes costs by behavior, rather than by function.

In the absorption approach to cost-plus pricing, we found that the cost base consists of the cost to produce a unit of product. By contrast, the contribution approach to cost-plus pricing defines the cost base in terms of a product's variable expenses. The cost base includes not just variable manufacturing expenses, but variable selling and admininstrative expenses as well. A markup designed to cover appropriate fixed costs and to provide the desired profit per unit is added to this variable expense base.

To illustrate, refer again to the cost data for the Ritter Company. The base to use in cost-plus pricing under the contribution approach would be $15, computed as follows:

Direct materials	$ 5
Direct labor	4
Variable overhead	4
Variable selling and administrative expenses	2
Total variable expenses	$15

Let us assume that the Ritter Company has found that a markup of 100 percent of variable expenses is adequate to cover allocable fixed expenses and to provide the desired profit per unit. A price quotation sheet prepared under this assumption is shown in Exhibit 12–6.

Notice again that even though this pricing method is termed *cost*-plus pricing, a portion of the costs are buried in the *plus,* or markup part of the formula. In this case, however, the buried costs are the fixed costs rather than the selling and administrative costs. Again, the reason for not including the fixed costs in the cost base can be traced to the time and difficulty that would be involved in any attempt to allocate. As a practical matter, there is no way to equitably allocate many common fixed costs, as discussed in Chapter 6. Any attempt to do so may result in less usable

Exhibit 12–6
Price quotation sheet—contribution basis

Direct materials	$ 5
Direct labor	4
Variable overhead	4
Variable selling and administrative expenses	2
Total variable expenses	$15
Markup to cover fixed expenses and desired profit— 100% of variable expenses	15
Target selling price	$30

cost data for pricing, rather than more usable data. In addition, many users of the contribution approach to pricing argue that keeping the cost base free of any element of fixed costs facilitates pricing in special and unusual situations. This point is discussed further in a following section dealing with special pricing problems.

Compare the contribution approach to cost-plus pricing in Exhibit 12–6 to the absorption approach in Exhibit 12–4. Although both approaches are employing the cost-plus concept, notice the difference in the way in which the two approaches handle the cost data, and structure the price quotation sheet. Also notice that the Ritter Company can attain the *same* $30 target selling price by using either costing method.

In order to conclude the Ritter Company example, let us again assume that the company produces and sells 10,000 units of product at a selling price of $30 each. The company's income statement as it would appear under the contribution approach is shown in Exhibit 12–7.

Exhibit 12–7

RITTER COMPANY Income Statement Contribution Basis		
Sales (10,000 units at $30)		$300,000
Less variable expenses (10,000 units at $15)		150,000
Contribution margin		$150,000
Less fixed expenses:		
Production	$70,000	
Selling and administrative	10,000	80,000
Net income		$ 70,000

Using cost-plus data

By far the most crucial element in the cost-plus pricing formulas is the percentage markup added to the cost base. We have found that under both the absorption and the contribution approaches to cost-plus pricing some elements of cost are buried in the markup figure. This means that the markup must be sufficient to cover these buried costs, as well as to provide the desired profit per unit. In some situations the percentage markup is more or less standard, and has developed over long years of experience and use. In other situations, however, no standard markups are available, and the markups must be developed by the firm itself. One way of doing this is to set markups according to companywide profit objectives, or according to some desired rate of return on investment.

To illustrate, assume that a firm has found that an investment of $2,000,000 is necessary in order to produce and market 50,000 units of product X each year. It will cost $30 to produce each unit of product X at a 50,000 unit level of activity, and total selling and administrative expenses are estimated to be $700,000. If the firm desires a 25 percent return on investment, then the required markup would be computed as follows:

Desired return on investment (25% × $2,000,000)	$ 500,000
Selling and administrative expenses	700,000
Total	$1,200,000 (*a*)
Cost to manufacture (50,000 units × $30)	$1,500,000 (*b*)
Required markup—(*a*) ÷(*b*)	80%

The selling price of a unit of product X would be $54:[2]

Cost to manufacture	$30
Markup—80% × $30	24
Target selling price per unit	$54

The problem with a rigid application of an approach such as this is that it tends to ignore the relationship between price and volume. For example, the competitive situation may be such for product X that a selling price of $54 would result in far less than 50,000 units being sold each year. On the other hand, demand may be so great that the company would be swamped with orders.

In order to make cost-plus pricing formulas workable, companies usually do three things. First, they rarely price a product exactly at the target price suggested by the cost-plus formula. The costs used in the formula serve as a basis for establishing prices at their *lower limit*—the actual final selling price may be much higher than this minimum target figure. Many people have the mistaken notion that price is purely a function of cost, when in reality cost serves in large part simply to define the lower limit that can be set. Noncost factors, such as competitive position, promotional strategy, packaging, and ability to achieve long-term product differentiation may permit a manager to set a price significantly higher than the minimum target figure provided by use of the cost formulas. The mark of real executives in pricing can be found in their ability to sense the market situation, and in knowing when price adjustments can and should be made. If the executives sense that their competitive position is strong, they will adjust the prices upward; if they sense a strengthening of opposing competitive forces, then they will either shade the prices downward or attempt to further differentiate the product.

Second, the price setter must recognize that just because a particular margin has been obtainable for the last 20 or 30 years there is no assurance that it will continue to be obtainable. For example, the neighborhood gro-

---

[2] For a detailed discussion of various approaches to computing markups, see A. D. H. Kaplan, Joel B. Dirlan, and Robert F. Lanzillotti, *Pricing in Big Business: A Case Approach* (Washington, D.C.: Brookings Institution, 1958).

cery stores suddenly discovered in the 1940s that the margins they had been obtaining for many decades were no longer obtainable because of the development of large chain supermarkets. In turn, the chain supermarkets have discovered in the 1970s that the margins they have enjoyed for nearly three decades are being undercut by the self-serve discount food outlets. In order to achieve target return on investment figures, managers are often required to trade-off some margin in order to achieve a higher turnover of assets, such as we considered in our ROI discussion in Chapter 10. This means that markups sometimes must be reduced, in the hope of stimulating the overall volume of sales.

Third, companies will not use the same markup for all product lines, but rather will vary the markup according to custom, need, or general industry practice. For example, one product line may carry a markup of 20 percent whereas another may carry a markup of 60 percent. This is typical of clothing and department stores, where the percentage markup varies by department and occasionally even by item. Jewelry generally has a high markup, whereas stockings carry a relatively low markup.

Why use cost data in pricing?

If pricing executives end up setting prices according to how they sense the market, then an obvious question at this point is why bother using cost data in the pricing decision? Several reasons can be advanced in favor of computing target selling prices by means of the cost-plus approach, even if the resulting prices aren't actually used. First, in making pricing decisions, the manager is faced with a myriad of uncertainties. Cost-plus target prices represent a *starting point,* a way of perhaps removing some of the uncertainties and shedding some light on others. By this means, the manager may be able more easily to feel his or her way through the thicket, and come up with a price that will be acceptable given the constraints at hand.

Second, cost might be viewed as a floor of protection, guarding the price setter from pricing too low and incurring losses. Although this line of reasoning is appealing and reassuring, the protection offered by the cost floor is more illusionary than real. For one thing, we have already noted that neither the absorption nor the contribution costing approaches include all costs in the cost base. For another thing, unit cost depends on volume. This is because many costs are fixed, and unit cost will therefore depend on the number of units produced and sold. Even though selling prices may be set above total costs, losses may still be incurred if the volume of sales is less than estimated, thereby forcing per unit costs upward to the point that they exceed the selling price.

Third, formula-based target selling prices may give the price setter some insights into competitors' costs, or help him to predict what a competitive price will be. For example, if a company is operating in an industry where 30 percent markups over cost to manufacture are common, then the company may be able to assume that this same pattern will hold for new products and thereby either predict competitors' prices or price in such a way as to gain quick acceptance of a new product line. On the other hand, by following standard markups over cost, a company may be able to largely *neutralize* the pricing issue, and concentrate on competing in other ways, such as in delivery or in credit terms.

Finally, many firms have such a wide range of products that they simply don't have time to do a detailed cost-volume-profit analysis on every item in every product line. Cost-plus pricing formulas provide a quick and direct way to at least a tentative price that can be further refined as time and circumstances permit.

PRICING NEW PRODUCTS

New products easily present the most challenging pricing problems, for the reason that the uncertainties involved are so great. If a new product is unlike anything presently on the market, then demand will be uncertain. If the new product is similar to existing products already being sold, uncertainty will exist as to the degree of substitution that will develop between the new product and the existing products. Uncertainty will also exist over ultimate marketing costs, and so forth. In order to reduce the level of these uncertainties, a firm will often resort to some type of experimental or test marketing.

Test marketing of products

Many firms have used test marketing with great success in order to gain data relative to the pricing decision. The approach is to introduce the new product in selected areas only, generally at different prices in different areas. By this means the company can gather data on the competition the product will encounter, on the relationship between volume and price, and on the contribution to profits that can be expected at various selling prices and volumes of sales. A price can then be selected that will result in the greatest overall contribution to profits, or that seems best in relation to the company's long-run objectives.

Of course, test marketing is not the same thing as the full-scale production and marketing of a product, but it can provide highly useful information that can help to ensure that the full-scale effort will be successful. An added benefit can be found in the fact that through test marketing it may be possible to contain any errors in pricing on a small scale, rather than nationwide.

Pricing strategies

Two basic pricing strategies are available to the price setter in pricing new products. These pricing strategies are known as *skimming pricing* and *penetration pricing.*

Skimming pricing involves setting a high initial price for a new product, with a progressive lowering of the price as time passes and as the market broadens and matures. The purpose of skimming pricing is to maximize short-run profits. In effect, it represents a direct application of the economist's pricing models discussed earlier in the chapter.

Penetration pricing involves setting low initial prices in order to gain quick acceptance in a broad portion of the market. It calls for the sacrifice of some short-run profits in order to achieve a better long-run market position. Whether a firm adopts the skimming or the penetration strategy will depend on what it is trying to accomplish, and on which approach appears to offer the greatest chance for success.

For example, many new products have a certain novelty appeal that causes demand to be quite price inelastic. In these cases, high initial prices are often set and maintained until competitors develop competing products and begin price cutting. As sales volume becomes more sensitive to sales price, prices are slowly reduced until the point is reached where a penetration price is possible that permits access to a mass market. A good example of this type of skimming strategy can be found in the marketing of electronic calculators. Prices of hand-sized calculators started at about $300 in the early 1970s and dropped to less than $25 in about three years' time, finally permitting access to a market so wide that it included the purchasing of calculators for use in weekly grocery shopping. Television sets, stereo sets, automobiles, electronic ovens, and some drug products all went through a similar skimming pricing period before prices were eventually lowered to a mass market penetration level.

One strong argument in favor of skimming pricing is that it offers some protection against unexpected costs in production and marketing of a product. If a new product is priced on a penetration basis and costs are unexpectedly high, then the company may be forced later to raise prices—not an easy thing to do when you are trying to gain wide market acceptance of a new product. On the other hand, if a new product is priced initially on a skimming level, the company has a layer of protection that can be used to absorb any unexpected costs or cost increases. Even if this later causes price reductions to be less than expected, the company will still be in the more favorable position of reducing prices rather than raising them.

Skimming pricing is most effective in those markets where entry is relatively difficult, because of the technology or investment required. The more easy market entry becomes, the less the likelihood that skimming can be carried off very effectively, or at least for a very long period of time.

For example, skimming pricing was possible for many years in the computer industry because of technological barriers to entry. By contrast, it is doubtful if skimming pricing was ever much of a factor in the marketing of household cleaning products.

Target costs and product pricing

Our discussion thus far has presumed that a product has already been developed, has been costed, and is ready to be marketed as soon as a price is set. In many cases, the sequence of events is just the reverse. That is, the company will already *know* what price should be charged, and the problem will be to *develop* a product that can be marketed profitably at the desired price. Even in this situation, where the normal sequence of events is reversed, cost is still a crucial factor. The company's approach will be to set *target costs* that can be used as guides in developing a product that can be sold within the desired price range.

This approach is used widely in the household appliance industry, where a company will determine in advance the price range in which it wants a particular product model to sell, and will then set about to develop the model. Component parts will be designed, and then costed item by item to see if the total cost is compatible with the target cost already set. If not, the parts will be redesigned and recosted, and features will be changed or eliminated, until the expected costs fall within the desired targets. Prototypes will then be developed, and again costs will be carefully analyzed to be sure that the desired targets are being met. In these types of situations, the accountant can be of great help to management by continually pointing out the relationships between cost and volume, by segregating relevant costs where needed, and by assisting in the organization and interpretation of cost data.

SPECIAL PRICING DECISIONS

When faced with a pricing decision, which pricing method should the manager use—the absorption approach illustrated in Exhibit 12–4 or the contribution approach illustrated in Exhibit 12–6? If all pricing decisions related to the pricing of *standard* products, the answer would be that it really wouldn't matter which method was used. We have already seen that the same target selling price for a standard product can be obtained using either method. The choice would probably depend on which method was otherwise being used to cost units of product. If the absorption method was otherwise in use, then it would be simpler to go ahead and use it as a basis for pricing decisions as well; the opposite would be the case if contribution costing was otherwise in use.

But all pricing decisions don't relate to standard products, or even to new standard products which fall in the same general category. Many pricing decisions relate to special or unusual situations. For example, a company may get a large order for a standard product but be asked to quote a special, one-time only price. Or a special order may come in from a foreign customer who wants a special price on a standard item on a continuing basis because his or her order represents business that the company otherwise wouldn't have. A company may have substantial excess capacity and be faced with the problem of pricing special products that are not a part of the regular line, and which are being produced on a limited basis. Finally, a company may be in a competitive bidding situation and forced to bid on many unlike jobs, some of which will be on a more or less continuing basis and others be one-time-only affairs.

All of these situations present *special* pricing problems of one kind or another. Many managers feel that special pricing problems such as those above can be much more easily handled by the contribution approach to pricing than by the absorption approach. The reasons are twofold. First, advocates of the contribution approach argue that it provides the price setter with much more detailed information than the absorption approach, and that this information is structured in a way which parallels the way in which the price setter is used to thinking—in terms of cost-volume-profit relationships. And second, it is argued that the contribution approach provides the price setter with a flexible framework that is immediately adaptable to *any* pricing problem, without the necessity of doing a lot of supplementary analytical work.

Pricing a special order

In order to illustrate the adaptability of the contribution approach to special pricing situations, and to show how the data it presents guides the price setter in decisions, let us assume the following price quotation sheets for the Helms Company:

Absorption method		Contribution method	
Direct materials	$ 6	Direct materials	$ 6
Direct labor	7	Direct labor	7
Overhead at 100% of direct labor	7	Variable overhead	2
Total cost to manufacture	$20	Variable selling and	
Markup—20%	4	administrative	1
Target selling price	$24	Total variable expenses	$16
		Markup—50%	8
		Target selling price	$24

These price quotation sheets relate to a vacuum pump which the Helms Company manufactures and markets through jobbers. The company has never been able to sell all that it can produce, and for this reason is constantly on the lookout for new business. Let us assume that the Helms Company has just been approached by a foreign distributor who wants to purchase 10,000 pumps at a price of $19 per pump. Should the company accept the offer?

THE ABSORPTION METHOD. The price quotation sheet prepared above by the absorption method is of little help in making the decision. If the Helms Company tries to relate the $20 "cost of manufacture" to the proposed price of $19, then the offer is clearly unattractive:

Sales (10,000 units at $19)	$190,000
Absorption cost to manufacture (10,000 units at $20)	200,000
Net loss from the order	($ 10,000)

On the other hand, since there is excess capacity in the plant, management may be tempted to accept the offer. The dilemma is that no one really *knows* from looking at the price quotation sheet which course of action is best. The pricing system doesn't provide the essential keys that are needed to move in an intelligent way. As a result, whatever decision is made will be made either on a "seat of the pants" basis, or only after much effort has been expended in trying to dig into the cost records for additional information.

THE CONTRIBUTION METHOD. By contrast, the price quotation sheet prepared by the contribution method provides the company with exactly the framework that it needs in making the decision. Since this price quotation sheet is organized by cost behavior, it dovetails precisely with cost-volume-profit concepts, and guides the decision maker in his or her decisions without the necessity of doing all kinds of added digging and analytical work in the cost records.

Consider the Helms Company data. Since the company has idle capacity (for which there apparently is no other use), fixed overhead costs are irrelevant in the decision over whether to accept the foreign distributor's offer. Any amount received over unit variable costs (and any *incremental* fixed costs) will increase overall profitability; therefore, rather than relating the proposed purchase price to the $20 "cost to manufacture," the company should relate it to the unit variable costs involved. This is easy to do if the regular price quotation sheet on a product is organized by cost behavior, such as shown above under the contribution method. In the case of the Helms Company, the unit variable costs are $16. Assuming that the unit variable costs associated with the special order will be the same as those associated with regular business, the analysis would be:

Sales (10,000 units at $19)	$190,000
Variable expenses (10,000 units at $16)	160,000
Contribution margin promised by the order (and also increased net income, if fixed costs don't change)	$ 30,000

In sum, by using the price quotation sheet prepared by the contribution method the Helms Company will be able to see a clear-cut, short-run advantage to accepting the foreign distributor's offer. Before any final decision can be made, however, the Helms Company will have to weigh long-run considerations very carefully, particularly the impact which accepting this offer might have on future efforts to secure a position in foreign markets. Accepting the $19 price might seriously undermine future negotiations with foreign dealers, and cause disruptions in the long-run profitability of the firm. The Helms Company may feel that it is better to forego the short-run $30,000 increase in contribution margin in order to protect its future long-run market position.

The essential point of our discussion is that the contribution approach to pricing contains a ready-made framework within which the price setter can operate in special pricing situations. By organizing costs in a way that is compatible with cost-volume-profit concepts, this approach to structuring price quotation sheets assists the manager in isolating those costs that are relevant in special pricing decisions, and guides the manager in those decisions from a cost point of view.

The variable pricing model

The contribution approach to pricing can be presented in general model form, as shown in Exhibit 12–8.

The contribution approach provides a ceiling and a floor between which the price setter operates. The ceiling represents the price that the manager would *like* to obtain, and indeed *must* obtain on the bulk of the sales over the long run. But under certain conditions, the model shows that the manager can move within the *range of flexibility* as far down as the floor of variable costs in quoting a price to a prospective customer. What are the conditions under which a price based on variable costs alone might be appropriate? We can note three:

1.   When idle capacity exists, such as in the case of the Helms Company.
2.   When operating under distress conditions.
3.   When faced with sharp competition on particular orders, under a competitive bidding situation.

When any of these conditions exist, it may be possible to increase overall profitability by pricing *some* jobs, products, or orders at *any amount* above

Exhibit 12–8
The contribution approach to pricing: A general model

Variable costs (detailed)	XXX	(Floor)
Fixed costs	XXX	Range of flexibility
Desired profit	XXX	
Target selling price	XXX	(Ceiling)

variable costs, even if this amount is substantially less than the normal markup.

We will now examine each of the three special conditions listed above more closely, to see how each relates to the range of flexibility depicted in Exhibit 12–8.

IDLE CAPACITY. There is no need to be concerned about the range of flexibility depicted in Exhibit 12–8 so long as a company can sell all that it can produce at regular prices. That is, no company is going to sell at less than regular prices if regular prices are obtainable.

However, a different situation exists if a company has idle capacity, and that idle capacity can't be used to expand regular sales at regular prices. Under these conditions, any use to which the idle capacity can be put that increases revenues more than variable costs (and any *incremental* fixed costs) will increase overall net income.

The use might come in the form of a special order for a regular product from a customer or source that the company normally does not supply (such as a foreign market). Or the use might come in the form of an order for a special product that the company normally does not produce. Or the use might come in the form of a modification of a regular product to meet a new customer's specifications, or to be sold under the customer's own brand name. In any of these situations, so long as the price received on the extra business exceeds the variable costs (and any *incremental* fixed costs) involved, overall net income will be increased by utilizing the idle capacity.

The Helms Company used earlier is a good example of the sort of situation we are talking about. The company has excess capacity, and there is no prospect of using the excess capacity for regular business. Under these conditions, nothing will be lost by quoting a price to the foreign distributor that is below full cost, or even relaxing the price down very close to the floor of variable costs, if necessary.

DISTRESS CONDITIONS. Occasionally a company is forced to operate under distress conditions, when the market for its product has been adversely affected in some way. For example, demand may virtually dry up overnight, forcing the company to drop its prices sharply downward. Under these conditions, any contribution which can be obtained above variable costs that will be available to help cover fixed costs may be preferable to ceasing operations altogether. If operations cease, then *no* contribution will be available to apply toward fixed costs.

COMPETITIVE BIDDING. The pricing model illustrated in Exhibit 12–8 is particularly useful in competitive bidding situations. Competition is often hot and fierce in situations where bidding is involved, so companies can't afford to be inflexible in their pricing. Unfortunately, many companies in competitive bidding situations refuse to cut prices in the face of stiff competition, adamantly stating that they price only on a "full cost" basis and don't want the business unless they can get a "decent" price for the work. There are several problems associated with taking this kind of a position on pricing. First, it involves circular reasoning. The so-called decent price is obtained by tacking some markup onto "full cost." But cost is dependent on *volume* of sales, which in turn is dependent on selling price.

Second, as discussed in Chapter 10, there are *two* determinants of profitability—margin and turnover. The "decent" price attitude ignores the turnover factor and focuses entirely on the margin factor. Yet many companies have demonstrated that a more modest margin combined with a faster turnover of assets can be highly effective from a profitability point of view. One way to increase turnover, of course, is to be flexible in bidding, by shading prices in those situations where competition is keen.

Finally, in those situations where fixed costs are high, a company can't *afford* to be inflexible in its pricing policies. Once an investment in plant and other fixed productive facilities has been made, a company's strategy must be to generate every dollar of contribution that it can to assist in the covering of these costs. Even if a company is forced to operate at an accounting loss, this might be preferable to having no contribution at all toward recovery of investment.

CRITICISMS OF THE CONTRIBUTION APPROACH TO PRICING

The major criticism leveled against the contribution approach to pricing is that it leads to suicidal underpricing and to eventual bankruptcy. It is argued that since the absorption approach to pricing includes an element of fixed overhead in the base on which prices are computed, it is superior to the contribution approach, which looks only at variable costs as a base. Including the fixed overhead element in the base under absorption costing is said to make it safer in terms of long-run pricing. Some feel that if variable costs alone are used in the pricing base, the manager may be misled into accepting *any* price over variable costs on a long-run basis for any product.

There are a number of weaknesses to this argument. We should note first that the absorption approach to pricing excludes just as many costs from the pricing base as does the contribution approach. It just excludes *different* costs. For example, the absorption approach doesn't consider selling and administrative costs at all in its base, since the base typically is made up entirely of "costs to manufacture." By contrast, the contribution approach does include variable selling and administrative expenses along with variable production expenses in developing a base for pricing.

Whether or not *any* pricing mechanism results in intelligent pricing decisions will depend in large part on the ability of the price setter to use the available data. As a practical matter, this means that pricing decisions must be restricted to managers who are qualified to make them. This point has been made very well in an NAA study of actual pricing practices:

No instance of unprofitable pricing attributable to direct costing was reported, but on the contrary, opinion was frequently expressed to the effect that direct costing had contributed to better pricing decisions. However, companies restrict product cost and margin data to individuals qualified to interpret such data and responsible for pricing policy decisions.[3]

On the other hand, no matter how expert a decision maker may be, the decisions will be faulty if the cost information with which he or she is working is irrelevant, unclear, or inadequate. Firms that have adopted the contribution approach to pricing have found that the old pricing system often led to incorrect pricing decisions because of faulty data:

Instances were cited in which management had unknowingly continued selling products below out-of-pocket cost or had decided to withdraw from the market when a substantial portion of the period costs could have been recovered. . . .

In one interview . . . when direct costing was introduced, analysis demonstrated that contracts which would have contributed to period costs had often been refused at times when the company had a large amount of idle capacity.[4]

THE ROBINSON-PATMAN ACT

In structuring a pricing policy firms must take care to keep their actions within the requirements of the Robinson-Patman Act. The act forbids quoting different prices to competing customers unless the difference in price can be traced directly to ". . . differences in the cost of manufacture, sale, or delivery resulting from the differing methods or quantities in which commodities are to such purchasers sold or delivered." Both the Federal Trade Commission and the courts have consistently held that "cost" is to be interpreted as full cost, and not just incremental or variable costs. This means that in the case of *competing* customers for the *same* goods, price differences cannot be defended on the basis of covering incremental costs alone. Note, though, that we are talking about *competing* customers for the *same* goods. We are not talking about a competitive bidding situation, nor are we talking about a situation in which idle capacity might be used to produce for a noncompeting market, or for some purpose other than production of regular products.

Many states prohibit the sale of goods or services below "cost." Cost is normally either specified as full cost, or so interpreted by the regulating agencies. These regulations all suggest that firms should keep careful

---

[3] Research Report No. 37, *Current Applications of Direct Costing* (New York: National Association of Accountants, January 1961), p. 55.

[4] Ibid.

records of their costs and of the way their prices are structured in order to be able to answer questions of regulatory bodies.

SUMMARY

The general pricing models of the economist contain the basic framework for pricing decisions. Since these models are conceptual in nature, and since the specific information required for their direct application rarely is available, firms normally rely on pricing formulas to implement the ideas the models contain. Pricing decisions can be divided into three broad groups:

1. Pricing standard products.
2. Pricing new products.
3. Pricing special orders.

Pricing of standard and new products is generally carried out through cost-plus pricing formulas. Such formulas require a cost base, to which a markup is added to derive a target selling price. Cost-plus pricing can be carried out equally well using either the absorption or contribution approaches.

Pricing of special orders is somewhat different, in that in some situations full costs may not be applicable in setting prices. Circumstances may exist in which the price setter may be justified in pricing simply on a basis of variable or incremental costs. In these special pricing situations, price setters often find the contribution approach, with its emphasis on cost behavior, more useful than the absorption approach, which may require considerable reworking of data in order to generate the information needed for a pricing decision.

KEY TERMS FOR REVIEW

Total revenue curve   **Cost-plus pricing**
Total cost curve   **Markup**
Marginal revenue   **Test marketing**
Marginal cost   **Skimming pricing**
Price elasticity   **Penetration pricing**
Monopoly   **Target costs**
Monopolistic competition   **Range of flexibility**
Oligopoly

QUESTIONS

12–1. Why does the economist depict a slowing down of the rate of increase in total revenue as more and more units are sold?

12–2. What is the optimum point of production and what is the optimum price to be charged for a product, as depicted by the total revenue and total cost curves?

12–3. According to the marginal revenue and marginal cost curves, what is the optimum point of production and what is the optimum price to charge for a product?

12–4. What is meant by price elasticity? Contrast a product that is price inelastic to a product that is price elastic.

12–5. Identify four limitations to the economic pricing models.

12–6. What costs are relevant in long-run pricing decisions?

12–7. What is meant by the term "cost-plus" pricing? Distinguish between the absorption and contribution approaches to cost-plus pricing.

12–8. In what sense is the term "cost-plus" pricing a misnomer?

12–9. "Full cost can be viewed as a floor of protection. If a firm always sets its prices above full cost, it will never have to worry about operating at a loss." Discuss.

12–10. Distinguish between skimming pricing and penetration pricing. Which strategy would you probably use if you were introducing a new product that was highly price inelastic? Why?

12–11. What are "target costs," and how do they enter into the pricing decision?

12–12. What problem is sometimes encountered under absorption costing in trying to price special orders?

12–13. Identify those circumstances under which the manager might be justified in pricing at any amount above variable costs.

12–14. Why will net income be maximized (or net loss minimized) when the contribution margin is maximized?

12–15. In what way does the Robinson-Patman Act influence pricing decisions?

EXERCISES

E12–1. Cost data relating to a product produced by the Bead Company are presented below:

	Per unit	Total
Direct materials	$5	
Direct labor	7	
Variable overhead	3	
Fixed overhead	5	$40,000
Variable selling and administrative expense	1	
Fixed selling and administrative expense	2	16,000

The costs above are based on an anticipated volume of 8,000 units produced and sold. The company has a policy of adding a markup of 20 percent of cost to manufacture to obtain target selling prices, or adding a markup of 50 percent of variable costs.

Required:

1. Compute the target selling price under the absorption approach.
2. Compute the target selling price under the contribution approach.

E12–2. Barker Company is considering the introduction of a new product. The company has gathered the following information:

Number of units to be produced each year	14,000
Unit cost to manufacture .... $	25
Projected annual selling and administrative expenses..................................	50,000
Estimated investment required by the company	750,000
Desired rate of return on investment	12%

The company uses cost-plus pricing.

Required:

1. Compute the required markup in percentage terms.
2. Compute the target selling price per unit.

E12–3. Fraser Company has a capacity of 150,000 motors per year. The company is presently producing and selling 130,000 motors per year at a selling price of $40 per motor. The cost of producing one motor at the 130,000-unit level of activity is given below:

	Per motor
Direct materials	$16
Direct labor	8
Overhead.............................	10
Total cost	$34

The company has a special order for 10,000 motors at a price of $33 each. Selling and administrative costs on the special order would be $2 per motor. The company's fixed overhead costs total $780,000 per year. The company has rejected the order, based on the following computations:

Selling price per motor		$33
Less costs per motor:		
Production cost (above)	$34	
Selling and administrative cost	2	36
Loss per motor		($ 3)

Required:

1. Should the company have accepted the order? Show computations.
2. Using the data given above, prepare a model price quotation sheet that could be used to guide the company in special pricing decisions. Explain how it would be used.

E12–4. Advance Technology, Inc., is anxious to enter the electronic calculator market. The company feels that in order to be competitive, the electronic calculator which it produces and sells must not be priced at more than $15. The company wants a 12 percent rate of return on investment. In order to produce 20,000 calculators a year, an investment of

$375,000 would be required. Selling and administrative expenses would total $75,000 per year.

Required:

Compute the target cost to manufacture one calculator.

E12–5. To a large extent, the selling price which must be obtained on a product will be dependent on the volume of units that can be sold. Consider the following data on a new product:

Variable production cost per unit	$	5
Variable selling and administrative expenses per unit		3
Fixed production cost (total)		120,000
Fixed selling and administrative expenses (total)		100,000
Desired markup		80%

The company uses absorption costing for product costing and for pricing.

Required:

1. What would be the target selling price per unit if the company can produce and sell (*a*) 30,000 units each period, (*b*) 60,000 units each period?
2. If the company charges the prices that you computed in (1) above, will it be assured that no losses will be sustained? Explain.

E12–6. The market research division of Delsey Company has stated that the company's new deluxe product line would be best received on the market at a selling price of $54 per unit. At this price, the market research division projects that 20,000 units could be sold. Costs associated with the new product line would be:

Direct materials	$	12
Direct labor		10
Variable overhead		4
Variable selling and administrative expenses		3
Fixed overhead (total)		200,000
Fixed selling and administrative expenses (total)		250,000
Desired markup (absorption basis)		75%

Required:

1. Based on the data given above, is $54 per unit an acceptable selling price to Delsey Company? Show computations.
2. What percentage markup does the $54 per unit selling price represent?

E12–7. The Ford Company is contemplating entry into a new market. Costs and other information associated with the new product are given below:

Projected annual sales in units		30,000
Projected variable costs per unit:		
Production	$	12
Selling and administrative		3
Projected fixed costs in total:		
Production		180,000
Selling and administrative		90,000
Projected investment required		500,000

As a first approximation for a selling price, the company normally uses a markup of 80 percent on variable costs.

Required:

1. Compute the target selling price, using the contribution approach.
2. Assume that the Ford Company will not add a new product line unless it promises a return on investment of at least 20 percent. On this basis, is the selling price you computed in (1) acceptable? Show computations.

PROBLEMS

P12–8. *Percentage markups and price quote sheets.* Aspen Company produces and markets a number of consumer products, including a toaster. Cost and revenue data on the toaster for 19x5, the most recent year, are given below:

	10,000 units sold	
	Total	Per unit
Sales	$300,000	$30
Cost of goods sold	180,000	18*
Gross margin	$120,000	$12
Selling and administrative expenses	70,000	7
Net income	$ 50,000	$ 5

* Contains $3 per unit in direct materials, and $4 in direct labor.

Fixed costs comprise $100,000 of cost of goods sold, and $50,000 of the selling and administrative expenses are fixed.

Required:

1. Compute the percentage markup being used by the company, based on absorption cost to manufacture, and prepare a model price quotation sheet (per unit).
2. Recast the income statement for 19x5 in the contribution format. Compute the percentage markup based on variable cost, and prepare a model price quotation sheet (per unit).
3. Assume that the company has sufficient capacity to produce 12,500 toasters each year. J-Mart, a regional discount chain located in the East, is willing to make a bulk purchase of 2,500 toasters at a price of $15 per toaster, if the toasters are imprinted with the J-Mart name. These toasters would not disturb regular sales.
   a. Using the model price quotation sheet prepared in (1) ábove, should the offer be accepted? Explain.
   b. Explain how the model price quotation sheet prepared in (2) above can be helpful to the manager in making special pricing decisions. Using this sheet as a guide, should the offer be accepted? Show computations.

P12–9. *Target costs and percentage markups.*   Auto Supply, Inc., is a producer and distributor of auto accessories. The company is anxious to enter the rapidly growing market for long-life batteries. The company feels that to be fully competitive, the battery which it produces and markets cannot be priced at more than $40. At this price, the company is certain that it can capture 5 percent of the present 2,000,000 battery sales made annually in its area.

A study has indicated that the following costs and other data would be associated with the new battery line:

Permanent investment required	$1,200,000
Annual marketing costs:	
Advertising	140,000
Commissions and other ($1.80 per battery)	180,000
Annual administrative costs (salaries)	40,000
Required rate of return on investment	20%

Required:

1. What is the target cost to manufacture one battery?
2. Assume that the target cost to manufacture one battery which you computed above consists of 70 percent variable manufacturing cost and 30 percent fixed manufacturing cost. What percentage markup does the $40 selling price represent under (*a*) the absorption approach to cost-plus pricing, and (*b*) the contribution approach?

P12–10. *Evaluating a special order.*   Briggs Company, a medium-sized producer of electric motors, is located in Pennsylvania. The company distributes its motors in the East Coast area. One of the company's most popular motors is the ES2A. A new plant, with an annual capacity of 500,000 motors, has just been constructed to produce the ES2A line. The company is producing and selling 300,000 ES2A motors each year, at the following cost per motor:

	Per ES2A motor
Direct materials	$20
Direct labor	14
Manufacturing overhead (60% fixed, based on	
300,000 motors produced)	10
Shipping expense	2
Sales commission	1
Total	$47

Other costs associated with the ES2A line are (fixed per year):

Selling	$200,000
Administration	100,000
Total fixed costs	$300,000

The ES2A motors are sold to East Coast distributors for $50 each. The president of Briggs Company is very anxious to expand sales of the ES2A line. He has just received an offer from a West Coast distributor to purchase 100,000 motors per year at a price of $43 per motor. Although there would be no sales commission on this order, the shipping expense per motor would increase by 50 percent. Fixed selling costs would increase by 25 percent.

Required:

1. If the president of Briggs Company accepts this special price offer, does it appear that he would be in violation of the Robinson-Patman Act?
2. On the basis of the cost data given, would you recommend that the offer be accepted or rejected? Show all computations.
3. What noncost matters should be considered before the offer is accepted or rejected?

P12–11. *Percentage markups and price quote sheets.* Dover Company produces and markets a number of consumer products, including a food blender. Cost and revenue data on the blender for the first quarter, 19x2, are given below:

| | 10,000 units sold | |
	Total	Per unit
Sales	$240,000	$24
Cost of goods sold	160,000	16*
Gross margin	$ 80,000	$ 8
Selling and administrative expenses	60,000	6
Net income	$ 20,000	$ 2

* Contains $5 per unit in direct materials, and $4 in direct labor.

Fixed costs comprise $60,000 of the cost of goods sold, and $40,000 of the selling and administrative expenses are fixed.

Required:

1. Compute the percentage markup being used by the company, based on absorption cost to manufacture, and prepare a model price quotation sheet (per unit).
2. Recast the income statement for the quarter in the contribution format. Compute the percentage markup based on variable cost, and prepare a model price quotation sheet (per unit).
3. Assume that the company has sufficient capacity to produce 12,000 blenders each quarter. Savemore, a regional discount chain, is willing to purchase 2,000 blenders each quarter at a price of $15 per blender. The blenders would be imprinted with the Savemore name, and would not affect regular sales.
   a. Using the model price quotation sheet prepared in (1) above, should the offer be accepted? Explain.
   b. Explain how the model price quotation sheet prepared in (2) above can be helpful to the manager in making special pricing decisions. Using this sheet as a guide, should the offer be accepted? Show computations.

P12–12. *Distress pricing.* The Matheson Mining Company purchased a mine for $1,000,000 in 19x1. The company then expended another $500,000 installing railroad tracks into the mine, setting up supporting beams, and purchasing equipment to process the ore coming out of the mine. The tracks, beams, and equipment were given a ten-year life. It was estimated that the mine contained 1,000,000 tons of ore. Active mining was started in 19x2, and continued through 19x5, with the following average yearly results:

Number of tons of ore mined per year	100,000
Mining costs per ton (exclusive of depletion and depreciation)	$4
Selling price per ton	7

In early 19x6, a competing company discovered massive deposits of the ore just a few miles from the Matheson Mining Company's mine. The result was that the market became flooded with ore, and the selling price dropped to $5 per ton. The president of the Matheson Mining Company made a few quick computations, and declared, "We'll have to close the mine. If we keep it open we'll lose $0.50 a ton for every ton of ore we mine and sell. At a $5 selling price it will be less costly to just close the doors and walk away from the place."

Required:

1. How did the president compute the $0.50 per ton loss?
2. Do you agree with the president's decision? Explain.

P12–13. *Distress pricing.* The Marks Toy Company produces and distributes a broad line of games and toys. The company has always used cost-plus pricing, computed by the absorption approach.

In 19x2, hula hoops became very popular with the 8-to-15-year-old set. In order to supply what appeared to be a large and quite permanent demand for a new toy, the company acquired new equipment in 19x2 at a cost of $600,000. The equipment was estimated to be capable of producing 3,000,000 hula hoops before it would have to be replaced. In 19x3, production began. The hula hoops were priced as follows (per unit):

Direct materials	$0.10
Direct labor	0.05
Overhead ($\frac{1}{3}$ variable)	0.30
Cost to manufacture	$0.45
Desired markup (60%)	0.27
Target selling price	$0.72

The selling and administrative expenses were:

Salaries and other fixed expenses (annual)	$15,000
Shipping cost per hula hoop	$0.05

In 19x3 and 19x4, the company produced and sold 300,000 hula hoops each year. In 19x5, it suddenly became apparent that hula hoops were more of a fad than a permanent market. Almost overnight, the selling price dropped to $0.40 per hula hoop.

The marketing manager has recommended that the company drop the hula hoop line and scrap the special equipment. "It would be insane to continue producing," she reasoned, "At our present level of activity and at a $0.40 selling price we would lose $0.15 on every unit we sold."

Required:

1. How did the marketing manager compute the $0.15 per unit loss?
2. Do you agree with her recommendation? Explain.
3. Assume that the company has 50,000 hula hoops in the warehouse unsold, and that no more hula hoops will be produced. What is the minimum selling price that the company could accept?

P12–14. *Contribution approach to pricing.* E. Berg and Sons build custom-made pleasure boats that range in price from $10,000 to $250,000. For the past 30 years, Mr. Berg, Sr., has determined the selling price of each boat by estimating the costs of material, labor, a prorated portion of the overhead, and adding 20 percent to these estimated costs.

For example, a recent price quotation was determined as follows:

Direct materials	$ 5,000
Direct labor	8,000
Overhead	2,000
	$15,000
Plus 20%	3,000
Selling price	$18,000

The overhead figure was determined by estimating total overhead costs for the year and allocating them at 25 percent of direct labor.

If a customer rejected the price and business was slack, Mr. Berg, Sr., would often be willing to reduce his markup to as little as 5 percent over estimated costs. Thus, average markup for the year is estimated at 15 percent.

Mr. Ed Berg, Jr., has just completed a course on pricing, and believes the firm could use some of the techniques discussed in the course. The course emphasized the contribution approach to pricing, and Mr. Berg, Jr., feels such an approach would be helpful in determining the selling prices of their custom-made pleasure boats.

Total overhead, which includes selling and administrative expenses for the year, has been estimated at $150,000, of which $90,000 is fixed and the remainder is variable in direct proportion to direct labor.

Required:

1. Assume the customer in the example rejected the $18,000 quotation and also rejected a $15,750 quotation (5 percent markup) during a slack period. The customer countered with a $15,000 offer.
   a. What is the difference in net income for the year between accepting or rejecting the customer's offer?

      b. What is the minimum selling price Mr. Berg, Jr., could have quoted without reducing or increasing company net income?

2. What advantages does the contribution approach to pricing have over the approach used by Mr. Berg, Sr.?
3. What possible dangers are there, if any, to the contribution approach to pricing?

(CMA, adapted)

P12–15. *Pricing strategy.* Seals, Sawbuck and Co. is trying to determine the proper pricing strategy to use on its new line of electronic ovens. The company purchases the ovens from a manufacturer according to the following price schedule:

Units purchased	Unit cost
Up to 20,000	$200
Excess over 20,000	180

The ovens are sold to retail consumers through retail outlets located in the western part of the country. Management has been presented with the following two marketing and pricing alternatives:

Alternative 1. Set the regular selling price at $240 per oven. At this price the company estimates that 20,000 ovens can be sold each year. All ovens would be sold at the regular price.

Alternative 2. Set the regular selling price at $240 per oven, but offer periodic "specials" at a price 10 percent off the regular price. The company estimates that 10,000 ovens could be sold at the special price, but that 30 percent of these sales would represent ovens that otherwise would have been sold at the regular price.

    Other costs associated with the ovens are:

Sales commission per oven	$ 12
Shipping cost per oven	5
Fixed costs (in total):	
Regular advertising	90,000
Advertising of "specials"	15,000
Allocated general overhead	150,000

Required:

1. Which alternative should the company accept? Show all computations in good form.
2. If the company accepts Alternative 2, what will be the net profit or loss realized from the periodic specials? Show computations.

P12–16. *Pricing a bid.* Garvey Instruments produces thermostats for industrial use. The company prices its thermostats by adding a markup of 75 percent to variable costs (so that the selling price is equal to 175 percent of variable costs). This pricing policy has worked very well over the years.

    Garvey Instruments has received an invitation to bid on a government order for 1,000 specially designed thermostats. The company has made the following cost estimates:

Direct materials	$ 70,000
Direct labor	50,000
Variable overhead	10,000
Allocated fixed overhead	20,000
Tools, dies, and other special production costs	30,000
Shipping costs	5,000
Special administrative costs	5,000
Total costs	$190,000
Cost per thermostat ($190,000 ÷ 1,000)	$190

Garvey Instruments is now operating at capacity. If the company takes on the government order, it will have to forego regular sales of $210,000.

Required:

1. In terms of contribution margin sacrificed, what is the opportunity cost of accepting the government order?
2. What is the lowest price that Garvey Instruments can bid on the government order, without sacrificing current profits?

P12–17. *Competitive bidding.* The Tolby Machine Company designs and produces machine tools to customer specifications. The bulk of the company's business is obtained by competitive bidding. In the latter part of 19x5, the company was invited (along with several other companies) to bid on an order of 50 specially designed jigs needed by a manufacturing firm.

The Tolby Machine Company was very happy to receive the invitation to bid, since business had been very slow for over a year with no prospects for the situation improving. The company estimated the following costs relating to the 50 jigs:

	Total	Per jig
Direct material	$ 50,000	$1,000
Direct labor	40,000	800
Variable overhead	10,000	200
Fixed overhead*	50,000	1,000
Design and cost study	5,000	100
Shipping	7,500	150
Total cost	$162,500	$3,250

* Allocated on a basis of machine-hours.

Based on these data, the company has submitted a bid of $3,900 per jig. The price quotation sheet used to compute the bid is shown below:

Direct materials	$1,000
Direct labor	800
Manufacturing overhead	1,200
Total cost to manufacture	$3,000
Markup desired—30%	900
Bid price per jig	$3,900

The manufacturer receiving the bid has replied that the bid is too high, and that no bid over $3,300 per jig will be considered. Upon hearing this, the president of the Tolby Machine Company stated, "That lets us out. Our cost is $3,250 per jig. At a bid price of $3,300 the profit we'd make wouldn't be worth the effort."

Required:

What would you advise the Tolby Machine Company to do? Show computations in good form.

P12–18. *Pricing and joint product decisions.* Midwest Mills has a plant that can either mill wheat into a cracked wheat cereal, or further mill the cracked wheat into flour. The company can sell all the cracked wheat cereal that it can produce at a selling price of $240 per ton. In the past, the company has sold only part of its cracked wheat as cereal, and has retained the rest for further milling into the flour product. The flour has been selling for $295 per ton, but recently the price has become unstable and has dropped to $265 per ton.

   Because of this price drop, the sales manager feels that the company should discontinue the milling of flour, and concentrate its entire milling capacity on the milling of cracked wheat to sell as cereal. (The same milling equipment is used for both products.) Her feeling is based on the following analysis:

	Cracked wheat cost per ton		Flour cost per ton
Raw materials	$200	Cost of cracked wheat used	
Direct labor	12	in milling of flour	$230
Overhead	18	Added milling costs:	
Total cost per ton	$230	Added materials	10
		Added labor	12
		Overhead	18
		Total cost per ton	$270

	Cracked wheat	Flour
Selling price per ton	$240	$265
Cost per ton (above)	230	270
Net profit (loss) per ton	$ 10	($ 5)

The sales manager argues that since the present $265 per ton price for the flour results in a $5 per ton loss, milling of flour should be discontinued, and should not be resumed until the price per ton rises above $270.

   The company assigns overhead to the two products on the basis of direct labor-hours. The same amount of time is required to either mill a ton of cracked wheat or to further mill a ton of cracked wheat into flour. Because of the nature of the plant, virtually all overhead costs are fixed. Materials and labor costs are variable.

Required:

1. Do you agree with the sales manager that the company should discontinue milling flour, and use the entire milling capacity to mill cracked wheat if the price of flour remains at $265 per ton? Support your answer with appropriate comments and computations.
2. What is the lowest price that the company should accept for a ton of flour? Again support your answer with appropriate comments and computations.

P12–19. *Special order; Capacity utilization.* Tiffany Company manufactures several different styles of jewelry cases. Management estimates that during the third quarter of 19x6 the company will be operating at 80 percent of normal capacity. Because the company desires a higher utilization of plant capacity, it will consider a special order.

Tiffany has received special-order inquiries from two companies. The first order is from JCP, Inc., which would like to market a jewelry case similar to one of Tiffany's cases. The JCP jewelry case would be marketed under JCP's own label. JCP, Inc., has offered Tiffany $5.75 per jewelry case for 20,000 cases to be shipped by October 1, 19x6. Cost data are given below for the Tiffany jewelry case which is similar to the jewelry case desired by JCP:

Regular selling price per unit	$9.00
Costs per unit:	
Raw materials	$2.50
Direct labor, 0.5 hrs. at $6	3.00
Overhead, 0.25 machine-hours at $4	1.00
Total costs	$6.50

According to the specifications provided by JCP, Inc., the special order case requires less expensive raw materials. Consequently, the raw materials will only cost $2.25 per case. Management has estimated that the remaining costs, labor time, and machine time will be the same as the Tiffany jewelry case.

The second special order was submitted by the Krage Co. for 7,500 jewelry cases at $7.50 per case. These jewelry cases would be marketed under the Krage label and would have to be shipped by October 1, 19x6. The Krage jewelry case is different from any jewelry case in the Tiffany line. The estimated costs per unit of this case are as follows:

Raw materials	$3.25
Direct labor, 0.5 hrs. at $6	3.00
Overhead, 0.5 machine-hours at $4	2.00
Total costs	$8.25

In addition, Tiffany will incur $1,500 in additional setup costs and will have to purchase a $2,500 special device to manufacture these cases; this device will be discarded once the special order is completed.

The Tiffany manufacturing capabilities are limited to the total machine-hours available. The plant capacity under normal operations is 90,000 machine-hours per year or 7,500 machine-hours per month. The budgeted fixed overhead for 19x6 amounts to $216,000. All manufacturing overhead costs (fixed and variable) are applied to production on the basis of machine-hours, at $4 per hour.

Tiffany will be able to use all of its excess capacity during the third quarter to work on special orders. Management does not expect any repeat sales to be generated from either special order. Company practice precludes Tiffany from subcontracting any portion of an order when special orders are not expected to generate repeat sales.

Required:

Should Tiffany Company accept either special order? Justify your answer and show your calculations. (Hint: It may be helpful to distinguish between fixed and variable overhead.)

(CMA, adapted)

P12–20. *Pricing a special order.* The Bestline Furniture Company has been operating at a loss of about $300,000 per year. Last year's income statement is typical:

Sales	$12,500,000
Cost of goods sold	6,000,000
Gross margin	$ 6,500,000
Operating expenses	6,800,000
Net loss	$(300,000)

The company's factory has a capacity of 100,000 machine-hours per year, but is being operated at a level of only 60,000 machine-hours. The company's fixed overhead costs total $840,000 per year. The variable overhead rate is $2 per machine-hour. (All overhead costs are allocated to production on a basis of machine-hours.)

Bestline has received an order from a large TV manufacturer for 10,000 TV cabinets per year. Although Bestline doesn't normally produce TV cabinets, it is considering the offer, since the company is anxious to increase the utilization of its plant. Bestline has determined the following information relating to the order:

1. It is will require two machine-hours to produce one TV cabinet.
2. Direct materials and direct labor per TV cabinet will total $70 and $20, respectively.
3. Total fixed overhead will not change.
4. Selling expenses will total $9 per cabinet.
5. The TV manufacturer's offer is for a selling price of $125 per cabinet.
6. Administrative expenses will increase by $10,000 per year.

The company has decided to reject the order, based on the following computation:

	Per TV cabinet	Total
Sales (10,000 cabinets)	$125	$1,250,000
Cost of goods sold	115	1,150,000
Gross margin	$ 10	$ 100,000
Operating expenses:		
Selling	$ 9	$ 90,000
Administrative	1	10,000
Total	$ 10	$ 100,000
Net income from the order	$–0–	$ –0–

The company has no alternative uses for its idle capacity.

Required:

1. Show the probable cost breakdown of the $115 cost of goods sold figure.

2. Based on the cost data, do you agree with the decision to reject the order? Show computations.

3. What is the lowest selling price that Bestline can accept per TV cabinet if it wants to eliminate the present net loss in the company as a whole?

Chapter 13

Capital budgeting decisions

The term *capital budgeting* is used to describe those actions relating to the planning and financing of capital outlays, such as for the purchase of new equipment, for the introduction of new product lines, and for the modernization of plant facilities. As such, capital budgeting decisions are a key factor in the long-run profitability of a firm. This is particularly true in those situations where a firm has only limited investment funds available, but has almost unlimited investment opportunities to choose from. The long-run profitability of the firm will depend on the skill of the manager in choosing those uses for limited funds which will provide the greatest return. This selection process is complicated by the fact that most investment opportunities are long term in nature, and the future is often distant and hard to predict.

To make wise investment decisions, managers need tools at their disposal which will guide them in comparing the relative advantages and disadvantages of various investment alternatives. We are concerned in this chapter with gaining understanding and skill in the use of these tools.

CAPITAL BUDGETING—AN INVESTMENT CONCEPT

Capital budgeting is an *investment* concept, since it involves a commitment of funds now in order to receive some desired return in the future. When speaking of investments, one is inclined to think of a commitment of funds into corporate stocks and bonds. This is just one type of investment, however. The commitment of funds by a business into inventory, equipment, and related uses is *also* an investment in that the commitment is made with the expectation of receiving some return in the future from the funds committed.

Typical capital budgeting decisions

What types of business decisions require capital budgeting analysis? Virtually any decision that involves an outlay now in order to obtain some return (increase in revenue or reduction in costs) in the future. Typical capital budgeting decisions encountered by the business executive are:

1. Cost reduction decisions. Should new equipment be purchased in order to reduce costs?
2. Plant expansion decisions. Should a new plant, warehouse, or other facilities be acquired in order to increase capacity and sales?
3. Equipment selection decisions. Would machine A, machine B, or machine C do the job best?
4. Lease or buy decisions. Should new plant facilities be leased or purchased?
5. Equipment replacement decisions. Should old equipment be replaced now or later?

Capital budgeting decisions tend to fall into two broad categories—screening decisions and preference decisions. Screening decisions are those relating to whether a proposed project meets some preset standard of acceptance. For example, a firm may have a policy of accepting cost reduction projects only if they promise a return of, say, 20 percent before taxes.

Preference decisions, by contrast, relate to selecting from among several *competing* courses of action. To illustrate, a firm may be considering five different machines to replace an existing machine on the assembly line. The choice as to which of the five machines to purchase is a *preference* decision.

In this chapter, we discuss ways of making screening decisions. The matter of preference decisions is reserved until the following chapter.

Characteristics of business investments

Some business investments are such that the original sum invested in a project is still existing at the time the project terminates. As an example, if a firm purchases land for $5,000, and rents it out at $750 a year for ten years, at the end of the ten-year term the land will still be intact, and should be salable for at least its purchase price. The computation of the rate of return on such an investment is fairly simple. Since the original investment itself will still be intact at the end of the ten-year period, each year's inflow of $750 is a return on the original $5,000 investment. The rate of return is therefore a straight 15 percent ($750 ÷ $5,000).

THE PROBLEM OF DEPRECIABLE ASSETS. A far more common kind of business investment is one that involves *depreciable* assets. An important characteristic of depreciable assets is that they generally have little or no resale value at the end of their useful lives. Thus, any returns provided by such assets must be sufficient to do two things:

1. Provide a return on the original investment.
2. Return the total amount of the *original investment* itself.

To illustrate, assume that the $5,000 investment in the preceding section was made in factory equipment rather than in land. Also assume that the equipment will reduce the firm's operating costs by $750 each year for ten years. Is the return on the equipment a straight 15 percent, the same as it was on the land? The answer is no. The return being promised by the equipment is much less than the return being promised by the land. The reason is that part of the yearly $750 inflow from the equipment must go to recoup the original $5,000 investment itself, since the equipment will be worthless at the end of its ten-year life. Only what remains after recovery of this investment can be viewed as a return *on* the investment over the ten-year period.

THE TIME VALUE OF MONEY. Another characteristic of business investments is that the returns which they promise are likely to extend over fairly long spans of time. Therefore, in approaching capital budgeting decisions it is necessary to employ techniques that recognize the time value of money. Any business leader would prefer to receive a dollar today than a year from now. The same concept applies in choosing between investment projects. Those that promise returns earlier in time are preferable over those that promise returns later in time.

The capital budgeting techniques that recognize these characteristics most fully are those involving *discounted cash flows.* We shall spend the remainder of this chapter illustrating the use of discounted cash flow methods of making capital budgeting decisions. Before discussing these methods, however, it will be helpful to consider the concept of *present value,* and the techniques involved in *discounting.*

THE CONCEPT OF PRESENT VALUE

The point was made above that a business leader would prefer to receive a dollar today than a year from now. There are two reasons why this is true. First, a dollar received today is more valuable than a dollar received a year from now. The dollar received today can be invested immediately, and by the end of a year will have earned some return, making the total amount in hand at the end of the year *greater* than the investment started with. The person receiving the dollar a year from now will simply have a dollar in hand.

Second, the future involves uncertainty. The longer people have to wait to receive a dollar, the more uncertain it becomes that they will ever get the dollar that they seek. As time passes, conditions change. The changes may be such as to make future payments of the dollar impossible.

Since money has a time value, the manager needs a method of determining whether a cash outlay made now in an investment project can be justified in terms of expected receipts from the project in future years. That is, the manager must have a means of expressing future receipts in present dollar terms, so that the future receipts can be compared *on an equivalent basis* with whatever investment is required in the project under consideration. The theory of interest provides managers with the means of making such a comparison.

The theory of interest

If a bank pays $105 one year from now in return for a deposit of $100 now, we would say that the bank is paying interest at an annual rate of 5 percent. The relationships involved in this notion can be expressed in mathematical terms by means of the following equation:

$$F_1 = P(1 + r) \tag{1}$$

where F_1 = the amount to be received in one year, P = the present outlay to be made, and r = the rate of interest involved.

If the present outlay is $100 deposited in a bank savings account that is to earn interest at 5 percent, then P = $100 and r = 0.05. Under these conditions, F_1 = $105, the amount to be received in one year.

The $100 present outlay can be called the *present value* of the $105 amount to be received in one year. It is also known as the *discounted value* of the future $105 receipt. The $100 figure represents the value in present terms of a receipt of $105 to be received a year from now, by an investor who requires a return of 5 percent on his money.

COMPOUNDING OF INTEREST. What if the investor wants to leave his or her money in the bank for a second year? In that case, by the end of the second year the original $100 deposit will have grown to $110.25:

Original deposit	$100.00
Interest for the first year:	
$100.00 × 0.05	5.00
Amount at the end of the first year	$105.00
Interest for the second year:	
$105.00 × 0.05	5.25
Amount at the end of the second year	$110.25

Notice that the interest for the second year is $5.25, as compared to only $5.00 for the first year. The reason for the greater interest earned during the second year is that, during the second year, interest is being paid *on interest*. That is, the $5 interest earned during the first year has been left in the account and has been added to the original $100 deposit in computing interest for the second year. This technique is known as *compounding* of interest. The compounding we have done is annual compounding. Interest can be compounded on a semiannual, quarterly, or even more frequent basis. Many savings institutions are now compounding interest on a daily basis. Of course, the more frequently compounding is done, the more rapidly the invested balance will grow.

How is the concept of compounding of interest expressed in equation form? It is expressed by taking Equation (1) and adjusting it to state the number of years, n, that a sum is going to be left deposited in the bank:

$$F_n = P(1 + r)^n \qquad (2)$$

where n = years.

If n = 2 years, then our computation of the value of F in 2 years will be:

$$F_2 = \$100(1 + 0.05)^2$$
$$F_2 = \$110.25$$

Exhibit 13–1
The relationship between present value and future value

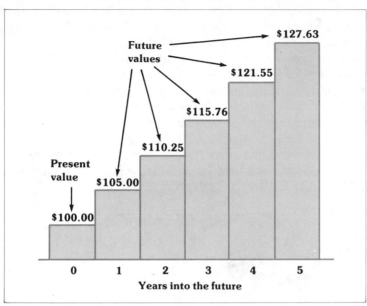

PRESENT VALUE AND FUTURE VALUE.   Exhibit 13–1 shows the relationship between present value and future value, as expressed in the theory of interest equations. As shown in the exhibit, if $100 is deposited in a bank at 5 percent interest, it will grow to $127.63 by the end of five years, if interest is compounded annually.

Computation of present value

An investment can be viewed in two ways. It can be viewed either in terms of its future value, or in terms of its present value. If we know the present value of a sum (such as our $100 deposit), we have seen that it is a relatively simple task to compute the sum's future value in n years by using Equation (2). But what if the tables are reversed, and we know the *future* value of some amount, but not its present value?

For example, assume that you are to receive $200 two years from now. You know that the future value of this sum is $200, since this is the amount that you will be receiving in two years. But what is the sum's present value—what is it worth *right now?* The present value of any sum to be received in the future can be computed by turning Equation (2) around, and solving for P:

$$P = \frac{F_n}{(1+r)^n}$$ (3)

In our example, $F = \$200$ (the amount to be received in the future), $r = 0.05$ (the rate of interest), and $n = 2$ (the number of years in the future the amount is to be received).

$$P = \frac{\$200}{(1 + 0.05)^2}$$

$$P = \frac{\$200}{1.1025}$$

$$P = \$181.40$$

As shown by the computation above, the present value of $200 to be received two years from now is $181.40, if an interest return of 5 percent is required. In effect, we are saying that $181.40 received *right now* is equivalent to $200 received two years from now, if the investor requires a return of 5 percent on his or her money. The $181.40 and the $200 are just two ways of looking at the same item.

The process we have just completed is sometimes called *discounting*. We have *discounted* the $200 to its present value of $181.40. Discounting of future sums to their present value is a common practice in business. A knowledge of the present value of a sum to be received in the future can be very useful to the manager, particularly in making capital budgeting decisions. However, we need to find a simpler way of computing present value than using Equation (3) every time we need to discount a future sum. The computations involved in using this equation are complex and time-consuming.

Fortunately, tables are available in which most of the mathematical work involved in the discounting process has been done. Table 13A–1 in the Appendix shows the discounted present value of $1 to be received at various periods in the future at various interest rates. The table indicates that the present value of $1 to be received two periods from now at 5 percent is 0.907. Since in our example we want to know the present value of $200, rather than just $1, we need to multiply the factor in the table by $200:

$$\$200 \times 0.907 = \$181.40$$

The answer we obtain is the same answer we got earlier using the formula in Equation (3).

Present value of a series of cash flows

Although some business investments are such that they involve a single sum to be received (or paid) at a single point in the future, other investments involve a *series* of cash flows. For example, assume that a firm has just purchased a government bond, in order to temporarily invest funds that are being held for future plant expansion. The bond will yield interest of $500 each year, and will be held for five years. What is the present value of the stream of interest receipts from the bond? As shown in Exhibit 13–2, the present value of this stream is $2,106.00, if we assume a discount rate of 6 percent compounded annually. The discount factors used in this exhibit were taken from Table 13A–1 in the Appendix.

EXHIBIT 13–2
Present value of a series of cash receipts

Year	Factor at 6% (Table 13A–1)	Interest received	Present value
1	0.943	$500	$ 471.50
2	0.890	500	445.00
3	0.840	500	420.00
4	0.792	500	396.00
5	0.747	500	373.50
			$2,106.00

Two points are important in connection with this exhibit. First, notice that the farther we go forward in time, the smaller the present value of the $500 interest receipt. The present value of $500 received a year from now is $471.50, as compared to only $373.50 for the $500 interest payment to be received five years from now. This point simply underscores the fact that money has a time value.

The second point is that even though the computations involved in Exhibit 13–2 are accurate, they have involved unnecessary work. The same present value of $2,106.00 could have been obtained more easily by referring to Table 13A–2 in the Appendix. Table 13A–2 contains the present value of $1 to be received each year over a *series* of years, at various interest rates. Table 13A–2 has been derived by simply adding the factors from Table 13A–1 together. To illustrate, we used the following factors from Table 13A–1 in the computations in Exhibit 13–2:

Year	Table 13A–1 factors at 6%
1	0.943
2	0.890
3	0.840
4	0.792
5	0.747
	4.212

The sum of the five factors above is 4.212. Notice from Table 13A–2 that the factor for $1 to be received each year for five years at 6 percent is also 4.212. If we use this factor, and multiply it by the $500 to be received each year, then we get the same present value of $2,106.00 that we obtained earlier in Exhibit 13–2:

$$\$500 \times 4.212 = \$2,106.00$$

Therefore, when dealing with a *series,* or stream, of cash flows, Table 13A–2 should be used. A series, or stream, of cash flows is known as an *annuity.*

DISCOUNTED CASH FLOWS—THE NET PRESENT VALUE METHOD

Earlier in the chapter the point was made that business investments have two distinguishing characteristics. The first is that they often involve depreciable assets, and the return which the assets provide must be sufficient to recoup the original investment itself as well as to provide a satisfactory yield on the investment. The second is that business investments are generally long term in nature, often spanning a decade or more. This characteristic lays heavy stress on the necessity to recognize the time value of money in business investment decisions.

If a capital budgeting method is to be fully useful to management, it must be capable of giving full recognition to *both* of the characteristics mentioned above. Although several methods of making capital budgeting decisions are in use, the ones that do the best job are those involving discounted cash flows. The discounted cash flow methods give full recognition to the time value of money, and at the same time provide for full recovery of any investment in depreciable assets. No other capital budgeting method is capable of performing *both* of these functions.

There are two approaches to making capital budgeting decisions by means of discounted cash flow. One is known as the net present value method, and the other is known as the time-adjusted rate of return (sometimes called the *internal rate of return*) method. Both methods are discussed in following sections.

The net present value method illustrated

The concepts involved in the net present value method are best understood by means of a concrete example. Let us assume the following data:

EXAMPLE A

The Harper Company is contemplating the purchase of a machine that is capable of performing certain operations that are now performed manually. The machine will cost $4,941 new, and it will last for five years. At the end of the five-year period the machine will have a zero scrap value. Use of the machine will reduce labor costs by $1,800 per year. The Harper Company requires a 20 percent return before taxes on all investment projects.

Should the machine be purchased? To answer this question it will be necessary first to isolate the cash inflows and cash outflows associated with the proposed project. In order to keep the example free of unnecessary complications, we have assumed only one cash inflow and one cash outflow. The cash inflow is the $1,800 annual reduction in labor costs. The cash outflow is the $4,941 initial investment in the machine.

The investment decision: The Harper Company must determine whether a cash investment now of $4,941 can be justified, if it will result in an $1,800 reduction in cost each year over the next five years, and if the company can get a 20 percent return on its money invested elsewhere.

To determine whether the investment is desirable, it will be necessary to discount the stream of annual $1,800 cost reductions to present value, and to compare this discounted present value to the cost of the new machine. Since The Harper Company requires a return of 20 percent on all investment projects, we will use this rate in the discounting process. Exhibit 13–3 gives a net present value analysis of the desirability of purchasing the machine.

Exhibit 13–3
Net present value analysis of a proposed project

Initial cost $4,941
Life of the project (years) 5
Annual cost savings $1,800
Salvage value .... –0–
Desired rate of return 20%

Item	Year(s) having cash flows	Amount of cash flow	20% factor	Present value of cash flows
Annual cost savings	1–5	$ 1,800	2.991*	$ 5,384
Initial investment	Now	(4,941)	1.000	(4,941)
Net present value				$ 443

* From Table 13A–2 in the Appendix.

According to the analysis, The Harper Company should purchase the new machine. The present value of the cost savings is $5,384, as compared to a present value of only $4,941 for the investment required (cost of the machine). Deducting the present value of the investment required from the present value of the cost savings gives a *net present value* of $443. Whenever the *net present value* is positive, as in our example, then an investment project is acceptable. Whenever the *net present value* is negative (the present value of the cash outflows exceed the present value of the cash inflows), then an investment project is not acceptable.

A full interpretation of the solution would be as follows: The new machine promises slightly more than the desired 20 percent rate of return. This is evident from the positive net present value of $443. The Harper Company could spend up to $5,384 for the new machine and still obtain the 20 percent rate of return it desires. The net present value of $443, therefore, shows the amount of "cushion" or "margin of error" which the company has in estimating the cost of the new machine. Alternatively, it also shows the amount of error that can exist in the present value of the cost savings, with the project remaining acceptable. That is, if the present value of the cost savings were only $4,941, rather than $5,384, the project would still promise the desired 20 percent rate of return.

Emphasis on cash flows

In organizing data for making capital budgeting decisions, the reader may have noticed that our emphasis has been on cash flows and not on accounting net income. The reason is that accounting net income is based on accrual concepts which ignore the timing of cash flows into and out of an organization. As we stated earlier in the chapter, from a capital budgeting standpoint the timing of cash flows is important, since a dollar received today is more valuable than a dollar received in the future. Therefore, even though the accounting net income figure is useful for many things, it must be ignored in those capital budgeting computations which involve discounted cash flow analysis. Instead of determining accounting net income, the manager must concentrate on identifying the specific cash flows associated with various investment projects, and on determining when these cash flows will take place.

In considering an investment project, what kinds of cash flows should the manager look for? Although the specific cash flows will vary from project to project, certain types of cash flows tend to recur, and should be looked for. Usually a cash outflow in the form of an initial investment of some type will be present. In addition, some projects require that a firm expand its working capital in order to service the greater volume of business that will be generated. Any such incremental working capital needs should be treated as part of the initial investment in a project. Also, many projects require periodic outlays for repairs and maintenance, and for additional operating costs.

On the cash inflow side, a project will normally either increase revenues or reduce costs. In regard to this point, notice that *a reduction in costs is equivalent to an increase in revenues,* so far as the ultimate impact on net income is concerned. Cash inflows are also frequently realized from salvage of equipment when a project is terminated. In addition, upon termination of a project, any working capital that is freed for use elsewhere should be treated as a cash inflow.

In summary, the following types of cash flows are common in business investment projects:

Cash outflows:
  Initial investment (including installation costs).
  Increased working capital needs.
  Repairs and maintenance.
  Incremental operating costs.

Cash inflows:
  Incremental revenues.
  Reductions in costs.
  Salvage value.
  Release of working capital.

Recovery of the original investment

When first introduced to present value analysis, students are often mystified by the fact that depreciation is not deducted in computing the profitability of a project. There are two reasons for not deducting depreciation.

First, depreciation is an accounting concept not involving a current cash outflow.[1] As discussed in the preceding section, discounted cash flow methods of making capital budgeting decisions focus on *flows of cash*. Although depreciation is a vital concept in computing accounting net income for financial statement purposes, it is not relevant in an analytical framework that focuses on flows of cash.

A second reason for not deducting depreciation is that discounted cash flow methods *automatically* provide for return of the original investment, thereby making a deduction for depreciation unnecessary. To demonstrate this point, let us assume the following data:

EXAMPLE B

The Carver Hospital is considering purchasing an attachment for its X-ray machine that will cost $3,170. The attachment will be usable for four years, after which time it will have no salvage value. It is estimated that the attachment will increase revenues from the X-ray department by $1,000 each year. The hospital's board of directors has instructed that no investments are to be made unless they promise an annual return of at least 10 percent.

A present value analysis of the desirability of purchasing the attachment is presented in Exhibit 13–4. Notice that the attachment promises exactly a 10 percent return on the original investment, since the net present value at a 10 percent discount rate is exactly zero.

---

[1] Although depreciation itself does not involve a cash outflow, it does have an effect on cash outflows for income taxes. We shall take a look at this effect in the following chapter, when we discuss the impact of income taxes on management planning.

Exhibit 13–4
Net present value analysis of x-ray machine attachment

Initial cost	$3,170
Life of the project (years)	4
Annual incremental revenues	$1,000
Salvage value	–0–
Desired rate of return	10%

Item	Year(s) having cash flows	Amount of cash flow	10% factor	Present value of cash flows
Annual incremental revenue	1–4	$ 1,000	3.170	$ 3,170
Initial investment	Now	(3,170)	1.000	(3,170)
Net present value				$ –0–

Each annual $1,000 cash inflow arising from use of the attachment is made up of two parts. One part represents a recovery of a portion of the original $3,170 paid for the attachment, and the other part represents a return *on* this investment. The breakdown of each year's $1,000 cash inflow between recovery *of* investment and return *on* investment is shown in Exhibit 13–5.

Exhibit 13–5
The Carver Hospital—breakdown of annual cash inflows

Year	(1) Investment outstanding during the year	(2) Cash inflow	(3) Return on investment (1) × 10%	(4) Recovery of investment during the year (2) – (3)	(5) Unrecovered investment at the end of the year (1) – (4)
1	$3,170	$1,000	$317	$ 683	$2,487
2	2,487	1,000	249	751	1,736
3	1,736	1,000	173	827	909
4	909	1,000	91	909	–0–
Total investment recovered				$3,170	

The first year's $1,000 cash inflow consists of a $317 interest return (10 percent) on the $3,170 original investment, plus a $683 return *of* that investment. Since the amount of the unrecovered investment decreases over the four years, the dollar amount of the interest return also decreases. By the end of the fourth year, all $3,170 of the original investment has been recovered.

Limiting assumptions

In working with discounted cash flows, at least two limiting assumptions are usually made. The first is that all flows of cash occur at the end of a period. This is somewhat unrealistic in that cash flows typically occur somewhat uniformly *throughout* a period. The purpose of this assumption is just to simplify computations.

The second assumption is that all cash flows generated by an investment project are immediately reinvested in another project. It is further assumed that the second project will yield a rate of return at least as large as the first project. Unless these conditions are met, the return computed for the first project will not be accurate. To illustrate, we computed a rate of return for the Carver Hospital in Exhibit 13–4 of 10 percent. Unless the funds released each period are immediately reinvested in another project yielding at least a 10 percent return, then the return computed for the X-ray attachment will be overstated.

Choosing a discount rate

In using the net present value method, it is necessary to choose some rate of return for discounting cash flows to present value. In Example A we used a rate of return of 20 percent before taxes, and in Example B we used a rate of return of 10 percent. These rates were chosen somewhat arbitrarily simply for sake of illustration.

As a practical matter, firms put much time and study into the choice of a discount rate. The rate generally viewed as being most appropriate is a firm's *cost of capital*. A firm's cost of capital is not simply the interest rate which it must pay for long-term debt. Rather, cost of capital is a broad concept, involving a blending of the costs of *all* sources of capital funds, both debt and equity. The mechanics involved in cost of capital computations are covered in finance texts, and will not be considered here.

Most finance people would agree that a before-tax cost of capital of 18 percent to 20 percent would be typical for an average industrial corporation. The appropriate after-tax figure would depend on the corporation's tax circumstances, but would probably average around 8 to 10 percent.

An extended example of the net present value method

EXAMPLE C

The Swinyard Company is contemplating adding a new product line. The new product line would be marketable for only five years, after which time it would have to be discontinued. The costs and revenues that would be associated with the new line are:

Cost of equipment required	$80,000
Working capital needed	70,000
Salvage value of the equipment in 5 years	10,000
Annual sales revenues	75,000
Annual out-of-pocket costs for salaries, advertising, etc.	45,000
Overhaul of the equipment required in 4 years	5,000

The Swinyard Company's cost of capital is 12 percent. Would you recommend that the new product line be introduced? Ignore income taxes.

This example involves several cash inflows and several cash outflows. The solution is given in Exhibit 13–6.

Exhibit 13–6
The net present value method—an extended example

			Years 1–5
Sales revenues			$75,000
Out-of-pocket costs			45,000
Annual net cash inflows			$30,000

Item	Year(s) having cash flows	Amount of cash flows	12% factor	Present value of cash flows
Purchase of equipment	Now	($80,000)	1.000	($80,000)
Working capital needed	Now	(70,000)	1.000	(70,000)
Overhaul of equipment	4	(5,000)	0.636	(3,180)
Annual net cash inflows from sales of the product line	1–5	30,000	3.605	108,150
Salvage value of the equipment	5	10,000	0.567	5,670
Working capital released	5	70,000	0.567	39,690
Net present value				$ 330

Notice particularly how the working capital is handled in the exhibit. Also notice how the sales revenues and out-of-pocket costs are handled.

Since the overall net present value is positive, the new product line should be added, assuming that there is no better use for the investment funds involved.

DISCOUNTED CASH FLOWS—THE TIME-ADJUSTED RATE OF RETURN METHOD

The time-adjusted rate of return (or *internal rate of return*) can be defined as the true interest yield promised by an investment project over its useful life. It can be computed by finding that discount rate which will equate the present value of the investment (cash outflows) required by a project with the present value of the returns (cash inflows) that the project promises. In other words, the time-adjusted rate of return is that discount rate which will cause the net present value of a project to be equal to zero.

The time-adjusted rate of return method illustrated

Finding a project's time-adjusted rate of return can be very helpful to a manager in making capital budgeting decisions. To illustrate, let us assume the following data:

EXAMPLE D

The Glendale School District is considering the purchase of a large tractor-pulled lawn mower. If the mower is purchased, it will replace hiring persons to mow with small, individual gas mowers. The large mower will cost $5,650 and will have a life of 10 years. It will have only a negligible scrap value, which can be ignored. The mower will provide a savings of $1,000 per year in mowing costs because of the labor it will replace.

To compute the time-adjusted rate of return promised by the new mower, it will be necessary to find that discount rate which will cause the net present value of the project to be equal to zero. How do we proceed to do this? The simplest and most direct approach is to divide the investment in the project by the expected annual cash inflow. This computation will give a factor that will be equal to the factor of the time-adjusted rate of return.

$$\frac{\text{Investment in the project}}{\text{Annual cash inflow}} = \text{Factor of the time-adjusted rate of return}$$

The factor can then be located in the present value tables, to see what rate of return it represents. We will now perform these computations for the Glendale School District's proposed project:

$$\frac{\$5,650}{\$1,000} = 5.650$$

The discount factor that will equate a series of $1,000 cash inflows with a present investment of $5,650 is 5.650. We need now to find this factor in Table 13A–2 in the Appendix, to see what rate of return it represents. If we refer to table 13A–2 and scan along the line for period 10, we find that a factor of 5.650 represents a 12 percent rate of return. Therefore, the time-adjusted rate of return promised by the mower project is 12 percent. We can prove this by computing the project's net present value, using a 12 percent discount rate. This computation is made in Exhibit 13–7.

Exhibit 13–7
Evaluation of the mower purchase using a 12 percent discount rate

		Initial cost	$5,650	
		Life of the project (years)	10	
		Annual cost savings	$1,000	
		Salvage value	–0–	

Item	Year(s) having cash flows	Amount of cash flow	12% factor	Present value of cash flows
Annual cost savings	1–10	$ 1,000	5.650	$ 5,650
Initial investment	Now	(5,650)	1.000	(5,650)
Net present value				$ –0–

Notice from Exhibit 13–7 that using a discount rate of 12 percent equates the present value of the annual cash inflows with the present value of the investment required in the project, leaving a zero net present value. The 12 percent rate, therefore, represents the time-adjusted rate of return promised by the project.

The problem of uneven cash flows

The technique just demonstrated works very well if a project's cash flows are even. But what if they are not? For example, what if a project will have some salvage value at the end of its life, in addition to the annual cash inflows? Under these circumstances, a trial-and-error process is necessary to find that rate of return which will exactly equate the cash inflows with the cash outflows. The trial-and-error process can be carried out by hand, or canned computer programs are available that can perform the necessary computations in seconds. In short, simply because cash flows are erratic or uneven will not in any way prevent a manager from determining a project's time-adjusted rate of return.

The process of interpolation

Interpolation is the process of finding odd rates of return that do not appear in published interest tables. It is important, since only rarely will a project have a nice, round rate of return that can be found directly in the present value tables. To illustrate, assume the following data:

Investment required	$6,000
Annual cost savings	1,500
Life of the project	10 years

What is the time-adjusted rate of return promised by this project? We can proceed as before, and find that the relevant factor is 4.000:

$$\frac{\text{Investment required}}{\text{Annual cost savings}} = \frac{\$6,000}{\$1,500} = 4.000$$

Looking in Table 13A–2 in the Appendix, and scanning along the line for period 10, we find that a factor of 4.000 falls just between a return of 20 percent and a return of 22 percent. To find the exact rate of return, we will need to interpolate, as follows:

		Present value factors
20% factor	4.192	4.192
True factor	4.000	
22% factor		3.923
Difference	0.192	0.269

$$\text{Time-adjusted rate of return} = 20\% + \left(\frac{0.192}{0.269} \times 2\%\right)$$

$$\text{Time-adjusted rate of return} = 21.4\%$$

Using the time-adjusted rate of return

Once the time-adjusted rate of return has been computed, what does the manager do with the information? The time-adjusted rate of return can be compared with the rate of return (usually the cost of capital) that the organization requires on its investment projects. If the time-adjusted rate of return is *greater* than the cost of capital, then the project is acceptable. If it is *less* than the cost of capital, then the project is rejected. A project is not a profitable undertaking if it can't provide a rate of return at least as great as the cost of the funds invested in it.

In the case of the Glendale School District example used earlier, let us assume that the District has set a minimum required rate of return of 10 percent on all projects. Since the mower promises a rate of return of 12 percent, it clears this hurdle, and would therefore be an acceptable investment.

THE COST OF CAPITAL AS A SCREENING TOOL

The cost of capital operates as a *screening* tool, helping the manager to screen out undesirable investment projects. When the time-adjusted rate of return method is being used, this screening takes the form of a *hurdle rate* which a project must clear for acceptance. The hurdle rate is the cost of capital itself. The time-adjusted rate of return promised by a project must be great enough to clear the cost of capital hurdle, or the project is rejected. We saw the application of this idea in the Glendale School District example above, where the hurdle was set at 10 percent.

The cost of capital also serves as a screening tool when the net present value method is used. In this case, the cost of capital becomes the *actual discount rate* used to compute the net present value of any proposed project, as discussed earlier. Any project yielding a negative net present value is rejected.

The operation of the cost of capital as a screening tool is summarized below.

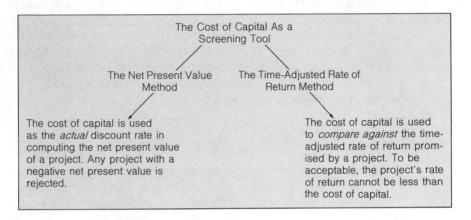

The Cost of Capital As a
Screening Tool

The Net Present Value
Method

The Time-Adjusted Rate of
Return Method

The cost of capital is used as the *actual* discount rate in computing the net present value of a project. Any project with a negative net present value is rejected.

The cost of capital is used to *compare against* the time-adjusted rate of return promised by a project. To be acceptable, the project's rate of return cannot be less than the cost of capital.

COMPARISON OF THE NET PRESENT VALUE AND THE TIME-ADJUSTED RATE OF RETURN METHODS

The net present value method has a number of advantages over the time-adjusted rate of return method of making capital budgeting decisions.

First, the net present value method is simpler to use. As explained earlier, the time-adjusted rate of return method often requires a trial-and-error process in trying to find the exact rate of return which will equate a project's cash inflows and outflows. No such trial-and-error process is necessary when working with the net present value method.

Second, using the net present value method makes it easier to adjust for risk. The point was made earlier in the chapter that the longer one has to wait for a cash inflow, the greater the risk that the cash inflow will never materialize. To show the greater risk connected with cash flows that are projected to occur many years in the future, firms often discount such amounts at higher discount rates than flows that are projected to occur earlier in time. For example, a firm might anticipate that a project will provide cash inflows of $10,000 per year for 15 years. If the firm's cost of capital is 18 percent before taxes, it might discount the first ten years' inflows at this rate, and then raise the discount rate to, say, 30 percent or 35 percent for the last five years. The raising of the discount rate would show the greater risk connected with the cash flows that are projected to be received far in the future.

No such selective adjustment of discount rates is possible under the time-adjusted rate of return method. About the only way to adjust for risk is to raise the hurdle rate that the rate of return for a project must clear for acceptance. This is a somewhat crude approach to the risk problem, in that it attaches the same degree of increased risk to *all* cash flows associated with a project—those that occur earlier in time as well as those that occur later in time.

Third, the net present value method provides more usable information than the time-adjusted rate of return method. The dollar net present value figure generated by the net present value method is viewed as being particularly useful for decision-making purposes. This point is considered further in the following chapter.

EXPANDING THE NET PRESENT VALUE APPROACH

So far we have confined all of our examples to the consideration of a single investment alternative. We will now expand the net present value approach to include two alternatives. In addition, we will integrate the concept of relevant costs into discounted cash flow analysis.

There are two ways that competing investment projects can be compared using the net present value method. One is the total-cost approach, and the other is the incremental-cost approach. Each approach is illustrated below.

The total-cost approach

The total-cost approach is the most flexible and most widely used method of making a net present value analysis of competing projects. To illustrate the mechanics of the approach, let us assume the following data:

EXAMPLE E

The Harper Ferry Company provides a ferry service across the Mississippi River. One of its ferryboats is in poor condition. The ferryboat can be renovated at an immediate cost of $20,000. Further repairs and an overhaul of the motor will be needed five years from now, at a cost of $8,000. In all, the ferry will be usable for ten years if this work is done. At the end of ten years, the ferry will have to be scrapped at a salvage value of approximately $5,000. The scrap value of the ferry right now is $7,000. It will cost $16,000 each year to operate the ferry, and revenues will total $25,000 annually.

As an alternative, The Harper Ferry Company can purchase a new ferryboat at a cost of $36,000. It will have a life of ten years, but will also require some repairs at the end of five years. It is estimated that these repairs will amount to $2,500. At the end of ten years, it is estimated that the ferry will have a scrap value of $5,000. It will cost $12,000 each year to operate the ferry, and revenues will total $25,000 annually.

The Harper Ferry Company requires a return of at least 18 percent before taxes on all investment projects.

Should the company purchase the new ferry, or renovate the old ferry? The solution is given in Exhibit 13–8.

Two points should be noted from the exhibit. First, observe that *all* cash inflows and *all* cash outflows are included in the solution under each alternative. No effort has been made to isolate those cash flows that are relevant to the decision, and those that are not relevant. The inclusion of all cash flows associated with each alternative gives the approach its name—the *total-cost* approach.

Second, notice that a net present value figure is computed for each

Exhibit 13–8
The total-cost approach to project selection

	New ferry	Old ferry
Annual revenues	$25,000	$25,000
Annual cash operating costs	12,000	16,000
Net annual cash inflows	$13,000	$ 9,000

Item	Year(s) having cash flows	Amount of cash flows	18% factor	Present value of cash flows
Buy the new ferry:				
Initial investment	Now	$(36,000)	1.000	$(36,000)
Repairs in 5 years	5	(2,500)	0.437	(1,093)
Net annual cash inflows	1–10	13,000	4.494	58,422
Salvage of the old ferry	Now	7,000	1.000	7,000
Salvage of the new ferry	10	5,000	0.191	955
Net present value				$ 29,284
Keep the old ferry:				
Initial repairs	Now	$(20,000)	1.000	$(20,000)
Repairs in 5 years	5	(8,000)	0.437	(3,496)
Net annual cash inflows	1–10	9,000	4.494	40,446
Salvage of the old ferry	10	5,000	0.191	955
Net present value				$ 17,905
Net present value in favor of buying the new ferry				$ 11,379

of the two alternatives. This is a distinct advantage of the total-cost approach, in that an unlimited number of alternatives can be compared side by side, to determine the most profitable course of action. For example, another alternative for The Harper Ferry Company would be to get out of the ferryboat business entirely. The net present value of this alternative could be computed if management desired, to compare with the alternatives shown in Exhibit 13–8. Still other alternatives might be open to the company. Once management has determined the net present value of each alternative it wishes to consider, that course of action can be selected which will be the most profitable. In the case at hand, given only the two alternatives, the data indicate the most profitable course is to purchase the new ferry.[2]

The incremental-cost approach

When only two alternatives are being considered, the incremental-cost approach offers a simpler and more direct route to a decision. Unlike the total-cost approach, it focuses only on differential costs.[3] The procedure is to pick out those costs and revenues that differ between the two alternatives being considered, and include only them in the discounted cash

Exhibit 13–9
The incremental-cost approach to project selection

Items	Year(s) having cash flows	Amount of cash flows	18% factor	Present value of cash flows
Incremental investment required to purchase the new ferry	Now	$(16,000)	1.000	$(16,000)
Repairs in 5 years avoided	5	5,500	0.437	2,403
Increased net annual cash inflows	1–10	4,000	4.494	17,976
Salvage of the old ferry	Now	7,000	1.000	7,000
Difference in salvage in 10 years	10	–0–	—	–0–
Net present value in favor of buying the new ferry				$ 11,379

---

[2] The alternative with the highest net present value is not always the best choice, although it is the best choice in this case. For further discussion, see the section titled "Preference Decisions—The Ranking of Investment Projects" in Chapter 14.

[3] Technically, the incremental-cost approach is misnamed, since it does focus on differential costs (that is, on both cost increases and decreases), rather than just on incremental costs. As used here, the term incremental costs should be interpreted broadly, to include both cost increases and decreases.

flow analysis. To illustrate, refer again to the data in Example E relating to The Harper Ferry Company. The solution using only differential costs is presented in Exhibit 13–9.

Two things should be noted from the data in this exhibit. First, notice that the net present value of $11,379 shown in Exhibit 13–9 agrees exactly with the net present value shown under the total-cost approach in Exhibit 13–8. This agreement should be expected, since the two approaches are just different roads to the same destination.

Second, notice that the costs used in Exhibit 13–9 are just mathematical differences between the costs shown for the two alternatives in the prior exhibit. For example, the $16,000 incremental investment required to purchase the new ferry in Exhibit 13–9 is the difference between the $36,000 cost of the new ferry and the $20,000 cost required to renovate the old ferry from Exhibit 13–8. The other figures in Exhibit 13–9 have been computed in the same way.

Least-cost decisions

Some decisions are such that revenues are not directly involved. For example, a company that makes no charge for delivery service may need to replace an old delivery truck, or a company may be trying to decide whether to lease or to buy its fleet of executive cars. In such cases, when the total-cost approach is used, the most desirable alternative will be the one that involves the least total cost, on a present value basis. To illustrate, assume the following data:

EXAMPLE F

The Val-Tek Company is considering the replacement of an old threading machine which is used in the manufacture of a number of products. A new threading machine is available on the market which could substantially reduce annual operating costs. Selected data relating to the old and to the new machines are presented below:

	Old machine	New machine
Purchase cost new	$20,000	$25,000
Salvage value now	3,000	—
Annual cash operating costs	15,000	9,000
Overhaul needed immediately	4,000	—
Salvage value in 6 years	–0–	5,000
Remaining life	6 years	6 years

The Val-Tek Company's cost of capital is 10 percent.

An analysis of the alternatives, using the total-cost approach, is provided in Exhibit 13–10.

Exhibit 13–10
The total-cost approach (least-cost decision)

Items	Year(s) having cash flows	Amount of cash flows	10% factor	Present value of cash flows
Buy the new machine:				
Initial investment	Now	$(25,000)	1.000	$(25,000)
Salvage of the old machine	Now	3,000	1.000	3,000
Annual cash operating costs.......	1–6	(9,000)	4.355	(39,195)
Salvage of the new machine	6	5,000	0.564	2,820
Present value of net cash outflows				$(58,375)
Keep the old machine:				
Overhaul needed now	Now	$(4,000)	1.000	$(4,000)
Annual cash operating costs	1–6	(15,000)	4.355	(65,325)
Present value of net cash outflows.....................				$(69,325)
Net present value in favor of buying the new machine				$ 10,950

As shown in the exhibit, the new machine promises the lowest present value of total costs. An analysis of the two alternatives using the incremental-cost approach is presented in Exhibit 13–11.

Exhibit 13–11
The incremental-cost approach (least-cost decision)

Items	Year(s) having cash flows	Amount of cash flows	10% factor	Present value of cash flows
Incremental investment required to purchase the new machine	Now	$(21,000)	1.000	$(21,000)
Salvage of the old machine	Now	3,000	1.000	3,000
Savings in annual cash operating costs	1–6	6,000	4.355	26,130
Difference in salvage value in 6 years	6	5,000	0.564	2,820
Net present value in favor of buying the new machine				$ 10,950

As before, the data going into this exhibit represent the differences between the alternatives as shown under the total-cost approach.

SUMMARY

Decisions relating to the planning and financing of capital outlays are known as capital budgeting decisions. Such decisions are of key importance to the long-run profitability of a firm, since large amounts of money are usually involved, and since whatever decisions are made may "lock-in" a firm for many years.

A decision to make a particular investment basically hinges on whether the future returns promised by the investment can be justified in terms of the present cost outlay that must be made. A valid comparison between the future returns and the present cost outlay is difficult because of the difference in timing involved. The cost outlay occurs now, and the returns usually come sometime in the future. This problem is overcome through use of the concept of present value, and through employment of the technique of discounting. The future sums are discounted to their present value, in order to be compared on a valid basis with current cost outlays. The discount rate used may be the firm's cost of capital, or it may be some arbitrary rate of return which the firm requires on all investment projects.

There are two ways of using discounted cash flow in making capital budgeting decisions. One is the net present value method, and the other is the time-adjusted rate of return method. The net present value method simply involves the choosing of a discount rate, and then the discounting of all cash flows to present value, as described in the preceding paragraph. If the present value of the cash inflows exceeds the present value of the cash outflows, then the net present value is positive, and the project is acceptable. The opposite is true if the net present value is negative. The time-adjusted rate of return method finds that discount rate which exactly equates the cash inflows and the cash outflows, leaving a zero net present value.

KEY TERMS FOR REVIEW

Capital budgeting

Screening decisions

Preference decisions

Time value of money

Compound interest

Discounting

Discounted cash flow

Present value

Annuity

Net present value

Time-adjusted rate of return

Internal rate of return

Discount rate

Discount factor

Cost of capital

Interpolation

Hurdle rate

Total-cost approach

Incremental-cost approach

APPENDIX: PRESENT VALUE TABLES

Table 13A–1
Present value of $1 $P = \dfrac{F_n}{(1+r)^n}$

Periods	4%	5%	6%	8%	10%	12%	14%	16%	18%	20%	22%	24%	26%	28%	30%	40%
1	0.962	0.952	0.943	0.926	0.909	0.893	0.877	0.862	0.847	0.833	0.820	0.806	0.794	0.781	0.769	0.714
2	0.925	0.907	0.890	0.857	0.826	0.797	0.769	0.743	0.718	0.694	0.672	0.650	0.630	0.610	0.592	0.510
3	0.889	0.864	0.840	0.794	0.751	0.712	0.675	0.641	0.609	0.579	0.551	0.524	0.500	0.477	0.455	0.364
4	0.855	0.823	0.792	0.735	0.683	0.636	0.592	0.552	0.516	0.482	0.451	0.423	0.397	0.373	0.350	0.260
5	0.822	0.784	0.747	0.681	0.621	0.567	0.519	0.476	0.437	0.402	0.370	0.341	0.315	0.291	0.269	0.186
6	0.790	0.746	0.705	0.630	0.564	0.507	0.456	0.410	0.370	0.335	0.303	0.275	0.250	0.227	0.207	0.133
7	0.760	0.711	0.665	0.583	0.513	0.452	0.400	0.354	0.314	0.279	0.249	0.222	0.198	0.178	0.159	0.095
8	0.731	0.677	0.627	0.540	0.467	0.404	0.351	0.305	0.266	0.233	0.204	0.179	0.157	0.139	0.123	0.068
9	0.703	0.645	0.592	0.500	0.424	0.361	0.308	0.263	0.225	0.194	0.167	0.144	0.125	0.108	0.094	0.048
10	0.676	0.614	0.558	0.463	0.386	0.322	0.270	0.227	0.191	0.162	0.137	0.116	0.099	0.085	0.073	0.035
11	0.650	0.585	0.527	0.429	0.350	0.287	0.237	0.195	0.162	0.135	0.112	0.094	0.079	0.066	0.056	0.025
12	0.625	0.557	0.497	0.397	0.319	0.257	0.208	0.168	0.137	0.112	0.092	0.076	0.062	0.052	0.043	0.018
13	0.601	0.530	0.469	0.368	0.290	0.229	0.182	0.145	0.116	0.093	0.075	0.061	0.050	0.040	0.033	0.013
14	0.577	0.505	0.442	0.340	0.263	0.205	0.160	0.125	0.099	0.078	0.062	0.049	0.039	0.032	0.025	0.009
15	0.555	0.481	0.417	0.315	0.239	0.183	0.140	0.108	0.084	0.065	0.051	0.040	0.031	0.025	0.020	0.006
16	0.534	0.458	0.394	0.292	0.218	0.163	0.123	0.093	0.071	0.054	0.042	0.032	0.025	0.019	0.015	0.005
17	0.513	0.436	0.371	0.270	0.198	0.146	0.108	0.080	0.060	0.045	0.034	0.026	0.020	0.015	0.012	0.003
18	0.494	0.416	0.350	0.250	0.180	0.130	0.095	0.069	0.051	0.038	0.028	0.021	0.016	0.012	0.009	0.002
19	0.475	0.396	0.331	0.232	0.164	0.116	0.083	0.060	0.043	0.031	0.023	0.017	0.012	0.009	0.007	0.002
20	0.456	0.377	0.312	0.215	0.149	0.104	0.073	0.051	0.037	0.026	0.019	0.014	0.010	0.007	0.005	0.001
21	0.439	0.359	0.294	0.199	0.135	0.093	0.064	0.044	0.031	0.022	0.015	0.011	0.008	0.006	0.004	0.001
22	0.422	0.342	0.278	0.184	0.123	0.083	0.056	0.038	0.026	0.018	0.013	0.009	0.006	0.004	0.003	0.001
23	0.406	0.326	0.262	0.170	0.112	0.074	0.049	0.033	0.022	0.015	0.010	0.007	0.005	0.003	0.002	
24	0.390	0.310	0.247	0.158	0.102	0.066	0.043	0.028	0.019	0.013	0.008	0.006	0.004	0.003	0.002	
25	0.375	0.295	0.233	0.146	0.092	0.059	0.038	0.024	0.016	0.010	0.007	0.005	0.003	0.002	0.001	
26	0.361	0.281	0.220	0.135	0.084	0.053	0.033	0.021	0.014	0.009	0.006	0.004	0.002	0.002	0.001	
27	0.347	0.268	0.207	0.125	0.076	0.047	0.029	0.018	0.011	0.007	0.005	0.003	0.002	0.001	0.001	
28	0.333	0.255	0.196	0.116	0.069	0.042	0.026	0.016	0.010	0.006	0.004	0.002	0.002	0.001	0.001	
29	0.321	0.243	0.185	0.107	0.063	0.037	0.022	0.014	0.008	0.005	0.003	0.002	0.001	0.001	0.001	
30	0.308	0.231	0.174	0.099	0.057	0.033	0.020	0.012	0.007	0.004	0.003	0.002	0.001	0.001	0.001	
40	0.208	0.142	0.097	0.046	0.022	0.011	0.005	0.003	0.001	0.001						

Table 13A-2
Present value of annuity of $1 in arrears

$$P_n = \frac{1}{r}\left[1 - \frac{1}{(1+r)^n}\right]$$

Periods	4%	5%	6%	8%	10%	12%	14%	16%	18%	20%	22%	24%	26%	28%	30%	40%
1	0.962	0.952	0.943	0.926	0.909	0.893	0.877	0.862	0.847	0.833	0.820	0.806	0.794	0.781	0.769	0.714
2	1.886	1.859	1.833	1.783	1.736	1.690	1.647	1.605	1.566	1.528	1.492	1.457	1.424	1.392	1.361	1.224
3	2.775	2.723	2.673	2.577	2.487	2.402	2.322	2.246	2.174	2.106	2.042	1.981	1.923	1.868	1.816	1.589
4	3.630	3.546	3.465	3.312	3.170	3.037	2.914	2.798	2.690	2.589	2.494	2.404	2.320	2.241	2.166	1.879
5	4.452	4.330	4.212	3.993	3.791	3.605	3.433	3.274	3.127	2.991	2.864	2.745	2.635	2.532	2.436	2.035
6	5.242	5.076	4.917	4.623	4.355	4.111	3.889	3.685	3.498	3.326	3.167	3.020	2.885	2.759	2.643	2.168
7	6.002	5.786	5.582	5.206	4.868	4.564	4.288	4.039	3.812	3.605	3.416	3.242	3.083	2.937	2.802	2.263
8	6.733	6.463	6.210	5.747	5.335	4.968	4.639	4.344	4.078	3.837	3.619	3.421	3.241	3.076	2.925	2.331
9	7.435	7.108	6.802	6.247	5.759	5.328	4.946	4.607	4.303	4.031	3.786	3.566	3.366	3.184	3.019	2.379
10	8.111	7.722	7.360	6.710	6.145	5.650	5.216	4.833	4.494	4.192	3.923	3.682	3.465	3.269	3.092	2.414
11	8.760	8.306	7.887	7.139	6.495	5.988	5.453	5.029	4.656	4.327	4.035	3.776	3.544	3.335	3.147	2.438
12	9.385	8.863	8.384	7.536	6.814	6.194	5.660	5.197	4.793	4.439	4.127	3.851	3.606	3.387	3.190	2.456
13	9.986	9.394	8.853	7.904	7.103	6.424	5.842	5.342	4.910	4.533	4.203	3.912	3.656	3.427	3.223	2.468
14	10.563	9.899	9.295	8.244	7.367	6.628	6.002	5.468	5.008	4.611	4.265	3.962	3.695	3.459	3.249	2.477
15	11.118	10.380	9.712	8.559	7.606	6.811	6.142	5.575	5.092	4.675	4.315	4.001	3.726	3.483	3.268	2.484
16	11.652	10.838	10.106	8.851	7.824	6.974	6.265	5.669	5.162	4.730	4.357	4.033	3.751	3.503	3.283	2.489
17	12.166	11.274	10.477	9.122	8.022	7.120	6.373	5.749	5.222	4.775	4.391	4.059	3.771	3.518	3.295	2.492
18	12.659	11.690	10.828	9.372	8.201	7.250	6.467	5.818	5.273	4.812	4.419	4.080	3.786	3.529	3.304	2.494
19	13.134	12.085	11.158	9.604	8.365	7.366	6.550	5.877	5.316	4.844	4.442	4.097	3.799	3.539	3.311	2.496
20	13.590	12.462	11.470	9.818	8.514	7.469	6.623	5.929	5.353	4.870	4.460	4.110	3.808	3.546	3.316	2.497
21	14.029	12.821	11.764	10.017	8.649	7.562	6.687	5.973	5.384	4.891	4.476	4.121	3.816	3.551	3.320	2.498
22	14.451	13.163	12.042	10.201	8.772	7.645	6.743	6.011	5.410	4.909	4.488	4.130	3.822	3.556	3.323	2.498
23	14.857	13.489	12.303	10.371	8.883	7.718	6.792	6.044	5.432	4.925	4.499	4.137	3.827	3.559	3.325	2.499
24	15.247	13.799	12.550	10.529	8.985	7.784	6.835	6.073	5.451	4.937	4.507	4.143	3.831	3.562	3.327	2.499
25	15.622	14.094	12.783	10.675	9.077	7.843	6.873	6.097	5.467	4.948	4.514	4.147	3.834	3.564	3.329	2.499
26	15.983	14.375	13.003	10.810	9.161	7.896	6.906	6.118	5.480	4.956	4.520	4.151	3.837	3.566	3.330	2.500
27	16.330	14.643	13.211	10.935	9.237	7.943	6.935	6.136	5.492	4.964	4.525	4.154	3.839	3.567	3.331	2.500
28	16.663	14.898	13.406	11.051	9.307	7.984	6.961	6.152	5.502	4.970	4.528	4.157	3.840	3.568	3.331	2.500
29	16.984	15.141	13.591	11.158	9.370	8.022	6.983	6.166	5.510	4.975	4.531	4.159	3.841	3.569	3.332	2.500
30	17.292	15.373	13.765	11.258	9.427	8.055	7.003	6.177	5.517	4.979	4.534	4.160	3.842	3.569	3.332	2.500
40	19.793	17.159	15.046	11.925	9.779	8.244	7.105	6.234	5.548	4.997	4.544	4.166	3.846	3.571	3.333	2.500

QUESTIONS

13–1. What is meant by the term "capital budgeting"?

13–2. Distinguish between capital budgeting screening decisions, and capital budgeting preference decisions.

13–3. What is meant by the term "time value of money"?

13–4. What is meant by the term "discounting," and why is it important to the business manager?

13–5. Why can't accounting net income figures be used in the net present value and time-adjusted rate of return methods of making capital budgeting decisions?

13–6. Why are discounted cash flow methods of making capital budgeting decisions superior to other methods?

13–7. What is net present value? Can it ever be negative? Explain.

13–8. One real shortcoming of discounted cash flow methods is that they ignore depreciation. Do you agree? Why or why not?

13–9. Identify two limiting assumptions associated with discounted cash flow methods of making capital budgeting decisions.

13–10. If a firm has to pay interest of 8 percent on long-term debt, then its cost of capital is 8 percent. Do you agree? Explain.

13–11. What is meant by an investment project's time-adjusted rate of return? How is the time-adjusted rate of return computed?

13–12. Explain how the cost of capital serves as a screening tool, when dealing with (a) the net present value method, and (b) the time-adjusted rate of return method.

13–13. Companies that invest in underdeveloped countries usually require a higher rate of return on their investment than they do when their investment is made in countries that are better developed, and that have more stable political and economic conditions. Some people say that the higher rate of return required in the underdeveloped countries is evidence of exploitation. What other explanation can you offer?

13–14. More risky investment proposals should be discounted at lower rates of return. Do you agree? Why or why not?

13–15. As the discount rate increases, the present value of a given future sum also increases. Do you agree? Explain.

13–16. Refer to Exhibit 13–6 in the text. Is the return promised by this investment proposal exactly 12 percent, slightly more than 12 percent, or slightly less than 12 percent? Explain.

13–17. If an investment project has a zero net present value, then it should be rejected since it will provide no return on funds invested. Do you agree? Why?

13–18. A machine costs $12,000. It will provide a cost savings of $2,000 per year. If the company requires a 14 percent rate of return, how many years will the machine have to be used to provide the desired 14 percent return?

EXERCISES

(Ignore income taxes on all exercises.)

E13–1. (The solution to this exercise is given below.) Each of the following situations is independent. Work out your own solution to each situation, and then check it against the solution provided.

1. John has just reached age 58. In 12 years he plans to retire. Upon retiring he would like to take an extended vacation, which he expects will cost at least $4,000. What lump-sum amount must he invest now in order to have the needed $4,000 at the end of 12 years if the desired rate of return is:

   a. 8 percent?

   b. 12 percent?

2. The Morgans would like to send their daughter to an expensive music camp at the end of each of the next five years. The camp costs $1,000 each year. What lump-sum amount would have to be invested now in order to have the $1,000 at the end of each year, if the desired rate of return is:

   a. 8 percent?

   b. 12 percent?

3. You have just received an inheritance from your father's estate. You can invest the money and either receive a $20,000 lump-sum amount at the end of ten years, or receive $1,200 at the end of each year for the next ten years. If the minimum desired rate of return is 12 percent, which alternative would you prefer?

Solution to Exercise 13–1.

1. a. The amount needed to be invested now would be the present value of the $4,000, using a discount rate of 8 percent. From Table 13A–1 in the Appendix, the factor for a discount rate of 8 percent for 12 periods is 0.397. Multiplying this discount factor times the $4,000 needed in 12 years will give the amount of the present investment required: $4,000 × 0.397 = $1,588.

   b. We will proceed as we did in Part (*a*) above, but this time use a discount rate of 12 percent. From Table 13A–1 in the Appendix, the factor for a discount rate of 12 percent for 12 periods is 0.257. Multiplying this discount factor times the $4,000 needed in 12 years will give the amount of the present investment required: $4,000 × 0.257 = $1,028.

   Notice that as the discount rate (desired rate of return) increases, the present value decreases.

2. This part differs from (1) in that we are now dealing with an annuity, rather than with a single future sum. The amount needed to be invested now will be the present value of the $1,000 needed at the end of each year for five years. Since we are dealing with an annuity, or series, of cash flows we must look in Table 13A–2 in the Appendix for the appropriate discount factor.

   a. From Table 13A–2 in the Appendix, the discount factor for 8 percent for five periods is 3.993. Therefore, the amount which must be invested now in order to have $1,000 available at the end of each year for five years is: $1,000 × 3.993 = $3,993.

b. From Table 13A–2 in the Appendix, the discount factor for 12 percent for five periods is 3.605. Therefore, the amount which must be invested now in order to have $1,000 available at the end of each year for five years is: $1,000 × 3.605 = $3,605.

Again notice that as the discount rate (desired rate of return) increases, the present value decreases. This is logical, since at a higher rate of return we would expect to have to invest less now than if a lower rate of return was being earned.

3. For this part we will need to refer to both tables in the Appendix. From Table 13A–1 we will need to find the discount factor for 12 percent for ten periods, and apply it to the $20,000 lump sum to be received in ten years. From Table 13A–2 we will need to find the discount factor for 12 percent for ten periods, and apply it to the series of $1,200 payments to be received over the ten-year period. Whichever alternative has the highest present value is the one that should be selected.

$20,000 × 0.322 = $6,440.
$ 1,200 × 5.650 = $6,780.

Thus, you would prefer to receive the $1,200 per year for ten years, rather than the $20,000 lump sum.

E13–2. Each of the following parts is independent.

1. Prudent Company contemplates that it will need a new warehouse in five years. The warehouse will cost $500,000 to build. What lump-sum amount should the company invest now in order to have the $500,000 available at the end of the five-year period? Assume that the company's desired rate of return is:

a. 10 percent.
b. 14 percent.

2. Jantzen Company can purchase a new milling machine that will save $2,000 annually in materials costs. If the machine will last for ten years, and have no salvage value, what is the maximum purchase price the Jantzen Company would be willing to pay, if the company's desired rate of return is:

a. 10 percent.
b. 14 percent.

3. JCP Company has just purchased a new packaging machine that cost $14,150. The machine is expected to save $2,500 annually in cash operating costs. If the company desires a rate of return of 14 percent on its investments, how many years must the machine be used in order to justify its purchase price? (Assume the machine will have no salvage value.)

E13–3. Consider each of the cases below independently.

1. Blair Company requires a 14 percent return on all investments. How much will the company be willing to pay for Machine A if the machine will save $8,000 per year for ten years?

2. Machine B has a projected life of 18 years. It is estimated that the machine will save $4,000 per year in operating costs. What is the machine's time-adjusted rate of return if it costs $29,000 new?

3. Assume that Machine C will yield a 16 percent time-adjusted rate

of return. It will last 15 years. If the machine costs $22,300 new, what are the annual cost savings?

E13–4. Consider each of the following cases independently:

1. Annual cash inflows that will arise from two competing investment opportunities are given below. Each investment opportunity will require the same initial investment. You desire a rate of return of 20 percent on funds invested. In terms of present values, which investment opportunity is best? Show computations.

Year	Investment X	Investment Y
1	$ 1,000	$ 4,000
2	2,000	3,000
3	3,000	2,000
4	4,000	1,000
	$10,000	$10,000

2. At the end of three years, when you graduate from college, your father has promised to give you a new car that will cost $4,500. What lump-sum amount must he invest now in order to have the $4,500 at the end of three years, if his desired rate of return is:
   a. 6 percent?
   b. 10 percent?

3. You want to spend $1,000 on a vacation at the end of the year for each of the next five years. What lump-sum amount must you invest now in order to have the needed $1,000 available at the end of each year for five years, if your desired rate of return is:
   a. 6 percent?
   b. 10 percent?

E13–5. 1. You have just learned that you are a beneficiary in the will of your late Aunt Susan. The executrix of her estate has given you three options as to how you may receive your inheritance:
   a. You may receive $50,000 immediately.
   b. You may receive $75,000 at the end of six years.
   c. You may receive $11,000 at the end of each year for six years.
   If your desired rate of return is 8 percent, which option would you prefer?

2. You can purchase an annuity now for $10,000. The annuity will pay you $8,000 per year for the eighth through tenth years in the future, after which it will terminate. If you require a rate of return of 12 percent, is the annuity an acceptable investment?

E13–6. Bill paid $12,000 for bonds which he purchased in 19x1. The bonds paid interest of $720 each year for five years, after which time Bill sold them for $12,400. Bill would like to earn a rate of return of at least 8 percent on all of his investments.

Required:

Did Bill earn an 8 percent return on the bonds? Show computations using the net present value format. (Round all dollar amounts to the nearest whole dollar.)

E13–7. Dayton Company has $15,000 to invest. The company is trying to decide between two alternative uses of the funds. The alternatives are:

	Invest in Project A	Invest in Project B
Investment required.................	$15,000	$15,000
Annual cash inflows	4,000	—
Single cash inflow at the end of 10 years	—	60,000
Life of the project	10 years	10 years

Dayton Company's cost of capital is 16 percent.

Required:

Which investment would you recommend the company accept? Show all computations using the net present value format.

E13–8. The Wriston Company has $100,000 to invest. The company is trying to decide between two alternative uses of the funds. The alternatives are:

	Invest in Alternative A	Invest in Alternative B
Cost of equipment required	$100,000	—
Working capital investment	—	$100,000
Annual net cash inflows	—	20,000
Single cash inflow at the end of 4 years	150,000	—
Life of the project	4 years	4 years

The equipment required in Alternative A will have no salvage value. The Wriston Company's cost of capital is 12 percent.

Required:

Which investment alternative (if either) would you recommend that the company accept? Show all computations, using the net present value format.

E13–9. The Pisa Pizza Parlor is investigating the purchase of a new delivery truck. The truck would cost $5,000 and have a five-year useful life. The truck would save $500 per year over the present method of delivering pizzas. In addition, it would result in delivery of about 1,000 more pizzas each year. The company realizes a contribution margin of $1 per pizza.

Required:

1. What would be the annual cash inflows associated with the new truck?
2. Compute the time-adjusted rate of return promised by the new truck. Interpolate to the nearest tenth of a percent.
3. In addition to the data given above, assume that the truck will have a $1,900 salvage value at the end of five years. Under these conditions, compute the time-adjusted rate of return to the nearest *whole* percent.

PROBLEMS

P13–10. *Net present value.* The Doughboy Bakery would like to buy a new bread mixer. The mixer the bakery is considering costs $12,000 new. It would last the bakery ten years, but would require a $5,000 overhaul at the end of the sixth year. After ten years, the mixer could be sold for $2,000.

The Doughboy Bakery estimates that it will cost $800 per year to operate the new mixer. It will replace an old mixer that costs $2,000 per year to operate. In addition, the new mixer will increase output by 18,000 loaves of bread per year. The company realizes a contribution margin of ten cents per loaf.

Required (Ignore income taxes):
1. What are the annual cash inflows that will be provided by the new bread mixer?
2. Assume that the company requires an 18 percent rate of return. What is the mixer's net present value? (Use the incremental-cost approach.)

P13–11. *Net present value.* The Barnes Company is contemplating the purchase of equipment to exploit a mineral deposit in land to which it has mineral rights. The projected cash flows that would be associated with the invest-ment are given below:

Cost of required equipment	$50,000
Net annual cash receipts	23,000
Working capital needed	10,000
Salvage value of equipment in 4 years	5,000
Overhaul of equipment needed in 3 years	8,000

The company estimates that the mineral deposit would be totally ex-hausted after four years' operation.

Required (Ignore income taxes):
Assume that the company's cost of capital is 20 percent. Would you recommend the project be undertaken? Use the net present value method.

P13–12. *Net present value analysis.* The Superior Pipe Company would like to purchase a new high-speed threading machine that costs $45,000. If purchased, the new machine will replace an old machine that will be sold for its scrap value of $5,000. The company is convinced that the new threading machine can produce the following annual cost savings:

Reduction in materials and supplies used	$7,000
Reduction in maintenance required	5,000

The new machine will require about $2,000 more labor cost annually to operate than the old machine, because of its more intricate mecha-nism. In addition, it will require an overhaul costing $6,000 at the end of six years' use. The new machine will be usable for eight years, after which time it will have a salvage value of $3,000. The Superior Pipe

Company requires a rate of return of at least 16 percent on investments of this type.

Required (Ignore income taxes):

Compute the new machine's net present value. Would you recommend purchase?

P13–13. *Time-adjusted rate of return; Sensitivity analysis.* The Big Piney Lumber Company has a saw that has been in use for many years. The saw has a zero disposal value. The company is considering the purchase of a new laser saw that would cost $27,000, but which could save $6,000 per year in cash operating costs and reduced waste. If the new laser saw is not purchased, the company can go on using the old saw almost indefinitely. The manufacturer estimates that the new laser saw will have a service life of ten years.

Required (Ignore income taxes):

1. Compute the time-adjusted rate of return on the new saw.
2. Since laser saws are very new, the management of the Big Piney Lumber Company is very unsure about the estimated ten-year useful life. Compute what the time-adjusted rate of return would be if the useful life of the laser saw was (*a*) 6 years, and (*b*) 15 years, instead of 10 years.
3. Assume that the life of the saw will be ten years as originally estimated, but that the annual cost savings will be only $4,000 rather than $6,000. Compute the time-adjusted rate of return.
4. Refer to the original data. Technology in the laser saw industry is moving so rapidly that management may not want to keep the new laser saw for more than five years. If disposed of at the end of five years, the laser saw would have a salvage value of $4,500. Compute the time-adjusted rate of return to the nearest *whole* percent, assuming that the saw is kept for only five years. If the company's cost of capital is 15 percent, would you recommend purchase? Explain.

P13–14. *Opening a small business; Net present value.* Ray Searle retires in six years. Mr. Searle has $50,000 to invest, and wants to open some type of small business operation which can be managed in the free time he has available from his regular occupation, and which can be closed easily when he retires. He is considering several investment alternatives, one of which is to open a self-service laundromat.

Mr. Searle has determined that it will cost $48,000 to purchase washers, dryers, and other equipment needed to open the laundromat. It will require another $2,000 in working capital investment to purchase an inventory of soap, bleaches, and related items, and to provide change for the change machines. The soap and related items will be sold to customers basically at cost.

Mr. Searle will charge $0.50 per use for the washers, and $0.25 per use for the dryers. A regular wash cycle will be 20 minutes, and a regular dryer cycle will be 15 minutes. Mr. Searle expects to gross a total of $550 each week from use of the washers, and $375 each week from use of the dryers. The only variable costs in the laundromat will be $0.06 per use for water and electricity for the washers, and $0.09 per use for gas and electricity for the dryers. Fixed costs are expected to be $1,000 per month for rent, $500 per month for cleaning, and $750 per month for maintenance, insurance, and other fixed costs.

The equipment will have about a 10 percent disposal value in six years. Mr. Searle has another investment alternative which will yield him a 12 percent rate of return.

Required (Ignore income taxes):

1. Assuming that the laundromat will be open 52 weeks a year, compute the expected net annual cash receipts from its operation (gross cash receipts less cash disbursements).
2. Would you advise Mr. Searle to open the laundromat? Show computations, using the net present value method of investment analysis. Round all dollar amounts to the nearest whole dollar.

P13–15. *Replacement decision.* The Bestline Furniture Store has the choice of overhauling its present delivery truck, or purchasing a new one. The company has assembled the following information:

	Present truck	New truck
Purchase cost new	$4,000	$5,000
Remaining book value	1,500	—
Overhaul needed now	2,000	—
Annual cash operating costs	3,500	2,000
Salvage value—now	1,000	—
Salvage value—5 years from now	250	1,000

If the company keeps the old delivery truck, it will have to be overhauled immediately at the cost shown above. With the overhaul, it can be made to last for five more years. If the new truck is purchased, it will be used for five years, after which it will be traded in on another truck. The company computes depreciation on a straight-line basis. All investment projects are evaluated on a basis of a 20 percent before-tax rate of return.

Required (Ignore income taxes):

1. Should the Bestline Furniture Store keep the old truck, or purchase the new one? Use the total-cost approach in making your decision. Round to the nearest whole dollar.
2. Redo (1), this time using the incremental-cost approach.

P13–16. *Net present value analysis; Incremental cost.* Craftsman Cabinets, Inc., is considering the purchase of new equipment to further automate its production line. Selected data relating to the new equipment are provided below:

Cost of the equipment	$50,000
Installation costs..........................	4,000
Salvage value in 10 years	5,000
Annual savings in maintenance costs	3,000
Annual increase in power costs	4,000
Life of the equipment	10 years

The savings in maintenance costs above would be for only the first five years in the life of the new equipment, after which time total maintenance costs would be the same as now. A number of workers can be discharged if the new equipment is purchased, resulting in a reduction of 2,400 hours in labor time worked annually, at a rate of $5 per hour. The company's cost of capital is 12 percent.

Required (Ignore income taxes):

1. Would you recommend that the new equipment be purchased? Show all computations, using the net present value format.
2. Assume that the new equipment is purchased. At the end of the first year, the cost analyst who prepared the data above tells you that some items haven't worked out as planned. Installation costs were $5,000, due to unforeseen problems; a rate increase granted to the power company has caused power costs to operate the equipment to be $500 more per year than planned; and the company has been able to reduce labor time by only 2,100 hours annually, rather than by 2,400 hours as planned. Assuming that all other items of cost data were accurate, did the company make a wise investment? Show computations, using the net present value format. (Hint: It might be helpful to place yourself back at the beginning of the first year, with the new data.)
3. If labor costs increase to $6 per hour, will this make the new equipment more or less desirable? Explain. No computations are necessary.

P13–17. *Investments in securities.* Ms. Paula Hill had $30,000 available for investment in 19x1. She used the $30,000 to purchase the following three securities during the year:

First investment. Ms. Hill purchased preferred stock at a cost of $8,000. The stock paid a 6 percent annual dividend. After four years, the stock was sold for $8,300.

Second investment. Ms. Hill purchased bonds at a cost of $10,000. The interest rate on the bonds was 7 percent, with the interest paid semiannually.[4] After four years, the bonds were sold for $9,800.

Third investment. Ms. Hill purchased common stock at a cost of $12,000. The stock paid no dividends, but was sold for $17,800 after four years.

Ms. Hill's goal is to earn a before-tax rate of return of 8 percent on her investments. Round all amounts to the nearest whole dollar.

---

[4] In discounting a cash flow that occurs semiannually, the procedure is to halve the discount rate and double the years. Use the same procedure in discounting the proceeds from the sale.

Required (Ignore income taxes):

1. On which investment(s) did Ms. Hill earn the desired 8 percent return? Show all computations, using discounted cash flow.
2. Considering all three investments together, did Ms. Hill earn the desired 8 percent return?

P13–18. *Lease or buy decision.* The Riteway Advertising Agency provides cars for its sales staff. In the past, the company has always purchased its cars outright from a dealer, and then sold the cars after two years' use. The company's present fleet is two years old, and will be sold very shortly. In order to provide a replacement fleet, the company is considering two alternatives:

Alternative 1. Purchase the cars outright, as in the the past, and sell the cars after two years' use. If this alternative is accepted, the following costs will be incurred on the fleet as a whole:

Purchase cost...................................	$45,000
Annual cost of servicing, taxes, and licensing	2,500
Repairs, first year of ownership	900
Repairs, second year of ownership	2,000

At the end of the two-year period, the cars could be sold for $12,000. Another fleet would then be purchased immediately, under the cost conditions indicated above. In all, a four-year time span would be covered by the two purchases.

Alternative 2. Lease the cars from a dealer under a four-year lease contract. The dealer would provide a new fleet of cars immediately, and then take these cars back and provide another new fleet at the end of the second year. The lease cost would be $22,300 per year (payable in installments throughout the year). As part of this lease cost, the dealer would provide all servicing and repairs, license the cars, and pay all taxes. At the end of the four-year period, the second fleet of cars would then revert back to the dealer, as owner.

If the fleet of cars is purchased, depreciation will be on a straight-line basis. The company's cost of capital is 14 percent.

Required (Ignore income taxes):

Would you advise the company to lease or buy its autos? Use the total-cost approach in your analysis.

P13–19. *Expansion of facilities; Net present value.* Quik-Lunch, Inc., operates a number of small sandwich-type food outlets in the downtown area of a large western city. The outlets are open for three hours each day, from 11 A.M. until 2 P.M., and serve a variety of hot and cold sandwiches, as well as salads, ice cream, and drinks. The outlets are open 260 days per year. One outlet is in a particularly favorable location, and is now serving an average of 250 customers each hour, and turning away another 300 customers each day, due to lack of facilities to handle them. A small dress shop next door has just gone out of business, and Quik-Lunch, Inc., is studying two ways this space might be used to satisfy the excess demand.

Alternative 1. The wall between the outlet and the dress shop can be torn out, and the outlet expanded. Remodeling and equipment would cost $250,000. If this is done, it is expected that all 300 customers now being turned away each day would use the new facilities. Studies show that the average customer takes 20 minutes to eat lunch, and spends an average of $2.30. The cost of the food to Quik-Lunch, Inc., is about $0.70 per serving.

Rent for the added space would be $12,000 per year; added salaries would be $45,000 per year; and added insurance, utilities, and other fixed costs would be $26,000 per year. Added working capital of $20,000 would be required for inventories and other working capital needs. The company can obtain a 15-year lease on the dress shop property. At the end of this time, the equipment would have a salvage value of $30,000.

Alternative 2. Vending machines can be placed in the dress shop space. This would entail only minor remodeling, at a cost (including equipment) of $80,000. An additional $12,000 would be required for inventories and other working capital needs. It is expected that two thirds of the customers now being turned away each day would use the vending service, and purchase $1.50 in food. The food would cost Quik-Lunch, Inc., an average of $0.45 per customer. Rent would still be $12,000 per year, as above, but salaries would be only $10,000 per year, and insurance, utilities, and other fixed costs would be only $15,000 per year. The vending equipment would have a salvage value of $5,000 in 15 years.

Required (Ignore income taxes):

1. Compute the expected net annual cash inflow from each alternative (cash receipts less cash disbursements).
2. Assume the company has a required rate of return of 12 percent. Compute the net present value of each alternative. (Use the total-cost approach, and round all dollar amounts to the nearest whole dollar.) Which alternative would you recommend?
3. Assume that the company decides to accept Alternative 2. At the end of the first year, the company finds that only one half of the customers who were being turned away from the regular outlet have been using the vending service. In light of this new information, did the company make the best choice between the alternatives? Show computations to support your answer. (Hint: It might be helpful to go back to the beginning of the first year under the vending alternative, with the new information.)

P13–20. *Rental property decision.* Earl Contino, professor of languages at an eastern university, owns an office building adjacent to the university campus. Professor Contino acquired the property ten years ago at a total cost of $525,000–$50,000 for the land, and $475,000 for the office building itself. He is uncertain whether it will be more profitable to keep the property and to continue to rent it, or to sell it to a realty investment company. His alternatives are:

Keep the property. Professor Contino has kept careful records of the income he has realized from the property. These records indicate the following annual revenues and expenses:

Annual rental revenues		$75,000
Annual operating expenses:		
Utilities	$14,000	
Depreciation	16,000	
Taxes and insurance	12,000	
Repairs and maintenance	8,000	50,000
Net income		$25,000

Professor Contino makes a $10,000 mortgage payment each year on the property. The mortgage will be paid off in eight more years. Professor Contino has been depreciating the building by the straight-line method, assuming a salvage value for the building of $75,000. He feels sure that the building can be rented for another 15 years. He also feels sure that 15 years from now the land will be worth three times what he paid for it.

Sell the property. A realty investment company has offered to purchase the property, by paying $175,000 immediately and $25,000 per year for 15 years. Control of the property would go to the reality company immediately. In order to sell the property, Professor Contino would need to pay the mortgage off, which can be done by a lump-sum payment of $65,000.

Required (Ignore income taxes):

Assume that Professor Contino desires an 8 percent rate of return. Would you recommend he keep or sell the property? Show computations, using discounted cash flow, and the total-cost approach.

P13–21. *Equipment replacement decision.* The JD Company purchased a new milling machine a year ago at a cost of $35,000. The machine will last the company ten more years, after which it will have no salvage value. The JD Company has just been approached by a sales representative selling a highly innovative computer-controlled milling machine that costs $50,000. The computer-controlled machine could increase the company's output by about 10 percent, while at the same time reduce per unit costs. The JD Company's engineering department has prepared the following comparative cost and revenue data:

	Present machine	Computer-controlled machine
Total annual revenues	$100,000	$110,000
Total annual expenses:		
Materials and supplies	$ 30,000	$ 28,000
Maintenance	8,000	12,000
Depreciation	3,000	4,800
Labor	45,000	37,000
Total	$ 86,000	$ 81,800
Net income per year	$ 14,000	$ 28,200

The computer-controlled machine would have a service life of ten years, after which it could be sold for $2,000 salvage. The present milling machine has a book value of $32,000, but it can be sold now for only $10,000.

Required (Ignore income taxes):

1. Use the total-cost approach to discounted cash flow analysis to determine whether the company should purchase the new machine. The company's desired rate of return is 18 percent.
2. Repeat the computations in (1), this time using the incremental-cost approach.

P13–22. *Lease or buy decision.* Rightway Stores, Inc., owns a nationwide chain of supermarkets. The company is going to open another store soon, and a suitable building site has been located in an attractive and rapidly growing area. The company has two choices as to how it can acquire the desired building and other facilities needed to open the new store. *Alternative 1.* The company can purchase the building site, construct the desired building, and purchase store fixtures. The total cost of these items would come to $415,000. This alternative would require the immediate payment of $250,000, and then $50,000 each year for the next four years (including interest). The company estimates that the property would be worth about $200,000 in 18 years, the length of time the company would want to occupy the property. *Alternative 2.* A large insurance company is willing to purchase the building site, construct a building, and install fixtures to Rightway Stores, Inc.'s specifications, and then lease the completed facility to Rightway Stores, Inc., for 18 years at annual lease cost of $48,000 (payable in installments throughout the year). The insurance company would require a $10,000 security deposit immediately which would be returned at the termination of the lease. The lease would be a ''net'' lease, in which Rightway Stores, Inc., would be required to pay all costs of insurance, taxes, and so on, associated with the property, the same as if Rightway Stores, Inc., were the owner of the property.

Rightway Stores, Inc., estimates that the annual costs of operating the store, exclusive of salaries and depreciation, would be:

Insurance	$ 6,000
Taxes (property)	18,000
Other	12,000
	$36,000

Rightway Stores, Inc.'s cost of capital is 16 percent.

Required (Ignore income taxes):

Using discounted cash flow, determine whether the company should lease or buy the desired store facilities. Use the total-cost approach.

P13–23. *Make or buy decision.* Enviroteck is now purchasing a component part, used in the manufacture of one of its products, from another company. The parts are purchased for $5 each, with a total volume of 20,000 parts being purchased each year. The engineering department of Enviro-teck has submitted a recommendation that the company begin to pro-duce this part in its own plant. The engineering department has supported its recommendation with the following information:

1. New equipment would have to be purchased to produce the part, at a total cost of $70,000. The equipment would have a ten-year life, and a $5,000 salvage value.
2. A lathe already owned by the company, but not in use, would also be used in production of the parts. The lathe would easily last for ten years, but would have no salvage value. Its present book value is $24,000.
3. Annual straight-line depreciation on the new equipment would be $6,500; on the presently owned lathe, $2,400.
4. If the parts are produced in Enviroteck's own plant, working capital of $20,000 would be needed to carry raw material and supplies inventories. However, the working capital required to carry finished parts could be reduced by $5,000.
5. Variable production costs per part would be:

Direct labor (0.5 hr at $4 per hour)	$2.00
Direct materials	2.20
Power, supplies, etc.	0.20
Total	$4.40

6. No other costs in Enviroteck's plant would be affected by the decision to manufacture the parts. The company applies general factory overhead to production on a basis of $2 per direct labor-hour.
7. The company requires a before-tax return of 18 percent on all investments.

Required (Ignore income taxes):

Do you agree with the engineering department's recommendation to produce the parts? Show computations, using the discounted cash flow total-cost approach.

P13–24. *C-V-P analysis and discounted cash flow.* Mercury Transit, Inc., has decided to inaugurate express bus service between its headquarters city and a nearby suburb (one-way fare, $0.50), and is considering the purchase of either 32- or 52-passenger buses, on which pertinent estimates are as follows:

	32-passenger bus	*52-passenger bus*
Number of each to be purchased	6	4
Useful life	8 years	8 years
Purchased price of each bus (paid on delivery)	$80,000	$110,000
Mileage per gallon	10	7½
Salvage value per bus	$ 6,000	$ 7,000
Drivers' hourly wage	$ 3.50	$ 4.20
Price per gallon of gasoline	$ 0.60	$ 0.60
Other annual cash expenses	$ 4,000	$ 3,000

During the four daily rush hours all buses will be in service and are expected to operate at full capacity (state law prohibits standees) in both directions of the route, each bus covering the route 12 times (six round trips) during the four-hour period. During the remainder of the 16-hour day, 500 passengers would be carried and Mercury Transit would operate only four buses on the route. Part-time drivers would be employed to drive the extra hours during the rush hours. A bus traveling the route all day would go 480 miles and one traveling only during rush hours would go 120 miles a day during the 260-day year.

Required (Ignore income taxes):
1. Prepare a schedule showing the computation of the estimated annual gross revenues from the new route for each alternative.
2. Prepare a schedule showing the computation of the estimated annual drivers' wages for each alternative.
3. Prepare a schedule showing the computation of the estimated annual cost of gasoline for each alternative.
4. Assume that your computations in (1), (2), and (3) are as follows:

	32-passenger bus	52-passenger bus
Estimated annual revenues	$365,000	$390,000
Estimated annual drivers' wages	67,000	68,000
Estimated annual cost of gasoline	32,000	36,000

Assuming that a minimum rate of return of 12 percent before income taxes is desired and that all annual cash flows occur at the end of the year, determine whether the 32- or the 52-passenger buses should be purchased. Use discounted cash flow, and the total-cost approach.

(CPA, adapted)

P13–25. *Discontinuing a department.* You have just been hired as a management trainee by Marley's Department Store. Your first assignment is to determine whether the store should discontinue its housewares department and expand its appliances department. The store's vice president feels that the housewares space could be better utilized selling appliances, since the appliances have a better markup and move more rapidly. The store's most recent income statement is presented below:

MARLEY'S DEPARTMENT STORE
Income Statement

	Appliances	Housewares	Clothing	Total
Sales	$400,000	$50,000	$200,000	$650,000
Cost of goods sold	280,000	40,000	110,000	430,000
Gross margin	$120,000	$10,000	$ 90,000	$220,000
Commissions	$ 40,000	$ 5,000	$ 20,000	$ 65,000
Depreciation	12,000	8,000	10,000	30,000
Other fixed expenses	20,000	8,000	15,000	43,000
Total expenses	$ 72,000	$21,000	$ 45,000	$138,000
Net income	$ 48,000	($11,000)	$ 45,000	$ 82,000

In the course of your analytical work you have determined the following information:

1. If the housewares department is discontinued, sales of appliances can be expanded by 25 percent. Sales of clothing will be unaffected.
2. The store fixtures being used in the housewares department could not be used in the expanded appliances department. These fixtures would have to be sold for their salvage value of $6,000. The fixtures will last for eight years more, after which they will have zero sale value.
3. Since appliances are much more expensive than housewares items, the store would have to expand its working capital investment in inventories and accounts receivable by $20,000.
4. The added level of appliance sales would carry the same proportionate variable expenses as current appliance sales.
5. Expanding the appliances department would require an expenditure of $60,000 for renovation and new fixtures. These fixtures would have an eight-year life and a $4,000 salvage value.
6. The store uses straight-line depreciation. If the fixtures now being used in the housewares department are sold, then all depreciation now being charged to that department will disappear.
7. The "other fixed expenses" in the housewares department represent the salary of a long-time employee, who will be retained regardless of whether the housewares department is retained or discontinued.
8. The store has a before-tax desired rate of return of 16 percent on all investments.

Required (Ignore income taxes):

Make a recommendation to the vice president as to whether the housewares department should be discontinued and the appliances department expanded. Use discounted cash flow, covering an eight-year period. Use the incremental-cost approach.

P13–26. *Equipment acquisition: Uneven cash flows.* Ellis Company is using a single Model 400 shaping machine in the manufacture of one of its products. The company is expecting to have a large increase in demand for the product, and is anxious to expand its productive capacity. Two possibilities are under consideration:

Alternative 1. Purchase another Model 400 shaping machine to operate along with the currently owned Model 400 machine.

Alternative 2. Purchase a Model 800 shaping machine, and use the currently owned Model 400 machine as standby equipment. The Model 800 machine is a high-speed unit, with double the capacity of the Model 400 machine.

The following additional information is available on the two alternatives:

1. All machines have a ten-year life from the time they are first used in production. Scrap value is nominal, and can be ignored. Straight-line depreciation is used.
2. The cost of a new Model 800 machine is $40,000.
3. The Model 400 machine now in use cost $18,000 three years

ago. Its present book value is $12,600, and its present market value is $10,000.

4. A new Model 400 machine costs $22,000 now. If the company decides not to buy the Model 800 machine, then the currently owned Model 400 machine will have to be replaced in seven years at a cost of $25,000. The replacement machine will have a market value of about $18,000 when it is three years old.

5. Production over the next ten years is expected to be:

Year	Production in units
1	40,000
2	50,000
3	60,000
4–10	65,000

6. The two models of machines are not equally efficient in output. Comparative variable costs per unit are:

	Model 400	Model 800
Materials per unit	$0.22	$0.40
Direct labor per unit	0.42	0.15
Supplies and lubricants per unit	0.06	0.05
Total variable cost per unit.............	$0.70	$0.60

7. The Model 400 machine is less costly to maintain than the Model 800 machine. Annual repairs and maintenance on a single Model 400 machine are $2,500.

8. Repairs and maintenance on a Model 800 machine, with a Model 400 machine used as standby, would total $3,800 per year.

9. No other factory costs will change as a result of the decision between the two machines.

10. The Ellis Company requires a before-tax rate of return of 20 percent on all investments.

Required (Ignore income taxes):

1. Which alternative should the company choose? Show computations, using discounted cash flow.

2. Suppose that the cost of labor increases by 10 percent. Would this make the Model 800 machine more or less desirable? Explain. No computations are needed.

3. Suppose that the cost of materials doubles. Would this make the Model 800 machine more or less desirable? Explain. No computations are needed.

Chapter 14

Further aspects of investment decisions

We continue our discussion of capital budgeting in this chapter by focusing on three new topics. First, we focus on income taxes and their impact on the capital budgeting decision. Second, we focus on methods of ranking competing capital investment projects, according to their relative desirability. And third, we focus on methods of making capital budgeting decisions, other than discounted cash flow.

INCOME TAXES AND CAPITAL BUDGETING

In our discussion of capital budgeting in the preceding chapter, the matter of income taxes was omitted for two reasons. First, many organizations have no taxes to pay. These organizations include schools, hospitals, and governmental units on local, state, and national levels. Use of capital budgeting techniques by these organizations will always be on a before-tax basis, as illustrated in the preceding chapter. Second, the topic of capital budgeting is sufficiently complex that it is best absorbed in small doses. Now that we have laid a solid groundwork in the concepts of present value and discounting, we can explore the effects of income taxes on capital budgeting decisions with little difficulty.

The concept of after-tax cost

If someone were to ask you how much the rent is on your apartment, you would probably answer with the dollar amount you pay out each month. If someone were to ask a business executive how much the rent is on the factory building, he or she might answer by stating a lesser figure than the dollar amount being paid out each month. The reason is that rent is a tax-deductible expense to a business firm, and expenses such as rent are often looked at on an *after-tax* basis, rather than a before-tax basis. The true cost of a tax-deductible item is not the dollars paid out, but the amount of payment that will remain after taking into consideration *any reduction in income taxes* that the payment will bring about. An expenditure net of its tax effect is known as *after-tax cost*.

After-tax cost is not a difficult concept. To illustrate the ideas behind it, assume that two firms, A and B, normally have sales of $15,000 each month, and cash expenses of $5,000 each month. Firm A is considering an advertising program that will cost $2,000 each month. The tax rate is 40 percent. What will be the after-tax cost to Firm A of the contemplated $2,000 monthly advertising expenditure? The after-tax cost is computed at the top of page 567 following.

	Firm A	Firm B
Sales	$15,000	$15,000
Expenses:		
Regular	$ 5,000	$ 5,000
New advertising program	2,000	–0–
Total	$ 7,000	$ 5,000
Net income before taxes	$ 8,000	$10,000
Income taxes (40 percent)	3,200	4,000
Net income	$ 4,800	$ 6,000
After-tax cost of the new advertising program.........	$1,200	

The after-tax cost of the advertising program would be only $1,200 per month. This figure must be correct, since it measures the difference in net income between the two companies, and since their income statements are identical except for the $2,000 in advertising paid by Firm A. In effect, a $2,000 monthly advertising expenditure would *really* cost Firm A only $1,200 *after taxes*.

A formula can be developed from these data that will give the after-tax cost of *any* cash expenditure. The formula is:

$$(1 - \text{Tax rate}) \times \text{Total amount paid} = \text{After-tax cost} \qquad (1)$$

We can prove the accuracy of this formula by applying it to Firm A's $2,000 advertising expenditure:

$$(1 - 0.40) \times \$2,000 = \$1,200 \text{ after-tax cost of the advertising program}$$

The concept of after-tax cost is very useful to the manager, since it measures the *actual* amount of cash that will be leaving a company as a result of a particular expenditure decision. In integrating income taxes into capital budgeting decisions, it will be necessary to place all revenue and expense items associated with a project on an after-tax basis.

In the case of revenues and other *taxable* cash receipts, the after-tax cash inflow can be obtained by a simple variation of the expenditure formula used above:

$$(1 - \text{Tax rate}) \times \text{Total amount received}$$
$$= \text{After-tax benefit (net cash inflow)} \qquad (2)$$

We emphasize the term *taxable* cash receipts above, since not all cash inflows are taxable. For example, the release of working captial at the termination of an investment project would not be a taxable cash inflow.

The concept of depreciation tax shield

The point was made in the preceding chapter that depreciation deductions in and of themselves do not involve cash flows. For this reason, depreciation deductions were ignored in Chapter 13 in all discounted cash flow computations.

Even though depreciation deductions do not involve cash flows, they do have an impact on the amount of income taxes that a firm will pay, and income taxes *do* involve cash flows. Therefore, as we now integrate income taxes into capital budgeting decisions, it will be necessary to consider depreciation deductions to the extent that they affect tax payments.

AN ILLUSTRATION.   To illustrate the effect of depreciation deductions on tax payments, let us compare two firms, X and Y. Both firms have annual sales of $20,000, and cash operating expenses of $10,000. In addition, Firm X has a depreciable asset, on which the depreciation deduction is $2,500 per year. The tax rate is 40 percent. A cash flow comparison of the two firms is given in Exhibit 14–1.

Exhibit 14–1
The impact of depreciation deductions on tax payments—
A comparison of cash flows

	Firm X	Firm Y
Sales	$20,000	$20,000
Expenses:		
Cash operating expenses	$10,000	$10,000
Depreciation expense	2,500	–0–
Total	$12,500	$10,000
Net income before taxes	$ 7,500	$10,000
Income taxes (40 percent)	3,000	4,000
Net income	$ 4,500	$ 6,000
Cash inflow from operations:		
Net income, as above	$ 4,500	$ 6,000
Add: The noncash deduction for depreciation	2,500	–0–
Total cash inflow	$ 7,000	$ 6,000
Greater amount of cash available to Firm X	$1,000	

Notice from the exhibit that Firm X's net cash inflow exceeds Firm Y's net cash inflow by $1,000. Also notice that in order to obtain Firm X's net cash inflow, it is necessary to add the $2,500 depreciation deduction back to the company's net income. This step is necessary since depreciation is a noncash deduction on the income statement.

Exhibit 14–1 presents an interesting paradox. Notice that even though Firm X's net cash inflow is $1,000 *greater* than Firm Y's, its net income is much *lower* than Firm Y's (only $4,500, as compared to Firm Y's $6,-000). The explanation for this paradox lies in the concept of the *depreciation tax shield.*

THE DEPRECIATION TAX SHIELD.   Firm X's greater net cash inflow comes about as a result of the *shield* against tax payments that is provided by depreciation deductions. Although depreciation deductions involve no outflows of cash, they are fully deductible in arriving at taxable income. In effect, depreciation deductions *shield* revenues from taxation, and thereby *lower* the amount of taxes that a company must pay.

In the case of Firm X above, the $2,500 depreciation deduction taken involved no outflow of cash to the firm. But yet this depreciation was fully deductible on the company's income statement, and thereby *shielded* $2,500 in revenues from taxation. Were it not for the depreciation deduction, the company's income taxes would have been $1,000 higher, since the entire $2,500 in shielded revenues would have been taxable at the regular tax rate of 40 percent (40 percent × $2,500 = $1,000). In effect, the depreciation tax shield *has reduced Firm X's taxes by $1,000,* permitting these funds to be retained within the company, rather than going to the tax collector. Viewed another way, we can say that Firm X has realized a $1,000 *cash inflow* (through reduced tax payments) as a result of its $2,500 depreciation deduction.

Because they shield revenues from taxation, depreciation deductions are generally referred to as a "depreciation tax shield." The reduction in tax payments made possible by the depreciation tax shield will always be equal to the amount of the depreciation deduction taken, multiplied by the tax rate. The formula is:

Depreciation deduction × Tax rate
$$= \text{Tax savings from the depreciation tax shield} \quad (3)$$

We can prove this formula by applying it to the $2,500 depreciation deduction taken by Firm X in our example:

$2,500 × 40% = $1,000 reduction in tax payments (shown as "Greater amount of cash available to Firm X" in Exhibit 14–1)

As we now integrate income taxes into capital budgeting computations, it will be necessary to consider the impact of depreciation deductions on tax payments, by showing the tax savings provided by the depreciation tax shield.

The best depreciation method

The most widely used depreciation methods are straight-line, sum-of-the-years'-digits, and double-declining balance. Which depreciation method is best? No categorical answer to this question is possible, since what is "best" will depend on the purpose of the deduction. For financial statement purposes one method may be best, in that it may provide for the most accurate matching of costs and revenues; for tax accounting purposes another method may be best, in that it may minimize the company's overall tax bill. As a practical matter, it is not uncommon for a company to depreciate an asset in more than one way according to how the resulting depreciation deduction is going to be used.

In a capital budgeting analysis, the depreciation method used will usually parallel the method used for income tax purposes. This generally will be either sum-of-the-years'-digits or double-declining balance, since these accelerated depreciation methods often are more advantageous than the straight-line method from a present value of tax savings point of view.

Exhibit 14–2
Tax shield effects of depreciation, on a present value basis

Cost of the asset	$100,000		
Life of the asset	4 years		
Salvage value	–0–		
Desired rate of return	15% after taxes		
Income tax rate	40%		

Method of depreciation		15% factor	Present value of tax savings
Straight-Line Depreciation:			
Annual depreciation ($100,000 ÷ 4 = $25,000):			
Depreciation deduction $25,000			
Multiply by 40% . . . . × 40%			
Income tax savings, years 1–4 . . . . $10,000		2.855	$28,550

Sum-of-the-Years'-Digits Depreciation:

Year	Multiplier*	Depreciation deduction	Tax shield: income tax savings at 40%	15% factor	Present value of tax savings
1 . . . . 4/10		$40,000	$16,000	0.870	$13,920
2 . . . . 3/10		30,000	12,000	0.756	9,072
3 . . . . 2/10		20,000	8,000	0.658	5,264
4 . . . . 1/10		10,000	4,000	0.572	2,288
					$30,544

Double-Declining Balance Depreciation:

Year	Book value	Rate† (%)	Depreciation deduction	Tax shield: income tax savings at 40%	15% factor	Present value of tax savings
1 . . . . . $100,000		50	$50,000	$20,000	0.870	$17,400
2 50,000		50	25,000	10,000	0.756	7,560
3 25,000		50	12,500	5,000	0.658	3,290
4 12,500		50	12,500	5,000	0.572	2,860
						$31,110

* The denominator for the sum-of-the-years'-digits method is: $1 + 2 + 3 + 4 = 10$
or

$$S = \frac{n(n+1)}{2} \qquad S = \frac{4(4+1)}{2} = 10$$

where S = sum of the years
n = life of the asset

† The percentage rate for the double-declining balance method is: $2 \times$ straight-line rate $= 2 \times 25\% = 50\%$. The asset is depreciated to zero salvage value in the 4th year.

To illustrate, refer to the data in Exhibit 14–2. This exhibit compares the three depreciation methods, in terms of the present value of the tax savings which they provide on a hypothetical asset costing $100,000.

As shown by the exhibit, the double-declining balance method provides the largest present value of tax savings, the sum-of-the-years'-digits method is second, and the straight-line method brings up the rear. This example goes far to explain why firms often prefer the accelerated depreciation methods over the straight-line method for tax purposes. Since the accelerated methods provide the bulk of their tax shield early in the life of an asset, the present value of the resulting tax savings will nearly always be greater than the present value of tax savings under the straight-line method.

The point should be emphasized that all three depreciation methods provide the *same total* dollars of tax savings in *absolute* terms. That is, each method provides $40,000 in *absolute* dollars of tax savings over the four-year life of the asset, as shown in the tabulation below:

Year	Straight-line	Sum-of-the-years'-digits	Double-declining balance
1	$10,000	$16,000	$20,000
2	10,000	12,000	10,000
3	10,000	8,000	5,000
4	10,000	4,000	5,000
Total dollars of tax savings	$40,000	$40,000	$40,000

The difference between the three depreciation methods lies in the *present value* of these tax savings. Notice that the accelerated methods provide most of their tax savings *early* in the life of the asset, as compared to the straight-line method. Since money has a time value, this earlier availability of the tax savings increases the present value of the total tax savings stream. In sum, by providing large depreciation tax shields early in the life of an asset, accelerated methods of depreciation defer taxes to the future, thereby making more dollars of cash available for use *now* in a business.

Comprehensive example of income taxes and capital budgeting

Armed with an understanding of the concepts of after-tax cost, after-tax revenue, and depreciation tax shield, we are now prepared to examine a comprehensive example of income taxes and capital budgeting. Assume the following data:

The Daily Globe newspaper has an auxiliary press that was purchased three years ago at a cost of $56,000. The press is being depreciated by the straight-

Exhibit 14-3
Comprehensive example of income taxes and capital budgeting: Total-cost approach

Item and computations			Year(s) having cash flows	Amount of cash flows	10% factor	Present value of cash flows
Buy the New Press:						
Initial investment			Now	$(50,000)	1.000	$(50,000)
Annual cash operating costs	$40,000					
Multiply by 1 − 40%	× 60%					
After-tax cost	$24,000		1–4	(24,000)	3.170	(76,080)
Depreciation deductions:						

Year	Multiplier	Depreciation deduction	*Tax shield: income tax savings at 40%*					
1	4/10	$20,000	$8,000	1	8,000	0.909	7,272
2	3/10	15,000	6,000	2	6,000	0.826	4,956
3	2/10	10,000	4,000	3	4,000	0.751	3,004
4	1/10	5,000	2,000	4	2,000	0.683	1,366

Item and computations			Year(s)	Amount	10% factor	PV
Salvage value, fully taxable since book value will be zero	$ 5,000					
Multiply by 1 − 40%	× 60%					
Net cash inflow	$ 3,000		4	3,000	0.683	2,049
Cash flow from disposal of the old press:						
Book value now ($56,000 − $24,000)	$32,000					
Sale price now	25,000	$25,000				
Loss on disposal	$ 7,000					
Income tax savings at 40%	× 40%	2,800				
Total cash inflow from disposal		$27,800	Now	27,800	1.000	27,800
Present value of costs						$(79,633)

Keep the Old Press:

Annual cash operating costs	$48,000				
Multiply by 1 − 40%	× 60%				
After-tax cost	$28,800	1-4	$(28,800)	3.170	$(91,296)
Depreciation deduction	$ 8,000				
Multiply by 40%	× 40%				
Income tax savings	$ 3,200	1-4	3,200	3.170	10,144
Salvage value, fully taxable since book value will be zero	$ 3,000				
Multiply by 1 − 40%	× 60%				
Net cash inflow	$ 1,800	4	1,800	0.683	1,229
Overhaul at end of year two	$ 8,000				
Multiply by 1 − 40%	× 60%				
After-tax cost	$ 4,800	2	(4,800)	0.826	(3,965)
Present value of costs					$(83,888)
Net present value in favor of purchasing the new press					$ 4,255

line method, with no provision for salvage value. The press will last four more years, but it will need an overhaul in two years at a cost of $8,000. The overhaul will be fully deductible for tax purposes when incurred. The operating costs of the press are $48,000 each year, exclusive of depreciation. Although no salvage value is being recognized for tax purposes, the press will have a salvage value of about $3,000 at the end of four more years.[1]

The Daily Globe is thinking about selling the old press and purchasing a new press. The old press can be sold right now for $25,000. A new press will cost $50,000, and will be used only four years, after which time it will be salable for $5,000. If the new press is purchased, it will be depreciated by the sum-of-the-years'-digits method. No salvage value will be recognized for tax purposes. The new press will cost $40,000 each year to operate.

The tax rate is 40 percent. The Daily Globe requires a return after taxes of 10 percent on all investments in fixed assets.

Should the Daily Globe keep its old press, or buy the new press? As explained in the preceding chapter, there are two ways to approach a capital budgeting decision such as this one—by the total-cost approach, or by the incremental-cost approach. Exhibit 14–3 contains the solution from the total-cost approach, and Exhibit 14–4 contains the solution from the incremental-cost approach.

Since the total-cost approach is more widely used than the incremental-cost approach, we will focus our discussion on it. The following points should be noted about the data and computations in Exhibit 14–3:

1. The initial investment of $50,000 in the new press is included in full, with no reductions for taxes. The tax effects of this investment are considered in the depreciation deductions.
2. Annual cash operating costs are kept separate from depreciation deductions. These are unlike items, and should not be mixed together. The annual cash operating costs are included in present value computations on an after-tax cost basis.
3. The tax savings provided by the depreciation deductions are included in present value computations in exactly the way illustrated and discussed earlier in the chapter (see Exhibit 14–2).
4. Since The Daily Globe does not consider salvage value when depreciating assets, book value at the end of four years will be zero for both the old and the new presses. Therefore, the entire salvage value in each case will be fully taxable. The net cash inflow to the company is computed by multiplying the salvage value by (1 − Tax rate), as discussed earlier in the chapter.
5. The computation of the cash inflow from the disposal of the old press is somewhat more involved than the other items in the exhibit. Note

---

[1] Section 167(f) of the *Internal Revenue Code* permits a taxpayer to ignore salvage value up to 10 percent of the cost of an asset in computing depreciation deductions. Therefore, if an asset cost $20,000, and had a salvage value of $3,000, only $1,000 of the salvage value would need to be recognized in computing depreciation deductions for tax purposes.

Exhibit 14–4
Comprehensive example of income taxes and capital budgeting: Incremental-cost approach

Item and computations			Year(s) having cash flows	Amount of cash flows	10% factor	Present value of cash flows
Initial investment			Now	$(50,000)	1.000	$(50,000)
Savings in annual cash operating costs		$8,000				
Multiply by 1 − 40%		× 60%				
Net annual savings		$4,800	1–4	4,800	3.170	15,216
Difference in depreciation:						

Year	New press	Old press	Difference	Tax savings at 40%					
1	$20,000	$8,000	$12,000	$4,800	1	4,800	0.909	4,363
2	15,000	8,000	7,000	2,800	2	2,800	0.826	2,312
3	10,000	8,000	2,000	800	3	800	0.751	600
4	5,000	8,000	(3,000)	(1,200)	4	(1,200)	0.683	(820)

Item and computations		Year(s) having cash flows	Amount of cash flows	10% factor	Present value of cash flows
Difference in salvage value:					
Salvage of the new press	$5,000				
Salvage of the old press	3,000				
	$2,000				
Multiply by 1 − 40%	× 60%				
Net cash inflow	$1,200	4	1,200	0.683	820
Disposal value now of the old press (see computations in Exhibit 14–3)		Now ...	27,800	1.000	27,800
Overhaul avoided in two years on the old press	$8,000				
Multiply by 1 − 40%	× 60%				
Net cash inflow	$4,800	2	4,800	0.826	3,964
Net present value in favor of purchasing the new press					$ 4,255

Note: The figures in this exhibit are derived from the *differences* between the two alternatives given in Exhibit 14–3.

that *two* cash inflows are connected with the disposal of the old press. The first is a $25,000 cash inflow in the form of the sale price. The second is a cash inflow of $2,800 resulting from the tax shield provided by the loss sustained on the sale. This tax shield functions in the same way as the tax shield provided by depreciation deductions. That is, the loss on disposal of the old press (the difference between the sale price of $25,000 and the book value of $32,000) is fully deductible from income in the year the loss is sustained. This loss shields income from taxation, thereby causing a reduction in the income taxes that otherwise would be payable. The tax savings resulting from the loss tax shield are computed by multiplying the loss by the tax rate (the same procedure as for depreciation deductions).

6. The overhaul of the old press is treated the same as any other cash expenditure, and included in the analysis on an after-tax cost basis.

7. Generally, any gains on sales of depreciable assets used in a business are taxed as ordinary income, just as losses are deductible as ordinary losses. Only under very narrow circumstances can such gains ever be taxed as capital gains, even in part. The tax laws in this matter are very complex, and expert tax advice should be sought if doubt exists as to the proper classification of a gain.

Finally, two points should be noted on an *overall* basis in both Exhibits 14–3 and 14–4. First, notice that all cash flows involving tax-deductible costs and taxable revenues have been placed on an after-tax basis, by multiplying the cash flow in each case by one minus the tax rate (1 — 40 percent). Second, notice that the depreciation deductions and loss deductions have been multiplied *by the tax rate itself* (40 percent) to determine the tax savings (cash inflow) resulting from the tax shield. *These two points should be studied with great care, until both are thoroughly understood.*

PREFERENCE DECISIONS—THE RANKING OF INVESTMENT PROJECTS

In the preceding chapter we indicated that there are two types of decisions to make relative to investment opportunities. These two types of decisions are screening decisions and preference decisions, respectively. Screening decisions have to do with whether or not some proposed investment is acceptable to a firm. We discussed ways of making screening decisions in the preceding chapter, where we studied the use of the cost of capital as a screening tool. Screening decisions are very important, in that many investment proposals come to the attention of management, and those that are not worthwhile must be screened out.

Preference decisions come *after* screening decisions, and attempt to answer the following question: "How do the remaining investment proposals, all of which have been screened and provide an acceptable rate of return, rank in terms of preference? That is, which one(s) would be *best* for the firm to accept?'' Preference decisions are much more difficult to make than screening decisions. The reason is that investment funds are usually limited, and this often requires that some (perhaps many) otherwise very profitable investment opportunities be foregone.

Preference decisions are sometimes called *ranking* decisions, or *rationing* decisions, because they attempt to ration limited investment funds among many competing investment opportunities. The choice may be simply between two competing alternatives, or many alternatives may be involved, which must be ranked according to their overall desirability. Either the time-adjusted rate of return method or the net present value method can be used in making preference decisions.

Time-adjusted rate of return method

When using the time-adjusted rate of return method to rank competing investment projects, the preference rule is: *The higher the time-adjusted rate of return, the more desirable the project.* If one investment project promises a time-adjusted rate of return of 18 percent, then it is preferable over another project which promises a time-adjusted rate of return of only 15 percent.

Ranking projects according to time-adjusted rate of return is widely used as a means of making preference decisions. The reasons are probably twofold. First, no additional computations are needed beyond those already performed in making the initial screening decisions. The rates of return themselves are used to rank acceptable projects. And second, the ranking data are easily understood by management. Rates of return are very similar to interest rates, which the manager works with every day.

Net present value method

If the net present value method is being used to rank competing investment projects, the net present value of one project cannot be compared directly to the net present value of another project, unless the investments in the projects are of equal size. For example, assume that a company is considering two competing investments, as shown below:

	Investment A	Investment B
Investment required	$50,000	$5,000
Present value of cash inflows	51,000	6,000
Net present value	$ 1,000	$1,000

Each project has a net present value of $1,000, but the projects are not equally desirable. A project requiring an investment of only $5,000, that produces cash inflows with a present value of $6,000, is much more desirable than a project requiring an investment of $50,000 that is capable of producing cash inflows with a present value of only $51,000. In order to compare the two projects on a valid basis, it is necessary in each case to divide the present value of the cash inflows by the investment required. The ratio which this computation yields is called the *profitability index*. The profitability indexes for the two investments above would be:

	Investment A	Investment B
Present value of cash inflows	$51,000 *(a)*	$6,000 *(a)*
Investment required.	$50,000 *(b)*	$5,000 *(b)*
Profitability index *(a) ÷ (b)*	1.02	1.20

The preference rule to follow when using the profitability index to rank competing investment projects is: *The higher the profitability index, the more desirable the project.* Applying this rule to the two investments above, Investment B should be chosen over Investment A.

In computing the investment in a project, the cash outlays should be reduced by any salvage recovered from sale of old equipment being re-placed. Investment in a project also includes any working capital that the project may require, as explained in the preceding chapter.

Comparing the preference rules

The profitability index is conceptually superior to the time-adjusted rate of return as a method of making preference decisions. This is because the profitability index will always give the correct signal as to the relative desirability of alternatives, even if the alternatives have different lives and different patterns of earnings. By contrast, if lives are unequal, the time-adjusted rate of return method can lead the manager to make incorrect decisions.

Assume the following situation:

Parker Company is considering two investment proposals, only one of which can be accepted. Project A requires an investment of $5,000, and will provide a single cash inflow of $6,000 in one year. Therefore, it promises a time-adjusted rate of return of 20 percent. Project B also requires an investment of $5,000. It will provide cash inflows of $1,360 each year for six years. Its time-adjusted rate of return is 16 percent. Which project should be accepted?

Although Project A promises a time-adjusted rate of return of 20 percent as compared to only 16 percent for Project B, Project A is not necessarily preferable over Project B. It is preferable *only* if the funds released at the end of the year under Project A can be reinvested at a high rate of return in some *other* project for the five remaining years. Otherwise, Project B, which promises a return of 16 percent over the *entire* six years, is more desirable.

Let us assume that the company in the example above has a cost of capital of 12 percent. The profitability index approach to ranking competing investment projects would rank the two proposals as follows:

	Project A	Project B
Present value of cash inflows:		
$6,000 received at the end of one year at 12 percent (factor of 0.893)	$5,358 *(a)*	
$1,360 received at the end of each year for six years at 12 percent (factor of 4.111)		$5,591 *(a)*
Investment required	$5,000 *(b)*	$5,000 *(b)*
Profitability Index *(a)* ÷ *(b)*	1.07	1.12

The profitability index indicates that Project B is more desirable than Project A. This is in fact the case if the funds released from Project A at the end of one year can be reinvested at only 12 percent (the cost of capital). Although the computations will not be shown here, in order for Project A to be more desirable than Project B, the funds released from Project A would have to be reinvested at a rate of return *greater* than 14 percent for the remaining five years.

OTHER APPROACHES TO CAPITAL BUDGETING DECISIONS

The discounted cash flow methods of making capital budgeting decisions are relatively new. They were first introduced on a widespread basis in the 1950s, although their appearance in business literature predates this period by many years. Discounted cash flow methods have gained widespread acceptance as accurate and dependable decision-making tools. Other methods of making capital budgeting decisions are also available, however, and are preferred by some managers.

The payback method

The payback method centers around a span of time known as the *payback period*. The payback period can be defined as the length of time that it takes for an investment project to recoup its own initial cost out of the cash receipts it generates. In business jargon, this period is sometimes spoken of as "the time that it takes for an investment to pay for itself." The basic premise of the payback method is that the more quickly the cost of an investment can be recovered, the more desirable is the investment.

The payback period is expressed in years. The formula used in computing the payback period is:

$$\text{Payback period} = \frac{\text{Investment required}}{\text{Net annual cash inflows}^*} \qquad (4)$$

* If new equipment is replacing old equipment, this becomes *Incremental* net annual cash inflow.

Notice from the formula that depreciation is ignored in computing the payback period. To illustrate the mechanics involved in payback computations, assume the following data:

The Concord Company needs a new milling machine. The company is considering two machines, Machine A and Machine B. Machine A costs $15,000 and will reduce annual operating costs by $5,000. Machine B costs only $12,000, but will also reduce annual operating costs by $5,000.

Required:
Which machine should be purchased? Make your calculations by the payback method.

$$\text{Machine A payback period} = \frac{\$15,000}{\$5,000} = 3.0 \text{ years}$$

$$\text{Machine B payback period} = \frac{\$12,000}{\$5,000} = 2.4 \text{ years}$$

According to the payback calculations, the Concord Company should purchase Machine B, since it has a shorter payback period than Machine A.

Evaluation of the payback method

The payback method is not a measure of profitability. It is a measure of how quickly investment dollars can be recouped. This is a major defect in the approach, since a shorter payback period is not always an accurate guide as to whether one investment is more desirable than another. To illustrate this point, consider again the two machines used in the example above. Since Machine B has a shorter payback period than Machine A, it *appears* that Machine B is more desirable than Machine A. But if we add one more piece of data, this illusion quickly disappears. Machine A has a projected ten-year life, and Machine B has a projected five-year life. It would take two purchases of Machine B to provide the same length of service as a single purchase of Machine A. Under these circumstances, Machine A would be a much better investment than Machine B, even though Machine B has a shorter payback period. Unfortunately, the payback method has no inherent mechanism for highlighting differences in useful life between investments for the decision maker. Such differences can be very subtle, and relying on payback alone can cause the manager to make incorrect decisions.

A further criticism of the payback method can be found in the fact that it does not consider the time value of money. A cash inflow to be received several years in the future is weighed equally with a cash inflow to be received right now. To illustrate, assume that for an investment of $8,000 you can purchase either of the two following streams of cash inflows:

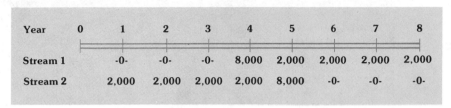

Year	0	1	2	3	4	5	6	7	8
Stream 1		-0-	-0-	-0-	8,000	2,000	2,000	2,000	2,000
Stream 2		2,000	2,000	2,000	2,000	8,000	-0-	-0-	-0-

Which stream of cash inflows would you prefer to receive in return for your $8,000 investment? Each stream has a payback period of 4.0 years. Therefore, if payback alone was relied on in making the decision, you would be forced to say that the streams are equally desirable. However, from point of view of the time value of money, Stream 2 is much more desirable than Stream 1.

On the other hand, under certain conditions, the payback method can be very useful to the manager. For one thing, it can help the manager to identify the "ball park" in weeding out investment proposals. That is, it can be used as a screening tool to help answer the question, "Should I consider this proposal further?" If a proposal doesn't provide at least some minimum payback period, then there might be no need to consider it further. In addition, the payback period is often of great importance to new firms that are "cash poor." When a firm is cash poor, a project with a short payback period, but low rate of return, might be preferred over another project with a high rate of return, but a long payback period. The reason is that the company may simply need a faster return of its cash investment.

Payback and uneven cash flows

When the cash inflows associated with an investment project are erratic or uneven, the simple payback formula which we outlined earlier is no longer usable, and the computations involved in deriving the payback period can be fairly complex. Consider the following data:

Year	Investment	Cash inflow
1	$4,000	$1,000
2		-0-
3		2,000
4	2,000	1,000
5		500
6		3,000
7		2,000
8		2,000

Exhibit 14–5
Payback and uneven cash flows

Year	(1) Beginning unrecovered investment	(2) Additional investment	(3) Total unrecovered investment (1) + (2)	(4) Cash inflow	(5) Ending unrecovered investment (3) – (4)
1	$4,000		$4,000	$1,000	$3,000
2	3,000		3,000	–0–	3,000
3	3,000		3,000	2,000	1,000
4	1,000	$2,000	3,000	1,000	2,000
5	2,000		2,000	500	1,500
6	1,500		1,500	3,000	–0–
7	–0–		–0–	2,000	–0–
8	–0–		–0–	2,000	–0–

What is the payback period on this investment? The answer is 5.5 years, but to obtain this figure it is necessary to balance off the cash inflows against the investment outflows on a *year-by-year* basis. The steps involved in this process are shown in Exhibit 14–5. By the middle of the sixth year, sufficient cash inflows will have been realized to recover the entire investment of $6,000 ($4,000 + $2,000).

The simple rate of return method

The simple rate of return method is another capital budgeting technique that does not involve discounted cash flows. The method is also known as the financial statement method, the unadjusted rate of return method, and the book value method. It derives its popularity primarily from the fact that it is supposed to parallel conventional financial statements in its handling of investment data.

Unlike other capital budgeting methods we have discussed, the simple rate of return method does not focus on cash flows. Rather, it focuses on accounting net income. The approach is to estimate the revenues that will be generated by a proposed investment, and then to deduct from these revenues all projected operating expenses associated with it, *including depreciation.* This net income figure is then related to the required investment in the project, as shown in the following formula:

$$\text{Simple rate of return} = \frac{[\text{Incremental revenue}] - \left[\begin{array}{c}\text{Operating expenses} \\ \text{(including depreciation)}\end{array}\right]}{\text{Initial investment}} \qquad (5)$$

Or, if the project is a cost reduction project, the formula becomes:

$$\text{Simple rate of return} = \frac{\text{Reduction in costs} - \text{Depreciation}}{\text{Initial investment}}$$

EXAMPLE

Brigham Tea, Inc., is a processor of a nontannic acid tea product. The company is contemplating the purchase of equipment for an additional processing line. The additional processing line would increase revenues by $10,000 per year. Cash operating expenses would be $4,000 per year. The equipment would cost $24,000 and have a 12-year life. No salvage value is projected.

Required:

1. Compute the simple rate of return.
2. Compute the time-adjusted rate of return, and compare it to the simple rate of return.

By applying the formula for the simple rate of return found in Equation (5), we can compute the simple rate of return to be 16.7 percent:

Simple rate of return =

$$\frac{\left[\begin{array}{c}\$10,000 \text{ incremental} \\ \text{revenues}\end{array}\right] - \left[\begin{array}{c}\$4,000 \text{ cash operating expenses} \\ + \$2,000 \text{ depreciation}\end{array}\right]}{\$24,000 \text{ initial investment}}$$

Simple rate of return = 16.7 percent

This rate, however, is far below the time-adjusted rate of return of approximately 23 percent:

Time-adjusted rate of return $= \dfrac{\$24,000}{\$6,000^*} =$ Factor of 4.000

Time-adjusted rate of return $=$ Approximately 23 percent from Table 13A-2, scanning across the 12-year line.

* $10,000 increased revenues, minus $4,000 cash expenses.

Criticisms of the simple rate of return

The most damaging criticism of the simple rate of return method is that it does not consider the time value of money. A dollar received ten years from now is viewed as being just as valuable as a dollar received today. Thus, the manager can be misled in attempting to choose between competing courses of action if the alternatives being considered have different cash flow patterns. Ignoring the time value of money tends to create a bias in favor of those investment projects which yield the bulk of their cash flows in later years.

A further criticism of the simple rate of return method is that it often proves to be misleading in its basic approach. The method is supposed to parallel conventional financial statements in its handling of data. Yet studies show that this parallel is rarely present.[2] The problem is that conventional accounting practice tends to write costs off to expense very quickly.

---

[2] See *Research Report 35, Return on Capital as a Guide to Managerial Decisions,* National Association of Accountants (December 1959), p. 64.

As a result, the net income and asset structure actually reflected on financial statements may differ substantially from comparable items in rate of return computations, wherein costs tend to be expensed less quickly. This disparity in handling of data is especially pronounced in those situations where rate of return computations are carried out by nonaccounting personnel.

The choice of an investment base

In our examples, we have defined the investment base for simple rate of return computations to be the entire initial investment in the project under consideration [see the formula in (5)]. Actual practice varies between using the entire initial investment, as we have done, and using only the *average* investment over the life of a project. As a practical matter, which approach one chooses to follow is unimportant. If the average investment is used, rather than the entire initial investment, then the resulting rate of return will be approximately doubled.

SUMMARY

Unless a company is a tax-exempt organization, such as a school or a governmental unit, income taxes should be considered in making capital budgeting computations. When income taxes are a factor in a company, cash expenditures must be placed on an after-tax basis by multiplying the expenditure by one minus the tax rate. Only the after-tax amount is used in determining the desirability of an investment proposal. Similarly, taxable cash inflows must be placed on an after-tax basis by multiplying the cash inflow by one minus the tax rate.

Although depreciation deductions do not involve a present outflow of cash in a company, they are valid expenses for tax purposes, and as such affect income tax payments. Depreciation deductions shield income from taxation, resulting in decreased taxes being paid. This shielding of income from taxation is commonly called a depreciation tax shield. The savings in income taxes arising from the depreciation tax shield are computed by multiplying the depreciation deduction by the tax rate itself. Since accelerated methods of depreciation provide the bulk of their tax shield early in the life of an asset, they are superior to the straight-line method of depreciation, from a present value of tax savings point of view.

Preference decisions relate to ranking two or more investment proposals according to their relative desirability. This ranking can be performed using either the time-adjusted rate of return or the profitability index. The profitability index, which is the ratio of the present value of a proposal's cash inflows to the investment required, is generally regarded as the best way of making preference decisions when discounted cash flow is being used.

Instead of using discounted cash flow, some companies prefer to use either payback or the simple rate of return in evaluating investment proposals. Payback is determined by dividing a project's cost by the annual cash inflows which it will generate, in order to find how quickly the original investment can be recovered. The simple rate of return is determined by dividing a project's accounting net income either by the initial investment in the project or by the average investment over the life of the project. Both payback and the simple rate of return can be useful to the manager, so long as they are used with a full understanding of their limitations.

KEY TERMS FOR REVIEW

After-tax cost   **Profitability index**
After-tax benefit   **Payback method**
Depreciation tax shield   **Simple rate of return method**

QUESTIONS

14–1.   Why is it important to understand capital budgeting on a before-tax basis, as well as on an after-tax basis?

14–2.   What is meant by after-tax cost, and how is the concept used in capital budgeting decisions?

14–3.   What is a depreciation tax shield, and how does it affect capital budgeting decisions?

14–4.   The three most widely used depreciation methods are straight-line, sum-of-the-years'-digits, and double-declining balance. Explain why a company might use more than one of these methods to depreciate the same asset.

14–5.   Ludlow Company is considering the introduction of a new product line. Would an increase in the income tax rate tend to make the new investment more or less attractive? Explain.

14–6.   Why are accelerated methods of depreciation superior to the straight-line method of depreciation, from an income tax point of view?

14–7.   Assume that an old piece of equipment is sold at a loss. From a capital budgeting point of view, what two cash inflows will be associated with the sale?

14–8.   Assume that a new piece of equipment costs $30,000. The tax rate is 40 percent. Should the new piece of equipment be shown in the capital budgeting analysis as a cash outflow of $30,000 or as a cash outflow of $18,000 ($30,000 times 1 − 40%)? Explain.

14–9.   Assume that a company has cash operating expenses of $15,000 and depreciation expense of $10,000. Can these two items be added together and treated as one in a capital budgeting analysis, or should they be kept separate? Explain.

14–10.   What is meant by the term "payback period?" How is the payback period determined?

14–11.   Distinguish between capital budgeting screening decisions, and capital budgeting preference decisions. Why are preference decisions more difficult to make than screening decisions?

14–12. What is the preference rule for ranking investment projects under time-adjusted rate of return?

14–13. What is the preference rule for ranking investment projects under the net present value method?

14–14. Can an investment with a profitability index of less than 1.00 be an acceptable investment? Explain.

14–15. What is the major criticism of the payback and simple rate of return methods of making capital budgeting decisions?

EXERCISES

E14–1. *a.* Reed Company now spends $50,000 each year on advertising. The company is contemplating increasing its advertising to $70,000 each year. What would be the after-tax cost of the increased advertising, if the company pays taxes of 45 percent on income?

b. Black Company has just purchased a new machine that will increase revenues by $30,000 per year. If the company pays combined income taxes at a 40 percent rate, what will be the annual after-tax cash inflow from revenues provided by the new machine?

c. Fisher Company has just purchased a new computer at a cost of $150,000. The computer has a five-year life, and salvage value is estimated at $10,000. The tax rate is 40 percent. What are the annual cash inflows resulting from the depreciation tax shield? Use straight-line depreciation, and ignore salvage value.

d. Repeat *(c),* this time using sum-of-the-years'-digits depreciation.

E14–2. *a.* Lavery Company has a machine with a book value of $18,000. If the company sells the machine for $12,000 what will be the effect on cash flows, after taxes? Assume a tax rate of 40 percent.

b. The Colver Company has just sold a piece of equipment for $8,000. The equipment had a book value of $5,000. What will be the effect of this sale on cash flows, after taxes? Assume a tax rate of 40 percent.

E14–3. Andy's Auto Rentals has just purchased a piece of car washing equipment at a cost of $30,000. Although the equipment will have a $2,000 salvage value at the end of its five-year life, salvage value is not considered in computing depreciation for tax purposes. The company uses sum-of-the-years'-digits depreciation, and the tax rate is 40 percent. Assume a discount rate of 8 percent, after taxes.

a. Compute the present value of the cash flows resulting from the depreciation tax shield each year.

b. Assume that the equipment is sold for its salvage value at the end of five years. What is the present value of the cash flows resulting from the sale, after taxes?

E14–4. The Dorsey Publishing Company is investigating the purchase of a new collating machine to replace a presently owned hand-operated collating machine. The new machine would cost $24,000, and have a ten-year life. Its scrap value in ten years would be $1,000.

If the new machine is purchased, the old machine will be kept and used on a standby basis. The operator of the old machine is paid a salary of $6,000 per year. If the new machine is purchased, the operator will be discharged, but given severance pay of $500. The severance pay will be paid and deducted for tax purposes in the first year of operation of the new machine. The company uses straight-line depreciation, and ignores salvage value in computing depreciation deductions.

Required:

Compute the net present value of the new collating machine, assuming the company requires an after-tax return of 10 percent on investments of this type. Use a tax rate of 40 percent.

E14–5.   A company is considering two investment alternatives. Relevant cost and revenue information on the two alternatives is given below:

	Alternative A	Alternative B
Investment in machinery and equipment...........	$20,000	—
Investment in working capital....................	—	$20,000
Net annual revenues or cost savings	5,000	5,000
Life of the project	8 years	8 years

At the end of eight years the equipment will have no salvage value. Straight-line depreciation will be used. At the end of eight years the working capital can be released for investment elsewhere. The company requires an after-tax return of 8 percent on all investments. The tax rate is 40 percent.

Required:

1.   Compute the net present value of each investment alternative.
2.   Compute the profitability index for each investment. Which alternative should be accepted? Rejected?

E14–6.   Nick's Novelties, Inc., is considering the purchase of a new type of pinball machine to place in amusement houses. The machines would cost $4,000 each, have a six-year useful life, and have an ultimate salvage value of $400 each. The company estimates that average annual revenues and expenses per machine would be:

Revenues from customers		$2,000
Operating expenses:		
Maintenance, taxes, etc.	$400	
Depreciation	600	
Commission to amusement house	500	1,500
Net income		$ 500

Required:

1.   Assume that Nick's Novelties, Inc., will not purchase new equipment unless it promises a payback period of less than 3.5 years. Would you recommend purchase of the pinball machines? Ignore taxes.

2. Assume that Nick's Novelties, Inc., will not purchase new equipment unless it promises a simple rate of return of at least 12 percent. Would you recommend purchase of the pinball machines? (Compute investment at initial cost.) Ignore taxes.

E14–7. The following data relate to a piece of equipment just purchased by the Darley Company:

Purchase cost $23,375
Annual cost savings that will be provided by
   the equipment......................... 5,000
Life of the equipment .... 15 years
Cost of capital of the company 16%

Required:

Compute the following (round computations to the nearest dollar):
a. The payback period. Ignore taxes.
b. The simple rate of return. Ignore taxes.

E14–8. Information on four investment proposals is given below.

Proposal number	Investment required	Present value of cash inflows	Net present value	Life (years)
1............	$ 8,000	$ 9,800	$1,800	5
2............	11,000	10,200	(800)	7
3............	7,000	9,100	2,100	6
4............	14,000	16,200	2,200	6

Required:

Rank the proposals in terms of preference.

E14–9. Ferre Company is contemplating the purchase of a new milling machine to increase output and reduce labor costs. Relevant data on the machine now being used and on the proposed new machine are given below:

	Present machine	Proposed new machine
Total annual revenues	$100,000	$115,000
Total annual expenses:		
Materials and supplies	$ 30,000	$ 32,000
Maintenance	8,000	15,000
Depreciation	3,000	4,800
Labor	45,000	40,000
Total	$ 86,000	$ 91,800
Net income per year	$ 14,000	$ 23,200

The new machine would have a service life of ten years, after which it could be sold for $2,000. The machine now being used has a book value of $32,000, but it can be sold for only $10,000. The president of the Ferre Company is unenthused about the new machine. She has made the following payback computation:

Cost of the new machine $50,000
Loss on the old machine ($32,000 − $10,000) 22,000
Total investment in the new machine $72,000

Net income promised by the new machine $23,200
Net income provided by the old machine 14,000
Incremental net income from the new machine .... $ 9,200

$$\frac{\$72,000}{\$9,200} = \underline{\underline{7.8 \text{ years}}}$$

The company will not make a purchase of new equipment unless it has a payback period of less than five years. Ignore income taxes.

Required:

1. What errors did the president make in her payback computation?
2. Compute a corrected payback period.

PROBLEMS

P14–10. *Net present value.* The Tyler Transport Company has just purchased a new barge for hauling freight on the Mississippi River. The barge cost $90,000. Other data are given below.

Net annual cash inflow (before taxes) expected
   from use of the new barge $28,000
Salvage value of the barge in 5 years (ignore
   in computing depreciation) 8,000
One-time-only inspection and seaworthiness
   certification cost (expensed in Year 1) 1,000

The company uses sum-of-the-years'-digits depreciation, and desires an after-tax return of 14 percent on all equipment. The tax rate is 40 percent.

Required:

Does the new barge promise at least the minimum desired rate of return? Show computations by the net present value method. Round to the nearest whole dollar.

P14–11. *Various depreciation methods; net present value.* Vitro Company has been offered a four-year contract to produce a key part for a governmental agency. The following costs and revenues would be associated with the contract:

Cost of special equipment $180,000
Working capital needed to
   carry inventories 15,000
Annual revenues under the contract 200,000
Annual out-of-pocket costs
   (excluding taxes) 131,000
Salvage value of the equipment in
   four years 10,000

The company's cost of capital is 12 percent. The tax rate is 40 percent.

Required:

1. Assume that the company uses straight-line depreciation, and ignores salvage value for tax purposes. Use discounted cash flow analysis to determine whether the contract should be accepted.

2. Assume that the company uses sum-of-the-years'-digits depreciation, and ignores salvage value for tax purposes. Use discounted cash flow analysis to determine whether the contract should be accepted. How do you explain the difference in rate of return between (1) and (2)?

P14–12. *Various depreciation methods; Profitability index.* Noble Company is considering two machines, only one of which can be purchased. Cost and other information on the two machines is given below:

	Machine 1	Machine 2
Cost of the machine	$10,000	$15,000
Annual savings in cash operating costs	4,200	5,700
Life of the machine	5 years	5 years
Depreciation method to be used	*	†

* Straight-line.
† Sum-of-years'-digits.

Neither machine will have any salvage value. The tax rate is 40 percent; the cost of capital is 10 percent. Round all figures to the nearest whole dollar.

Required:

1. Compute the net present value of each machine. Based on these data, which machine should be purchased?

2. Compute the profitability index for each machine. Based on the profitability index, which machine should be purchased?

P14–13. *Net present value analysis.* Fran's Travel Service is located in a large western city. The company specializes in recreational travel, and is considering the purchase of a large bus to provide sightseeing tours of the area. A 40-passenger bus can be purchased for $36,750. After six years' use the bus will be traded in on a replacement or sold for $3,500. The costs of operating the bus for a single season are estimated as follows:

Salaries	$ 6,000
Maintenance	1,100
Fuel	9,500
Promotion	3,000
Licenses and taxes	400
Insurance	2,000
Total	$22,000

The travel service estimates that the tours would average two full bus loads a day, for a 150-day season. The cost for a tour would average

$2.50 per person. The management of Fran's Travel Service feels that the investment in the bus would have to yield a return of at least 10 percent, after taxes, to make the venture worthwhile. The company uses sum-of-the-years'-digits depreciation, and ignores salvage value in computing depreciation deductions. The tax rate is 40 percent.

Required:

1. Compute the net cash inflow (before taxes) each season from operating the bus.
2. By use of the net present value method, determine whether the bus should be purchased.

P14–14. *Depreciation methods and rate of return.* John Belmont, manufacturing vice president of Atlantic Industries, has been anxious for some time to purchase a new piece of equipment for use in the plant. The equipment would cost $360,000 and have an eight-year life. It would have a final salvage value of $20,000.

Mr. Belmont has just received an analysis from his staff indicating that the equipment will not provide the 12 percent after-tax rate of return required by the company. In making this analysis, Mr. Belmont's staff estimated that the new equipment would generate net income before taxes of $43,000 per year. Straight-line depreciation of $45,000 per year was deducted in arriving at the $43,000 figure. The company does not consider salvage value in computing depreciation deductions. The tax rate is 40 percent.

The controller of Atlantic Industries has told Mr. Belmont that he should instruct his staff to use sum-of-the-years'-digits depreciation in their analysis. Somewhat irritated by this suggestion, Mr. Belmont replied, "You accountants and your fancy bookkeeping methods! What difference does it make what depreciation method we use—we have the same investment, the same income, and the same total depreciation either way. That equipment just doesn't measure up to our rate of return requirements. How you make the bookkeeping entries for depreciation won't change that fact."

Required:

1. Compute the net present value of the new equipment, using straight-line depreciation.
2. Compute the net present value of the new equipment, using sum-of-the-years'-digits depreciation.
3. Explain to Mr. Belmont how the depreciation method used can affect the rate of return generated by an investment project.

P14–15. *Equipment replacement decision.* The Coral Lake Resort has recently purchased 30 new motorized golf carts for use on its exclusive golf course. The carts cost the resort considerably more than had been planned, and the manager of the resort is now wondering if they will provide the 14 percent after-tax rate of return that the resort's board of directors requires on all equipment purchases. The manager has asked you to make the necessary computations to determine if the 14 percent

rate of return will be realized. You have determined the following information:

1. The total cost of the carts was $40,000. The carts will have a $4,000
    salvage value in ten years.
2. Thirty old golf carts were sold that had a total book value of $8,000.
    The sale price totaled $5,000. Depreciation on the old carts would
    have totaled $800 per year for the next ten years.
3. The board of directors insists that straight-line depreciation be used
    on all equipment. Salvage value is not considered in computing
    depreciation deductions.
4. The 30 new golf carts are expected to generate net income each
    year of $8,000 (before depreciation and income taxes) above what
    the old carts would have generated.
5. The Coral Lake Resort's income tax rate is 40 percent.
6. The 30 new carts will require an overhaul at the end of the sixth
    year, costing a total of $5,000.

Required:

Use discounted cash flow to determine whether the new golf carts will
provide the required 14 percent rate of return. Round to the nearest
whole dollar. Use the incremental-cost approach.

P14–16. *Simple rate of return and payback.* Bostitch Company uses a large
stapling machine in the manufacture of one of its products. The machine
is well built, and could last the company for at least another eight years.
Bostitch Company has learned that a smaller but equally productive
stapling machine is now on the market that could provide some savings
in annual operating costs over the present machine. Comparative cost
data on the two machines are given below:

	Old machine	New machine
Original cost	$18,000	$16,500
Remaining useful life	8 years	8 years
Salvage value in 8 years	–0–	500
Annual depreciation	1,500	2,000
Annual operating costs excluding depreciation	9,000	5,600

The company deducts salvage value in computing depreciation charges.
If the new machine is purchased, the old machine will be scrapped at
a negligible scrap value.

Required:

1. Compute the simple rate of return promised by the new machine.
    If the company requires a minimum return of 10 percent on initial
    investment, would you recommend purchase? Ignore taxes.
2. Assume that a used equipment dealer will give the company $5,000
    cash for the old stapling machine. Under these conditions, what
    would you say the "cost" would be of the new machine? Compute
    the simple rate of return. Ignore taxes.

3. Refer to the original data. Compute the payback period for the new machine. If the company requires a payback period of no more than five years, would you recommend purchase of the new machine? Ignore taxes.

4. If the company can get $5,000 cash for the old stapling machine, as stated in (2) above, what would be the payback period for the new machine? Ignore taxes.

P14–17. *Equipment replacement decision.* A medium-sized manufacturing company has been concerned for some time about the cost of its data processing operations. The company now has a manual system in operation, but is considering the purchase of a small computer in order to reduce data processing costs. The following information is available:

1. The company's present manual system involves the following direct cash expenses each month:

Salaries	$6,000
Forms and supplies	500
Payroll taxes and other . . .	2,000
Total	$8,500

2. The equipment associated with the manual system is fully depreciated, and has zero salvage value.

3. Several of the employees associated with the manual system would have to be discharged. They would be given severance pay of $10,000, which would be paid and fully tax deductible in the first year of operation of the new computer.

4. The new computer would cost $90,000, and have a 10 percent salvage value in three years.

5. The company uses sum-of-the-years'-digits depreciation, and considers salvage value fully in computing depreciation deductions. (Thus, the book value of the computer would be $9,000 at the time of sale.)

6. The annual costs of operating the new computer would be:

Salaries	$45,000
Forms and supplies	7,100
Payroll taxes and other	3,700
Total	$55,800

7. The company's after-tax cost of capital is 10 percent. Assume a tax rate of 40 percent.

Required:

1. Compute the annual savings in cash expenses that will be provided by the new computer.

2. Decide whether the new computer should be purchased, using discounted cash flow. Use the incremental-cost approach; round computations to the nearest whole dollar.

P14–18. *Payback; Simple rate of return; Discounted cash flow; Profitability index.* Sal's Soda Shop is investigating the purchase of a new soft ice cream dispensing machine that is capable of dispensing several different flavors at one time. The machine costs $10,000. It will have an eight-year life, and a $2,000 scrap value. The following annual operating results are expected if the machine is purchased:

Increase in annual revenues		$8,000
Increase in expenses:		
Operating expenses	$5,900	
Depreciation	1,000	6,900
Net income before taxes		$1,100
Income taxes (30%)		330
Net income		$ 770

Sal's Soda Shop expects an after-tax return of 10 percent on all equipment purchases. Straight-line depreciation will be used. Notice that salvage value is considered in computing depreciation deductions (therefore, the book value of the machine will be $2,000 at the time of sale).

Required:

1. What is the after-tax payback period on the new machine?
2. What is the after-tax simple rate of return on the new machine? Is it an acceptable investment?
3. Using discounted cash flow, determine whether the machine will provide the minimum 10 percent return required by Sal's Soda Shop. Round computations to the nearest whole dollar.
4. Compute the new machine's profitability index.

P14–19. *Payback; Simple rate of return; Net present value; Profitability index.* Essex Company is considering the replacement of an old lathe with a newer model in order to save costs. The following analysis has been made:

Annual cash operating costs—old lathe	$30,000
Annual cash operating costs—new lathe	24,000
Annual cash savings	$ 6,000
Annual depreciation—new lathe	4,000
	$ 2,000
Income tax (40%)	800
Annual increase in net income	$ 1,200

The new lathe would cost $20,000 and have a 10 percent salvage value. Salvage value has been ignored in computing depreciation deductions.

Required:

1. Assume that the company will not purchase new equipment unless it has an after-tax payback period of three years or less. Should the new lathe be purchased?
2. Compute the after-tax simple rate of return promised by the new lathe. If the company has a 10 percent cost of capital, is the new lathe acceptable?
3. Assume again that the cost of capital is 10 percent. Using discounted

cash flow, determine whether the new lathe should be purchased. (The old lathe is fully depreciated.)

4. Compute the new lathe's profitability index.

P14–20. *Preference ranking of investments proposals.* Sperry Company is investigating five different investment opportunities. The company's cost of capital is 10 percent. Information on the five investment proposals under study is given below:

Proposal number	Invest- ment required	Present value of the cash inflows, at a 10% rate	Net present value	Life of the project (years)	Time- adjusted rate of return (percent)
1	$24,000	$28,360	$4,360	6	16
2	18,000	21,669	3,669	12	14
3	15,000	18,674	3,674	6	18
4	18,000	20,918	2,918	3	19
5	17,000	16,013	(987)	6	8

Required:

1. Compute the profitability index for each investment proposal.
2. Rank the five proposals according to preference, in terms of:
   a. Time-adjusted rate of return.
   b. Profitability index.
3. Which ranking do you prefer? Why?

P14–21. *Depletion; Uneven cash flows.* The Augusta Mining Company has an opportunity to purchase the mineral rights on a piece of land for $100,000. Other information relevant to this investment opportunity is given below:

1. The land contains 50,000 tons of mineral deposits. If the rights to these mineral deposits are purchased, extraction of the deposits will proceed as follows:

Year	Tons mined and sold
1	4,000
2	8,000
3	20,000
4	10,000
5	8,000

2. If the mineral rights are purchased, the $100,000 cost would be depleted on a basis of the number of tons mined and sold each year.
3. The selling price of the mineral would be $20 per ton. This price is expected to remain unchanged for quite some time.
4. Equipment costing $50,000 would have to be purchased to mine the mineral deposits. The equipment would have only nominal residual value when extraction was complete. The company uses straight-line depreciation.

5. Annual out-of-pocket costs for salaries, insurance, utilities, and so on, would total $30,000.
6. Variable out-of-pocket costs for supplies, labor, overhead, selling expense, and so on, would total $12 per ton.
7. After all mineral extraction was completed, the company would have to spend $60,000 to restore the land to its natural condition.
8. The Augusta Mining Company's after-tax cost of capital is 12 percent. The company's tax rate is 45 percent.

Required:

Determine whether the company should purchase the mineral rights and proceed with mining, as outlined above. Use discounted cash flow in your analysis. Round to the nearest whole dollar.

P14–22. *Comparison of the total-cost and incremental-cost approaches.*   Cache Dairies, Inc., is considering the purchase of a new milk separator. The separator would cost $120,000. After five years' use the separator could be sold for $12,000, but this salvage value would not be considered in computing annual depreciation deductions. The new separator would provide considerable savings in annual operating costs, as shown below:

	Old separator	New separator
Salaries	$34,000	$24,000
Supplies...........................	6,000	5,000
Utilities	8,000	6,000
Cleaning and maintenance	22,000	5,000
Total annual operating costs	$70,000	$40,000

If the new separator is purchased, the old separator will be sold for its present salvage value of $30,000. If the new separator is not purchased, the old separator will be used for five more years, then scrapped for a $2,000 salvage. The old separator's present book value is $50,000. The old separator is being depreciated by the straight-line method, with salvage value ignored for depreciation purposes. The new separator would be depreciated by the sum-of-the-years'-digits method. If kept and used, the old separator would require repairs costing $40,000 in one more year. These repairs would be expensed in full. Cache Dairies, Inc.'s after-tax cost of capital is 18 percent. The tax rate is 40 percent.

Required:

1. Determine whether the new milk separator should be purchased, using the total-cost approach to discounted cash flow. Round to the nearest whole dollar.
2. Repeat (1), this time using the incremental approach to discounted cash flow.

P14–23. *Comparison of the total-cost and incremental-cost approaches.*   The Queensway Touring Lines is considering replacing the boiler system in one of its smaller touring boats. As a new management trainee with the company, you have been given responsibility for making the decision.

You have gathered the following information relative to the boiler system now in operation on the boat, and relative to the proposed new boiler system:

	Old boiler system	*New boiler system*
Cost of the system new	$11,000	$ 9,450
Accumulated depreciation to date	5,000	—
Remaining life	6 years	6 years
Salvage value now	4,000	—
Salvage value in six years	500	900
Annual operating costs, excluding		
depreciation	24,000	22,000
Repairs needed in three years	2,000	—
Depreciation method used	*	†

* Straight-line.
† Sum-of-years'-digits.

The Queensway Touring Lines does not consider salvage value in computing depreciation deductions. The change in boiler systems would have no effect on total annual revenues from the touring boat. If the new boiler system is installed, the old system will be sold for its current salvage value. The company requires an after-tax return of 8 percent on all investments. Assume a tax rate of 40 percent.

Required:

1. Using the total-cost approach to discounted cash flow, determine whether the new boiler system should be installed on the touring boat. Round to the nearest whole dollar.
2. Repeat (1), this time using the incremental-cost approach to discounted cash flow.

P14–24. *A comparison of investment alternatives.* Paul Corso is a professor in a large western university. Professor Corso has just received an inheritance of $100,000 from his father's estate, and he is wondering how he can best invest the sum between now and the time of his retirement at age 65. Professor Corso's position with the university pays him a salary of $25,000 per year. This salary is expected to remain unchanged if Professor Corso stays with the university until his retirement in 12 years. Professor Corso is considering two alternatives for investing his inheritance.

Alternative 1. The first alternative would be to purchase $100,000 in municipal bonds, which would mature in 12 years. The bonds would bear interest at 8 percent, which would be tax-free and paid semiannually. (In discounting a cash flow that occurs semiannually, the procedure is to halve the interest rate and double the periods.) This alternative would permit Professor Corso to stay with the university.

Alternative 2. The second alternative would be to purchase a business of his own, which he would operate. Professor Corso could purchase a well-established retail store for $100,000. The following information relates to this alternative:

1. Of the purchase price, $48,000 would be for fixtures and other depreciable items. The remainder would be for inventory and other working capital items.
2. The store building would be leased. At the end of 12 years, if Professor Corso could not find someone to buy out the business, it would be necessary to pay $2,000 to the owner of the building in order to break the lease.
3. Straight-line depreciation would be used on the depreciable items. These items would have negligible residual value in 12 years.
4. Sales would average $112,000 per year. Out-of-pocket costs, including rent on the building, would total $76,500 per year (exclusive of income taxes).
5. Since Professor Corso would operate the store himself, it would be necessary for him to leave the university if this alternative is selected. Professor Corso's tax rate is 30 percent.

Required:

Advise Professor Corso as to which alternative he should select. Use discounted cash flow in your analysis. Round to the nearest whole dollar. Use an after-tax rate of return of 8 percent, and the total-cost approach.

P14–25. *Fast-food operation; Effects of write-offs.* R. Haskins and C. Bobbins have formed a corporation to franchise a quick food system for shopping malls. They have just completed experiments with the prototype machine which will serve as the basis for the operation, and they feel certain that the food it prepares will be well received by the public. However, because the system is new and untried publicly, they have decided to conduct a pilot operation in a nearby mall. If it proves successful, they will aggressively market franchises for the system throughout the nation.

The income statements below represent their best estimates of income from the mall operation for the next four years. At the end of the four-year period they intend to sell the pilot operation and concentrate on the sale and supervision of franchises for the system. Based on the income stream projected, they believe the pilot operation can be sold for $120,000; the income tax liability from the sale will be $20,000.

		Year ending December 31		
	19x5	*19x6*	*19x7*	*19x8*
Sales	$140,000	$160,000	$190,000	$220,000
Less: Cost of goods sold	$ 70,000	$ 80,000	$ 95,000	$110,000
Wages....................	14,000	20,000	30,000	40,000
Supplies	3,000	3,300	3,400	4,200
Personal property taxes	1,000	1,200	1,600	1,800
Annual rental charge	12,000	12,000	12,000	12,000
Depreciation	10,000	10,000	10,000	10,000
Development costs	20,000	20,000	20,000	20,000
Total expenses	$130,000	$146,500	$172,000	$198,000
Net income before taxes	$ 10,000	$ 13,500	$ 18,000	$ 22,000
Income taxes at 40%	4,000	5,400	7,200	8,800
Net income after taxes	$ 6,000	$ 8,100	$ 10,800	$ 13,200

The following additional information is available on the pilot operation:

a. The shopping mall requires tenants to sign a ten-year lease. Three years' rental is payable at the beginning of the lease period with annual payments at the end of each of the next seven years (starting with the first year). The advance payment will apply to the last three years under the lease.

b. The cost of building an operational machine for the pilot operation will be $110,000. The machine will have a salvage value of $10,000 at the end of its ten-year life. Straight-line depreciation will be used for statement purposes, and sum-of-the-years'-digits depreciation will be used for tax purposes. Salvage value will be ignored for tax purposes.

c. An earlier prototype machine cost $200,000 to develop and build in 19x3. It is not usable for commercial purposes. However, since it was the early basis for the system it is being amortized against revenues at $20,000 per year. The same amount will be deducted for tax purposes.

Required:

1. Compute the before-tax net cash inflow from operations for each year.
2. Haskins and Bobbins want to employ discounted cash flow techniques to determine whether the pilot mall operation is a sound investment. Compute the net present value of the contemplated investment, using a minimum desired rate of return of 16 percent after taxes.

(CMA, adapted)

PART THREE

SELECTED TOPICS FOR FURTHER STUDY

Chapter 15

Service department cost allocations

As stated in Chapter 1, most organizations have one or more service departments which carry on critical auxiliary services for the entire organization. In this chapter we look more closely at service departments, and consider how their costs are handled for product costing and for other purposes.

THE NEED FOR COST ALLOCATION

Departments within a firm can be divided into two broad classes: (1) producing departments, and (2) service departments. Producing departments would include those departments where work is done directly on the product of the organization such as milling, assembly, and painting. Service departments do not engage directly in production. Rather, they provide services or assistance that facilitate the activities of the producing departments. Examples of such services would include internal auditing, cafeteria, personnel, cost accounting, production planning, and medical facilities.

Although service departments do not engage directly in production, the costs they incur are generally viewed as being just as much a part of the cost of a company's finished products as are materials, labor, and overhead.

The predetermined overhead rate revisited

In Chapters 3 and 9 we found that indirect costs such as lubricants, depreciation, and property taxes are allocated to finished products through manufacturing overhead by means of the predetermined overhead rate. Basically, the same procedure is used in the matter of service department costs. That is, before the output of a producing department is charged with overhead costs, the predetermined overhead rate must be expanded to include a provision for the cost of services provided by the various service departments throughout the firm. This process of allocation to the producing departments, and subsequent reallocation to finished products by means of the predetermined overhead rate, can be illustrated as in Exhibit 15–1.

Perhaps this allocation process can be seen most clearly by referring to the flexible budget of a producing department. Recall from our discussion in Chapter 9 that the flexible budget forms the basis for computing predetermined overhead rates. Normally, allocated costs from service departments to producing departments are included directly in the latters' flexible budgets, as shown in Exhibit 15–2. By this process, producing departments are able to routinely consider service department costs in the computation of predetermined overhead rates. (Notice the computation of the predetermined overhead rate at the bottom of Exhibit 15–2.)

Exhibit 15–1
Allocation of service department costs to finished products

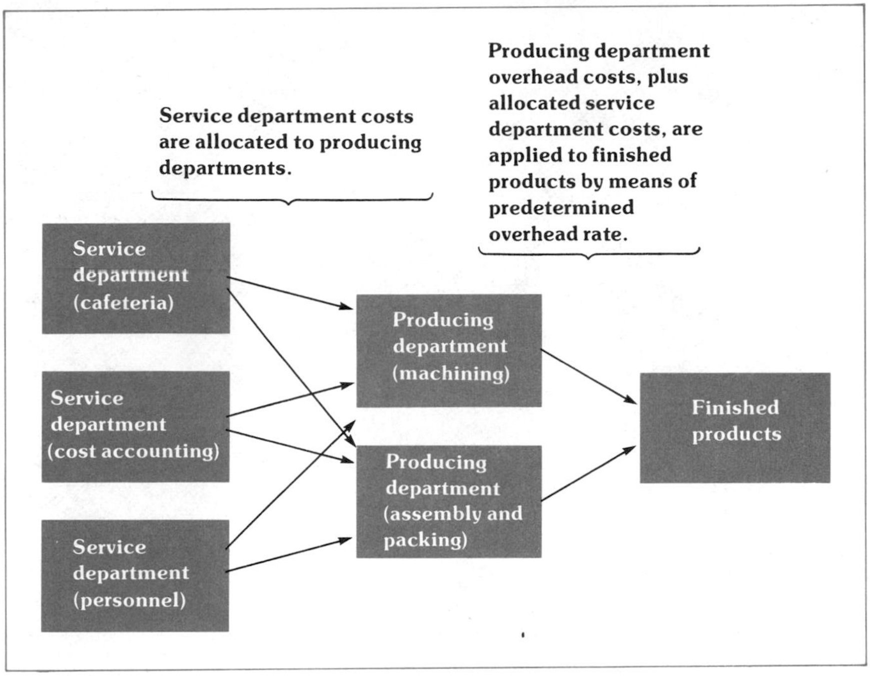

Equity in allocation

The major question which we must consider in this chapter is: How does the manager determine how much service department cost is to be allocated to each of the various producing departments? This is an important question, since the amount of service department cost allocated to a particular department will affect that department's overhead rate, and, hence, the amount of overhead cost borne by the products moving through the department. As we shall see, there are many factors to be considered if allocations are to be equitable as between departments.

GUIDELINES FOR COST ALLOCATION

There are several basic guidelines to follow in service department cost allocation. These guidelines relate to (1) selecting the proper allocation base, (2) allocating the costs of interdepartmental services, (3) allocating costs by behavior, and (4) avoiding certain allocation pitfalls. These topics are covered in order in the following four sections.

Exhibit 15–2
Flexible budget containing allocated service department costs

SUPERIOR COMPANY
Flexible Budget—Milling Department

Budgeted Direct Labor-Hours 5,000

	Cost formula (per direct labor-hour)	Direct labor-hours		
		4,000	5,000	6,000
Variable overhead costs:				
Indirect labor	$0.20	$ 800	$ 1,000	$ 1,200
Indirect materials	0.10	400	500	600
Utilities	0.05	200	250	300
Allocation—Cafeteria	*0.15*	*600*	*750*	*900*
Total	$0.50	$ 2,000	$ 2,500	$ 3,000
Fixed overhead costs:				
Depreciation		$ 4,000	$ 4,000	$ 4,000
Property taxes		1,000	1,000	1,000
Allocation—Cafeteria		*1,500*	*1,500*	*1,500*
Allocation—Personnel Department		*2,000*	*2,000*	*2,000*
Total		$ 8,500	$ 8,500	$ 8,500
Total overhead costs		$10,500	$11,000	$11,500

$$\text{Predetermined overhead rate} = \frac{\$11,000}{5,000 \text{ DLH}} = \$2.20 \text{ per direct labor- hour}$$

Selecting allocation bases

Costs of service departments are allocated to producing departments by means of some type of allocation base. Allocation bases are selected which reflect as accurately as possible the benefits to be received by the various producing departments from the services involved. A number of such bases may be selected according to the nature of the services. Examples of allocation bases in common use include the following:

Cafeteria	Number of employees.
Medical facilities	Periodic analysis of cases handled, number of employees, hours worked.
Materials handling	Hours of service, volume handled.
Building and grounds	Square or cubic footage occupied.
Engineering	Periodic analysis of services rendered, direct labor-hours.
Production planning and control	Periodic analysis of services rendered, direct labor-hours.
Cost accounting	Labor-hours.
Power	Metered usage, capacity of machines.

| Personnel and employment . . . . | Number of employees, turnover of labor, periodic analysis of time spent. |
| Receiving, shipping, and stores . . . . . . | Units handled, number of requisition and issue slips, square or cubic footage occupied. |

Notice that the allocation bases being spoken of here are *not* for purposes of computing predetermined overhead rates; rather, they are for allocating service department costs *to* producing departments.

Once allocation bases are chosen they tend to remain unchanged for long periods of time. Selection of an allocation base represents a *major policy decision* that is reviewed normally only at very infrequent intervals, or when it appears that some major inequity exists.

As we noted earlier, the way in which service department costs are allocated to producing departments will have a heavy influence on the way in which products are costed, so the selection of an allocation base is no minor decision. Criteria for making selections may include: (1) direct, traceable benefits from the service involved, as measured, for example, by the number of service orders handled; (2) the extent of facilities provided, as measured, for example, by the square footage of space occupied; and (3) the ease of making an allocation. In regard to the latter point, complex allocation computations run the risk of yielding negative returns. That is, if allocation computations become too complex, the cost of the computation may exceed any benefits it is trying to bring about. Allocation formulas should be simple and easily understood by all involved, particularly by the managers to whom the costs are being allocated.

Interdepartmental services

Many service departments provide services for each other, as well as for producing departments. The Cafeteria, for example, provides food for all employees, including those assigned to other service departments, and in turn may receive services from the Custodial Department or from Personnel. There are two approaches to handling the costs of services between departments. The first, called the *step method,* provides for allocation of a department's costs to other service departments, as well as to producing departments, in a sequential manner. The second, called the *direct method,* ignores the cost of services between departments, and allocates all service department costs directly to producing departments.

STEP METHOD. In allocating by the step method, some sequence of allocation must be chosen. The sequence typically begins with the department which provides the greatest amount of service to other departments. After its costs have been allocated, the process continues, step-by-step, ending with the department providing the least amount of services to other service departments. This step procedure is illustrated graphically in Exhibit 15–3.

Exhibit 15–3
Graphical illustration—Step method

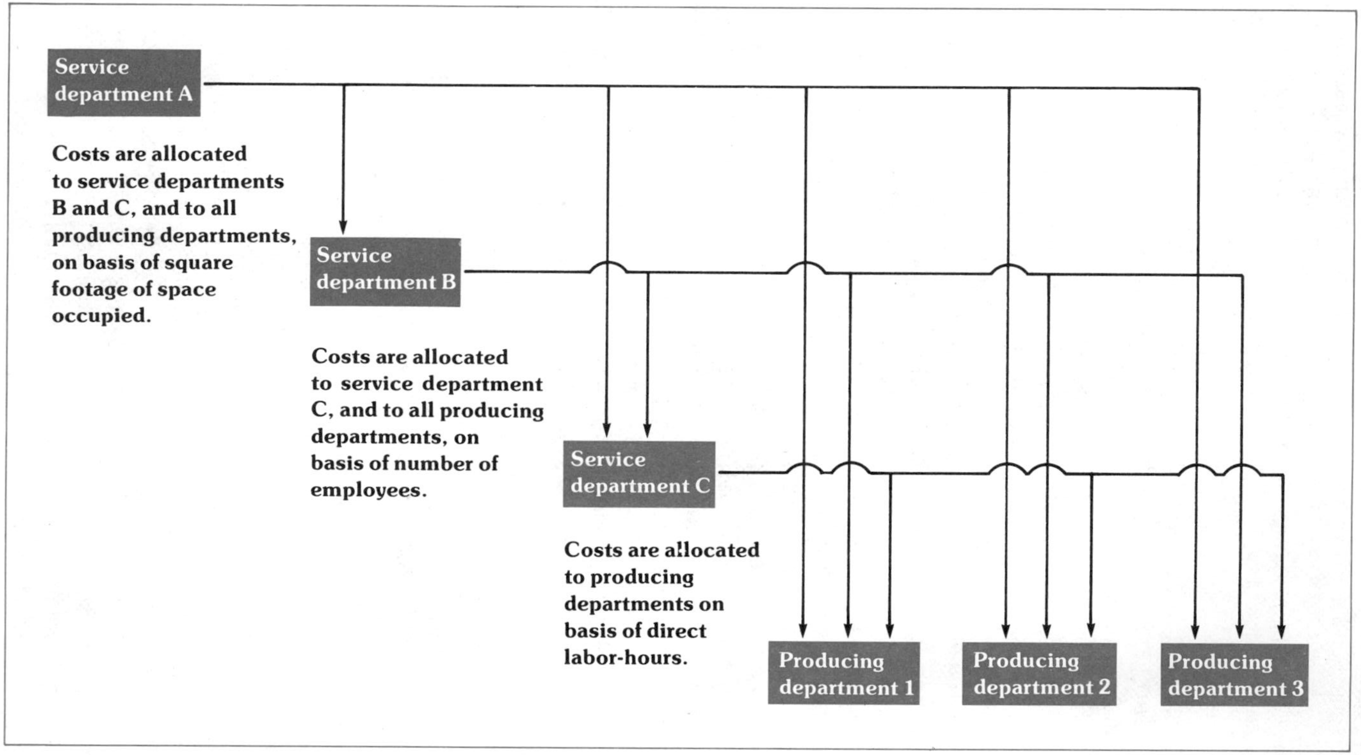

Service department A

Costs are allocated to service departments B and C, and to all producing departments, on basis of square footage of space occupied.

Service department B

Costs are allocated to service department C, and to all producing departments, on basis of number of employees.

Service department C

Costs are allocated to producing departments on basis of direct labor-hours.

Producing department 1

Producing department 2

Producing department 3

To provide a numerical example of the step method, assume the following data:

| | Service departments | | Producing departments | | |
	Factory administration A	Custodial services B	Machining 1	Assembly 2	Total
Overhead costs before allocation	$200,000	$45,000	$200,000	$300,000	$745,000
Labor-hours	—	5,000	10,000	25,000	40,000
Proportion	—	1/8	2/8	5/8	8/8
Space occupied—sq. ft.	10,000	—	50,000	40,000	100,000
Proportion	10%	—	50%	40%	100%

The costs of Factory Administration are allocated first, on a basis of labor-hours in other departments. The costs of Custodial Services are then allocated, on a basis of square footage of space occupied. Allocations by the step method are shown in Exhibit 15–4.

Exhibit 15–4
Step method of allocation

| | Department | | | | |
	A	B	1	2	Total
Overhead costs before allocation	$200,000	$45,000	$200,000	$300,000	$745,000
Allocation:					
Department A costs: (1/8, 2/8, 5/8)	(200,000)	25,000	50,000	125,000	
Department B costs: (5/9, 4/9)*		(70,000)	38,889	31,111	
Total overhead after allocations	$ –0–	$ –0–	$288,889	$456,111	$745,000

* Based on 50,000 + 40,000 = 90,000.

Note from the exhibit that the costs of Department A are borne by another service department, Department B, as well as by the producing departments. Also note that the costs of Department A which have been allocated to Department B *are included with Department B costs,* and the total ($45,000 + $25,000) is allocated only to *subsequent* departments. That is, no part of Department B's costs are reallocated back to Department A, even though Department B may have provided services for Department A during the period. This is a key idea associated with the step method: Once a service department's costs have been allocated out, no costs are subsequently reallocated back to it.

Note further from the exhibit that after the allocations have been made all overhead costs are contained in the producing departments. These totals will form the basis for preparing predetermined overhead rates in the producing departments for the period.

DIRECT METHOD.   The direct method is much simpler than the step method, in that services between departments are ignored, and all allocations are made directly to producing departments. Exhibit 15–5 illustrates the direct method, using the data provided earlier.

Exhibit 15–5
Direct method of allocation

	Department				
	A	B	1	2	Total
Overhead costs before allocation	$200,000	$45,000	$200,000	$300,000	$745,000
Allocation:					
Department A costs: (2/7, 5/7)*	(200,000)		57,143	142,857	
Department B costs: (5/9, 4/9)†		(45,000)	25,000	20,000	
Total overhead after allocations	$ –0–	$ –0–	$282,143	$462,857	$745,000

* Based on 10,000 + 25,000 = 35,000.
† Based on 50,000 + 40,000 = 90,000.

Although simpler than the step method, the direct method is less accurate since it ignores interdepartmental services. This can be a major defect, in that predetermined overhead rates can be affected if the resulting errors in allocation are significant. In turn, incorrect overhead rates can lead to distorted product costs, and to ineffective pricing. Even so, many firms use the direct method because of its ease of application.

Allocating costs by behavior

Whenever possible, service department costs should be separated into fixed and variable classifications and allocated separately. This approach is necessary to avoid possible inequities in allocation, as well as to provide more useful data for planning and control of departmental operations.

VARIABLE COSTS.   Variable costs represent direct costs of providing services, and will generally vary in total in proportion to fluctuations in the level of service consumed. Food cost in a cafeteria would be a variable cost, for example, and one would expect this cost to vary proportionately with the number of persons using the cafeteria over a given period of time. As a general rule, variable costs should be charged to consuming departments according to whatever activity base controls the incurrence of the cost involved. If, for example, the variable costs of a service department are incurred according to the number of machine-hours worked in producing departments, then they should be allocated to producing departments on that basis. By this means, the departments directly responsible for the incurrence of servicing costs are required to bear them, and in proportion to their actual usage of the cost involved.

Technically, the assigning of variable servicing costs to consuming departments can more accurately be termed "charges" than allocations, since the service department is actually charging the consuming departments at some fixed rate per unit of service provided. In effect, the service department is saying, "I'll charge you X dollars for every unit of my service that you consume. You can consume as much or as little as you desire; the total charge you bear will vary proportionately."

FIXED COSTS. The fixed costs of service departments represent the cost of having long-run service capacity available. As such, these costs are most equitably allocated to consuming departments on a basis of *predetermined lump-sum amounts.*

When a service department is first established, some basic capacity is built into it according to the observed needs of the other departments which it will service. This basic capacity may reflect the peak-level needs of the other departments, or it may reflect their long-run average or "normal" servicing needs. Depending on how much servicing capacity is provided for, it will be necessary to make a commitment of resources to the servicing unit, which will be reflected in its fixed costs. It is generally felt that these fixed costs should be borne by the consuming departments whose servicing needs have made the creation of the service department necessary, and that the costs should be borne in proportion to the individual servicing needs which have been provided for. That is, if available capacity in the service department has been provided to meet the peak-period needs of consuming departments, then the fixed costs of the service department should be allocated in predetermined lump-sum amounts to consuming departments on this basis. If available capacity has been provided only to meet "normal" or long-run average needs, then fixed costs should be allocated on this basis.

Once set, allocations should not vary from period to period, since they represent each consuming department's "fair share" of having a certain level of service capacity available and on line. The fact that a consuming department does not need peak-level or even a "normal" level of servicing every period is immaterial; if it requires such servicing at certain times then the capacity to deliver it must be available. It is the responsibility of the consuming department to bear the cost of that availability.

To illustrate this idea, assume that Novak Company has just organized a Maintenance Department to service all machines in the Cutting, Assembly, and Finishing Departments. In determining the capacity that should be built into the newly organized Maintenance Department, the company recognized that the various producing departments would have the following peak-period needs for maintenance:

Department	Peak-period maintenance needs in terms of number of hours of maintenance work required	Percent of total hours
Cutting Department	300	30%
Assembly Department	600	60
Finishing Department	100	10
	1,000	100%

Therefore, in allocating the Maintenance Department fixed costs to the producing departments, 30 percent should be allocated to the Cutting Department, 60 percent to the Assembly Department, and 10 percent to the Finishing Department. These lump-sum allocations *will not change* from period to period unless there is some shift in servicing needs due to structural changes in the organization.

Pitfalls in allocating fixed costs

Rather than allocate fixed costs in predetermined lump-sum amounts, some firms allocate them by use of a *variable* allocation base. What's wrong with this practice? The answer is that it can create serious inequities between departments. The inequities will arise from the fact that the fixed costs allocated to one department will be influenced heavily by what happens in *other departments.*

To illustrate, assume that a company has one service department and two producing departments. The service department costs are all fixed. Contrary to good practice, the company allocates these fixed costs to producing departments on the basis of machine-hours (a variable base). Selected cost data for two years are given below:

	Year 1	Year 2
Service department cost (all fixed)	$30,000(*a*)	$30,000(*a*)
Producing Department A machine-hours	15,000	15,000
Producing Department B machine-hours	15,000	5,000
Total machine-hours	30,000(*b*)	20,000(*b*)
Allocation rate per machine-hour: (*a*) ÷ (*b*)	$1.00	$1.50

Notice that Department A maintained a production level of 15,000 machine-hours in both years. On the other hand, Department B allowed its production to drop off from 15,000 hours in Year 1 to only 5,000 hours in Year 2. The service department costs that would have been allocated to the two departments over the two-year span are given on the following page:

```
Year 1:
    Department A: 15,000 hours at $1.00 . . . . . . . . . . . . . . . . .  $15,000
    Department B: 15,000 hours at $1.00 . . . . . . . . . . . . . . . . .   15,000
        Total cost allocated  . . . . . . . . . . . . . . . . . . . . . . . . . .  $30,000

Year 2:
    Department A: 15,000 hours at $1.50 . . . . . . . . . . . . . . . . .  $22,500
    Department B: 5,000 hours at $1.50 . . . . . . . . . . . . . . . . . .    7,500
        Total cost allocated  . . . . . . . . . . . . . . . . . . . . . . . . . .  $30,000
```

In Year 1 the two producing departments share the service department costs equally. In Year 2, however, the bulk of the service department costs are allocated to Department A. This is not because of any increase in activity in Department A; rather, it is because of the inefficiency in Department B, which did not maintain its activity level during Year 2. Even though Department A maintained the same level of efficiency in both years, the use of a variable allocation base has caused it to be penalized with a heavier cost allocation because of what has happened in *another* department.

This kind of inequity is almost inevitable when a variable allocation base is used to allocate fixed costs. The manager of Department A will be incensed at the inequity forced on his department, but he will feel powerless to do anything about it. The result will be a loss of confidence in the system, and the accumulation of a considerable backlog of ill-feeling.

Should actual or budgeted costs be allocated?

Should a service department allocate its *actual* costs to producing departments, or should it allocate its *budgeted* costs? The answer is that budgeted costs should be allocated. What's wrong with allocating actual costs? Allocating actual costs burdens the producing departments with the inefficiencies of the service department managers. If actual costs are allocated, then any lack of cost control on the part of the service department manager is simply buried in a routine allocation to other departments.

Any variance over budgeted costs should be retained in the service department and closed out against cost of goods sold along with producing department variances. Producing department managers rarely complain about being allocated a portion of service department costs, but they complain bitterly if they are forced to absorb service department inefficiencies.

Guidelines for allocating service department costs

By way of summary, we can note five key points to remember about allocating service department costs:

1. Where feasible, the distinction between variable and fixed costs in service departments should be maintained.

2. Variable costs should be allocated at the budgeted rate, according to whatever activity measure (machine-hours, direct labor-hours, number of employees) controls the incurrence of the cost involved.
   a. If the allocations are being made at the beginning of the year, they should be based on the budgeted activity level planned for the consuming departments. The allocation formula would be:

   Budgeted rate × Budgeted activity = Cost allocated

   b. If the allocations are being made at the end of the year, they should be based on the actual activity level which has occurred during the year. The allocation formula would be:

   Budgeted rate × Actual activity = Cost allocated

   Allocations made at the beginning of the year would be to provide data for computing predetermined overhead rates in the producing departments. Allocations made at the end of the year would be to provide data for comparing actual performance against planned performance.

3. Fixed costs represent the cost of having service capacity available. Where feasible, these costs should be allocated in predetermined lump-sum amounts. The lump-sum amount going to each separate department should be in proportion to the servicing needs that gave rise to the investment in the service department in the first place. (This might be either peak-period needs for servicing, or long-run average needs.) Budgeted fixed costs, rather than actual fixed costs, should always be allocated.

4. If it is not feasible to maintain a distinction between variable and fixed costs in a service department, then the costs of the department should be allocated to consuming departments according to that base which appears to provide the best measure of benefits received.

5. Where feasible, reciprocal services between departments should be recognized.

IMPLEMENTING THE ALLOCATION GUIDELINES

We will now show the implementation of these guidelines by the use of specific examples. We will focus first on the allocation of costs for a single department, and then develop a more extended example where multiple departments are involved.

Basic allocation techniques

The Silex Company has a Maintenance Department that provides maintenance service for two producing departments. Variable servicing costs are budgeted at $0.10 per machine-hour. Fixed costs are budgeted at $10,000 per year. Budgeted and peak-period machine-hours are:

	Budgeted hours	Peak period hours
Producing Department A	12,000	18,000
Producing Department B	10,000	12,000
Total hours	22,000	30,000

The amount of service department cost that would be allocated to each producing department at the beginning of the year would be:

	Producing Department A	Producing Department B
Variable cost allocation:		
$0.10 × 12,000 hours	$1,200	
$0.10 × 10,000 hours		$1,000
Fixed cost allocation:		
60%* × $10,000	6,000	
40%* × $10,000		4,000
Total cost allocated	$7,200	$5,000

* 18,000 hours ÷ 30,000 hours = 60%.
  12,000 hours ÷ 30,000 hours = 40%.

As explained earlier, these allocations would be placed on the flexible budgets of the producing departments, to be included in the computation of predetermined overhead rates.

At the end of the year, the management of Silex Company may want to make a second allocation, this time based on actual activity, in order to compare actual performance for the year against planned performance. Assume that year-end records show that actual service department costs for the year were: variable, $2,760; and fixed, $10,800. We will assume that one producing department worked more hours during the year than planned, and the other one worked less hours than planned:

	Budgeted hours (see above)	Actual hours
Producing Department A	12,000	14,000
Producing Department B	10,000	9,000
Total hours	22,000	23,000

The amount of service department cost chargeable to each producing department would be:

	Producing Department A	Producing Department B
Variable cost allocation:		
$0.10 × 14,000 hours	$1,400	
$0.10 × 9,000 hours		$ 900
Fixed cost allocation:		
60% × $10,000	6,000	
40% × $10,000		4,000
Total cost allocated	$7,400	$4,900

Notice that the variable cost is allocated according to the budgeted rate ($0.10) times the *actual activity,* and the fixed cost is allocated according to the original budgeted amount. As stated in the guidelines earlier, allocations are always based on budgeted rates and amounts in order to avoid the passing on of inefficiency from one department to another. Thus, a portion of the year-end service department costs will not be allocated, as shown below:

	Variable	Fixed
Total costs incurred	$2,760	$10,800
Costs allocated above	2,300*	10,000
Spending variance—not allocated ...	$ 460	$ 800
* $0.10 × 23,000 actual hours = $2,300		

These variances will be closed out to cost of goods sold, along with the manufacturing variances for the year.

An extended example

The Proctor Company has three service departments, Building Maintenance, Cafeteria, and Inspection. The company also has two producing departments, Shaping and Assembly. The service departments provide services to each other, as well as to the producing departments. Types of costs in the service departments, and bases for allocation are:

Department	Type of cost	Base for allocation
Building Maintenance	Fixed costs	Square footage occupied
Cafeteria	Variable costs Fixed costs	Number of employees 10% to Inspection, 40% to Shaping, and 50% to Assembly.
Inspection	Variable costs Fixed costs	Direct labor-hours 70% to Shaping, and 30% to Assembly.

The Proctor Company allocates service department costs by the step method, in the following order:

1. Building Maintenance.
2. Cafeteria.
3. Inspection.

Assume the following budgeted cost and operating data for 19x1:

	Variable cost	Fixed cost
Building Maintenance	—	$15,000
Cafeteria	$100 per employee	40,000
Inspection	$0.12 per direct labor-hour	20,000

	Number of employees	Direct labor-hours	Square footage of space occupied (sq. ft.)
Building Maintenance	—*	—	500
Cafeteria	—*	—	1,000
Inspection	30	—	500
Shaping	240	40,000	4,750
Assembly	355	56,000	8,750
Totals	625	96,000	15,500

* Although there are employees in both of these service departments, under the step method costs are only allocated *forward*—never backward. For this reason, the costs of the cafeteria will be allocated *forward* on the basis of the number of employees in the inspection, shaping, and assembly departments.

Using these data, cost allocations to the producing departments would be as shown in Exhibit 15–6. To save space, we have placed the producing departments' flexible budget overhead costs on the exhibit, and computed the predetermined overhead rates there.

No distinction made between fixed and variable costs

As stated in the guidelines given earlier, in some cases it may not be feasible to maintain a distinction between fixed and variable service department costs. We noted there that in such cases the costs should be allocated to producing departments according to that base which appears to provide the best measure of benefits received. An example of such an allocation was given earlier in Exhibit 15–4 where we first illustrated the step method. The reader may wish to turn back and review this example before reading on.

Should all costs be allocated?

For product costing purposes, the general rule is that all service department costs which are incurred as a result of specific services provided to producing departments should be allocated back to these departments and added to product costs via the predetermined overhead rate. The

Exhibit 15–6

THE PROCTOR COMPANY
Beginning-of-Year Cost Allocations for Purposes
of Preparing Predetermined Overhead Rates

	Building maintenance	Cafeteria	Inspection	Shaping	Assembly
Variable costs to be allocated	$ -0-	$62,500	$ 8,520	—	—
Cafeteria allocation at $100 per employee:					
30 employees × $100		(3,000)	3,000		
240 employees × $100		(24,000)		$ 24,000	
355 employees × $100		(35,500)			$ 35,500
Inspection allocation at $0.12 per direct labor-hour:					
40,000 DLH × $0.12			(4,800)	4,800	
56,000 DLH × $0.12			(6,720)		6,720
Totals	$ -0-	$ -0-	$ -0-	$ 28,800	$ 42,220
Fixed costs to be allocated	$15,000	$40,000	$20,000		
Building Maintenance allocation at $1 per square foot:*					
1,000 sq. ft. × $1	(1,000)	$ 1,000			
500 sq. ft. × $1	(500)		$ 500		
4,750 sq. ft. × $1	(4,750)			$ 4,750	
8,750 sq. ft. × $1	(8,750)				$ 8,750
Cafeteria allocation:†					
10% × $41,000		(4,100)	4,100		
40% × $41,000		(16,400)		16,400	
50% × $41,000		(20,500)			20,500
Inspection allocation:‡					
70% × $24,600			(17,220)	17,220	
30% × $24,600			(7,380)		7,380
Totals	$ -0-	$ -0-	$ -0-	$ 38,370	$ 36,630
Total allocated costs	$ -0-	$ -0-	$ -0-	$ 67,170	$ 78,850

Other flexible budget costs at the planned activity level	220,000	340,000
Total overhead costs	$287,170	$418,850 (a)
Budgeted direct labor-hours	40,000	56,000 (b)
Predetermined overhead rate (a) ÷ (b)	$7.18	$7.48

* Square footage of space .... 15,500 sq. ft.
  Less Building Maintenance space .... 500 sq. ft.
  Net space for allocation .... 15,000 sq. ft.

$$\frac{\text{Building Maintenance fixed cost } \$15,000}{\text{Net space for allocation } 15,000 \text{ sq. ft.}} = \$1/\text{sq. ft.}$$

† Cafeteria fixed costs $40,000
  Allocated from Building Maintenance 1,000
  Total cost to be allocated $41,000

Allocation percentages are given in the problem.

‡ Inspection fixed costs $20,000
  Allocated from Building Maintenance 500
  Allocated from Cafeteria 4,100
  Total cost to be allocated $24,600

Allocation percentages are given in the problem.

only time when this general rule is not followed is in those situations where, in the view of management, allocation would result in an undesirable behavioral response from producing departments. There are some servicing costs, for example, which are clearly beneficial to producing departments, but which the departments may not utilize as fully as they should, particularly in times of cost-economizing. Internal auditing is a good example of such a cost. Utilization of internal audit services may be very beneficial to producing departments in terms of improving overall efficiency, reducing waste, and assuring adherence to departmental policies. But if a department knows that it will be charged for the internal audit services it uses, it may be less inclined to take advantage of benefits involved, especially if the department is feeling some pressure to trim costs. In short, the departmental manager may opt for the near-term benefit of avoiding a direct charge, in lieu of the long-term benefit of reduced waste and greater efficiency.

To avoid discouraging use of a service that is helpful to the entire organization, some firms make no charge for the service at all. These managers feel that by making such services a "free" commodity, departments will be more inclined to take full advantage of their benefits.

Other firms take a somewhat different approach. They agree that charging according to usage may discourage utilization of such services as internal auditing, but they argue that such services should not be free. Instead of providing free services, these firms take what is sometimes called a "retainer fee" approach. Each department is charged a flat amount each year, regardless of how much or how little of the service it utilizes. The thought is that if a department knows that it is going to be charged a certain amount for internal audit services, *regardless of usage,* then it probably will utilize the services at least to that extent.

Beware of sales dollars as an allocation base

Over the years, sales dollars have been a favorite allocation base for service department costs. One reason is that sales dollars are simple, straightforward, and easy to work with. Another reason is that people tend to view sales dollars as being a measure of well-being, or "ability to pay," and, hence, as being a measure of how extensively costs can be absorbed from other parts of the organization.

Unfortunately, sales dollars often constitute a very poor allocation base, for the reason that sales dollars vary from period to period whereas the costs being allocated are often largely *fixed* in nature. As discussed earlier, if a variable base is used to allocate fixed costs, inequities can result as between departments since the costs being allocated to one department will depend in large part on what happens in *other* departments. For example, a letup in sales effort in one department will shift allocated costs off of it onto other, more productive departments. In effect, the departments putting forth the best sales efforts are penalized in the form of higher allocations, simply because of inefficiencies elsewhere that are beyond their control. The result often is bitterness and resentment on the part of the managers of the better departments.

Consider the following situation encountered by the author:

A large men's clothing store has one service department and three sales departments—suits, shoes, and accessories. The service department's costs are allocated to the three sales departments according to sales dollars. A recent period showed the following allocation:

	Suits	Shoes	Accessories	Total
Sales by department...............	$78,000	$18,000	$24,000	$120,000
Percentage of total sales	65%	15%	20%	100%
Allocation of service department costs, based on percentage of total sales.....................	$19,500	$ 4,500	$ 6,000	$ 30,000

In a following period the manager of the suit department launched a very successful program to expand sales to over $100,000 in his department. Sales in the other two departments remained unchanged. Total service department costs also remained unchanged, but the allocation of these costs changed substantially, as shown below:

	Suits	Shoes	Accessories	Total
Sales by department	$108,000	$18,000	$24,000	$150,000
Percentage of total sales	72%	12%	16%	100%
Allocation of service department costs, based on percentage of total sales	$ 21,600	$ 3,600	$ 4,800	$ 30,000
Increase (or decrease) from prior allocation	$ 2,100	$ (900)	$ (1,200)	—

The manager of the suit department complained very bitterly that as a result of his succesful effort to expand sales in his department, he was being forced to carry a larger share of the service department costs. On the other hand, the managers of the departments that showed no improvement in sales were being relieved of a portion of the costs which they had been carrying. Yet there had been no change in the amount of services provided for any department.

The manager of the suit department viewed the increased service department cost allocation to his department as a penalty for his outstanding performance, and wondered whether his efforts had really been worthwhile after all in the eyes of top management.

Sales dollars should be used as an allocation base only in those cases where there is a direct causal relationship between sales dollars and the service department costs being allocated. In those situations where service department costs are fixed in nature, they should be allocated according to the guidelines discussed earlier in the chapter.

SUMMARY

Service departments are organized to provide some needed service in a single, centralized place, rather than to have all units within the organization provide the service for themselves. Although service departments do not engage directly in production, the costs which they incur are vital to the overall productive effort, and therefore are properly included as part of the cost of a company's finished products.

Service department costs are charged to producing departments by an allocation process. In turn, the producing departments include the allocated costs within their flexible budgets, from which predetermined overhead rates are computed for product costing purposes.

In order to avoid inequity in allocations, variable and fixed service department costs should be allocated separately. The variable costs should be allocated according to whatever activity measure controls their incurrence. The fixed costs should be allocated in predetermined lump-sum amounts according to either the peak-period or the long-run average servicing needs of the consuming departments. Budgeted costs should always be allocated, rather than actual costs, in order to avoid the passing on of inefficiency between departments. Any variances between budgeted and actual service department costs should be kept within the service departments for analysis purposes, and then written off to cost of goods sold along with the manufacturing variances.

KEY TERMS FOR REVIEW

Service department   **Step method**
Allocation base   **Direct method**
Interdepartmental services **Retainer fee approach**

QUESTIONS

15–1. What is the difference between a service department and a producing department? Give several examples of service departments.

15–2. How do service department costs enter into the final cost of finished products?

15–3. What are interdepartmental service costs? How are such costs handled for allocation purposes?

15–4. What guidelines should govern the allocation of fixed service department costs to producing and other departments? The allocation of variable service department costs?

15–5. "A variable base should never be used in allocating fixed service department costs to producing departments." Explain.

15–6. In what way are service department costs similar to costs such as lubricants, utilities, and factory supervision?

15–7.   Why might it be desirable to not allocate some service department costs to producing departments?

15–8.   What is the purpose of the "retainer fee" approach to cost allocation?

15–9.   "Units of product can be costed equally well with or without allocations of service department costs." Do you agree? Why or why not?

15–10. What criteria are relevant to the selection of allocation bases for service department costs?

EXERCISES

E15–1. The Clark Company has a Maintenance Department which performs needed maintenance work on the equipment in the company's Machining and Assembly Departments. The Maintenance Department has sufficient capacity to handle peak-period needs of 40,000 machine-hours in Machining, and 10,000 machine-hours in Assembly. At this level of activity budgeted maintenance costs would total $40,000, consisting of $0.30 per hour variable cost and $25,000 total fixed cost.

During the coming year, 19x2, 30,000 machine-hours are budgeted to be worked in Machining, and 10,000 in Assembly.

Required:

Compute the amount of maintenance cost which should be allocated to Machining and Assembly at the beginning of 19x2.

E15–2. Precision Plastics operates a medical services unit for its employees. The variable costs of the medical services unit are allocated to using departments on a basis of the number of employees in each department. Budgeted and actual data for 19x8 are given below:

Variable Costs—19x8

	Budgeted	*Actual*
Medical Services Unit	$100/employee	$105/employee

Number of Employees—Using Departments

	Mainte-nance depart-ment	*Producing departments*		
		1	*2*	*3*
Budgeted number of employees	20	200	700	300
Actual number of employees	21	198	704	295

Required:

Determine the amount of medical services cost that should be allocated to each of the four using departments at the end of 19x8.

E15–3. The Bonneville Corporation has two service departments, janitorial services and cafeteria. The fixed costs of the two service departments are allocated on the following bases:

Service department	*Basis for allocation*
Janitorial Services ..	Square footage of floor space occupied.

Floor space is occupied as follows:

Cafeteria	3,000 sq. ft.
Producing Department A	30,000 sq. ft.
Producing Department B	67,000 sq. ft.

Cafeteria .... Producing Department A–30%
Producing Department B–70%

The fixed costs of janitorial services total $25,000 each year. The fixed costs of the cafeteria total $75,000 each year. The company uses the step method of allocation.

Required:

1. Show the allocation of the fixed costs of janitorial services.
2. Show the allocation of the fixed costs of the cafeteria.

E15–4. Castile Company has three service departments and two producing departments. Selected data on the five departments follow:

	Service departments			*Producing departments*		
	A	*B*	*C*	*1*	*2*	*Total*
Overhead costs	$10,000	$8,000	$6,000	$50,000	$80,000	$154,000
Number of employees ...	100	20	80	350	550	1,100
Square feet of space occupied	800	1,000	1,200	3,000	4,000	10,000
Labor-hours	300	300	1,400	2,000	6,000	10,000

The company allocates service department costs by the step method, in the following order: A (number of employees); B (space occupied); C (labor-hours). The company makes no distinction between fixed and variable service department costs.

Required:

Using the step method, make the necessary allocations of service department costs.

E15–5. Refer to the data for Castile Company in Exercise 15–4. Assume that the company allocates service department costs by the direct method, rather than by the step method. Under this assumption, how much overhead cost would be chargeable to each producing department? Show computations in good form.

E15–6. In practice, factory service department costs are allocated to producing departments in many ways. For example, some firms allocate all service department costs, whereas other firms allocate only the variable costs. Some firms allocate only the budgeted costs, and other firms allocate full actual costs. In some cases, these allocations are made on the basis of a specified rate per unit of activity, and in other cases the allocations are in block sums. The allocation rates are sometimes computed in advance (predetermined), and at other times the rates are set only after all of the costs of the period have been accumulated.

Below are four plans for allocating service department costs to producing departments. Evaluate each plan.

1. Allocate all service department costs, based on an activity measure such as machine-hours. A single allocation rate is used for both variable and fixed costs, which is set after-the-fact; i.e., on actual costs of the period.
2. The same plan as in (1) above, except the allocation rate is predetermined (set in advance).
3. Allocate budgeted service department costs (fixed and variable) in block sums to using departments.
4. Allocate both fixed and variable service department costs, but allocate them separately. In each case, allocate budgeted costs based on predetermined (but separate) rates per unit of activity, such as per machine-hour.

E15–7. Service Department A provides maintenance service for producing departments X and Y. The cost of this service is allocated to producing departments on a basis of machine-hours. Cost and operating data for 19x5 are given below:

Service Department A

	Budget	Actual
Variable costs .	$10,000	$13,200
Fixed costs	50,000	49,800

Producing Departments X and Y

	Machine-hours		
	Long-run average	Budget–19x5	Actual–19x5
Department X	100,000	80,000	85,000
Department Y	150,000	120,000	135,000

Required:

1. Assume that it is the beginning of 19x5. An allocation of service department cost must be made to the producing departments to assist in computing predetermined overhead rates. How much budgeted service department cost would be allocated to each producing department?
2. Assume that it is now the end of 19x5. Management would like data to assist in comparing actual performance against planned performance in both the producing and service departments.
    a. How much of the actual service department cost would be allocated to each producing department?
    b. How much of the actual service department cost would remain in the service department as a spending variance?

PROBLEMS

P15–8. *Various allocation methods.* The Dearborn Motor Company has a Truck Division and an Auto Division. A single company cafeteria serves the employees of both divisions. The costs of operating the cafeteria are budgeted at $50,000 per month, plus $3 per meal served. The cafeteria has a capacity to serve 40,000 meals per month—based on peak needs of 26,000 meals per month in the Auto Division, and 14,000 meals per month in the Truck Division.

During June, the Auto Division has estimated that it will need 18,000 meals served and the Truck Division has estimated that it will need 12,000 meals served.

Required:

1. How much cafeteria cost should be allocated to each division at the beginning of June, for flexible budget planning purposes?
2. Assume that it is now the end of June. Cost records in the cafeteria show that actual fixed costs for the month totaled $52,000 and meal costs totaled $78,000. Due to unexpected layoffs of employees during the month, only 12,000 meals were served to the Auto Division. Another 12,000 meals were served to the Truck Division. How much of the actual cafeteria costs for the month should be allocated to each division? (Management uses these end-of-month allocations to compare actual performance against planned performance.)
3. Refer to the data in (2) above. Assume that the company follows the practice of allocating *all* cafeteria costs to the divisions in proportion to the number of meals served to each division during the month. On this basis, how much cost would be allocated to each division for June?
4. What criticisms can you make of the allocation method used in (3) above?
5. If managers know that fixed costs are going to be allocated on a basis of long-run average usage, what will be their probable strategy in planning meetings with other divisional managers? As a member of top management, how would you move to neutralize any undesirable strategy ploys?

P15–9. *End-of-year cost allocations.* A company's factory has three producing departments, a maintenance department, and a steam electric power plant. The steam electric power plant provides electricity for the producing departments and for the maintenance department.

The 19x1 budget for the power plant shows budgeted fixed costs of $50,000, and budgeted variable costs of $0.02 per kilowatt-hour produced.

The following data show the long-run demand for power in each department, the power budgeted for 19x1, and the actual power consumed during 19x1.

	Long-run demand (kwh.)	Budgeted for 19x1 (kwh.)	Actual power used in 19x1 (kwh.)
Maintenance Department	30,000	25,000	25,000
Producing Department 1	280,000	250,000	160,000
Producing Department 2	540,000	540,000	540,000
Producing Department 3	150,000	85,000	75,000
Total	1,000,000	900,000	800,000

As shown above, the steam electric power plant actually generated 800,000 kilowatt-hours of power during 19x1. Actual costs of the power plant in providing this power are given below:

Actual fixed costs $51,000
Actual variable costs 17,600
Total $68,600

Required:

Assume that management makes an allocation of power service cost at the end of each year to the four departments listed above, in order to compare actual performance against budgeted performance. How much of 19x1's $68,600 actual power service cost should be allocated to each department?

P15–10. *End-of-month cost allocations.* The Power Services Department in a factory provides electrical power for other departments. The power budget is $9,520 per month. Of this amount, $2,500 is considered to be a fixed cost. Actual costs for the month of April amounted to $9,300.

Power consumption in the factory is measured by kilowatt hours (kwh.) used. The monthly power requirements of the factory's other four departments are as follows (in kwh.):

	Producing departments		Service departments	
	A	B	X	Y
Needed at capacity production	10,000	20,000	12,000	8,000
Budgeted	8,000	15,000	8,000	5,000
Used during April	8,000	13,000	7,000	6,000

Required:

Assume that management makes an allocation of power service cost at the end of each month to the four departments listed above, in order to compare actual performance against budgeted performance. How much of April's $9,300 actual power service cost should be allocated to each department? (You may assume that there was no variance in the fixed cost during the month.)

P15–11. *Cost allocation in a hospital; Step method.* Pleasant View Hospital has three service departments—Food Services, Administrative Services, and X-Ray Services. The costs of these departments are allocated by the step method, using the bases and in the order shown below:

Service department	Costs incurred	Base for allocation
Food Services	Variable	Meals served
	Fixed	Full capacity needs—meals
Administrative Services	Variable	Files processed
	Fixed	10% X-Ray, 20% Outpatient Clinic, 30% OB Care, and 40% General Hospital
X-Ray Services	Variable	X-rays taken
	Fixed	Analysis of long-term usage

Estimated cost and operating data for all departments in the hospital for the forthcoming month are presented in the following table:

	Food services	Admin. services	X-ray services	Out-patient clinic	OB care	General hospital	Total
Variable costs	$ 73,150	$ 6,800	$38,100	$11,700	$ 14,850	$ 53,400	$198,000
Fixed costs	48,000	33,040	59,520	26,958	99,738	344,744	612,000
Total costs	$121,150	$39,840	$97,620	$38,658	$114,588	$398,144	$810,000
Files processed	—	—	1,500	3,000	900	12,000	17,400
X-rays taken	—	—	—	1,200	350	8,400	9,950
Long-term average X-ray needs	—	—	—	1,560	360	10,080	12,000
Meals served	—	1,000	500	—	7,000	30,000	38,500
Meals served at capacity	—	1,000	500	—	8,500	40,000	50,000

All billing in the hospital is done through the Outpatient Clinic, OB Care, or General Hospital. The hospital's administrator wants the costs of the three service departments allocated to these three billing centers.

Required:

Prepare the cost allocation desired by the hospital administrator. Include under each billing center the direct costs of the center, as well as the costs allocated from the service departments.

P15–12. *Cost allocation: Step method versus direct method.* Budgeted costs for the various departments of Burns Company for the coming period are as follows:

Factory Administration	$50,000
Personnel	15,000
Custodial Services	17,350
Machine Maintenance	5,800
Machining—overhead	83,325
Assembly—overhead	98,525
Total cost	$270,000

The company follows the practice of allocating service department costs to producing departments. Bases for allocation are to be chosen from the following (allocate departments in the order listed):

	Direct labor-hours	Number of employees	Square feet of space occupied	Labor-hours	Machine-hours
Factory Administration*	—	30	4,000	—	—
Personnel	—	5	1,000	2,000	—
Custodial Services	—	5	2,000	2,000	—
Machine Maintenance	—	15	5,000	6,000	—
Machining	15,000	60	30,000	30,000	50,000
Assembly	30,000	120	40,000	60,000	10,000
	45,000	235	82,000	100,000	60,000

* Allocated on a labor-hour base.

The company does not make a distinction between fixed and variable service department costs; allocations are made to using departments according to that base which appears to provide the best measure of benefits received.

Required:

1. Allocate service department costs to using departments by the step method. Then compute predetermined overhead rates for Machining and Assembly, based on direct labor-hours.
2. Repeat (1) above, this time using the direct method. Again compute predetermined overhead rates for both Machining and Assembly.
3. Assume that the company doesn't want to bother with allocating service department costs, and simply wants to compute a single plantwide overhead rate based on total overhead costs (both service department and producing department) divided by total direct labor-hours. Compute the appropriate overhead rate.
4. Hours required in Machining and Assembly to complete two jobs are given below:

	Direct labor-hours	
Job	Machining	Assembly
101 5		30
102 35		4

Using the overhead rates computed in (1), (2), and (3) above, compute the amount of overhead cost that would be assigned to each job if overhead rates were developed using the step method, the direct method, and the plantwide method.

P15–13. *Allocation of computer center costs in a university.* A large western university has a central computer system that handles the bulk of the computer needs of the administrative, teaching, and research functions of the university. The computer system is housed in a centrally located, specially constructed facility, and contains the finest in technology available both in terms of equipment and trained personnel. Virtually all costs associated with the computer system are fixed. The personnel assigned to the computer center are on flat annual salaries, and the equipment is all leased at flat monthly rates. The only variable costs associated with the computer center are paper and utilities which tend to be very nominal in comparison to the fixed costs.

Up until two years ago, the university had never attempted to allocate the use of computer time among the various university functions of administration, teaching, and research. The computer center was simply open to any users, who, after obtaining clearance for their projects (which required the approval and signature of the chairpersons, deans, and so on, to whom the users were responsible) and being assigned a user number, were permitted to use the computer facilities to the extent they desired. This procedure seemed to work very well. Generally, the computer center was able to handle all user requests for computer time. In those periods when user requests exceeded the computer capacity, some projects were deferred for a day or two until the computer time became available. One factor that made the system work well was that users were willing to let the computer center supervisors schedule projects which had no particular time constraint to "slow" periods, such as between terms and in the summer months.

Two years ago, the university hired a retired, very successful business executive to develop a budgeting system for the university. One of his first steps was to set up a system of controls over the computer center. Essentially, this involved the allocation of computer time as between administration, teaching, and research uses. This allocation was made in the form of a specified dollar amount of computer time which was allocated to each prospective user for a particular year. The rate per computer hour of use was determined by taking the total costs associated with the computer center (salaries of personnel, leasing costs, estimated depreciation of the building, and so forth) and dividing this figure by the maximum computer time available. Each prospective user was then allocated a certain dollar amount of computer time. This allocation was based on the user's prior year's use of computer facilities (the computer center had always kept track of the use of computer time for information and planning purposes). This pattern was to hold in future years, with each year's allocation of computer time being based on the prior year's usage. However, users had the right to petition the computer committee at any time for increases in their allocation.

Although the computer center supervisors were not happy about the thought of the new controls, they were willing to go along with the new plan. For one thing, it was argued by those setting up the allocation plan that the new plan would "put the monkey on the users' backs" in determining what was and what was not a "good" use of computer time. Since there now was a cost associated with computer use, they argued, users would be forced to evaluate each project carefully to determine which projects were justified and which were not in terms of the cost involved. As the business executive who developed the new plan explained, "This way we let the market decide how the computer should be used."

By the end of the first year under the new plan, several developments had taken place in the computer center. For the first time ever, demand for computer time far exceeded the time available. Particularly during the last few months of the year, users complained that they were unable to get adequate "turnaround" from the computer center to keep critical projects rolling. These users petitioned the computer committee for the right to take a portion of their allocated computer funds and go outside the university to process their data. Generally, these requests were denied. By the end of the year, the computer committee had received many requests from users for increases in computer allocations. In addition, grumbling was heard from some users, who complained that certain other users "thought that the computer belonged to them."

In their report to the university president at the end of the first year, those who had developed the allocation plan stated, ". . . the computer center is now under control." They pointed out the greatly increased demand for computer center services, explaining that this increased demand was a function of a growing awareness on the part of users of the value of the computer to the university community. They stated that these valuable services would continue to be controlled on a strict cost basis.

Required:

1. What do you think was the cause of the "greatly increased demand for computer center services" during the first year under the new plan?
2. Do you agree that the new plan resulted in a "cost" being associated with computer use, whereas no such cost existed before? What problems of cost justification might be encountered in a university that would not in a business firm?
3. Should the users who requested the right to take their allocated funds and go outside the university for computer services have been permitted to do so? Explain.
4. What changes, if any, would you recommend in the allocation plan?

P15–14. *Cost allocation: Step method versus direct method; Pricing.*   The Ashley Company has budgeted costs in its various departments as follows for the coming period:

Factory Administration	$ 45,000
Custodial Services	35,150
Personnel	25,950
Engineering	49,200
Machining—overhead	251,380
Assembly—overhead	133,320
Total costs	$540,000

The company allocates service department costs to other departments, in the order listed below. Bases for allocation are to be chosen from the following:

	Number of employees	Total labor-hours	Square feet of space occupied	Direct labor-hours	Machine-hours
Factory Administration*	20	—	5,000	—	—
Custodial Services..............	4	3,000	2,000	—	—
Personnel	5	5,000	3,000	—	—
Engineering	25	22,000	10,000	—	—
Machining	40	30,000	50,000	20,000	60,000
Assembly	60	90,000	40,000	80,000	20,000
	154	150,000	110,000	100,000	80,000

* Basis for allocation is total labor-hours.

Machining and Assembly are producing departments; the other depart-ments all act in a service capacity. The company does not make a distinction between fixed and variable service department costs; alloca-tions are made to using departments according to that base which ap-pears to provide the best measure of benefits received.

Required:

1. Allocate service department costs to using departments by the step method. Then compute predetermined overhead rates in the produc-ing departments, using a machine-hours basis in Machining and a direct labor-hours basis in Assembly.
2. Repeat (1) above, this time using the direct method. Again compute predetermined overhead rates in Machining and Assembly.
3. Assume that the company doesn't want to bother with allocating service department costs, and simply wants to compute a single plantwide overhead rate based on total overhead costs (both service department and producing department) divided by total direct labor-hours. Compute the appropriate overhead rate.
4. Assume that the company wants to bid on a job during the year that will require machine and labor time as follows:

	Machining time—hours	Direct-labor time— hours
Machining Department	200	60
Assembly Department....................	20	100
Total hours	220	160

a. Using the overhead rates developed under the step method in (1) above, compute the overhead that would be assigned to the job.
b. Using the overhead rate developed under the plantwide method

in (3) above, compute the overhead that would be assigned to the job.

5. Assume that the job being bid on in (4) will require $700 in materials and $800 in direct labor cost, and that the company prices its jobs at 150 percent of total cost to manufacture. Compute the price that would be bid on the job under the step method and the plantwide method of computing overhead rates.

P15–15. *Service department allocations, predetermined overhead rates, and unit costs.* Apsco Company has two service departments and two producing departments. The service departments are Medical Services and Maintenance. Estimated monthly cost and operating data for the coming year are given below. These data have been prepared for purposes of computing predetermined overhead rates in the producing departments.

	Medical services	Mainte-nance	Producing A	Producing B
Direct labor cost	—	—	$ 30,000	$ 40,000
Maintenance labor cost	—	$ 5,000	—	—
Direct materials	—	—	50,000	80,000
Maintenance materials	—	7,536	—	—
Medical supplies	$ 3,630	—	—	—
Miscellaneous overhead costs....................	7,500	6,000	104,000	155,000
Total costs	$11,130	$18,536	$184,000	$275,000
Direct labor hours	—	—	6,000	10,000
Number of employees: Presently employed	3	8	38	64
Long-run employee needs	3	10	60	80
Floor space occupied— square feet..............	800	1,500	8,000	12,000

The Apsco Company allocates service department costs to producing departments for product costing purposes. The step method is used, starting with Medical Services. Allocation bases for the service departments are:

Department	Cost	Base for allocation
Medical Services	Variable	Presently employed workers
	Fixed	Long-run employee needs
Maintenance	Variable	Direct labor hours
	Fixed	Square footage of floor space occupied

The behavior of various costs is shown on the following page:

	Medical services	Maintenance
Maintenance labor cost	—	V
Maintenance materials	—	V
Medical supplies	V	—
Miscellaneous overhead costs	F	F

V = Variable.
F = Fixed.

Required:

1. Show the allocation of the service department costs for the purpose of computing predetermined overhead rates.
2. Compute the predetermined overhead rate to be used in each of the producing departments (overhead rates are based on direct labor-hours).
3. Assume that production in Department B is planned at 20,000 units for the month. Compute the planned cost of one unit of product in Department B.

P15–16. *Allocating service department costs.* The Murray Iron Works, Inc., has two producing departments, Department A and Department B, and three service departments. The service departments, and the bases on which their costs are allocated to using departments, are listed below:

Department	Cost	Allocation base
Building and Grounds	Fixed	Square footage occupied
Medical Services	Variable	Number of employees
	Fixed	Employee needs at full capacity
Equipment Maintenance	Variable	Machine-hours
	Fixed	40% to Department A
		60% to Department B

Service department costs are allocated to using departments by the step method, in the order shown above. The company has developed the cost and operating data given in the following table, for purposes of preparing predetermined overhead rates in the two producing departments:

	Building and grounds	Medical services	Equipment maintenance	Dept. A	Dept. B	Total
Variable costs	$ –0–	$22,200	$ 2,850	$146,000	$320,000	$ 491,050
Fixed costs	88,200	60,000	24,000	420,000	490,000	1,082,200
Total	$88,200	$82,200	$26,850	$566,000	$810,000	$1,573,250
Budgeted employees	6	4	30	450	630	1,120
Employee needs at capacity	8	4	45	570	885	1,512
Square footage of space occupied	600	500	1,400	12,000	15,500	30,000
Budgeted machine-hours	—	—	—	16,000	18,500	34,500

Required:

1. Show the allocation of service department costs to using departments for purposes of preparing predetermined overhead rates in departments A and B.
2. Assuming that predetermined overhead rates are set on a basis of machine-hours, compute the predetermined overhead rate for each producing department.
3. Assume the following *actual* data for the year for the Medical Services Department:

Actual variable costs $24,794
Actual employees for the year:
    Building and Grounds   6
    Medical Services   4
    Equipment Maintenance   32
    Department A 460
    Department B 625
                                   1,127

Compute the amount of end-of-year Medical Services variable cost that should be allocated to each department. (Management uses these end-of-year allocations to compare actual performance against planned performance.)

P15–17. *Determining allocation bases.* Bonn Company recently reorganized its computer and data processing activities. The small installations located within the accounting departments at its plants and subsidiaries have been replaced with a single Data Processing Department at corporate headquarters responsible for the operations of a newly acquired large-scale computer system. The new department has been in operation for two years and has been regularly producing reliable and timely data for the past 12 months.

Because the department has focused its activities on converting applications to the new system and producing reports for the plant and subsidiary managers, little attention has been devoted to the costs of the department. Now that the department's activities are operating relatively smoothly, company management has requested that the manager of the Data Processing Department recommend a cost accumulation system to facilitate cost control and the development of suitable rates to charge users for computer service.

For the past two years, the departmental costs have been totaled into one figure. The costs have then been allocated to user departments on the basis of computer time used. For example, the schedule below reports the costs and charging rate for computer service for 19x5:

DATA PROCESSING DEPARTMENT
Costs for the Year Ended December 31, 19x5

1.	Salaries and benefits	$ 622,600
2.	Supplies	40,000
3.	Equipment maintenance contract	15,000
4.	Insurance	25,000
5.	Heat and air conditioning	36,000
6.	Electricity	50,000
7.	Equipment and furniture depreciation	285,400
8.	Building improvements depreciation	10,000
9.	Building occupancy and security	39,300
10.	Corporate administrative charges	52,700
	Total costs	$1,176,000
	Computer-hours for user processing*	2,750
	Hourly rate ($1,176,000 ÷ 2,750)	$ 428

* Use of available computer-hours:

Testing and debugging programs	250
Set-up of jobs	500
Processing jobs	2,750
Down-time for maintenance	750
Idle time	742
Total computer-hours	4,992

The manager of the Data Processing Department recommends that the department costs above be accumulated by five activity centers within the department: Systems Analysis, Programming, Data Preparation, Computer Operations (processing of data), and Administration. She then suggests that the costs of the Administration activity should be allocated to the other four activity centers before a separate rate for charging users is developed for each of these first four centers. That is, the department would no longer have a single charging rate, but four separate rates, one each for Systems Analysis, Programming, Data Preparation, and Computer Operations.

To assist in determining how the department's costs should be allocated between the five proposed activity centers within the department, the Data Processing Department manager has provided the following information relative to the department's costs (numbers are keyed to the cost items listed above):

1. Salaries and benefits—this account records the salary and benefit costs of all employees in the department.
2. Supplies—this account records punch card costs, paper costs for printers, and a small amount for miscellaneous other costs.
3. Equipment maintenance contracts—this account records charges for maintenance contracts; all equipment is covered by such contracts.
4. Insurance—this account records the cost of insurance covering the equipment and the furniture in the department.
5. Heat and air conditioning—this account records a charge from the corporate heating and air-conditioning department estimated to be the incremental costs to meet the special needs of the computer facility.

6. Electricity—this account records the charge for electricity based upon a separate meter within the department.
7. Equipment and furniture depreciation—this account records the depreciation charges for all owned equipment and furniture in the department.
8. Building improvements—this account records the amortization charges for the building changes required to provide proper environmental control and electrical service for the computer equipment.
9. Building occupancy and security—this account records the computer department's share of the depreciation, maintenance, and heat and security costs of the building; these costs are allocated to the department on the basis of square feet occupied.
10. Corporate administrative charges—this account records the Data Processing Department's share of the corporate administrative costs. They are allocated to the department on the basis of number of employees in the department.

Required:

1. For each of these ten cost items, state whether or not it should be distributed (allocated) to the five proposed activity centers, and for each cost item that should be distributed, recommend the basis to be used in the distribution. Justify your conclusion in each case.
2. Assume that the costs of one activity center, Computer Operations (processing of data), will be charged to the user departments on the basis of computer-hours. Using the analysis of computer utilization shown as a footnote to the department cost schedule presented in the problem, determine the total number of hours that should be employed to determine the charging rate for Computer Operations. Justify your answer.

(CMA, adapted)

Chapter 16

"How well am I doing?" — Financial statement analysis

No matter how carefully prepared, all financial statements are essentially historical documents. They tell what *has happened* during a particular year or series of years. The most valuable information to most users of financial statements, however, concerns what probably *will happen* in the future. The purpose of financial statement analysis is to assist statement users in *predicting the future* by means of comparison, evaluation, and trend analysis.

THE IMPORTANCE OF STATEMENT ANALYSIS

Virtually all users of financial data have concerns that can be resolved to some degree by the predictive ability of statement analysis. The stockholders are concerned, for example, about matters such as whether they should hold or sell their stocks, about whether the present management group should remain or be replaced, and about whether the company should have their approval to sell a new offering of senior debt. The creditors are concerned about matters such as whether income will be sufficient to cover the interest due on their bonds or notes, and about whether prospects are good for their obligations to be paid at maturity. The managers are concerned about matters such as dividend policy, availability of funds to finance future expansion, and the probable future success of operations under their leadership.

The thing about the future that statement users are most interested in predicting is profits. It is profits, of course, that provide the basis for an increase in the value of the stockholder's stock, and that encourage the creditor to risk his or her money in an organization. And it is largely profits that make future expansion possible. The dilemma is that profits are uncertain. For this reason, one must have certain analytical tools to assist in interpreting the key relationships and trends that serve as a basis for judgments of potential future success. Without financial statement analysis, the story that key relationships and trends have to tell may remain buried in a sea of statement detail.

In this chapter we consider some of the more important ratios and other analytical tools used by analysts in attempting to predict the future course of events in business organizations.

Importance of comparisons

Not only are financial statements historical documents, but they also are essentially static documents. They speak only of the events of a single period of time. However, statement users are concerned not just with the present, but with what the *trend of events* has been (and will be) over time. For this reason, financial statement analysis directed toward a single period is of limited usefulness. The results of financial statement analysis are of value only when viewed in *comparison* with the results of other periods, and in some cases, with the results of other firms. It is only through comparison that one can gain insight into trends, and make intelligent judgments as to their significance.

Unfortunately, comparisons between firms within an industry are often made difficult by differences in accounting methods in use. For example, if one firm values its inventories by Lifo and another firm values its inventories by average cost, then direct dollar-for-dollar comparisons between the two firms may not be possible. In such cases, comparisons can still be made, but they must focus on data in a broader, more relative sense. Although the analytical work required here may be tougher, it often is necessary if the manager is to have any data available for comparison purposes.

The need to look beyond ratios

There is a tendency for the inexperienced analyst to assume that ratios are sufficient in themselves as a basis for judgments about the future. Nothing could be further from the truth. The experienced analyst realizes that the best prepared ratio analysis must be considered tentative in nature, and never conclusive in itself. Rather than an end, ratios should be viewed as a *starting point,* as indicators of what to pursue in greater depth. They raise many questions, but rarely answer any by themselves.

To solidify his or her judgments, the analyst must take a careful look at industry trends, technological changes in process or anticipated, changes in consumer tastes, changes in economic factors both regionally and nationally, and at changes taking place within the firm itself. A recent change in a key management position, for example, might rightly serve as a basis for much optimism about the future, even though the past performance of the firm may have been very mediocre.

STATEMENTS IN COMPARATIVE AND COMMON-SIZE FORM

As stated above, few figures appearing on financial statements have much significance standing by themselves. It is the relationship of one figure to another, and the amount and direction of change from one point in time to another, that is important in financial statement analysis. How does the analyst key in on significant relationships? How does the analyst dig out the important trends and changes in a company? Three analytical techniques are in widespread use:

1. Dollar and percentage changes on statements.
2. Common-size statements.
3. Ratios.

All three techniques are discussed in following sections.

Dollar and percentage changes on statements

A good beginning place in financial statement analysis is to put statements in comparative form. This consists of little more than putting two or more years' data side by side. Statements cast in comparative form will underscore movements and trends, and may give the analyst many valuable clues as to what to expect in the way of financial and operating performance in the future. Comparative financial statements for Brickey

Exhibit 16–1

BRICKEY ELECTRONICS COMPANY Comparative Balance Sheet December 31, 19x1, and December 31, 19x2 ($000)			Increase (decrease)	
	19x2	19x1	Amount	Per-cent
Assets				
Current Assets:				
Cash	$ 1,000	$ 2,570	$(1,570)	(61.1)
Accounts receivable, net	6,000	4,000	2,000	50.0
Inventory	8,000	10,000	(2,000)	(20.0)
Prepaid expenses	500	200	300	150.0
Total Current Assets	$15,500	$16,770	$(1,270)	(7.6)
Property and Equipment:				
Land	$ 4,000	$ 4,000	–0–	–0–
Buildings and equipment, net	9,500	6,000	3,500	58.3
Total Property and Equipment	$13,500	$10,000	$ 3,500	35.0
Total Assets	$29,000	$26,770	$ 2,230	8.3
Liabilities and Stockholders' Equity				
Current Liabilities:				
Accounts payable	$ 6,000	$ 4,200	$ 1,800	42.9
Accrued payables	500	300	200	66.7
Current portion of bonds payable	500	500	–0–	–0–
Total Current Liabilities	$ 7,000	$ 5,000	$ 2,000	40.0
Long-term Liabilities:				
Bonds payable, 5%	7,500	8,000	(500)	(6.3)
Total Liabilities	$14,500	$13,000	$ 1,500	11.5
Stockholders' Equity:				
Preferred stock, $100 par, 6%, $100 liquidation value	$ 2,000	$ 2,000	–0–	–0–
Common stock, $10 par	6,000	6,000	–0–	–0–
Additional paid-in capital	1,000	1,000	–0–	–0–
Total Paid-in Capital	$ 9,000	$ 9,000	–0–	–0–
Retained earnings	5,500	4,770	730	15.3
Total Stockholders' Equity	$14,500	$13,770	$ 730	5.3
Total Liabilities and Equity	$29,000	$26,770	$ 2,230	8.3

Electronics Company, a hypothetical firm, are shown in Exhibits 16–1 and 16–2.

HORIZONTAL ANALYSIS. Comparison of two or more years' financial data is known as *horizontal analysis.* Horizontal analysis is greatly facilitated by showing changes between years in both dollar *and* percentage form, as has been done in Exhibits 16–1 and 16–2. Showing changes in dollar form helps the analyst to zero in on key factors which have affected profitability or financial position. For example, observe in Exhibit 16–2 that sales

Exhibit 16–2

BRICKEY ELECTRONICS COMPANY
Comparative Income Statement and Reconciliation
of Retained Earnings
For the Year Ended December 31, 19x1, and December 31, 19x2
($000)

			Increase (decrease)	
	19x2	*19x1*	*Amount*	*Percent*
Sales	$52,000	$48,000	$4,000	8.3
Cost of goods sold	36,000	31,500	4,500	14.3
Gross margin	$16,000	$16,500	$ (500)	(3.0)
Operating expenses:				
Selling expenses	$ 7,000	$ 6,500	$ 500	7.7
Administrative expenses	5,000	5,200	(200)	(3.8)
Total operating expenses	$12,000	$11,700	$ 300	2.6
Net operating income	$ 4,000	$ 4,800	$ (800)	(16.7)
Interest expense	375	400	(25)	(6.3)
Net income before taxes	$ 3,625	$ 4,400	$ (775)	(17.6)
Less income taxes	2,175	2,640	(465)	(17.6)
Net income	$ 1,450	$ 1,760	$ (310)	(17.6)
Dividends to preferred stockholders, $6 per share (see Exhibit 16–1)	120	120		
Net income remaining for common stockholders	$ 1,330	$ 1,640		
Dividends to common stockholders ($1 per share)	600	600		
Net income added to retained earnings	$ 730	$ 1,040		
Retained earnings, beginning of year	4,770	3,730		
Retained earnings, end of year	$ 5,500	$ 4,770		

for 19x2 were up $4 million over 19x1, but that this increase in sales was more than negated by a $4.5 million increase in cost of goods sold.

Showing changes between years in percentage form helps the analyst to gain *perspective,* and to gain a feel for the *significance* of the changes that are taking place. One would have a different perspective of a $1 million increase in sales if the prior year's sales were $2 million than he would if the prior year's sales were $20 million. In the first situation the increase would be 50 percent—undoubtedly a significant increase for any firm. In the second situation the increase would be only 5 percent—perhaps a reflection of just normal growth.

TREND PERCENTAGES. Horizontal analysis of financial statements can also be carried out by computing trend percentages. Trend percentages state several years' financial data in terms of a base year. The base year equals 100 percent with all other years stated as some percentage of this base. To illustrate, assume that Glacor Company has reported the following sales and income data for the past five years:

	19x5	19x4	19x3	19x2	19x1
Sales	$725,000	$700,000	$650,000	$575,000	$500,000
Net income	$ 99,000	$ 97,500	$ 93,750	$ 86,250	$ 75,000

By simply looking at these data one can see that both sales and net income have increased over the five-year period reported. But how rapidly have sales been increasing, and have the increases in net income kept pace with the increases in sales? By looking at the raw data alone it is difficult to answer these questions. The increases in sales and the increases in net income can be put into proper perspective by stating them in terms of trend percentages, with 19x1 as the base year. These percentages are given below:

	19x5	19x4	19x3	19x2	19x1
Sales	145%	140%	130%	115%*	100%
Net income	132%	130%	125%	115%	100%

    * $575,000 ÷ $500,000 = 115%.

Notice that the growth in sales dropped off somewhat between 19x3 and 19x4, and dropped off even more between 19x4 and 19x5. Also notice that the growth in net income has not kept pace with the growth in sales. In 19x5 sales are 1.45 times greater than in 19x1, the base year; however, in 19x5 net income is only 1.32 times greater than in 19x1.

Common-size statements

Key changes and trends can also be highlighted by the use of common-size statements. A common-size statement is one that shows the separate items appearing on it in percentage form, rather than in dollar form. Each item is stated as a percentage of some total of which that item is a part. Preparation of common-size statements is known as *vertical analysis.*

THE BALANCE SHEET. One application of the vertical analysis idea is to state the separate assets of a company as percentages of total assets. A common-size statement of this type is shown in Exhibit 16–3 for Brickey Electronics Company.

Exhibit 16–3

	19x2	19x1	Common-size percentages 19x2	19x1
BRICKEY ELECTRONICS COMPANY Common-Size Comparative Balance Sheet December 31, 19x1, and December 31, 19x2 ($000)				
Assets				
Current Assets:				
Cash	$ 1,000	$ 2,570	3.4	9.6
Accounts receivable, net	6,000	4,000	20.7	14.9
Inventory	8,000	10,000	27.6	37.4
Prepaid expenses	500	200	1.7	0.7
Total Current Assets	$15,500	$16,770	53.4	62.6
Property and Equipment:				
Land	$ 4,000	$ 4,000	13.8	14.9
Buildings and equipment, net	9,500	6,000	32.8	22.5
Total Property and Equipment	$13,500	$10,000	46.6	37.4
Total Assets	$29,000	$26,770	100.0	100.0
Liabilities and Stockholders' Equity				
Current Liabilities:				
Accounts payable	$ 6,000	$ 4,200	20.7	15.7
Accrued payables	500	300	1.7	1.1
Current portion of bonds payable	500	500	1.7	1.9
Total Current Liabilities	$ 7,000	$ 5,000	24.1	18.7
Long-term Liabilities:				
Bonds payable, 5%	7,500	8,000	25.9	29.9
Total Liabilities	$14,500	$13,000	50.0	48.6
Stockholders' Equity:				
Preferred stock, $100 par, 6%, $100 liquidation value	$ 2,000	$ 2,000	6.9	7.5
Common stock, $10 par	6,000	6,000	20.7	22.4
Additional paid-in capital	1,000	1,000	3.4	3.7
Total Paid-in Capital	$ 9,000	$ 9,000	31.0	33.6
Retained earnings	5,500	4,770	19.0	17.8
Total Stockholders' Equity	$14,500	$13,770	50.0	51.4
Total Liabilities and Equity	$29,000	$26,770	100.0	100.0

Notice from Exhibit 16–3 that placing all assets in common-size form clearly shows the relative importance of the current assets as compared to the noncurrent assets. It also shows that significant changes have taken place in the *composition* of the current assets over the last year. Notice, for example, that the receivables have increased in relative importance, and that both cash and inventory have declined in relative importance. Judging from the sharp increase in receivables, the deterioration in the cash position may be a result of inability to collect from customers.

THE INCOME STATEMENT.   Another application of the vertical analysis idea is to place all items on the income statement in percentage form in terms of total sales. A common-size statement of this type is shown in Exhibit 16–4.

Exhibit 16–4

	19x2	19x1	19x2	19x1
BRICKEY ELECTRONICS COMPANY Common-Size Comparative Income Statement For the Year Ended December 31, 19x1, and December 31, 19x2 ($000)			Common-size percentages	
Sales	$52,000	$48,000	100.0	100.0
Cost of goods sold	36,000	31,500	69.2	65.7
Gross margin	$16,000	$16,500	30.8	34.3
Operating expenses:				
Selling expenses	$ 7,000	$ 6,500	13.5	13.5
Administrative expenses	5,000	5,200	9.6	10.8
Total operating expenses	$12,000	$11,700	23.1	24.3
Net operating income	$ 4,000	$ 4,800	7.7	10.0
Interest expense	375	400	0.7	0.8
Net income before taxes	$ 3,625	$ 4,400	7.0	9.2
Income taxes (60%)	2,175	2,640	4.2	5.5
Net income	$ 1,450	$ 1,760	2.8	3.7

By placing all items on the income statement in common size in terms of sales, it is possible to see at a glance how each dollar of sales is distributed between the various costs, expenses, and profits. For example, notice from Exhibit 16–4 that in 19x2, 69.2 cents out of every dollar of sales was needed to cover cost of goods sold, and that only 2.8 cents out of every dollar of sales remained for profits.

Common-size statements are also very helpful in pointing out efficiencies and inefficiencies that otherwise might go unnoticed. To illustrate, in 19x2 Brickey Electronics Company's selling expenses increased by $500 over 19x1. A glance at the common-size income statement shows, however, that on a relative basis selling expenses were no higher in 19x2 than in 19x1. In each year they represented 13.5 percent of sales.

RATIO ANALYSIS—THE COMMON STOCKHOLDER

The common stockholder has only a residual claim on profits and assets of a corporation. It is only after all creditor and preferred stockholder claims have been satisfied that the common stockholder can step forward and receive a distribution of profits, or assets in liquidation. A measure of the common stockholder's well-being, therefore, provides some perspective of the depth of protection available to others associated with a firm.

Earnings per share

An investor buys and retains a share of stock with the thought in mind of a return coming in the future either in the form of dividends or in the form of capital gains. Since earnings form the basis for dividend payments, as well as the basis for any future increases in the value of shares, investors are always extremely interested in a company's reported earnings per share. Probably no single statistic is more widely quoted or relied upon in investor actions than earnings per share, although it has some inherent dangers, as discussed below.

The computation of earnings per share is made by dividing net income remaining for common shareholders by the number of common shares outstanding. "Net income remaining for common shareholders" is equal to the net income of a company, reduced by the dividends due to the preferred shareholders.

$$\frac{\text{Net income} - \text{Preferred dividends}}{\text{Common shares outstanding}} = \text{Earnings per share}$$

Using the data in Exhibits 16–1 and 16–2, we see that the earnings per share for Brickey Electronics Company for 19x2 would be:

$$\frac{\$1,450,000 - \$120,000}{600,000 \text{ shares}} = \$2.22 \tag{1}$$

Two problems can arise in connection with the computation of earnings per share. The first arises whenever an extraordinary gain or loss appears as part of net income. The second arises whenever a company has convertible securities on its balance sheet. These problems are discussed in the following two sections.

Extraordinary items and earnings per share

If a company has extraordinary gains or losses appearing as part of net income, *two* earnings-per-share figures must be computed—one showing the earnings per share resulting from *normal* operations, and one showing the earnings-per-share impact of the *extraordinary* items. This approach to computing earnings per share accomplishes three things. First, it helps statement users to recognize extraordinary items for what they are—unusual events that probably will not recur. Second, it eliminates the distorting influence of the extraordinary items from the basic earnings-per-share figure. And third, it helps statement users to properly assess the *trend* of *normal* earnings per share over time. Since one would not expect the extraordinary or unusual items to repeat year after year, they should be given less weight in judging earnings performance than is given to profits resulting from normal operations.

In addition to reporting extraordinary items separately, the accountant also reports them *net of their tax effect.* By "net of their tax effect" we mean that whatever impact the unusual item has on income taxes is *deducted from* the unusual item on the income statement. Only the net, after-tax, gain or loss is used in earnings-per-share computations.

To illustrate these concepts, let us assume a fire loss of $4,000, and the following additional items of revenue and expense:

Incorrect Approach		
Sales		$50,000
Cost of goods sold		30,000
Gross margin		$20,000
Operating expenses:		
Selling expenses	$5,000	
Administrative expenses	8,000	
Fire loss	4,000	17,000
Net income before taxes		$ 3,000
Income taxes (40%)		1,200
Net income		$ 1,800

Extraordinary gains and losses should not be included with normal items of revenue and expense. This distorts a firm's normal income producing ability.

Correct Approach		
Sales		$50,000
Cost of goods sold		30,000
Gross margin		$20,000
Operating expenses:		
Selling expenses	$5,000	
Administrative expenses	8,000	13,000
Net operating income		$ 7,000
Income taxes (40%)		2,800
Net income before extraordinary item		$ 4,200
Extraordinary item:		
Fire loss, net of tax		(2,400)
Net income		$ 1,800

Reporting the extraordinary item separately and net of its tax effect leaves the normal items of revenue and expense unaffected.

Original loss		$4,000
Less reduction in taxes at a 40% rate		1,600
Loss, net of tax		$2,400

The fire loss is fully deductible for tax purposes. Therefore, this deduction will reduce the firm's taxable income by $4,000. If taxable income is $4,000 lower, then income taxes will be $1,600 *less* (40% × $4,000) than they *otherwise* would have been. In other words, the fire loss of $4,000 *saves* the company $1,600 in taxes that otherwise would have been paid. The $1,600 savings in taxes is deducted from the loss that caused it, leaving a net loss of only $2,400.

Extraordinary *gains* will *increase* taxes. The increased taxes are deducted from the extraordinary item, leaving only the net gain that will remain after the added taxes are paid.

To continue our illustration, assume that the company above has 2,000 shares of common stock outstanding. Earnings per share would be reported as follows:

Earnings per share on common stock:
On net income before extraordinary item ($4,200 ÷ 2,000 shares)* $2.10
On extraordinary item, net of tax ($2,400 ÷ 2,000 shares) .... (1.20)
Net earnings per share $0.90

* Sometimes called the *primary* earnings per share.

In sum, computation of earnings per share as we have done above is necessary to avoid misinterpretation and misunderstanding of a company's normal income producing ability. Reporting *only* the flat $0.90 per share figure would be misleading and perhaps cause investors to regard the company less favorably than they should.

Fully diluted earnings per share

A problem sometimes arises in trying to determine the number of common shares to use in computing earnings per share. Until recent years, the distinction between common stock, preferred stock, and debt was quite clear. The distinction between these securities has now become somewhat diffused, however, due to a growing tendency to issue convertible securities of various types. Rather than simply issuing common stock, firms today often issue preferred stock or bonds that carry a *conversion feature* allowing the purchaser to convert holdings into common stock at some future time.

When convertible securities are present in the financial structure of a firm, the question arises as to whether they should be retained in their unconverted form, or whether they should be treated as common stock, in computing earnings per share. The American Institute of Certified Public Accountants has taken the position that convertible securities should be treated *both* in their present and prospective forms. This requires the presentation of *two* earnings-per-share figures for firms that have convertible securities outstanding, one showing earnings per share assuming no conversion into common stock, and the other showing full conversion into common stock. The latter earnings-per-share figure is said to show earnings on a *fully diluted* basis.

To illustrate, let us assume that the preferred stock of Brickey Electronics Company in Exhibit 16–1 is convertible into common on a basis of five shares of common for each share of preferred. Since 20,000 shares of preferred are outstanding, conversion would require issuing an additional 100,000 shares of common stock. Earnings per share on a fully diluted basis would be:

$$\frac{\text{Net income before preferred dividends}}{(600{,}000 \text{ original shares} + 100{,}000 \text{ converted shares})}$$

$$= \frac{\$1{,}450{,}000}{700{,}000 \text{ shares}} = \$2.07 \quad (2)$$

In comparing Equation (2) with Equation (1), we can note that the earnings-per-share figure has dropped by $0.15. Although the impact of full dilution is relatively small in this case, it can be very significant in situations where large amounts of convertible securities are present.

Price earnings ratio

The relationship between the market price of a share of stock and the stock's current earnings per share is often quoted in terms of a *price/earnings* ratio. If we assume that the market price of Brickey Electronics Company's stock is $45 per share, the company's price/earnings ratio would be computed as follows:

$$\frac{\text{Market price}}{\text{Earnings per share}} = \text{Price/earnings ratio}$$

$$\frac{\$45.00}{\$2.22 \text{ See Equation (1)}} = 20.3 \quad (3)$$

The price/earnings ratio is 20.3; that is, the stock is selling for about 20.3 times its current earnings per share.

The price/earnings ratio is widely used by investors as a general guideline in gauging stock values. Investors increase or decrease the price/earnings ratio that they are willing to accept for a share of stock according to how they view its *future prospects.* Companies with ample opportunities for growth generally have high price/earnings ratios, with the opposite being true for companies with limited growth opportunities. If investors decided that Brickey Electronics Company had greater than average growth prospects, they might be willing to let the price/earnings ratio for the company rise to 25. In that case we would expect the company's stock to begin selling for about $55 per share ($2.22 EPS × 25.0 P/E ratio).

Dividend payout and yield ratios

Investors hold shares of one stock in preference to shares of another stock because they anticipate that the first stock will provide them with a more attractive return. The return sought after isn't always dividends. Many investors prefer not to receive dividends. Instead, they prefer to have the company retain all earnings and reinvest them internally in order to support growth. Such stocks, loosely termed "growth stocks," often enjoy rapid upward movement in market price. On sale of the stock, investors can then reap their return in the form of capital gains, which receive very favorable treatment from an income tax point of view. Other investors prefer to have a dependable, current source of income through regular dividend payments, and prefer not to gamble on the fortunes of stock prices to provide a return on their investment. Such investors seek out stocks with consistent dividend records and payout ratios.

THE DIVIDEND PAYOUT RATIO. The dividend payout ratio gauges the portion of current earnings being paid out in dividends. Investors seeking capital gains would like this ratio to be small, whereas investors who seek dividends prefer it to be large. The ratio is computed by relating dividends per share to earnings per share for common stock:

$$\frac{\text{Dividends per share}}{\text{Earnings per share}} = \text{Dividend payout ratio}$$

For Brickey Electronics Company, the dividend payout ratio for 19x2 was:

$$\frac{\$1.00 \text{ (see Exhibit 16–2)}}{\$2.22 \text{ [see Equation (1)]}} = 45\% \tag{4}$$

There is no such thing as a "right" payout ratio, even though it should be noted that the ratio tends to be somewhat the same for the bulk of firms within a particular industry. Industries with ample opportunities for growth at high rates of return on assets tend to have low payout ratios, and the reverse tends to be true for industries with limited reinvestment opportunities.

THE DIVIDEND YIELD RATIO. The dividend yield ratio is obtained by dividing the current dividends per share by the current market price per share:

$$\frac{\text{Dividends per share}}{\text{Market price per share}} = \text{Dividend yield ratio}$$

If we continue the assumption of a market price of $45 per share for Brickey Electronics Company stock, the dividend yield is:

$$\frac{\$1.00}{\$45.00} = 2.2\% \tag{5}$$

In making this computation, note that we used the current market price of the stock, rather than the price the investor paid for the stock initially (which might be above or below the current market). By using current market price, we recognize the opportunity cost[1] of the investment in terms

---

[1] Opportunity cost can be defined as the potential benefit that is lost or sacrificed when the choice of one course of action requires the giving up of an alternative course of action.

of its yield. That is, this is the yield that would be lost or sacrificed if the investor sells the stock for $45 and buys a new security in its place.

Return on total assets

Managers have two basic responsibilities in managing a firm—*financing* responsibilities and *operating* responsibilities. Financing responsibilities relate to how one *obtains* the funds needed to provide for assets in an organization. Operating responsibilities relate to how one *uses* the assets once they have been obtained. Proper discharge of both responsibilities is vital to a well-managed firm. However, care must be taken not to confuse or mix the two in assessing the performance of a manager. That is, whether funds have been obtained partly from creditors and partly from stockholders or entirely from stockholders should not be allowed to influence one's assessment of *how well* the assets have been employed since being received by the firm.

The return on total assets ratio is a measure of how well assets have been employed; that is, it is a measure of operating performance. The formula is:

$$\frac{\text{Net income} + \text{Interest expense}}{\text{Average total assets}} = \text{Return on total assets}$$

By adding interest expense back to net income we derive a figure that shows earnings before any distributions have been made to either creditors or stockholders. Thus we eliminate the matter of how the assets were financed from influencing the measurement of how well the assets have been employed.

The return on total assets for Brickey Electronics Company for 19x2 would be (from Exhibits 16–1 and 16–2):

Net income	$ 1,450,000	
Add back interest expense	375,000	
Total	$ 1,825,000	(a)
Assets, beginning of year	$26,770,000	
Assets, end of year	29,000,000	
Total	$55,770,000	
Average total assets $55,770,000 ÷ 2	$27,885,000	(b)
Return on total assets (a) ÷ (b)	6.5%	(6)

Brickey Electronics Company has earned a return of 6.5 percent on average assets employed over the last year.

Return on common stockholders' equity

One of the primary reasons for operating a corporation is to generate income for the benefit of the common stockholders. One measure of a company's success in this regard is the rate of return which it is able to generate on the common stockholders' equity:

$$\frac{\text{Net income} - \text{preferred dividends}}{\begin{array}{l}\text{Average common stockholders' equity (average} \\ \text{total stockholders' equity} - \text{preferred stock)}\end{array}}$$

= Return on common stockholders' equity

For Brickey Electronics Company, the return on common stockholders' equity is 11.0 percent for 19x2, as shown below:

Net income	$ 1,450,000	
Deduct preferred dividends	120,000	
Net income remaining for common stockholders	$ 1,330,000	(a)
Average stockholders' equity	$14,135,000*	
Deduct preferred stock.................................	2,000,000	
Average common stockholders' equity....................	$12,135,000	(b)
Return on common stockholders' equity (a) ÷ (b)	11.0%	(7)

* $13,770,000 + $14,500,000 = $28,270,000; $28,270,000 ÷ 2 = $14,135,000.

Compare the return on common stockholders' equity above (11.0 percent) to the return on total assets computed in the preceding section (6.5 percent). Why is the return on common stockholders' equity so much higher? The answer lies in the principle of *leverage* (sometimes called "trading on the equity").

THE CONCEPT OF LEVERAGE. Leverage involves the securing of funds for investment at a *fixed rate of return* to the suppliers of the funds, normally with the thought in mind of enhancing the well-being of the common stockholders. If the assets in which the funds are invested are able to earn at a rate of return *greater* than the fixed rate of return required by the suppliers of the funds, then leverage is *positive* and the common stockholders benefit.

For example, assume that a firm is able to earn a return of 8 percent on its assets. If that firm can borrow from creditors at a 5 percent interest rate in order to expand its assets, then the common stockholders can benefit from positive leverage. The borrowed funds invested in the business will earn at a rate of 8 percent, but the interest cost of the funds will be only 5 percent. The difference will go to the common stockholders.

We can see this concept in operation in the case of Brickey Electronics Company. Notice from Exhibit 16–1 that the company's bonds payable bear a fixed interest rate of 5 percent. The company's total assets (which would contain the proceeds from the original sale of these bonds) are generating a rate of return 6.5 percent, as we computed earlier. Since the return on total assets (6.5 percent) is greater than the fixed interest cost of the bonds (5 percent), leverage is positive, and the difference accrues to the benefit of the common stockholders. This explains in part why the return on common stockholders' equity (11.0 percent) is greater than the return on total assets (6.5 percent).

SOURCES OF LEVERAGE. Leverage can be obtained from several sources. One source is long-term debt, such as bonds payable or notes payable. Two additional sources are current liabilities and preferred stock. Current liabilities are always a source of positive leverage in that funds are provided for use in a company with no interest return required by the short-term creditors involved. For example, when a company acquires inventory from a supplier on account, the inventory is available for use in the business, yet the supplier requires no interest return on the amount owed to him.

Preferred stock can also be a source of positive leverage so long as the preferred dividend payable to the preferred shareholders is less than the rate of return being earned on total assets employed. In the case of Brickey Electronics Company, positive leverage is being realized on the preferred stock. Notice from Exhibit 16–1 that the preferred dividend rate is only 6 percent, whereas the assets in the company are earning at a rate of 6.5 percent, as computed earlier. Again, the difference goes to the common stockholders, thereby helping to bolster their return to the 11.0 percent computed above.

Unfortunately, leverage is a two-edged sword. If assets are unable to earn a high enough rate to cover the interest costs of debt, or to cover the preferred dividend due to the preferred stockholders, *then the common stockholder suffers.* The reason is that part of the earnings from the assets which the common stockholder has provided to the company will have to go to make up the deficiency to the long-term creditors or to the preferred stockholders, and he or she will be left with a smaller return than otherwise would have been earned. Under these circumstances, leverage is said to be *negative.*

THE IMPACT OF INCOME TAXES. Long-term debt and preferred stock are not equally efficient in generating positive leverage. The reason is that interest on long-term debt is tax deductible, whereas preferred dividends are not. This makes long-term debt a much more effective source of positive leverage than preferred stock.

To illustrate this point, assume that a company is considering two ways of financing a $100,000 expansion of its assets:

1. $50,000 from an issue of common stock, and $50,000 from an issue of preferred stock bearing a dividend rate of 8 percent.
2. $50,000 from an issue of common stock, and $50,000 from an issue of bonds bearing an interest rate of 8 percent.

Assuming that the company can earn an additional $15,000 each year before interest and taxes as a result of the expansion, the operating results under each of the two alternatives would be:

	Alternative 1	Alternative 2
Earnings before interest and taxes	$15,000	$15,000
Deduct interest expense (8% × $50,000)	—	4,000
Net income before taxes	$15,000	$11,000
Deduct income taxes (40%)	6,000	4,400
Net income	$ 9,000	$ 6,600
Deduct preferred dividends (8% × $50,000)	4,000	—
Net income remaining for common	$ 5,000	$ 6,600 (a)
Common stockholders' equity	$50,000	$50,000 (b)
Return on common stockholders' equity (a) ÷ (b)	10%	13.2%

Notice that the return to the common stockholders under Alternative 2 (where bonds are issued) is higher than it is under Alternative 1 (where preferred stock is issued). The reason is that the interest expense on the bonds is tax deductible, whereas the dividends on the preferred stock are not.

If the company in our hypothetical example above was earning a return on total assets of 12 percent, would leverage be positive or negative? Leverage would be negative in the case of Alternative 1, since the return on common stockholders' equity would be less than the return on total assets. Leverage would be positive in the case of Alternative 2, since the return on common stockholders' equity would be greater than the return on total assets.

THE DESIRABILITY OF LEVERAGE.   The leverage principle amply illustrates that prudent use of debt in the capital structure can substantially benefit the common shareholder. For this reason, most companies today try to keep a certain level of debt within the organization—at least a level equal to that which is considered to be "normal" within the industry. Occasionally one comes across a company which boasts of having no debt outstanding. Although there may be good reasons for a company having no debt, in view of the benefits that can be gained from positive leverage the possibility always exists that such a company is short-changing its stockholders. As a practical matter, many companies, such as commercial banks and other financial institutions, rely heavily on leverage to provide an attractive return on their common shares.

Book value per share

Another statistic frequently used in attempting to assess the well-being of the common shareholder is book value per share:

$$\frac{\text{Stockholders equity} - \text{Preferred stock}}{\text{Number of common shares outstanding}} = \text{Book value per share}$$

The book value of Brickey Electronics Company common stock is:

$$\frac{\$14,500,000 - \$2,000,000}{600,000 \text{ shares}} = \$20.83 \qquad (8)$$

If this book value is compared with the $45 market value which we have assumed in connection with the Brickey Electronics Company stock, then the stock appears to be badly overpriced. It is not necessarily true, however, that a market value in excess of book value is an indication of overpricing. As we discussed earlier, market prices are geared toward future earnings and dividends. Book value, by contrast, purports to reflect nothing about the future earnings potential of a firm. As a practical matter, it is actually geared to the *past,* in that it reflects the balance sheet carrying value of already completed transactions.

Of what use, then, is book value? Unfortunately, the answer must be that it is of limited use so far as being a dynamic tool of analysis is concerned. It probably finds its greatest application in situations where large amounts of liquid assets are being held in anticipation of liquidation. Occasionally, some use is also made of book value per share in attempting to set a price on the shares of closely held corporations.

RATIO ANALYSIS—THE SHORT-TERM CREDITOR

Although the short-term creditor is always well advised to keep an eye on the fortunes of the common shareholder, as expressed in the ratios of the preceding section, the focus of attention is normally channeled in another direction. The creditor is concerned with the near-term prospects of having obligations paid on time. As such, the creditor is much more interested in cash flows and in working capital management than he or she is in how much accounting net income a company is reporting.

Working capital

The excess of current assets over current liabilities is known as working capital. The working capital for Brickey Electronics Company is given below:

	19x2	19x1
Current assets	$15,500,000	$16,770,000
Current liabilities	7,000,000	5,000,000
Working capital	$ 8,500,000	$11,770,000

The amount of working capital available to a firm is of considerable interest to short-term creditors, *since it represents assets financed from long-term capital sources that do not require near-term repayment.* Therefore, the greater the working capital, the greater the cushion of protection available to short-term creditors, and the greater the assurance that short-term debts be paid when due.

Although it is always comforting to short-term creditors to see a large working capital balance, their joy becomes full only after they have been satisfied that the working capital is turning over at an acceptable rate of speed, and that their obligations could be paid even under stringent operating conditions. The reason is that a large working capital balance standing by itself is no assurance that debts will be paid when due. Rather than being a sign of strength, a large working capital balance may simply mean that stagnant or obsolete inventory is building up. Therefore, to put the working capital figure into proper perspective, it must be supplemented with other analytical work. The following four ratios (the current ratio, the acid-test ratio, the accounts receivable turnover, and the inventory turnover) should all be used in connection with an analysis of working capital.

The current ratio

The elements involved in the computation of working capital are frequently expressed in ratio form. This ratio is known as the current ratio:

$$\frac{\text{Current assets}}{\text{Current liabilities}} = \text{Current ratio}$$

For Brickey Electronics Company, the current ratio for 19x1 and 19x2 would be:

$$\begin{array}{cc} 19\text{x}2 & 19\text{x}1 \\ \dfrac{\$15,500,000}{\$\ 7,000,000} = 2.21 \text{ to } 1 & \dfrac{\$16,770,000}{\$\ 5,000,000} = 3.35 \text{ to } 1 \qquad (9) \end{array}$$

Although widely regarded as a measure of short-term debt-paying ability, the current ratio must be interpreted with a great deal of care. A *declining* ratio, as above, might be a sign of a deteriorating financial condition. On the other hand, it might be the result of a paring out of obsolete inventories or other stagnant assets. An *improving* ratio might be the result of an unwise stockpiling of inventory, or it might point up an improving financial situation. In short, the ratio is useful, but tricky to interpret. To avoid a blunder, the analyst must take a hard look at the individual items of assets and liabilities involved.

The general rule of thumb calls for a current ratio of 2 to 1. This rule, of course, is subject to many exceptions, depending on the industry and the firm involved. Some industries can operate quite successfully on a current ratio of slightly over 1 to 1. The adequacy of a current ratio depends heavily on the *composition* of the assets involved. For example, although Company X and Company Y below both have current ratios of 2 to 1, one could hardly say that they are in comparable financial condition. Company Y most certainly will have difficulty meeting its obligations as they come due.

	Company X	Company Y
Current Assets:		
Cash	$ 50,000	$ 5,000
Accounts receivable	50,000	5,000
Inventory	70,000	160,000
Prepaid expenses	5,000	5,000
Total	$175,000	$175,000
Current Liabilities	$ 87,500	$ 87,500
Current Ratio	2 to 1	2 to 1

Acid-test ratio

A much more rigorous test of a company's ability to meet its short-term debts can be found in the acid-test, or quick ratio. Merchandise inventory and prepaid expenses are excluded from the total of current assets, leaving only the more liquid (or "quick") assets to be divided by current liabilities:

$$\frac{\text{Cash} + \text{Marketable securities} + \text{Accounts receivable}}{\text{Current liabilities}} = \text{Acid-test ratio}$$

The ratio is designed to measure how well a company can meet its obligations without having to liquidate or depend too heavily on its inventory. Since inventory is not an immediate source of cash, and may not even be salable in times of economic stress, it is generally felt that to be properly protected each dollar of liabilities should be backed by at least $1 of quick assets. Thus, an acid-test ratio of 1 to 1 is broadly viewed as being adequate in many firms.

The acid-test ratios for Brickey Electronics Company for 19x1 and 19x2 are given below:

	19x2	19x1	
Cash	$1,000,000	$2,570,000	
Accounts receivable	6,000,000	4,000,000	
Total quick assets	$7,000,000	$6,570,000	
Current liabilities	$7,000,000	$5,000,000	
Acid-test ratio	1 to 1	1.3 to 1	(10)

Although Brickey Electronics Company has an acid-test ratio for 19x2 that is within the acceptable range, an analyst might be very concerned about several disquieting trends revealed in the company's balance sheet. Notice that short-term debts are rising while the cash position seems to be deteriorating. Perhaps the weakened cash position is a result of the greatly expanded volume of accounts receivable. One wonders why the accounts receivable have been allowed to increase so rapidly in so brief a time.

In short, as with the current ratio, to be used intelligently the acid-test ratio must be interpreted with one eye on its basic components.

Accounts receivable turnover

The accounts receivable turnover ratio is frequently used in conjunction with an analysis of working capital, since it provides at least a rough gauge as to how well receivables are turning into cash. The accounts receivable turnover is computed by dividing sales by the average accounts receivable balance during a period. The turnover figure can then be divided into 365 to determine the average number of days being taken to collect an account.

The accounts receivable turnover for Brickey Electronics Company for 19x2 is:

Accounts receivable:	
Beginning of year	$ 4,000,000
End of year	6,000,000
	$10,000,000
Average balance for year	$ 5,000,000

$$\frac{\text{Sales}}{\text{Average accounts receivable balance}} = \frac{\$52,000,000}{\$5,000,000} = 10.4 \text{ times} \qquad (11)$$

The average number of days taken during 19x2 to collect an account would be:

$$\frac{365 \text{ days}}{\text{Accounts receivable turnover}} = \frac{365}{10.4 \text{ times}}$$

$$= 35 \text{ days average collection period} \quad (12)$$

Whether the average of 35 days taken to collect an account is good or bad depends on the credit terms Brickey Electronics Company is offering to its customers. If credit terms are 30 days, then a 35-day average collection period would be viewed as being very good. Most customers will tend to withold payment for as long as credit terms will allow and may even go over a few days. This factor, added to the ever present few slow accounts, can cause the average collection period to exceed normal credit terms by a week to ten days, and should not be a matter for too much alarm.

On the other hand, if the company's credit terms are 10 days, then a 35-day average period may be a cause for some concern. The long collection period may be a result of the presence of many old accounts of doubtful collectibility, or it may be a result of poor day-to-day credit management. The firm may be making sales with inadequate credit checks on the companies to whom the sales are being made, or perhaps no follow-ups are being made on slow accounts.

Inventory turnover

The inventory turnover ratio measures how many times a company's inventory has been sold during the year. It is computed by dividing the cost of goods sold by the average level of inventory on hand:

$$\frac{\text{Cost of goods sold}}{\text{Average inventory}} = \text{Inventory turnover}$$

The average inventory figure is usually computed by taking the average of the beginning and ending inventory figures. Since Brickey Electronics Company has a beginning inventory figure of $10,000,000 and an ending inventory figure of $8,000,000, its average inventory for the year would be $9,000,000. The company's inventory turnover for 19x2 would be:

$$\frac{\text{Cost of goods sold}}{\text{Average inventory}} = \frac{\$36,000,000}{\$9,000,000} = 4 \text{ times} \qquad (13)$$

The number of days that it takes to sell the entire inventory one time can be determined by dividing 365 by the number of times the inventory turns over during the year:

$$\frac{365}{\text{Inventory turnover}} = \frac{365 \text{ days}}{4 \text{ times}} = 91\tfrac{1}{4} \text{ days} \qquad (14)$$

Grocery stores tend to turn their inventory over very quickly, perhaps as often as every 12 to 15 days. On the other hand, jewelry stores tend to turn their inventory over very slowly, perhaps only a couple of times each year.

If a firm has a turnover that is much slower than the average for its industry, then there may be obsolete goods on hand, or inventory stocks may be needlessly high. Excessive inventories simply tie up funds that could be used elsewhere in operations. Managers often argue that they must buy in very large quantities in order to take advantage of the best discounts being offered. But these discounts must be carefully weighed against the added costs of insurance, taxes, financing, and risks of obsolescence and deterioration that carrying added inventories bring.

An inventory turnover that is substantially faster than the average usually is an indication that inventory levels are inadequate.

RATIO ANALYSIS—THE LONG-TERM CREDITOR

The position of long-term creditors differs from that of short-term creditors in that they are concerned with both the near-term *and* the long-term ability of a firm to meet its commitments. They are concerned with the near term since whatever interest they may be entitled to is normally paid on a current basis. They are concerned with the long term from the point of view of the eventual retirement of their holdings. Since the long-term creditor is usually faced with somewhat greater risks than the short-term creditor, firms are often required to make various restrictive covenants for the long-term creditor's protection. Examples of such restrictive covenants would include the maintenance of minimum working capital levels, and restrictions on payment of dividends to common stockholders. Although these restrictive covenants are in widespread use, they must be viewed as being a poor second to *prospective earnings* from the point of view of assessing protection and safety. Creditors do not want to go to court to collect their claims; they would much prefer staking the safety of their claims for interest and eventual repayment of principal on an orderly and consistent flow of funds from operations.

Times interest earned

The most common measure of the ability of a firm's operations to provide protection to the long-term creditor is the times interest earned ratio. It is computed by dividing earnings *before* interest expense and income taxes by the yearly interest charges that must be met:

$$\frac{\text{Earnings before interest expense and income taxes}}{\text{Interest expense}}$$

$$= \text{Times interest earned}$$

For Brickey Electronics Company, the times interest earned ratio for 19x2 would be:

$$\frac{\$4,000,000}{\$375,000} = 10.7 \text{ times} \tag{15}$$

Earnings before income taxes must be used in the computation since interest expense deductions come *before* income taxes are computed. Income taxes are secondary to interest payments in that the latter have first claim on earnings. Only those earnings remaining after all interest charges have been provided for are subject to income taxes.

Various rules of thumb exist to gauge the adequacy of a firm's times interest earned ratio. Generally, earnings are viewed as adequate to protect long-term creditors if the times interest earned ratio is 2 or more. Before making a final judgment, however, it would be necessary to look at a firm's long-run *trend* of earnings, and to decide how vulnerable the firm is to cyclical changes in the economy.

The debt/equity ratio

Although long-term creditors look primarily to prospective earnings and budgeted cash flows in attempting to gauge the risk of their position, they cannot ignore the importance of keeping a reasonable balance between the portion of assets being provided by creditors and the portion of assets being provided by the stockholders of a firm. This balance is measured by the debt/equity ratio:

$$\frac{\text{Total liabilities}}{\text{Stockholders equity}} = \text{Debt/equity ratio}$$

	19x2	19x1
Total liabilities	$14,500,000	$13,000,000 (*a*)
Stockholders equity	$14,500,000	$13,770,000 (*b*)
Debt/equity ratio (*a*) ÷ (*b*)	1 to 1	0.94 to 1

(16)

The debt/equity ratio indicates the amount of assets being provided by creditors for each dollar of assets being provided by the owners of a company. In 19x1, creditors of Brickey Electronics Company were providing $0.94 of assets for each $1.00 of assets being provided by stockholders. By 19x2, however, creditors were providing just as much in assets to the company as were its owners.

It should come as no surprise that creditors would like the debt/equity ratio to be relatively low. The lower the ratio, the larger the amount of assets being provided by the owners of a company, and the greater the buffer of protection to creditors. By contrast, common stockholders would like the ratio to be relatively high, since through leverage common stockholders can benefit from the assets being provided by creditors.

In most industries norms have developed over the years that serve as guides to firms in their decisions as to the "right" amount of debt to include in the capital structure. Different industries face different risks. For this reason, the appropriate level of debt for firms in one industry is no necessary guide to the appropriate level of debt for those in a different industry.

SUMMARY

The data contained in financial statements represent a quantitative summary of a firm's operations and activities. If a manager is skillful at taking these statements apart, he or she can learn much about a company's strengths, its weaknesses, its developing problems, its operating efficiency, its profitability, and so forth.

Many analytical techniques are available to assist managers in taking financial statements apart, and to assist them in assessing the direction and importance of trends and changes. In this chapter we have discussed three such analytical techniques—dollar and percentage changes in statements, common-size statements, and ratio analysis. In the following chapter we continue our discussion of statement analysis by focusing on two new topics, funds flow and cash flow, and on their usefulness to the manager in his or her attempts to assess how well the firm is doing.

KEY TERMS FOR REVIEW

Horizontal analysis	Return on stockholders' equity
Common-size statements	Leverage
Vertical analysis	Book value per share
Earnings per share	Working capital
Fully diluted earnings per share	Current ratio
	Acid-test ratio
Price/earnings ratio	Accounts receivable turnover
Dividend payout ratio	Inventory turnover
Dividend yield ratio	Times interest earned
Return on total assets	Debt/equity ratio

QUESTIONS

16–1. What is the basic objective in looking at trends in financial ratios and other data? Rather than looking at trends, to what other standard of comparison might a statement user turn?

16–2. What is meant by the term "leverage"?

16–3. The president of a medium-sized plastics company was recently quoted in a business journal as stating, "We haven't had a dollar of interest-paying debt in over ten years. Not many companies can say that." As a stockholder in this firm, how would you feel about its policy of not taking on interest-paying debt?

16–4. "Preferred stock always results in negative leverage." Do you agree? Explain.

16–5. Distinguish between horizontal and vertical analysis of financial statement data.

16–6. If you were a long-term creditor of a firm, would you be more interested in the firm's long-term or short-term debt paying ability? Why?

16–7. A young college student once complained to the author, "The reason that corporations are such big spenders is that Uncle Sam always picks up part of the tab." What did he mean by this statement?

16–8. What is meant by the yield on a common stock investment? In computing yield why do you use current market value rather than original purchase price?

16–9. What pitfalls are involved in computing earnings per share? How can these pitfalls be avoided?

16–10. A company seeking a line of credit at a bank was turned down. Among other things, the bank stated that the company's 2 to 1 current ratio was not adequate. Give reasons why a 2 to 1 current ratio might not be adequate.

16–11. What is meant by reporting an extraordinary item on the income statement net of its tax effect? Give an example of an extraordinary gain net of its tax effect, and an extraordinary loss net of its tax effect. Assume a tax rate of 40 percent.

16–12. In financial analysis, rather than computing ratios, why not simply study the underlying financial data? What dangers are there is using ratios?

16–13. Assume that two companies in the same industry have equal earnings. Why might these companies have different price-earnings ratios? If a company has a price/earnings ratio of 20 and reports earnings per share for the current year of $4, at what price would you expect to find the stock selling on the market?

16–14. Weaver Company experiences a great deal of seasonal variation in its business activities. The company's high point in business activity is in June; its low point is in January. During which month would you expect the current ratio to be highest? At what point would you advise the company to end its fiscal year? Why?

16–15. Distinguish between a manager's *financing* and *operating* responsibilities. Which of these responsibilities is the return on total assets ratio designed to measure?

EXERCISES

E16–1. The financial statements of Pead Sales, Inc., are given below:

PEAD SALES, INC.
Balance Sheet
June 30, 19x5

Assets

Cash	$ 7,500
Accounts receivable, net	28,000
Merchandise inventory	45,000
Prepaid expenses	2,500
Plant and equipment, net	104,000
Total Assets	$187,000

Equities

Current liabilities	$ 36,000
Long-term liabilities (8%)	50,000
Common stock, $10 par	40,000
Retained earnings	61,000
Total Equities	$187,000

PEAD SALES, INC.
Income Statement
For the Year Ended June 30, 19x5

Sales	$224,000
Cost of goods sold	180,000
Gross margin	$ 44,000
Operating expenses	24,000
Net operating income	$ 20,000
Interest expense	4,000
Net income before taxes	$ 16,000
Income taxes	6,400
Net income	$ 9,600

Accounts receivable and inventory remained relatively constant during the year.

Compute the following:

a. Current ratio.

b. Acid-test ratio. (Industry average: 1.2 to 1.)

c. Debt/equity ratio.

d. Accounts receivable turnover in days. (Terms: 2/10; n/30.)

e. Inventory turnover. (Industry average: 75 days.)

f. Times interest earned.

g. Book value per share.

E16–2. Refer to the financial statements for Pead Sales, Inc., in Exercise 16–1. In addition to these statements, assume that Pead Sales, Inc., paid dividends of $1.50 per share during the year ended June 30, 19x5. Also assume that the company's stock had a market price of $30 on June 30. Compute the following:

a. Earnings per share.

b. Dividend payout ratio.

c. Dividend yield ratio.

d. Price/earnings ratio.

E16–3. Refer to the financial statements for Pead Sales, Inc., in Exercise 16–1. Assets at the beginning of the year totaled $183,400, and the stockholders' equity totaled $97,400.

Required:

1. Compute the return on total assets.

2. Compute the return on common stockholders' equity.

3. Was financial leverage positive or negative for the year? Explain.

E16–4. Consider the following income statement data for the Hilty Company:

HILTY COMPANY
Income statement

	This year	Last year
Sales	$690,000	$620,000
Cost of goods sold	448,500	372,000
Gross margin	$241,500	$248,000
Selling expenses	$ 69,000	$ 62,000
Administrative expenses	124,200	124,000
Total expenses	$193,200	$186,000
Net operating income	$ 48,300	$ 62,000

Required:

1. Express each year's income statement in common-size percentages.
2. Comment briefly on the changes between the two years.

E16–5. The Halver Company has reported the following asset, liability, and sales data for the past five years:

	19x5	19x4	19x3	19x2	19x1
Cash	$ 40,000	$ 45,000	$ 55,000	$ 60,000	$ 50,000
Accounts					
receivable	380,000	340,000	270,000	230,000	200,000
Inventory	625,000	600,000	575,000	550,000	500,000
Total	$1,045,000	$ 985,000	$ 900,000	$ 840,000	$ 750,000
Current					
liabilities	$ 400,000	$ 362,000	$ 325,000	$ 275,000	$ 250,000
Sales	$1,875,000	$1,800,000	$1,725,000	$1,650,000	$1,500,000

Required:

1. Express the asset, liability, and sales data in trend percentages. Use 19x1 as the base year.
2. Comment on the results of your analysis.

E16–6. Selected financial data for Arby Company are given below:

Interest paid on long-term debt	$ 9,600
Net income after interest and taxes	68,000
Total assets	850,000
Long-term debt (8% interest rate)	120,000
Preferred stock, $100 par, 8%	150,000
Total stockholders' equity	650,000

Answer the following:

a. What is the return on total assets?
b. What is the return on common stockholders' equity?
c. Is leverage positive or negative? Explain.

E16–7. The Austin Company's condensed income statement is given below:

AUSTIN COMPANY
Income Statement
For the Year Ended September 30, 19x6

Sales..	$400,000
Cost of goods	300,000
Gross margin	$100,000
Operating expenses	60,000
Net income before taxes..........................	$ 40,000
Income taxes (40%)	16,000
Net income	$ 24,000

Included in the operating expenses above is a $14,000 loss resulting from flood-damaged merchandise.

Required:

1. Redo the company's income statement, showing the loss net of tax.
2. Assume that the company has 10,000 shares of common stock outstanding. Compute the earnings per share.

E16–8. Rusco Products had a current ratio of 2.5 to 1 on December 31 of the current year. On that date its assets were:

Cash		$ 60,000
Accounts receivable	$150,000	
Less allowance for uncollectible		
accounts	15,000	135,000
Inventory		250,000
Prepaid expenses		5,000
Plant and equipment, net		350,000
Total assets		$800,000

Required:

1. What was the company's working capital on December 31?
2. What was the company's quick ratio on December 31?
3. The company paid an account payable of $30,000 immediately after December 31.
   a. What effect did this transaction have on the current ratio? Show computations.
   b. What effect did this transaction have on working capital? Show computations.

PROBLEMS

P16–9. *Comprehensive problem on ratio analysis.* You have just been hired as a loan officer at Slippery Rock State Bank. Your supervisor has given you a file containing a request from Lydex Company for a $50,000, five-year loan. Financial statement data on the company for the last two years are given below:

LYDEX COMPANY
Comparative Balance Sheets

	This year	Last year
Assets		
Current assets:		
Cash	$ 16,000	$ 21,000
Marketable securities	–0–	5,000
Accounts receivable, net	45,000	30,000
Inventory	65,000 ·	40,000
Prepaid expenses	4,000	3,000
Total current assets	$130,000	$ 99,000
Plant and equipment, net	155,000	151,000
Total assets	$285,000	$250,000

LYDEX COMPANY
Comparative Balance Sheets (Continued)

	This year	Last year
Liabilities and Stockholders' Equity		
Current Liabilities	$ 65,000	$ 44,000
Note payable, 9%	60,000	50,000
Total liabilities	$125,000	$ 94,000
Stockholders' equity:		
Preferred stock, 6%, $30 par value	$ 30,000	$ 30,000
Common stock, $20 par value	100,000	100,000
Retained earnings	30,000	26,000
Total stockholders' equity	$160,000	$156,000
Total liabilities and equity	$285,000	$250,000

LYDEX COMPANY
Comparative Income Statements

	This Year	Last Year
Sales	$262,500	$208,000
Less cost of goods sold	210,000	165,000
Gross margin	$ 52,500	$ 43,000
Less operating expenses	29,100	26,500
Net operating income	$ 23,400	$ 16,500
Less interest expense	5,400	4,500
Net income before taxes	$ 18,000	$ 12,000
Less income taxes (40%)	7,200	4,800
Net income	$ 10,800	$ 7,200
Dividends paid:		
Preferred dividends	$ 1,800	$ 1,800
Common dividends	5,000	2,400
Total dividends paid	$ 6,800	$ 4,200
Net income retained	$ 4,000	$ 3,000
Retained earnings, beginning of year	26,000	23,000
Retained earnings, end of year	$ 30,000	$ 26,000

J. C. Stearns, who just a year ago was appointed president of Lydex Company, argues that although the company has had a "spotty" record in the past, it has "turned the corner," as evidenced by a 25 percent jump in sales and by a greatly improved earnings picture between last year and this year. Stearns also points out that investors generally have recognized the improving situation at Lydex, as shown by the increase in market value of the company's common stock, which is currently selling for $22 per share (up from $10 per share last year). Stearns feels that with his leadership and with the modernized equipment that the $50,000 loan will permit the company to buy, profits will be even stronger in the future. Stearns has a reputation in the industry for being a good manager who runs a "tight" ship.

Not wanting to botch your first assignment, you decide to generate all the information that you can about the company. You determine that the following ratios are typical of firms in Lydex Company's industry:

Current ratio .... 2.3 to 1
Acid-test ratio .... 1.2 to 1

Average age of receivables . . . . 42 days
Inventory turnover . . . . 66 days
Return on assets 6.0%
Debt/equity ratio . . . . 0.65 to 1
Times interest earned 6.5
Price/earnings ratio 16

Required:

1. You decide first to assess the rate of return which the company is generating. Compute the following for both this year and last year:

   a. The return on total assets. (Total assets at the beginning of last year were $218,000.)

   b. The return on common equity. (Common stock outstanding has not changed for several years.)

   c. Is the company's leverage positive or negative? Explain.

2. You decide next to assess the well-being of the common stockholders. For both this year and last year, compute:

   a. The earnings per share.

   b. The fully diluted earnings per share. The preferred stock is convertible into common at the rate of 2.5 shares of common for each share of preferred.

   c. The dividend yield ratio for common.

   d. The dividend payout ratio for common.

   e. The price/earnings ratio. How do investors regard Lydex Company as compared to other firms in the industry? Explain.

   f. The book value per share of common. Does the difference between market value per share and book value per share suggest that the stock at its current price is a bargain? Explain.

3. You decide, finally, to assess creditor ratios to determine both short-term and long-term debt paying ability. For both this year and last year, compute:

   a. The current ratio.

   b. The acid-test ratio.

   c. The average age of receivables. (The accounts receivable at the beginning of last year totaled $26,000.)

   d. The inventory turnover. (The inventory at the beginning of last year totaled $32,000.)

   e. The debt/equity ratio.

   f. The number of times interest was earned.

4. Evaluate the data computed in (1) to (3) above, and using any additional data provided in the problem, make a recommendation to your supervisor as to whether the loan should be approved.

P16–10. *Common-size financial statements.* Refer to the financial statement data for Lydex Company, given in Problem 16–9.

Required:

For both this year and last year:

1. Present the balance sheet in common-size format.

2. Present the income statment in common-size format down through net income.

3. Comment on the results of your analysis.

P16–11. *Trend and common-size statements combined with selected ratios.* Financial statements for Beakins Company follow:

BEAKINS COMPANY
Comparative Income Statements
For the Years Ended December 31, 19x6, 19x7, and 19x8
($000)

	19x8	19x7	19x6
Sales	$4,000	$3,500	$3,000
Cost of goods sold	2,600	2,170	1,800
Gross margin	$1,400	$1,330	$1,200
Selling expenses	$ 560	$ 525	$ 480
Administrative expenses	480	315	180
Total expenses	$1,040	$ 840	$ 660
Net income before taxes	$ 360	$ 490	$ 540
Income taxes	144	196	216
Net income	$ 216	$ 294	$ 324

BEAKINS COMPANY
Comparative Balance Sheets
As of December 31, 19x6, 19x7, and 19x8
($000)

	19x8	19x7	19x6
Assets			
Current assets	$ 500	$ 600	$ 750
Long-term investments	100	200	250
Plant and equipment (net)	5,500	3,500	2,500
Total Assets	$6,100	$4,300	$3,500
Liabilities and Capital			
Current liabilities	$ 400	$ 300	$ 250
Long-term liabilities	2,000	1,000	500
Capital stock	2,500	2,000	2,000
Retained earnings	1,200	1,000	750
Total Liabilities and Capital	$6,100	$4,300	$3,500

Required:

1. Compute the working capital for each of the three years.
2. Compute the current ratio for each of the three years.
3. Compute the debt/equity ratio for each of the three years.
4. Express the income statement data in common-size percentages.
5. Express the balance sheet data in trend percentages.
6. Comment on any significant information revealed by your work in (1) through (5) above.

P16–12. *Effect of various transactions on working capital, current ratio, and acid-test ratio.* Dunn Company's working capital accounts at December 31, 19x6, are given below:

Cash	$ 50,000
Marketable securities	30,000
Accounts receivable (net)	200,000
Inventory	210,000
Prepaid expenses	10,000

```
Accounts payable ....................    150,000
Notes due within one year ............     30,000
Accrued liabilities ..................     20,000
```

During 19x7, Dunn Company completed the following transactions:

x. Paid a cash dividend previously declared, $12,000.
a. Issued additional shares of capital stock for cash, $100,000.
b. Sold inventory costing $50,000 for $80,000, on account.
c. Wrote off uncollectible accounts in the amount of $10,000.
d. Declared a cash dividend, $15,000.
e. Paid accounts payable, $50,000.
f. Borrowed cash on a short-term note with the bank, $35,000.
g. Sold inventory costing $15,000 for $10,000 cash.
h. Purchased inventory on account, $60,000.
i. Paid off all short-term notes due, $30,000.
j. Purchased fixed assets for cash, $15,000.
k. Sold marketable securities costing $18,000 for cash, $15,000.
l. Collected cash on accounts receivable, $80,000.

Required:

1. Compute the following amounts and ratios as of December 31, 19x6:
   a. Working capital.
   b. Current ratio.
   c. Acid-test ratio.
2. For 19x7, indicate the effect of each of the transactions given above on working capital, the current ratio, and the acid-test ratio. Give the effect in terms of increase, decrease, or none. Item (*x*) is given below as an example of the format to use:

	The effect on		
Transaction	Working capital	Current ratio	Acid-test ratio
(*x*)	None	Increase	Increase

P16–13. *Extraordinary gains and losses, and earnings per share.* Cox Bros., Inc., has 10,000 shares of no par common stock outstanding. The company's income statement for 19x7 as prepared by the company's accountant is given below:

```
Sales .......................              $200,000
Cost of goods sold .............            120,000
Gross margin ................              $ 80,000
Less operating expenses:
  Selling expenses ............  $15,000
  Administrative expenses .......  30,000
  Loss from obsolete inventory ...  20,000      65,000
Income before taxes ............           $ 15,000
Income taxes (40 percent) .......            6,000
Net income ..................              $  9,000
```

The earnings per share for Cox Bros., Inc., common stock over the past three years is given below:

	19x6	19x5	19x4
Earnings per share—common	$1.80	$1.50	$1.20

Required:

1. Consider the income statement as prepared by the company's accountant. Why might an investor have difficulty interpreting this statement so far as determining Cox Bros., Inc.'s ability to generate normal after-tax earnings?
2. Recast Cox Bros., Inc.'s income statement in better form, showing the inventory loss net of tax.
3. Assume that rather than having a $20,000 loss from obsolete inventory the company has a $20,000 gain from sale of unused plant. Redo the income statement, showing the gain net of tax.
4. Using the income statements which you prepared in (2) and (3) above, compute the earnings per share of common stock.
5. Explain how your computation of earnings per share would be helpful to an investor trying to evaluate the trend of Cox Bros., Inc.'s earnings over the past few years.

P16–14. *Leverage through the use of long-term debt.* (Note to the instructor: Problems 16–15 and 16–16 delve more deeply into the financial statements presented in this problem. Together, Problems 16–14, 16–15, and 16–16 provide a comprehensive coverage of the financial ratios presented in this chapter. All or any of them can be assigned—each is independent of the others. The numbers have been simplified for ease of computation.)

MEREDITH, INC.
Income Statement and Reconciliation of Retained Earnings
For the Years Ended December 31, 19x1 and 19x2

		19x2		19x1
Sales		$23,500		$20,500
Cost of goods sold		16,000		14,000
Gross margin		$ 7,500		$ 6,500
Selling expense	$2,000		$1,900	
Administrative expense	3,600	5,600	3,200	5,100
Net operating income		$ 1,900		$ 1,400
Interest expense		400		280
Net income before taxes		$ 1,500		$ 1,120
Income taxes (40%)		600		448
Net income		$ 900		$ 672
Dividends paid:				
Preferred		$ 75		$ 75
Common		525		375
Total dividends		$ 600		$ 450
Net income retained		$ 300		$ 222
Retained earnings, beginning of year		5,050		4,828
Retained earnings, end of year		$ 5,350		$ 5,050

MEREDITH, INC.
Comparative Balance Sheets
December 31, 19x1 and 19x2

	19x2	19x1
Assets		
Current Assets:		
Cash	$ 600	$ 590
Accounts receivable (net)	2,900	1,900
Inventories	5,100	3,200
Prepaid expenses	100	100
Total Current Assets	$ 8,700	$ 5,790
Fixed assets, net	6,315	5,600
Other assets	785	1,410
Total Assets	$15,800	$12,800
Liabilities and Stockholders' Equity		
Current Liabilities	$ 3,600	$ 2,400
Bonds payable, 8%, due in 10 years	$ 5,000	$ 3,500
Stockholders' equity:		
Preferred stock, 5%, $10 par value	$ 1,500	$ 1,500
Common stock, $0.50 par value	350	350
Retained earnings	5,350	5,050
Total Stockholders' Equity	$ 7,200	$ 6,900
Total Liabilities and Equity	$15,800	$12,800

Required:

Compute the following for 19x2:
1. Return on average total assets.
2. Return on common equity. Explain fully why the return on average total assets differs from the return on common equity.

P16–15. *Common stockholder ratios.* Refer to the financial statements in Problem 16–14.

Required:

Compute the following for 19x2:
1. Earnings per share.
2. Assume that each share of preferred is convertible into two shares of common. What is the fully diluted earnings per share?
3. Meredith, Inc.'s common stock is selling at 12½. What is the dividend yield ratio?
4. What is the dividend payout ratio?
5. What is the price/earnings ratio? The average price/earnings ratio for firms in Meredith, Inc.'s industry is 15. How do investors regard Meredith, Inc., as compared to other firms in the industry? Explain.
6. Book value per share of common. Does the difference between the 12½ market price and the book value which you have computed suggest that the stock is overpriced? Explain.

P16–16. *Creditor ratios, and comparison to industry averages.* Refer to the financial statements in Problem 16–14 for Meredith, Inc. Meredith, Inc., is a manufacturer of machine tools. The company is contemplating issuing another $2,000 in bonds in order to finance a remodeling of its existing plant. The bonds would bear interest at 10 percent. Some stockholders are reluctant to approve additional long-term debt, due to the fact that the machine tools industry is subject to wide ranging fluctuations in sales and profits. Typical ratios for firms in the machine tools industry are given below:

Current ratio 2.5
Acid-test ratio 1.2
Average age of receivables . . . . 30 days
Inventory turnover . . . . 5.0 times
Times interest earned . . . . 8.0 times
Debt/equity ratio . . . . 0.70 to 1

Required:

1. Assume that you have been approached by a group of stockholders in Meredith, Inc. They present you with the "typical ratios" given above, and ask that you compute these ratios for Meredith, Inc., for both 19x1 and 19x2. (The inventory balance two years ago was $2,500; the accounts receivable balance two years ago was $1,700.)
2. Comment on the performance of Meredith, Inc., as compared to industry averages, and make a recommendation to the stockholders as to whether they should approve the proposed additional $2,000 in long-term debt.

P16–17. *Effect of leverage on the return on common equity.* Mr. H. P. Barney and several other investors are in the process of organizing a new company to produce and distribute a household cleaning product. Mr. Barney and his associates feel that $500,000 would be adequate to finance the new company's operations, and the group is studying three methods of raising this amount of money. The three methods are:

Method A: All $500,000 obtained through issue of common stock.
Method B: $250,000 obtained through issue of common stock, and the other $250,000 obtained through issue of $100 par value, 6% preferred stock.
Method C: $250,000 obtained through issue of common stock, and the other $250,000 obtained through issue of bonds carrying an interest rate of 6%.

Mr. Barney and his associates are confident that the company can earn $75,000 each year before interest and taxes. The tax rate is 40 percent.

Required:

1. Assuming that Mr. Barney and his associates are correct in their earnings estimate, compute the net income that would go to the common stockholders under each of the financing methods listed above.
2. Using the income data computed in (1) above, compute the return on common equity under each of the three methods.
3. Why do methods B and C provide a greater return on common

equity than method A? Why does method C provide a greater return on common equity than method B?

P16–18.   *Determining the effect of transactions on various financial ratios.*   In the right-hand column below certain financial ratios are listed. Opposite each ratio to the left is a business transaction or event relating to the operating activities of Beaver Company.

Business transaction or event	Ratio
1. Issued a common stock dividend to common stockholders.	Earnings per share.
2. Paid accounts payable.	Debt/equity ratio.
3. Purchased inventory on open account.	Acid-test ratio.
4. Wrote off an uncollectable account against the Allowance for Bad Debts.	Current ratio.
5. The market price of Beaver Company common stock increased from 24½ to 30. Earnings per share remained unchanged.	Price/earnings ratio.
6. The market price of Beaver Company common stock increased from 24½ to 30. The dividend paid per share remained unchanged.	Dividend yield ratio.
7. The company declared a cash dividend.	Current ratio.
8. Sold inventory on account at cost.	Acid-test ratio.
9. The company issued bonds with an interest rate of 8 percent. The company's return on assets is 10 percent.	Return on common stockholders' equity.
10. The Beaver Company's net income decreased by 10 percent between last year and this year. Long-term debt remained unchanged.	Times interest earned.
11. A previously declared cash dividend was paid.	Current ratio.
12. The market price of the company's common stock dropped from 24½ to 20. The dividend paid per share remained unchanged.	Dividend payout ratio.
13. $100,000 in obsolete inventory was written off as a loss.	Inventory turnover ratio.
14. Sold inventory for cash at a profit.	Debt/equity ratio.
15. Changed customer credit terms from 2/10, n/30 to 2/15, n/30 to comply with a change in industry practice.	Accounts receivable turnover ratio.
16. Issued a dividend on common stock.	Book value per share.
17. The market price of the company's common stock increased from 24½ to 30.	Book value per share.

Required:

Indicate the effect that each business transaction or event would have on the ratio listed opposite to it. State the effect in terms of increase, decrease, or no effect on the ratio involved, and give the reason for your choice of answer. In all cases, assume that the current assets exceed the current liabilities both before and after the event or transaction. Use the following format for your answers:

Effect on ratio	Reason for increase, decrease, or no effect
1.	
Etc.	

P16–19. *Extraordinary loss net of tax, and earnings per share.* Marsha Green is upset. As president of Green Enterprises, she is very concerned that the unusual potential of Green Enterprises be properly portrayed to investors, particularly since the company will be making a public offering of its stock in a few months. The chief accountant at Green Enterprises has just presented the following income statement to Ms. Green for the company's recent fiscal year:

GREEN ENTERPRISES
Income Statement
For the Year Ended January 31, 19x8

		Amount	Percent
Sales		$8,000,000	100.0
Cost of goods sold		5,000,000	62.5
Gross margin		$3,000,000	37.5
Operating expenses:			
Selling expenses	$ 500,000		
Administrative expenses	800,000		
Other expenses	1,500,000	2,800,000	35.0
Net operating income		$ 200,000	2.5
Income taxes (40%)		80,000	1.0
Net income		$ 120,000	1.5

When Ms. Green saw the income statement, she moaned, "Just look at that, a net income of only 1.5 percent of sales, and the industry average is 5 percent! When investors see this statement, they'll die laughing! We might as well forget about that stock offering this year. And all because of a fire in an old building that we were going to dump anyway." The fire that Ms. Green was referring to was a fire in an antiquated factory building that the company had moved out of several years ago. The building had a book value of $1,500,000 and was uninsured. The loss is shown under "other expenses" on the income statement above.

Required:

1. Redo the income statement for Green Enterprises in a format that will provide investors with a better perspective of the company's normal operating ability.
2. Assume that Green Enterprises has 200,000 shares of common stock outstanding. Compute the earnings per share as it should be presented in the company's annual report.

P16–20. *Interpretation of ratios.* Thorpe Company is a wholesale distributor of professional equipment and supplies. The company's sales have averaged about $900,000 annually for the three-year period 19x3–x5. The firm's total assets at the end of 19x5 amounted to $850,000.

   The president of Thorpe Company has asked the controller to prepare a report summarizing the financial aspects of the company's operations for the past three years. This report will be presented to the board of directors at their next meeting.

   In addition to comparative financial statements, the controller has decided to present a number of relevant financial ratios that can assist in the identification and interpretation of trends. At the request of the controller, the accounting staff has calculated the following ratios for the three-year period 19x3–x5:

	19x3	19x4	19x5
Current ratio	2.00	2.13	2.18
Acid-test ratio	1.20	1.10	0.97
Accounts receivable turnover	9.72	8.57	7.13
Percent of total debt to total assets	44%	41%	38%
Ratio of sales to fixed assets (sales divided by fixed assets)	1.75	1.88	1.99
Sales as a percent of 19x3 sales (trend analysis)	100%	103%	106%
Gross margin percentage	40.0%	38.6%	38.5%
Net income to sales	7.8%	7.8%	8.0%
Return on total assets	8.5%	8.6%	8.7%
Return on common stockholders' equity	15.1%	14.6%	14.1%
Inventory turnover	5.25	4.80	3.80
Percent of long-term debt to total assets	25%	22%	19%

In the preparation of his report, the controller has decided first to examine the financial ratios independently of any other data to determine if the ratios themselves reveal any significant trends over the three-year period.

Required:

Answer the following questions. Indicate in each case which ratio(s) you used in arriving at your conclusion.
1. The current ratio is increasing while the acid-test ratio is decreasing. Using the ratios provided, identify and explain the contributing factor(s) for this apparently divergent trend.
2. In terms of the ratios provided, what conclusion(s) can be drawn regarding the company's use of financial leverage during the 19x3–x5 period?
3. Using the ratios provided, what conclusion(s) can be drawn regarding the company's net investment in plant and equipment?

(CMA, adapted)

P16–21. *Comprehensive problem on ratio analysis, with comparisons to industry averages.* Selected financial data from the financial statements of two companies selling similar products are given below.

Data from the Current Year-End Balance Sheets

	Company A	Company B
Cash	$ 15,000	$ 10,000
Accounts receivable	49,500	89,500
Inventory	55,000	117,000
Plant and equipment, net	150,000	240,000
Total Assets	$269,500	$456,500
Current liabilities	$ 56,900	$101,000
Bonds payable	75,000	100,000
Preferred stock, 6%, $100 par	35,000	40,000
Common stock, $10 par	50,000	100,000
Retained earnings	52,600	115,500
Total Liabilities and Capital	$269,500	$456,500

Data from the Current Year-End Income Statements

	Company A	Company B
Sales	$500,000	$700,000
Cost of goods sold	325,000	455,000
Interest expense	6,000	8,000
Net income before taxes	30,000	45,000
Net income	18,000	27,000
Tax rate	40%	40%

Beginning-of-the-Year Data

	Company A	Company B
Accounts receivable........................	$ 45,500	$ 85,500
Inventory	51,000	113,000
Total assets	250,000	425,000
Total stockholders' equity	131,300	246,900

Other Selected Data

	Company A	Company B
Dividends paid:		
Preferred	$ 2,100	$ 2,400
Common	9,600	16,000
Market price per share (common)	48	45

Industry Averages

Current ratio	2.1 to 1
Acid test ratio	1.1 to 1
Accounts receivable turnover	10.0 times
Inventory turnover	5.7 times
Times interest earned	6 times
Debt/equity ratio	0.9 to 1
Dividend yield	4%
Price/earnings ratio	15
Dividend payout ratio	60%
Return on total assets	9%
Return on common equity	15.5%

Required:

1. Compute the following ratios for each company:
   a. Current ratio.
   b. Acid-test ratio.
   c. Accounts receivable turnover.
   d. Average collection period for receivables.
   e. Inventory turnover.
   By use of these ratios, (f) tell which company is the better short-term credit risk and why.
2. Compute the following ratios for each company:
   a. Times interest earned.
   b. Debt/equity ratio.
   By use of these ratios and any ratios from (1), above, (c) tell which company could better take on *additional* long-term debt and why.
3. Compute the following ratios for each company:
   a. Earnings per share.
   b. Dividend yield ratio.
   c. Price/earnings ratio.

> d. Dividend payout ratio.
> e. Return on total assets.
> f. Return on common equity.
>
> By use of these ratios and any data from (1) and (2) above, (g) tell which company's stock is the better buy and why.

P16–22. *Interpretation of already completed ratios.* Before purchasing shares of stock in a company, Sally Perkins always investigates the company thoroughly. She presently is interested in the stock of Plunge Enterprises, and has assembled the following data on the company:

	19x3	19x2	19x1
Current ratio	2.8:1	2.5:1	2.1:1
Acid-test ratio	0.7:1	0.9:1	1.4:1
Accounts receivable turnover	8.7 times	9.5 times	10.4 times
Inventory turnover	5.1 times	5.7 times	6.8 times
Sales trend	125.0	112.0	100.0
Dividends paid per share	Unchanged over the three years		
Dividend yield	5%	4%	3%
Dividend payout ratio	40%	50%	60%
Return on total assets	6.8%	6.1%	5.7%
Return on common equity	7.9%	5.8%	4.7%

Sally wants answers to a number of questions about the trend of events in Plunge Enterprises over the last three years. However, all she has to go on is a copy of the current year's (19x3) financial statements, and the ratios given above. Sally's questions are:

a. Is the market price of the company's stock going up or down?
b. Is the amount of the earnings per share increasing or decreasing?
c. Is the price/earnings ratio going up or down?
d. Is the company employing leverage to the advantage of the common stockholder?
e. Is it becoming easier for the company to pay its bills as they come due?
f. Are customers paying their accounts at least as fast now as they were in 19x1?
g. Is the total of the accounts receivable increasing?
h. Is the level of inventory remaining constant?

Required:

Answer each of Sally's questions, using the data given above. In each case, explain how you arrived at your answer.

Chapter 17

"How well am I doing?" — Statement of changes in financial position

Three major statements are prepared annually by most companies—
an income statement, a balance sheet, and a statement of changes in
financial position. The statement of changes in financial position is less
well known than the income statement or balance sheet, but many view
it as being equal in importance. In this chapter our focus is on the development of the statement and on its use as a tool for assessing the well-
being of a company.

THE PURPOSE OF THE STATEMENT

The purpose of the statement of changes in financial position is to show
the sources and uses of working capital during an accounting period.
The statement is used by managers, investors, and creditors alike to answer
such questions as: Why have current assets decreased? What use was
made of net income during the period? How was the company's plant
expansion financed? Is the company's dividend policy in balance with
its operating policies?

An example of the statement

An example of a well-prepared statement of changes in financial position
is presented in Exhibit 17–1. This statement has been extracted from a
recent annual report of Standard Brands Incorporated, a highly diversified,
international company dealing in high-quality food products.

Notice that the statement differs considerably from both the income
statement and balance sheet formats with which you are familiar, although
key elements from both the income statement and the balance sheet are
represented in it. Three things in particular should be noted about the
construction of the statement: first, notice that the statement deals with
changes in working capital; second, notice that net income is a key item
on the statement, and that it is adjusted for depreciation and other "non-
fund" charges; and third, notice that a major part of the statement consists
of changes which have taken place in various noncurrent balance sheet
accounts, such as plant and equipment, long-term debt, and capital stock.

More will be said in later sections about the construction of the statement.
For the moment let's look at the statement from point of view of what it
tells about the policies and overall management of Standard Brands Incorporated. First, observe that dividends are well-balanced with net income,
representing about a 50 percent payout ratio in both 1976 and 1977.
Second, observe that in both years the bulk of the company's "Sources
of Working Capital" came from operations, and primarily from the net .
income component of operations. This shows that most of the funds needed
to support the company's growth are being generated internally, rather
than being obtained primarily from outside sources. Third, observe that
in 1976 the company made substantial additions to property, plant and

Exhibit 17-1

Consolidated Statement of Changes in Financial Position
Standard Brands Incorporated and Subsidiary Companies

($000 omitted)

	Year Ended December 31,	
	1977	1976
Sources of Working Capital:		
From Operations		
Net Income	$ 68,554	$ 67,587
Depreciation and Amortization	28,785	23,865
Other Non-Fund Charges—Net	4,077	10,598
Total from Operations	101,416	102,050
Decrease in Notes Receivable	—	6,322
Increase in Long-Term Debt	54,504	2,382
Disposition and Retirement of Property, Plant and Equipment	5,060	20,022
Common and Treasury Stock Issued in Connection with Stock Option, Incentive and Employee Ownership Plans and Acquisitions	1,552	3,273
	162,532	134,049
Uses of Working Capital:		
Additions to Property, Plant and Equipment	49,765	89,394
Dividends	36,118	34,072
Decrease in Long-Term Debt	12,636	45,103
Cost of Acquisitions less Working Capital Acquired	29,858	—
Other Items—Net	1,108	(1,268)
	129,485	167,301
Increase (Decrease) in Working Capital	$ 33,047	$ (33,252)
Changes in Working Capital Represented by:		
Increase (Decrease) in Current Assets		
Cash	$ 4,464	$(9,860)
Marketable Securities	14,318	(33,265)
Receivables	51,864	3,072
Inventories	7,496	52,547
Prepaid Expenses	1,119	(1,188)
	79,261	11,306
Decrease (Increase) in Current Liabilities		
Notes and Loans Payable	22,120	(45,337)
Current Maturities—Long-Term Debt	(1,365)	6,903
Accounts Payable and Accrued Expenses	(42,830)	(1,624)
United States and Foreign Taxes on Income	(24,139)	(4,500)
	(46,214)	(44,558)
	$ 33,047	$ (33,252)

Source: *Annual Report.*

equipment ($89 million), while at the same time retiring a substantial amount of long-term debt ($45 million). These uses of working capital, when combined with the $34 million in dividends paid, exceeded the sources of working capital for the year, causing overall net working capital to decrease by $33 million.

But then in 1977 the company bolstered its working capital position by issuing $54 million in long-term debt. These funds, when added to the strong showing from operations for the year (another $101 million), provided sufficient working capital to permit the company to make further additions to plant and equipment ($49 million), to retire $12 million in long-term debt, to expend $29 million to acquire assets of other companies, and then to add $33 million back to working capital accounts. Moreover, this expansion and recapitalization was all accomplished while maintaining a consistent and reasonable dividend policy. In short, this statement provides every indication that Standard Brands Incorporated is a stable, growing, well-managed organization. This is the purpose of the statement of changes in financial position—to draw out those key changes from the income statement and balance sheet which will provide clues as to an organization's policies and financial management.

Alternate titles to the statement

In published corporate reports the statement of changes in financial position is occasionally labeled as a *statement of sources and uses of working capital,* as a *statement of sources and application of funds,* or simply as a *funds statement.* The term *statement of changes in financial position* is preferred, and should be used in published reports. For convenience in writing, however, the term "funds statement" has the advantage of brevity, and so will be used to some extent in the remaining pages of this chapter.

SOURCES AND USES OF WORKING CAPITAL

Now that we have an understanding of what the funds statement looks like and what it is designed to accomplish, we are prepared to analyze its construction. Notice from Exhibit 17–1 that the funds statement has two major sections, one titled "Sources of Working Capital" and the other titled, "Uses of Working Capital." Several sources and several uses can be identified, as discussed in the two following sections.

Sources of working capital

There are three major sources of working capital in an organization. They are:

1. Profitable operations.
2. Long-term financing.
3. Sales of plant, equipment, or other noncurrent assets.

PROFITABLE OPERATIONS. By far, operations represents the most significant continuing source of working capital in most firms. If a company is not able to generate significant amounts of funds from its operations over time, then difficulties in maintaining an adequate working capital balance almost invariably develop. This is because there are limits to the amount of funds which can be obtained through long-term financing or other means. Thus, operations generally must be depended on as the key source of additions to working capital from year to year. For this reason many managers feel that the funds provided by operations represents the best leading indicator as to the economic health and well-being of an organization.

LONG-TERM FINANCING. From time to time it becomes necessary for a company to bolster its working capital position by turning to external sources of funds, such as Standard Brands did in 1977. The two chief sources of long-term investment funds are sales of capital stock and issues of long-term debt. Notice from Exhibit 17–1 that Standard Brands sold small amounts of common stock in both 1976 and 1977, in addition to issuing $54 million in long-term debt in 1977. These issues all represented sources of working capital for the company.

SALES OF ASSETS. Although sales of plant, equipment, and various other noncurrent assets (such as patents, leaseholds, and franchises) also constitute sources of working capital, these kinds of transactions are fairly infrequent, and cannot be relied upon as a significant or continuing source of funds to an organization. The reason is obvious—if an organization sells off its assets, it will cease to exist. Thus, the "Sources of Working Capital" section from Exhibit 17–1 contains only a nominal amount of funds provided from disposition or retirement of property.

Uses of working capital

The major uses of working capital in an organization are basically the opposite of its sources, with one additional item. The uses are:

1. Unprofitable operations.
2. Retirement of long-term financing.
3. Purchase of plant, equipment, or other noncurrent assets.
4. Declaration of dividends.

UNPROFITABLE OPERATIONS. If operations are unprofitable, then a firm will suffer a net outflow of resources, resulting in a depletion of working capital for the period. Note, however, that even if the income statement shows a net loss for the year, the funds provided by operations can still be positive. This can happen, for example, if the depreciation charge deducted on the income statement is greater than the net loss reported on the bottom line. To illustrate, assume that the depreciation deduction for the year is $50,000, and that the net loss shown on the income statement is $35,000. Under the "Sources of Working Capital" section of the funds statement, we would find:

Net income (loss) .... $(35,000)
Add: depreciation   50,000
   Funds from operations..................... $ 15,000

Thus, the company would show a positive amount of funds provided by operations, even though a loss was sustained for the year. As this example suggests, the *composition* of the funds provided by operations is equally as important as the amount provided.

RETIREMENT OF LONG-TERM FINANCING.   If a firm decides to retire capital stock or long-term debt, then working capital is drained out of the organization, and must be entered under the "Uses of Working Capital" section of the funds statement. Although Standard Brands did not retire any capital stock during 1976 or 1977, we have already noted that the company did retire large amounts of long-term debt, entering the retirements under "Uses of Working Capital" for the reason just stated. Generally, any decision to retire capital stock or to retire long-term debt will be made only after much advance planning, to be sure that the working capital position of the company is not impaired in the process. In this regard, notice that Standard Brands' retirements of long-term debt are closely correlated with its new issues, both totaling about $57 million over the two-year period.

PURCHASE OF ASSETS.   A much more common drain on working capital comes in the form of acquisitions of property, plant, and equipment. Investment in these areas is more or less continuous in most firms, and can represent a major use of funds if purchases in a particular year are especially large. The danger comes from expanding more rapidly than operations and long-term financing will permit, with a resulting drain on working capital. We have already noted that Standard Brands made major acquisitions of property, plant, and equipment during 1976 and 1977. However, these acquisitions appear to have created no major problems in the company since they were covered adequately by funds provided by operations and by funds provided through new issues of long-term debt.

DECLARATION OF DIVIDENDS.   Finally, the declaration of dividends represents a major use of working capital. A company's dividend policy must be an integral part of its overall financial planning, since a dividend policy that is poorly coordinated with plant expansion and with other uses of funds can be disastrous even to a profitable firm. Notice that we emphasize the "declaration" of dividends—not the payment of dividends—as having the effect on working capital. This is because the declaration of dividends increases current liabilities, and thus reduces working capital. The later payment of the dividend so declared will have no effect on the working capital balance, as explained in a following section.

Summary of sources and uses

To summarize, those transactions which will result in either a source or a use of working capital have a common identifying characteristic: they involve a change in a noncurrent balance sheet account which also affects a current asset or a current liability account in some way. Reread the preceding sentence before going on. Refer again to the funds statement in Exhibit 17–1. Run your finger down the sources and uses of working capital shown there. Notice in each case that the item involved represents a change in a noncurrent balance sheet account (asset, liability, or equity) which has affected the company's current assets or current liabilities in some way.

With this thought in mind, we can summarize below the major sources and uses of working capital discussed in this section:

Sources of working capital:
1. Profitable operations.
2. Long-term financing.
3. Sales of plant, equipment, or other noncurrent assets.

Uses of working capital:
1. Unprofitable operations.
2. Retirement of long-term financing.
3. Purchase of plant, equipment, or other noncurrent assets.
4. Declaration of dividends.

In order to prepare a funds statement, therefore, one simply analyzes the noncurrent asset, liability, and equity accounts to see what effect the changes in them had on the company's working capital during the period.

No effect on working capital

There are two groups of transactions that have no effect on working capital, and therefore do not appear on the funds statement. The first group consists of transactions affecting only current asset and current liability accounts. For example, the collection of an account receivable will have no effect on the total amount of working capital in an organization. This is because the amount involved is simply transferred from one current asset account (Accounts Receivable) into another current asset account (Cash), with the total amount of working capital left unchanged.

Likewise, the payment of a current liability (such as dividends payable) has no effect on working capital, since both current assets and current liabilities are reduced by an equal amount. In short, if a transaction affects *only* current asset and/or current liability accounts it will not change the total amount of working capital available and therefore will not appear on the funds statement.

The second group consists of transactions involving *only noncurrent* accounts. For example, the issue of a stock dividend has no effect on working capital. Amounts are simply transferred from Retained Earnings, one noncurrent account, into Capital Stock, another noncurrent account. Working capital is not affected, because current assets neither leave nor come into an organization as a result of a stock dividend. Another example of a transaction affecting only noncurrent accounts would be the issue of capital stock in exchange for new fixed assets. Since neither current asset nor current liability accounts are disturbed by such a transaction, it will have no effect on a company's working capital. As a practical matter, however, most analysts would prefer to show the stock-for-fixed assets transaction *as if* two separate transactions had occurred—first, *as if* a sale of capital stock had occurred, and second, *as if* the cash from the sale had been used to acquire fixed assets (even though no cash actually

Exhibit 17–2

EXAMPLE COMPANY
Balance Sheet
December 31, 19x1 and 19x2

	19x2	19x1
Assets		
Current Assets:		
Cash	$ 200	$ 150
Accounts receivable	600	300
Inventory	600	700
Total Current Assets	$1,400	$1,150
Fixed Assets:		
Plant and equipment	$ 900	$ 700
Less accumulated depreciation	(200)	(150)
Net Fixed Assets	$ 700	$ 550
Long-term investments	$ 300	$ 400
Total Assets	$2,400	$2,100
Equities		
Current Liabilities:		
Accounts payable	$ 800	$ 400
Taxes payable	50	100
Total Current Liabilities	$ 850	$ 500
Bonds payable	$ 150	$ 500
Stockholders' Equity:		
Capital stock	$ 800	$ 700
Retained earnings	600	400
Total Stockholders' Equity	$1,400	$1,100
Total Liabilities and Stockholders' Equity	$2,400	$2,100

was involved in the fixed asset acquisition). By treating the single transaction as two separate *as if* transactions, it becomes possible to present the elements involved as part of an overall funds flow analysis, whereas treating it simply as an exchange of stock for fixed assets would tend to conceal it from view.[1]

THE FUNDS STATEMENT—AN ILLUSTRATION

In order to pull together the ideas considered thus far we will turn to the financial statements of Example Company presented in Exhibits 17–2, 17–3, and 17–4, and prepare a funds statement. The numbers in these exhibits have been simplified for ease of computation and discussion.

Exhibit 17–3

EXAMPLE COMPANY Income Statement For the Year Ended December 31, 19x2		
Sales		$900
Cost of goods sold		200
Gross margin		$700
Operating expenses:		
Selling expense	$100	
Administrative expense	150	
Depreciation expense	50	
Total expenses		300
Net income		$400

Exhibit 17–4

EXAMPLE COMPANY Statement of Retained Earnings For the Year Ended December 31, 19x2	
Retained earnings, December 31, 19x1	$400
Add: Net income	400
	$800
Deduct: Dividends paid	200
Retained earnings, December 31, 19x2	$600

Three basic steps to the funds statement

There are three basic steps to follow in preparing a funds statement:

1. Find the change which has taken place in working capital during the year.

---

[1] For organizations preparing funds statements for inclusion in annual reports the *as if* treatment explained above is a requirement. See APB Opinion 19, *Reporting Changes in Financial Position* (New York: American Institute of Certified Public Accountants, March 1971), p. 373.

2. Analyze the change which has taken place in each *noncurrent balance sheet account,* to determine if the change resulted in a source or a use of working capital.

3. Total the sources and uses of working capital obtained in Step 2. The difference between the total sources and the total uses should equal the change in working capital obtained in Step 1.

Statement of changes in working capital

The starting point in a funds statement is to see what change has taken place in the working capital balance during the year. Notice from Exhibit 17–1 that Standard Brands made such an analysis on its funds statement, showing the current asset and current liability components of working capital at the bottom of the statement. We will now do the same thing for Example Company, to see what its change in working capital was during the year. The analysis is presented in Exhibit 17–5.

Exhibit 17–5

EXAMPLE COMPANY
Statement of Changes in Working Capital
For the Year Ended December 31, 19x2

	19x2	19x1	Working capital increase (decrease)
Current Assets:			
Cash	$ 200	$ 150	$ 50
Accounts receivable	600	300	300
Inventory	600	700	(100)
Total	$1,400	$1,150	$ 250
Current Liabilities:			
Accounts payable	$ 800	$ 400	$(400)
Taxes payable	50	100	50
Total	$ 850	$ 500	$(350)
Working capital	$ 550	$ 650	$(100)

The Statement of Changes in Working Capital shows that working capital decreased by $100 during the year. As stated earlier, the causes of this decrease can be determined by analyzing the changes which have taken place during the year in the noncurrent balance sheet accounts, and deciding whether these changes resulted in sources or uses of working capital.

Changes in noncurrent balance sheet accounts

So far as the end result is concerned, it makes no difference which noncurrent account we analyze first, nor does it matter in which order we proceed. This is simply a matter of choice. Since operations usually represents the most significant source of funds, most analysts prefer to start with an analysis of the retained earnings account (which contains the period's net income).

RETAINED EARNINGS. From the balance sheet in Exhibit 17–2 we can see that Retained Earnings increased by $200 during 19x2 (going from $400 at the end of 19x1 to $600 at the end of 19x2). To determine the cause of this change, we need to look at another exhibit—Exhibit 17–4—which contains an analysis of the Retained Earnings account. We can see from this exhibit that the $200 increase in Retained Earnings is a net result of $400 in net income for the year, and $200 in dividends declared and paid during the year. From our earlier discussion on sources and uses of working capital, we know that these two items would be classified as a source and as a use, respectively, on the funds statement:

```
Sources of Working Capital:
  From operations:
     Net income . . . . . . . . . . . . . . . . . . . . . . . . . . . . . . . . . . .  $400
Uses of Working Capital:
  To pay dividends . . . . . . . . . . . . . . . . . . . . . . . . . . . . . . . .  $200
```

PLANT AND EQUIPMENT. We can now proceed through the other noncurrent balance sheet accounts, to determine the impact of their changes on the company's working capital position. Plant and equipment has increased by $200 during the year (going from $700 in 19x1 to $900 in 19x2). From our earlier discussion, we know that a purchase of property, plant and equipment represents a use of funds:

```
Sources of Working Capital:
  From operations:
     Net income . . . . . . . . . . . . . . . . . . . . . . . . . . . . . . . . . . .  $400
Uses of Working Capital:
  To pay dividends . . . . . . . . . . . . . . . . . . . . . . . . . . . . . . . .  $200
  To purchase plant and equipment . . . . . . . . . . . . . . . . . . .   200
```

ACCUMULATED DEPRECIATION. The accumulated depreciation account has increased by $50 during 19x2. Looking at the income statement for Example Company in Exhibit 17–3, we can see that this $50 is a result of a $50 charge for depreciation expense. Since depreciation is an expense that does not require a present outflow of funds, any depreciation charges on the income statement must be added back to net income. This permits the company to see the total amount of funds provided by operations during the period. (We saw this process take place on the funds statement of Standard Brands in Exhibit 17–1.) For Example Company, the computation would be:

Sources of Working Capital:		
From operations:		
Net income		$400
Add: Depreciation		*50*
Total funds from operations		$450
Uses of Working Capital:		
To pay dividends		$200
To purchase plant and equipment		200

The mechanics of adding depreciation back to net income on the funds statement often leads people to the hasty conclusion that depreciation is a source of funds. We must state emphatically that depreciation is not a source of funds. We add it back to net income for the reason that it required no funds outlay during the period, but yet was deducted as an expense in arriving at net income. Thus, by adding it back we are able to cancel out its effect, thereby leaving as part of net income only those items of revenue and expense which did affect the funds position during the period.

Certain other charges on the income statement also reduce net income without involving an outflow of funds. These charges include depletion of natural resources, deferred income taxes, and amortization of goodwill, patents, and leaseholds. Like depreciation, they must be added back to net income in determining the amount of funds provided by operations during a period.

LONG-TERM INVESTMENTS. Example Company's balance sheet in Exhibit 17–2 shows a $100 decrease in long-term investments during 19x2. Long-term investments would generally consist of securities (stocks and bonds) of other companies which are being held for some reason or other. If the amount of these investments decreases during a period, the most likely conclusion is that they were sold. From our earlier discussion of sources and uses of working capital, we know that the sale of a noncurrent asset is a source of funds:

Sources of Working Capital:		
From operations:		
Net income		$400
Add: Depreciation		50
Total funds from operations		$450
From sale of long-term investments		*100*
Uses of Working Capital:		
To pay dividends		$200
To purchase plant and equipment		200

BONDS PAYABLE. Bonds payable decreased by $350 during 19x2 (going from $500 in 19x1 to $150 in 19x2). From our earlier discussion, we know that a retirement of long-term debt represents a use of funds:

```
Sources of Working Capital:
  From operations:
    Net income ...................................  $400
    Add: Depreciation ...........................    50
        Total funds from operations .................  $450
    From sale of long-term investments ...............   100
Uses of Working Capital:
  To pay dividends ...............................  $200
  To purchase plant and equipment .................   200
  To retire bonds payable .........................   350
```

CAPITAL STOCK. Exhibit 17–2 shows that the capital stock account increased by $100 during 19X2. The most likely explanation of this increase is that the company issued more shares of stock during the year. An issue of stock represents a source of funds:

```
Sources of Working Capital:
  From operations:
    Net income ...................................  $400
    Add: Depreciation ...........................    50
        Total funds from operations .................  $450
    From sale of long-term investments ...............   100
    From sale of capital stock .......................   100
Uses of Working Capital:
  To pay dividends ...............................  $200
  To purchase plant and equipment .................   200
  To retire bonds payable .........................   350
```

The completed funds statement

We can now organize the results of our analytical work into statement form. Using the data which we have developed, a completed funds statement for Example Company is presented in Exhibit 17–6 on page 694.

Notice from the exhibit that we have computed a total for both the sources of working capital and the uses of working capital. Also notice that the difference between these two totals ($100) equals the change in working capital derived earlier in Exhibit 17–5. Thus, by analyzing the company's noncurrent balance sheet accounts we have been able to determine why working capital decreased during the year.

Uses of the funds statement

The funds statement is highly regarded as a management planning tool. Although it deals in historical costs, any lack of forward planning, coordination, or balance in working toward long-run objectives becomes quickly evident in the story it has to tell. For example, a company may have as its stated objective to double plant capacity in five years, using

Exhibit 17–6

```
                          EXAMPLE COMPANY
                 Statement of Changes in Financial Position
                    For the Year Ended December 31, 19x2

Sources of Working Capital:
  From operations:
    Net income  . . . . . . . . . . . . . . . . . . . . . . . . . . . . . . .    $400
    Add: Depreciation . . . . . . . . . . . . . . . . . . . . . . . . . . .      50
        Total funds from operations . . . . . . . . . . . . . . .         $450
From sale of long-term investments . . . . . . . . . . . . . . .           100
From sale of capital stock . . . . . . . . . . . . . . . . . . . . . . .    100
        Total sources . . . . . . . . . . . . . . . . . . . . . . . . . . .   $650
Uses of Working Capital:
  To pay dividends . . . . . . . . . . . . . . . . . . . . . . . . . . . . .   $200
  To purchase plant and equipment . . . . . . . . . . . . . . . . .          200
  To retire bonds payable . . . . . . . . . . . . . . . . . . . . . . . .     350
        Total uses . . . . . . . . . . . . . . . . . . . . . . . . . . . . .   $750
Decrease in Working Capital . . . . . . . . . . . . . . . . . . . . . .      ($100)
```

only funds provided through operations. If the company at the same time is paying dividends equal to earnings and is retiring large amounts of long-term debt, the discrepancy between long-run plans and current actions will be highlighted very quickly on the funds statement.

Some of the more significant ways in which managers use the funds statement include:

1. To coordinate dividend policy with other actions of the company.
2. To plan the financing of additional plant and equipment, the financing of new product lines, and the financing of new marketing outlets.
3. To find ways of strengthening a weak working capital position, and thereby strengthening credit lines.
4. To check the implementation of plans and policies.

A WORKING PAPER APPROACH TO THE FUNDS STATEMENT

The procedure relied on to this point of simply developing a funds statement through logic has allowed us to concentrate our efforts on learning basic concepts, with a minimum of effort expended on mechanics. For many firms, this simple logic procedure is completely adequate as a means of developing a funds statement.

Some companies, however, have balance sheets that are so complex that working papers are needed to help organize the changes in noncurrent

Exhibit 17–7

UNIVERSAL COMPANY
Balance Sheet
December 31, 19x1 and 19x2

	19x2	19x1
Assets		
Current Assets:		
Cash	$ 1,000	$ 2,000
Accounts receivable, net	9,000	4,000
Inventory	10,000	12,000
Total Current Assets	$20,000	$18,000
Plant and equipment (Note 1)	$38,500	$30,000
Less: Accumulated depreciation	(10,500)	(9,000)
Net plant and equipment	$28,000	$21,000
Intangible assets:		
Patents	$ 2,000	$ 2,500
Total Assets	$50,000	$41,500
Liabilities and Stockholders' Equity		
Current Liabilities:		
Accounts payable	$ 7,000	$ 4,000
Accrued liabilities	4,000	2,500
Taxes payable	1,000	1,500
Total Current Liabilities	$12,000	$ 8,000
Mortgage payable	$ 7,500	$ 4,000
Stockholders' Equity:		
Common stock	$11,000	$10,000
Preferred stock	4,500	7,500
Retained earnings	15,000	12,000
Total Stockholders' Equity	$30,500	$29,500
Total Liabilities and Stockholders' Equity	$50,000	$41,500

Note 1: Equipment which had cost $1,500 new, and on which there was accumulated depreciation of $1,000, was sold during the year for its book value of $500.

accounts into statement form. A number of working paper approaches to the funds statement are available. The one we have chosen to illustrate relies on the use of T-accounts to assist in analysis and organization of data. In order to illustrate the T-account approach to working paper preparation, we will use the financial statements of Universal Company found in Exhibits 17–7 and 17–8.

The statement of changes in working capital

The starting point of our analytical work will again be the preparation of a Statement of Changes in Working Capital.

UNIVERSAL COMPANY
Statement of Changes in Working Capital
For the Year Ended December 31, 19x2

	19x2	19x1	Working capital—Increase or (decrease)
Current Assets:			
Cash	$ 1,000	$ 2,000	$(1,000)
Accounts receivable	9,000	4,000	5,000
Inventory	10,000	12,000	(2,000)
Total	$20,000	$18,000	$ 2,000
Current Liabilities:			
Accounts payable	$ 7,000	$ 4,000	$(3,000)
Accrued liabilities	4,000	2,500	(1,500)
Taxes payable	1,000	1,500	500
Total	$12,000	$ 8,000	$(4,000)
Working Capital	$ 8,000	$10,000	$(2,000)

Universal Company has suffered a $2,000 decrease in its working capital during 19x2. As before, our objective will be to determine the *causes* of this change in the working capital balance. Also as before, our basic analytical approach will be to review the changes in noncurrent accounts. The only function the T-accounts will serve will be to assist us in the mechanical process of *organizing* our information as it develops.

Exhibit 17–8

UNIVERSAL COMPANY
Statement of Income and Reconciliation of Retained Earnings
For the Year Ended December 31, 19x2

Sales		$85,000
Cost of goods sold		62,500
Gross margin		$22,500
Less operating expenses (Note 2)		15,250
Income before taxes		$ 7,250
Income tax expense		3,000
Net income		$ 4,250
Retained earnings, beginning		12,000
Total		$16,250
Less dividends distributed:		
Cash dividends, preferred	$ 250	
Stock dividends, common	1,000	1,250
Retained earnings, ending		$15,000

Note 2: Operating expenses contain $2,500 of depreciation expense, and $500 of patent amortization expense.

The T-account approach

In Exhibit 17–9, we have prepared a T-account for each of the noncurrent accounts found on Universal Company's balance sheet. In these T-accounts we have entered the beginning and ending balances of the noncurrent accounts. The exhibit also contains a T-account titled "Working Capital," which we will use to accumulate the sources and uses of working capital as they develop through our analysis of the noncurrent account changes.

The procedure is to make entries directly in the T-accounts to explain the actions that have caused the changes in the various noncurrent account balances. To the extent that changes in the noncurrent accounts have affected working capital, appropriate entries are made in the T-account representing working capital.

Exhibit 17–9
T-accounts showing changes in noncurrent account balances—Universal Company

Working Capital		
Sources		Uses

Plant and Equipment			Accumulated Depreciation		
Bal.	30,000			Bal.	9,000
Bal.	38,500			Bal.	10,500

Patents			Mortgage Payable		
Bal.	2,500			Bal.	4,000
Bal.	2,000			Bal.	7,500

Common Stock			Preferred Stock		
	Bal.	10,000		Bal.	7,500
	Bal.	11,000		Bal.	4,500

Retained Earnings		
	Bal.	12,000
	Bal.	15,000

Exhibit 17-10
T-accounts after completion of all noncurrent account analysis—Universal Company

Working Capital

Sources		Uses	
(1) 4,250		(2) 250	To pay cash dividends
(4) 500		(5) 10,000	To purchase equipment
(6) 2,500		(9) 3,000	To retire preferred stock
(7) 500			
(8) 3,500			

From operations: Net income
From sale of equipment
From operations: Depreciation
From operations: Patent amortization
From issue of mortgage note

Plant and Equipment

Bal.	30,000		
(5)	10,000	(4)	1,500
Bal.	38,500		

Accumulated Depreciation

		Bal.	9,000
(6)	1,000	(6)	2,500
		Bal.	10,500

Patents

| Bal. | 2,500 | (7) | 500 |
| Bal. | 2,000 | | |

Common Stock

		Bal.	10,000
		(3)	1,000
		Bal.	11,000

Preferred Stock

		Bal.	7,500
(9)	3,000		
		Bal.	4,500

Retained Earnings

		Bal.	12,000
(2)	250	(1)	4,250
(3)	1,000		
		Bal.	15,000

Mortgage Payable

		Bal.	4,000
		(8)	3,500
		Bal.	7,500

Explanation of entries:
(1) To record net income for the year.
(2) To record payment of a cash dividend.
(3) To record a stock dividend.
(4) To record the sale of equipment.
(5) To record the purchase of equipment.
(6) To record depreciation expense for the year.
(7) To record patent amortization expense for the year.
(8) To record the issue of a mortgage note.
(9) To record retirement of preferred stock.

RETAINED EARNINGS. As we mentioned earlier in the chapter, the Retained Earnings account is generally the most useful starting point in developing a funds statement. Exhibit 17–8 presents a detail of the change in the Retained Earnings account of Universal Company. We can note from the exhibit that net income of $4,250 was added to retained earnings during 19x2, and that dividends of $1,250 were charged against retained earnings. The dividends consisted of $250 in cash dividends and $1,000 in stock dividends.

Entries have been made in the T-accounts in Exhibit 17–10 to show the effect of these activities on the company's working capital, as follows: Entry (1) shows the increase in retained earnings that resulted from the net income reported for 19x2, and the corresponding increase that would have come about in working capital:

Working Capital—Sources 4,250		
Retained Earnings	4,250	(1)

Entry (2) records the payment of cash dividends on preferred stock, and the corresponding drain on working capital:

Retained Earnings 250		
Working Capital—Uses	250	(2)

Entry (3) records the distribution of a stock dividend to common stockholders. A stock dividend has no effect on working capital. It simply capitalizes a portion of retained earnings, and results in no outflow of assets:

Retained Earnings 1,000		
Common Stock	1,000	(3)

The reader should trace these three entries into the T-accounts in Exhibit 17–10.

Notice from the exhibit that these three entries fully explain the change which has taken place in the Retained Earnings account during the period. We can now proceed through the remainder of the noncurrent accounts, analyzing the change between beginning and ending balances in each one, and recording the appropriate entries in the T-accounts.

PLANT AND EQUIPMENT. Notice from the T-accounts that the Plant and Equipment account has increased by $8,500 during the year. This increase could simply represent $8,500 in plant and equipment purchases. On the other hand, there may have been retirements or sales during the year that are concealed in this net change.

From the footnote to the balance sheet we find that certain items of equipment were, indeed, sold during 19x2, at a sale price of $500. The entry to record this sale and its effect on working capital would be:

```
Working Capital—Sources ...........................   500
Accumulated Depreciation ......................... 1,000
     Plant and Equipment ...........................            1,500  (4)
```

How much did the company expend on plant and equipment purchases during the year? Overall, we know that the Plant and Equipment account increased by $8,500. Since this $8,500 increase is what remains *after* the $1,500 retirement of equipment recorded above, then purchases during the year must have amounted to $10,000 ($10,000 − $1,500 = $8,500 net increase). Entry (5) records these purchases in the T-accounts:

```
Plant and Equipment............................. 10,000
     Working Capital—Uses .........................          10,000  (5)
```

ACCUMULATED DEPRECIATION.   Footnote 2 on Universal Company's income statement indicates that depreciation expense totaled $2,500 for the year. The entry in the T-accounts would be:

```
Working Capital—Sources (Operations) ................ 2,500
     Accumulated Depreciation .......................          2,500  (6)
```

This entry, along with Entry (4) above, explains the change in the accumulated depreciation account for the year.

PATENTS.   Footnote 2 on Universal Company's income statement indicates that $500 of patent amortization expense was charged against earnings for the year. As stated earlier, amortization expense is similar to depreciation expense, and is handled the same way on the funds statement. The entry would be:

```
Working Capital—Sources (Operations) ...................   500
     Patents .........................................            500  (7)
```

MORTGAGE PAYABLE.   The company obtained funds during the year by increasing the amount of its mortgage debt. The entry in the T-accounts would be:

```
Working Capital—Sources ........................... 3,500
     Mortgage Payable ..............................            3,500  (8)
```

COMMON STOCK.   The increase in the Common Stock account is explainable in this example by the $1,000 in stock dividends issued to common stockholders. This issue was recorded in the T-accounts earlier in Entry (3). More commonly, an increase in the Common Stock account will be the result of an issue of additional shares of stock, which will be a source of working capital.

PREFERRED STOCK.   Since we have no contrary information, we will have to assume that the $3,000 decrease in the Preferred Stock account is a result of repurchase and retirement of shares. Entry (9) records the repurchase:

Preferred Stock	3,000	
Working Capital—Uses	3,000	(9)

The completed funds statement

The T-accounts in Exhibit 17–10 now contain the final results of our analysis of Universal Company's noncurrent balance sheet accounts. All that now remains is to organize these data into statement form, which is done in Exhibit 17–11. The reader should review this statement carefully, and as an exercise, state in his or her own words what caused working capital in Universal Company to decrease by $2,000 during the year.

Exhibit 17–11

UNIVERSAL COMPANY Statement of Changes in Financial Position For the Year Ended December 31, 19x2		
Sources of Working Capital:		
From operations:		
Net income	$ 4,250	
Add: Depreciation	2,500	
Patent amortization	500	
Total from operations	$ 7,250	
From sale of equipment	500	
From issue of mortgage note	3,500	
Total sources	$11,250	
Uses of Working Capital:		
To pay cash dividends	$ 250	
To purchase equipment	10,000	
To retire preferred stock	3,000	
Total uses	13,250	
Decrease in Working Capital	$ (2,000)	

FOCUSING ON CHANGES IN CASH

In preparing a statement of changes in financial position, some firms prefer to focus on cash, rather than to focus on working capital. The purpose of the statement then becomes to explain what has caused cash to increase or to decrease during a period.

A statement with its emphasis on changes in cash (often called a "cash flow" statement) can be particularly useful to a firm that is experiencing cash problems. The statement can show a firm what its sources of cash were during a period, and show how the cash was used. Such information can be very helpful in planning cash needs, and in maintaining overall control of cash activities.

An example of a cash flow statement is presented in Exhibit 17–12. This statement has been extracted from a recent annual report of Pet Incorporated, an internationally known company dealing in high-quality

Exhibit 17–12

Pet Incorporated and Subsidiaries

Consolidated Changes in Financial Position (In thousands)

Years Ended March 31

	1977	1976
Source of funds		
Net earnings	$27,035	$23,676
Depreciation	17,960	16,177
Deferred income taxes	1,007	1,450
Total from operations	$46,002	$41,303
Common stock issued for company acquired	3,688	
Disposals of plant and equipment	2,885	2,288
Increase in payables and accruals	2,615	6,261
Lease-purchase agreement	2,400	
Decrease in investments and other assets	1,308	2,168
Other items, net	86	(702)
	$58,984	$51,318
Use of funds		
New plants, facilities and equipment	$20,927	$18,485
Properties and businesses of companies acquired	1,890	1,572
Cash dividends	11,699	11,097
Increase (decrease) in inventories	10,992	(19,177)
Decrease in long-term debt	6,933	7,581
Capital stock purchased for treasury	2,806	
Decrease in notes payable and current portion of long-term debt	1,910	10,656
Increase in accounts and notes receivable	444	8,497
Rescission of Glaser/Medicare		4,024
	$57,601	$42,735
Increase in cash and short-term investments	$ 1,383	$ 8,583

Source: *Annual Report.*

food products. The major difference between the cash flow statement presented here and the funds statement presented earlier for Standard Brands Incorporated is that the cash flow statement includes changes in Current Asset and Current Liability accounts (such as Accounts Receivable, Inventories, and Accounts Payable), as well as changes in noncurrent balance sheet accounts.

What activities have an impact on cash?

In our earlier discussion, when we focused on working capital, we found that changes in the noncurrent balance sheet accounts contained the key as to why working capital changed during a period. As we now focus on cash, we will again analyze changes in the noncurrent accounts. But, as suggested by the items included on Pet Incorporated's statement, we must go a step further. We must also analyze changes in the Current Asset and Current Liability accounts, and include them on the statement as well. The reason is that changes in the Current Asset and Current Liability accounts have just as much effect on cash as do changes in the noncurrent accounts. The major sources and uses of cash, as reflected on the funds statement, are presented in the following two sections.

Sources of cash

Cash can be increased by:

1. Profitable operations.
2. Sales of capital stock.
3. An increase in *any* liability account (current or noncurrent).
4. A decrease in *any* asset account (current or noncurrent).

Only items (3) and (4) require any further explanation.

INCREASE IN ANY CURRENT LIABILITY. In the normal course of events, short-term creditors extend credit to a firm, are paid off, re-extend credit, and are paid off again, on a continuing basis period after period. Most firms depend on these short-term creditors as a major source of financing, and for this reason try to keep the turnover going smoothly. If management should make a decision, however, to defer paying short-term creditors, then the volume of accounts due would expand. The result would be that cash that otherwise would have gone to pay creditors would be kept in the organization, and would be available to use internally. By this line of reasoning, one can see that *increases* in amounts due to short-term creditors represent a *source* of cash to a firm.

This can be seen from Pet Incorporated's statement in Exhibit 17–12. Notice that the "Increase in payables and accruals" is included as a source of cash.

DECREASE IN ANY CURRENT ASSET. Current assets such as inventory and accounts receivable represent an investment of cash. If the level of investment in any current asset is reduced, then cash is freed to flow back into the cash account. Therefore, a decrease in a current asset (such as inventory or accounts receivable) should be entered on the cash flow statement in the "sources of cash" section.

Uses of cash

Cash can be decreased by:

1. Unprofitable operations.
2. Retirement of capital stock or payment of dividends.
3. A decrease in *any* liability account (current or noncurrent).
4. An increase in *any* asset account (current or noncurrent).

As before, only items (3) and (4) require any explanation.

DECREASE IN ANY CURRENT LIABILITY.   We stated in the preceding section that if payments to creditors are deferred the resulting increase in current liabilities represents a source of cash to an organization. By this same line of reasoning, if payments to creditors are accelerated so that overall current liabilities *decrease,* the result will be a net outflow of cash. Therefore, in preparing a cash flow statement, a reduction in a current liability account should be treated as a use of cash.

This can be seen from Pet Incorporated's statement in Exhibit 17–12, where the "Decrease in notes payable and current portion of long-term debt" is treated as a use of cash.

INCREASE IN ANY CURRENT ASSET.   An increase in a current asset account also represents a use of cash on the cash flow statement. A decision on the part of management, for example, to expand the volume of inventory being carried will cause a drain on the cash account, as cash is tied up in investment in inventory. In like manner, a decision to liberalize credit terms will result in an expanded volume of receivables as customers take longer to pay. The build-up of receivables will result in decreased cash being available internally. This can be seen from Pet Incorporated's statement, where both the increase in inventories and the increase in accounts receivable are treated as uses of cash.

Managers often fail to recognize that an expansion of inventory or receivables represents just as much of an investment decision as a decision to expand the size of the plant and equipment. As a practical matter, an investment in inventories or in receivables can be just as illiquid as an investment in plant and equipment. Once inventories are built up, there always is a reluctance to trim them back down, particularly if customers become used to the greater variety of selection available. And once customers get used to taking longer to pay, it is an extremely difficult task to speed collections up again.

The cash flow statement—An illustration

A cash flow statement for Universal Company is presented in Exhibit 17–13. This statement has been prepared from the financial statements of Universal Company used earlier in the chapter.

Exhibit 17–13

UNIVERSAL COMPANY
Statement of Changes in Financial Position
For the Year Ended December 31, 19x2

Sources of cash:	
From operations:	
Net income	$ 4,250
Add: Depreciation	2,500
Patent amortization	500
Total from operations	$ 7,250
From reduction of inventory	2,000
From sale of equipment	500
From expansion of current liabilities	4,000
From issue of mortgage note	3,500
Total sources	$17,250
Uses of cash:	
To pay cash dividends	$ 250
To expand accounts receivable	5,000
To purchase equipment	10,000
To retire preferred stock	3,000
Total uses	$18,250
Decrease in cash	$ (1,000)

The $1,000 decrease in cash shown in the exhibit agrees with the decrease in cash shown on Universal Company's balance sheet in Exhibit 17–7. We can summarize the cause of this cash decrease as follows: During 19x2 Universal Company's major sources of cash were: from operations, $7,250; from reduction of inventories, $2,000; from expansion of current liabilities, $4,000; and from issue of long-term debt, $3,500. The total of these sources of cash were insufficient to cover all of the uses of cash during the year. The major uses of cash were: to expand accounts receivable, $5,000; to purchase equipment, $10,000; and to retire preferred stock, $3,000. The result was an overall reduction of $1,000 in cash available to the firm.

Working papers to support the statement are presented in Exhibit 17–14. The only difference between these working papers and the ones prepared earlier is that these contain changes in the current asset and current liability accounts, as well as changes in the noncurrent accounts.

Exhibit 17-14
T-account working papers—cash flow statement

Cash

Sources		Uses	
(1)	4,250	(2)	250
(5)	2,000	(4)	5,000
(6)	500	(7)	10,000
(8)	2,500	(12)	3,000
(9)	500		
(10)	4,000		
(11)	3,500		

From operations: Net income — To pay cash dividends
From reduction of inventory — To expand accounts receivable
From sale of equipment — To purchase equipment
From operations: Depreciation — To retire preferred stock
From operations: Patent amortization
From expansion of current liabilities
From issue of mortgage note

Accounts Receivable

Bal.	4,000		
(4)	5,000		
Bal.	9,000		

Inventory

Bal.	12,000	(5)	2,000
Bal.	10,000		

Accounts Payable

		Bal.	4,000
		(10)	3,000
		Bal.	7,000

Patents

Bal.	2,500	(9)	500
Bal.	2,000		

Common Stock

		Bal.	10,000
		(3)	1,000
		Bal.	11,000

Mortgage Payable

		Bal.	4,000
		(11)	3,500
		Bal.	7,500

Plant and Equipment

Bal.	30,000	(6)	1,500
(7)	10,000		
Bal.	38,500		

Accrued Liabilities

		Bal.	2,500
		(10)	1,500
		Bal.	4,000

Preferred Stock

(12)	3,000	Bal.	7,500
		Bal.	4,500

Accumulated Depreciation

(6)	1,000	Bal.	9,000
		(8)	2,500
		Bal.	10,500

Taxes Payable

(10)	500	Bal.	1,500
		Bal.	1,000

Retained Earnings

(2)	250	Bal.	12,000
(3)	1,000	(1)	4,250
		Bal.	15,000

SUMMARY

The statement of changes in financial position is one of the three major statements prepared by business firms. Its purpose is analytical, in that it attempts to explain how working capital has been provided and how it has been used during an accounting period. As such, it is a very useful tool in attempting to assess "how well" a firm is doing, and to assess the quality of its management.

If a firm has been experiencing a cash problem, the statement of changes in financial position can be made to focus on changes in cash, rather than on changes in working capital. If working capital is the focus of the statement, then any change in working capital can be explained by an analysis of the noncurrent accounts. If cash is the focus of the statement, then any change in cash can be explained by an analysis of *all* other accounts, current as well as noncurrent.

KEY TERMS FOR REVIEW

Funds statement	**Funds from operations**
As if **transactions**	**Cash flow statement**
Nonfund charges	

APPENDIX: MODIFIED CASH FLOW STATEMENT

When preparing a cash flow statement, some managers prefer a format which adjusts all changes in current assets and current liabilities through the income statement, rather than presenting these changes as separate items on the cash flow statement itself. This results in a cash flow statement which is identical to the funds statement, except for the "funds from operations" figure.

An illustration

To illustrate, we will prepare a cash flow statement for Universal Company, using this modified format. The procedure required for adjusting changes in the current asset and current liability accounts through the income statement is presented in Exhibit 17–15. Notice that this adjustment process changes the income statement to a cash basis.

Using the "net cash flow from operations" figure derived in Exhibit 17–15, we present a cash flow statement for Universal Company in Exhibit 17–16.

Observe that once the "net cash flow from operations" figure is obtained, the noncurrent balance sheet accounts are analyzed in the same way we did earlier in the chapter.

Exhibit 17–15
Income statement adjusted to a cash basis

Revenue or expense item	Plus or minus adjustments to derive cash basis	Illustration— Universal Company
Revenue (as reported on the income statement):		$85;000
Adjustments to cash basis:		
1. Increase in accounts receivable	−	−5,000
2. Decrease in accounts receivable	+	
Revenue adjusted to cash basis		$80,000
Cost of goods sold (as reported on the income statement):		$62,500
Adjustments to cash basis:		
3. Increase in inventory	+	
4. Decrease in inventory	−	−2,000
5. Increase in accounts payable	−	−3,000
6. Decrease in accounts payable	+	
Cost of goods sold adjusted to cash basis		57,500
Operating expenses (as reported on the income statement):		$15,250
Adjustments to cash basis:		
7. Increase in accrued liabilities	−	−1,500
8. Decrease in accrued liabilities	+	
9. Increase in prepaid expenses	+	
10. Decrease in prepaid expenses	−	
11. Period's depreciation, amortization, and depletion ($2,500 + $500)	−	−3,000
Operating expenses adjusted to cash basis		10,750
Income tax expense (as reported on the income statement):		$ 3,000
Adjustments to cash basis:		
12. Increase in accrued taxes payable	−	
13. Decrease in accrued taxes payable	+	+ 500
14. Increase in deferred income taxes	−	
15. Decrease in deferred income taxes	+	
Income taxes adjusted to cash basis		3,500
Net cash flow from operations		$ 8,250

Exhibit 17–16

UNIVERSAL COMPANY
Statement of Changes in Financial Position
For the Year Ended December 31, 19x2

Sources of cash:		
Net cash flow from operations	$ 8,250	
From sale of equipment	500	
From issue of mortgage note	3,500	
Total sources	$12,250	
Uses of cash:		
To pay cash dividends	$ 250	
To purchase equipment	10,000	
To retire preferred stock	3,000	
Total uses	$13,250	
Decrease in cash	$ (1,000)	

Exhibit 17-17. T-account working papers—modified cash flow statement

Cash

Sources		Uses	
From operations:		(4) 5,000	Increase in accounts receivable
Net income	(1) 4,250		
Decrease in inventory	(5) 2,000		
Depreciation	(8) 2,500		
Patent amortization	(9) 500		
Increase in current liabilities	(10) 4,000		
Net cash flow from operations	8,250		
From sale of equipment	(6) 500	(2) 250	To pay cash dividends
From issue of mortgage note	(11) 3,500	(7) 10,000	To purchase equipment
		(12) 3,000	To retire preferred stock

Accounts Receivable

Bal.	4,000		
(4)	5,000		
Bal.	9,000		

Inventory

Bal.	12,000	(5)	2,000
Bal.	10,000		

Accounts Payable

		Bal.	4,000
		(10)	3,000
		Bal.	7,000

Plant and Equipment

Bal.	30,000	(6)	1,500
(7)	10,000		
Bal.	38,500		

Accumulated Depreciation

(6)	1,000	Bal.	9,000
		(8)	2,500
		Bal.	10,500

Patents

Bal.	2,500	(9)	500
Bal.	2,000		

Accrued Liabilities

		Bal.	2,500
		(10)	1,500
		Bal.	4,000

Taxes Payable

(10)	500	Bal.	1,500
		Bal.	1,000

Common Stock

		Bal.	10,000
		(3)	1,000
		Bal.	11,000

Preferred Stock

(12)	3,000	Bal.	7,500
		Bal.	4,500

Retained Earnings

(2)	250	Bal.	12,000
(3)	1,000	(1)	4,250
		Bal.	15,000

Mortgage Payable

		Bal.	4,000
		(11)	3,500
		Bal.	7,500

Working paper procedure

Adjustment of the income statement to a cash basis is not necessary if working papers are prepared, since the working papers will make this adjustment automatically. To illustrate, working papers are presented in Exhibit 17–17 from which the modified cash flow statement in Exhibit 17–16 could have been prepared. Notice that these working papers automatically compute the $8,250 "net cash flow from operations" figure needed for the statement. Thus, the adjustment of the income statement to a cash basis, such as illustrated in Exhibit 17–15, is needed only if working papers are *not* prepared.

QUESTIONS

17–1. What is the purpose of the funds statement?

17–2. To the layman, "funds" means cash. Yet when business executives speak of funds they generally have working capital in mind. Why do business executives think of funds in terms of working capital, rather than in terms of cash?

17–3. How does a funds statement differ from a cash flow statement?

17–4. What are the major sources of working capital, and what are the major uses of working capital?

17–5. In determining "funds provided by operations," why is it necessary to add depreciation back to net income? What other income statement items must also be added back to net income in determining "funds provided by operations"?

17–6. What two groups of transactions have no effect on working capital? Give an example from each group.

17–7. During the current year, a company declared but did not pay a cash dividend of $50,000 and a 5 percent stock dividend. How will these two items be treated on the current year's funds statement?

17–8. Under what conditions would the cash flow statement be more useful to a firm than a funds statement? Under what conditions is the funds statement most useful?

17–9. An outside member of the board of directors of a small, but rapidly growing manufacturing company is puzzled by the fact that the company is very profitable, but yet never seems to have enough cash to pay its bills on time. Explain to the director how a company can be profitable, yet experience shortages of cash. The company pays no dividends.

17–10. Able Company started the year with $100,000 in accounts receivable. The company ended the year with only $80,000 in accounts receivable. Was this decrease in accounts receivable a source of funds to the company on the funds statement? Explain.

17–11. Appleby Company had a net loss for the year, but yet its funds statement shows a *positive* amount of funds provided by operations. How is this possible?

17–12. A business executive once stated, "Depreciation is one of our biggest sources of funds." Do you agree that depreciation is a source of funds? Explain.

17–13. Lido Company acquired a building in exchange for $100,000 in bonds due in ten years. Should this noncash, nonworking capital exchange be included on the funds statement? Explain.

17–14. (Appendix) A merchandising company showed $250,000 cost of goods sold on its income statement. Its beginning inventory was $75,000 and its ending inventory was $60,000. Accounts payable were $50,000 at the beginning of the year and $40,000 at the end of the year. Compute the cost of goods sold adjusted to a cash basis.

17–15. (Appendix) Company X shows operating expenses of $150,000 on its income statement. Depreciation for the period totaled $30,000. Accrued liabilities totaled $16,000 at the beginning of the year, and $25,000 at the end of the year. Prepaid expenses totaled $10,000 at the beginning of the year, and $15,000 at the end of the year. Compute the operating expenses adjusted to a cash basis.

EXERCISES

E17–1. Comparative financial statement data for Shay Company are presented below:

	December 31	
	19x5	*19x4*
Balance Sheet Data		
Current assets	$ 25	$20
Fixed assets	100	85
Accumulated depreciation	(30)	(20)
Long-term investments	10	10
Total Assets	$105	$95
Current liabilities	$ 16	$10
Bonds payable	5	8
Common stock, no par	65	60
Retained earnings	19	17
Total Equities	$105	$95
Other Selected Data		
Net income reported	$ 7	
Cash dividends declared and paid	5	
Depreciation expense	10	

Required:

1. Prepare a statement of changes in working capital.
2. Prepare a funds statement for 19x5.

E17–2. For each of the following transactions, state whether the items involved would appear on the funds statement for the period. For those items appearing on the funds statement, state whether each item would be a source of working capital or a use of working capital, and where appropriate state the dollar amount of the source or use.

1. Sold 500 shares of $100 par value common stock for $110 per share.
2. Retired fully depreciated equipment which had an original cost of $8,000.
3. Purchased $100,000 in inventory on account.
4. Sold fixed assets for $5,000 that had an original cost of $12,000 and accumulated depreciation of $7,000.
5. Declared a cash dividend, $15,000.
6. Purchased $15,000 in fixed assets on a 60-day, 6% note.
7. Amortized goodwill on the income statement, $7,000.
8. Paid the cash dividend in (5).
9. Declared and issued a 5% stock dividend in common on common.
10. $25,000 in long-term debt, due within the next year, was reclassified from a long-term liability status to a current liability status.

E17–3.   Comparative financial statement data for Wiley Company follow:

	December 31	
	19x7	*19x6*
Cash	$ 3	$ 6
Accounts receivable, net	32	24
Inventory	50	40
Plant and equipment	230	200
Accumulated depreciation	(65)	(50)
Total Assets	$250	$220
Accounts payable	$ 40	$ 36
Common stock	150	145
Retained earnings	60	39
Total Equities	$250	$220

For 19x7, the company reported net income as follows:

Sales	$275
Cost of goods sold	150
Gross margin	$125
Operating expenses	90
Net income	$ 35

Dividends of $14 were declared and paid during 19x7. Depreciation expense for the year was $15.

Required:

Prepare a cash flow statement for 19x7, showing the reason(s) for the decrease in cash for the year.

E17–4.   State whether each of the following transactions results in (1) a source of funds, (2) a use of funds, or (3) has no effect on funds. Define funds as working capital.

a. A sale of long-term investments.

b. Retirement of capital stock.

    c. Net income reported for the period.

    d. Purchase of new equipment.

    e. Declaration and issue of a stock dividend.

    f. Sale of capital stock for par.

    g. Retirement of fully depreciated equipment.

    h. Sale of old equipment for its salvage value.

    i. Depreciation charged for the period.

    j. Retirement of long-term debt.

    k. Collection of an account receivable.

    l. Purchase of inventory on account.

   m. Amortization of a patent.

    n. Declaration and payment of a cash dividend.

    o. Reclassification of long-term debt to a current liability status.

    p. Issue of capital stock in exchange for a piece of land.

E17–5. The following information has been extracted from the annual reports of Texon Company:

	December 31	
	19x2	*19x1*
Plant and equipment	$50,000	$38,000
Accumulated depreciation—plant and equipment	21,000	20,000
Net income (loss)	(5,000)	6,000
Depreciation expense	6,000	4,500
Goodwill amortization	2,000	2,000

During 19x1 the company sold equipment which had an original cost of $8,000 for its book value of $3,000.

Required:

1. For 19x2, compute the funds provided by operations. Define funds as working capital.

2. For 19x2, compute the plant and equipment purchases.

E17–6. (Appendix) The income statement for Erie Company for the current year is given below:

ERIE COMPANY
Income Statement

Sales	$150,000
Cost of goods sold	90,000
Gross margin	$ 60,000
Operating expenses	40,000*
Income before taxes	$ 20,000
Income taxes	8,000
Net income	$ 12,000

*Includes $7,500 depreciation.

Amounts from selected balance sheet accounts follow:

	Beginning of year	End of year
Accounts receivable	$30,000	$40,000
Inventory	45,000	54,000
Prepaid expenses	6,000	8,000
Accounts payable	28,000	35,000
Accrued liabilities	8,000	5,000
Income taxes payable	2,500	2,000
Deferred income taxes	4,000	6,000

Required:

Adjust the company's income statement to a cash basis. Show all computations.

PROBLEMS

P17–7. *Funds statement without working papers.* Comparative financial statements for Eaton Company follow:

EATON COMPANY
Balance Sheets
December 31, 19x4 and 19x5

	19x5	19x4
Assets		
Cash	$ 3	$ 1
Accounts receivable	6	3
Inventory	10	14
Equipment	15	10
Accumulated depreciation	(5)	(3)
Land	9	10
Long-term investments	7	5
Total Assets	$45	$40
Equities		
Accounts payable	$ 7	$ 4
Accrued liabilities	2	3
Bonds payable	8	11
Common stock	12	9
Retained earnings	16	13
Total Equities	$45	$40

EATON COMPANY
Income Statements
For the Years Ended December 31, 19x4 and 19x5

	19x5	19x4
Sales	$27	$20
Cost of goods sold	12	9
Gross margin	15	11
Operating expenses*	8	6
Net income	7	5
Beginning retained earnings	13	11
Total	20	16
Deduct cash dividends	4	3
Ending retained earnings	$16	$13

* Includes $2 depreciation expense each year.

Required:

1. Prepare a statement of changes in working capital for 19x5.
2. Prepare a funds statement for 19x5.

P17–8.   *Cash flow statement without working papers.* Refer to the financial statement data for Eaton Company in Problem 17–7.

Required:

Prepare a cash flow statement for Eaton Company for 19x5.

P17–9.   *Funds statement without working papers.* Saxon Company's balance sheet accounts at the end of Years 1 and 2 are given below:

	Year 2	Year 1
Debits		
Cash	$ 5,000	$ 11,000
Accounts receivable, net	16,500	10,000
Inventory	35,000	25,000
Prepaid expenses	2,500	4,000
Plant and equipment	175,000	160,000
Long-term investments	16,000	20,000
Total	$250,000	$230,000
Credits		
Accumulated depreciation	$ 36,000	$ 28,000
Accounts payable	25,000	21,500
Accrued liabilities	3,000	4,500
Bonds payable	28,000	16,000
Common stock	100,000	110,000
Retained earnings	58,000	50,000
Total	$250,000	$230,000

The company's income statement for Year 2 follows:

SAXON COMPANY
Income Statement
For Year 2

Sales	$120,000
Cost of goods sold	75,000
Gross margin	45,000
Operating expenses..	30,000
Net income	$ 15,000

There were no sales or retirements of equipment during Year 2. Dividends paid totaled $7,000 for Year 2, and depreciation expense totaled $8,000.

Required:

1. For Year 2, prepare a statement of changes in working capital.
2. Prepare a funds statement for Year 2.

P17–10. *Cash flow statement without working papers.* Refer to the financial statement data for Saxon Company in Problem 17–9. Lynn Collins, president of Saxon Company, views the cash account at the end of Year 2 to be at a "crises" level. Collins can't understand why cash declined so sharply during the year, particularly since net income was at a record high.

Required:

Prepare a cash flow statement for Year 2, and explain to the president the cause(s) of the sharp decline in cash available.

P17–11. *Funds statement without working papers.* Foxboro Company's bond indenture agreement requires that the company maintain a working capital balance at least equal to the amount of bonds outstanding at any point in time. Accordingly, the company monitors its working capital position with considerable care. Selected information on the company is given below:

1. Balance sheet accounts at the end of the current and preceding year:

	Current year	Preceding year
Cash	$ 4,500	$ 12,000
Accounts receivable	17,000	9,500
Inventory	36,500	25,000
Prepaid expenses	1,500	3,500
Plant and equipment	180,000	155,000
Long-term investments	15,000	20,000
Total	$254,500	$225,000
Accumulated depreciation	$ 50,000	$ 38,000
Accounts payable	26,500	22,000
Accrued liabilities	3,000	4,500
Bonds payable, 10%	30,000	15,000
Deferred income taxes	14,000	10,000
Common stock, $5 par	100,000	112,500
Retained earnings	31,000	23,000
Total	$254,500	$225,000

2. The company's income statement for the current year:

FOXBORO COMPANY
Income Statement
For the Current Year

Sales	$250,000
Cost of goods sold	180,000
Gross margin	$ 70,000
Operating expenses	45,000
Income before taxes	$ 25,000
Income tax expense	10,000
Net income	$ 15,000

3. The company paid $7,000 in dividends during the current year.
4. There were no sales or retirements of fixed assets during the current year. Depreciation for the current year totaled $12,000.

Required:

1. Prepare a statement of changes in working capital for the current year.
2. Prepare a funds statement for the current year.
3. Management estimates that net income next year will be about the same as for the current year. Next year the company would like to expand the plant by an additional $25,000. No additional issue of bonds is anticipated. Does it appear that the company will be able to expand its plant as desired?

P17–12. *Cash flow statement without working papers.* Refer to the data for Foxboro Company contained in Problem 17–11. M. J. Perry, president of Foxboro Company, considers $8,000 to be a minimum cash balance for operating purposes. As can be seen from the balance sheet data, only $4,500 in cash was available at the end of the current year. The sharp decline in cash is puzzling to Perry, particularly in view of the fact that working capital is up and the company had a good net income showing for the year.

Required:

1. Prepare a cash flow statement for the current year.
2. Explain to the president the chief cause(s) for the decline in the company's cash position.

P17–13. *Funds statement.* In early 19x5 Mr. Robert Miller was made president of the Bestway Sales Company. Mr. Miller is widely regarded as a hard-hitting sales executive, but he has little patience with financial matters. After many years of no sales growth, sales rose about 10 percent in 19x5 through Mr. Miller's leadership. This resulted primarily from an increase during the year in the number of distribution warehouses available to service customer needs. Mr. Miller plans further expansion of the company's warehouse facilities in 19x6, providing adequate funding can be made available through the company's bank.

Comparative balance sheet data for 19x4 and 19x5 are presented at the top of page 718.

The company's income statement for 19x5 follows:

BESTWAY SALES COMPANY
Income Statement
For the Year 19x5

Sales	$1,000,000
Cost of goods sold	750,000
Gross margin	$ 250,000
Operating expenses	200,000
Net income	$ 50,000

The following additional information is available for 19x5:

1. Fully depreciated equipment with an original cost of $50,000 was retired during the year. The equipment had a negligible scrap value.

BESTWAY SALES COMPANY
Comparative Balance Sheets
For the Years 19x5 and 19x4

December 31

	19x5	*19x4*
Cash	$ (5,000)	$ 40,000
Accounts receivable	100,000	75,000
Inventory	225,000	180,000
Prepaid expenses	5,000	10,000
Total current assets	$325,000	$305,000
Plant and equipment	890,000	800,000
Accumulated depreciation	(350,000)	(325,000)
Goodwill	35,000	40,000
Total Assets	$900,000	$820,000
Accounts payable	$163,000	$145,000
Accrued liabilities	12,000	15,000
Total current liabilities	$175,000	$160,000
Long-term debt	150,000	120,000
Common stock	375,000	370,000
Retained earnings	200,000	170,000
Total equities	$900,000	$820,000
Working capital	$150,000	$145,000

2. Cash dividends paid during 19x5 totaled $20,000.
3. The goodwill is being amortized against earnings.

The company's bank has requested that it be provided with a balance sheet, an income statement, and a funds statement in support of the company's application for additional long-term financing.

Required:

1. Prepare a statement of changes in working capital for 19x5.
2. Prepare T-account working papers for a funds statement.
3. Prepare a funds statement for 19x5.
4. As the company's banker, what additional information might you want relating to the company's activities during 19x5?

P17–14. *Cash flow statement.* Refer to the data for the Bestway Sales Company in Problem 17–13. Robert Miller, president of the Bestway Sales Company, was shocked when he received the 19x5 balance sheet data showing that the company's cash account was overdrawn. He was all the more perplexed when he noted from the statements that the company's working capital had increased during the year. After mulling over the statements for awhile, he exclaimed, "These statements just don't make sense. We've had the most profitable year in our history, our working capital is up, but yet we don't have a dime in the bank. It looks like the more we make, the poorer we get."

Assume you are the chief financial officer of the Bestway Sales Company, and that it is your responsibility to explain to Mr. Miller what happened to the company's cash during 19x5.

Required:

1. Prepare T-account working papers for a cash flow statement.
2. Prepare a cash flow statement for 19x5.
3. Write a brief memo to Mr. Miller explaining the chief causes of the decrease in cash during the year.

P17–15. *Cash Flow Statement.* (Appendix) Refer to the data for the Bestway Sales Company in Problem 17–13. Upon receiving the financial statements illustrated in the problem, the Bestway Sales Company's bank requested a cash flow statement so that they could see the reasons for the dramatic reduction in cash during the year.

Required:

1. Prepare T-account working papers for a cash flow statement. Use the working paper format illustrated in Exhibit 17–17 in the Appendix to the chapter.
2. Prepare a cash flow statement for 19x5.
3. Write a brief memo to the bank, explaining the chief causes of the decrease in cash during the year.

P17–16. *Funds statement.* Marcroft Company had a poor year during 19x7. The company suffered a net loss for the year, and saw its current ratio slip from 3.0 to 2.5. The drop in the current ratio is of particular concern to management, since substantial long-term financing was obtained during the year to bolster the working capital position. Comparative balance sheets for the last two years are given below:

MARCROFT COMPANY
Balance Sheets
December 31, 19x6 and 19x7

	19x7	*19x6*
Current Assets:		
Cash	$ 15,000	$ 10,000
Accounts receivable	45,000	48,000
Inventory	90,000	80,000
Total	$150,000	$138,000
Buildings and equipment	$210,000	$190,000
Less: Accumulated depreciation	65,000	52,000
Net buildings and equipment	$145,000	$138,000
Investments in subsidiaries	$ 15,000	$ 9,000
Total Assets	$310,000	$285,000
Current Liabilities:		
Accounts payable	$ 50,000	$ 35,500
Accrued liabilities	10,000	10,500
Total	$ 60,000	$ 46,000
Bonds payable	$ 80,000	$ 50,000
Stockholders' equity:		
Common stock	$120,000	$125,000
Retained earnings	50,000	64,000
Total Stockholders' Equity	$170,000	$189,000
Total Liabilities and Equity	$310,000	$285,000
Current ratio	2.5 to 1	3.0 to 1

The company's income statement for 19x7:

MARCROFT COMPANY
Income Statement
For the Year Ended December 31, 19x7

Sales	$375,000
Cost of goods sold	260,000
Gross margin	$115,000
Operating expenses	124,000
Net loss	$ (9,000)

The following additional information is available for the year:

a. The company has the longest unbroken dividend record in its industry. To maintain this record, cash dividends of $3,500 were declared
and paid during the year.

b. Equipment with an original cost of $12,000 was sold for its book
value of $3,000.

c. During the year, the company repurchased the stock of a dissident
stockholder. The stockholder was paid $6,500 for stock that had
a carrying value of $5,000 on the company's books. The excess
was charged against retained earnings.

Management would like a complete analysis of working capital to
accompany the 19x7 annual report.

Required:

1. Prepare a statement of changes in working capital.
2. Prepare T-account working papers for a funds statement.
3. Prepare a funds statement for 19x7, in good form.

P17–17. *Cash flow statement.* See the data for Marcroft Company in Problem
17–16. Marcie Shaw, a stockholder, is puzzled over the company's
financial statements. After studying the statements for a few moments,
she commented, "There's something wrong here. The company lost
$9,000 for the year, and paid $3,500 in cash dividends. But yet the
cash account increased by $5,000. It seems to me that the cash account
should have decreased."

Required:

1. Prepare T-account working papers for a cash flow statement.
2. Prepare a cash flow statement for 19x7, in good form.
3. Prepare a short memo explaining to Marcie the reason(s) why the
cash account increased during the year.

P17–18. *Cash flow statement.* (Appendix) Refer to the financial statement data
for Marcroft Company in Problem 17–16. Gerri Allen, president of Marcroft Company, is elated that the company's cash position improved
during the year, although she is puzzled as to why it happened. Ms.
Allen observed, "With our $9,000 operating loss, continued payment
of dividends, and large equipment purchases I was sure we would end
the year with almost nothing in the bank. But I find our cash position
stronger than it has ever been. I would like a detailed analysis of exactly
what happened in the cash account during the year."

Required:

1. Prepare T-account working papers for a cash flow statement. Use the working paper format illustrated in Exhibit 17–17 in the Appendix to the chapter.
2. Prepare a cash flow statement for 19x7.
3. Write a brief memo to Ms. Allen, explaining the chief cause(s) of the increase in cash during the year.

P17–19. *Funds statement.* Royal Company's 19x5 annual report contained the following balance sheet data:

ROYAL COMPANY
Balance Sheets
For the Years 19x5 and 19x4

	December 31,	
	19x5	19x4
Assets		
Current Assets:		
Cash	$ 9,000	$ 9,500
Accounts receivable, net	31,000	26,000
Inventory	80,000	75,000
Prepaid expenses	4,500	4,000
Total Current Assets	$124,500	$114,500
Property and equipment:		
Land	$ 50,000	$ 50,000
Buildings and equipment	518,000	440,000
Total	$568,000	$490,000
Less: Accumulated depreciation	112,500	90,000
Net Property and Equipment	$455,500	$400,000
Investments	$ 20,000	$ 35,500
Total Assets	$600,000	$550,000
Liabilities and Stockholders' Equity		
Current Liabilities:		
Accounts payable	$ 48,000	$ 40,000
Accrued liabilities	9,000	12,000
Taxes payable	3,000	4,000
Total Current Liabilities	$ 60,000	$ 56,000
Notes payable	$ 90,000	$120,000
Deferred income taxes	$ 50,000	$ 42,000
Stockholders' equity:		
Common stock	$320,000	$250,000
Retained earnings	80,000	82,000
Total Stockholders' Equity	$400,000	$332,000
Total Liabilities and Equity	$600,000	$550,000

The following additional information has been gleaned from the company's annual report:

1. The net income for 19x5 was $48,000.
2. Depreciation expense during 19x5 was $40,000.

3. Cash dividends declared and paid during the year totaled $20,000.
4. Fully depreciated equipment with an original cost of $10,000 was written off during the year.
5. Stock dividends of $30,000 were declared and distributed during 19x5.
6. Equipment with a book value of $4,500 was sold at book value for cash.
7. Four thousand shares of common stock were issued during 19x5, at an issue price of $10 per share.

Required:

1. Prepare a statement of changes in working capital for 19x5.
2. Prepare T-account working papers for a funds statement for the year 19x5.
3. Prepare a funds statement for 19x5, in good form.

P17–20. *Funds statement and current ratios.* Members of the board of directors of Janax Products are very pleased with the company's operating performance for 19x2. Net income has more than doubled from the previous year, although sales increased by only 60 percent. Comparative income statements for the last two years are given below:

JANAX PRODUCTS
Income Statements
For the Years Ended June 30, 19x1 and 19x2

	19x2	*19x1*
Sales	$8,000,000	$5,000,000
Cost of goods sold	3,700,000	2,500,000
Gross margin	$4,300,000	$2,500,000
Operating expenses	2,900,000	1,900,000
Income before taxes	$1,400,000	$ 600,000
Income tax expense	500,000	200,000
Net income	$ 900,000	$ 400,000

Although the board members are pleased with the company's operating record, they are disappointed and puzzled over the company's financial condition at the end of 19x2. For the first time in many years Janax Products has a current ratio that is below the industry average of 2.2 to 1. This concerns the board members for two reasons. First, the president of Janax Products is new, 19x2 being his first full year directing the company's affairs. And second, the board is contemplating the issue of a sizable amount of bonded debt to replace the long-term notes now outstanding, and the board members feel certain that any further erosion of the current position will surely put this move in jeopardy. Comparative balance sheet data are given at the top of page 723.

The chairman of the board has asked that you prepare an analysis showing what happened to the company's working capital during 19x2.

JANAX PRODUCTS
Comparative Balance Sheets
June 30, 19x1 and 19x2

Assets

Current Assets:	19x2	19x1
Cash	$ 450,000	$ 500,000
Accounts receivable, net	1,150,000	900,000
Inventory	3,100,000	2,200,000
Prepaid expenses	50,000	50,000
Total Current Assets	$4,750,000	$3,650,000
Property and equipment:		
Land	$ 500,000	$ 200,000
Plant and equipment	5,500,000	4,890,000
Total	$6,000,000	$5,090,000
Less: Accumulated depreciation	1,900,000	1,500,000
Net property and equipment	$4,100,000	$3,590,000
Stock of affiliated companies	$ 350,000	$ 160,000
Total Assets	$9,200,000	$7,400,000

Liabilities and Stockholders' Equity

Current Liabilities:		
Accounts payable	$1,775,000	$1,360,000
Income taxes payable	200,000	100,000
Notes payable—current portion	500,000	—
Total Current Liabilities	$2,475,000	$1,460,000
Long-term notes	$1,250,000	$1,750,000
Deferred taxes	$ 400,000	$ 250,000
Stockholders' Equity:		
Common stock	$3,500,000	$2,800,000
Retained earnings	1,575,000	1,140,000
Total Stockholders' Equity	$5,075,000	$3,940,000
Total Liabilities and Equity	$9,200,000	$7,400,000
Current Ratio	1.9 to 1	2.5 to 1

The following information is available:

a. Cash dividends declared and paid during the year totaled $265,000.

b. The company issued $190,000 of its own stock in exchange for an equal amount of stock in an affiliated company.

c. Fully depreciated equipment costing $100,000 new was retired and removed from the books.

d. A stock dividend of $200,000 was declared and issued during the year.

e. A $300,000 fabricating plant was acquired during 19x2 by giving $200,000 in the company's common stock and $100,000 in cash to cover the purchase price.

f. Depreciation expense for 19x2 totaled $650,000.

g. Unneeded equipment with an original cost of $350,000 was sold for its book value of $200,000.

h. Five thousand shares of common stock were issued at $22 per share. The stock is no par.

j. Some $500,000 in long-term notes were reclassified during the year to a current liability status, since these notes will fall due within a few months.

Required:

1. Prepare a schedule of changes in working capital.
2. Prepare T-account working papers for a funds statement.
3. Prepare a funds statement for 19x2, in good form.
4. Based on your work in (1) to (3) above, comment to the board of directors on whether a problem exists in relation to the company's working capital.

Index

A

Absorption costing, 56
  and changes in production, 225–27
  and changes in sales, 223–25
  compared to direct costing, 219–21
  and CVP analysis, 227–28
  income statement, 220, 224, 226
  and pricing, 491–92
Accounting information, 11–12
Accounts receivable turnover, 659
Acid-test ratio, 658
Administrative costs, 26
After-tax cost, 566–67
Allocation bases for service department costs, 606–7
Annuity, 529
Application of overhead, 60, 68–69
  predetermined overhead rate, 61–62, 74–76, 360–61, 604
  using estimated data, 61
Avoidable costs, 432

B

Balance sheet
  budgeted, 271–72
  in common size form, 645
  manufacturing firm, 29
  merchandising firm, 29
Bill of materials, 309
Book value
  and cost relevance, 433–34
  per share, 655
Break-even analysis
  and absorption costing, 227–28
  defined, 163
  equation technique, 173
  graph technique, 175
  limiting assumptions, 183–84
  and sales mix, 182
  unit contribution technique, 174–79
Break-even chart, 175–80
Budget committee, 260
Budget period, 257
Budget variance, overhead, 362–63

Budgeting; *see* Budgets
Budgets
  advantages of, 255–56
  balance sheet, 271–72
  capital, 257
  cash, 260–61, 269–70
  definition of, 254
  direct labor, 266
  direct materials, 264–65
  flexible, 348
  human relations, 259–60
  income statement, 271
  manufacturing overhead, 266–67
  master, 254, 260–61
  plans of management, 12
  preparation of, 262–74
  sales, 260, 263
  self-imposed, 257–58
  selling and administrative expense, 268–69
Burden; *see* Factory overhead

C

Capital budgeting
  and discounted cash flow, 529–45
  and income taxes, 571–76
  an investment concept, 522
  and payback, 579–82
  and simple rate of return, 582–83
  typical decisions, 522–23
Capital budgets, 257, 522–23
Cash budget
  illustrated, 269–70
  importance of, 260–61
Cash flow statement, 701–10
Certificate in management accounting, 17–18
Clearing account, 68–69
C/M ratio, 165
Commissions, 181
Committed fixed costs, 126–27
Common costs
  in decision making, 432–33, 439
  definition of, 37, 211
  and net income, 214
Common-size statements, 644–46

Constraint equations
 in linear programming, 452–53
 in minimization problems, 456
 purpose of, 451
Continuous budgets, 257
Contribution approach, 140
 advantages of, 229
 to cost allocation, 208–17
 and CVP analysis, 163–80
 to the income statement, 141
 and joint product decisions, 448–50
 and make or buy decisions, 444–46
 and pricing, 493
 and product line decisions, 438–40
 restrictions to use, 228
 and scarce resource use, 446–47
 and segmented reporting, 208–17
Contribution format, 140, 220
Contribution margin, 141, 163
 and fixed costs, 141, 162–66
 as a planning tool, 168–80
 and pricing decisions, 499–504
 and sales mix, 183
 and scarce resources, 446–48
 by segments, 209, 216
 per unit, 163
Contribution margin ratio
 and break-even analysis, 174, 182
 defined, 165
Control chart, 325
Controllable costs, 37
Controller, 8–9
Controlling by management, 5
Conversion cost, 25
Cost of capital
 definition of, 534
 as a screening tool, 538–39
Cost of goods manufactured, 28, 70–71, 73
Cost of goods sold, 28, 71, 73, 75–76
Cost allocation
 by the contribution approach, 208–17
 of service department costs, 604–22
 using normalized overhead rates, 89
 using predetermined overhead rates, 61–63,
  68–69, 74–76
 using sales dollars, 620–21
Cost centers, 397
Cost curves, economic
 limitations of, 488–90
 marginal revenue and cost, 486–87
 total revenue and cost, 484–85
Cost formula, 132, 137, 350
Cost-plus pricing
 and absorption costing, 491
 and contribution costing, 493
 limitations of, 494–95
Cost structure, 166
Cost-volume-profit analysis
 and absorption costing, 227–28
 basic concepts, 162–80

Cost-volume-profit analysis—*Cont.*
 definition, 162
 and direct costing, 221
 limiting assumptions, 183–84
Cost-volume-profit graph, 175–77
Costing systems
 absorption, 64–78
 direct, 217–28
 job order, 57, 64–78
 process, 57, 79–88
 standard, 306–30
Costs
 controllable, 37
 differential, 38
 direct and indirect, 36, 211
 fixed, 36, 125–27
 incremental, 168–80
 inventoriable, 30
 manufacturing, 24–25
 nonmanufacturing, 26, 70
 opportunity, 39, 411, 445
 period, 26
 product, 27, 30–33
 relevant, 432–33
 sunk, 39, 432
 variable, 35, 120, 122
Current ratio, 657
Curvilinear costs, 124

D

Debt/equity ratio, 662
Decentralization, 6
 measuring performance under, 397–405
 and responsibility accounting, 390–97
 and transfer pricing, 405–12
Decision making
 a function of management, 4–5
 under rationing of capital, 576–79
 using CVP analysis, 168–72
 using discounted cash flow, 529–38
 using linear programming, 451–56
 using payback, 579–82
 using relevant costs, 432–46
 using segmented statements, 208–17
 using simple rate of return, 582–84
Declining balance depreciation, 569
Denominator activity, 360
Depreciation
 and the funds statement, 691–92
 methods, 569–71
 tax shield effects of, 567–68
Differential costs, 38, 432–50
Direct costing, 218–20
Direct costs, 36, 211
Direct labor, 25, 60, 66–67
Direct labor budget, 261–66
Direct materials, 25, 58, 64–66
Direct materials budget, 261, 264–65
Direct method, 607
Discount rate, setting of, 534

Discounted cash flow
  net present value method, 529–35
  time-adjusted rate of return method, 535–38
Discounting, illustrated, 527–29
Discretionary fixed costs, 127
Dividend payout ratio, 651
Dividend yield ratio, 651
Divisional autonomy, 412

E

Earnings per share, 647
  and extraordinary items, 647–49
  fully diluted, 649–50
Economic order quantity
  formula approach, 278–79
  graphical approach, 278
  and the reorder point, 279–80
  tabulation approach, 276–77
Economic order range, 278
Efficiency variance
  for labor, 312, 318
  for overhead, 312, 319, 356
Elasticity of demand, 487
Employee time tickets, 60
Engineering approach to cost study, 139–40
Equivalent units of production, 81–82

F

Factory burden; *see* Factory overhead
Factory overhead, 25
Feedback, 12
Fifo cost flow, 85, 87
Financial accounting, comparision to managerial
  accounting, 13–16
Financial statements
  manufacturing firm, 28
  merchandising firm, 28
Finished goods inventory, 29
Fixed costs
  allocation, 611–12
  definition, 36, 125
  and direct costing, 219–22
  importance of, 162–64
  relevant range, 128–29
  trend toward, 126
  types of, 126–27
Fixed overhead variances
  budget, 362–63
  denominator activity, 360
  volume, 362–64
Flexible budgets
  characteristics of, 348
  and fixed costs, 358
  illustrated, 350–52
  measure of activity, 352
Funds statement, 682–701

G–H

Generally accepted accounting principles, 14
High-low method, 131–33

Horizontal analysis, 643
Human relations and budgets, 259–60

I

Ideal standards, 307
Idle time, 33
Income statement
  absorption basis, 28, 76, 220, 224, 226
  budgeted, 271
  contribution basis, 141, 162–68
  direct costing basis, 220, 224, 226
  manufacturing firm, 29
  merchandising firm, 29
  segmented, 209, 216
Incremental analysis
  and capital budgeting, 542–43
  and CVP decisions, 168–80
  and joint product decisions, 449
  and make or buy decisions, 442–46
  and pricing, 500–504
  and product line decisions, 438–42
  and relevant costs, 432–38
  and scarce resources, 449–50
Incremental costs, 38; *see also* Incremental
  analysis
Indirect costs, 36, 211
Indirect labor, 25, 33, 66–67
Indirect materials, 25, 65–66
Information, the need for, 5, 16
Interest, theory of, 524
Internal rate of return, 529
Interpolation, 537–38
Inventoriable costs, 30
Inventories
  finished goods, 29
  manufacturing firm, 30–33
  merchandise, 29
  merchandising firm, 29, 32
  raw materials, 29
  work in process, 29
Inventory, costs associated with, 275
Inventory control systems
  economic order quantity, 275–79
  reorder point, 279–80
  safety stock, 280–81
Inventory turnover, 660
Investment centers
  defined, 397
  measuring performance in, 397–405
  and transfer pricing, 405–12

J

Job order costing, 57
  flows of costs, 64–78
  job cost sheet, 59, 62
Joint product costs, 448–49
Joint products, 448

K–L

Kinked demand curve, 489
Labor costs, 33–34

Labor efficiency variance, 312, 318
Labor rate variance, 312, 317–18
Labor time tickets, 60
Lead time, 280
Least-cost decisions, 543–44
Least squares method, 131, 135–38, 143–44
Leverage
    definition of, 653
    the desirability of, 655
    illustrated, 653
    the impact of income taxes on, 654–55
    operating, 167
    sources of, 654
Line and staff, 7–8
Line functions, 7–8
Linear programming
    applications of, 457
    characteristics of, 451
    graphical approach, 451–56
    and scarce resources, 447
    simplex approach, 456
Linearity assumption, 124

M

Make or buy decisions, 442–46
Management
    need for information, 11
    the work of, 4–6
Management by exception
    determining exceptions, 323–25
    using standard costs, 306
Managerial accounting
    comparison to financial accounting, 13–16
    expanding role of, 16–17
Manufacturing costs, 24–25
Manufacturing overhead, 25, 60, 67–68,
        74–76
Manufacturing overhead budget, 261, 266–67
Margin, on sales, 399
Marginal cost, 486–87
Marginal revenue, 486–87
Marketing costs, 26
Master budget
    definition, 254
    a network, 260–61
    preparation of, 262–74
Materials price variance, 313–15
Materials quantity variance, 312, 316
Materials requisition form, 58
Merchandise inventory, 29
Mixed costs
    analysis of, 131–38
    behavior of, 130
    definition, 130
Monopolistic competition, 488
Monopoly, 488
Moving average cost flow, 86–87
Multiple overhead rates, 77–78
Multiple regression analysis, 139

N

Net present value method, 529–35
    choosing a discount rate, 534
    compared to rate of return method, 539–40
    extended example, 540
    and income taxes, 571–76
    incremental cost approach, 542
    limiting assumptions, 534
    preference decisions, 577
    total cost approach, 540–41
Nonmanufacturing costs, 26, 70
Normalized overhead rate, 89

O

Objective function, 451
Objectives, setting of, 2
Oligopoly, 489
Operating budgets, 257
Operating leverage, 167
Opportunity costs
    defined, 39
    and make or buy, 445–46
    and transfer pricing, 411
Organization chart, 7, 391
Organizational structure, 6–7
Organizations
    basic similarities, 9
    definition, 2
    line and staff, 7–8
    objectives, 2–3
    structure, 6
    types, 9
Organizing and directing, 4–5
Overapplied overhead, 74–76
Overhead
    analysis of, 312, 319
    application of, 60–62, 67–69, 74–76
    defined, 25
    flexible budgets, 350–52
    normalized rates, 89
    predetermined rates, 61–63, 68–69, 74–76
    problems with, 74–76
Overhead variances
    fixed budget, 362–63
    fixed volume, 362–64
    variable efficiency, 312, 319, 356
    variable spending, 312, 319–20, 355
Overtime premium, 34

P

Parallel processing, 79–80
Payback method, 579–82
Payroll fringe benefits, 34
Penetration pricing, 498
Performance report, 12, 314, 316, 351, 353–58,
        392
Period costs, 26
Perpetual budgets, 257
Planning, the need for, 4–5

Planning and control
  cycle, 6
  differences between, 255
Practical standards, 307
Predetermined overhead rate, 61–63, 68–69, 74–
  76, 360–61, 604
Preference decisions
  using net present value, 577–78
  using profitability index, 578
  using time-adjusted rate of return, 577
Present value
  and annuities, 527–29
  computation of, 526–28
  the concept of, 524
  and the theory of interest, 524–26
Present value tables, 546–47
Price/earnings ratio, 650
Price variances
  general model, 312
  labor rate, 312, 317
  materials price, 313–15
  overhead spending, 319
Pricing, 484–505
  economic framework, 484–90
  new products, 497–99
  special decisions, 499–504
  standard products, 490–96
Pricing strategies
  penetration pricing, 498
  skimming pricing, 498–99
Prime costs, 25
Process costing, 57
  measuring output, 81
  processing centers, 79–80
  production reports, 86, 88
  unit costs, 79, 82
Processing centers
  parallel, 79
  sequential, 79
Product costs, 27, 30–33
  and direct costing, 218
  and job order costing, 64–78
  and pricing decisions, 491–94
  and process costing, 79–88
Product line analysis, 438–42
Production
  budget, 263–64
  order, 63
  report, 86, 88
  run size, 279
Profit centers, 397
Profit-graph, 177–80
Profit/volume ratio; see P/V ratio
Profitability index, 578
P/V ratio, 165

Q

Quantity variances
  general model, 312
  labor efficiency, 312, 318

Quantity variances—*Cont.*
  materials quantity, 312, 316
  overhead efficiency, 312, 319

R

Range of flexibility, 502
Ranking projects
  by net present value, 577–78
  by profitability index, 578
  by time-adjusted rate of return, 577
Rationing decisions, 576–79
Ratios
  accounts receivable turnover, 659
  acid-test, 658
  book value, 655–56
  current, 657
  debt/equity, 662
  dividend payout, 651
  dividend yield, 651–52
  earnings per share, 647–50
  inventory turnover, 660
  price/earnings, 650
  return on common stockholders' equity, 652–
   53
  return on total assets, 652
  times interest earned, 661
Raw materials inventory, 29
Regression line, 134–35
Relevant costs
  and cost precision, 433
  defined, 432
  and depreciation, 435
  and joint products, 448–49
  and make or buy decision, 442–46
  and product line decision, 438–42
  and scarce resources, 449
Relevant range, 124
Reorder point, 279–80
Residual income, 404–5
Responsibility accounting, 256, 311, 390
Responsibility centers, 390, 396–97
Retainer fee approach, 620
Return on common stockholders' equity, 652–53
Return on investment
  controlling the, 400–401
  defined, 398
  factors underlying, 399–400
  formula, 399
Return on total assets, 652
Robinson-Patman Act, 505

S

Safety stock, 279–82
Sales budget
  illustrated, 263
  importance of, 260
Sales forecasting, 261–62
Sales mix, 181–83
Scattergraph method, 131, 134–35

Segment margin
   defined, 213
   and product line decisions, 438–42
   uses of, 213
Segmented income statement, 209, 216
Segmented reporting, 208–17
Segments of an organization
   defined, 208
   illustrated, 209
   types of, 217
Self-imposed budget
   advantages of, 258–59
   defined, 257
Selling and administrative expense, budget, 261,
      268–69
Selling costs, 26
Sequential processing centers, 79–80
Service department
   allocating costs of a, 604–22
   allocation bases of a, 606–7
   definition of a, 604
Simple rate of return, 582–83
Skimming pricing, 498
Spending variance, 312, 319–20, 355
Split-off point, 448
Staff functions, 7–8
Standard cost card, 311
Standard costs
   advantages of, 311
   defined, 306
   ideal versus practical, 307
   for labor, 309–10
   for materials, 308–9
   for overhead, 310
   setting standards, 307–10
Standard hours, 317
Standard quantity, 313
Statement of changes in financial position; see
      Funds statement
Statement analysis
   horizontal, 643
   importance of, 640–41
   limitations of, 641
   ratio, 646–63
   trend, 644
   vertical, 644–46
Static budget, 348–49
Step method, 607
Step-variable costs, 123–24, 129
Straight-line depreciation, 569–71
Strategic planning, 3–4
Suboptimization, 412
Sum-of-the-years'-digits depreciation, 569–71
Sunk costs, 39, 432

                          T

Target costs, 499
Target net profits, 180
Tax shield, depreciation, 567–68

Test marketing, 497
Time-adjusted rate of return method, 536–39
Time tickets, 60
Times interest earned, 661
Total cost approach, 540–42
Transfer pricing
   at cost, 406
   guidelines for, 408
   at market price, 407–10
   the need for, 406
   at negotiated market price, 410–11
   and opportunity costs, 411
   at variable cost, 407
Trend percentages, 644
Turnover of assets, 399

                          U

Unavoidable costs, 432
Underapplied overhead, 74–76
Unit costs, 56, 63–64, 267
   absorption basis, 64
   direct costing basis, 218–20
   for pricing, 491–93
   and process costing, 79, 82

                          V

Variable costs
   activity base, 121
   allocation, 610–11
   definition, 35, 120
   types of, 122
Variable pricing, 502–4
Variance analysis
   fixed overhead, 362–65
   a general model of, 311–12
   labor, 317–19
   materials, 313–16
   on performance reports, 314, 316
   variable overhead, 320
Variances
   defined, 312
   fixed overhead budget, 362–63
   fixed overhead volume, 362–64
   labor efficiency, 318
   labor rate, 317–18
   materials price, 313–15
   materials quantity, 312, 316
   variable overhead efficiency, 319–20
   variable overhead spending, 319–20
Vertical analysis, 644–46
Volume variance, 362–64

                        W–Z

Work in process inventory, 29, 65–66
Work of management, 4–6
Working capital, 656
   sources and uses, 684–87
   statement of changes in, 690
Zero-base budgeting, 272